3 simple ways Checkpoint helps you make sense of all those taxes.

1 — Intuitive Web-based design makes it fast and simple to find what you need.

2 — A comprehensive collection of primary tax law, cases and rulings along with analytical insight you simply can't find anywhere else.

3 — Because more tax pros use Checkpoint® than any other resource today!

Checkpoint®
Look no further

For technical support call: **1-800-423-0563**

Visit our Web site at: **www.RIAhome.com**

RIA
A THOMSON COMPANY

© 2001 RIA RIA is a trademark used herein under license. All other names and trademarks are the property of their respective owners. 4-9880-2/02-01

West's Federal Tax Research
Sixth Edition

William A. Raabe, Ph.D., C.P.A.
Capital University

Gerald E. Whittenburg, Ph.D., C.P.A.
San Diego State University

Debra L. Sanders, Ph.D., C.P.A.
Washington State University

John C. Bost, J.D.
San Diego State University

Australia · Canada · Mexico · Singapore · Spain · United Kingdom · United States

West's Federal Tax Research, 6e
William A. Raabe, Gerald E. Whittenburg, Debra L. Sanders, and John C. Bost

Editor-in-Chief:
Jack W. Calhoun

Vice President/Team Director:
Melissa S. Acuña

Acquisition Editor:
Jennifer L. Codner

Developmental Editor:
Carol Bennett

Senior Marketing Manager:
Julie Lindsay

Production Editor:
Salvatore N. Versetto

Manufacturing Coordinator:
Doug Wilke

Production House:
Litten Editing and Production

Compositor:
Parkwood Composition Service, Inc.

Printer:
Phoenix Color
Hagerstown, Maryland

Design Project Manager:
Rick A. Moore

Cover Designer:
Rick A. Moore

Cover Image:
© digitalvision

Media Developmental Editor:
Sally Nieman

Media Production Editor:
Lora I. Craver

COPYRIGHT © 2003
by South-Western, a division of Thomson Learning. Thomson Learning™ is a trademark used herein under license.

Printed in the United States of America
2 3 4 5 04 03

For more information
contact South-Western,
5191 Natorp Boulevard,
Mason, Ohio 45040.
Or you can visit our Internet site at:
http://www.swcollege.com

ALL RIGHTS RESERVED.
No part of this work covered by the copyright hereon may be reproduced or used in any form or by any means—graphic, electronic, or mechanical, including photocopying, recording, taping, Web distribution or information storage and retrieval systems—without the written permission of the publisher.

For permission to use material from this text or product, contact us by
Tel (800) 730-2214
Fax (800) 730-2215
http://www.thomsonrights.com

Library of Congress Cataloging-in-Publication Data

West's federal tax research/William A. Raabe ... [et al.].—6th ed.
   p. cm.
Includes index.
ISBN 0-324-12385-X (hardcover)
   1. Taxation—Law and legislation—United States—Legal research. I. Raabe, William A.

KF241.T38 W47 2003
343.7304'072—dc21   2001055066

This book is dedicated to our parents

William A. and Shirley Raabe
Irene M. Whittenburg
Dola and Jack Cairo
Warren L. and Sara L. Bost

who first taught us to respect and question authority

About the Authors

William A. Raabe, PhD, CPA, is the founding Dean of the Capital University (OH) School of Management. He is a leader among business school tax faculty in incorporating developments in technology into curricula for the educational development of tax professionals.

Dr. Raabe's teaching and research interests focus on multijurisdictional taxation and financial planning, and he is recognized as the leader among business-school academics in the fields of state and local income, sales, and property taxation. Dr. Raabe is the author or editor of approximately twenty book titles, including *West Federal Taxation,* and the *Multistate Corporate Tax Guide.* He has received university-wide recognition as the winner of the AMOCO Foundation Award for Teaching Excellence, and the Wisconsin Institute of CPAs named him the Educator of the Year.

Gerald E. Whittenburg, PhD, CPA, EA, is a Professor in the School of Accountancy at San Diego State University. A graduate of the University of Houston, Dr. Whittenburg's teaching and research interests include individual and corporate taxation, pension plans, and tax research methodology.

Dr. Whittenburg is also an author of *West's Income Tax Fundamentals.* In addition, he has published articles in journals such as *Advances in Taxation, Practical Tax Strategies, Taxes—The Tax Magazine, Journal of Taxation of Investments, Journal of Taxation of Employee Benefits, Journal of Taxation of Financial Institutions, Valuation Strategies, Journal of Small Business Strategy, The Tax Adviser,* and *Journal of Accounting Education.* Professor Whittenburg's professional designations include Certified Public Accountant (CPA) and Enrolled Agent (EA). He has received numerous teaching awards, including the Trustee's Outstanding Faculty Award for the entire California State University System. Recently, Dr. Whittenburg spent a sabbatical at the University of Adelaide in Australia. In his picture, he is shown with "Pumpkin" the koala.

About the Authors

Debra L. Sanders, PhD, CPA, is a professor in the Washington State University School of Accounting, Information Systems and Business Law. She has received numerous awards for outstanding teaching, research, and service including the Boeing Distinguished Faculty Research Award, the Shell Corporation Outstanding Teacher Award, and the College of Business and Economics Outstanding Service Award.

Dr. Sanders, a graduate of Arizona State University, publishes in both academic and professional journals. Her work has appeared in the academic journals *Behavioral Research in Accounting, National Tax Journal, The Journal of the American Taxation Association, Advances in Taxation,* and *The International Journal of Accounting.* Professional journals that have published her articles include *Taxation for Accountants, Taxation for Lawyers, The Review of Taxation of Individuals, Taxes, The Tax Adviser, and Journal of Financial Planning.*

Brief Contents

PART 1
The Tax Research Environment 1

1. Introduction to Tax Practice 2
2. Tax Research Methodology 35

PART 2
Primary Sources of Federal Tax Law 63

3. Constitutional and Legislative Sources 64
4. Administrative Regulations and Rulings 91
5. Judicial Interpretations 117

PART 3
Computer Research Tools 151

6. Electronic and Printed Tax Services 152
7. Electronic and Printed Legal Services 199
8. Citators and Other Finding Devices 239
9. Journals, Newsletters, and Internet News Sources 277

PART 4
Implementing the Research Tools 313

10. Communicating Research Results 314
11. Tax Planning 339
12. Working with the IRS 364
13. Tax Practice and Administration: Sanctions, Agreements, and Disclosures 392

Appendix A: Time Value of Money Tables 436

Appendix B: Standard Tax Citations 440

Appendix C: IRS Circular 230 444

Glossary 483

Index 497

Contents

Preface xiv

Part 1: The Tax Research Environment 1

1: Introduction to Tax Practice 2

Elements of Tax Practice 3
Tax Compliance 3 | Tax Planning 4 | Tax Litigation 4 | Tax Research 4

Rules and Ethics in Tax Practice 5
Circular 230 5 | AICPA Code of Professional Conduct 10 | Statements on Standards for Tax Services 15 | ABA Model Code of Professional Responsibility 19

Nonregulatory Ethics 20
Morality 21 | Social Responsibility 21 | Business Ethics 21 | Other Ethical Standards 22

Tax Research by Certified Public Accountants 23
Historical Developments 24 | CPAs and Other Nonattorneys 25

Summary 26 | Tax Tutor 26 | Key Words 26 | Discussion Questions 26 | Exercises 29 | Research Cases 32

2: Tax Research Methodology 35

Outline of the Tax Research Process 36

Step 1: Establish the Facts 36 | Step 2: Identify the Issues 38 | Step 3: Locate Authority 41 | Step 4: Evaluate Authority 44 | Step 5: Develop Conclusions and Recommendations 44 | Step 6: Communicate the Recommendations 44

Overview of Computerized Tax Research 45
Online and CD-ROM Systems 46 | Benefits of Using a Computerized Tax Service 46 | Factors in Choosing a Computerized Tax Service 49 | Using a Computer in Tax Research 50 | Step 1: State the Issue as a Question 50 | Step 2: Identify the Keywords 51 | Step 3: Construct a Computer Research Query 51 | Step 4: Select a Database and Execute the Search 52 | Step 5: Interpret and Refine the Search 52 | IRS Web Site Research 53

Summary 53 | Tax Tutor 54 | Key Words 54 | Discussion Questions 55 | Exercises 57 | Research Cases 60

Part 2: Primary Sources of Federal Tax Law 63

3: Constitutional and Legislative Sources 64

Sources of Federal Tax Law 65

History of U.S. Taxation 65

U.S. Constitution 67

Tax Treaties 67

The Legislative Process 70
Where to Find Committee Reports 73

***Internal Revenue Code* 74**
Organization of the Internal Revenue Code 75 | Where to Find the Internal Revenue Code 78

Interpreting the *Internal Revenue Code* 80

Summary 84 | Tax Tutor 84 | Key Words 84 | Discussion Questions 84 | Exercises 85 | Research Cases 88

4: Administrative Regulations and Rulings 91

Regulations 92
Temporary Regulations 93 | Effective Date of Regulations 94 | Citing a Regulation 94 | Assessing Regulations 95 | Locating Regulations 96

Revenue Rulings 96
Revenue Ruling Citations 97 | Locating Revenue Rulings 99

Revenue Procedures 99

Letter Rulings 101

Private Letter Rulings 101 | Technical Advice Memoranda 102 | Determination Letters 102 | Public Inspection of Written Determinations 103 | Written Determination Numbering System 103 | Locating Written Determinations 104

Other IRS Pronouncements 104
Acquiescences and Nonacquiescences 104 | *Internal Revenue Bulletin* 105 | *Bulletin Index-Digest System* 105 | Chief Counsel Memoranda 107 | Announcements and Notices 108 | Miscellaneous Publications 108

Summary 110 | Tax Tutor 110 | Key Words 110 | Discussion Questions 111 | Exercises 113 | Research Cases 115

5: Judicial Interpretations 117

Federal Court System 118
Legal Conventions 119 | Tax Court 121 | District Courts 130 | Court of Federal Claims 131 | Court of Appeals 132 | Supreme Court 134

Case Briefs 136

The Internet and Judicial Sources 139
Computer Tax Service Example 139

Summary 139 | Tax Tutor 141 | Key Words 143 | Discussion Questions 143 | Exercises 145 | Research Cases 146

Part 3: Computer Research Tools 151

6: Electronic and Printed Tax Services 152

Published Versus Electronic 153
Currency 154 | Accessing Information 154

Computer Services 155

The Research Process 155
Illustrative Example 155 | Approaching the Research Problem 156 | Assessing Computerized Tax Information 156

RIA Checkpoint 157
Keyword Search 158 | Cite Search 161 | Contents Search 165

CCH Tax Research Network 167
Keyword Search 167 | Cite and Contents Searches 169 | State Tax Search 170

Kleinrock 171

Published Services 176

Annotated Services 176

Entering Compilation Volumes 176 | Keyword Search 178 | Code Section Search 180 | Case Name Search 183 | Other Pathways into the Compilations 184 | CCH Annotated Service 185 | RIA Compilations 187

Topical Services 187
Nature of Topical Tax Services 188 | RIA *Coordinator* and *Analysis* 189

Summary 190 | Tax Tutor 191 | Key Words 192 | Discussion Questions 192 | Exercises 194 | Research Cases 196 | Extensive Case 198

7: Electronic and Printed Legal Services 199

Lexis 200
Selecting and Searching a Database 200 | Documents 202 | Academic Universe 205

BNA 205
Portfolios 207 | Other Tax Products 209

Tax Analysts 212
TaxBase 213 | Other Tax Products 214

Westlaw 217
Data and Access 218 | Searching Westlaw 219 | State Searches 222

Other Legal Services 224
Mertens Service 225 | Bittker & Lokken Service 226

Internet Sites 227

Summary 228 | Tax Tutor 229 | Key Words 229 | Discussion Questions 229 | Exercises 230 | Research Cases 234 | Advanced Cases 236 | Extensive Case 237

8: Citators and Other Finding Devices 239

Basic Research Goals 240

Citators 240
What Is a Citator? 241 | Commercial Citators 242 | *RIA Citators* 243 | *CCH Citator* 253 | Shepard's and Lexis Citation Services 258 | Westlaw Citator System 264

Summary 268 | Tax Tutor 269 | Key Words 269 | Discussion Questions 270 | Exercises 271 | Research Cases 275

9: Journals, Newsletters, and Internet News Sources 277

Nature of Tax and Law Periodicals 278

Citing Print and Electronic Articles 278

Types of Tax Periodicals 279

Annual Proceedings 279 | Scholarly Reviews 281 | Professional Tax Journals 282 | Tax Newsletters 283

Locating Relevant Tax Articles 293
CCH *Federal Tax Articles* 293 | WG&L *Index to Federal Tax Articles* 294 | Shepard's Indexes 297 | LexisNexis Academic Universe 297 | Other Law and Accounting Indexes 300 | General Indexes 301 | Other Resources 302

Internet Sites 303

Summary 303 | Tax Tutor 303 | Key Words 304 | Discussion Questions 305 | Exercises 306 | Research Cases 310

Part 4: Implementing the Research Tools 313

10: Communicating Research Results 314

Communications and the Tax Professional 315

The Heart of Tax Research Communication: The File Memo 317

Evaluating the Sources of Law 320

Client Letters 322

Comprehensive Illustration of Client File 324

Oral Presentations of Research Results 328

Summary 332 | Tax Tutor 333 | Key Words 333 | Tax Research Assignments 333 | Problems 334 | Research Cases 336 | Advanced Cases 337

11: Tax Planning 339

Economics of Tax Planning, Avoidance, and Evasion 340

Tax Rate Terminology 342
Tax Base 342 | Tax Rates 343

Tax Planning in Perspective 345

Fundamentals of Tax Planning 346
Avoiding Income Recognition 348 | Postponing Income Recognition 349 | Changing Tax Jurisdictions 350 | Controlling Classification of Income 351 | Spreading Income Among Related Taxpayers 351

Departing from the Fundamentals 352

Exploiting Inconsistencies in the Statute 353
Inconsistencies between Transactions 353 | Inconsistencies between Taxpayers 353 | Inconsistencies between Years 354

Avoiding Tax Traps 355
Statutory Tax Traps 355 | Judicial Tax Traps 356

Tax Planning Illustrations 358

Summary 359 | Tax Tutor 360 | Key Words 360 | Exercises 360 | Problems 361 | Extended Cases 362

12: Working with the IRS 364

Organization of the Internal Revenue Service 365
IRS National Office 366 | IRS Service Centers 367 | Taxpayer Assistance Orders 368 | Local Taxpayer Advocates 369

Taxpayer Rights 369

The Audit Process 372
Preliminary Review of Returns 373 | Selection of Returns for Examination 374

Examinations 377
Correspondence Examinations 377 | Office Examinations 379 | Field Examinations 379 | Dealing with an Auditor 380 | Conclusion of Examination 381 | Thirty-Day Letter 381 | File a Protest or Go Straight to Court? 382

The Appeals Process 382
Appeals Conference 383 | Ninety-Day Letter 383 | Entering the Judicial System 384

Summary 385 | Tax Tutor 385 | Key Words 389 | Discussion Questions 389 | Exercises 390 | Problems 391

13: Tax Practice and Administration: Sanctions, Agreements, and Disclosures 392

Taxpayer Penalties 393
Civil Penalties 394 | Criminal Penalties 403

Penalties on Return Preparers 405
Definition of Return Preparer 405 | Definition of Return Preparation 406 | Preparer Disclosure Penalties 406 | Preparer Conduct Penalties 407

Injunctions 413
Action to Enjoin Income Tax Return Preparers 413 | Action to Enjoin Promoters of Abusive Tax Shelters 413

Interest 413
Interest-Computation Conventions 413 | Applicable Interest Rate 417

Statutes of Limitations 417
Nature of Statutes of Limitations 417 | Assessment 417 | Collection 419 | Claim for Refund or Credit 419 | Suspension of Period of Assessment and Collection 421 | Mitigation of Statute of Limitations 422

Statutory Agreements 422
Closing Agreements 422 | Offers in Compromise 423

Summary 425 | Tax Tutor 425 | Key Words 425 | Discussion Questions 427 | Exercises 428 | Problems 430 | Research Cases 432

Appendix A: Time Value of Money Tables 436

Appendix B: Standard Tax Citations 440

Appendix C: IRS Circular 230 444

Glossary 483

Index 497

Preface

We are pleased to offer the sixth edition of this popular text, which has been prepared as a comprehensive, stand-alone reference tool for the reader who wishes to become proficient in the practice of Federal tax research. It is written for readers who are familiar with the fundamentals of the Federal income and transfer tax law, at a level that typically is achieved on the completion of two comprehensive introductory courses in taxation in either (1) the accounting program in a business school or (2) second- or third-year courses in a law school.

Accordingly, the text is most appropriate for (1) upper-level accounting students in a business school (i.e., seniors in a four-year program or those in the fifth year of a 150-hour program) who desire additional information concerning the practice of taxation; (2) those who are enrolled in a nontax graduate program in business administration (e.g., an MBA or MS—management program) and would like further practical training in the functions of taxation in today's business environment; (3) second- or third-year law school students, especially those who desire a more detailed and pragmatic introduction to a specialized tax practice; (4) those who are commencing a graduate degree program in taxation, in either a business school or a law school, and require a varied and sophisticated introduction to the procedures of tax research and to the routine functions and implications of a tax practice; and (5) practicing accountants and attorneys who need an introduction, updating, or refresher relative to tax practice and research as an element of their career paths.

STRUCTURE AND PEDAGOGY

Sensing that existing textbooks too often ignore the detailed, pragmatic approach that today's students require in developing effective and efficient tax research skills, the authors have employed an unprecedented degree of "hands-on" tax research analysis throughout the text. This book does not stop, as do so many others, with a discussion of tax research procedures or of the sources of the Federal tax law; nor does it try to satisfy with a mere sampling of the pertinent tax reference materials. Rather, its pedagogy reflects the authors' conviction that the reader must be engaged in a series of exercises that require individualized experience with the most important elements of the Federal tax law.

This conviction is evident in the most important aspects of the structure of the book.

- An extremely readable style encourages the student to complete and understand even the most complex aspects of tax research and practice.
- Hundreds of exercises and discussion questions are provided that require the reader personally to explore the reference materials of the well-developed tax library in developing solutions. Responding to requests from our audience, several Extended Research Cases are new to this edition.
- TAX TUTOR—online tutorials located under student resources at the web site **http://raabe.swcollege.com** reinforce the tax research information covered in each chapter.
- Assignments require the reader to construct case briefs, file memos, client letters, and other elements of a comprehensive client file.
- Hundreds of pages of reproductions and illustrations have been excerpted from the most important tax reference materials.
- Summary charts, diagrams, and other study aids are interspersed throughout the text that summarize the elements of the primary and secondary sources of the Federal tax law and allow for development of the reader's own research routines and techniques.
- A serious review of state and local tax research opportunities is provided, reflecting the importance of this type of tax work in today's practice.
- An extensive introduction is provided that details the necessary aspects of tax practice, including preparer penalties, statutes of limitation, interest conventions, and return selection for IRS audit.
- A tax planning orientation to tax practice is developed in a manner that is unequaled in other texts of this sort.
- Attention is paid to other developments that affect those who conduct tax research, including revisions to codes of ethics, IRS organizational structure and enforcement functions, and other principles that control tax practice.

COMPUTER ORIENTATION

The unprecedented coverage in earlier editions of this text relative to the computer-oriented tools available to tax researchers was extremely well received. Accordingly, and in light of the growing importance of these tools for the practitioner, the discussion of such materials has been expanded yet again in this edition, and now perhaps exceeds our discussions of the traditional paper-based resources. This orientation is demanded by our audience, and it remains the greatest innovation of this text to the tax literature. Our extensive review involves a close look at Internet and CD-ROM-based research and other developments that have extended the boundaries of tax research.

USING THE TEXT

Although various instructors may wish to alter the specific sequence in which the chapters of the text are examined, several comments relative to the effective use of the book are in order.

The text's exercises, cases, and advanced cases offer enough variety in both difficulty and subject matter that they may be assigned to individual readers, or to student groups of two or three, for their optimal use. The instructor also should consider giving each student in the course a different research case to complete, thereby both discouraging joint work and reducing the strain on the pertinent library resources.

Given both the nature of the tax research process and the limited tax library resources that are available to most firms and universities, the instructor must take care (1) to assign discussion materials for which the necessary resources are available and (2) to work through the assignment him- or herself, to ascertain that one's target solution to the assignment reflects the very latest in the development of the Federal tax law.

Deliberation relative to several of the research cases could be delayed until the discussion concerning a specific electronic research service, which will provide additional illustrations. Alternatively, the reader could be encouraged to rework a previous assignment once the computerized tax reference tools have been introduced.

Other pedagogical support for the text will help to maintain this text's preeminence in providing instructors with teaching tools that assist in delivering this difficult course.

- Up-to-date solutions to the various chapter-end questions, exercises, cases, and advanced cases.
- Lecture notes and outlines, augmented by professional-quality transparency masters.
- An extensive test bank and an expanded set of in-class quizzes for use in classroom discussion.
- PowerPoint slides, tax links, and updated material provided at the text's home page **(http://raabe.swcollege.com)** on the Web.
- Access to thousands of primary source documents on RIA Checkpoint that accompanies the text.
- An Instructor's Resource CD-ROM (ISBN 0-324-12389-2) contains the Instructor's Manual, Solutions Manual, Test Bank, and E-Lectures.

ACKNOWLEDGEMENTS AND THANKS

The authors welcome your comments and suggestions for further improvements to this text. Please feel free to use the following addresses to convey these remarks.

William A. Raabe
Dean, School of Management
Capital University
Bexley, OH 43209
(614) 236-6510
E-mail: wraabe@capital.edu

Gerald E. Whittenburg
San Diego State University
San Diego, CA 92182-8221
E-mail: gwhitten@mail.sdsu.edu

Debra L. Sanders
Department of Accounting and Business Law
Washington State University
Pullman, WA 99164-4729
E-mail: dsanders@wsu.edu

The authors are grateful to the many instructors and students who assisted in the development of this text, both by their use thereof and by their resulting constructive criticisms. In addition, we have benefited from the contributions of the professional reviewers of the text, listed below, for their numerous contributions of both substance and style. Any errors, of course, are the sole responsibilities of the authors.

Glenn S. Freed,
University of Alabama at Birmingham

Roger L. Lirely,
Western Carolina University

Frank M. Messina,
University of Alabama at Birmingham

Janet Trewin,
Drexel University

Donald T. Williamson,
American University

William A. Raabe
Gerald E. Whittenburg
Debra L. Sanders
John C. Bost

Part 1

The Tax Research Environment

Chapter 1: Introduction to Tax Practice

Chapter 2: Tax Research Methodology

1

Introduction to Tax Practice

LEARNING OBJECTIVES

- Describe the elements of modern tax practice in the United States
- Distinguish between open and closed transactions
- Identify sources of legal and ethical standards that guide those who engage in tax practice
- Examine in detail the major collections of ethical standards that bear upon tax practitioners today
- Place tax issues in a broader context of ethics and morality
- Understand the limitations on tax research by CPAs and other nonattorneys

CHAPTER OUTLINE

Elements of Tax Practice
  Tax Compliance
  Tax Planning
  Tax Litigation
  Tax Research
Rules and Ethics in Tax Practice
  Circular 230
    Who May Practice
    Enrolled Agents
    Limited Practice without Enrollment
    Tax Return Preparers
    Conduct before the IRS
    Due Diligence
    Contingent and Unconscionable Fees
    Solicitation and Advertising
    Tax Return Positions
  AICPA Code of Professional Conduct
    Independence
    Integrity and Objectivity
    General Standards
    Compliance with Standards
    Accounting Principles
    Confidential Client Information
    Contingent Fees
    Acts Discreditable
    Advertising and Other Forms of Solicitation
    Commissions and Referral Fees
    Form of Organization and Name
  Statements on Standards for Tax Services
    Tax Return Positions
    Answers to Questions on Returns
    Certain Procedural Aspects of Preparing Returns
    Use of Estimates
    Departure from a Position Previously Concluded in an Administrative Proceeding or Court Decision
    Knowledge of Error: Return Preparation
    Knowledge of Error: Administrative Proceedings
    Form and Content of Advice to Taxpayers
  ABA Model Code of Professional Responsibility
Nonregulatory Ethics
  Morality
  Social Responsibility
  Business Ethics
  Other Ethical Standards
Tax Research by Certified Public Accountants
  Historical Developments
  CPAs and Other Nonattorneys

Chapter 1 Introduction to Tax Practice

In simple terms, taxation is the process of collecting revenue from citizens to finance government activities. In a modern technological society such as that of the United States, however, taxation comprises an interaction among several disciplines that is far from simple. The tax system is derived from law, accounting, economics, political science, and sociology (Exhibit 1–1). Principles of economics, sociology, and political science provide the environment, while law and accounting precepts are applied in a typical tax practice.

Tax policy questions concerning the effects that a specified tax law change will have on economic growth, the effects of projected inflation on the implementation of the tax law and vice versa, and the effects of the tax law on the United States' balance of payments are addressed by economists. Political scientists, economists, and sociologists, alternatively, examine issues such as who bears the ultimate burden of a tax, how a tax bill becomes law (including practical effects of the legislative process), the social equity of a tax, and whether a tax is discriminatory. Attorneys interpret (and often create) taxation statutes, and accountants apply the tax laws to current or prospective economic transactions.

ELEMENTS OF TAX PRACTICE

The tax laws of a democratic country such as the United States are created by a political process. In recent years, the result of this political process has been a law that levies taxes on income, sales, estates, gifts, and other items that usually are reflected by the accounting process. Thus, tax practice can be described as the application of tax legislation to specific accounting situations. The elements of modern tax practice can be separated into four (admittedly overlapping) categories: compliance, planning, litigation, and research.

Tax Compliance

In general, **tax compliance** consists of the gathering of pertinent information, evaluation and classification of such information, and the filing of necessary tax returns. Tax compliance also includes other functions necessary to satisfy government requirements, such as representation at a client's Internal Revenue Service (IRS) audit. Commercial tax preparers, enrolled agents, attorneys, and certified public accountants

Exhibit 1–1
Elements of Taxation

(CPAs) all perform tax compliance to some extent. Noncomplex individual, partnership, and corporate tax returns often are completed by commercial tax preparers. Enrolled agents, attorneys, and CPAs usually are involved in the preparation of more complex tax returns; in addition, they provide tax planning services and represent their clients before the IRS. The elements of tax compliance and administration are examined in more detail in later chapters.

TAX PLANNING

Tax planning is the process of arranging one's financial affairs to optimize tax liabilities. There is nothing inherently illegal or immoral in the avoidance of taxation according to the tax system's rules. The eminent jurist Learned Hand best expressed this doctrine in the dissenting opinion of *Commissioner v. Newman*, 159 F.2d 848 (CA-2, 1947):

> *Over and over again, courts have said that there is nothing sinister in so arranging one's affairs as to keep taxes as low as possible. Everybody does so, rich or poor, and all do right, for nobody owes any public duty to pay more than the law demands: taxes are enforced extractions, not voluntary contributions.*

However, whereas **tax avoidance** is the legitimate object of much of modern tax practice, **tax evasion** constitutes the illegal nonpayment of a tax and cannot be condoned. Fraudulent acts of this sort are unrelated to the professional practice of tax planning.

Tax planning can be divided into two major categories: **open transactions** and **closed transactions.** In an open transaction, the tax practitioner maintains some degree of control over the attendant tax liability because the transaction is not yet completed; for example, the title to an asset that has not yet passed. If desired, some modifications to an incomplete transaction can be made to receive more favorable tax treatment. In a closed transaction, however, all of the pertinent actions have been completed; therefore, tax planning may be limited to the presentation of the facts to the government in the most favorable, legally acceptable manner possible.

In recent years, the use of computers has greatly enhanced tax planning. By using electronic spreadsheets and other programs, the tax practitioner can perform a "what if" sensitivity analysis of an open-fact transaction.

TAX LITIGATION

A specialized area within the practice of law is the concentration on **tax litigation.** Litigation is the process of settling a dispute with another party (here, usually the IRS) in a court of law (here, a Federal court). Typically, a tax attorney handles tax litigation that progresses beyond the initial appeal of an IRS audit result. Accountants and other financial advisors can also serve in a support capacity. Later chapters contain additional discussions of the various opportunities and strategies available in tax litigation.

TAX RESEARCH

Tax research is undertaken to answer taxation questions. The tax research process includes the (1) identification of pertinent issues, (2) determination of proper authorities, (3) evaluation of the appropriateness of these authorities, and (4) application of these authorities to specific facts. Tax research techniques are examined in Chapters 2 through 10 of this text.

RULES AND ETHICS IN TAX PRACTICE

A person who prepares tax returns for monetary or other compensation, or who is licensed to practice in the tax-related professions, is subject to various statutes, rules, and codes of professional conduct. All tax practitioners are regulated by ***Circular 230, Regulations Governing the Practice of Attorneys, Certified Public Accountants, Enrolled Agents, Enrolled Actuaries, and Appraisers before the Internal Revenue Service***. The ethical conduct of an attorney is also governed by the laws of the state(s) in which he or she is licensed to practice. Most states have adopted, often with some modification, guidelines that are based on the **American Bar Association (ABA)** *Model Code of Professional Responsibility* or the newer ABA *Model Rules of Professional Conduct*. CPAs who are members of the **American Institute of Certified Public Accountants (AICPA)** must follow its *Code of Professional Conduct* and any other rules generated by the state board(s) of accountancy. The AICPA has also produced a series of *Statements on Standards for Tax Services*, which contain advisory guidelines for CPAs who prepare tax returns.

Although CPAs who are not members of the AICPA are not bound by the *Code of Professional Conduct* and the *Statements on Standards for Tax Services*, those rules and standards are a useful source of guidance for all members of the profession. Statutory tax law also specifies certain penalties and other rules of conduct that apply to everyone (e.g., attorneys, CPAs, and enrolled agents) in addition to their respective professional standards, and also to commercial tax preparers who are not attorneys, CPAs, or enrolled agents. Chapter 13 addresses these rules. The basic sources of rules and ethics for tax practitioners are summarized in Exhibit 1–2.

CIRCULAR 230

Circular 230, which constitutes Part 31 of the Treasury Department Regulations, is designed to provide protection to taxpayers and the IRS by requiring tax preparers

Exhibit 1–2 Sources of Rules and Ethics for Tax Practitioners

Source	Issued By	Binding Upon
ABA Model Code of Professional Responsibility	American Bar Association	Attorneys at law
AICPA Code of Professional Conduct	American Institute of CPAs	Certified public accountants who are AICPA members
Circular 230	Internal Revenue Service	Those in practice before the IRS
Statements on Standards for Tax Services	American Institute of CPAs	Certified public accountants who are AICPA members
Internal Revenue Code	U.S. Congress	Tax preparers

to be technically competent and to adhere to ethical standards. *Circular 230* contains the following definition of **practice before the IRS** in Section 10.2 of Subpart A.

> *... matters connected with presentation to the Internal Revenue Service or any of its officers or employees relating to a client's rights, privileges, or liabilities under laws or regulations administered by the Internal Revenue Service. Such presentations include the preparation and filing of necessary documents, correspondence with and communications to the Internal Revenue Service, and the representation of a client at conferences, hearings and meetings.*

Under this definition, practice before the IRS consists primarily of the representation of clients during audit procedures, such as a meeting with a revenue agent on behalf of a client to establish the correctness of a taxpayer's return. The preparation of tax returns or the furnishing of information to the IRS in response to a request for such information is not considered practice before the IRS. (Tax return preparation rules are addressed by various statutes discussed in Chapter 13.) *Circular 230* also states who may conduct such a practice and sets forth the disciplinary procedures that apply.

Who May Practice

Under Section 10.3, Subpart A, of *Circular 230,* the following individuals may practice before the IRS.

1. Attorneys
2. Certified public accountants
3. Enrolled agents
4. Enrolled actuaries

To qualify under this rule, an attorney must be a member in good standing of the bar of the highest court in any state, possession, territory, commonwealth, or the District of Columbia. Likewise, CPAs and enrolled actuaries must be qualified to practice in any state, possession, territory, commonwealth, or the District of Columbia. No further substantive examination is required.

Enrolled Agents

Individuals who are not attorneys or certified public accountants can qualify to practice before the Internal Revenue Service by becoming an enrolled agent (EA). An **enrolled agent** is someone who has either passed a special Internal Revenue Service examination (currently given once a year, in October) or worked for the IRS for five years. The procedures for becoming an enrolled agent are detailed in *Circular 230,* Subpart A, § 10.4, § 10.5, and § 10.6. Enrolled agents have the same rights as attorneys and certified public accountants to represent clients before the Internal Revenue Service. Under *Circular 230,* an enrolled agent must renew his or her enrollment card on a three-year cycle. For each enrollment cycle, enrolled agents, like attorneys and CPAs, must meet certain continuing education requirements as defined in Subpart A, § 10.6. For an EA's enrollment card to be renewed, he or she must complete seventy-two hours (i.e., an average of twenty-four hours per year) of qualifying continuing education for each three-year enrollment period. In addition, a minimum of sixteen hours of continuing education credit must be completed during each year of an enrollment cycle. Subpart A, § 10.6(f) defines what qualifies as continuing education for enrolled agents.

Circular 230 allows an individual to be an attorney or CPA and an enrolled agent simultaneously. Being both an EA and an attorney or CPA might be useful to certain tax practitioners who practice across state lines. For example, a CPA in Texas who is also an enrolled agent can practice in any state. The enrolled agent's card is effectively a national license to practice before the Internal Revenue Service anywhere in the United States (including territories). In addition, most state taxing agencies grant an enrolled agent the right to practice before that state agency.

Limited Practice without Enrollment

In *Circular 230,* the Internal Revenue Service has authorized certain individuals to practice without being an attorney, CPA, or enrolled agent. Individuals (with proper identification) can represent themselves under § 10.7(a) and participate in Internal Revenue Service rule making as provided for under § 10.7(b). In addition, under § 10.7(c), individuals (with proper identification and authorization, IRS Form 2848) are allowed to represent taxpayers in the following special situations.

1. An individual may represent a member of his or her immediate family.
2. A regular full-time employee of an individual employer may represent the employer.
3. A general partner or regular full-time employee of a partnership may represent the partnership.
4. A bona fide officer or regular full-time employee of a corporation (including a parent, subsidiary, or other affiliated corporation), an association, or organized group may represent the corporation, association, or organized group.
5. A trustee, receiver, guardian, personal representative, administrator, executor, or regular full-time employee of a trust, receivership, guardianship, or estate may represent the trust, receivership, guardianship, or estate.
6. An officer or regular employee of a governmental unit, agency, or authority may represent the governmental unit, agency, or authority in the course of his or her official duties.
7. An individual may represent any individual or entity before personnel of the Internal Revenue Service who are outside the United States.

Tax Return Preparers

Any person who signs a tax return as having prepared it for a taxpayer is authorized to conduct "limited practice" before the Internal Revenue Service (with proper taxpayer authorization) under § 10.7(c)(viii). *Circular 230* requires that such person must not be disbarred or suspended from practice before the Internal Revenue Service or his or her profession. A tax return preparer can make an appearance as the taxpayer's representative only before the Examination Division of the IRS. A return preparer may not represent a taxpayer before any other Internal Revenue Service division, including the Appeals and Collection Divisions [IRS Publication 947]. In addition, the following actions are outside the authority of an unenrolled preparer [Rev. Proc. 81-38, 1981-1 C.B. 386].

1. Executing a claim for refund for the taxpayer
2. Receiving checks in payment of any refund of taxes, penalties, or interest for the taxpayer
3. Agreeing to later assessment or collection of taxes than is provided for by the applicable statute of limitations

4. Executing closing agreements with respect to tax liability or other specific matters for the taxpayer
5. Executing waivers of restriction on assessment or collection of a tax deficiency

Conduct before the IRS

Subpart B of *Circular 230* provides the rules of conduct for those individuals authorized to practice before the Internal Revenue Service. Attorneys, CPAs, and enrolled agents must observe the following rules of conduct when practicing before the IRS.

1. A tax practitioner must furnish information, on request, to any authorized agent of the Internal Revenue Service, unless the practitioner has reason to believe that the request is of doubtful legality or the information is privileged [§ 10.20(a)].
2. A tax practitioner must provide the Director of Practice of the IRS, on request, any information concerning the violation of any regulation pertaining to practice before the Internal Revenue Service. The tax practitioner must testify in a disbarment or suspension proceeding, unless there is reason to doubt the legality of the request or the information is privileged [§ 10.20(b)].
3. A tax practitioner who knows of client noncompliance, error, or omission with regard to the tax laws must advise the client of that noncompliance, error, or omission [§ 10.21].
4. A tax practitioner must exercise due diligence in preparing tax returns and other documents submitted to the Internal Revenue Service [§ 10.22].
5. Practitioners must not unreasonably delay matters before the Internal Revenue Service [§ 10.23].
6. Practitioners must not accept assistance from or employ a disbarred or suspended person or a former Internal Revenue Service employee disqualified from practice under another rule or U.S. law [§ 10.24].
7. Partners of government employees cannot represent anyone for which the government employee-partner has (or has had) official responsibility [§ 10.25]. For example, a CPA firm with an IRS agent as a partner cannot represent any taxpayer that is (or was in the past) assigned to the IRS agent/partner.
8. No former government employee shall, subsequent to his or her government employment, represent anyone in any matter administered by the Internal Revenue Service if such representation would violate other U.S. laws [§ 10.26].
9. No tax practitioner may act as a notary public for his or her clients [§ 10.27].
10. Fees for tax work must not be contingent or unconscionable [§ 10.28], and a practitioner must not negotiate a taxpayer's refund check [§ 10.31].
11. No tax practitioner can represent conflicting interests before the Internal Revenue Service unless he or she has the express consent of the directly interested parties [§ 10.29].
12. Tax practitioners who issue tax shelter opinion letters must comply with the complex requirements of § 10.33 of *Circular 230*.

Due Diligence

Section 10.22 of *Circular 230* requires tax practitioners to use due diligence in preparing tax returns and in their practice before the IRS. Due diligence is not defined in *Circular 230*. However, the Second Circuit in *Harary v. Blumenthal*, 555 F.2d 1113 (CA-2, 1977), has held that due diligence requires that the tax practitioner be honest with his or her client in connection with all IRS-related matters. In the view of the IRS, the failure to exercise due diligence involves conduct that is more than a simple error, but less than willful and reckless misconduct (*Coursebook Training 994-102,* IRS, December 1992). In determining if a practitioner has exercised due diligence, the IRS uses several factors, including the nature of the error, the explanation of the error, and other standards that apply (for example, the AICPA *Statements on Standards for Tax Services* that are discussed later in this chapter). In essence, due diligence means a tax practitioner should use reasonable effort to comply with the tax laws.

Example 1–1 Judy is a CPA who fails to include rental income on a tax return she completed for a client. The omitted rental income was from a new rental property purchased by the client this year and therefore had not been reported on prior years' tax returns. The taxpayer did not mention the new rental property to Judy in any communications with her. Under these circumstances, Judy has exercised due diligence in preparing the tax return. However, if Judy also kept the rental income records for the new rental property and still omitted the income from the tax return, she would not be exercising due diligence.

Contingent and Unconscionable Fees

Tax practitioners are prohibited from charging **contingent fees** on an original tax return by § 10.28(b) of *Circular 230*. Examples of contingent fees include a fee that is based on a percentage of the refund on a tax return or a fee that is a percentage of tax "saved." Although contingent fees are prohibited for the preparation of an original return, a practitioner may charge a contingent fee for an amended return or a claim for refund (other than a claim for refund made on an original return). The tax practitioner must reasonably anticipate, at the time of the fee arrangement, that the amended return will receive a substantive review by the IRS.

Example 1–2 Oak Corporation has been audited by the IRS for its tax return filed two years ago. The controller of the company completed the original return. The IRS is asserting that Oak underpaid its taxes by $100,000. Oak contacted Joe, a CPA, and engaged him to handle the appeals process with the IRS. In this situation, Joe can use a contingent fee arrangement. (For instance, Joe's fee could be 30 percent of any amount by which he could get the IRS to reduce the assessment.)

Section 10.28(a) also prohibits a tax practitioner from charging an unconscionable fee. This term is not defined in *Circular 230*. If a tax practitioner charges a fee that is out of line with some measure of the value of the service provided to a client, then the fee would be unconscionable. For example, a CPA could not charge a fee of $10,000 to an unsophisticated taxpayer (such as an elderly person) for simple tax work that most CPAs would complete for less than $500.

Solicitation and Advertising

An attorney, CPA, or enrolled agent may use public communication to obtain clients under § 10.30 of Subpart B. Types of public communication allowed by this provision include billboards, telephone books, and advertisements in newspapers, on radio, and on television. However, such public communications must not contain false, fraudulent, unduly influencing, coercive, or unfair statements or claims. If done in a dignified manner, examples of items that a practitioner may communicate to the public include (1) his or her name, address, and telephone number, (2) names of individuals associated with the practitioner, (3) a factual description of services offered, (4) credit cards accepted, (5) foreign language ability, (6) membership in professional organizations, (7) professional licenses held, and (8) a statement of practice limitations. Attorneys, CPAs, and enrolled agents also must observe any applicable standards of ethical conduct adopted by the American Bar Association (ABA), the American Institute of CPAs (AICPA), and the National Association of Enrolled Agents (NAEA).

Tax Return Positions

Tax practitioners under *Circular 230* must meet certain standards with respect to advice given to clients on tax return positions. Under § 10.34, a practitioner must not sign a tax return if he or she determines that the return contains a position that does not have a **realistic possibility** of being sustained on its merits if challenged by the Internal Revenue Service. The realistic possibility standard is met if analysis of the tax return position by a reasonable and well-informed person knowledgeable in the tax law(s) would lead such person to conclude that the position has approximately a one in three (or greater) likelihood of being sustained on its merits [§ 10.34(a)(4)].

A practitioner may recommend a position on a tax return that does not meet the realistic possibility standard if the position is not frivolous and the position is *disclosed* on the tax return. A frivolous position is one that is patently improper under the tax law. When analyzing the merits of a tax return position, the authorities applicable under IRC § 6662 and Reg. § 1.6662 should be used to decide if the realistic possibility standard has been met. See Chapter 13 for further discussion of pertinent restrictions on tax return positions. The complete text of *Circular 230* can be found on the IRS's website at:

http://ftp.fedworld.gov/pub/irs-utl/cir230.pdf

AICPA Code of Professional Conduct

Members of the American Institute of Certified Public Accountants (AICPA) are subject to the Institute's *Code of Professional Conduct*. The Code is relevant to all of the professional services performed by CPAs, including those services provided in the practice of public accounting, private industry, government, or education. It was previously referred to as the AICPA *Code of Ethics*. Changes adopted in 1988 were believed necessary to reflect the significant changes in the profession and the environment in which CPAs practice, although the basic tenets of ethical and professional conduct remained the same. One of the most significant changes was the expansion of the rules to apply to all members in all fields of practice, except where the wording of the rule limits the application to a specified field of practice. Under the prior *Code of Ethics*, only members engaged in the practice of public accounting were required to observe all of the rules. Other members, such as those in the fields of education, government, and industry, were subject only to the rules requiring integrity and objectivity and the rule prohibiting members from performing acts discreditable to the profession.

In addition, the rule prohibiting a CPA in public practice from engaging in a business or an occupation concurrently with the practice of public accounting, which would create a conflict of interest in rendering professional services, was deleted from the *Code of Professional Conduct*. The members of the Institute felt that such conflicts of interest are effectively prohibited under new Rule 102, Integrity and Objectivity.

The *Code of Professional Conduct* was designed to provide its members with the following.

1. A comprehensive code of ethical and professional conduct
2. A guide for all members in answering complex questions
3. Assurance to the public concerning the obligations and responsibilities of the accounting profession

The AICPA *Code of Professional Conduct* consists of two integral sections: the principles and the rules. The principles provide a foundation on which the rules are based. The principles suggest that a CPA should strive for behavior above the minimal level of acceptable conduct required by law and regulations. In addition to expressing the basic tenets of ethical and professional conduct, the principles are intended to provide a framework for the certified public accountant's responsibilities to the public, clients, and colleagues. Included are guidelines concerning the member's responsibility to perform professional services with integrity, objectivity, and independence.

The rules consist of a set of enforceable ethical standards that have been approved by a majority of the members of the AICPA. These rules are broad in nature and apply to all of the professional services that a CPA performs, whether in the practice of public accounting or in the fields of education, industry, or government. The only exceptions to the rules occur when their wording indicates that their application is limited to a specified field of practice only, or with respect to certain activities of those who are practicing in another country. In the latter case, however, the CPA must adhere to the ethical standards of the foreign country.

Any failure to follow the rules under the *Code of Professional Conduct* may result in the offender receiving admonishment, suspension, or expulsion from membership in the AICPA. The rules apply not only to the CPA, but also to those employees who are under his or her supervision, partners or shareholders in the practice of the CPA, and any others who act on the CPA's behalf (even if they are not compensated for their activities). As previously discussed, the *Code of Professional Conduct* is applicable to all of the professional services performed by a CPA, including services rendered in the fields of public accounting, such as tax and management advisory services, education, industry, and government.

In addition to the principles and rules, the *Code of Professional Conduct* provides for three additional promulgations. These are interpretations of rules, ethics rulings, and "ethics features." *Interpretations of Rules* are issued by the Division of Professional Ethics of the AICPA. They provide additional detailed guidelines for the scope and application of the rules. These guidelines are enforceable, and the CPA must be prepared to justify any departure from them.

The Division of Professional Ethics of the AICPA also issues *ethics rulings* to further explain the application and interpretation of the rules of conduct and to provide interpretations of the rules in specific circumstances. A member who, in similar circumstances, departs from the findings of these ethics rulings must be prepared to justify such departure. In addition, the Division of Professional Ethics publishes a column in the *Journal of Accountancy* dealing with issues of professional ethics.

These informal articles are intended to address issues raised in questions submitted by members of the AICPA. The questions and answers contained in the articles are not considered formal rulings by the AICPA.

Rule 101: Independence

Under Rule 101, a CPA (or CPA firm) in public practice must be independent of the enterprise for which professional services are being provided. **Independence** is required not only for opinions on financial statements, but also for certain other reports and services where a body of the AICPA has promulgated standards requiring independence. A CPA is not independent if one or more financial relationships exist with a client during the period of professional engagement or at the issuing of the opinion. Thus, independence is impaired if a CPA:

1. has any direct or material indirect financial interest in the client's enterprise;
2. has any jointly held material investment with the client or with its officers, directors, or principal stockholders;
3. has any loan to or from the client, an officer of the client, or any principal stockholder of the client, except for loans, such as home mortgages, that were obtained under normal lending procedures;
4. is an officer, director, employee, or underwriter of the client during the period that is covered by the financial statements, during the period of the professional engagement, or at the time of expressing an opinion; or
5. is related as a trustee, executor, or administrator of any estate that holds a direct or material indirect financial interest in the client.

These independence standards also apply to a CPA who is restricted to doing tax work in a partnership with other CPAs who are examining related financial statements. For instance, a tax partner in a CPA firm should not own stock in a client whose financial statements are audited by her partners in the firm, even though she may have nothing to do with the audit of that client's statements.

Rule 102: Integrity and Objectivity

All professional services by a CPA should be rendered with objectivity and integrity, avoiding any conflict of interest. A CPA should not knowingly misrepresent facts or subordinate his or her judgment to that of others in rendering any professional services. For example, in a tax practice, the CPA may be requested to follow blindly the guidelines of a government agency or the demands of an audit client. Rule 102 prohibits such blind obedience. Prior to the most recent revision of Rule 102, a CPA in tax practice could resolve doubt in favor of the client. This phrase was omitted in the revised language because resolving doubt in favor of a client in an advocacy engagement is not considered as impairing integrity or objectivity and thus need not be specifically "allowed."

Rule 201: General Standards

The CPA must comply with the following general standards, as well as any interpretations of such standards, of the AICPA *Code of Professional Conduct*.

1. The CPA must be able to complete all professional services with professional competence.
2. The CPA must exercise due professional care in the performance of all professional services.

3. The CPA shall adequately plan and supervise the performance of all professional services.
4. The CPA must obtain sufficient relevant data to afford a reasonable basis for any conclusion or recommendation in connection with the performance of any professional services.

The standard requiring "professional competence" recognizes the need for members of the profession to commit to a program of professional development, learning, and improvement. Such a program of professional continuing education is also recognized in the standard of "due professional care."

Rule 202: Compliance with Standards
A CPA, whether providing tax, management advisory, audit, review, compilation, or other professional services, must comply with all standards promulgated by bodies designated by the AICPA Council.

Rule 203: Accounting Principles
A CPA is prohibited from expressing an opinion that financial data of an entity conform with Generally Accepted Accounting Principles if those statements or other financial data contain any material departure from the profession's technical standards. In some cases where a departure is present but the financial statement or other financial data would have been misleading without that departure, a member may be able to comply with this rule by describing the departure, the effect of the departure, and the justification for it.

Rule 301: Confidential Client Information
A CPA in the practice of public accounting must not disclose confidential client data without the specific consent of the client. Rule 301 does not, however, apply:

1. if there is a conflict with Rules 202 (Compliance with Standards) and 203 (Accounting Principles) as set forth by the AICPA *Code of Professional Conduct;*
2. if the CPA is served with an enforceable subpoena or summons, or must comply with applicable laws and government regulations;
3. if there is a review of a CPA's practice under AICPA or state society authorization; or
4. if the CPA is responding to an inquiry of an investigative or disciplinary body of a recognized society, or where the CPA is initiating a complaint with a disciplinary body.

In connection with this rule, members of the investigative bodies who may be exposed to confidential client information are precluded from disclosing such information.

Rule 302: Contingent Fees
A CPA in public practice cannot charge or receive a contingent fee for any professional services from a client for whom the CPA or the CPA's firm performs audit, review, or compilation work. For example, a fee schedule of $5,000 for a qualified audit opinion and $35,000 for an unqualified opinion would not be allowed. Rule 302 also prohibits a CPA from preparing an original or amended tax return, or claim for a tax refund for a contingent fee.

A contingent fee is defined here as a fee established for the performance of any service pursuant to an arrangement in which no fee will be charged unless a specified finding or result is attained, or in which the amount of the fee is otherwise dependent on the finding or result of such service. Solely for purposes of this rule, fees are not regarded as being contingent if fixed by courts or other public authorities, or, in tax matters, if determined based on the results of judicial proceedings or the findings of governmental agencies.

Rule 501: Acts Discreditable

A CPA must not commit an act that is discreditable to the profession. This rule is not specific as to what constitutes a discreditable act; however, violations have been found when the CPA committed a felony, failed to return client records after a client requested them, signed a false tax return, or issued a misleading audit opinion.

Rule 502: Advertising and Other Forms of Solicitation

A CPA in public practice cannot seek clients through false, misleading, or deceptive advertising or other forms of solicitation. In addition, solicitation by the use of coercion, overreaching, or harassing conduct is not allowed. The Institute has placed no restrictions as to the type, media, or frequency of a CPA's advertisements, or on the artwork that is associated with them. Under Rule 502, an activity would be prohibited:

1. if it created false or unjustified expectations of favorable results;
2. if it implied the ability to influence any court, tribunal, regulatory agency, or similar body or official;
3. if it contains a representation that specific professional services in current or future periods will be performed for a stated fee, estimated fee, or fee range when it was likely, at the time of the representation, that such fees would be substantially increased and the prospective client was not advised of that likelihood; or
4. if it contains any other representations that would be likely to cause a reasonable person to misunderstand or be deceived.

For example, a radio spot that states a CPA firm "can beat the IRS every time" would be in violation of Rule 502.

Rule 503: Commissions and Referral Fees

A CPA in public practice cannot charge or receive a commission or referral fee from a client for whom the CPA or the CPA's firm performs audit, review, or compilation work. Thus, under Rule 503, a CPA who does only tax or other nonaudit work for a client may accept or pay a commission. The CPA must, however, disclose the commission to the client or other party in the transaction. In addition, a member who accepts or pays a referral fee for recommending or referring any service of a CPA must disclose that fact.

Rule 505: Form of Organization and Name

CPAs may practice public accounting only in the form of organization permitted by state law or regulation whose characteristics conform to resolutions of the AICPA Council. Under Rule 505, a CPA cannot practice under a firm name that is misleading. The names of one or more past owners may be included in the firm name of a successor organization. In addition, all partners or members of a firm must be members of the AICPA if a firm is to designate itself as "Members of the AICPA."

STATEMENTS ON STANDARDS FOR TAX SERVICES

To assist CPAs, the AICPA has issued a series of statements as to what constitutes appropriate standards for tax practice. These *Statements on Standards for Tax Services (SSTS)* delineate a CPA's responsibilities to his or her clients, the public, the government, and the profession. In August 2000, the SSTS replaced a set of prior statements called the *Statements on Responsibilities in Tax Practice* (STRP). Unlike the STRP, which was advisory in nature, the SSTS is a set of enforceable standards. They are intended to specifically address the problems inherent in the tax practitioner's dual role in serving the client and the public. The statements are intended to supplement, rather than replace, the AICPA *Code of Professional Conduct* and *Circular 230*. They are designed to address the development of tax practice as an integral part of a CPA's practice and the changing environment in which tax practitioners must operate, including the rapidly changing tax laws.

SSTS No. 1: Tax Return Positions

In providing professional services that involve tax return positions, a member should have a good-faith belief that a recommended position has a realistic possibility of being sustained if challenged; otherwise, such a position should not be recommended by the member. A member may reach a conclusion that a position is warranted based on existing law and regulations, as well as on other sources such as well-reasoned articles by tax specialists, treatises, IRS General Counsel Memoranda and written determinations, and explanations of revenue acts as prepared by the Joint Committee on Taxation. The tax professional should be aware that in this statement the members of the AICPA have adopted a standard that is similar to the substantial authority standard of IRC § 6662; however, the statement specifically states that the member may reach a conclusion based on authority as specified in the statement without regard to whether such sources are treated as "authority" under IRC § 6662. Thus, a member who is in compliance with SSTS No. 1 may still lack substantial authority for taking a position under § 6662. In cases where a taxpayer insists on a specific position, a member may sign the return even though the position does not meet the above standard, provided that (1) the position is adequately disclosed on the return by the taxpayer, and (2) the position is not "frivolous." Under no circumstances should a member recommend a tax return position that is exploitative or frivolous.

In cases where the member believes that the taxpayer may have some exposure to a penalty, the statement suggests that the member advise the taxpayer of such risk. Where disclosure of a position on the tax return may mitigate the possibility of a taxpayer penalty under the *Internal Revenue Code*, the member should consider recommending that the taxpayer disclose the position on the return.

SSTS No. 2: Answers to Questions on Returns

Before signing a return as the preparer, a member should make a reasonable effort to obtain from the taxpayer appropriate answers to all questions on the taxpayer's tax return. Where the taxpayer leaves a question on the return unanswered and reasonable grounds exist for not answering the question, the member need not provide an explanation for the omission. The possibility that an answer to a question may prove disadvantageous to the taxpayer, however, does not justify omitting the answer.

Reasonable grounds may exist for omitting an answer to a question on a return. For example, such an omission is acceptable where:

1. the pertinent data are not readily available and are not significant to the determination of taxable income (or loss) or the tax liability;
2. the taxpayer and member are genuinely uncertain as to the meaning of the question on the return; or
3. an answer to a question is voluminous (however, assurance should be given on the return that the data can be supplied upon examination).

In relying for reasonable grounds on the fact that an answer is voluminous, the taxpayer and member should be aware of a relevant IRS district newsletter, which states that a notation on Form 1120 and related schedules that information will be provided on request is not considered acceptable (*IRS Brooklyn District Newsletter* No. 47, 10/89).

SSTS No. 3: Certain Procedural Aspects of Preparing Returns

In preparing or signing a return, the member ordinarily may rely without verification on information that the taxpayer or a third party has provided, unless such information appears to be incorrect, incomplete, or inconsistent. A more formal audit-like review of documents or supporting evidence is generally not required for a member to sign the tax return. Where material provided by the taxpayer appears to be incorrect or incomplete, however, the member should obtain additional information from the taxpayer. In situations where the statutes require that specific conditions be met, the member should determine, by inquiry, whether the conditions have been met. For example, the Code and Regulations impose substantiation requirements for the deduction of certain expenditures. In such a case, the member has an obligation to make appropriate inquiries.

Although members are not required to examine supporting documents, they should encourage the taxpayer to provide such documents when deemed appropriate; for example, in the case of deductions or income from a pass-through entity, such as a partnership.

The member should make proper use of the prior year's tax return when feasible to gather information about the taxpayer and to help avoid omissions and errors with respect to income, deductions, and credit computations.

SSTS No. 4: Use of Estimates

A member may prepare tax returns that involve the use of the taxpayer's estimates if it is impractical to obtain exact data and if the estimated amounts appear reasonable to the member. In all cases, the estimated information must be supplied by the taxpayer; however, the member may provide advice in connection with the estimate. When the taxpayer's estimates are used, they should be presented in such a manner as to avoid the implication of greater accuracy than exists. Situations where the use of estimates may be appropriate include cases where the keeping of precise records for numerous items of small amounts is difficult to achieve, where data are not available at the time of filing the tax return, or when certain records are missing.

The use of estimates in making pertinent accounting judgments where such use is not in conflict with the *Internal Revenue Code* is not prohibited under this statement; such judgments are acceptable and expected. For example, the income tax Regulations permit the use of a reasonable estimate for accruals if exact amounts are not known.

Although in most cases the use of estimates does not necessitate that the item be specifically disclosed on the taxpayer's return, disclosure should be made where failure to do so would result in misleading the IRS about the accuracy of the return. For example, disclosure may be necessary where the taxpayer's records have been destroyed in a fire or where the taxpayer has not received a Schedule K-1 from a pass-through entity at the time the return is filed. Tax practitioners should make their taxpayers aware that the tax law does not allow estimates of certain income and expenditure items, and that more restrictive substantiation requirements apply in cases of certain expenditures, such as travel and entertainment expenses.

SSTS No. 5: Departure from a Position Previously Concluded in an Administrative Proceeding or Court Decision

The recommendation by a member as to the treatment of an item on a tax return should be based on the facts and the law as they are evaluated at the time during which the return is prepared or signed by the member. Unless the taxpayer is bound by the IRS to the treatment of an item in later years, such as by a closing agreement, the disposition of an item in a prior year's audit, or as part of a prior year's court decision, the member is not prevented from recommending a different treatment of a similar item in a later year's return. Thus, a member may sign a return that contains a departure from a treatment required by the IRS in a prior year, provided that the member adheres to the standards in SSTS No. 1.

In most cases, a member's recommendation as to the treatment of an item on a tax return will be consistent with the treatment of a similar item consented to in a prior year's **administrative proceeding** or as a result of the prior year's court decision. In deciding whether a recommendation contrary to the prior treatment is warranted, the member should consider the following.

1. Neither the IRS nor the taxpayer is bound to act consistently with respect to the treatment of an item in a prior proceeding; however, the IRS tends to act consistently in similar situations.
2. The standards under SSTS No. 1, Tax Return Positions, must be followed. In determining whether such standards can be met, the member must consider the existence of an unfavorable court decision and the taxpayer's consent in an earlier administrative proceeding.
3. In some cases, the taxpayer's consent to the treatment of an item in a prior administrative or judicial proceeding may have been due to a desire to settle the issue or a lack of supporting data, whereas in the current year these factors no longer exist.
4. The tax climate may have changed for a given issue since the prior court decision was reached or the prior administrative hearing concluded.

SSTS No. 6: Knowledge of Error: Return Preparation

The member must advise the taxpayer promptly, whether or not the member prepared or signed the return in question, when he or she learns of an error in a previously filed tax return or becomes aware that a required return was not filed. Such advice should include a recommendation for appropriate measures the taxpayer should take. However, the member is neither obligated to inform the IRS of the situation, nor may he or she do so without the taxpayer's permission, except as provided by law.

If the member is requested to prepare the current year's return, and the taxpayer has not taken action to correct an error in a prior year's return, the member should consider whether to proceed with the preparation of the current year's return. If the current year's return is prepared, the member should take reasonable steps to ensure that the error is not repeated.

A member may advise a taxpayer, either orally or in writing, as to the correction of errors in the prior year's return. In a case where there is a possibility that the taxpayer may be charged with fraud, the taxpayer should be referred to an attorney. If a member discovers the error during an audit or other nontax engagement, he or she should refer the taxpayer to the tax return preparer. If the item in question has an insignificant effect on the taxpayer's tax liability, the item should not be considered an "error" under this statement. In addition, the term "error" does not include a situation where the taxpayer's position satisfied the standards under SSTS No. 1 at the time the return was filed.

SSTS No. 7: Knowledge of Error: Administrative Proceedings

When a member represents a taxpayer in an administrative proceeding (such as an audit), and the member is aware of an error other than one that has an insignificant effect on the taxpayer's tax liability, the member should request the taxpayer's agreement to disclose the error to the IRS. Lacking such an agreement with the taxpayer, the member may be under a duty to withdraw from the engagement and may consider terminating the professional relationship with the taxpayer. Disclosure, once agreed on, should be made in a timely manner to avoid misleading the IRS.

SSTS No. 8: Form and Content of Advice to Taxpayers

In providing tax advice to taxpayers, the member must use judgment that reflects professional competence and serves the taxpayer's needs. The member must assume that any advice given will be used to determine the manner of reporting items on the taxpayer's tax return; therefore, the member should ensure that the standards under SSTS No. 1 are satisfied. When providing advice that will be relied on by third parties, the member's responsibilities may differ. Neither a standard format nor guidelines have been issued or established that would cover all situations and circumstances involving written or oral advice from a member. When giving such advice to taxpayers, in addition to exercising professional judgment, the member should consider each of the following.

1. The importance of the transaction and the amounts involved
2. The specific or general nature of the taxpayer's inquiry
3. The time available to develop and submit the advice
4. The technical complications that are presented
5. The existence of authority and precedents
6. The tax sophistication of the taxpayer
7. The possibility of seeking legal advice

Written communication is recommended in important, unusual, or complicated transactions, while oral advice is acceptable in more typical situations. In the communication, the member should advise the taxpayer that the advice reflects his or her professional judgment based on the current situation and that subsequent developments may affect previous advice, such as stating that the position of authorities is subject to change (see Chapter 10).

Chapter 1 Introduction to Tax Practice

When subsequent developments affect the advice that a member has previously communicated to a taxpayer, the member is under no obligation to initiate further communication of such developments to the taxpayer unless a specific agreement has been reached with the taxpayer, or the member is assisting in the application of a procedure or plan relative to such advice.

Exhibit 1–3 summarizes the main topic of each of the AICPA *Statements on Standards for Tax Services*. The complete text of the SSTS can be found on the AICPA web site at:

http://www.aicpa.org/members/div/tax/exsumsts2.htm

ABA MODEL CODE OF PROFESSIONAL RESPONSIBILITY

In 1969, the American Bar Association (ABA) adopted a revised set of guidelines for professional conduct, the *Model Code of Professional Responsibility*. The Code includes nine *canons*, which may be thought of as statements of principles. Canon 6, for instance, requires an attorney to represent a taxpayer competently. Each canon is followed by a series of *ethical considerations* (ECs), which in turn are supported by *disciplinary rules* (DRs). The ethical considerations are aspirational in character, setting forth objectives toward which all attorneys are to strive. The disciplinary rules set forth minimum standards of conduct. Any failure to abide by the disciplinary rules may subject the attorney to disciplinary procedures and punishment.

In nearly all jurisdictions, the ABA Model Code was adopted by the appropriate policy agency, although sometimes modifications were made. In August 1983, the ABA adopted the *Model Rules of Professional Conduct*, which, in a majority of the states, have substantially replaced the Model Code as the guide for attorney professional conduct.

Exhibit 1–3
Summary of AICPA *Statements on Standards for Tax Services*

Statement	Summary of Contents
1	Enumerates the standards for professional services that involve tax positions
2	Explains how a member should handle answering questions on a tax return
3	Describes procedural aspects of preparing tax returns
4	Defines when a member can use the taxpayer's estimates in preparing a tax return
5	Explains what a member should do about items on a current return when similar items were audited on a prior year's return or were the subject of a judicial hearing
6	States what a member should do upon learning about an error in a prior year's tax return
7	Gives the procedure to follow if an error is discovered during an audit
8	Establishes standards for the giving of tax advice to taxpayers

The ABA has a Standing Committee on Ethics and Professional Responsibility that answers questions concerning ethics and professional conduct. Requests for opinions from the committee should be directed to the American Bar Association Center for Professional Responsibility in Chicago.

Neither the ABA Model Code nor the Model Rules have the force of law. Each was designed to be adopted by the appropriate agencies that govern the practice of law in the states. In many jurisdictions, the state supreme court is charged with policing the practice of law; in other states, the legislature bears this responsibility. Attorneys should consult their own jurisdiction's ethical guidelines to determine whether the provisions of the ABA Model Code or the Model Rules, or some modification of these doctrines, have been adopted.

The American Bar Association has not amended the Model Rules in more than twenty years. A commission called "Ethics 2000" has been established by the ABA to review the rules and to propose any needed adjustments. The specific charge of the Ethics 2000 Committee is to (1) conduct a comprehensive study and evaluate the ethical and professionalism precepts of the legal profession; (2) examine and evaluate the ABA *Model Rules of Professional Conduct* and the rules governing professional conduct in state and federal jurisdictions; (3) conduct original research, surveys, and hearings; and (4) formulate recommendations for action. The report of the Ethics 2000 Committee was released in November 2000. The current status of the ABA Model Rules and the Ethics 2000 Committee report can be found on the ABA web site at:

http://www.abanet.org/cpr/mrpc/mrpc_toc.html

NONREGULATORY ETHICS

There is substantially more to ethical behavior than just following the rules of ethics or conduct of professional organizations such as the AICPA or the ABA. Professional ethical behavior is the result of the interaction of personal morality, social responsibility, business ethics, and other general **ethical standards**. See Exhibit 1–4.

Exhibit 1–4
Ethical Behavior Sources

MORALITY

The subject of morality fills tens of thousands of books. Publications as diverse as the Bible and popular novels examine morality in one way or another. When something is judged to be morally right or wrong (or good or bad), the underlying standards on which such judgments are based are called moral standards.

According to some people's moral standards, cheating "just a little" in computing a tax liability is morally acceptable. Most people in the United States believe that everyone cheats a little on their taxes. Cheating significantly may be viewed differently, but where is the dividing line between morally "okay" tax cheating and morally wrong tax evasion? Under the self-assessed tax system in the United States, different moral standards provide different answers—from complete honesty to various degrees of dishonesty. The tax practitioner must be ready to work with clients holding various systems of morality and to accept the consequences of the moral choices made, including the possibility of losing a client, paying fines and penalties to the IRS, or even going to jail.

SOCIAL RESPONSIBILITY

The tax practitioner must be aware of social responsibility in areas such as environmental protection, equal opportunity, and occupational safety. Since World War II, society has held the business world increasingly responsible for meeting certain noneconomic standards. In 1970, Milton Friedman, the Nobel Prize-winning economist, said that the "social responsibility" of business is merely to increase profits. But the prevailing sentiment today is that business and the professions should return something to society to make it better, not just to make a profit. For the tax practitioner, this could mean going beyond the minimum legal responsibility to provide equal opportunity in the hiring of employees by making special recruitment efforts, or it could mean volunteering time to help charitable organizations with their tax problems.

BUSINESS ETHICS

In recent years, one of the major topics in the business world has been the question of business ethics. There are many people who think that ethics has application only in the personal life, not in the business or professional life. Like Milton Friedman, they think the business of business is to make a profit. This view is popular because (1) people who work in business or professions must concern themselves with producing goods and services to earn a profit, and (2) it is easier to measure profit than to make value judgments. People are more comfortable discussing problems in terms of profits, not the ethical impact of the entity and its actions. Few business and professional people are trained in ethical analysis, and, therefore, they usually are not familiar with how to evaluate a problem in terms of ethics.

That business and professional organizations have ethical responsibilities is readily apparent to anyone who reads the popular press. The lawsuits brought on by the savings and loan failures of the late 1980s and against the Big Five accounting firms in the last two decades are prime examples of society holding business to a standard of ethical conduct. Most of the Big Five will settle lawsuits against them for millions of dollars for what was, in part, a business ethics failure.

OTHER ETHICAL STANDARDS

The study of nonregulatory ethics could be expanded to cover such other issues as public policy, religious beliefs, and cultural values, issues that are beyond the scope of this text. Most of such topics would be addressed in a university course on ethics or business ethics. A tax practitioner can expand his or her understanding of the application of ethics to accounting and business situations by referring to the books on the following reading list:

- Armstrong, Mary Beth, *Ethics and Professionalism for CPAs* (Cincinnati: South-Western Publishing Co., 1993).
- Brooks, Leonard J., *Professional Ethics for Accountants* (Minneapolis/St. Paul: West Publishing Co., 1995).
- Bucholz, Rogene, *Fundamental Concepts and Problems in Business Ethics* (Englewood Cliffs, NJ: Prentice Hall, 1989).
- Collins, Denis, and Thomas O'Rourke, *Ethical Dilemmas in Accounting* (Cincinnati: South-Western Publishing Co., 1994).
- Donaldson, Thomas, *Corporations and Morality* (Englewood Cliffs, NJ: Prentice Hall, 1983).
- Velasquez, Manuel, *Business Ethics*, 2d ed. (Englewood Cliffs, NJ: Prentice Hall, 1988).

The following are examples of nonregulatory ethics dilemmas that could arise in a business, accounting, or tax setting:

Example 1-3 Hilary is a CPA who is a sole practitioner. This year, one of her clients, Gold Corporation, opened a new division in Europe. This is a long-time client of Hilary's, and she is anxious to keep it. However, Hilary has no experience in international tax and would not be able to give Gold the kind of tax advice needed for the new division. The ethical question is whether Hilary should inform the client of her lack of knowledge in this area and risk losing the client, or whether she should remain silent and "wing it" on the international tax issues. What should Hilary do in this situation?

Example 1-4 Patrick is a CPA who is a partner in a successful local CPA practice. The state in which Patrick lives has a forty-hour annual continuing professional education (CPE) requirement. If the CPE requirement is not met, a CPA will have his or her license suspended and will not be able to practice. Patrick is approached by the Flight-by-Night CPE Company about signing up for some of their CPE courses. The company representative tells Patrick that they will report that Patrick attended the courses so that he gets the CPE credit, even if he does not attend. Because Patrick is overloaded with work, he considers this a "low hassle" way to get his CPA license renewed. Would it be ethical for Patrick to obtain his CPE credit this way?

Example 1-5 Devona is an auditor in the Boston office of a large international CPA firm. She is sent on an inventory observation for a new client of the Houston office of the firm. The Houston office gives her a six-hour budget for the job. When she arrives at the client's office, Devona discovers that the Houston office has substantially underestimated the size of inventory to be counted. The client has a $20,000,000 inventory comprised of more than 6,000 different items. The client plans to take twenty hours to complete the count. Devona is up for promotion, and she does not want to have a negative personnel review because she overran the budget on this job. Therefore, she considers spending the budgeted six hours on the observation and signing off in the audit work papers that she completely observed the inventory. Devona thinks this would be OK since she perceives there is only a small risk of a material misstatement of the inventory. Would it be ethical for Devona to do this?

Example 1–6 Last year, one of Andy's clients, Trout Corporation, had a significant tax problem. Andy needed thirty-five hours of research time to arrive at an answer to Trout's problem. This year, another of Andy's clients, Bass Corporation, had the same problem. Because of his experience with Trout, Andy could solve Bass's tax problem in three hours. The ethical question is whether Andy should bill Bass for three hours or thirty-five hours of professional consulting time. There are two ways to look at this situation. Andy only spent three hours on the job, so he should only bill for three hours of time. Yet, there is "value" in Andy already knowing the approach to take on the Bass matter, so perhaps he should bill for that knowledge and not just for the actual time spent working on the problem. What should Andy do in this situation?

Example 1–7 Betty is negotiating a transaction on behalf of one of her clients, John Carp. During the process, Betty becomes aware that the other party to the transaction does not adequately understand the tax consequences of the proposed transaction, which are highly favorable to Carp. In fact, if the transaction were completed as proposed, the other side would suffer significant negative tax consequences. Ethically, should Betty inform the other party of the potential negative tax consequences of the proposed transaction?

As shown in the above examples, the application of ethics to business situations is not clear-cut. In many situations, doing what is right may not be possible. The tax practitioner is constantly faced with challenges on how to apply proper business ethics on a daily basis.

TAX RESEARCH BY CERTIFIED PUBLIC ACCOUNTANTS

Over the years, the tax community has addressed the issue of whether the practice of tax by a CPA or other nonattorney constitutes the **unauthorized practice of law.** The problem stems from the tax law itself, passed in 1913. The provisions of early tax law called for an income tax, but the statute was not specific about the accounting methods to be used in implementing it. In fact, not until 1954 was a formal statutory effort made to address accounting issues in the computation of taxable income. For this reason, many attorneys avoided tax work, allowing CPAs to fill the void and provide taxpayers with most of the professional-quality tax work.

When a CPA resolves an issue in most nonroutine tax situations, he or she is, to some extent, solving a legal problem. The issue is not whether the CPA is rendering legal service but, rather, how much legal service is provided. When does the CPA cross the mythical boundary and begin an unauthorized practice of law? Neither these professions nor the courts have promulgated binding guidelines on this issue. Instead, the Federal agencies seem to have taken the lead in attempting to solve this problem.

Historical Developments

Lowell Bar Association v. Loeb, 315 Mass. 176, S2 N.E.2d 27 (1943), addressed the issue of the unauthorized practice of law by nonattorneys engaged in tax practice. The Lowell Massachusetts Bar Association sued Birdie Loeb, a commercial tax preparer, for her preparation of simple wage-earner tax returns. On appeal, the court held that the preparation of "simple" tax returns did not constitute the unauthorized practice of Massachusetts law because tax return preparation could not be identified as strictly within the legal discipline. Tax practice includes interaction among various disciplines, including law, accounting, economics, political science, and others.

Subsequent courts attempted to adopt the *Lowell* "wholly within the field of law" test in other jurisdictions, but they found that defining the boundaries of the legal profession was so difficult and the 1943 opinion was so general and vague that the *Lowell* precedent was of little value in other situations.

Probably the best known case concerning a tax accountant's unauthorized practice of law is *Bercu,* 299 N.Y. 728, 87 N.E.2d 451 (1949). Bercu was an accountant who consulted with a client concerning whether sales taxes that were accrued, but not yet paid, could be deducted on a tax return. The taxpayer who requested this advice was not one of Bercu's regular clients. Bercu advised the client that the sales tax could be deducted when it was paid. Bercu presented a bill to the client and, when it was not paid, sued the client to collect the fees.

Ultimately, the State Court of New York held that it was not proper for Bercu to render services in such a situation. The Court indicated that Bercu could have provided this type of service and answered the sales tax question had it been incidental to the tax return work he regularly performed for his clients.

This "incidental to accounting practice" test became the chief issue in several subsequent cases concerning the unauthorized practice of law. In a Minnesota case, *Gardner v. Conway,* 234 Minn. 468, 48 N.W.2d 788 (1951), a person who was neither an attorney nor a CPA attempted to answer difficult and substantial questions of law. The court held that the practitioner improperly gave advice to the client and rejected the "incidental to practice" test as an approach to providing guidelines for the definition of tax practice.

In a California case, *Agran v. Shapiro,* 127 Cal. App.2d Supp. 807, 273 P.2d 619 (1954), CPA Agran prepared returns, performed research, and represented his clients before the IRS. Agran's preparation of Shapiro's return involved extensive research—including more than 100 court cases, Code sections, and Regulations—concerning a question involving the proper treatment of a net operating loss. Upon completion of the work, the CPA presented his bill and, when he was not paid, sued Shapiro to collect. Agran was found by the court to have engaged in the unauthorized practice of law and, therefore, was unable to collect his fees. In its decision, the California Superior Court relied on *Gardner v. Conway* and rejected the "incidental to practice" test that Agran used in his defense. The Court did not decide, however, whether the authorization to practice before the IRS preempted the right of the state to regulate tax practice.

In *Sperry v. Florida,* 373 U.S. 379, 83 S.Ct. 1322 (1963), the U.S. Supreme Court held that a Federal statute that admitted nonattorneys to practice before Federal agencies (in this case, the Patent Office) took precedence over state regulation. In late 1965, Congress enacted Public Law 89-332, amending prior law and allowing CPAs to practice before the IRS. Although this law added to the force of the *Sperry* decision as it applied to CPAs, *Sperry* still provides for the preemption of Federal regulations and statutes in matters of practice before other Federal agencies.

In 1981, the AICPA and the ABA held a conference for attorneys and CPAs to address some of these definitional questions relative to tax practice and the unauthorized practice of law. The stated purpose of this session was to "promote understanding between the professions in the interests of the client [taxpayers] and the general public." This National Conference of Lawyers and CPAs issued a statement in November 1981, reaffirming that client [taxpayers] are best served when attorneys and CPAs work together in tax practice. The text of the statement identifies eight areas related to income taxation and three areas related to estate and gift planning in which such professional cooperation should be encouraged. The statement lacks any form of exclusionary language. Indeed, it asserts the following:

Frequently, the legal and accounting phases (of tax practice) are so intertwined that they are difficult to distinguish. This is particularly true in the field of income taxation, where questions of law and accounting are often inextricably intertwined. (For a complete discussion of this conference statement, see the Journal of Accountancy, *August 1982).*

CPAs and Other Nonattorneys

Currently, CPAs and other nonattorneys who practice tax law before the IRS are in little danger of entering into the unauthorized practice of law provided they avoid providing general legal services. This can be accomplished if CPAs and other nonattorneys do not themselves engage in the following kinds of general law activities.

- Expressing a legal opinion on any nontax matter
- Drafting wills or trust instruments
- Drafting contracts
- Drafting incorporation papers
- Drafting partnership agreements

Taxpayers can draft any of these documents themselves without the services of an attorney. If a CPA's client wishes to handle personal legal affairs in this manner, the CPA (exercising caution) can render professional advice without running afoul of the case law concerning the unauthorized practice of law.

As long as CPAs and other nonattorneys stay within the practice of tax, and do not cross over into the practice of general law, the control exercised by *Circular 230* and the code should ensure that virtually all tax compliance, planning, and research activities that are provided by adequately trained nonattorney CPAs constitute the "authorized practice of law."

SUMMARY

In addition to the tax return preparation statutes that are discussed in Chapter 13, CPAs, attorneys, enrolled agents, and others who practice before the IRS are faced with various sets of overlapping rules of conduct. *Circular 230* applies to anyone who practices before the IRS. In addition, members of the legal and public accounting professions are subject to codes of ethics and conduct. Similarly, cultural codes of morality and social responsibility form general boundaries relative to acceptable behavior by a taxpayer or tax professional. When engaged in tax practice, one always must be aware of the appropriate rules of conduct that apply and conduct oneself in accordance with those rules.

TAX TUTOR

Reinforce the tax research information covered in this chapter by completing the online tutorials located at the Federal Tax Research web site:

http://raabe.swcollege.com

KEY WORDS

By the time you complete this chapter, you should be comfortable discussing each of the following terms. If you need additional review of any of these items, return to the appropriate material in the chapter or consult the glossary to this text.

Administrative Proceeding
American Bar Association (ABA)
American Institute of Certified
   Public Accountants (AICPA)
Circular 230
Closed Transaction
Contingent Fees
Enrolled Agent
Ethical Standards
Independence

Open Transaction
Practice before the IRS
Realistic Possibility
Tax Avoidance
Tax Compliance
Tax Evasion
Tax Litigation
Tax Planning
Tax Research
Unauthorized Practice of Law

DISCUSSION QUESTIONS

1. In a modern, industrial society, the tax system is derived from several disciplines. Identify the disciplines that play this role in the United States. Explain how each of them affects the U.S. tax system.
2. The elements of tax practice fall into what four major categories?
3. What is tax compliance as practiced in the United States? Give several examples of activities that can be classified as tax compliance.

4. Several groups of individuals do most of the tax compliance work in the United States. Identify these groups and describe briefly the kind of work that each group does. In this regard, be sure to define the term "enrolled agent."
5. What is tax planning? Explain the difference between tax evasion and tax avoidance, and the role of each in professional tax planning.
6. Tax planning falls into two major categories, the "open" transaction and the "closed" transaction. Discuss each type of transaction, and describe how each affects tax planning.
7. What is tax litigation? What type of tax practitioner typically handles tax litigation on a taxpayer's behalf?
8. Define tax research. Briefly describe the tax research process.
9. Who issues *Circular 230*? Which tax practitioners are regulated by it?
10. CPAs must follow the rules of *Circular 230*. In addition, CPAs in tax practice are subject to two other sets of ethical rules. Give the name and the issuer of both of these sets of rules.
11. The term "practice before the IRS" includes the representation of clients in the United States Tax Court for cases being handled under the "small tax case procedure." True or false? Explain your answer. (IRS adapted)
12. The rules that govern practice before the IRS are found in *Circular 230*. Discuss what entails practice before the IRS, and state which section of *Circular 230* contains the definition.
13. Leigh, who is not an enrolled agent, attorney, or CPA, is employed by Rose, a CPA. One of Rose's clients has been notified that his 1997 income tax return has been selected for audit by the IRS. Rose had prepared the return and signed it as preparer. Rose has been called out of town on a family emergency and would like for Leigh to represent the client. Leigh cannot represent the client even if she has Rose's written authority to do so and has the client's power of attorney. True or false? Explain your answer. (IRS adapted)
14. Regular full-time employees are allowed to represent certain organizations before the Internal Revenue Service without being an attorney, CPA, or enrolled agent. Name the organizations that can be represented by full-time employees, and cite where you found that authority in *Circular 230*.
15. A practitioner could be suspended from practice before the IRS if the practitioner employs, accepts assistance from, or shares fees with any person who is under disbarment or suspension from practice before the IRS. True or false? Explain your answer. (IRS adapted)
16. Tax practitioners must not sign a tax return under *Circular 230* if the return takes a position that does not have a "realistic possibility" of being sustained by the Internal Revenue Service.
    a. What is a realistic possibility as defined by the Internal Revenue Service?
    b. Is it possible for a tax practitioner to sign a tax return that takes a position that does not meet the realistic possibility standard? If so, what must be done to allow the tax practitioner to sign the tax return?
17. Under *Circular 230*, may an attorney, CPA, or enrolled agent advertise on televison? On the Internet? If so, what standards are applied to the advertisements?
18. Can a tax practitioner who is a CPA form a CPA partnership with an IRS agent who is also a CPA? What limits (if any) would be placed on such a partnership?

19. If a tax practitioner finds an error in a prior year's tax return, what action must he or she take (if any) under *Circular 230*? What subpart and section addresses this situation?
20. Practicing CPAs generally are subject to the AICPA *Code of Professional Conduct*. What is its stated purpose?
21. The rules under the AICPA *Code of Professional Conduct* are a group of enforceable ethical standards. Broad in nature, they generally apply to all of the services that are performed by a CPA who is an AICPA member. Identify the two situations in which the application of the rules may be limited.
22. In what situation may a CPA under the AICPA *Code of Professional Conduct* accept a commission?
23. Under Rule 101 (Independence), a CPA (or CPA firm) in public practice must be independent of the enterprise for which professional services are being provided. Discuss situations in which the CPA's independence may be impaired.
24. Under Rule 102 (Integrity and Objectivity), a CPA who is engaged in tax practice may resolve a doubtful area in favor of his or her client. Explain.
25. A CPA must meet certain qualitative standards under Rule 201 (General Standards). Discuss the four general standards of this rule.
26. In each of the following independent situations, state which AICPA *Code of Professional Conduct* (if any) is violated by a CPA in public practice.
    a. The CPA opens a tax practice and names the new firm "Jill's Super Tax."
    b. In return for recommending a certain investment to an *audit* client, a CPA receives a 5 percent commission from the broker who sells the investments.
    c. A taxpayer is being assessed by the IRS for an additional $100,000 of tax. The CPA offers to represent the taxpayer for a fee that is equal to 25 percent of any amount by which he can get the IRS to reduce its assessment.
    d. A CPA places an advertisement in the local newspaper that states that she is the "Best CPA in the Western World." The advertisement further states that, because of her great skill, the CPA has considerable influence with the IRS and the United States Tax Court.
    e. A CPA partnership has eight partners, six of whom are members of the AICPA. On its letterhead, the firm designates itself as "Members of the AICPA."
    f. A CPA who is not in public practice is convicted of helping to run a large illegal drug operation.
27. Under Rule 301 of the AICPA *Code of Professional Conduct,* a CPA must not disclose confidential client data without the specific consent of the client. Under what conditions might a disclosure of confidential information without the client's consent be appropriate?
28. What are the *Statements on Standards for Tax Services*? Who issues them? Discuss their principal objectives.
29. What guidelines does SSTS No. 1 provide for a tax practitioner regarding tax return positions?
30. According to SSTS No. 2, a tax return should be signed by a member only after reasonable effort has been made to answer all of the questions on the return that apply to the taxpayer. What are some of the reasonable grounds under which a member may sign a return as the preparer even though some of the pertinent questions remain unanswered?

31. What guidelines are provided by SSTS No. 3 as to the reliance by a member on information supplied by the taxpayer for use in preparing the taxpayer's return?
32. A member may use estimates in completing a tax return according to SSTS No. 4. When might the use of estimates be considered appropriate?
33. Last year a taxpayer was audited by the IRS and an item of deduction on the tax return was disallowed. On this year's tax return, the taxpayer would like to deduct a similar item. Discuss the circumstances under which a member may allow the taxpayer to take the deduction on the current year's return and still be in compliance with SSTS No. 5. Under what conditions must special disclosure be made by the member?
34. When a member learns of an error in a previously filed tax return or learns of an error during an audit, how is he or she to respond and still be in compliance with SSTS No. 6 and No. 7?
35. What situations are addressed by SSTS No. 8?
36. Differentiate between the ABA *Model Code of Professional Responsibility* and that organization's *Model Rules of Professional Conduct*.
37. Who sets ethical rules for attorneys in the various states?
38. How does the term "the unauthorized practice of law" apply to CPAs?
39. List several services or products that a CPA or enrolled agent purposely should not make a part of a tax practice, so as to minimize exposure to a charge of the unauthorized practice of law.

EXERCISES

40. Summarize what is discussed in each of the following sections of *Circular 230*.
    a. Subpart A, § 10.4(b)
    b. Subpart B, § 10.21
    c. Subpart B, § 10.26
    d. Subpart B, § 10.32
41. Summarize what is discussed in each of the following sections of *Circular 230*.
    a. Subpart C, § 10.51(b)
    b. Subpart A, § 10.6(e)
    c. Subpart A, § 10.2(e)
    d. Subpart B, § 10.28
42. Which subpart and section of *Circular 230* discusses each the following topics?
    a. Solicitation
    b. Negotiation of a taxpayer's refund checks
    c. Depositions
    d. Authority to disbar or suspend from practice before the Internal Revenue Service
43. Which subpart and section of *Circular 230* discusses each the following topics?
    a. Conflicting interests
    b. Tax shelter opinions
    c. Disreputable conduct
    d. Assistance from disbarred or suspended persons

44. Summarize what is discussed in each of the following rules of the AICPA *Code of Professional Conduct*. Give a simple example of a transaction or an action relevant to each rule.
    a. Article VI, ¶ .01
    b. Rule 201, ¶ .02 201-1
    c. Rule 502, ¶ .03 502-2
    d. Rule 504, ¶ .01
45. Summarize what is discussed in each of the following *Statements on Standards for Tax Services*.
    a. SSTS No. 1
    b. SSTS No. 4
    c. SSTS No. 6
46. What is the precedent-setting value of each of the following cases?
    a. *Lowell Bar Association v. Loeb*
    b. *Bercu*
    c. *Sperry v. Florida*
47. Ms. E is an enrolled agent who prepared the tax returns for Mr. A and Mr. B (buyer and seller, respectively). Ms. E may not, under any circumstances, represent A and B before the IRS with regard to this buy and sell transaction. True or false? Explain your answer. (IRS adapted)
48. A full-time employee of a sole proprietorship may represent his or her employer in an examination by the IRS without being an enrolled agent, attorney, or CPA. True or false? Explain your answer. (IRS adapted)
49. An unenrolled agent who has not prepared the tax return of John Gomez may represent John before an IRS revenue agent in the conduct of an examination, provided that the unenrolled agent has written authorization from John. True or false? Explain your answer. (IRS adapted)
50. Enrolled agents, attorneys, and CPAs shall exercise due diligence in preparing or assisting in the preparation of documents and other papers relating to IRS matters. True or false? Explain your answer. (IRS adapted)
51. Which of the following statements may not be used when an enrolled agent advertises?
    a. Name, address, and office hours
    b. Names of associates of the firm
    c. Claims of quality of service that cannot be verified
    d. Membership in professional organizations

    Explain your answer. (IRS adapted)
52. The Director of Practice may take into consideration a petition for reinstatement from any person disbarred from practice before the IRS after a period of how many years?
    a. Never
    b. 2 years
    c. 3 years
    d. 5 years

    Explain your answer. (IRS adapted)
53. Inclusion of which of the following statements in a CPA's advertisement is *unacceptable* under the AICPA *Code of Professional Conduct*?
    a. Julie Adams, Certified Public Accountant, Fluency in Spanish and French

Continued

b. Julie Adams, Certified Public Accountant, MBA, Big State University, 1992
c. Julie Adams, Certified Public Accountant, Free Initial Consultation
d. Julie Adams, Certified Public Accountant, I Always Win IRS Audit

Explain your answer.

54. Which of the following situations would most likely result in a violation of the practitioner's ethical standards?
   a. A CPA is controller of a bank and grants permission to the bank to use his "CPA" title in the listing of the bank officers in the bank's publications.
   b. A CPA who is also a member of the bar represents on her letterhead that she is both an attorney and a CPA.
   c. A CPA, the sole shareholder in a professional accountancy corporation, uses the term "and company" in his firm's title.
   d. A CPA who writes a newsletter on financial management topics grants permission to the publisher to solicit subscriptions.

   Explain your answer.

55. Which of the following situations would provide an acceptable case for using a taxpayer's estimated figure in the preparation of a federal income tax return?
   a. The taxpayer has the necessary data available, but is busy with a pressing public offering and has not had the time to look through her records for the information.
   b. The data are not available at the time of filing the return, and the estimated amounts appear reasonable to the CPA.
   c. The taxpayer has the data available at the time for filing the return but feels that the data do not fairly represent the results of her business operation and therefore desires to use an "estimate."
   d. The taxpayer, relying on the income tax regulations that allow the use of reasonable estimates under certain circumstances, desires to use an estimate to determine the amount of his deduction for entertainment expenses.

   Explain your answer.

56. According to the AICPA *Code of Professional Conduct,* CPAs in tax practice who are representing a taxpayer in a formal controversy with the government are permitted to receive contingent fees because
   a. this practice establishes fees that are commensurate with the value of the services rendered.
   b. attorneys who are in tax practice customarily set contingent fees.
   c. determinations by tax authorities are a matter of judicial proceedings that do not involve third parties.
   d. the consequences are based on the findings of judicial proceedings or the findings of a government agency.

   Explain your answer.

57. The AICPA *Code of Professional Conduct* states that a CPA shall not disclose any confidential information in the course of a professional engagement, except with the consent of the client. This rule should be understood to preclude a CPA from responding to an inquiry that is received from
   a. an investigative body of a state CPA society.
   b. the Trial Board of the AICPA.
   c. a CPA-shareholder of the taxpayer corporation.
   d. an AICPA voluntary quality review body.

   Explain your answer.

58. A taxpayer's records are destroyed by fire. A CPA prepares the tax return based on estimates and other indirect information she has obtained. Under the *Statements on Standards for Tax Services,* she should
    a. disclose the use of estimates to the IRS.
    b. not disclose the use of estimates to the IRS.
    c. charge the taxpayer a double fee.
    d. not prepare a return based on estimates.
    e. have an attorney prepare the return.

    Explain your answer.

59. With regard to the categories of individuals who may practice before the IRS under *Circular 230*, which of the following statements is correct?
    a. Only enrolled agents, attorneys, or CPAs may represent trusts and estates before any officer or employee of the IRS.
    b. An individual who is not an enrolled agent, attorney, or CPA and who signs a return as having prepared it for the taxpayer may, with proper authorization from the taxpayer, appear as the taxpayer's representative, with or without the taxpayer, at an IRS Appeals Office conference with respect to the tax liability of the taxpayer for the taxable year or period covered by the return.
    c. Under the limited practice provision in *Circular 230*, only general partners may represent a partnership.
    d. Under the limited practice provision in *Circular 230*, an individual who is under suspension or disbarment from practice before the IRS may not engage in limited practice before the IRS.

    Explain your answer. (IRS adapted)

60. If an enrolled agent, attorney, or CPA knows that a client has not complied with the revenue laws of the United States with respect to a matter administered by the IRS, the enrolled agent, attorney, or CPA is required under *Circular 230* to
    a. do nothing until advised by the client to take corrective action.
    b. advise the client of the noncompliance.
    c. immediately notify the IRS.
    d. advise the client and notify the IRS.

    Explain your answer. (IRS adapted)

RESEARCH CASES

61. You are a CPA in practice who has just obtained a new client. Another CPA did the tax returns for the prior three years. The client has operated his business as an S corporation during the three-year period. After starting work on this year's tax return, you notice that the S corporation has an October 31 fiscal year-end. After examining the file, you discover that three years ago, when the S corporation adopted the fiscal tax year, a § 444 election was not made. In addition, the S corporation has not maintained the proper required "minimum deposit account" with the IRS.

    The client wants your advice on what to do now. You determine that there are three options: (1) you can do nothing and hope the IRS doesn't find out, (2) you can notify the IRS of the mistake and pay any interest and penalties, or (3) you can elect a calendar year and hope the IRS doesn't notice the current invalid fiscal year. What potential nonregulatory ethical issues do you see in this situation that could influence your decision on any recommendation?

62. You are a CPA in practice and have a long-term client who is involved in a nasty divorce proceeding with her husband. The client has assets she deposited in a bank account in the Grand Cayman Islands. There is U.S.-taxable interest on the deposits. Because she does not want her husband to know about the deposits, she asks you to report the interest on her tax return in such a way that it will not "tip off" her husband to the existence of the account. You can handle this request by reporting the interest through the Schedule C (instead of Schedule B) on her tax return and thus avoid making the source of the income known. What potential nonregulatory ethics issues do you see in this situation?

63. Ahi Corporation is one of your clients in Hawaii. The company had a good year last year and owes the IRS $100,000,000, due on March 15. There are no penalties or interest due to the IRS. One of Ahi's employees approaches you with the following plan to benefit from the so-called "float" on the large payment due to the government. First, Ahi Corp. will courier its tax return and payment to the U.S. Virgin Islands. There, the tax return will be mailed to the IRS Service Center in Fresno by certified mail on the return's due date, March 15. By doing this, the employee thinks it will take at least six days for the tax return to reach the IRS and for them to cash the $100,000,000 check. Ahi can earn 7 percent after tax on its money, so the interest earned during these six days because of the float is $19,178 per day [($100,000,000 $\times$ .07) / 365 days]. Thus, the total interest earned on the float for six days would be $115,068 ($19,178 $\times$ 6 days).
    a. Would you recommend Ahi complete this transaction?
    b. What potential ethics issues do you see in this situation?

64. John Haddock owns 75 percent of Haddock Corporation. The other 25 percent of the stock is held by John's wife, Marsha. You are a tax manager assigned to prepare the corporate tax return for Haddock. While working on the return, you note that Haddock Corp. pays rent to John for a building he owns with his son, John, Jr. The rent being paid is at least three times the normal rate for rentals of similar property in that area of town. You report this observation to the partner on the engagement. She tells you that it is all right to deduct the payments because Haddock Corp. has been doing it for several years. Under your firm's policy, managers sign the tax return for clients.
    a. Would you sign this tax return?
    b. What potential ethics issues do you see in this situation?

65. You are negotiating a transaction for your client, Shark Corporation. Parties on the other side of the deal ask you for information about the structural stability of a building, which is a significant part of the transaction. Coleman, Shark's tax director, tells you to say "everything is OK," when, in reality, the building has substantial hidden damage. Coleman tells you to say this because it would be more favorable to Shark's position in the transaction.
    a. How would you respond to Coleman's request?
    b. What if you have already told the other side that the building is OK when you learn about the problems?
    c. What other potential ethics issues do you see in this situation?

66. Big CPA Firm has many partners in one of its local offices. Two of these partners are Tom, a tax partner, and Alice, an audit partner. Because of the size of the office, Tom and Alice do not know each other very well.

Continued

Tom has a tax client, Anchovy Corporation, that is in severe financial trouble and may have to file for bankruptcy. Anchovy is a customer of Sardine Corporation, one of Alice's audit clients. Accounts receivable on Sardine's books from Anchovy are significant. If Anchovy goes bankrupt, it could cause serious problems for Sardine. Alice is unaware of the bad financial condition of Anchovy.
   a. Can Tom disclose to Alice the problems at Anchovy?
   b. What if Anchovy goes under and takes Sardine with it?
   c. What potential ethics issues do you see in this situation?

67. You are the tax manager in a CPA office. One of your clients, Snapper Corporation, is also an audit client of the firm. The CFO of Snapper invites you and the audit manager for a one-week deep-sea fishing trip to Mexico, all expenses to be paid by Snapper. The audit manager says that you both should go and just not tell your supervisor at the CPA firm any details (like who paid the expenses) about the trip.
   a. Would you go on the trip?
   b. Would you tell your supervisors at the CPA firm if the audit manager went on the trip without you?
   c. What other potential ethics issues do you see in this situation?

68. Clara comes to an attorney's office in need of assistance with her husband's estate. Her husband, Phil, a factory worker, had been a saver all his life and owned approximately $1,500,000 in stocks and bonds. Clara is relatively unsophisticated in financial matters, so the attorney agrees to handle the estate for 17 percent of the value of the estate. The normal charge for such work is 3–5 percent of the estate. The widow agrees to the 17 percent arrangement. The attorney then hires CPA Charles for $10,000 to compute Phil's estate tax on Form 706 and to prepare other appropriate documents.
   a. Does Charles have any responsibility to inform the widow that she is being significantly overcharged by the attorney?
   b. What potential ethics issues do you see in this situation?

69. Darlene works for Big CPA Firm. When she was being interviewed, Darlene was told by a partner in the firm that she was not to underreport her time spent on various engagements. However, after working for a few months, she discovers that everyone in her office "eats time." Because she is not eating time like everyone else, Darlene is always overbudget. She is beginning to get a reputation as a "budget buster." As a result, none of the senior tax staff wants her on their engagements. She is getting the worst clients and bad reviews from the people for whom she works. It appears that unless she starts eating time, Darlene's future with the firm is limited.
   a. What would you recommend Darlene do?
   b. What potential ethics issues do you see in this situation?

70. Freya is an accountant working on the tax return of a high-tech client. After reviewing the work papers, she discovers that there is a pattern of double billing the U.S. Navy for various projects done by the tax client. She brings this to the attention of her manager on the job, and he tells her that it is not the CPA firm's business what the client does since this is not an audit engagement.
   a. What would you recommend Freya do at this point?
   b. What potential ethics issues do you see in this situation?

2

Tax Research Methodology

LEARNING OBJECTIVES

- Recognize the importance of a systematic approach to tax research
- Delineate and elaborate on the steps of the tax research process
- Appreciate the importance of gathering pertinent facts and identifying research issues
- Discuss the sources of the federal tax law
- Identify how computer resources affect the conduct of tax research

CHAPTER OUTLINE

Outline of the Tax Research Process
    Step 1: Establish the Facts
    Step 2: Identify the Issues
        Tax Research as an Iterative Process
    Step 3: Locate Authority
    Step 4: Evaluate Authority
    Step 5: Develop Conclusions and Recommendations
    Step 6: Communicate the Recommendations
Overview of Computerized Tax Research
    Online and CD-ROM Systems

Benefits of Using a Computerized Tax Service
Factors in Choosing a Computerized Tax Service
Using a Computer in Tax Research
    Step 1: State the Issue as a Question
    Step 2: Identify the Keywords
    Step 3: Construct a Computer Research Query
    Step 4: Select a Database and Execute the Search
    Step 5: Interpret and Refine the Search
IRS Web Site Research

The overriding purpose of tax research is to find solutions to the tax problems of one's clients or employer. The process is similar to that of traditional legal research. The researcher must find authority, evaluate the usefulness of that authority, and apply the results of the research to a specific situation.

One can identify two essential tax research skills. The first is the ability to use certain mechanical techniques to identify and locate the tax authorities that relate to solving a problem. The second entails a combination of reasoning and creativity and is more difficult to learn. A tax researcher must begin with native intelligence and imagination and add training and experience properly to apply the information found. Creativity is necessary to explore the relevant relationships among the circumstances and problems at hand to find a satisfying (and defensible) solution. In many cases, no legal authority will exist that is directly on point for the problem. If such a situation exists, the researcher must combine seemingly unrelated facts, ideas (including those that he or she has derived from previous research work), and legal authority to arrive at a truly novel conclusion. This creative ability of the researcher often spells the difference between success and failure in the research process.

OUTLINE OF THE TAX RESEARCH PROCESS

As the tax problems of the client become more significant, the related tax research can become time consuming and thus expensive to the client. A moderate tax research problem often takes up to eight or ten hours of research time, and the bill for these services may approach or even exceed $2,000. Because of the costs that are involved, the tax researcher must work as efficiently as possible to obtain the solution to the client's problem. The researcher needs a framework for the research process, so that he or she does not waste time and effort in arriving at a solution to the problem.

The tax research process can be broken down into six major steps (Exhibit 2–1). Tax researchers (especially those without a substantial amount of experience at the task) must approach the resolution of a tax problem in a structured manner, so that the analysis of the problem will be thorough and the solution complete.

STEP 1: ESTABLISH THE FACTS

All tax research begins with an evaluation of the client's factual situation. To find the solution to a problem, the researcher must understand fully all of the facts that could affect the related tax outcome. Many beginning tax researchers make the mistake of attempting to research a problem before they completely understand all of the relevant facts and circumstances.

Moreover, a tax researcher may approach the tax research process so rigidly that he or she ignores new factual questions that arise during the other steps of the research task. As Exhibit 2–1 illustrates, the tax researcher may engage in several rounds of fact gathering, including those necessitated by additional tax questions that arise as he or she is searching for or evaluating pertinent tax authority. These research "feedback loops" are not endless, although they might appear to be. The best tax researcher is one who can balance the need for efficiency against the need for thoroughness.

Exhibit 2–1

Steps in Tax Research

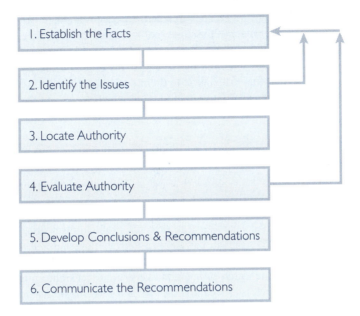

Significant tax facts that often influence the client's situation include:

1. the client's tax entity, for example, individual, corporation, trust;
2. the client's family status and stability;
3. the client's past, present, and projected marginal tax rates;
4. the client's place of legal domicile and citizenship;
5. the client's motivation for the transaction;
6. relationships among the client and other parties who are involved in the transaction;
7. whether special tax rules apply to the taxpayer due to the type of business in which the taxpayer is engaged (he or she is a farmer, fisherman, or long-term contractor); and
8. whether the transaction is proposed or completed.

Fact gathering can present many practical problems for the researcher. Often, the client will (wittingly or not) omit information that is vital to a solution. He or she may not believe that the information is important or may have personal reasons for not conveying the information to the practitioner. In such cases, the researcher must persist until all of the available information is known. In some cases, facts that initially appear to be irrelevant may prove to be important as the research project progresses. The researcher, therefore, should pay attention to and record all details that the client discloses. Efficient tax research cannot be completed until the factual situation is clear; without all of the facts at hand, the researcher could make costly false starts that, when additional pertinent facts become known, must be discarded or redone, often at the client's (or, worse, at the researcher's) expense.

In gathering facts relative to a research problem, the researcher also must be aware of the nontax considerations that are pertinent to the client's situation. For example, the client may have economic constraints (such as cash flow problems) that could preclude the implementation of certain solutions. In addition, the client may have personal preferences that will not accommodate the best tax solution to the problem. For instance, assume that the client could reduce his own income and estate tax liability by making a series of gifts to his grandchildren. However, because the client does not trust the financial judgment of the grandchildren, he does not want to make any such gifts to them during his lifetime. Accordingly, the researcher must look for alternative methods by which to reduce the client's total family tax burden.

STEP 2: IDENTIFY THE ISSUES

A combination of education, training, and experience is necessary to enable the researcher to identify successfully all of the issues with respect to a tax problem. In some situations, this step can be the most difficult element of a tax research problem.

Issues in a closed-fact tax research problem often arise from a conflict with the IRS. In such a case, one can easily ascertain the issue(s). Research of this nature usually consists of finding support for an action that the client has already taken.

In most research projects, however, the researcher must develop the list of issues. Research issues can be divided into two major categories, namely, fact issues and law issues. **Fact issues** are concerned with information having an objective reality, such as the dates of transactions, the amounts involved in an exchange, reasonableness, intent, and purpose. **Law issues** arise when the facts are well established, but it is not clear which portion of the tax law applies to the issue. The application of the law might not be clear because of an apparent conflict among code sections, because a genuine uncertainty as to the meaning of a term as used in the *Internal Revenue Code* may exist, or because there are no provisions in the law that deal directly with the transaction at hand.

When undertaking a research project where the issue may end up being challenged in court, the researcher must be sure to address all of the issues in the tax return. The legal concept of *collateral estoppel* bars relitigation on the same facts or the same issues. Therefore, the practitioner must make sure that his or her case is researched fully, and that no issues that could be resolved in the client's favor have been overlooked. If such an issue is not addressed in the original case, it may be lost forever.

In many situations, a research project may encompass several tax years. The researcher must be aware of any fact or law changes that occur during the period that might affect the results of the research project. The pertinent facts or law may be subject to changes that will cause the researcher to arrive at different conclusions and recommendations, depending on the tax year involved. For example, at one time, the question of whether property qualified for the regular investment credit was a common problem encountered by the tax practitioner. Since the investment credit was repealed for most property placed in service after 1985, subject to transitional rules for certain property, defining "qualified property" is no longer an issue for most taxpayers. Because the transitional rules and the recapture rules still apply where the investment credit was claimed, though, the researcher must still be aware of the provisions.

Seemingly simple situations can often generate many tax research issues. In the process of identifying tax issues, the researcher might discover that additional facts are necessary to provide sufficient answers for the new questions. The taxpayer in the following example is used to illustrate the potential for complexities in merely identifying tax research issues.

Example 2-1 The KML Medical Group of Houston would like to hire a new physician from Atlanta. However, the new physician owns a home in Georgia on which she will sustain a loss if it is sold in the current housing market. KML approached the Happy Care Hospital, the institution at which the group practices, and asked whether they would reimburse the new physician for the loss to facilitate her move to Texas. The hospital agreed to reimburse the physician this year for her $20,000 realized loss.

A tax researcher might address or clarify at least the following issues in making recommendations concerning tax treatment of the reimbursement.

- Why did the hospital reimburse the physician?
- Is there any parent-subsidiary relationship between the hospital and the KML Medical Group?
- Do any members of the KML Medical Group have an equity or debt interest in the hospital?
- Does the reimbursement constitute gross income to the physician?
- If the reimbursement does constitute gross income to the physician, is it treated as active, passive, or investment income?
- Is the new physician classified as an employee of the hospital?
- Should the hospital report the payment to the physician on a Form 1099 or W-2?
- Should the hospital withhold any income or FICA tax on the reimbursement?
- Can the hospital deduct the reimbursement as a trade or business expense?
- Should the physician consider the reimbursement and/or the loss on the sale of her residence in computing her moving expense deduction?
- If the reimbursement is considered gross income to the physician, when should the amount be included in the physician's income?
- Is the reimbursement subject to any restrictions such as the physician's continued employment? For how long?
- Is the reimbursement to the physician considered an additional amount realized on the sale of her residence?
- Can the reimbursement be considered a gift from the hospital to the physician?

Imagine how the question concerning whether the physician's gross income (if any) was ordinary income might lead to the further questions concerning her potential employee status, income tax and FICA withholding, and reporting issues.

Tax Research as an Iterative Process

The process of tax research is iterative in the sense that, once an answer is found, it often causes a new issue to appear and thus requires the gathering of more information. In other words, the tax research process is not strictly linear. This relationship between facts, issues, and answers is illustrated in Exhibit 2–2. The linear tax research process requires *mechanical skills* and *critical thinking*. Mechanical techniques are gained and sharpened through both knowledge and experience. *Knowledge* is usually gained through education in universities and other formal class work. *Experience* is obtained through working in the field and dealing with real tax problems on a recurring basis. Critical thinking is the hardest skill for the researcher to develop. To some

Exhibit 2–2

Interactions among Research Facts, Issues, and Solutions

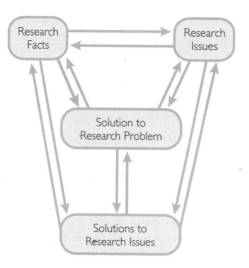

extent it depends on native ability, but a person can be taught the elements of logical analysis and can learn to watch for common pitfalls in evaluating information. Being able to analyze and solve a problem is something the tax researcher must master if he or she is to earn a living in this field. Knowledge is useless when it cannot be applied to solve the problem at hand. The following example illustrates how both mechanical skills and critical thinking are used to solve a tax research problem.

Example 2–2 This year, Chris Lee, a client of your CPA firm, sold stock in Slippery Bank (a publicly traded company with a limited market) to Kolpin Corporation for $100,000. Chris has records that show the stock was acquired ten years ago and has a basis of $135,000. He personally owns 30 percent of Kolpin Corporation. At first glance, the tax researcher would conclude that Chris would have a capital loss of $35,000, which would be deductible against his current-year long-term capital gains of $50,000. This situation appears to be very straightforward. The problem could become complex, though, if someone at the CPA firm asked questions about the other owners of Kolpin. What if Chris's wife, Judy Lee, owns Kolpin stock? The researcher must back up in the research process and gather more facts to determine how many shares she owns.

Suppose Judy Lee owns 25 percent of the Kolpin stock. Now the tax practitioner (you) is faced with new facts and issues; § 267 of the *Internal Revenue Code* suggests that the loss might be disallowed. By looking at § 267(b)(2), you would find that losses between an individual and a corporation are disallowed if "more than 50 percent in value of the outstanding stock of which is owned directly or indirectly, by or for such individual." You then need to know what is "indirect ownership." Looking further in the Code, you would find in § 267(c), "An individual shall be considered as owning the stock owned, directly or indirectly, by or for his family." Finally, in § 267(c)(4), you would discover, "The family of an individual shall include only his brother and sisters (whether by whole or half blood), spouse, ancestors, and lineal descendants."

Armed with this new information, it becomes clear that Chris is a related party to Kolpin Corporation within the meaning of § 267. He owns more than 50 percent of the stock, 30 percent directly and 25 percent indirectly through his wife. As a result, the $35,000 capital loss is not allowed to Chris, and he cannot use it to offset his other capital gains.

STEP 3: LOCATE AUTHORITY

Once facts have been gathered and the issues defined, the tax researcher must locate legal authority that relates to the issue(s). Authority comes from many sources, including Congress, the courts, and the IRS. Since the inception of the 1913 tax law, several hundred thousand pages of such authority have been produced. To solve a given problem, the researcher must find the appropriate authority in this massive amount of information.

In general, tax authority can be classified as either primary or secondary authority. **Primary authority** comes from statutory, administrative, and judicial sources. **Statutory sources** include the U.S. Constitution, tax treaties, and tax laws passed by Congress. Statutory authority is the basis for all tax provisions. The Constitution grants Congress the power to impose and collect taxes, and also authorizes the creation of treaties with other countries. The power of Congress to implement and collect taxes is summarized in the *Internal Revenue Code*, the official title of U.S. tax law. The *Internal Revenue Code* constitutes the basis for all tax law and, therefore, the basis for arriving at solutions to all tax questions.

The other primary sources of the tax law, administrative and judicial authority, function primarily to interpret and explain the application of the provisions of the *Internal Revenue Code* and the intent of Congress. **Administrative sources** include the various rulings of the Treasury Department and the IRS. These are issued in the form of Regulations, Revenue Rulings, and other pronouncements. **Judicial sources** consist of the collected rulings of the various courts on federal tax matters. The primary sources of the tax law will be discussed in greater detail in Chapters 3, 4, and 5. **Secondary authority** consists of unofficial sources of tax information. Examples of secondary authority include tax services, journals, textbooks and treatises, and newsletters. The distinction between primary and secondary sources of authority has become more important since the enactment of IRC § 6662, which imposes a penalty on substantial understatements of tax, except where the taxpayer has "substantial authority" for the position taken on the return. The regulations under § 6662 specify the sources of "substantial authority" to include the provisions of the *Internal Revenue Code*, temporary and final Regulations, court cases, administrative pronouncements, tax treaties, and congressional intent as reflected in committee reports. This list was expanded by the Committee Report for the Revenue Reconciliation Act of 1989 to include Proposed Regulations, Private Letter Rulings, Technical Advice Memoranda, Actions on Decisions, General Counsel Memoranda, Information or Press Releases, Notices, and any other similar documents published by the IRS in the *Internal Revenue Bulletin*. Treatises and articles in legal periodicals, however, are not considered substantial authority under this statute.

Secondary authority is useful when conflicting primary authority exists, when there appears to be no extant primary authority, or when the researcher needs an explanation or clarification of the primary authority. During the past fifteen years, as the support staff of government agencies and (especially) Federal courts has decreased in number or otherwise become inadequate, more dependence has been placed on the secondary authorities of the tax law, even by the IRS, the Treasury Department, and the court system. The beginning researcher must be careful, though, not to rely too heavily on secondary authority, and always to read any pertinent primary authority that is referred to in the secondary sources.

Because of the vast amount of tax authority that is available, the tax researcher would have a tremendous problem in undertaking a tax research problem for a client if it were not for commercial **tax services** and treatises. Several publishers have produced coordinated sets of reference materials that organize the tax authority into a usable format, making the *Internal Revenue Code* much more accessible. These commercial tax services are useful in that they often provide simplified explanations with footnote citations, as well as examples illustrating the application of the law. These tax services may lead the tax researcher, via the footnote references, to the primary source that is pertinent to the question at hand.

Traditionally, tax services have been classified as either annotated or topical. The annotated services are organized in *Internal Revenue Code* section order, while the topical services are arranged by topic, as defined by the publisher's editorial staff. However, the use of computers has significantly blurred the differences between the organization of commercial tax services. With computer hypertext linking, any of the tax services can be used from a Code or topical orientation. Exhibit 2–3 includes a listing of the current major commercial tax services. The tax services are discussed in greater detail in later chapters.

In 1992, Prentice Hall (and Maxwell Macmillan, an associated publisher) sold its annotated tax reporter and other research items to the Research Institute of America (RIA). RIA has renamed and continued the former annotated Prentice Hall tax reporter, as well as its original topical reporter *(Tax Coordinator)*. As the new products are phased into existing shelf space, some of the items mentioned in this book as produced by RIA, especially older material, may still appear in tax libraries as Prentice Hall or Maxwell Macmillan publications.

Court decisions are published in sets of bound volumes called *court reporters*. Depending on the court involved, the reporters are produced by the Government Printing Office (GPO), West Publishing Company, Research Institute of America (RIA), and Commerce Clearing House (CCH). Exhibit 2–4 lists the common court reporters that contain tax cases frequently used in tax research. Chapter 5 discusses in greater detail the means by which to find court cases in these reporters.

Exhibit 2–3 Major Tax Services

Publisher	Title of Tax Service	Orientation
Research Institute of America (RIA)	*Tax Coordinator 2d*	Topic
Research Institute of America (RIA)	*United States Tax Reporter*	Code
Commerce Clearing House (CCH)	*Standard Federal Tax Reporter*	Code
Commerce Clearing House (CCH)	*Federal Tax Service*	Topic
Bureau of National Affairs (BNA)	*Tax Management Portfolios*	Topic
West Group	*Mertens Law of Federal Income Taxation*	Topic

Exhibit 2–4
Common Court Reporters Used in Tax Research

Publisher	Court Reporter Title
Research Institute of America	*American Federal Tax Reports (AFTR)*
Research Institute of America	*TC Memorandum Decisions*
West Publishing Co.	*Federal Supplement*
West Publishing Co.	*Federal Reporter*
West Publishing Co.	*Supreme Court Reporter*
Commerce Clearing House	*United States Tax Cases (USTC)*
Commerce Clearing House	*Tax Court Memorandum Decisions*
Government Printing Office	*Tax Court of the U.S. Reports*
Government Printing Office	*Tax State Reports*

Both CCH and RIA provide "citators" as part of their tax services. A citator is a reference source that enables the researcher to follow the judicial history of court cases. The citators are discussed in detail in Chapter 8. The GPO prints many of the pronouncements of the IRS. The primary publication for IRS authority is in a set of bound volumes titled the *Cumulative Bulletin*. Chapter 4 includes a detailed discussion concerning the use of this authority.

Tax journals are another source of information that can be useful. By reading tax journals, a tax practitioner can become aware of many current problem areas in taxation. She can also increase her awareness of recent developments in the tax law, tax compliance matters, and tax planning techniques and opportunities. Numerous journals, ranging from law reviews to *Cosmopolitan,* publish articles on current tax matters. The tax researcher typically is interested in publications devoted to scholarly and professional discussions of tax matters. Among these publications, each tax journal usually is written for a specific group of readers. Chapter 9 further examines the major tax journals and explains how to locate articles of interest to the tax practitioner. Exhibit 2–5 lists several useful tax journals, their publishers, and the target readership of each.

Exhibit 2–5 Selected Tax Journals

Journal	Publisher	Target Readership
Journal of Taxation	Warren, Gorham & Lamont—RIA	Sophisticated tax practitioners
Practical Tax Strategies	Warren, Gorham & Lamont—RIA	Tax practitioners in general practice
Estate Planning	Warren, Gorham & Lamont—RIA	Practitioners who are interested in estate and gift tax matters
The Tax Adviser	American Institute of CPAs	Members of AICPA and other tax practitioners
TAXES	Commerce Clearing House	General tax practitioners

Step 4: Evaluate Authority

After the researcher has located authority that deals with the client's problem, he or she must evaluate the usefulness of that authority. All tax authority does not carry the same precedential value. For example, the Tax Court could hold that an item should be excluded from gross income at the same time that an outstanding IRS Revenue Ruling asserts the item is taxable. The tax researcher must evaluate the two authorities and decide whether to recommend that his or her client report the disputed item.

In the process of evaluating the authority for the issue(s) under research, new issues not previously considered by the researcher may come to light. If this is the case, the researcher may be required to gather additional facts, find additional pertinent authority, and evaluate the new issues. This loop is illustrated in Exhibit 2–1.

Step 5: Develop Conclusions and Recommendations

After several iterations of the first four steps of the tax research process, the researcher must arrive at his or her conclusions for the tax issues raised. Often, the research will not have resulted in a clear solution to the client's tax problems, perhaps because of unresolved issues of law or incomplete descriptions of the facts. In addition, the personal preferences of the client must also be considered. The "ideal" solution for tax purposes may be entirely impractical because of other factors that are integral to the tax question. In any of these cases, the tax practitioner must use professional judgment in making recommendations based on the conclusions drawn from the tax research process.

Where unresolved issues exist, the researcher might inform the client about alternative possible outcomes of each disputed transaction, and give the best recommendation for each. If the research involved an open-fact situation, the recommendation might detail several alternative courses of future action (e.g., whether to complete the deal, or how to document the intended effects of the transaction). In many cases, the researcher may find it appropriate to present his or her recommendation of the "best" solution from a tax perspective, as well as one or more alternative recommendations that may be much more workable solutions. In any case, the researcher will want to discuss with the client the pros and cons of all reasonable recommendations and the risks associated with each course of action.

Step 6: Communicate the Recommendations

The final step in the research process is to communicate the results and recommendations of the research. The results of the research effort usually are summarized in a memorandum to the client file and in a letter to the client. Both of these items usually contain a restatement of the pertinent facts as the researcher understands them, any assumptions the researcher made, the issues addressed, the applicable authority, and the practitioner's recommendations. An example of the structure of a simple tax research memo is shown in Exhibit 2–6. The memorandum to the file usually contains more detail than does the letter to the client.

In any event, the researcher must temper his or her communication of the research results so that it is understandable by the intended reader. For instance, the researcher should use vastly different jargon and citation techniques in preparing an

Exhibit 2–6
Tax Research Memo
Sample Format

Over & Short CPAs
San Francisco, CA

Relevant Facts:
_____
_____
_____
_____
_____

Specific Issues:
_____
_____
_____
_____
_____

Conclusions:
_____
_____
_____
_____
_____

Support:
_____
_____
_____
_____
_____

Actions to be Taken:
_____ Discuss with client. Date discussed: _____
_____ Prepare a memo or letter to the client.
_____ Explore other fact situations.
_____ Other action. Describe

Preparer: _____
Reviewer: _____

article for the *Journal of Taxation* than in preparing a client memo for a businessperson or layperson who is not sophisticated in tax matters. Chapter 10 provides additional guidelines and formats for client memoranda and other means of delivering the results of one's research.

OVERVIEW OF COMPUTERIZED TAX RESEARCH

The body of knowledge that encompasses the field of taxation has been growing at a phenomenal pace for the past fifteen years. Since 1975, Congress has enacted more than a dozen major tax and revenue bills that have had a significant effect on U.S. taxpayers. In addition, each year hundreds of new Treasury Regulations, court decisions, Revenue and Private Letter Rulings, Revenue Procedures, and Technical Advice Memoranda are issued.

The avalanche of tax-related information is not expected to decrease during the foreseeable future. The abundance of available information, as well as the complexity of the tax laws that have been enacted since 1975, has made it even more difficult and time consuming to conduct thorough and effective research concerning a tax-related issue.

Whenever a diligent tax professional is providing advice or other services to a client, he or she must be cognizant of the latest legislative changes and judicial decisions. Furthermore, he or she must be able to draw upon, and sort through, the vast body of established tax knowledge and to apply statutes and administrative and judicial rulings to the current tax issue.

Computers have significantly changed how tax research is conducted. The vast amount of storage available on a computer, coupled with the computer's fast retrieval of information, has made it an invaluable tool for tax research. The tax practitioner has two chief ways to find computer information for tax research purposes: (1) **online** and **CD-ROM** subscription systems and (2) online free (nonsubscription) **Internet** sites.

Althought Part III of this text discusses computerized tax research in detail, an overview of the subject is presented below.

ONLINE AND CD-ROM SYSTEMS

Computerized tax online services are accessible through the Internet and several public telecommunications networks. The materials that are available through the use of these services are contained in databases that are stored at centralized computer locations. These databases may be accessed from remote locations with the use of a variety of compatible video display terminals and keyboards. Usually, they can be accessed via compatible commercial (including personal) computers that the user already owns. The personal computer's (PC) function keys typically perform all of the services that are required by the search software. Some popular online and CD-ROM subscription systems are shown in Exhibit 2–7 and examples of online free Internet sites are shown in Exhibit 2–8.

Electronic online tax research systems are relatively simple to operate. Normally, the user will have no trouble utilizing the system after he or she has devised an effective search command or query. Once the user is satisfied with the composition of his or her search query in an online system, it is transmitted over a telecommunications network to a central computer, where it is processed and documents are identified that satisfy the search request. The text of the retrieved documents is then transmitted to the user and displayed on his or her terminal. After the documents are received, the user must evaluate them and decide whether further research is required. Any documents that are displayed on the terminal may be printed in the researcher's office or saved as a file on a PC and retained for future reference.

BENEFITS OF USING A COMPUTERIZED TAX SERVICE

Traditional tax research usually begins with the consultation of topical and annotated tax services or tax-related text. In most instances, the user first must consult a topical index to locate the appropriate page or pages on which to begin his or her research. However, any time that a printed tax service is accessed by way of its topical index, the user is relying on someone else's judgment (i.e., the service's editors) or

Exhibit 2–7 Examples of Online and CD-ROM Subscription Systems

Name	Description
RIA Checkpoint	A web-based computerized tax research service that contains all the RIA material on Federal, state, local, and international taxation. Checkpoint contains all RIA analytical material such as the *Tax Coordinator 2d* and the *United States Tax Reporter*. All public domain information such as the code and regulations, U.S. tax treaties, IRS publications and pronouncements, and court cases are available on Checkpoint. Also available on CD-ROM as RIA OnPoint.
CCH Tax Research Network	A web-based Internet system that contains all of CCH's tax services and other Federal and state legal and tax information. All government documents (IRS publications, court cases, etc.) are available on this system.
Kleinrock's	The Code, the Regulations, *Cumulative Bulletins*, Tax Court Regular decisions (since 1954), Tax Court Memo decisions and other court cases (since 1987), and all IRS publications. Also available on CD-ROM.
Tax Analysts	The Code, the Regulations, *Cumulative Bulletins*, Court Regular decisions (since 1954). Tax Court Memo decisions and other court cases (since 1985), *Circular 230*, and all IRS publications.
LexisNexis	The largest of the commercial computer-based information systems. Besides containing all Federal and state legal and tax research material, Lexis has extensive libraries of newspapers, magazines, journals, patent records, and medical, economic, and accounting databases.
Westlaw	Offered by the major legal publisher, this system contains all Federal and state legal sources including court cases, administrative releases, and statutory information. All government documents (IRS publications, court cases, etc.) are also available on this system. Also available on CD-ROM.

performance (e.g., the filing staff of the library for proper treatment of update material) as to what is important with respect to the specific topic. Moreover, the desired information may not be located, even if it exists and has been filed properly, because the keyword for which the user is looking is not the same word that was used by the editor in the index to discuss the issue that is the subject of the search. It is also possible that, when the index was prepared, the topic of the search was ignored because it was not as important a topic as it is today.

The primary benefit of using a computerized tax service is that such a resource makes it possible for the *user* to index any significant term, that is, by using it as a search term in a query. By creating his or her own indexes, the researcher is not bound by the limitations that are imposed in manually accessing tax materials through a printed service or text. Once the central computer or CD is accessed with a proper search request, the service's software will electronically scan the designated files and retrieve all of the documents that contain the word or words included in the query. Thus, the user is able to bypass the predefined list of topics that constitute the subject's index and perform his or her search directly on the documents themselves.

Another benefit of using a computerized tax research system is that the user can tailor his or her query to fit the requirements of a specific tax problem. Because the

Exhibit 2-8 Examples of Online Free Internet Sites

Site Name	Internet Address	Description
Will Yancey's Home Page	http://www.willyancey.com	One of the best indexes available to other tax, accounting, and legal web sites. There are hundreds of links to commercial, Federal government, state, local, and international web sites.
Internal Revenue Service	http://www.irs.ustreas.gov	The best free site where taxpayers can find tax forms, instructions, publications, and other IRS information.
Practitioners Pub. Co.	http://www.ppcnet.com	An excellent site that contains a free newsletter, free common tax forms, and an index to other Internet tax resources.
Ernst & Young	http://www.ey.com	A web site that contains a large amount of tax and accounting information from the staff of E&Y.
Deloitte & Touche	http://www.dtonline.com	The D&T web site contains a large amount of tax and accounting information from the staff of D&T.
Thomas	http://thomas.loc.gov	Legislative information from the Library of Congress.

user defines the precise specifications of the query, computerized research is exceptionally flexible. Each search request can be made as specific or as broad as desired, depending on the issue to be researched. If they are properly structured, computerized search queries can result in the research process being conducted with greater speed and thoroughness, and they can reduce the amount of time spent on that phase of the research task.

Such speed and flexibility is best realized as the researcher moves among pertinent tax documents. Most of the electronic services allow this capability through **hypertext** linking. Generally, when a hypertext link is indicated, typically through a different color for the text or a special character like a caret, the user can move to the related document so indicated with a click of the mouse or keyboard. For instance, the researcher could be reading a court case that refers to § 2032A. By clicking on the hypertext link character, he or she is taken directly to the text of the code section for direct perusal of the statutory language. Similarly, links can be made to pertinent regulations or to similar court documents in a manner that has no parallel in the traditional paper-oriented world of tax research. As the underlying documents become more voluminous, the importance of moving among the documents quickly is met only with an electronic research base.

Online services are updated much faster than printed tax services. A researcher generally is able to retrieve recent court decisions and administrative rulings from a computerized service one or more weeks before his or her library will receive updated print material containing the same case or ruling. In addition, the computerized services include one or more of the daily tax news summaries, including those written by the editorial staff of the producer of the service itself, or by other tax service organizations, such as BNA's *Daily Tax Report* or Tax Analysts' *Tax Notes Today*. In this regard, a computerized tax service allows a tax researcher to stay on top of the latest news and developments without incurring additional subscription costs for the stand-alone services.

Computerized services are particularly useful in researching case law. Every word that is contained in a case is included in the database of the computerized service. Thus, the user can save time by directly accessing only those cases that contain the key terms of his or her search. For example, all of the cases that deal with unreasonable compensation can be accessed within minutes, simply by using *unreasonable compensation* as a search request. In addition, the research is probably more thorough this way than it would be by traditional methods because the user will be able to retrieve all of the cases that are included in the library that is accessed, not just those that are included in a legal index or digest.

An additional benefit of using a computerized tax service is that certain documents may be obtained only from the central computer library. For example, full printed transcripts of Actions on Decision and slip opinions normally are not published. However, these documents often may be obtained from the databases of computerized commercial tax services.

A computerized research service also can be used to obtain regularly published documents to which the researcher does not have access. For example, the full text of Private Letter Rulings is available on most computerized tax research databases. Thus, by using a computerized service, a tax practitioner can obtain only the ruling needed, without subscribing to an expensive loose-leaf service for the entire year.

FACTORS IN CHOOSING A COMPUTERIZED TAX SERVICE

In *Computer-Assisted Legal and Tax Research* (Prentice-Hall), Thomas and Weinstein propose that a potential subscriber consider the following factors when choosing a computerized tax database:

- *Database contents:* Does the service provide specialty libraries that will be important in the researcher's work and that are unavailable elsewhere?
- *Search capabilities:* While the search commands and requirements are similar among the commercial tax services, some of the electronic services allow direct reviews of editorial information, and others encompass the Shepard's citations service.
- *Training:* Each of the services offers some level of educational training, either at the user's office or at a regional training center. The proximity, depth, and quality of such seminars may differ among services and across the country.
- *Customer support:* Other forms of contact with the user, such as to develop more sophisticated search techniques or to provide necessary repair services, should be available to the subscriber.
- *Price:* One must consider the cost of the time required to perform the research itself, as well as that of necessary equipment or special software.

In the past, tax practitioners were faced with a choice of either a variable-cost online computer service (e.g., Lexis, Westlaw) or a fixed-cost CD-ROM tax service (e.g., RIA OnPoint). Recently, however, the advent of the **World Wide Web**-based fixed-cost tax service (e.g., RIA Checkpoint) has changed what is the optimal computer tax subscription for many tax practitioners. With a web-based tax service, tax practitoners have all the features (e.g., fast updates, large databases) of the variable-cost online system with the fixed-cost structure of a CD-ROM system. In addition, a web-based computer tax service does not require any additional hardware since most tax practitioners already have the hardware for tax return preparation and word processing. Because of all its inherit advantages, the web-based tax service will probably become the standard source for current and archival tax research material.

USING A COMPUTER IN TAX RESEARCH

In the first part of this chapter, we presented a model of the tax research process. In this model, steps 1 and 2 of the tax research model are to (1) establish the facts and (2) identify the issues related to the research question(s). The next step in the research model is to locate tax authority with which to solve the research question. In most situations, the tax researcher is going to use a computer to find the required authority (or to conclude that there is no authority on the subject). The process of finding tax authority using a computer can be broken down into several steps, as shown in Exhibit 2–9.

STEP 1: STATE THE ISSUE AS A QUESTION

After the tax researcher has established the facts and identified the issues that he or she needs to resolve, the issues should be stated as a question to be answered. For example, suppose the researcher has a client who is a self-employed attorney. As part of her trade or business, the attorney incurs substantial travel expenses during the year. She has learned that if she buys airline tickets in advance and extends her visit over a Saturday night, she will receive a large savings on airfare. Usually, an extra day of meals and lodging can save many hundreds of dollars in her airfare travel expenses. In the current year, she has spent $4,000 in extra Saturday night expenses to save $12,000 in airfare. The research question in this situation could be stated as:

Are the additional travel costs (primarily meals and lodging) of staying over a Saturday night in order to save substantial amounts on the business airfare deductible?

Exhibit 2–9
Steps in the Computer Research Process

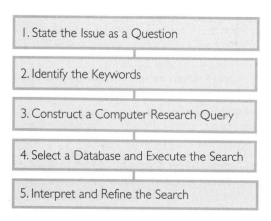

STEP 2: IDENTIFY THE KEYWORDS

Once the research question has been stated, the researcher must next identify the keywords to construct a proper query in the next step. In the above research question, the keywords would be as follows:

- meals and lodging
- travel
- Saturday
- deductible
- airfare

The researcher is looking for words that, when entered into a computer, will find tax authority that is "on point." If the correct keywords are not identified, tax researchers cannot find the authority needed or could be led down blind alleys.

STEP 3: CONSTRUCT A COMPUTER RESEARCH QUERY

Computer tax research systems use a **query** in order to begin the search for the authority needed by the researcher. The construction of the query varies for each commercial computer tax research system; however, there are many similarities between the systems. All tax computer research systems recognize various types of connectors to construct a research query. Generally, computer tax services, such as **RIA Checkpoint,** have ten to fifteen search connectors available, but most tax research searches can be accomplished by using several basic connectors. The syntax of the four most useful connectors in RIA Checkpoint are shown in Exhibit 2–10.

In addition, RIA Checkpoint and other computer tax services allow the use of wildcard (universal) character(s). For example, in RIA Checkpoint, an "*" (asterisk) at the end of a root word finds all variations of that word. Thus, the word "deduct*" will find deduct, deducted, deduction, deductible, etc. Other computer tax services use similar methods to construct tax research queries.

Computer tax services are continually being updated. Users should check the appropriate help menu of whichever computer tax service is being used to determine how to construct a query and to find other new features.

Exhibit 2–10
Selected RIA Checkpoint Search Connectors

Connector	Example	Description
and	stock and securities	Finds documents with both the term stock and the term securities in them.
or	stock or securities	Finds documents with either the term stock or the term securities in them.
/n	stock/15 securities	Finds documents where the term stock is within 15 words of the term securities.
not	stock not securities	Finds documents with the term stock, but not the term securities.

STEP 4: SELECT A DATABASE AND EXECUTE THE SEARCH

Once the query is constructed, the researcher must log on to and choose a database to search. Each computer tax research system contains numerous databases. As an example, RIA Checkpoint contains the following databases (among many others):

- All Federal Databases
- Federal Editorial Material
- *Federal Tax Coordinator 2d* (a tax service)
- Source Material: Cases
- Source Material: Code, Committee Reports, Regulations, Tax Treaties
- Source Material: IRS Rulings and Releases
- Source Material: Tax Court and Federal Procedural Rules
- WG&L Journals

Continuing our example of the deductibility of Saturday night expenses, we could choose to search *"All Federal Databases"* using a query such as: *travel /25 Saturday*. See Exhibit 2–11. If we executed this search on RIA Checkpoint, we would find several references to the fact that the IRS has issued Private Letter Ruling 9237014 that states the extra expenses for staying over a Saturday to get a lower airfare are deductible as part of the expenses of the business trip.

STEP 5: INTERPRET AND REFINE THE SEARCH

After executing a computer tax search, often the research is going to have too little or too much information. If there is too little information, the search query has to be

Exhibit 2–11
RIA Checkpoint Query and Database Selection Screen

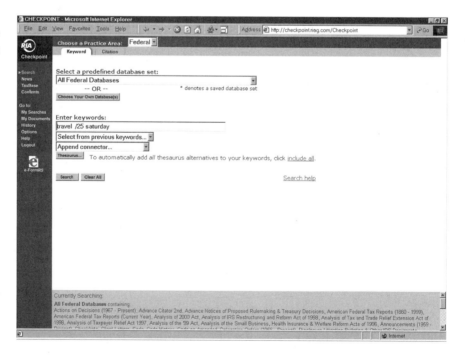

broadened. For example, other keywords may have to be used or proximity connectors may have to be relaxed. On the other hand, if the researcher has too much information, the search query has to be tightened. For example, more unique keywords may have to be used or proximity connectors may have to be used or narrowed.

Computer tax services (e.g., Lexis, Westlaw, Kleinrock's, CCH Tax Research Network) have their own format for conducting tax searches. However, they all use the same basic steps in executing such searches. In all computer tax systems, the researcher has to state the issue, select the keywords, construct a query, choose a database, execute a search, and interpret and refine the search.

IRS WEB SITE RESEARCH

The IRS maintains an excellent web site where someone interested in tax information can conduct limited tax research. While the IRS web site is not a full-service site, it does contain searchable and downloadable tax information such as tax forms, instructions, publications (e.g., Publication 17), and other IRS information. The IRS web site also has a limited search engine that uses three basic connectors and recognizes wild card characters. The connectors used by the search engine are (1) "and," (2) "or," and (3) "not." There is currently no proximity connector in the search engine, but hopefully the IRS will add one in the future.

The wildcards "*" and "?" are also allowed by the IRS search engine. Using these wildcards, you can find documents that contain words that have similar spellings but are not stemmed variants. For example, air* finds documents that contain air, airline, and airhead. Entering "?at" finds documents that contain cat and hat, while "??at" finds documents that contain that and chat.

Example 2–3 Last year, Doris' daughter and her (worthless) husband moved into her home. This year, Doris has supported both of them for the entire year. Doris would like to know if she can claim a dependency exemption for her son-in-law. Doris could go to the IRS web site **(http://www.irs.ustreas.gov)** and click the search button. She could then search terms such as "son-in-law" and "dependent." See Exhibit 2–12. The IRS search engine should return several IRS Publications (e.g., Pub 501) that will inform Doris she can claim a deduction for her son-in-law.

SUMMARY

Tax research is a complex process. The researcher must complete all of the steps in the research process to arrive at a solution to or recommendation for the client's tax problem. Moreover, the steps delineated in Exhibit 2–1 (or iterations of them) must be completed in their proper order to minimize the possibility of errors in evaluating the authority, arriving at conclusions, or making recommendations. If the process is abbreviated, the researcher risks failure to properly serve the client. This could result in the payment of unnecessary taxes by the client, or in the payment of damages by the tax practitioner to the client.

EXHIBIT 2-12

Example of IRS Site Search

TAX TUTOR

Reinforce the tax research information covered in this chapter by completing the on-line tutorials located at the Federal Tax Research web site:

http://raabe.swcollege.com

KEY WORDS

By the time you complete this chapter, you should be comfortable discussing each of the following terms. If you need additional review, return to the material in the chapter or consult the glossary to this text.

Administrative Sources	Online System
CD-ROM System	Primary Authority
Collateral Estoppel	Query
Fact Issue	RIA Checkpoint
Hypertext	Secondary Authority
Internal Revenue Code	Statutory Sources
Internet	Tax Journal
Judicial Sources	Tax Service
Law Issue	World Wide Web
LexisNexis	

DISCUSSION QUESTIONS

1. What is the purpose of tax research?
2. What are the basic steps in conducting tax research? Briefly discuss each step in the tax research process.
3. What are the two chief tax research skills, as identified in this text? Explain the importance of each basic skill.
4. The tax researcher must find the facts as the first step in tax research. Give examples of the kind of factual information that a tax practitioner might want to obtain.
5. What are some of the potential pitfalls in the first step of the tax research process?
6. In each of the following independent situations, indicate whether the item generally would be a tax (T) or a nontax (NT) consideration in solving a tax research or tax planning problem.
   a. The taxpayer would like to set up a private foundation to reduce her annual income tax liability.
   b. The taxpayer has a very poor cash flow because of prior investments; therefore, he has a limited ability to make "tax-advantaged" investments.
   c. The taxpayer wants to transfer as much of her property to her grandchildren as possible. However, she does not want any of the property to fall into the hands of the grandchildren's mother (her daughter-in-law).
   d. The taxpayer lived through the Great Depression of the 1930s and does not like investments with any risk, such as owning stocks or bonds.
   e. The taxpayer likes to maintain highly liquid investments, such as money market funds and certificates of deposit in insured banks and savings and loan institutions.
   f. The taxpayer hates to pay Federal taxes. He will take any legal action to avoid paying any Federal income, estate, or gift taxes.
7. Identify and briefly describe the two major types of tax research issues.
8. What is *collateral estoppel?* How does it affect tax research and planning?
9. Tax law provisions tend to change over time. Explain how this might affect tax research and planning.
10. In the tax research process, the researcher has an obligation to the client to evaluate authority. Do the precedents in all tax authority carry the same value? Explain.
11. Primary tax authority can be classified as statutory, administrative, or judicial. Briefly describe each.
12. Classify each of the following items as a primary (P) or secondary (S) tax research authority.
    a. The *Internal Revenue Code*
    b. A Tax Court case
    c. A textbook on corporate taxation
    d. Treasury Regulations
    e. An IRS Revenue Ruling
    f. An article in *Journal of Taxation*

Continued

g. *Taxes on Parade* (a newsletter)
h. A Supreme Court decision on a tax matter

13. Briefly characterize and distinguish between annotated tax services and topical tax services.
14. Classify each of the following commercial tax services as either an annotated service (A) or a topical service (T).
    a. CCH's *Standard Federal Tax Reporter*
    b. RIA's *Tax Coordinator*
    c. BNA's *Tax Management Portfolios*
    d. *Mertens Law of Federal Income Taxation*
    e. CCH's *Federal Tax Service*
    f. RIA's *United States Tax Reporter*
15. Where can one find published court decisions?
16. Who publishes each of the following court reporters?
    a. *Tax Court Memorandum Decisions*
    b. *United States Reports*
    c. *TC Memorandum Decisions*
    d. *Federal Reporter*
    e. *Supreme Court Reporter*
    f. *Federal Supplement*
    g. *American Federal Tax Reports*
    h. *Tax Court of the U.S. Reports*
    i. *United States Tax Cases*
17. What kind of information can be found in a citator?
18. Name the primary bound publication where IRS pronouncements can be found.
19. Tax practitioners use the term "tax service" all the time. What is a tax service?
20. What is the target readership of each of the following tax journals?
    a. *TAXES*
    b. *Journal of Taxation*
    c. *Practical Tax Strategies*
    d. *The Tax Adviser*
    e. *Estate Planning*
21. Specific items of tax authority have different "values" in helping the tax researcher to solve his or her problem. Explain this statement and describe how it applies to the tax research process.
22. Step 5 in the tax research process is concerned with reaching a conclusion or making a recommendation. If one has not found a clear answer to a tax research problem, how is a conclusion or recommendation to be reached?
23. The final step in the research process typically involves a memorandum to the client file and/or a letter to the client communicating the results of the research. List the items that should be found in the body of both of these documents.
24. It has been said that the tax research process is more circular than linear. Do you agree with this statement? Explain your answer.
25. What is deemed to be substantial authority under the § 6662 Regulations? Why is this important?
26. Describe an online tax research system. What are two advantages of such a system over a standard printed tax service?
27. What is computerized tax research, and why is it necessary for the tax professional to be able to use computerized techniques to conduct tax research?

28. What are the disadvantages of using a computerized tax service?
29. List four benefits of using a computerized service to conduct your tax research.
30. What are the major steps in developing an effective computerized tax research query?
31. If you were researching an issue and the computer informed you that it had located 1,000 pertinent documents, what would you do to reduce the number of retrieved documents to a more reasonable number?
32. What are the search connectors discussed in the text used by RIA Checkpoint? Describe how each operates.
33. For the following RIA Checkpoint databases state if they generally contain primary or secondary authority: (1) *Federal Tax Coodinator 2d,* (2) Source Material Cases, (3) Source Material IRS Rulings and Releases, and (4) WG&L Journals.
34. What is the Internet address of the Internal Revenue Service's server?
35. What are the connectors used by the IRS web site search engine?
36. What are the two "wildcards" used by the IRS web site search engine. Explain how each operates.

EXERCISES

37. Use your university's tax library (or other library assigned by your instructor) to discover the breadth of tax journal offerings. List any five tax journals and the publisher of each.
38. The purpose of this exercise is for you to locate publications that frequently are used in tax research. Give the call number and location (i.e., floor, room, stack, etc.) in your library, and the major color of the binding of the publication, for each of the following references. If a publication is not available, state that it is not.
    a. RIA's *United States Tax Reporter*
    b. CCH's *Standard Federal Tax Reporter*
    c. BNA's *Tax Management Portfolios*
    d. *Mertens Law of Federal Income Taxation*
    e. RIA's *Tax Coordinator 2d*
39. Find out whether each of the following court reporters is available in your library. Give the call number and location (i.e., floor, room, stack, etc.) for each reference. If a reporter is not available, state that it is not.
    a. *American Federal Tax Reports*
    b. *United States Tax Cases*
    c. *Tax Court of the U.S. Reports*
    d. *Tax Court Memorandum Decisions*
    e. *United States Reports*
    f. *Federal Reporter, 3d Series*
40. Determine if each of the following tax journals is available in your library. What is the most current issue in your library? List the author(s) and title of any two articles from the most recent issue.
    a. *Journal of Taxation*
    b. *Practical Tax Strategies*
    c. *Journal of International Taxation*
    d. *The Tax Adviser*
    e. *TAXES*

41. Is the *Internal Revenue Code* found in separate volumes in each of the following tax services? If so, in how many volumes?
    a. CCH's *Standard Federal Tax Reporter*
    b. BNA's *Tax Management Portfolios*
    c. RIA's *Tax Coordinator 2d*
42. Find a copy of the *Cumulative Bulletin* in your university's library. By looking in a volume, list three different tax research sources published in a *Cumulative Bulletin*.
43. Locate a copy of the *American Federal Tax Reports* in your library. List two courts that have decisions published in this court reporter.
44. Locate a copy of CCH's *United States Tax Cases* in your library. List two courts which have decisions published in this court reporter.
45. In your university's library, locate the CCH and RIA citators. How many volumes does each contain?
46. Determine if your campus has any of the following online or CD-ROM tax research services available for student use. If a service is available on your campus, describe how you would gain access to that system for research projects in your tax classes. If a service is not available on your campus, state where you might be able to find it.
    a. Kleinrock's
    b. Lexis
    c. RIA Checkpoint
    d. Westlaw
    e. CCH Tax Research Network
47. Go to the IRS web page **(http://www.irs.ustreas.gov)** and print out a copy of the most recent Instructions for Form 3903 of Form 1040. You may first need to download the Adobe Acrobat Reader (© Adobe Systems) software to be able to view or print the form. The software is provided free of charge by Adobe through a link on the IRS page.
48. Go to Will Yancey's home page **(http://www.willyancey.com)** and give the complete web address for each of the following sites:
    a. The California Franchise Tax Board
    b. The New York Department of Taxation and Finance
    c. The American Institute of CPAs (AICPA)
49. Go to the Practitioners Publishing Co. web site **(http://www.ppcnet.com)** and locate the most recent Practitioners *Tax Action Bulletin*. Print out a copy of the bulletin.
50. Go to the IRS Web page **(http://www.irs.ustreas.gov)** and find the most recent IRS Publication 1542, Per Diem Rates. What is the maximum per diem rate for lodging and meals and incidental expenses (M&IE) for each of the following towns:
    a. Tucson, Arizona
    b. Palm Springs, California
    c. San Antonio, Texas
51. Jennifer owns 200 acres of land on which she grows flowers for sale to local nurseries. Her adjusted basis in the land is $30,000. She receives condemnation proceeds of $20,000 from the state for ten acres of her land on which a new freeway will be built. The state also pays her $30,000 for the harmful effects that the increased auto exhausts might have on her flowers. List as many tax research issues

as you can to determine the tax consequences of these transactions. Do not attempt to answer any of the questions you raise. Simply identify the research issues.

52. Joey parked his car on the top of a hill when he went to watch the X games in San Diego. He did not properly set his brakes or curb the wheels when he parked the car. When he returned from the games, he found his car had rolled down the hill, smashed into Nick's house, and injured Nick, who was watching TV in his den. Joey does not have car insurance. List as many tax research issues as you can to determine the tax consequences of this accident. Do not attempt to answer any of the questions you raise. Simply identify the research issues.

53. John and Marsha are married and filed a joint return for the past year. During that year, Marsha was employed as an assistant cashier at a local bank and, as such, was able to embezzle $75,000, none of which was reported on their joint return. Before the defalcation was discovered, Marsha disappeared and has not been seen or heard from since. List as many tax research issues as you can to determine the tax consequences of this crime. Do not attempt to answer any of the questions you raise. Simply identify the research issues.

54. In the current year, Dave receives stock worth $125,000 from his employer. The stock is restricted and cannot be sold by Dave for seven years. Dave estimates the stock will be worth $300,000 after the seven years. List as many tax research issues as you can to determine the tax consequences of this transaction. Do not attempt to answer any of the questions you raise. Simply identify the research issues.

55. On December 1, 20x1, Ericka receives $18,000 for three months' rent (December, January, and February) of an office building. List as many tax research issues as you can to determine the tax consequences of this transaction. Do not attempt to answer any of the questions you raise. Simply identify the research issues.

56. Formulate a search query to determine whether your client is required to include in gross income the proceeds from a redemption of a tax-exempt bond, purchased in 1988 and called by the school district this year. Redemption proceeds were $90,000, and the 1988 purchase price on the secondary market was $76,000. Give an example of a computer search query using only the following RIA Checkpoint connectors: "and," "or," "/n," and "not."

57. Formulate a search query to determine the provisions of the United States' treaty with Germany relative to fellowship income received by a business student during a summer internship with the German Department of Price Controls. Give an example of a computer search query using only the following RIA Checkpoint connectors: "and," "or," "/n," and "not."

58. Formulate a search query to determine whether your client is required to capitalize fringe benefits and general overhead that is attributable to employees who are building an addition to your client's factory during a "slack time" at work. Give an example of a computer search query using only the following RIA Checkpoint connectors: "and," "or," "/n," and "not."

59. Formulate a search query to determine whether your client can retroactively elect to change its accounting method. Give an example of a computer search query using only the following RIA Checkpoint connectors: "and," "or," "/n," and "not."

60. Formulate a search query to find all of the cases in which the word *constructive* occurs within ten words of the word *dividend*. Give an example of a computer query using only the following RIA Checkpoint connectors: "and," "or," "/n," and "not."

RESEARCH CASES

61. Sam Manuel has been employed on a full-time basis as an electrical engineer for the past three years. Prior to obtaining full-time employment, he was self-employed as an inventor of complex electronic components. During this period of self-employment, most of his projects produced little income, although several produced a significant amount of revenue.

    Due to the large expenditures necessary and the failure of the majority of the products to produce a profit, Sam was forced to seek full-time employment. After obtaining full-time employment, he continued to work long hours to perfect several of his inventions. He continued to enjoy relatively little success with most of his products, but certain projects were successfully marketed and generated a profit. For the last two years, Sam's invention activity has generated a net loss.

    a. List as many possible tax research issues as you can to determine whether the losses may be deducted.
    b. After completing your list of tax research issues, list the keywords you might use to construct a computer tax research query.

62. Matthew Broadway was a partner in the law firm of Johnson and Smith, a partnership of twenty partners, for the past ten years. Without the knowledge or consent of the other partners, Matthew worked on a highly complicated acquisition and merger project for six months, at all times using the resources of the law firm. Several months later, the firm for which Matthew provided the professional services made out a check for $300,000 to the firm of Johnson and Smith. Matthew insisted that the fee should rightly be his, while the firm disputed his claim. As a result of the dispute, the fee was held in escrow until the following year when the dispute was settled.

    The dispute was settled with Matthew agreeing to withdraw from the partnership. Included as part of the withdrawal agreement was a clause that specified he would receive $45,000 of the $300,000 fee, with the law firm retaining the remainder. Six months later, Matthew received a total payment of $125,000, which included the $45,000 fee, from Johnson and Smith.

    a. List as many possible tax research issues as you can to determine the tax treatment of the $125,000 payment received by Matthew.
    b. After completing your list of tax research issues, list the keywords you might use to construct a computer tax research query.

63. Juanita Sharp purchased a large parcel of property for $120,000. A short time after purchasing the property, Sharp submitted plans for the division of the parcel into six lots and the construction of three single-family residences on three of the lots. The city permits required that the property be divided into six lots and that street improvements and water and sewer access be provided. Sharp spent $22,000 for the street, water, and sewer improvements. As a result of the improvements, the value of each of the three vacant lots increased by $1,000, based on an appraisal completed subsequent to the completion of the improvements. The costs of constructing the three single-family residences totaled $200,000.

    a. List as many possible tax research issues as you can to determine how the original purchase price of $120,000, the $22,000 cost of the improvements, and the $200,000 cost of the construction of the homes should be allocated to the basis of each of the lots for purposes of determining gain or loss on the sale of the lots.

b. After completing your list of tax research issues, list the keywords you might use to construct a computer tax research query.

64. Tom and Donna were divorced three years ago. At the time of their divorce, they owned a highly appreciated residence. Tom remained half-owner of the house, but moved out and allowed Donna to continue living in the house. In the current year, Tom and Donna sold the house for $300,000. Last year, Tom purchased a new house for $190,000.

   a. List as many possible tax research issues as you can to determine tax treatment(s) available to Tom on the sale and purchase of the residence.

   b. After completing your list of tax research issues, list the keywords you might use to construct a computer tax research query.

65. Your client, Barney Green, and his wife, Edith, attended a three-day program in Honolulu, entitled "Financial, Tax, and Investment Planning for Investors." The Greens went to Hawaii several days early so that they could get adjusted to jet lag and be ready for the seminar. The $3,000 cost of the trip included the following expenses.

First-class air fare	$1,200
Hotel (7 days)	800
Program fee	300
Meals and other expenses	700

The Greens have records to substantiate all of the above expenditures in a manner that is acceptable under IRC § 274.

   a. List as many possible tax research issues as you can to determine whether the Greens can deduct any or all of the $3,000 of expenditures on their current-year tax return.

   b. After completing your list of tax research issues, list the keywords you might use to construct a computer tax research query.

   c. Execute a computer search using your query. For simplicity, select the IRS Taxpayer Information Publications (TIPS) database from whichever computer tax service you use. Summarize your findings.

66. Ban Vallew was divorced in 1981. He has a son, Katt, by this marriage, who is in the custody of his ex-wife. Katt Vallew has a history of emotional disturbance. He has been sent to a psychiatrist for several years for this problem. This year he has become so disturbed, manifesting violence at home and school, that he had to be sent to a special school in Arizona for problem children. This school is very expensive ($2,000 per month), the cost of which Ban pays for. Ban would like to determine whether he is entitled to the medical expenses deduction (over 7.5 percent of adjusted gross income) for the cost of sending his son to this special school.

   a. List as many possible tax research issues as you can to determine tax treatment(s) available to Ban on the payments to the special school.

   b. After completing your list of tax research issues, list the keywords you might use to construct a computer tax research query.

   c. Execute a computer search using your query. For simplicity, select the IRS Taxpayer Information Publications (TIPS) database from whichever computer tax service you use. Summarize your findings.

67. Linda Larue suffered from arthritis. Her chiropractor advised her that she needed to swim daily to alleviate her pain and other symptoms. Consequently, Linda and her husband, Philo, purchased for $100,000 a new home that had a swimming pool, after selling their old home for $85,000. If the Larues had constructed a pool at their former residence, it would have cost $15,000 to build, and it would have increased the value of their home by $8,000.
   a. List as many possible tax research issues as you can to determine whether the Larues can deduct any of their current-year expenditures for Linda's arthritis.
   b. After completing your list of tax research issues, list the keywords you might use to construct a computer tax research query.
   c. Execute a computer search using your query. For simplicity, select the IRS Revenue Rulings database from whichever computer tax service you use. Summarize your findings.

Part 2

Primary Sources of Federal Tax Law

Chapter 3:   Constitutional and Legislative Sources

Chapter 4:   Administrative Regulations and Rulings

Chapter 5:   Judicial Interpretations

Constitutional and Legislative Sources

LEARNING OBJECTIVES

- Outline the primary and secondary sources of the federal tax law
- Describe in detail the nature and structure of the statutory sources of the tax law, including the Constitution, tax treaties, and the *Internal Revenue Code*
- Delineate how statutory tax law is created and how tax research resources are generated in this process
- Determine how to locate the statutory sources of the tax law
- Discuss how the tax researcher can carefully interpret the *Internal Revenue Code*

CHAPTER OUTLINE

Sources of Federal Tax Law
History of U.S. Taxation
U.S. Constitution
Tax Treaties
The Legislative Process
    Where to Find Committee Reports
Internal Revenue Code
    Organization of the *Internal Revenue Code*
    Where to Find the *Internal Revenue Code*
Interpreting the *Internal Revenue Code*

In Chapter 2, we provided an overview of tax research methodology, presenting the steps that are necessary to complete a federal tax research project in a timely manner. In addition, we presented an introductory discussion concerning the materials used in conducting research.

In this chapter, we take a closer look at the tax research process. We will outline the primary and secondary sources of Federal tax law, examine in some detail the primary statutory sources of Federal tax law, learn how to locate selected provisions thereof, and find out how these laws may pertain to a client's problem. Following a short look at the history of the Federal tax law, we will examine the statutory sources of income tax laws, including the U.S. Constitution, tax treaties, and other revenue laws that Congress has passed.

SOURCES OF FEDERAL TAX LAW

The sources of the Federal tax law can be classified as **primary authorities** or **secondary authorities.** Chapters 3 through 9 of this text include detailed examinations of these various sources, discussing their nature, location, and use in the tax research process. The sources of the Federal tax law to be examined here are presented in outline form in Exhibit 3–1. In particular, we will examine the **statutory sources** of the U.S. Constitution, tax treaties, and the *Internal Revenue Code*. The reader should refer to this outline while reading this text to maintain perspective as to the relationships between each of the sources discussed.

HISTORY OF U.S. TAXATION

Although the Massachusetts Bay Colony enacted an income tax law in 1643, the first U.S. income tax was not created until the Civil War. An income tax law was passed at that time to help the North pay for the cost of fighting the war. This Federal income tax law was passed on August 5, 1861. Although the tax was not generally enforced, some limited collections were made under the law.

This first Federal income tax was levied at the rate of a modest 3 percent on income between $600 and $10,000, and 5 percent on marginal incomes in excess of $10,000. Later, in 1867, the rate was a flat 5 percent of income in excess of $1,000. The Civil War income taxes were allowed to expire in 1872. In 1894 another income tax act was passed by Congress. By this time, however, the income tax had become an important political issue. The southern and western states generally favored the tax, and the eastern states generally opposed it because the tax had developed into an important element of the Populist political movement. In *Pollock v. Farmers' Loan and Trust Co.*, 157 U.S. 429, 15 S.Ct. 673 (1895), the Supreme Court held that the income tax was unconstitutional because it was a constitutionally prohibited "direct tax."

The supporters of the income tax decided to amend the Constitution so that there would be no question as to the constitutionality of a Federal income tax. The proposed amendment was sent to the states on July 12, 1909, by the Sixty-first Congress; it was ratified on February 3, 1913. The new Sixteenth Amendment to the Constitution stated:

The Congress shall have the power to lay and collect taxes on incomes, from whatever source derived, without apportionment among the several States, and without regard to any census or enumeration.

Exhibit 3–1

Primary and Secondary Sources of Federal Tax Law

Primary Sources	**Secondary Sources**

Statutory sources
    U.S. Constitution
    Tax treaties
	Tax services
	    Annotated services
	    Topical services

Internal Revenue Code
    Language of the statute
    Legislative history and intent
	Tax journals and newsletters
	Tax textbooks and treatises

Administrative sources
    Treasury Regulations
    Revenue Rulings
    Revenue Procedures
    Other written determinations
    Miscellaneous IRS publications	

Judicial sources
    Supreme Court
    Courts of Appeals
    Entry-level courts
    Tax Court
    Tax Court, Small Cases Division
    Claims Courts
    District Courts	

Before the Sixteenth Amendment was ratified, Congress passed a corporate income tax in 1909. This tax also was challenged at the Supreme Court level, in *Flint v. Stone Tracy Co.* 220 U.S. 107, 31 S.Ct. 342 (1911). The Court held that this tax was constitutional because it was a special form of excise tax using income as its base, rather than a (prohibited) direct income tax.

In recent years, the income tax has been attacked in the courts on the basis that it is unconstitutional. For instance, some protesters have asserted that, since the U.S. currency no longer is based on the gold standard, the Sixteenth Amendment's measure of income, and therefore the tax itself, is invalid. Others have asserted that the Federal income tax law forces the taxpayer to surrender his or her Fifth Amendment rights against self-incrimination. Federal courts, however, have denied virtually all of the protesters' challenges.

As a result of inflation and other economic turbulence of the 1970s and early 1980s, such tax protests increased rapidly, and Congress passed several new laws to discourage them. For instance, a taxpayer is subject to a $500 fine if he or she files a "frivolous" tax return as a form of protest against the IRS or the U.S. budgetary process. This fine would be levied, for example, when the taxpayer files a blank tax return accompanied by a note suggesting that the Federal income tax is unconstitutional or that the taxpayer wishes to protest against tax revenues going to the creation of nuclear weapons. To date, a number of lower courts have upheld the constitutionality of this fine [e.g., *Schull,* 842 USTC ¶ 9529 (D.C., Va.)].

The Tax Court can impose a penalty, not to exceed $25,000, if the taxpayer brings a "frivolous" matter before the Court. Under §§ 6673 and 6702, a frivolous matter is where the intent is to delay the revenue collection process and where the proceedings are found to be groundless, or where the taxpayer unreasonably failed to pursue available administrative remedies. Sanctions can also be imposed against tax practitioners.

U.S. CONSTITUTION

The Constitution of the United States is the source of all of the Federal laws of the country, including both tax and nontax provisions. In addition to the Sixteenth Amendment, however, the Constitution contains other provisions that bear upon the taxation process. For example, the Constitution provides that Congress may impose import taxes but not export taxes. Moreover, the constitutional rights of due process and of the privacy of the citizen apply in tax, as well as nontax, environments.

The Constitution also requires that taxes imposed by Congress apply uniformly throughout the United States. For instance, it would be unconstitutional for Congress to impose one Federal income tax rate in California and another rate in Vermont. Moreover, except as provided by the Sixteenth Amendment, the Constitution still bars per capita and other direct taxes, unless the revenues that are generated from these taxes are apportioned to the population of the states from which they were collected.

The Federal courts have upheld the constitutionality of the estate and gift taxes because they are in the form of excise taxes on (the transfer of) property, rather than direct taxes on individuals. Thus, one can conclude that, for better or worse, most future judicial challenges to the constitutionality of the elements of the federal tax structure probably will be fruitless.

One can find copies of the U.S. Constitution in many textbooks, encyclopedias, dictionaries, and in publications such as *The World Almanac* and the *Information Please Almanac*. The Constitution is also reproduced in Volume One of the *United States Code*, as published by the Government Printing Office.

The U.S. Constitution can also be found at various nonsubscription Internet sites. Examples (see Exhibit 3–2) of such sites would be:

http://www.nara.gov/exhall/charters/constitution/conmain.html
http://lcweb2.loc.gov/const/const.html

TAX TREATIES

Tax treaties are agreements negotiated between countries concerning the treatment of entities subject to tax in both countries. The United States has entered into treaties with most of the major Western countries of the world. The overriding purpose of such treaties (also known as *tax conventions*) is to eliminate the "double taxation" that the taxpayer would face if his or her income were subject to tax in both countries. In such a case, a U.S. citizen who has generated income from an investment in the United Kingdom (U.K.) usually would be allowed a credit on her U.S. income tax return to the extent of any related U.K. taxes that she paid.

Exhibit 3–2

Example of U.S. Constitution from the Internet

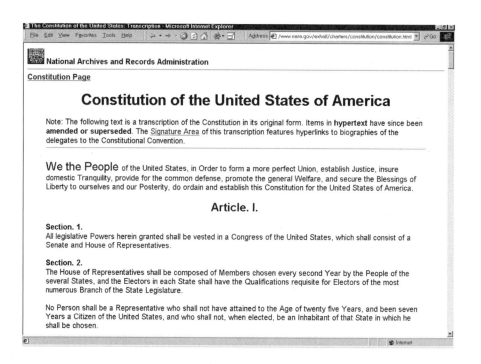

Any tax matter can be covered in a tax treaty with another country. Many times, there are multiple tax treaties with a given country. For example, one treaty will address income tax issues, while another treaty covers estate tax, and a third treaty addresses excise taxes. An example of a portion of a tax treaty is shown as Exhibit 3–3. In addition to the tax treaties, the U.S. government enters into nontax international agreements that are not formal tax treaties; however, in many respects they function like one. Along with other provisions, these agreements address tax issues involving the parties associated with the agreement. Examples of such international agreements include the North American Free Trade Agreement (NAFTA) and the General Agreement on Tariffs and Trade (GATT).

The Constitution provides that "Laws of the United States which shall be made in pursuance thereof; and all Treaties made, or which shall be made, under the Authority of the United States, shall be the supreme Law of the Land." An *Internal Revenue Code* provision and a provision under a treaty will sometimes conflict. In such a case, both of the provisions cannot represent the law; the one adopted later in time generally controls.

Example 3–1 Treaty Override. Prior to 1980, the United States negotiated treaties with several countries that allowed foreign taxpayers to sell U.S. real estate and not pay tax on gains. Under these treaties, nonresident aliens and foreign corporations could avoid U.S. taxes on real estate if the gains were treated as capital gains and were not effectively connected with the conduct of a U.S. business. Because of this

Exhibit 3–3

Tax Treaty Excerpt

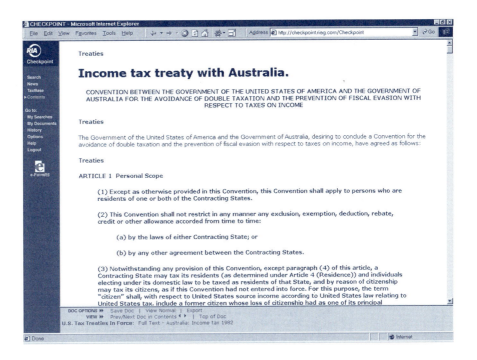

favorable treatment for foreign investors, many U.S. farmers felt foreign investors were bidding up the price of farmland in the United States. This and other concerns led Congress to pass the Foreign Investment in Real Property Tax Act (FIRPTA) of 1980. Under § 897, FIRPTA makes gains and losses by nonresident aliens and foreign corporations taxable by treating such transactions as effectively connected with a U.S. trade or business. This provision overrides any treaties in effect at that time by making foreign capital gains on real property taxable for transactions after 1984. If an existing treaty was renegotiated prior to 1985, the new treaty could designate a different effective date for § 897; however, the designated effective date could not be more than two years after the signing of the renegotiated treaty.

This later-in-time rule appears to be a simplistic approach to the complex interaction of the Code and treaty provisions. The courts have presented interpretive guidelines to be used in resolving interstatutory conflicts. One such guideline is that, where possible, equal effect should be given to both statutes; congressional intent to repeal a statute should not be assumed. A significant judicial history also exists for the interaction of treaties and the Code. In fact, as with conflicts between statutes, courts usually attempt to reconcile the apparent conflict in a way that gives consideration to both the treaty and the Code provisions.

The equality of the two types of provisions is indicated in § 7852(d) of the Code, which provides that neither a treaty nor a law shall be given preferential status by reason of its being a treaty or a law. The language of both the Code and the

Constitution make this clear. The only codified exception to this rule is that treaty provisions in effect in 1954 and which conflicted with the 1954 Code as originally enacted are given precedence over the existing provisions of the 1954 Code, but not over later amendments to the Code. Section 894 states that due regard shall be given to any treaty obligation of the United States that applies to the taxpayer when applying the provisions of the *Internal Revenue Code*.

Treaties are authorized by the Constitution. Under Article II, Section 2, of the Constitution, the President of the United States is allowed to enter into treaties with other countries after receiving the advice and consent of the Senate. The President may also enter into other international agreements that have effects on the Federal tax structure. Such agreements need not be ratified by the Senate; however, they are implemented by Congress in accordance with existing Federal laws.

Treaties may be terminated in several ways. They may expire because of a specific Congressional time limitation, be superseded by a newer treaty, or be terminated by the countries' mutual actions.

Tax researchers often find it necessary to examine the provisions of tax treaties. Exhibit 3–4 shows where to find tax treaties in a traditional tax library.

Treaties are an important source of Federal law, including tax law. When dealing with a research problem that has international connotations, the researcher must locate, read, and evaluate any tax treaty that applies to the client's problem. The researcher cannot rely on the more typical sources of tax research information because these references usually address only domestic tax precedents.

THE LEGISLATIVE PROCESS

To understand how to research tax issues, the tax researcher must have a grasp of the Federal legislative process. The tax law of the United States, like automobiles and hot dogs, is created in a multistep process. At each stage in the creation of a tax law, Congress generates additional items of information, each of which may be useful in addressing a client's tax problem.

Exhibit 3–4
Examples of Where to Find Tax Treaties

Title	Publisher
Computer Sources:	
RIA Checkpoint	Research Institute of America
Westlaw	West Group
CCH Tax Research Network	Commerce Clearing House
Kleinrock's	Kleinrock Publishing Co.
Lexis	LexisNexis
Printed Sources:	
Tax Coordinator 2d	Research Institute of America
Tax Treaties Service	Commerce Clearing House
Tax Treaties Service	Warren, Gorham & Lamont
United States Code Annotated	West Group

Most tax legislation begins in the House of Representatives. In the House, tax law changes are considered by the Ways and Means Committee. Upon approval by this committee, the bill is sent to the full House of Representatives for its approval. The bill then is sent to the Senate, where it is referred to the Finance Committee. When the Finance Committee approves the bill, the proposal is considered by the entire Senate.

If any differences between the House and Senate versions of the tax bill exist (which is almost always the case), the bill is referred to a Joint Conference Committee, where these differences are resolved. The compromise bill must be approved by both houses of Congress before it is forwarded to the President. If the President signs the bill, the new provisions are incorporated into the ***Internal Revenue Code.*** If the bill is vetoed by the President, however, it is not enacted, unless Congress overrides the veto with a sufficient revote. Exhibit 3–5 summarizes the usual steps of the legislative process as it is encountered relative to tax legislation.

At each step in the legislative process, the appropriate committee of Congress produces a **Committee Report,** which explains the elements of the proposed changes and the reasons for each of the proposals. These Committee Reports are an important tool for tax researchers. In many situations where the tax law is unclear, or when recent legislation has been passed, they can provide insight concerning the meaning of a specific phrase of the statute or of the intention of Congress concerning a certain provision of the law. Committee Reports typically result from the deliberations of the Ways and Means Committee, the Finance Committee, and the Joint Conference Committee. A "General Explanation" of tax legislation occasionally is prepared by the Joint Committee on Taxation (the "Blue Book"). Exhibit 3–6 reproduces a portion of such a Committee Report.

Exhibit 3–5
Legislative Process to Amend the Tax Law

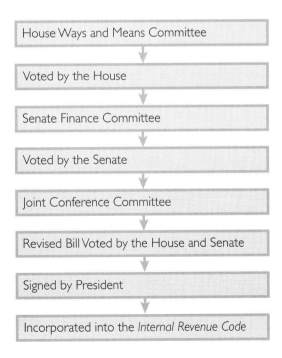

Exhibit 3–6 Committee Report Excerpt

H. Rep. 105-599: INTERNAL REVENUE SERVICE RESTRUCTURING AND REFORM ACT OF 1998 [Paperless Electronic Filing (sec. 203 of the House bill and sec. 2003 of the Senate amendment)]

PAPERLESS ELECTRONIC FILING (SEC. 203 OF THE HOUSE BILL AND SEC. 2003 OF THE SENATE AMENDMENT)

PRESENT LAW

Code Section 6061 requires that tax forms be signed as required by the Secretary. The IRS will not accept an electronically filed return unless it has also received a Form 8453, which is a paper form that contains signature information of the filer.

A return generally is considered timely filed when it is received by the IRS on or before the due date of the return. If the requirements of Code Section 7502 are met, timely mailing is treated as timely filing. If the return is mailed by registered mail, the dated registration statement is prima facie evidence of delivery.

The IRS periodically publishes a list of the forms and schedules that may be electronically transmitted, as well as a list of forms, schedules, and other information that cannot be electronically filed.

HOUSE BILL

The House bill requires the Secretary to develop procedures that would eliminate the need to file a paper form relating to signature information. Until the procedures are in place, the provision authorizes the Secretary to provide for alternative methods of signing all returns, declarations, statements, or other documents or to waive the signature requirement. An alternative method of signature would be treated identically, for both civil and criminal purposes, as a signature on a paper form.

The provision also provides rules for determining when electronic returns are deemed filed and for authorization for return preparers to communicate with the IRS on matters included on electronically filed returns.

The provision requires the Secretary to establish procedures, to the extent practicable, to receive all forms electronically for taxable periods beginning after December 31, 1998.

EFFECTIVE DATE: Date of enactment.

SENATE AMENDMENT

Same as the House bill, with the following exceptions: (1) The Senate amendment deletes the provision permitting the Secretary to waive the signature requirement. (2) The Secretary of the Treasury must establish procedures for all tax forms, instructions, and publications created in the most recent 5-year period to be made available electronically on the Internet in a searchable database not later than the date such records are available to the public in printed form. (3) The Secretary of the Treasury must, to the extent practicable, establish procedures for other taxpayer guidance to be made available electronically on the Internet in a searchable database not later than the date such guidance is available to the public in printed form.

EFFECTIVE DATE: Generally effective on the date of enactment. The provision which relates to Internet access to IRS forms, instructions, publications, and guidance is effective for taxable periods beginning after December 31, 1998.

CONFERENCE AGREEMENT

The conference agreement follows the Senate amendment, except as follows. The Secretary is permitted to waive the signature requirement, but only returns signed or subscribed under alternative methods prescribed by the Secretary (not including waiver) are entitled to be treated as though signed or subscribed. The provision that requires the Secretary, to the extent practicable, to receive all forms electronically applies to taxable periods after December 31, 1999. The provision relating to authorizing return preparers to communicate with the IRS on matters included on electronically filed returns is clarified.

Committee Reports generally are referred to by public law number. Every bill that Congress passes is assigned such a number. For example, the Tax Reform Act of 1986 was designated as P.L. 99-514. Public Law is abbreviated as "P.L." in this context. The prefix of the numerical designation (here, 99) refers to the session of Congress that passed the law. The suffix of the Public Law number (here, 514) indicates that this was the 514th bill that this session of Congress adopted.

Congressional sessions last for two years; therefore, the researcher may find it useful to construct a method by which to identify the two-year period in which a tax law was passed. The recent sessions of Congress are identified as follows.

Congressional Sessions	Years
One-hundred-sixth	1999–2000
One-hundred-seventh	2001–02
One-hundred-eighth	2003–04
One-hundred-ninth	2005–06
One-hundred-tenth	2007–08
One-hundred-eleventh	2009–10

Through 1999, to convert a session number into the second year of the applicable congressional session, multiply the session number by 2 and subtract 112 (the number of years from 1788 to 1900). Thus, the second year of the One-hundredth Congress was 1988 [$(100 \times 2) - 112 = 88$]. For the year 2000 and after, substitute 212 (the number of years from 1788 to 2000) for 112 in the formula. For example, the second year of the One-hundred-eighth Congress is 2004 [$(108 \times 2) - 212 = 04$].

WHERE TO FIND COMMITTEE REPORTS

When a new tax law is passed, the pertinent Committee Reports are printed in the Internal Revenue Service's weekly *Internal Revenue Bulletin*. The weekly IRS reports are reorganized and published every six months in the *Cumulative Bulletin*. However, the texts of the 1954 Committee Reports relative to the *Internal Revenue Code* are found not in the *Cumulative Bulletin*, but in the *United States Code Congressional and Administrative News*. Finally, all of the pre-1939 Revenue Act Committee Reports are reprinted in the 1939 *Cumulative Bulletin*. Exhibit 3–7 summarizes the locations and publishers of the most important tax-related Committee Reports.

The Committee Reports and other legislative items can also be found at various nonsubscription Internet sites. Examples of such sites would be:

http://thomas.loc.gov
http://www.house.gov/jct
http://www.house.gov/ways_means/
http://www.senate.gov/~finance/

Commerce Clearing House and the Research Institute of America both publish, usually in paperback form, a collection of Committee Reports (or excerpts thereof) whenever a major new tax law is passed. If a tax researcher wants to find the Committee Reports that underlie a statutory provision, he or she also can use reference

Exhibit 3–7

Location of Committee Reports

Publication	Publisher
Computer Sources:	
RIA Checkpoint	Research Institute of America
Westlaw	West Group
CCH Tax Research Network	Commerce Clearing House
Kleinrock's	Kleinrock Publishing Co.
Lexis	LexisNexis
Printed Sources:	
Cumulative Bulletin	Government Printing Office
Public Law Legislative History	Commerce Clearing House
Primary Sources (since 1968)	Bureau of National Affairs

materials that are included in the bodies of most of the commercial tax services or in the index to the *Cumulative Bulletin*.

The Committee Reports Findings List in Commerce Clearing House's *Citator*, Volume M–Z, is a good place for the tax researcher to locate Committee Reports by P.L. number. See Part 3 of this text for a detailed review of the use of citators.

In addition to the Committee Reports, the Floor Debate Report may be of value to the tax researcher. The Floor Debate Report includes a summary of what was said from the floor of the House or Senate concerning the proposed bill. It may include some detailed or technical information that is excluded from the Committee Report. The Floor Debate Report is included in the *Congressional Record* for the day of the debate.

INTERNAL REVENUE CODE

After the Sixteenth Amendment was ratified in 1913, Congress passed a series of self-contained revenue acts, each of which formed the entire income tax law of the United States. For about two decades, Congress passed such a free-standing revenue act every year or two. By the 1930s, however, this series of revenue acts, and the task of rewriting the entire tax statute so often, had become unmanageable. Thus, in 1939, Congress replaced the revenue acts with the *Internal Revenue Code of 1939*, the first fully organized Federal tax law.

Although the concept of a free-standing tax code, as part of the entire *United States Code*, was a good idea, the organization of the *Internal Revenue Code of 1939* left little room to accommodate subsequent changes to the law. Accordingly, the 1939 Code was replaced with a reorganized, more flexible codification in 1954. Due to extensive revisions to the Code that were made as part of the Tax Reform Act of 1986, the statute was renamed the *Internal Revenue Code of 1986*. Thus, although the statute still follows the 1954 numbering system and organization, the official title of the extant U.S. tax law is the *Internal Revenue Code of 1986, as Amended*.

The principal sources of tax laws of the United States since 1913, then, have been identified as follows.

Period	Principal U.S. Tax Law
1913–39	Periodic Revenue Acts
1939–54	*Internal Revenue Code of 1939*
1954–86	*Internal Revenue Code of 1954*
1986–Present	*Internal Revenue Code of 1986*

Many provisions of the 1939 Code were carried over to the *Internal Revenue Code of 1954* without substantive change; some of these sections were adopted into the Code verbatim, although all of the sections were renumbered as part of the 1954 reorganization.

The *Internal Revenue Code* is part of the *United States Code,* which is a codification of all of the Federal laws of the United States. The elements of the *United States Code* are organized alphabetically and assigned title numbers. Accordingly, the *Internal Revenue Code* constitutes Title 26 of the *United States Code;* its neighbors in the *U.S. Code* include "Insane Asylums" and "Intoxicating Liquors."

ORGANIZATION OF THE *INTERNAL REVENUE CODE*

The *Internal Revenue Code* is organized into several levels or subdivisions, as follows.

1. Subtitles
2. Chapters
3. Subchapters
4. Parts
5. Subparts
6. Sections
7. Subsections

Subtitles of the Code are assigned a capital letter to identify them (currently A through I are used). Generally, each subtitle contains all of the tax provisions that relate to a well-defined area of the tax law. Exhibit 3–8 identifies the subtitles of the current Code. The tax researcher spends most of his or her time working with Subtitles A, Income Taxes; B, Estate and Gift Taxes; and F, Procedure and Administration. The other subtitles typically are used only from time to time for special research problems.

Each subtitle contains a number of chapters, numbered, although not continuously, from 1 through 98. These chapter numbers do not start over at each subtitle; rather, they are used in ascending order throughout the Code. Thus, for example, there is only one Chapter 11 in the *Internal Revenue Code,* not nine of them. Each chapter contains the tax provisions that relate to a more narrowly defined area of the tax law than is addressed by the subtitles. Most of the subtitles include several chapters. Exhibit 3–9 examines the numbering system of the chapters of the *Internal Revenue Code,* concentrating on selected important chapters.

The chapters of the *Internal Revenue Code* are further divided into subchapters. Typically a subchapter contains a group of provisions that relates to a fairly specific area of the tax law. Subchapters sometimes are divided into parts, which may be divided into subparts. Letters are used to denote subchapters, and the lettering scheme starts over with each chapter. Thus, there may be a Subchapter A in each chapter.

Exhibit 3–8

Subtitles of the *Internal Revenue Code*, as Amended

Subtitle	Tax Law Included
A	Income Taxes
B	Estate and Gift Taxes
C	Employment Taxes
D	Miscellaneous Excise Taxes
E	Alcohol; Tobacco; Miscellaneous Excise Taxes
F	Procedure and Administration
G	Joint Committee on Taxation
H	Presidential Election Campaign Financing
I	Trust Funds

Many times, tax practitioners use the subchapter designation as a shorthand reference to identify a certain area of taxation. For example, Subchapter C of Chapter 1 of Subtitle A of the *Internal Revenue Code* includes many of the basic corporate income tax provisions. Thus, when a tax practitioner wants to refer to a corporate tax matter, he or she often simply identifies it as a "Subchapter C" issue. Exhibit 3–10 identifies the subchapters of Chapter 1 (Income Taxes) of the Code.

Most of the Code's subchapters are divided into parts. The parts provide a natural grouping of provisions that address essentially the same issue. Not all subchapters are divided into parts, and occasionally the parts are not numbered consecutively. For instance, the parts of Chapter 1, Subchapter A (i.e., normal income taxes), are

Part I	Tax on Individuals
Part II	Tax on Corporations
Part III	Changes in Rates during a Taxable Year
Part IV	Credits against Tax
Part VI	Alternative Minimum Tax
Part VII	Environmental Tax

Exhibit 3–9

Key Chapters of the *Internal Revenue Code*

Chapter	Subjects Included
1	Normal Taxes and Surtaxes
2	Self-Employment Tax
6	Consolidated Returns
11	Estate Taxes
12	Gift Taxes
61	Administration/Information
79	Definitions

Exhibit 3–10
Subchapters of Chapter 1 (Normal Taxes), Subtitle A (Income Taxes), *Internal Revenue Code*

Subchapter	Topic(s) Included
A	Determination of Tax Liability
B	Computation of Taxable Income
C	Corporate Distributions and Adjustments
D	Deferred Compensation
E	Accounting Periods and Methods
F	Tax-Exempt Organizations
G	Corporate Accumulations/Personal Holding Companies
H	Banking Institutions
I	Natural Resources
J	Income Taxation of Estates and Trusts
K	Partnerships and Partners
L	Insurance Companies
M	Mutual Funds
N	International Taxation
O	Property Transactions
P	Capital Gains and Losses
Q	Readjustment of Tax between Years and Special Limitations
R	[Repealed]
S	S Corporations and Shareholders
T	Cooperatives and Patrons
U	[Repealed]
V	Bankruptcy Effects

The most important division of the *Internal Revenue Code* for the tax researcher is the section, because the Code is arranged so that its primary unit is the section number. The sections currently are numbered 1 through 9602, although not all of the numbers are used. Each section number is used only once in the Code. The researcher can refer to a specific provision of the *Internal Revenue Code* by its section number and not be concerned about duplication in another part of the law. Indeed, the most common element of the jargon of the tax practitioner community is the Code section number, and tax researchers must learn to identify important tax provisions merely by the corresponding section number.

Code sections can be divided into various smaller elements for the convenience of the drafter or user of the section. A section can contain subsections, paragraphs, subparagraphs, and clauses. Sections are denoted by numbers (1, 2, etc.), subsections by lowercase letters (a, b, etc.), paragraphs by numbers, subparagraphs by capital letters (A, B, etc.), and clauses by lowercase roman numerals (i, ii, etc.). In citing a Code section, one uses parentheses for each division that occurs after the section number. Exhibit 3–11 provides a specific interpretation of a Code section citation.

Although there are thousands of Code sections, certain ones contain basic principles that affect most tax situations (Exhibit 3–12). The tax researcher should be familiar with this group of Code sections for efficient analysis of his or her clients' tax problems.

WHERE TO FIND THE *INTERNAL REVENUE CODE*

The amended *Internal Revenue Code* can be found in several places. National publishers such as Research Institute of America (RIA), West, and Commerce Clearing House (CCH) publish paperback versions of the Code for use by tax practitioners. In addition, the text of the Code may be found in most commercial tax services and as Title 26 of the *United States Code*.

The type of tax service will indicate the probable location of the original language of the Code in the service. Typically, an annotated tax service (refer to Chapter 2 to review this definition) will include the text of the Code with the related section's discussion. On the other hand, a topical tax service typically reproduces the text of the Code in an appendix to pertinent chapters or volumes of the service.

The *U.S. Code* and the *Internal Revenue Code* (which is Title 26 of the *U.S. Code*) can also be found at various nonsubscription Internet sites. An example of such site would be:

http://uscode.house.gov/

Occasionally, a tax researcher needs to refer to a source that originated from the *Internal Revenue Code of 1939*. Many of the provisions of the 1986 (and 1954) Code can be found in the 1939 Code. Exhibit 3–13 gives examples of 1986 Code sections and their 1939 Code equivalents.

Other useful indices to the Code itself are provided by the editors of the tax services. For example, several useful tables are included in the Code volumes of the Commerce Clearing House tax service. In Cross-Reference Table 1, 1939 Code sections are cross-referenced to their 1954 (and 1986) counterparts. In Table 2 of the CCH service, current Code sections are cross-referenced to the 1939 Code.

Table III of this feature cross-references the Code sections within the current Code. These three tables can be useful to the tax researcher when he or she needs to find a 1939 Code section number, perhaps in interpreting a court case that addresses a pre-1954 Code issue, or in identifying situations where a Code section is referred to elsewhere in the current Code, or perhaps to find out whether other Code sections provide information bearing on the section being reviewed.

Most tax services also contain information about the history of each Code section. Typically, at the end of the text of each Code section the editors include a list of the Public Laws that have altered or amended the section. This listing generally includes a reference to the section as it existed prior to amendment, as well as the effective date of the amendment to the law. The tax researcher must be careful to consider the impact of any such amendments. Exhibit 3–14 illustrates the Public Law history with respect to a specific Code section.

One other publication will prove to be valuable if the researcher is addressing issues that predate the 1954 Code. *Seidman's Legislative History of Federal Income*

Exhibit 3–11
Interpreting a Code Section Citation

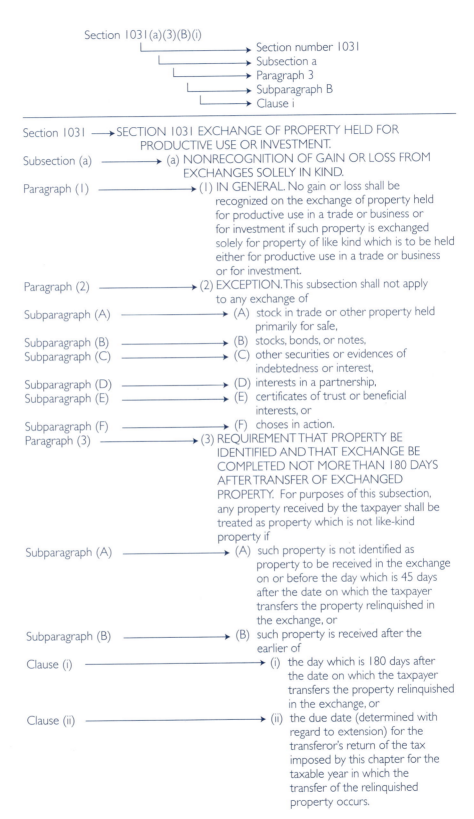

Exhibit 3–12
Some Important Code Sections

Section Number	Contents
1	Individual Tax Rates
11	Corporate Tax Rates
61	Definition of Gross Income
62	Deductions for Adjusted Gross Income
162	Trade or Business Deductions
163	Interest Deduction
164	Deduction for Taxes
165	Losses
167, 168	Depreciation, Cost Recovery
212	Production-of-Income Expenses

Tax Laws details the historical evolution of the early tax law. It explains how certain provisions evolved into their current form in the Code.

INTERPRETING THE *INTERNAL REVENUE CODE*

One of the greatest problems for a tax researcher is the interpretation of the *Internal Revenue Code*. Often, Code provisions are long, interrelated, and confusing. For example, several sentences in the Code exceed 300 words; one of them exceeds 400

Exhibit 3–13
Examples of 1986 Code Sections Derived from the 1939 Code

1986 Code Section	1939 Code Section
§ 61, Gross income defined	§ 22(a)
§ 71, Alimony and separate maintenance payments	§ 22(k)
§ 103, Interest on state and local bonds	§ 22(b)(4)
§ 151, Allowance of deductions for personal exemptions	§ 25(b)
§ 162, Trade or business expenses	§ 23(a)(1)
§ 172, Net operating loss deduction	§ 122
§ 212, Expenses for production of income	§ 23(a)(2)
§ 301, Distributions of property	§ 22(e), 115(a), (b), (d), (e)
§ 316, Dividends defined	§ 115(a) and (b)
§ 701, Partners, not partnership, subject to tax	§ 181

Exhibit 3–14 1989–1999 P.L. Amendments to Section 1031

In 1999, P.L. 106-36, Sec. 3001(c)(2)(A), substituted "assumed [as determined under section 357(d)] a liability of the taxpayer" for "assumed a liability of the taxpayer or acquired from the taxpayer property subject to a liability" in subsec. (d).... Sec. 3001(c)(2)(B), deleted "or acquisition (in the amount of the liability)" after "such assumption" in subsec. (d), effective for transfers after 10/31/98.

In 1997, P.L. 105-34, Sec. 1052(a), amended subsec. (h), effective for transfers after 6/8/97, in tax. yrs. end. after 6/8/97. Sec. 1052(b)(2) of this Act provides:

"(2) Binding contracts. The amendment made by this section shall not apply to any transfer pursuant to a written binding contract in effect on June 8, 1997, and at all times thereafter before the disposition of property. A contract shall not fail to meet the requirements of the preceding sentence solely because—

"(A) it provides for a sale in lieu of an exchange," or

"(B) the property to be acquired as replacement property was not identified under such contract before June 9, 1997."

Prior to amendment, subsec. (h) read as follows:

"(h) Special rule for foreign real property."

"For purposes of this section, real property located in the United States and real property located outside the United States are not property of a like kind."

In 1990, P.L. 101-508, Sec. 11701(h), substituted "Section 267(b) or 707(b)(1)" for "Section 267(b)", in para. (f)(3), effective for transfers after 8/3/90.

—P.L. 101-508, Sec. 11703(d)(1), added the last sentence to para. (a)(2), effective for transfers after 7/18/84.

In 1989, P.L. 101-239, Sec. 7601(a), added subsecs. (f)-(h), effective for transfers after 7/10/89, in tax. yrs. end. after 7/10/89, except as provided in Sec. 7601(b)(2) of this Act, which reads as follows:

"(2) Binding contract. The amendments made by this section shall not apply to any transfer pursuant to a written binding contract in effect on July 10, 1989, and at all times thereafter before the transfer."

words. In researching a client's tax problem, one must read each Code section that might apply. Many times, a single phrase or clause in the section may prevent the client from being subject to the provision or may contain other unexpected implications for the client's situation.

A researcher, in his or her initial review, may find the topical index, which is included by most publishers of the Code, a useful tool in locating a starting point or the relevant Code section. In reading, interpreting, and evaluating a selected Code section, the tax researcher must be especially critical of the language used throughout the section. Many, if not most, Code sections contain a general rule, followed by specific conditions that must be satisfied in order to apply the provision, and situations under which the taxpayer is excepted from the general rule. In some cases, the exceptions to the general rule are further modified to provide for exceptions to the general exceptions. Moreover, some exceptions to a Code section are addressed not within the same section, but in another section of the Code. Therefore, all relevant provisions must be read carefully.

In addition to being aware of the required conditions for application of a section, as well as the exceptions thereto, the researcher must be aware of the definitions of terms used in the section; pertinent definitions may be given within the section or in some other provision of the Code. These definitions may be significantly different from the common use of the term.

In § 7701, the text defines many of the terms used throughout the Code, but these definitions may be superseded by material contained within the applicable Code section. In addition, the researcher may need to look beyond the Code such as to the Regulations or other authority, to determine the conditions that a specific term may encompass. In all cases, the researcher should avoid jumping to premature conclusions until a thorough analysis of all relevant Code sections has been completed.

The tax researcher must be careful not to overlook words that connect phrases, such as "and" and "or." These words have very different logical meanings, and, even when the words are "hidden" at the end of the previous clause or subparagraph, they may significantly change the outcome of a research project. The word "and" is conjunctive; the word "or" is disjunctive. If the word "and" lies between two phrases, both of them must be true for the provision to apply to the client's problem. However, if the word "or" lies between two phrases, then only one of them must be true for the provision to apply.

The researcher also must be careful with words that modify percentage or dollar amounts. The phrases "less than 50%," "more than 50%," and "not less than 50%" have very different meanings in determining whether the provisions of a section apply. The researcher also must distinguish between such terms as "30 days" and "one month," because they usually identify different time periods.

Example 3–2 Conflicting Code Sections. Paul is a roofing contractor and has a truck he uses 100 percent of the time in his business. The truck cost $35,000 three years ago, and Paul has claimed ACRS of $24,920 on the truck, which leaves him an adjusted basis of $10,080. Paul sells the truck for $22,080 resulting in a gain of $12,000 on the truck. How is he to treat this gain for tax purposes?

In the *Internal Revenue Code,* Paul finds that when depreciable property used in a trade or business [§ 1231(b)] is sold, the gain is treated as a long-term capital gain [§ 1231(a)]. Thus, he might report the gain on his tax return as a long-term capital gain. However, in § 1245(a), Paul discovers that gain on depreciable personal property (in this case, the truck) is ordinary income to the extent of depreciation claimed since 1961. Thus, § 1245 would indicate the gain is ordinary, not long-term capital.

How is the problem resolved? In § 1245(d), Paul finds a directive that the recapture provision "shall apply notwithstanding any other provision of this subtitle [of the Code]." As a result, he must report the gain as ordinary income on his tax return, not long-term capital gain.

If Paul had read only § 1231 of the Code and not § 1245, he would have arrived at a different conclusion about the gain. In many situations, when Code sections conflict, the resolution of the conflict may not be as easy as in this example.

When analyzing a provision that recently has been changed by Congress, a researcher must be very careful to cross-reference all of the uses of terms whose definitions have been affected by the new law. Often, Congress does not use the care necessary to ascertain that all of the "loose ends" of the new provisions have been tied up. In recent years, almost every major change in the tax law has been followed by a "technical corrections act" to remove errors in implementing and interpreting the new provisions of the law, as well as to clarify problems that arise in integrating the new provisions with the existing provisions of the Code. Most of these corrections are identified by practitioners whose clients' situations are adversely affected by a given reading of the amended law; thus, the typical technical corrections act testifies as much to the thoroughness of the practitioners' research as to shoddy drafting of the law by Congress.

Because the provisions of the *Internal Revenue Code* change frequently, the researcher must be aware of the effective dates of the various changes to the law. A provision may not go into effect immediately upon its adoption by Congress. The date of the act with which the change in law is passed is not always indicative of the effective date of the provision. Often, various provisions under the same tax law will become effective on different dates and, in fact, may have effective dates that precede the date of the tax act. Similarly, when a provision of the tax law is deleted from the Code, the provision may be left in effect for a designated period of time before it actually expires. Transitional rules may also apply. The effective date for a change in the tax law usually may be found in the explanation of the Public Laws, which follows the pertinent Code section (see, for example, Exhibit 3–14). In some cases, the researcher may need to look to the explanation under another Code section for the effective date of a provision. The researcher must be careful to align the client's facts with the effective law at the pertinent dates, or a serious mistake could be made in the research conclusion.

Finally, the tax researcher must be aware that not *all* of the answers to a tax question will be found in the Code. The Code may be silent concerning the problem at hand, the application of Code language to the fact situation at hand may not be clear, or Code sections may appear to be in conflict. Thus, the researcher must look for an answer from other sources, such as tax treaties, administrative rulings (see Chapter 4), judicial decisions (see Chapter 5), or secondary sources of the law (see Chapters 6 through 9). Alternatively, the controlling law may be found in other parts of the Code, such as tariff or bankruptcy laws. Exhibit 3–15 lists examples of Federal laws other than the Code that affect specific tax matters.

Exhibit 3–15

Examples of Federal Laws Other Than the *Internal Revenue Code* That May Affect a Tax Transaction

Administrative Procedure Act

Alaska Native Claims Settlement Act

Atomic Energy Act Tax Provision

Bank Holding Company Act of 1956

Civil Rights Attorneys' Fees Awards Act of 1976

Financial Institutions Reform, Recovery, and Enforcement Act of 1989

Metric Conversion Act of 1975

Merchant Marine Act: Capital Construction Fund

New York City Pension Act

Organic Act of Guam

SUMMARY

The three major sources of statutory tax law are the Constitution, tax treaties, and the *Internal Revenue Code*. The tax researcher must thoroughly understand each of these sources and the interrelationships among them. The Constitution is the basis for all Federal laws. The tax treaties are agreements between countries, negotiated by the President and approved by the Senate, that cover taxpayers subject to the tax laws of both countries. Tax treaties generally have a lesser or complementary authority compared with the *Internal Revenue Code*. The greatest volume of tax statutes is found in the *Internal Revenue Code,* which is Title 26 of the *United States Code.* The Code contains the tax laws that Congress has passed, and it is the basic document for most U.S. tax provisions.

TAX TUTOR

Reinforce the tax research information covered in this chapter by completing the online tutorials located at the Federal Tax Research web site:

http://raabe.swcollege.com

KEY WORDS

By the time you complete this chapter, you should be comfortable discussing each of the following terms. If you need additional review of any of these items, return to the appropriate material in the chapter or consult the glossary to this text.

Committee Report
Internal Revenue Code
Primary Authority

Secondary Authority
Statutory Sources
Tax Treaty

DISCUSSION QUESTIONS

1. What are the three primary statutory sources of U.S. Federal tax law?
2. Discuss the effect of *Pollock v. Farmers' Loan and Trust Co.* on the development of U.S. income tax laws.
3. The Sixteenth Amendment to the Constitution had a significant effect on the U.S. income tax. What was it?
4. What did the U.S. Supreme Court hold in *Flint v. Stone Tracy Co.* in 1911?
5. Tax protestors who file "frivolous" tax returns or bring "frivolous" proceedings before the U.S. Tax Court are subject to certain fines or other penalties. What are the grounds for imposing each penalty? What is the maximum amount of each penalty?
6. Discuss the powers of taxation that are granted to Congress by the U.S. Constitution. Are any limits placed on the powers of Congress to so tax?

7. Have the Federal courts ever held Federal estate and gift taxes to be unconstitutional?
8. What is a tax treaty? Explain the purpose of a tax treaty. What matters generally are covered in a tax treaty?
9. How is a tax treaty terminated?
10. When an *Internal Revenue Code* section and a tax treaty provision appear to conflict, which usually prevails?
11. Describe the ratification process for a tax treaty between the United States and another country.
12. The tax researcher must be able to find descriptions of tax treaties to solve certain tax problems. List at least five different publications and their publishers that provide this information. State whether each publication gives the complete text of the treaty or just a summary.
13. Briefly summarize the usual steps of the legislative process for development of Federal tax legislation.
14. As a bill proceeds through Congress, various Committee Reports are generated. List the three Committee Reports that typically are prepared for a new tax law.
15. When are Committee Reports useful to a tax researcher?
16. What is a Public Law number? In P.L. 100-203, what do the "100" and the "203" indicate?
17. Where would a tax researcher find pertinent Committee Reports? List at least four publications and their publishers that include tax-related Committee Reports. Is there an index that would help a tax researcher locate a specific Committee Report? If so, where might such an index be found?
18. In addition to the Committee Reports, which are a by-product to the development of tax legislation, what other report may be of value to the tax researcher analyzing a new provision of the tax law? Why?
19. Discuss the evolution of today's *Internal Revenue Code*.
20. The *Internal Revenue Code* is Title 26 of the *United States Code*. How is the *Internal Revenue Code* subdivided?
21. How are the subtitles of the *Internal Revenue Code* identified? What generally is contained in a subtitle?
22. In the citation § 101(a)(2)(B), what does the "a" stand for? What do the "2" and the "B" indicate to a tax researcher?
23. Not all statutory tax laws are found in the *Internal Revenue Code*. Is this statement true or false? Discuss briefly.
24. Discuss briefly the events leading to the passage of the Sixteenth Amendment to the U.S. Constitution.

EXERCISES

25. What is found in each of the following subtitles of the *Internal Revenue Code?*
    a. Subtitle B
    b. Subtitle F
    c. Subtitle A
    d. Subtitle C
26. Each subtitle of the *Internal Revenue Code* contains several chapters. How are chapters identified? What generally is included in a chapter of the Code?

27. Identify the general content of each of the following chapters of the *Internal Revenue Code*.
    a. Chapter 11
    b. Chapter 61
    c. Chapter 1
    d. Chapter 12
28. Chapters of the *Internal Revenue Code* are subdivided into subchapters. How are subchapters identified? What generally is contained in a subchapter?
29. What is the general content of each of the following subchapters of the *Internal Revenue Code?*
    a. Subchapter C
    b. Subchapter K
    c. Subchapter S
    d. Subchapter E
30. Subchapters of the *Internal Revenue Code* sometimes contain parts. How are such parts identified? What is contained in a typical part?
31. The most important division of the *Internal Revenue Code* is the section. Sections usually are subdivided into various smaller elements. Name several of these elements and state how they are denoted.
32. Do section numbers repeat themselves or is each one unique?
33. Identify the general contents of each of the following *Internal Revenue Code* sections.
    a. § 61
    b. § 162
    c. § 1
    d. § 212
34. Use a computer tax service (e.g., RIA Checkpoint, Lexis, Kleinrock's, etc.) to answer the following questions.
    a. Which computer service did you use?
    b. What is the general content of *Internal Revenue Code* § 28?
    c. What is the general content of *Internal Revenue Code* § 141?
    d. What is the general content of *Internal Revenue Code* § 166?
    e. Print a copy of any one of the above Code sections and attach it to your assignment.
35. Use a computer tax service (e.g., RIA Checkpoint, Lexis, Kleinrock's, etc.) to answer the following questions.
    a. Which computer tax service did you use?
    b. What is the general content of *Internal Revenue Code* § 117?
    c. What is the general content of *Internal Revenue Code* § 165?
    d. What is the general content of *Internal Revenue Code* § 304?
    e. Print a copy of any one of the above Code sections and attach it to your assignment.
36. Name several locations where a tax researcher would find the text of the current *Internal Revenue Code.*
37. If a tax researcher wants to know if there is an equivalent 1939 Code section for a specific 1986 Code section, how would he or she locate it?
38. One important problem that faces a tax researcher is interpretation of the *Internal Revenue Code.* Comment on each of the following interpretation problems.

Continued

Chapter 3 Constitutional and Legislative Sources

a. Exceptions to a Code section
b. Words that connect phrases, such as "and" and "or"
c. Recent changes in the Code
d. Effective dates
e. Words that modify percentages, dollar amounts, or time

39. Comment on the statement, "All tax questions can be answered using the *Internal Revenue Code*."

40. Does the United States have an income tax treaty with any of the following countries? If it does, in what year was the treaty signed? State where you found this information.
    a. Japan
    b. United Kingdom
    c. Egypt
    d. Germany

41. Does the United States have an estate tax treaty with any of the following countries? If it does, in what year was the treaty signed? State where you found this information.
    a. Canada
    b. Finland
    c. Hungary
    d. Italy

42. Use a computer tax service (e.g., RIA Checkpoint, Lexis, Kleinrock's, etc.) to locate § 117 of the *Internal Revenue Code*. Answer the following questions.
    a. Which computer tax service did you use?
    b. How many subsection(s) does § 117 include?
    c. How many paragraph(s) does § 117(b) include?
    d. How many subparagraph(s) does § 117(d)(2) include?
    e. Print a copy of this section and attach it to your assignment.

43. Use a computer tax service (e.g., RIA Checkpoint, Lexis, Kleinrock's, etc.) to locate § 385 of the *Internal Revenue Code*. Answer the following questions.
    a. Which computer tax service did you use?
    b. How many subsection(s) does § 385 include?
    c. How many paragraph(s) does § 385(b) include?
    d. Print a copy of this section and attach it to your assignment.

44. When was each of the following sections originally enacted? State how you obtained this information.
    a. § 843
    b. § 131
    c. § 469
    d. § 263A

45. In which subtitle, chapter, and subchapter of the 1986 Code are each of the following sections found?
    a. § 32
    b. § 172
    c. § 2039
    d. § 6013

46. List the first three section numbers and titles of each of the following subchapters of Chapter 1 of the *Internal Revenue Code*.

Continued

a. Subchapter B
b. Subchapter E
c. Subchapter J
d. Subchapter S

47. Identify the equivalent section of the 1954 Code for each of the following sections of the 1939 Code. If there is no equivalent section, say so.
    a. § 1
    b. § 113(a)
    c. § 22(a)
    d. § 115(a)
    e. § 181

48. Use a computer tax service (e.g., RIA Checkpoint, Lexis, Kleinrock's, etc.) to locate the following Code sections. What other Code sections reference each of the sections you found? State which computer tax service you used to complete this assignment.
    a. § 72
    b. § 307
    c. § 446

49. Name the article and section of the U.S. Constitution that gives Congress the power to tax.

50. Enumerate the Code sections that contain the chief tax law provisions on the following topics.
    a. S corporations
    b. Personal holding company tax
    c. Gift tax
    d. Tax accounting methods

51. Use a nonsubscription Internet site to determine how many Senators are on the Senate Finance Committee. Who is the Chair of the Finance Committee? State where you found this information.

52. Use a nonsubscription Internet site to determine how many Representatives are on the House Ways and Means Committee. Who is the Chair of the Ways and Means Committee? State where you found this information.

53. Use a nonsubscription Internet site to determine what is contained in each of the following. State where you found this information.
    a. U.S. Const. art. I, § 9 cl. 3
    b. U.S. Const. art. I, § 8 cl. 1
    c. U.S. Const. art. II, § 2 cl. 2

54. Locate and print the first page of a House Way and Means Committee Report using only a nonsubscription Internet site. State where you found this information.

RESEARCH CASES

55. Private G.I. Jane was a soldier in the Gulf War. Her salary was $1,300 per month, and she was in the war zone for eight months. How much of her salary is taxable for the eight months? In answering this case, use only the *Internal Revenue Code* for your research. *Computer search keywords:* combat, pay, officers, enlisted

56. Carol received a gift of stock from her favorite uncle. The stock had a fair market value of $30,000 and a basis to the uncle of $10,000 at the date of the gift. How much is taxable to Carol from this gift? In answering this case, use only the *Internal Revenue Code* for your research. *Computer search keywords:* gift, gross income, exclusion

57. Maria is an independent long-haul trucker. She receives a speeding ticket for $125, which she pays. Can Maria deduct the ticket on Schedule C? In answering this case, use only the *Internal Revenue Code* for your research. *Computer search keywords:* fines, penalties, deduction

58. Julie loaned her friend Nathan $2,500. Nathan did not repay the debt and skipped town. Can Julie claim any deduction? In answering this case, use only the *Internal Revenue Code* for your research. *Computer search keywords:* loss, bad debt, worthless

59. In December of 20x1, Ann's twelve-year-old cousin, Susan, came to live with her after Susan's parents met an untimely death in a car accident. In 20x2, Ann provided all normal support (e.g., food, clothing, education) for Susan. Ann did not formally adopt Susan. If Susan lived in the household for the entire year, can Ann claim a dependency exemption for her cousin for the 20x2 tax year? In answering this case, use only the *Internal Revenue Code* for your research. *Computer search keywords:* dependent, household, support

60. John and Maria support their twenty-one-year-old son, Bill. The son earned $10,500 last year working in a part-time job. Bill went to college part time in the spring semester of the current year. To complete his degree, Bill started school full time in the fall. The fall semester at Bill's college runs from August 20 to December 20. Can John and Maria claim Bill as a dependent on the current year's tax return, even if Bill earns $9,000 gross income? Assume any dependency test not mentioned has been met. In answering this case, use a computer tax service with only the *Internal Revenue Code* database selected. State your keywords and which computer tax service you used to arrive at your answer.

61. George and Linda are divorced and own a house from the marriage. Under the divorce decree, Linda pays George $3,000 per month alimony. Since the real estate market has collapsed in the area where they live, George and Linda cannot sell the house. Since they are still friends, they decide to live in separate wings of the house until the real estate market recovers. If George and Linda live together for the entire current year, can Linda claim a deduction for the alimony paid to George? In answering this case, use a computer tax service with only the *Internal Revenue Code* database selected. State your keywords and which computer tax service you used to arrive at your answer.

62. Juan sold IBM stock to Richard for a $10,000 loss. Richard is the husband of Juan's sister. How much of the loss can Juan deduct in the current year if Juan's taxable income is $55,000 and he has no other capital transactions? In answering this case, use a computer tax service with only the *Internal Revenue Code* database selected. State your keywords and which computer tax service you used to arrive at your answer.

63. Tex is a rancher. This year her herd of cattle was infested with hoof-and-mouth disease and had to be destroyed. Tex's insurance policy reimburses her for an amount in excess of the tax basis in the cattle, thereby creating an "insurance gain." After receiving the insurance proceeds, Tex buys a new herd of cattle. Can Tex defer the recognition of this insurance gain on the destroyed herd? In

answering this case, use a computer tax service with only the *Internal Revenue Code* database selected. State your keywords and which computer tax service you used to arrive at your answer.

64. Betty owed Martha $5,000. In payment of this debt, Betty transferred to Martha a life insurance policy on Betty, with a cash surrender value of $5,000. The face value of the policy is $100,000. Martha names herself as beneficiary of the policy and continues to make the premium payments. After Martha has paid $15,000 in premiums, Betty dies and Martha collects $100,000. Is any of the $100,000 Martha received taxable? In answering this case, use a computer tax service with only the *Internal Revenue Code* database selected. State your keywords and which computer tax service you used to arrive at your answer.

65. On May 1, Rick formed a new corporation, Red, Inc. He spent $3,000 in legal fees and paid the state $600 in incorporation fees to set up Red Corporation. Red Corporation started operating its business on May 10. Can Rick or Red Corporation deduct either of these organizational fees? In answering this case, use a computer tax service with only the *Internal Revenue Code* database selected. State your keywords and which computer tax service you used to arrive at your answer.

66. This year, there were massive brush fires in the interior of Mexico. Amy gave $10,000 to the Mexican Relief Foundation, which is located in Mexico City. The funds were used to provide food, clothing, and shelter to the victims of the Mexican fires. Is Amy's charitable contribution deductible for income tax purposes? In answering this case, use a computer tax service with only the *Internal Revenue Code* database selected. State your keywords and which computer tax service you used to arrive at your answer.

67. Curtis is fifty years old and has an IRA with substantial funds in it. His son, Curtis, Jr., was accepted to Yale University upon graduating from high school. Curtis had not planned for this and needs to draw $25,000 per year out of his IRA to help pay the tuition and fees at Yale. What are the tax consequences of the withdrawals from the IRA? In answering this case, use a computer tax service with only the *Internal Revenue Code* database selected. State your keywords and which computer tax service you used to arrive at your answer.

68. Dennis is an executive of Gold Corporation. He receives a one-for-one distribution of stock rights for each share of common stock he owns. On the date of distribution the stock rights have a fair market value of $2 per right and the stock has fair market value of $20 per share. Dennis owns 10,000 shares of the stock with a basis of $5 per share. If Dennis does not make any special elections with regards to the stock rights, what is his basis in the rights? In answering this case, use a computer tax service with only the *Internal Revenue Code* database selected. State your keywords and which computer tax service you used to arrive at your answer.

4

Administrative Regulations and Rulings

LEARNING OBJECTIVES

- Identify the most important administrative sources of the Federal tax law
- Distinguish among the structure, nature, and purpose of Regulations, Revenue Procedures, and IRS Rulings
- Describe how to locate, and how to interpret, the precedential value of administrative sources of the tax law
- Explain the elements of common citations for Regulations and other IRS pronouncements
- Detail the contents and publication practices of the *Internal Revenue Bulletin* and the *Cumulative Bulletin*

CHAPTER OUTLINE

Regulations
   Temporary Regulations
   Effective Date of Regulations
   Citing a Regulation
   Assessing Regulations
   Locating Regulations
Revenue Rulings
   Revenue Ruling Citations
   Locating Revenue Rulings
Revenue Procedures
Letter Rulings
   Private Letter Rulings
   Technical Advice Memoranda
   Determination Letters
   Public Inspection of Written Determinations
   Written Determination Numbering System
   Locating Written Determinations
Other IRS Pronouncements
   Acquiescences and Nonacquiescences
   Internal Revenue Bulletin
   Bulletin Index-Digest System
      Contents of the System
   Chief Counsel Memoranda
   Announcements and Notices
   Miscellaneous Publications

The Treasury Department is charged with administering the tax laws of the United States. In accomplishing this task, it makes various pronouncements to explain the *Internal Revenue Code*. Administrative pronouncements of this type constitute one of the major categories of primary tax authority. Thus, to properly research a client's tax problem, the tax researcher must understand what the various rulings represent, their significance, and their location.

The Secretary of the Treasury has the general responsibility for administering the tax law. The Secretary is a member of the President's cabinet and is not to be confused with the Treasurer of the United States. The Treasurer is another official in the Treasury Department, but is not concerned directly with tax matters.

The Internal Revenue Service is a division of the Treasury Department. It is assigned to manage day-to-day operations associated with administration of the provisions of the *Internal Revenue Code*. The chief operating official of the IRS is the Commissioner of Internal Revenue, a presidential appointee. The Treasury Secretary delegates most of the administrative responsibilities for the tax law to the IRS Commissioner.

To facilitate the IRS's administration of the tax laws, the Code authorizes the Treasury Secretary (or his or her delegate) to prescribe the Rules and Regulations necessary to administer the Code. According to § 7805(a),

Except where such authority is expressly given by this title to any person other than an officer or employee of the Treasury Department, the Secretary shall prescribe all needful rules and regulations for the enforcement of this title, including all rules and regulations as may be necessary by reason of any alteration of law in relation to internal revenue.

This section gives the IRS general authority to issue binding Rules and Regulations concerning Title 26 of the *United States Code*. In practice, most of the IRS's pronouncements are written by IRS staff or by the office of the Chief Counsel of the IRS, who is an assistant General Counsel of the Treasury Department.

The tax researcher must be especially familiar with the four major types of pronouncements that may be forthcoming under this authority, namely, Regulations, Revenue Rulings, Revenue Procedures, and Letter Rulings. Each of these categories of rulings is issued for a different purpose and carries a different degree of authority. The first three of these categories generally are published by the IRS, while the Letter Rulings (and other pronouncements) typically are not published by any government agency. The remainder of this chapter addresses the nature and location of each of these administrative pronouncements.

REGULATIONS

The **Regulations** constitute the IRS's and, thereby, the Treasury's official interpretation of the *Internal Revenue Code*. Regulations are issued in the form of **Treasury Decisions (TDs),** which are published in the *Federal Register* and, sometime later, in the *Internal Revenue Bulletin,* discussed later in this chapter. At least thirty days before a TD is published in final form, however, it must be issued in proposed form, allowing interested parties time to comment on it. As a result of the comments received during this process of public hearings, the IRS may make changes in the TD before its final publication.

Before and during the hearings process, the TDs are referred to as **Proposed Regulations** and, unlike Final Regulations, do not have the effect of law. After the hearings are completed, and changes (if any) have been made to the text of the TD, the TD is published in final form. Final Regulations are integrated with previously approved TDs and constitute the full set of IRS Regulations. After this integration has occurred, the TD designation usually is dropped, and the pronouncement simply is referred to as a "Regulation."

Observers have identified two distinct categories of Regulations, general and legislative. **General Regulations** are issued under the general authority granted to the IRS to interpret the language of the Code, usually under a specific Code (or Committee Report) directive of Congress, and with specific congressional authority. An example can be found under § 212, Expenses for the Production of Income. This short Code section has many pages of interpretive Regulations, providing taxpayers with operational rules for applying this provision to tax situations.

With respect to **Legislative Regulations,** the IRS is directed by Congress to fulfill effectively a law-making function and to specify the substantive requirements of a tax provision. Regulations that are ordered by the Code in this manner essentially carry the authority of the statute itself and are not easily challenged by taxpayers. Such authority is granted because, in certain (especially technical) areas of the tax law, Congress cannot or does not care to address the detailed or complex issues that are associated with an otherwise-defined tax issue. Accordingly, Congress directs the IRS to pronounce Regulations on the matter. For example, Congress delegated to the IRS the authority to prescribe Regulations necessary to carry out the provisions of § 135, which grants an exclusion for interest on certain U.S. savings bonds used for higher education expenses, including Regulations requiring record keeping and information reporting. Another example of this legislative authority is found in § 385, which directs the IRS to prescribe Regulations to distinguish debt from equity in "thinly capitalized" corporations. Legislative Regulations bear the greatest precedential value of any IRS pronouncement.

TEMPORARY REGULATIONS

In addition to Proposed and Final Regulations, the IRS periodically issues **Temporary Regulations** in response to a Congressional or judicial change in the tax law or its interpretation. Temporary Regulations are not subject to the public-hearings procedure that typifies the development of a Final Regulation, and they are effective immediately upon publication. Although they are effective immediately, the IRS must simultaneously issue the Regulations in proposed form; the Temporary Regulations expire three years after issuance pursuant to the statute (IRC § 7805). Temporary Regulations are issued to provide the taxpayer with immediate guidance concerning a new provision of the law, perhaps concerning filing requirements that must be satisfied immediately or the clarification of definitions and terms.

Until a Temporary Regulation is replaced with the Final Regulation under a Code section, the tax researcher should treat the Temporary Regulation as though it were final. Thus, Temporary Regulations are fully in effect and must be followed until they are superseded, whereas Proposed Regulations, having been issued only to solicit comments and to expose the IRS's proposed interpretation of the law, need not be followed as if they were law.

Effective Date of Regulations

In general, under § 7805(b), a new Regulation can be effective on the date on which such Regulation is filed with the *Federal Register*. However, there are certain situations in which a Regulation can be effective retroactively. These are:

- The Regulation is filed or issued within 18 months of the date of the enactment of the statutory provision to which the regulation relates.
- The Regulation is designed to prevent abuse by taxpayers.
- The Regulation corrects a procedural defect in the issuance of a prior Regulation.
- The Regulation relates to internal Treasury Department policies, practices, or procedures.
- The Regulation may apply retroactively by congressional directive.
- The Commissioner also has the power to allow taxpayers to elect to apply new Regulations retroactively.

In situations where a Regulation applies retroactively, it technically can apply starting with the date of the underlying Code section to which it relates. However, the statute of limitations may limit the application of a retroactive Regulation in many situations.

Citing a Regulation

Tax practitioners use a uniform system for citing specific Regulations. Each Regulation is assigned a unique number by the Treasury, which is broadly based on the Code section being interpreted in that Regulation. An example of this citation system appears in Exhibit 4–1. The number to the left of the period in a Regulation citation indicates the type of issue that is addressed in the pronouncement. The most commonly encountered types of Regulations include the following.

1.	Income Tax
20.	Estate Tax
25.	Gift Tax
31.	Employment Tax
301.	Procedural Matters

By being familiar with this arbitrary numbering system used by the Regulations, the tax researcher immediately can identify the general issue that is addressed in a pronouncement. Note that these numbers indicating the type of issue addressed in the Regulation do not necessarily correspond to the chapter numbers of the Code sections that address the same issues.

The number to the immediate right of the period in the citation of a Regulation indicates the Code section to which the Regulation relates. In the Exhibit 4–1 example of a full citation, one can determine that this is an income tax Regulation dealing with § 262 of the *Internal Revenue Code*. The numbers and letters to the right of the section number denote the Regulation number and smaller divisions of the pronouncement. Regulation numbers typically are consecutive, starting with 0 or 1, and follow the general order of the issues that are addressed in the corresponding Code section. The Regulation numbers, paragraphs, and so on, do not necessarily correspond, however, to the subsection or other division designations of the underlying Code section.

Exhibit 4–1
Interpreting a Regulation Citation

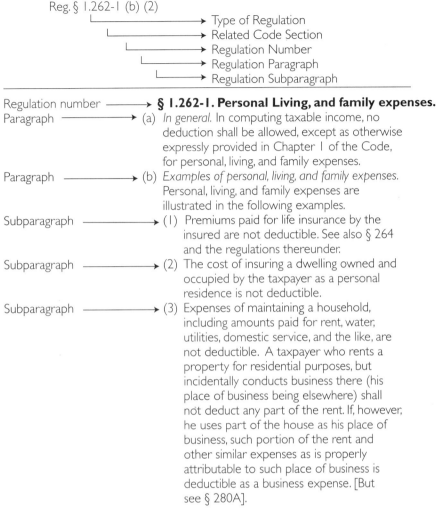

The numbering system for Temporary Regulations is similar to the numbering system for the Final and Proposed Regulations; however, usually the reference to or citation of a Temporary Regulation will include a "T" designating the temporary nature of the Regulation. An example of a citation for a Temporary Regulation under Code Section 280H is:

Reg. Sec. 1.280H-1T(b)(3).

ASSESSING REGULATIONS

In the course of tax practice, the researcher occasionally will be faced with a question concerning the validity of a Regulation. If the practitioner disagrees with the scope or language of the Regulation, he or she bears the burden of proof of showing that the Regulation is improper. This can be difficult. Many Regulations simply restate the

Code or Congressional Committee Reports; they are known as "hard and solid" Regulations. Moreover, because of the authority delegated to the IRS, Legislative Regulations have the full force and effect of law. Finally, the Supreme Court views General Regulations as also having the force and effect of law, unless they conflict with the statute [*Maryland Casualty Co. v. U. S.,* 251 U.S. 342 (1920)]. Thus, a taxpayer challenge to a Regulation typically must assert an improper exercise of IRS power, or an overly broad application of a rule.

In questioning the provisions of a Regulation, the tax researcher must be aware of several accuracy penalties Congress has enacted in the *Internal Revenue Code*. For example, § 6662 assesses a penalty equal to 20 percent of any underpayment of tax where the underpayment is found to be due to "negligence," which includes any failure to make a reasonable attempt to comply with the Code or any evidence of disregard of Treasury Rules or Regulations. Thus, if a practitioner chooses to ignore an administrative element of the tax law, he or she must possess substantial authority to do so to avoid this penalty or others of its kind. See Chapter 13 for a more detailed examination of these provisions.

LOCATING REGULATIONS

When Treasury Decisions are final, they are published in the ***Internal Revenue Bulletin*** (IRB), a weekly newsletter of the IRS. Twice a year, the IRBs, reorganized by Code section, are bound into a set of volumes titled the ***Cumulative Bulletin,*** which becomes the permanent IRS location of the Regulations.

Most commercial tax services also reproduce the Regulations in their materials; annotated services usually include the text adjacent to the language of the Code and the related court case notes, and topical services usually provide an appendix that includes the edited Regulations for the volume or chapter that discusses the pertinent issue. Paperback or hardbound editions of the tax Regulations also are available from several commercial publishers, including Research Institute of America (RIA), West Publishing Company, and Commerce Clearing House (CCH), typically as a companion to a similar edition of the Code. Exhibit 4–2 shows common places where the tax researcher can find the Regulations and most other sources of administrative tax research material.

REVENUE RULINGS

Revenue Rulings are second to Regulations as important administrative sources of the Federal tax law. A Revenue Ruling is an official pronouncement of the National Office of the IRS; it deals with the application of the Code and Regulations to a specific factual situation, usually one that has been submitted by a taxpayer. Thus, most Revenue Rulings indicate how the IRS will treat a given taxpayer transaction. Revenue Rulings do not carry the force and effect of Regulations.

Revenue Rulings provide excellent sources of information; in fact, they are published chiefly for the purpose of guiding taxpayers. Therefore, even for a tax researcher whose client did not submit the original request for the Ruling, the result of the Ruling is of value if it concerns a transaction similar in nature, structure, or effect to the client's situation. Reliance should, however, not be placed on a Revenue

Exhibit 4–2
Sources of Administrative Tax Law

Computer Sources:	
RIA Checkpoint	Research Institute of America
Westlaw	West Publishing Co.
CCH Tax Research Network	Commerce Clearing House
Kleinrock's	Kleinrock Publishing Co.
Lexis	LexisNexis
Printed Sources:	
Tax Coordinator 2d	Research Institute of America
United States Code Annotated	West Publishing Co.
Standard Federal Tax Reporter	Commerce Clearing House
Cumulative Bulletin	Government Printing Office
Public Law Legislative History	Commerce Clearing House
Primary Sources (since 1968)	Bureau of National Affairs

Ruling if it has been affected by subsequent legislation, Regulations, Rulings, or court decisions.

Revenue Rulings adhere to a general internal structure, as illustrated in Exhibit 4–3. The typical structure is as follows.

1. *Issue:* A statement of the issue in question.
2. *Facts:* The facts on which the Revenue Ruling is based.
3. *Law and analysis:* The IRS's application of current law to the issue in the Revenue Ruling.
4. *Holding:* How the IRS will treat the transaction.

Multiple Revenue Rulings (e.g., 59 in 2000) are released by the IRS each year. Each is identified by the year in which it was released and the number for that year. The IRS publishes them in the weekly *Internal Revenue Bulletin* and, later, in the *Cumulative Bulletin*.

REVENUE RULING CITATIONS

Revenue Rulings bear both a temporary and a permanent citation. The temporary citation is structured as follows.

>Rev. Rul. 2000-7, 2000-9 I.R.B. 712

where:

>2000-7 is the Revenue Ruling number (the 7th Revenue Ruling of 2000).
>2000-9 is the weekly issue of the *Internal Revenue Bulletin* (the 9th week of 2000).
>I.R.B. is the abbreviation for the *Internal Revenue Bulletin*.
>712 is the page number.

Exhibit 4–3 Revenue Ruling

REV. RUL. 2000-7

ISSUE

If the retirement and removal of a depreciable asset occurs in connection with the installation or production of a replacement asset, are the costs incurred in removing the retired asset required to be capitalized under Section 263(a) or 263A as part of the cost of the replacement asset?

FACTS

The assets of X, a telephone company, include telephone poles A and B. X placed Pole A in service in 1979 on land it owned. X placed Pole B in service in 1982 on land owned by Y under the terms of an easement permitting X to have one pole on Y's land. In 2000, X undertakes a project to replace telephone poles in the service area in which Pole A is situated. As part of that project, X incurs costs in 2000 in removing and discarding Pole A and installing a new telephone pole, Pole C, in the same location. X also undertakes a second project to replace telephone poles in the service area in which Pole B is situated. X installs a new telephone pole, Pole D, on Y's land, but not in the same location as Pole B. As part of this second project and to comply with the easement, X incurs costs in 2000 in removing and discarding Pole B.

LAW AND ANALYSIS

Section 162 of the *Internal Revenue Code* and Section 1.162-1 of the Income Tax Regulations generally allow a deduction for all the ordinary and necessary expenses paid or incurred during the taxable year in carrying on any trade or business.

Section 165 allows as a deduction any loss sustained during the taxable year and not compensated for by insurance or otherwise. For the allowance under Section 165(a) of losses arising from the permanent withdrawal of depreciable property from use in a trade or business or in the production of income, Section 1.165-2(c) cross references Section 1.167(a)-8(a), which permits, in part, a loss from physical abandonment of retired property.

Under Sections 263(a) and 1.263(a)-1(a), no deduction is allowed for capital expenditures, such as amounts paid for new buildings or for permanent improvements or betterments made to increase the value of any property. Section 1.263(a)-2(a) provides that capital expenditures include the costs of acquisition, construction, or erection of buildings, machinery and equipment, furniture and fixtures, and similar property having a useful life substantially beyond the taxable year.

Section 263A generally requires taxpayers that are producing real or tangible personal property to capitalize direct material costs, direct labor costs, and indirect costs that are properly allocable to the produced property. Section 263A(g)(1) provides that, for purposes of Section 263A, the term "produce" includes construct, build, install, manufacture, develop, or improve.

* * *

HOLDING

If the retirement and removal of a depreciable asset occurs in connection with the installation or production of a replacement asset, the costs incurred in removing the retired asset are not required to be capitalized under Section 263(a) or 263A as part of the cost of the replacement asset.

DRAFTING INFORMATION

The principal author of this revenue ruling is Beverly Katz of the Office of Assistant Chief Counsel (Income Tax and Accounting). For further information regarding this revenue ruling contact Ms. Katz at (202) 622-4950 (not a toll-free call).

The permanent citation for the same Revenue Ruling would be as follows.

Rev. Rul. 2000-7, 2000-1 C.B. 712

where:

2000-7 is the Revenue Ruling number (the 7th Revenue Ruling of 2000).
2000-1 is the volume number of the *Cumulative Bulletin* (Volume 1 of 2000).
C.B. is the abbreviation for the *Cumulative Bulletin.*
712 is the page number.

Once the pertinent *Cumulative Bulletin* is published, the temporary citation is normally no longer used.

In July 1999, the IRS started continuously numbering the pages in the *Internal Revenue Bulletin*. Thus, the page number in the IRB is the same as that in the CB after June 1999. Also, before 2000, Revenue Rulings were given a two-digit identification number instead of the current four-digit number (e.g., Rev. Rul. 98-23).

LOCATING REVENUE RULINGS

Generally, the tax researcher must examine every applicable Revenue Ruling before a tax research project is complete. Revenue Rulings can be found at most of the locations (i.e., published and computer tax services, the *Cumulative Bulletin,* and some Internet sites) shown in Exhibit 4–2. Prior to 1953, Revenue Rulings were known by different names, including Appeals and Review Memorandum (ARM), General Counsel's Memorandum (GCM), and Office Decision (OD). These early rulings still may have some application in client situations if the IRS has not revoked them or modified them in any way. A tax researcher cannot ignore such rulings simply because they are old.

The current status of a Revenue Ruling or other IRS ruling can be checked in the most current index to the *Cumulative Bulletin*. In addition, several of the printed commercial tax services, (i.e., Research Institute of America and Commerce Clearing House) present a variety of finding lists and other references with which to examine the status of a ruling. Later chapters of this text demonstrate the use of a tax service with respect to subsequent developments concerning IRS rulings.

REVENUE PROCEDURES

Revenue Procedures deal with the internal practice and procedures of the IRS in the administration of the tax laws. They constitute the IRS's way of releasing information to taxpayers. For example, when the IRS releases specifications for facsimile tax forms generated by a computer service, or informs the public about areas in which it will no longer issue Revenue Rulings, it issues a Revenue Procedure to that effect. Although a Revenue Procedure may not be as useful as a Regulation or a Revenue Ruling in the direct resolution of a tax research problem, the practitioner still should be familiar with all of the pertinent Procedures.

Revenue Procedures are issued in a manner similar to that for Revenue Rulings. They are first published in the weekly *Internal Revenue Bulletin* and later are included in the bound edition of the *Cumulative Bulletin*. The IRS issues approximately 50 to 60 Revenue Procedures per year (e.g., there were 50 in 2000).

A Revenue Procedure is cited using the same system as that for Revenue Rulings, that is, adopting first a temporary and then a permanent citation. In this regard, the temporary citation refers to the location of the Procedure in the *Internal Revenue Bulletin,* and the permanent citation denotes its location in the *Cumulative Bulletin.* Thus, a typical Revenue Procedure would have the following permanent citation.

Rev. Proc. 2001-21, 2001-1 C.B. 742

A Revenue Procedure is reproduced in Exhibit 4–4. Revenue Procedures can be found in the same publications in which Revenue Rulings are located.

Exhibit 4–4 Revenue Procedure Excerpt

REV. PROC. 2000-34

SECTION 1. PURPOSE

This revenue procedure provides guidance for submitting the information required under Section 6501(c)(9) of the *Internal Revenue Code* and Section 301.6501(c)-1(f) of the Procedure and Administration Regulations to adequately disclose a gift if the information was not initially submitted with a gift tax return filed for the calendar year in which the gift was made. The period of limitations on assessment under Section 6501(a) will commence to run with respect to such a gift when the taxpayer adequately discloses the gift on an amended gift tax return filed pursuant to this revenue procedure. The period of assessment will generally expire 3 years after the date such amended return is filed.

SECTION 2. BACKGROUND

Under Section 6501(c)(9), as amended by the Taxpayer Relief Act of 1997, 1997-4 (Vol. 1) C.B. 1, 69, and the Internal Revenue Restructuring and Reform Act of 1998, P.L. 105-206, 112 Stat. 685, if the value of a gift is required to be shown on a gift tax return but is not disclosed on the return, or on a statement attached to the return, in a manner adequate to apprise the Internal Revenue Service of the nature of the transfer, the period of limitations on assessment of gift tax with respect to the gift will not begin to run. If the transfer is adequately disclosed on the gift tax return and the period of limitations on assessment of gift tax has expired, then, under Section 2504(c), the value of the gift cannot be adjusted for purposes of determining "prior taxable gifts" and the current gift tax liability and, under Section 2001(f), the value of the gift cannot be adjusted for purposes of determining "adjusted taxable gifts" and the estate tax liability.

* * *

SECTION 3. SCOPE

This revenue procedure applies where the donor filed a federal gift tax return [Form 709, United States Gift (and Generation-Skipping Transfer) Tax Return] for the appropriate calendar year but failed to adequately disclose a gift because the gift was not reported on the return or because the information required under Section 301.6501(c)-1(f)(2) for the gift was not submitted with the return. This revenue procedure does not apply in any situation where Section 6501(c)(1), (c)(2), or (c)(3) applies.

SECTION 4. PROCEDURE

To commence the running of the period of limitations on assessment with respect to a gift that was not adequately disclosed on a Federal gift tax return, the donor must file an amended gift tax return for the calendar year in which the gift was made.

LETTER RULINGS

The tax researcher is also interested in the *letter rulings* that are issued by the IRS in several forms, including Private Letter Rulings, Determination Letters, and Technical Advice Memoranda. The IRS does not publish these items in any official collection, but they are available from several commercial sources, as will be discussed later in this chapter.

PRIVATE LETTER RULINGS

The National Office of the IRS issues **Private Letter Rulings** in response to a taxpayer's request for the IRS's position on a specified tax issue. The IRS has authority to decline to issue Letter Rulings under certain conditions, such as where the problem is one of an inherently factual nature. The content, format, and procedures that are used for Revenue Rulings apply with respect to Private Letter Rulings. The IRS does not publish its reply in the *Internal Revenue Bulletin* or *Cumulative Bulletin*, however. Rather, it sends its response only to the taxpayer who submitted the request. An excerpt of a Private Letter Ruling is shown in Exhibit 4–5.

The process is as follows. The taxpayer asks the IRS to disclose its interpretation of the Code, Regulations, and pertinent court cases for a transaction the taxpayer describes; the description should include a statement of the business purpose for the transaction. For instance, if two corporations plan to merge, one of them might request a Private Letter Ruling to find out whether the IRS believes that the Code's tax-favored reorganization provisions will apply to the anticipated merger. In many cases, if the IRS asserts that the transaction will not receive a treatment favorable to

Exhibit 4–5
Private Letter Ruling Excerpt

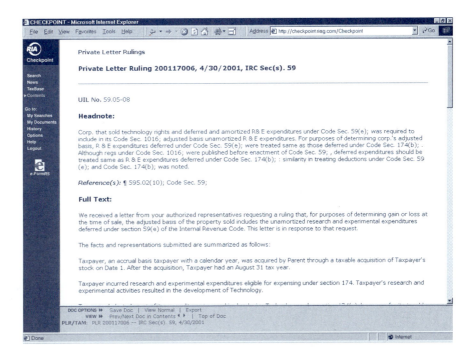

the taxpayer, it will suggest means by which the transaction could be restructured to obtain the favorable treatment.

As mentioned, a Private Letter Ruling is issued only to the taxpayer who requested the ruling. However, under Reg. § 1.6662-4(d)(3)(iii), Private Letter Rulings are included in the list of authorities constituting "substantial authority" upon which a taxpayer may rely to avoid certain statutory penalties. Letter Rulings are, in any case, an important source of information, because they indicate how the IRS may treat a similar transaction.

Private Letter Rulings also constitute an important IRS stimulus for new Revenue Rulings. When the IRS comes across an unusual transaction that it believes to be of general interest, or when it receives a flurry of Letter Ruling requests concerning very similar factual situations, a Private Ruling may be converted into Revenue Ruling form and published in official administrative sources. The IRS must notify the taxpayer of its intention to disclose the ruling, and the taxpayer has the right to protest such disclosure. Before publication, all aspects of the new ruling, including the statement of facts, are purged of any reference to the taxpayer's name or other identifying information.

TECHNICAL ADVICE MEMORANDA

A **Technical Advice Memorandum** is issued by the IRS's National Office, making it similar in this regard to the Private Letter Ruling and different from the Determination Letter. The Technical Advice Memorandum, however, concerns a completed transaction. Whereas a Private Letter Ruling typically is requested by a taxpayer prior to completing a transaction or filing a tax return, a Technical Advice Memorandum usually is requested by an agent when a question arises during an audit that cannot be answered satisfactorily by the local office.

Similar to the Private Letter Ruling, a Technical Advice Memorandum applies strictly to the taxpayer for whose audit it was requested, and it cannot be relied on by other taxpayers. However, again, the information that is contained in the memorandum may be useful to the tax researcher for the insight that it gives concerning the thinking of the IRS relative to a given problem area in taxation.

These memoranda are not included in any official IRS publication, but they are open for public inspection, as we will discuss next. If the facts or the holding of a Technical Advice Memorandum are felt by the IRS to be of general interest, the memorandum may be converted into Revenue Ruling format and published by the IRS in the *Internal Revenue Bulletin* and the *Cumulative Bulletin*.

DETERMINATION LETTERS

A **Determination Letter** is similar in purpose and nature to a Private Letter Ruling, except that it is issued by the office of the local IRS district director, rather than by the National Office of the IRS. Because a Determination Letter is issued by a lower-level IRS official, it usually deals with issues and transactions that are not overtly controversial. For instance, the trustee of a pension plan might request a Determination Letter to ascertain whether the plan is qualified for the Code's tax-favored deferred compensation treatment.

Determination Letters usually relate to completed transactions rather than to the proposed transactions that typically lead to the issuance of a Private Letter Ruling. Determination Letters are not included in any official IRS publication, but they may be available to the tax researcher from other sources.

Public Inspection of Written Determinations

The public can receive copies of any unpublished IRS Letter Rulings under § 6110(f). Included under this provision are Private Letter Rulings, Determination Letters, and Technical Advice Memoranda. Before any public inspection is allowed, however, the IRS is required by § 6110(c) to remove the taxpayer's name and any other information that might be used by a third party to identify the taxpayer. In addition, the IRS is required to purge the document of any items that could affect national defense or foreign policy, trade secrets, financial information, data relative to the regulation of financial institutions, geographical data, and items that could invade personal privacy. If the taxpayer opposes the disclosure of the written determination, he or she can bring the matter before the IRS and the Tax Court prior to the scheduled disclosure under § 6110(f).

Once all of the required data have been removed from the written determination, it must be made open for public inspection at such places as the Treasury Secretary designates in the Regulations. Information of this type is available in Washington, D.C., and at selected other locations.

IRC § 6110 specifically limits the precedential value of any of these written determinations. Overall, such pronouncements may not be cited as authority in a tax matter by either the taxpayer or the IRS. However, Letter Rulings can be used as "examples" of IRS treatment of similar factual patterns when dealing with the IRS. For example, tax practitioners could suggest that a Letter Ruling be used as guidance in an instant situation. However, keep in mind that an IRS agent does not have to follow a Letter Ruling issued to a different taxpayer because under § 6110, it has limited precedential value.

In 1989, Congress expanded the list of authorities on which taxpayers may rely to avoid certain understatement of tax penalties to include Private Letter Rulings, Technical Advice Memoranda, Actions on Decisions, General Counsel Memoranda, and other similar documents published by the IRS in the *Internal Revenue Bulletin*. The Committee Report expressed a general intent to broaden the list of authorities on which a taxpayer may rely to avoid penalties; however, it does not appear that Congress intended to change the general precedential value of these pronouncements with respect to determining a taxpayer's tax liability.

Written Determination Numbering System

Because the IRS issues thousands of Letter Rulings per year, it assigns a nine-digit document number to each written determination for identification purposes. The first four digits indicate the year in which the ruling was issued, the next two numbers denote the week, and the last three digits indicate the number of the ruling for the week. Thus, a lengthy but unique identifier is created for each pronouncement. For example, the number of a Letter Ruling can be interpreted as follows.

Ltr. Rul. 200117024

where:

2001 is the year the Ruling is issued.
17 is the week of the year the Ruling is issued.
024 indicates that this is the 24th Ruling issued that week.

Before the year 2000, only a two-digit date was used to signify the year in which the ruling was issued (e.g., 9814026).

LOCATING WRITTEN DETERMINATIONS

The tax researcher needs access to written determinations to complete many tax research projects. Selected written determinations can be found in summary form in the major tax services. However, if the tax researcher needs access to the full text of written determinations, a computer tax database is the best approach. Consult Exhibit 4–2 for the online computer tax databases that contain the full text of IRS written determinations.

OTHER IRS PRONOUNCEMENTS

The IRS issues several other types of information that can be of value to the tax researcher, including acquiescences and nonacquiescences, the *Internal Revenue Bulletin*, the *Bulletin Index-Digest System*, Chief Counsel Memoranda, and other miscellaneous publications.

ACQUIESCENCES AND NONACQUIESCENCES

When the IRS loses an issue or decision in court, the Commissioner may announce an acquiescence or nonacquiescence to the decision. An **acquiescence** indicates that the court decision, although it was adverse to the IRS, will be followed in similar situations. The Commissioner determines, at his or her own discretion, the degree of similarity required before the IRS will follow the result that is unfavorable to itself.

A **nonacquiescence** indicates that the IRS disagrees with the adverse decision in the case and will follow the decision only for the specific taxpayer whose case resulted in the adverse ruling. If the IRS wishes to express agreement with only part of the decision that is settled in the taxpayer's favor, the Commissioner may nonacquiesce with respect to certain issues. Finally, an acquiescence or nonacquiescence is not issued if the IRS prevails in a court case, because it likely agrees with all pertinent holdings.

Nonacquiescence may indicate to the tax practitioner that the IRS is likely to challenge a similar decision for the taxpayer in a case that has a similar factual situation. However, the issuance of an acquiescence does not necessarily mean that the IRS agrees with the adverse decision, but only that it will not pursue the matter in a (similar and) subsequent case. Each of these items of information can be useful when the practitioner prepares for, or anticipates, a court challenge to the client's position in a tax matter.

As mentioned, if the IRS has acquiesced to a case, then the taxpayer can rely on that decision as precedent that will be followed by agents for similar fact patterns. However, if the IRS has nonacquiesced, the taxpayer must evaluate whether to pursue a similar fact pattern in court. Such factors as the cost of litigation plus the probability of winning must be appraised before proceeding with a case similar to one with which the IRS has nonacquiesced.

Occasionally, the IRS changes (with an attendant retroactive effect on taxpayers) its acquiescence or nonacquiescence position by withdrawing the original pronouncement. For example, in *U.S. v. City Loan and Savings,* 287 F.2d 612 (CA-6, 1961), the court allowed the IRS to withdraw an acquiescence on an issue-by-issue, but not taxpayer-by-taxpayer, basis. This change may occur after only a short time passes or many years later. Such a change in the IRS's position typically is accompanied by a brief explanation of the reason for the change—for example, because of a contrary holding in a subsequent court case or a change in the agency's policy concerning the issue.

IRS acquiescence decisions are driven by related litigation costs, revenue effects, and administrative and policy directives. IRS acquiescences and nonacquiescences are published in the *Internal Revenue Bulletin* and thereafter, in the *Cumulative Bulletin*. Exhibit 4–6 reproduces an acquiescence from the *Cumulative Bulletin* in which the IRS indicates its position on a case. A citator (see Chapter 8) also can be used to locate acquiescence and nonacquiescence decisions.

The index to the *Internal Revenue Bulletin* lists acquiescences and nonacquiescences alphabetically and in Code section order. After the IRS issues such a pronouncement, any reference to the citation for the case includes either the abbreviation "Acq" or "Nonacq" (or, occasionally, "NA") to indicate the subsequent development.

INTERNAL REVENUE BULLETIN

The IRS's official publication for its pronouncements is the *Internal Revenue Bulletin* (IRB). Most IRS Revenue Rulings and Revenue Procedures, and the agency's acquiescences and nonacquiescences to regular Tax Court decisions, first are published in the IRB. This reference bulletin also includes the following information, all of which can be useful to the tax researcher.

- New tax laws, issued by Congress as Public Laws
- Committee Reports underlying tax statutes
- Procedural rules
- New tax treaties
- Treasury Decisions (which become Regulations)
- Other notices

Interested parties can subscribe to the *Internal Revenue Bulletin* by contacting the Internal Revenue Service. Alternatively, some of the commercial tax services include subscriptions to, or reproductions of, all of the issues of the *Internal Revenue Bulletin*.

BULLETIN INDEX-DIGEST SYSTEM

The IRS also produces the **Bulletin Index-Digest System,** a comprehensive index of matters that it has published since 1952 in the *Internal Revenue Bulletin*. This resource is available from the Government Printing Office on a subscription basis and

Exhibit 4–6 Action on Decision

ACTION ON DECISION 2000-004

May 10, 2000

Subject: *Smith, Algerine Est v Com.,* (1999; CA5) 84 AFTR 2d 99-7393, 198 F2d 515

Issue: Whether post-death events should be considered in determining the amount deductible under Internal Revenue Code Section 2053(a)(3) for claims against the estate that are contingent or contested at the date of death.

Discussion: Decedent died on November 16, 1990. At her death, Exxon had a claim against the estate that was being adjudicated in a United States District Court. In February 1991, the court ruled in favor of Exxon and referred the case to a Special Master to determine the amount of the liability. In April 1991, Exxon presented to the estate its $2,482,719 damages calculation. The executors deducted that amount on the estate tax return, which was filed in July 1991. On February 10, 1992, the estate settled the claim for $681,840 and paid this amount on or about March 10, 1992. The Commissioner determined that the estate was only entitled to a deduction for the amount actually paid, and the estate filed a petition in the United States Tax Court.

The Tax Court upheld the Commissioner's determination that the claim against the estate should be limited to the amount actually paid. The Tax Court held that, "[w]here a claim is disputed, contingent, or uncertain as of the date of the decedent's death, the estate is not entitled to a deduction until the claim is resolved and it is determined what amount, if any, will be paid. It is this latter amount that is allowed as a deduction." 108 T.C. at 419.

The United States Court of Appeals for the Fifth Circuit reversed, holding that the amount deductible was the fair market value of the claim on the date of death, rather than the amount paid to settle the claim as argued by the government, or the full amount of the claim as argued by the estate. The Fifth Circuit relied on the decision in *Ithaca Trust v. United States,* 279 U.S. 151, 155 (1929) [7 AFTR 8856]. In that case, the Supreme Court concluded that a post-death event (the premature death of the life tenant of a charitable remainder trust) should not be taken into account in determining the amount of the charitable deduction allowable under the predecessor to Section 2055. The Fifth Circuit remanded the case to the Tax Court to determine the value of the claim at the date of death with the instruction that the court was "neither to admit nor consider evidence of post-death occurrences when determining the date-of-death value of Exxon's claim." 198 F.3d at 526.

* * *

We nonacquiesce in the Fifth Circuit's opinion that disputed claims against the estate at the date of death are to be valued without reference to post-death events. We accept, however, the precedential effect of the Fifth Circuit's opinion in cases appealable to the Fifth Circuit and will follow it with respect to cases within the Fifth Circuit, if the opinion cannot be meaningfully distinguished.

Recommendation: Nonacquiescence

---

contains a variety of finding lists that accommodate alternate methods of IRB research. The *Bulletin Index-Digest System* consists of four separate services.

Service #1. Income Tax, Publication 641
Service #2. Estate and Gift Taxes, Publication 642
Service #3. Employment Taxes, Publication 643
Service #4. Excise Taxes, Publication 644

Each of these services consists of a basic volume and the latest cumulative supplement. The cumulative supplements are issued quarterly for the Income Tax service, and semiannually for the other three services. About every two years a new basic volume is published to consolidate the materials of the existing basic volume and the ever-increasing supplemental materials.

Contents of the System

The *Bulletin Index-Digest System* contains separate finding lists for Revenue Rulings, Revenue Procedures, Public Laws that amend the *Internal Revenue Code*, and Treasury Decisions that amend the pertinent Regulations. In addition, the system includes a number of special lists to identify other items that may be of interest to the tax researcher, such as the following.

- Supreme Court decisions
- Certain Tax Court decisions
- Revenue Rulings and Revenue Procedures issued under tax conventions
- Miscellaneous items that are published in the IRB
- Lists of Revenue Rulings and Revenue Procedures
- Actions relative to published Revenue Rulings and Revenue Procedures
- Public Laws that have been published in the IRB
- Tax conventions and related items that have been published in the IRB

A major portion of the *Bulletin Index-Digest System* consists of digests, that is, brief summaries, of (1) Revenue Procedures and Revenue Rulings, arranged alphabetically under topical headings and subheadings; (2) Supreme Court decisions and adverse-to-the-government Tax Court decisions to which the Commissioner has announced acquiescence or nonacquiescence; and (3) executive orders, Treasury Department orders, delegation orders, and certain other miscellaneous items that have been published in the *Cumulative Bulletin*. Each such digest is preceded by descriptive "keywords" that further identify the subject matter of the item, and each digest is followed by a citation to both the Code and/or Regulations section under which the item was published and the *Cumulative Bulletin* in which the full text of the cited item may be found.

This arrangement of digests under topical headings allows the practitioner to use a "subject matter" approach to find Revenue Rulings and most other items that are pertinent to the research task. Public Laws, Treasury Decisions, and tax conventions are not digested in this publication. Thus, the user can employ only the system's finding lists for determining whether any such items are relevant to the taxpayer's tax issue.

The *Bulletin Index-Digest System* does not contain a Code section finding list for Revenue Rulings, Revenue Procedures, Supreme Court decisions, or Actions on Decisions of the Tax Court that relate to the 1939 Code. One must use a commercial tax service, or some other available resource, to cross-reference the section numbers of the 1939 Code to those of the current edition. Digests of such items, however, include citations to the relevant 1939, 1954, and 1986 Code and Regulation material.

Again, in using the *Bulletin Index-Digest System,* one always must be sure to examine the most recent cumulative supplement to the service. The release dates of both the basic volume and the supplement itself are printed on the front cover of the publication.

CHIEF COUNSEL MEMORANDA

The office of the IRS's Chief Counsel periodically generates memoranda that may be of use to the tax researcher. Although the IRS does not publish these memoranda in any official document, they are available from commercial publishers. A **Technical Memorandum** (TM) is prepared in the production of a Proposed Regulation. A **General Counsel's Memorandum** (GCM) is generated upon the request of the IRS, typically as a means to assist in the preparation of Revenue Rulings and Private Letter Rulings. An **Action on Decision** (AOD) is prepared when the IRS loses a case in a court. The text of the AOD recommends the action, if any, that the IRS should take in response to the adverse decision (see Exhibit 4–6). In addition to the above documents, the Chief Counsel's office gives various forms of advice to IRS offices and personnel. These documents are called *Field Service Advice (FSAs)*, *Chief Counsel Advice (CCAs)*, *Chief Counsel Notices (CCNs)*, and *Service Center Advice (SCAs)*. All of these documents are available for public inspection and can be found on most computer-based tax services such as RIA Checkpoint.

ANNOUNCEMENTS AND NOTICES

The IRS issues **Announcements and Notices** concerning items of general importance to taxpayers. For example, at year-end, the IRS will issue a Notice to announce the mailing of the new tax-form packages to taxpayers or changes on the Forms 1040, 1040A, and 1040EZ. Exhibit 4–7 reproduces a typical Notice. Notices are generally considered more important than Announcements by the IRS, and thus they are published in the permanent, bound volumes of *Cumulative Bulletins*. Announcements are not published in the *Cumulative Bulletin;* however, they are published in the weekly *Internal Revenue Bulletin*.

Notices also are used to announce new provisions of the tax law that may affect a large number of taxpayers. For example, several Notices were issued in 1984 concerning the requirement that tax shelter partnerships obtain registration numbers from the IRS. Similarly, Notices regularly are used to announce the standard mileage rate that is used to compute taxpayers' deductions for the business use of automobiles. Important Notices are reproduced in the body of most of the commercial tax services' publications.

MISCELLANEOUS PUBLICATIONS

The IRS publishes numerous general and specialized documents to help taxpayers. Some of the more common ones include the following.

Publication 17, *Your Federal Income Tax*
Publication 225, *Farmer's Tax Guide*
Publication 334, *Tax Guide for Small Business*
Publication 519, *U.S. Tax Guide for Aliens*
Publication 589, *Tax Information on S Corporations*

Each of these documents is available directly from the IRS, both in print and electronic formats. See Exhibit 4–8 for an IRS Publication excerpt from the IRS web site. In addition, several of the commercial tax publishers offer copies of these lay-oriented *Publications*. Furthermore, any library that is designated as a government depository receives all of these documents. Finally, many of the above Publications can be ordered from the IRS in Spanish-language editions.

Although the IRS Publications contain useful information, the tax researcher must be careful when relying on them. IRS Publications typically do not cite the

Exhibit 4–7 IRS Notice

NOTICE 2001-7
REPORTING OF GROSS PROCEEDS PAYMENTS TO ATTORNEYS

This notice informs taxpayers that the Internal Revenue Service intends to further delay the effective date of the regulations proposed under Section 6045(f) of the *Internal Revenue Code* (relating to the reporting of payments of gross proceeds to attorneys). Under this extension, the rules in Section 1.6045-5 will apply to payments made during the first calendar year that begins at least two months after the date of publication of the final regulations in the *Federal Register*.

    Section 1021 of the Taxpayer Relief Act of 1997, 1997-4 (Vol. 1) C.B. 1, 136, added Section 6045(f) of the Code, which requires information reporting for payments made in the course of a trade or business to attorneys in connection with legal services (whether or not such services are performed for the payor). Section 6045(f) applies to payments made after December 31, 1997. The notice of proposed rulemaking (NPRM) under Section 6045(f) was published in the *Federal Register* on May 21, 1999 (64 F.R. 27730), 1999-1 C.B. 1193. Section 1.6045-5(h) of the proposed Income Tax Regulations provides that the rules in Section 1.6045-5 apply to payments made after December 31, 1999. However, Notice 99-53, 1999-2 C.B. 565, extended the effective date of Section 1.6045-5 to payments made after December 31, 2000.

    Because the Service is continuing to study the many comments regarding the NPRM under Section 6045(f), the Service intends to further delay the effective date of Section 1.6045-5. Accordingly, when finalized, the rules in Section 1.6045-5 will apply to payments made during the first calendar year that begins at least two months after the date of publication of the final regulations in the *Federal Register*. Nevertheless, payments of gross proceeds to attorneys made after December 31, 1997, are and continue to be reportable on Form 1099-MISC pursuant to Section 6045(f); only the effective date of the regulations that interpret Section 6045(f) will be delayed. Taxpayers may continue to rely on the NPRM as a safe harbor providing a reasonable interpretation of the statute.

EFFECT ON OTHER DOCUMENTS

Notice 99-53 is modified, and, as modified, is superseded.

DRAFTING INFORMATION

The principal author of this notice is Sara Paige Shepherd of the Office of the Associate Chief Counsel, Procedure and Administration (Administrative Provisions and Judicial Practice). For further information regarding this notice contact Ms. Shepherd at (202) 622-4910 (not a toll-free number).

Code, Regulations, or other authority on which the information included therein is based. In fact, the IRS disclaims any responsibility for damages that the taxpayer may suffer in erroneously relying on its Publications, and it may, in fact, take positions that are contrary to those that are included in the Publications in certain court cases or appeals hearings.

    These documents are prepared from the government's point of view. For instance, if a lower court has ruled against the IRS on a given matter that is addressed in a Publication, the text of the document probably will not mention the possibility that the IRS's official position will be found to be incorrect on appeal. Although IRS Publications can be the source of some basic information that is useful for laypersons, or in a tax compliance context, the tax researcher should not rely on or cite such a reference in a professional research report.

Exhibit 4–8
IRS Publication 3 (Armed Forces Tax Guide) Excerpt

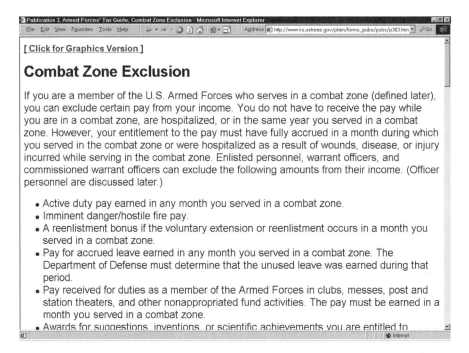

SUMMARY

Administrative pronouncements provide the tax researcher with a significant amount of information from and about the IRS. The primary IRS pronouncements that are of interest to the tax researcher include the Regulations, Revenue Rulings, Revenue Procedures, and Letter Rulings. The tax practitioner who performs competent research must be aware of the content and format of each of these items, know how to locate them, appreciate the precedential value of each, and understand how each might affect the client's tax problem. Exhibit 4–9 summarizes the most commonly encountered IRS pronouncements.

TAX TUTOR

Reinforce the tax research information covered in this chapter by completing the on-line tutorials located at the Federal Tax Research web site:

http://raabe.swcollege.com

KEY WORDS

By the time you complete this chapter, you should be comfortable discussing each of the following terms. If you need additional review of any of these items, return to the appropriate material in the chapter or consult the glossary to this text.

Chapter 4 Administrative Regulations and Rulings

Exhibit 4–9 Common IRS Pronouncements

Pronouncement	Purpose
Regulation	The official Treasury or IRS interpretation of a portion of the *Internal Revenue Code*
Revenue Ruling	The IRS's application of the tax law to a specific fact situation
Revenue Procedure	A statement of IRS practice or procedure that affects taxpayers or the general public
Private Letter Ruling	Statement issued by the National Office of the IRS at a taxpayer's request, applying the tax law to a proposed transaction
Determination Letter	Statement issued by the District Director in response to a taxpayer request, concerning the application of the tax law to a specific completed transaction
Acquiescence	Acceptance by the IRS of a Tax Court decision
Treasury Decision	The means by which a Regulation is promulgated or amended
Technical Advice Memorandum	A letter ruling issued on a completed transaction, usually during an audit

Acquiescence	Nonacquiescence
Action on Decision	Private Letter Ruling
Announcements and Notices	Proposed Regulation
Bulletin Index-Digest System	Regulation
Cumulative Bulletin	Revenue Procedure
Determination Letter	Revenue Ruling
General Counsel's Memorandum	Technical Advice Memorandum
General Regulation	Technical Memorandum
Internal Revenue Bulletin	Temporary Regulation
Legislative Regulation	Treasury Decision

DISCUSSION QUESTIONS

1. What department and agency of the U.S. government has the responsibility to administer the Federal tax laws?
2. Section 7805(a) of the *Internal Revenue Code* authorizes the IRS to perform what activities?
3. The IRS issues numerous pronouncements. Name the four that are the most important in conducting Federal tax research.
4. Define the terms *Regulation* and *Treasury Decision*. Where are Treasury Decisions published so that interested parties can comment on them?
5. "A tax researcher should not ignore Proposed Regulations." Comment on this statement.
6. Define and distinguish between *General* and *Legislative* Regulations.
7. In the citation, Reg. § 1.212-3, what do the "1," the "212," and the "3" indicate?

8. Give the number that is associated with each of the following categories of Regulations.
   a. Estate Tax Regulations
   b. Income Tax Regulations
   c. Gift Tax Regulations
   d. Procedural Regulations
   e. Employment Tax Regulations
9. What are Temporary Regulations? What weight do they carry in the tax researcher's analysis?
10. The burden of proof is on the taxpayer to prove that a provision of the Regulations is improper. How could this affect one's tax research?
11. In general, what is the effective date of a new Regulation?
12. Give at least three locations where a tax researcher can find the complete text of a Regulation.
13. What is a Revenue Ruling?
14. Describe the structure of a typical Revenue Ruling.
15. Where are Revenue Rulings initially published by the IRS? Where are the rulings permanently published in hardbound editions?
16. Explain each of the elements of this citation: Rev. Rul. 2000-15, 2000-1 C.B. 774.
17. What resources are available to help the tax researcher who wishes to check the current status of a Revenue Ruling?
18. Of what relevance to the tax practitioner is a Revenue Procedure?
19. Where can a tax researcher find copies of Revenue Procedures?
20. Construct the permanent citation for the fifth Revenue Procedure of 2001, which was published in the second week of the year. It is published on page 164 of the appropriate document.
21. Identify three types of letter rulings that are of interest to the tax researcher. Indicate whether each of these rulings is published by the IRS.
22. Which office of the IRS issues Private Letter Rulings? Who requests such a ruling? What kinds of issues are addressed therein?
23. Sometimes a Private Letter Ruling is generalized and included in an official IRS publication. What form does this recast private ruling take?
24. What is a Determination Letter? Which office of the IRS issues Determination Letters? What kinds of issues are addressed therein?
25. What is a Technical Advice Memorandum? Who requests it? What kinds of issues are addressed therein? Does the IRS include Technical Advice Memoranda in any official publication?
26. Discuss the precedential value of Private Letter Rulings, Determination Letters, and Technical Advice Memoranda. What role do these items play in conducting tax research?
27. Which IRS documents are open to public inspection under § 6110?
28. What is the precedential value of an IRS written determination under § 6110?
29. Explain each of the elements of this citation: Ltr. Rul. 9615032.
30. Where can a tax researcher find copies of written determinations?
31. The most important IRS publications are the *Internal Revenue Bulletin* and the *Cumulative Bulletin*. How often is each of these documents published? Name six items that typically are published in the *Cumulative Bulletin*.
32. Explain each of the elements of this citation: Rev. Proc. 2000-41, 2000-2 C.B. 371.

33. Answer the following questions about this citation: Reg. § 20.2039-1(a).
    a. What does the "20" stand for?
    b. What does the "2039" stand for?
    c. What does the "1" stand for?
    d. What does the "(a)" stand for?
34. Distinguish between a citation with "IRB" in it and one with "CB" in it.
35. Discuss the difference between a Revenue Ruling and a Revenue Procedure.
36. In what publication(s) would a tax researcher find the official listing of the IRS acquiescences and nonacquiescences to a Tax Court decision?
37. Can the IRS change its mind on acquiescences or nonacquiescences?
38. The IRS's *Bulletin Index-Digest System* consists of four separate services. What are they?
39. What is the purpose of each of the following?
    a. Technical Memorandum (TM)
    b. General Counsel's Memorandum (GCM)
    c. Action on Decision (AOD)
40. Describe each of the following.
    a. Publication 17
    b. Publication 463
    c. Publication 502
41. What is an IRS Notice? When is it used? In your opinion, could a tax practitioner rely on an IRS Notice as authority for a tax return position?
42. Why should the tax researcher exercise caution in relying on an IRS publication, such as published instructions to tax forms, in undertaking a research project?

EXERCISES

43. Locate Revenue Ruling 99-56. Explain the effect of that ruling on previous Treasury Department pronouncements.
44. Briefly describe the subject of each of the following Letter Rulings. State the type (Private Letter Ruling (PLR), Field Service Advice (FSA), Service Center Advice (SCA), etc.) of each Letter Ruling.
    a. 200034026
    b. 200113016
    c. 200113020
    d. 200113023
45. What is the current status of each of the following IRS pronouncements?
    a. Notice 2001-26
    b. Revenue Ruling 2000-41
    c. Revenue Procedure 89-31
    d. Announcement 99-110
46. What is the subject of each of the following IRS Notices?
    a. 89-114
    b. 99-51
    c. 2000-28

47. What is the subject matter of each of the following Technical Advice Memoranda?
    a. 9015001
    b. 199914034
    c. 200005005
48. Briefly describe the subject matter of each of the following Treasury Decisions.
    a. 8346
    b. 8780
    c. 8915
49. For each of the following Code sections, how many Treasury Regulations have been issued? Give the total number of such Regulations and the number of the last Regulation.
    a. § 102
    b. § 143
    c. § 301
    d. § 385
50. What is the current status of each of the following Revenue Rulings?
    a. Rev. Rul. 95-35
    b. Rev. Rul. 94-17
    c. Rev. Rul. 87-34
51. Locate the pronouncement at 1989-1 C.B. 76.
    a. What is the number assigned to this written determination?
    b. What is the issue(s) addressed in this written determination?
    c. What is the holding in this written determination?
52. Locate the pronouncement at 2000-2 C.B. 333.
    a. What is the number assigned to this written determination?
    b. What is the subject matter discussed in this written determination?
53. A member of a tax-exempt business league makes deposits into a strike fund. The contribution reverts to the taxpayer if the fund is terminated. Are these deposits tax deductible?
    Database to search: IRS Letter Rulings
    Keywords: business, league, strike, fund
54. Can proceeds from a life insurance policy be included in a decedent's gross estate if the policy was purchased by an S corporation for an employee-shareholder?
    Databases to search: the Code and IRS Letter Rulings
    Keywords: Sec. 2042, life, insurance, estate, inclusion
55. Is a veterinary medical corporation a "personal service corporation" for purposes of the required use of the flat 34 percent tax rate?
    Database to search: Revenue Rulings
    Keywords: veterinary, personal, service, corporation
56. Are homeowners who claim an itemized deduction for interest paid on adjustable rate mortgages (ARMs) and then receive refunds in a later year required to show the refunds as taxable income?
    Database to search: Notices
    Keywords: adjustable, rate, mortgage, refund
57. Are points paid by home buyers on VA and FHA loans deductible in the year the house is purchased?
    Database to search: Revenue Procedures
    Keywords: loan, origination, fees, VA, FHA

RESEARCH CASES

58. Lance asks you to explain why his employer, the Good Food Truck Stop, an establishment that employs more than thirty waiter/waitresses, included $2,400 in tip income on his Form W-2 for the year. Lance always has kept track of the tips he actually received, and he has reported them in full on his tax return.
   Partial list of research material: § 6053; Rev. Proc. 86-2, 1986-1 C.B. 560

59. Joe incurred $38,000 of investment interest expense in the current year. He also generated $35,000 in dividend income and had a $65,000 passive loss for the year. What is the amount of Joe's interest deduction?
   Partial list of research material: § 163; Reg. § 1.163-8T; Announcement 87-4, 1987-3 I.R.B. 17

60. Georgia won the Massachusetts lottery, which means that she will receive $28,000 a year for the next thirty years. Georgia purchased the lucky ticket in March, and it was selected the winner in June. Georgia regularly spent $100 a month on lottery tickets, one-third for Massachusetts tickets and two-thirds for Vermont tickets.
   a. What is Georgia's gross income from this prize?
   b. Is there any corresponding deduction?
   Partial list of research material: § 74; Rev. Rul. 78-140, 1978-1 C.B. 27

61. Dieter won the lottery this year, which means that he will receive $400,000 a year for the next thirty years. The present value of Dieter's prize is about $3,750,000. Conscious of the tax benefits of income shifting, Dieter irrevocably assigned one-fifth of every annuity payment to his daughter Heidi. What are the effects of these events on Dieter's taxable income?
   Partial list of research material: § 74; Rev. Rul. 58-127, 1958-1 C.B. 42

62. Ace High and Lady Luck live together and have pooled their funds for several months to purchase food and other household necessities and to buy an occasional state lottery ticket. Ace used part of these pooled funds to buy a lottery ticket that won $3,000,000. When they discovered that the lottery proceeds could be paid only to one recipient under state law, Ace and Lady executed a "separate ownership agreement." The agreement created an equal interest in the ticket for both Ace and Lady. Must Ace pay gift tax on the transfer of a one-half interest in the ticket to Lady? What is the value of the gift?
   List of research material: Ltr. Rul. 9217004.

63. Shaky Savings & Loan has a depositor named Olive who opened an account last year. At that time, Olive gave Shaky her Social Security number as a taxpayer identification number (TIN). The IRS notified Shaky that Olive's Social Security number was invalid. This year, Shaky asked Olive for a corrected number, which she provided. Later this year, the IRS notified Shaky that the new Social Security number also was invalid. What should Shaky do at this point about backup withholding on Olive's account? Prepare (in good form) a research memorandum to the file.

64. Alpine Corporation is a qualified small business corporation eligible to elect S corporation status. Albert is a shareholder in Alpine. On February 1 of the current year, Albert dies before signing the proper S corporation election form. The stock passes to Albert's estate. Ellen is appointed executor of Albert's estate on May 1 of the current year. On March 10 of the current year, Alpine filed Form

2553, the election form to be an S corporation, properly signed by all March 10 shareholders, and Ellen (the executrix) on behalf of Albert. Is this a valid S corporation election? Prepare (in good form) a research memorandum to the file.

65. Joe Bacillus, owns Bacillus's Italian Restaurant. A friend of Joe's who owns a sports bar comes to Joe and wants to form a partnership with Joe to buy an old building, renovate it, and then move both the restaurant and the sports bar into it along with other tenants. Joe would like to make this investment. He needs approximately $200,000 for his share of the buy-in of the partnership that will purchase, renovate, and manage the building. However, because of other recent large expenses, Joe finds himself cash short at the present time. His only large liquid asset is his self-directed IRA, which currently owns $225,000 in stock and bonds. Joe proposes that he direct the IRA to sell the securities and to use the proceeds to invest in the building renovation partnership. Conduct appropriate research (including a computer search) to determine if Joe's plan is workable. Prepare (in good form) a research memorandum to the file.

66. The Pima and Southern Railroad (PSRR) is a small railroad operating in rural Arizona. It exists by carrying freight to remote areas of the southwest. This year the PSRR needs to replace a 30-mile section of its track. The PSRR has bids from a contractor to replace the track for the following amounts:

Cost of new track	$5,000,000
Installing new track	3,000,000
Road bed grading and improvements	2,500,000
Removing old track (net of salvage)	1,500,000
Total	$12,000,000

The old track is fully depreciated, and the cost shown is net of $200,000 salvage value received for the scrap metal. The new track is an improved type, and it is expected to last 35–40 years. The controller of PSRR, Casey Jones, comes to you and wants to know the tax treatment of the above expenditures. He specifically wants to know if any costs can be deducted or if all must be capitalized and written off over a period of years. He is also concerned about any potential problems with the uniform capitalization rules under Section 263A. Prepare (in good form) a research memorandum to the file.

5

Judicial Interpretations

LEARNING OBJECTIVES

- Describe the structural relationship among the Federal courts that hear taxation cases
- Detail the constitution of, and procedures concerning, each element of the Federal court system hearing tax cases
- Use proper citation conventions for each of the courts that hear tax cases
- State where tax court cases are published for use by tax researchers
- Describe conditions under which the practitioner might choose each of the trial-level courts for a client's litigation
- Work with the format and content of a court case brief

CHAPTER OUTLINE

Federal Court System
    Legal Conventions
        Burden of Proof
        Tax Confidentiality Privilege
        Common Legal Terminology
    Tax Court
        Tax Court Decisions
        Small Cases Division
        Locating Tax Court Decisions
        Tax Court Rule 155
        Scope of Tax Court Decisions

    District Courts
        Locating District Court Decisions
    Court of Federal Claims
        Locating Court of Federal Claims Decisions
    Courts of Appeals
        Locating Court of Appeals Decisions
    Supreme Court
        Locating Supreme Court Decisions
Case Briefs
The Internet and Judicial Sources
    Computer Tax Service Example

Since the adoption of the Sixteenth Amendment to the Constitution in 1913, more than 50,000 Federal court decisions have been rendered concerning litigation between taxpayers and the Internal Revenue Service. These cases constitute the third primary source of Federal tax law. Such court cases are of special interest to the tax researcher because they typically are concerned with controversial areas of taxation. In this chapter, we will examine the Federal court system, learn to locate various Federal tax judicial decisions, and discuss the use of those decisions in solving tax research problems.

FEDERAL COURT SYSTEM

When a taxpayer and the Internal Revenue Service cannot reach an agreement concerning a specific tax matter using the administrative review process (i.e., audits and appeals, which are discussed in Chapter 12), the dispute may be settled in the Federal courts. Either the taxpayer or the IRS may initiate legal proceedings in the Federal court system. A taxpayer may decide to initiate proceedings as a final attempt to recover an overpayment of tax the IRS refuses to refund or to reverse a deficiency assessment determined by the IRS. Alternatively, the IRS may initiate proceedings to assert its claim to a deficiency, to enforce collection of taxes, or to impose civil or criminal penalties on the taxpayer.

Judicial decisions are the third primary source of the tax law. The *Internal Revenue Code* is the basis for Federal tax laws, and the administrative pronouncements of the IRS interpret provisions of the Code and explain their application. Frequently, however, additional issues and questions arise regarding the proper interpretation or intended application of the law that are not answered either in the law itself or in the administrative pronouncements. The judicial system is left with the task of resolving these questions. In this process, additional tax law is generated that can carry the full force of the statute itself. Often, recurring litigation in an area of innovative or unexpected judicial decisions regarding tax matters will result in Congress enacting legislation codifying certain judicial decisions. The practitioner must be familiar with the workings of this judicial system, which has the ability to stimulate tax laws and influence future legislative developments. In addition, in the event an issue is litigated in the court system, the tax practitioner must be familiar with the precedential value of court cases and the process for review of the court's decision.

Most disagreements with the Internal Revenue Service are resolved through the administrative process of appeals. Judicial decisions should be given significant weight in arriving at a conclusion or recommendation to a tax problem; however, caution should be exercised when it is apparent from the IRS's prior actions that a given position is almost certain to result in litigation. The costs of litigation, in terms of both money and time, may be prohibitive for certain taxpayers.

All litigation between a taxpayer and the government begins in a trial court. If the decision of the trial court is not satisfactory to one of the parties, the trial court decision may be appealed to an appellate court. The appellate court will review the trial court decision, often hear new evidence and arguments, and then either uphold the trial court's decision, modify it in some way, or reverse it.

The Federal court system consists of three trial courts and two levels of appellate courts. The three trial courts are the U.S. Tax Court, the U.S. District Courts, and the U.S. Court of Federal Claims. The two appellate courts are the U.S. Court of Appeals and the U.S. Supreme Court. Each of the trial courts has different attributes and is designed to serve in a different capacity in the Federal judicial system. Exhibit 5–1 diagrams the existing Federal court system. An appeal from any of the three trial courts is to the appropriate U.S. Court of Appeals. The parties have no direct access to the Supreme Court.

LEGAL CONVENTIONS

Burden of Proof

In most litigation, the party initiating the case has the burden of convincing the court that he is correct with respect to the issue. Historically, however, in most civil tax cases the *Internal Revenue Code* placed the burden of proof on the taxpayer, whether or not he or she initiated the case, except in cases of such items as hobby losses, fraud with intent to evade tax, and the accumulated earnings tax.

In 1998, the tax law was changed to shift the burden of proof to the IRS in a few situations. The IRS now has the burden of proof in any court proceeding on income, gift, estate, or generation-skipping tax liability with respect to factual issues, provided the taxpayer (1) introduces credible evidence of the factual issue, (2) maintains records and substantiates items as presently required under the Code and Regulations, and (3) cooperates with reasonable IRS requests for meetings, interviews, witnesses, information, and documents. For corporations, trusts, and partnerships with net worth exceeding $7 million, the burden of proof remains on the taxpayer. These rules apply only to those IRS–taxpayer disputes arising in connection with audits that began after the IRS Restructuring and Reform Act of 1998 was signed into law.

The burden of proof also automatically shifts to the IRS in two situations:

- If the IRS uses statistics to reconstruct an individual's income, or
- If the court proceeding against an individual taxpayer involves a penalty or addition to tax.

When reading a published opinion, the tax researcher should note whether the decision was based on the IRS's or the taxpayer's failure to meet a needed evidentiary

Exhibit 5–1
Federal Court System—Tax Cases

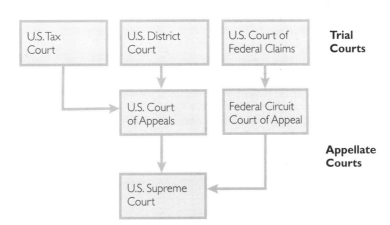

burden, or whether the IRS or the taxpayer established his or her position with sufficient proof. The first situation should be considered a weaker precedent than the second. Understanding the "strength" of a court decision is an important part of tax research.

Tax Confidentiality Privilege

The IRS Restructuring and Reform Act of 1998 extends the existing attorney–client privilege of confidentiality in tax matters to nonattorneys authorized to practice before the IRS (e.g., CPAs and enrolled agents), as identified in Chapter 1. The nonattorney–client privilege may be asserted only in a *noncriminal tax* proceeding before the IRS or Federal courts. The nonattorney–client privilege does not extend to written communications between a tax practitioner and a corporation in connection with the promotion of any tax shelter.

Certified public accountants and enrolled agents need to understand the rules regarding tax confidentiality as they have been applied to lawyers so as to be aware of the privilege limits. For example, privileged communication usually does not apply to the preparation of tax returns, the giving of accounting or business advice, or tax accrual workpapers. Unlike the attorney–client privilege, the nonattorney–client privilege does not automatically apply to state tax situations.

Common Legal Terminology

Some of the common legal terms likely to be encountered by the tax researcher follow.

ad hoc For one particular or special purpose; for example, an ad hoc committee might be formed to solve a certain problem.

ad valorem According to value; used in taxation to designate an assessment of taxes based on property value.

appellant The party who appeals a decision, usually to a higher court.

bona fide In good faith and without fraud or deceit.

certiorari (writ of) The process by which the U.S. Supreme Court agrees to hear a case, based on the appeal of a lower court decision by one of the parties involved in that decision.

collateral estoppel When an issue of fact has been determined by valid judgment, that issue cannot be litigated again by the same parties in future litigation.

covenant An agreement or promise to do or not to do something.

de jure In law or lawful; legitimate.

de facto In fact or reality; by virtue of accomplishment or deed.

defendant In civil proceedings, the party who is responding to the complaint; usually the one who is being sued in some matter.

deposition A written statement of a witness under oath, normally taken in question-and-answer form.

dictum (dicta) A statement or remark in a court opinion that is not necessary to support the decision.

en banc A decision by all the judges of a court instead of a single judge or a selected set of judges.

enjoin To command or instruct with authority; a judge can enjoin someone to do or not to do some act.

habeas corpus (writ of) The procedure for determining if the authorities can hold an individual in custody.

nolo contendere A party does not want to fight or continue to maintain a defense; the defendant will not contend a charge made by the government; "no contest."

non obstante veredicto (n.o.v.) Notwithstanding the verdict; a judgment that reverses the determination of a jury.

nullity Something in law that is void; an act having no legal force.

parol evidence The doctrine that renders any evidence of a prior understanding of the parties to a contract invalid if it contradicts the terms of a written contract.

plaintiff The one who initially brings a lawsuit.

per curiam A decision of the whole court, instead of just a limited number of judges.

prima facie At face value; something that is obvious and does not require further support.

res judicata The legal concept that bars relitigation on the same set of facts. Because of this concept, taxpayers must make sure that all of the issues they want (or do not want) to be litigated are included in a case. Once the case is decided, it cannot be reopened.

slip opinion An individual court decision published separately shortly after the decision is rendered.

vacate A reversal or abandonment of a prior decision of a court.

TAX COURT

The U.S. **Tax Court** is a specialized trial court that hears only Federal tax cases. Established under § 7441 of the *Internal Revenue Code*, its jurisdiction is limited to cases concerning the various *Internal Revenue Code*s and Revenue Acts that were adopted after February 26, 1926. Before 1943, the Tax Court was known as the **Board of Tax Appeals** (BTA); it was an administrative board of the Treasury Department rather than a true judicial court. In 1943, the BTA became the U.S. Tax Court, an administrative court, and in 1969 its status was upgraded to that of a full judicial court, with enforcement powers.

Nineteen judges hear Tax Court cases. Each judge is appointed to a fifteen-year term by the President of the United States, with the advice and confirmation of the Senate. This appointment must be based solely on the grounds of the judge's fitness to perform the duties of the office. A Tax Court justice may be removed from his or her position by the President, after notice and opportunity for public hearing, because of inefficiency, neglect of duty, or malfeasance in office, but for no other reason.

To alleviate the heavy case load of the appointed Tax Court judges, the Chief Judge of the Court periodically designates additional special trial judges to hear pertinent cases for a temporary period. Limited primarily by the budget granted by Congress, these temporary appointments are useful in decreasing the waiting period for taxpayers who wish to be heard before the Court. The decisions of these special judges carry the full authority of the U.S. Tax Court.

Tax Court judges are tax law specialists, not generalists. Typically, they have acquired many years of judicial or tax litigation experience before being appointed to the Tax Court. Thus, if a taxpayer wants to argue a technical tax issue with the IRS, the Tax Court usually is the best trial-level forum in which to try the case. Tax Court judges are better able to understand such issues than would a judge in a more general court.

The U.S. Tax Court is a national court, based in Washington, D.C. Its jurisdiction is not limited to a specific geographical region, as is the case with some other Federal courts. Taxpayers need not travel to Washington, D.C., to have a case tried before the Tax Court because some of its judges travel throughout the country and are available to hear taxpayer cases in every major city of the United States several times every year. See Exhibit 5–2 for a list of cities where the Tax Court holds trials.

Exhibit 5–2 Tax Court Trial Locations

ALABAMA:
 Birmingham
 Mobile
ALASKA:
 Anchorage
ARIZONA:
 Phoenix
ARKANSAS:
 Little Rock
CALIFORNIA:
 Los Angeles
 San Diego
 San Francisco
COLORADO:
 Denver
CONNECTICUT:
 Hartford
DISTRICT OF COLUMBIA:
 Washington
FLORIDA:
 Jacksonville
 Miami
 Tampa
GEORGIA:
 Atlanta
HAWAII:
 Honolulu
IDAHO:
 Boise
ILLINOIS:
 Chicago
INDIANA:
 Indianapolis
IOWA:
 Des Moines

KENTUCKY:
 Louisville
LOUISIANA:
 New Orleans
MARYLAND:
 Baltimore
MASSACHUSETTS:
 Boston
MICHIGAN:
 Detroit
MINNESOTA:
 St. Paul
MISSISSIPPI:
 Biloxi
 Jackson
MISSOURI:
 Kansas City
 St. Louis
MONTANA:
 Helena
NEBRASKA:
 Omaha
NEVADA:
 Las Vegas
 Reno
NEW JERSEY:
 Newark
NEW MEXICO:
 Albuquerque
NEW YORK:
 Buffalo
 New York City
 Westbury
NORTH CAROLINA:
 Winston-Salem

OHIO:
 Cincinnati
 Cleveland
 Columbus
OKLAHOMA:
 Oklahoma City
OREGON:
 Portland
PENNSYLVANIA:
 Philadelphia
 Pittsburgh
SOUTH CAROLINA:
 Columbia
TENNESSEE:
 Knoxville
 Memphis
 Nashville
TEXAS:
 Dallas
 El Paso
 Houston
 Lubbock
 San Antonio
UTAH:
 Salt Lake City
VIRGINIA:
 Richmond
WASHINGTON:
 Seattle
 Spokane
WEST VIRGINIA:
 Charleston/Huntington
WISCONSIN:
 Milwaukee

Note: The Court sits in about fifteen other cities to hear Small Tax Cases. A list of such cities is contained in a pamphlet entitled "Election of Small Tax Case Procedure and Preparation of Petitions," a copy of which may be obtained from the Clerk of the Court.

When a case is heard before the Tax Court, it almost always is presented before only one of the nineteen Tax Court judges. Taxpayers cannot request jury trials before this court. After the judge hears the case, he or she prepares a decision that is reviewed by the Chief Judge of the court. In most instances, the trial judge's opinion stands, but the Chief Judge can designate the opinion for review by the other members of the Tax Court. Upon their agreement with the decision, the opinion is released.

If the case involves an unusual, important, or novel issue, more than one judge, or the entire Tax Court, might hear the case. This rare occurrence is identified as an *en banc* sitting of the court.

For a case to be heard, the taxpayer must petition the Court within ninety days of the IRS's mailing of a notice and demand for payment of the disputed amount. The taxpayer need not pay the disputed tax liability before the case is heard.

Tax Court Decisions

The Tax Court issues two kinds of decisions: regular and memorandum. A **Regular decision** (about 150 cases per year) generally involves a new or unusual point of law, as determined by the Chief Judge of the court. If the chief judge believes that the decision concerns only the application of existing law or an interpretation of facts, the decision is issued as a **Memorandum decision** (500–600 cases per year). Over the years, however, this classification scheme has not always been strictly followed by the Court. Many of its Memorandum decisions address significant points of law or other issues important to the tax researcher. Accordingly, one should not ignore Memorandum decisions. If issues or points of law pertinent to the problem at hand are addressed, both Regular and Memorandum decisions of the Tax Court should be considered by the taxpayer.

Because the Tax Court is a national court, it hears cases that may be appealed to Courts of Appeals (discussed later in this chapter) in different geographical regions, or *circuits*. Because these Courts of Appeals occasionally disagree on tax issues, the Tax Court is faced with a dilemma. For example, one Court of Appeals may have held that a specific item is deductible in computing taxable income, while another has held against such a deduction. Which precedent should the Tax Court follow? Under *Golsen*, 54 T.C. 742 (1970), the Tax Court will follow the Court of Appeals that has direct jurisdiction over the taxpayer in question. If the Court of Appeals that has jurisdiction over the taxpayer has not ruled on the matter, the Tax Court will decide the case on the basis of its own interpretation of the disputed provision. This *Golsen* **rule** means the Tax Court may reach opposite decisions, based on identical facts, for taxpayers differentiated solely by the geographical area in which they live. The tax researcher must be aware of the *Golsen* rule in analyzing cases that may be affected by it.

Small Cases Division

The Tax Court maintains a **Small Cases Division,** which is similar to a small claims court. If the amount of a disputed deficiency, including penalties, or claimed overpayment does not exceed $50,000, a taxpayer may be heard before the Small Cases Division, upon approval of the Tax Court. The hearing is conducted as informally as possible, and the taxpayer may represent him- or herself, that is, acting *pro se*. (Of course, the taxpayer may be represented by an attorney if he or she so desires.) Neither elaborate written briefs nor formal oral arguments are required in the Small Cases Division.

At any time before a decision is final, the Tax Court may interrupt a Small Cases hearing and transfer the case to the regular Tax Court for trial. This might occur, for example, when important facts or issues of law, more suitably heard in the more formal Tax Court context, become apparent only after the Small Cases proceedings have begun.

Small Cases decisions are not officially published. Nevertheless, they are available for review by tax researchers and taxpayers (see Exhibit 5–3). Small Cases Division decisions cannot be used as precedents when dealing with the IRS; however, they do provide insight into how the Tax Court has treated similar tax situations. The decision of the Small Cases judge is final and may not be appealed by the taxpayer or the government.

Locating Tax Court Decisions

Tax Court regular decisions are published by the Government Printing Office (GPO) in a set of bound reporters called the *Tax Court of the United States Reports*. These volumes are cited as "T.C." The Board of Tax Appeals had its own reporter, called the *United States Board of Tax Appeals,* cited as "B.T.A."

Memorandum decisions are not published by the GPO. They are included in special-decision reporters that are published by Commerce Clearing House (CCH) and by Research Institute of America (RIA). The CCH reporter is titled *Tax Court Memorandum Decisions,* cited as "TCM," and the RIA reporter is known as *RIA Tax Court Memorandum Decisions,* cited as "RIA T.C. Memo." The Tax Court reporter is published twice a year, and both of the memorandum-case reporters are published once a year.

Because many months may elapse between the release of a Tax Court decision and its publication in a bound reporter, such decisions receive both a temporary and a permanent citation. The **temporary citation** is structured as follows.

Hillman, D. H., 114 T.C. ____, No. 6 (2000), where:

114 is the volume number.
T.C. is the abbreviation for the Tax Court Reporter.
____ indicates the page number, which is to be determined later.
No. 6 is the number of the case.
(2000) is the year of the decision.

The temporary citation includes no page number for the case because the opinion has not yet been published. All proper citations either italicize or underline the name of the court case; major elements of the citation are separated by commas. The **permanent citation** for the same case is reported as follows.

Hillman. D. H., 114 T.C. 103 (2000), where:

114 is the volume number.
T.C. is the abbreviation for the Tax Court Reporter.
103 is the page number.
(2000) is the year of the decision.

Most court case citations include the names of both parties involved. This convention is ignored for most Tax Court citations, however, because all such cases involve the taxpayer bringing suit against the government to avoid payment of disputed tax liabilities. Thus, a traditional citation for the above case would be *Hillman v. U.S.* (or, more precisely, *David H. Hillman v. Commissioner*). Nonetheless, common practice allows the tax researcher to omit the reference to the defendant in the action

Exhibit 5–3 Tax Court Small Case Excerpt

EDWARD M. FIELDS v. COMMISSIONER, Docket No. 17174-98S., T.C. Summary Opinion 2001-35, Filed March 20, 2001

Pursuant to *Internal Revenue Code* Section 7463(b), this opinion may not be treated as precedent for any other case.

James Charles Frooman, for petitioner. *Gary R. Shuler, Jr.,* for respondent.

CARLUZZO, Special Trial Judge:

Respondent determined a deficiency of $2,593 in petitioner's 1995 Federal income tax. The issue for decision is whether petitioner is entitled to deduct, as trade or business expenses, tuition costs and related expenses incurred in attending the Golf Academy of the South.

Background

This case was submitted fully stipulated, and the stipulated facts are so found. Petitioner resided in Mason, Ohio, at the time the petition was filed.

During 1995, petitioner was employed in a variety of ways. According to the stipulation of facts, he "worked full time in construction and was self-employed as a golf instructor and worked at golf courses in the pro shops."

Beginning in 1994, petitioner enrolled as a student at the Golf Academy of the South (the academy). The academy is accredited as a business school by the Accrediting Council for Independent Colleges and Schools, Washington, D.C.; it is licensed by the State Board of Independent Postsecondary, Vocational, Technical, Trade and Business Schools, Florida Department of Education. Successful graduates of its 2-year program are awarded a specialized associate degree in business. Courses offered by the academy are approved for the training of veterans and persons eligible for VA educational benefits. Subject to certain conditions and limitations, the academy accepts educational credits earned at other accredited educational institutions. Credits earned at the academy are transferable; according to its catalog, "Academy graduates can expect to earn a bachelor's degree in two academic years" at another educational institution.

In April 1995, petitioner was awarded a specialized associate degree in business from the academy. At the time, he held no other undergraduate degrees.

During 1995, petitioner paid tuition costs and related expenses of $9,986.43 incurred in connection with his enrollment at the academy (the education expenses). On a Schedule C, Profit or (Loss) From Business, included with his timely filed 1995 Federal income tax return, petitioner: (1) Listed his principal business or profession as "golf instructor"; (2) reported gross income of $2,010; (3) deducted total expenses (including the education expenses) of $16,297.52; and (4) reported a net loss of $14,287.52.

Discussion

On the Schedule C included with his 1995 return, petitioner deducted the education expenses as trade or business expenses paid in connection with his employment as a golf instructor. In general, Section 162(a) allows a deduction for all ordinary and necessary expenses incurred in carrying on a trade or business. Expenditures made by an individual for education that maintains or improves the skills required by the individual in the individual's trade or business are deductible as ordinary and necessary business expenses. See Sec. 1.162-5(a), Income Tax Regs. No deduction is allowed, however, if the education is part of a program of study that will lead to qualifying the individual in a new trade or business.

* * *

In this case, we find that the education expenses were incurred in the course of study that would lead to qualifying petitioner, who held no prior undergraduate degrees, in trades or businesses other than as a golf instructor. It follows that the education expenses are not deductible, and we so hold. Respondent's adjustment in this regard is therefore sustained.

Reviewed and adopted as the report of the Small Tax Case Division.

On the basis of the foregoing and to reflect the agreement of the parties on other adjustments.

Decision will be entered under Rule 155.

(i.e., the government), because such reference could be inferred from the notation for the court in which the lawsuit is heard.

Once the GPO publishes the decision in the permanent bound edition of the regular Tax Court cases, the temporary citation becomes obsolete. The same citation procedure is used with respect to Board of Tax Appeals cases, substituting "B.T.A." for the "T.C." identification. Indeed, this procedure for disclosing the citation for a case (i.e., Name–Volume Number–Reporter–Page Number–Year) is common among all American courts. Exhibit 5–4 is an example of a regular Tax Court decision, reproduced from the GPO Tax Court reporter.

Exhibit 5–4 Tax Court Opinion

JOHN W. and FAYTHE A. MILLER, Petitioners v. COMMISSIONER OF INTERNAL REVENUE, Respondent (114 T.C. 511)

Docket No. 12310-98. Filed June 23, 2000.

Ps claimed dependency exemptions on their 1996 joint Federal income tax return without furnishing SSNs for their children, as required under Sec. 151(e), I.R.C. Ps seek relief from the SSN requirement because of their religious beliefs in opposition to using SSN's. Held: the SSN requirement is the least restrictive means of achieving the Government's compelling interests in implementing the Federal tax system in a uniform, mandatory way and in detecting fraud in regard to dependency exemptions. Accordingly, neither the Free Exercise Clause of the First Amendment to the Constitution nor the Religious Freedom Restoration Act of 1993, Pub. L. 103-141, Sec. 2, 107 Stat. 1488, provides a basis for excepting Ps from the SSN requirement.

John W. and Faythe A. Miller, pro se.

Elizabeth A. Owen, for respondent.

OPINION

LARO, Judge: This case is before the Court fully stipulated. See *Rule 122*. Petitioners petitioned the Court to redetermine respondent's determination of a $1,391 deficiency in Federal income tax for 1996.

The issue in this case is whether requiring petitioners to provide Social Security numbers (SSNs) for their dependent children as a condition to allowing their dependency deductions violates petitioners' right to free exercise of religion. We hold that it does not.

Unless otherwise indicated, Section references are to the *Internal Revenue Code* in effect for the year in issue. Rule references are to the Tax Court Rules of Practice and Procedure. Dollar amounts are rounded to the nearest dollar.

BACKGROUND

The stipulation of facts and the exhibits submitted therewith are incorporated herein by this reference. Petitioners resided in Sugar Land, Texas, when the petition was filed.

Petitioners are the natural parents of two children, whom they claimed as dependents on their 1996 Federal income tax return. At the end of 1996, petitioners' children were 8 and 5 years old. Rather than provide SSNs for their children on their return, petitioners attached a notarized affidavit declaring their religious objection to the use of identifying numbers for their children.

Petitioners believe that SSNs are universal numerical identifiers to be equated with the "mark of the Beast" warned against in the Bible at Revelation 13:16-17. Petitioners both have SSNs and used them on their 1996 tax return but wish to avoid obtaining SSNs for their children.

Petitioners' religious objections extend only to universal identifiers and not to numbers issued for a discrete purpose. Accordingly, petitioners have offered to obtain Individual Taxpayer Identification Numbers (ITINs) for their children and provide the ITINs on their return. Respondent, however, refuses to issue ITINs to petitioners' children because respondent takes the position that Treasury regulations permit issuance of ITINs only to those who are ineligible to receive SSNs.

Exhibit 5–4 Tax Court Opinion—Continued

Except for the requirement that petitioners include their children's SSNs on their return, petitioners have met all the statutory requirements for claiming dependency exemptions in 1996. Respondent concedes that petitioners have a sincerely held religious belief which opposes the use of SSNs for their minor children, but respondent denies that he is required to accommodate that belief in administering the dependency exemption.

DISCUSSION

I. The SSN Requirement

Under Section 151, taxpayers are entitled to claim an exemption for each dependent child. However, Section 151(e) provides: "No exemption shall be allowed under this section with respect to any individual unless the TIN of such individual is included on the return claiming the exemption." Thus, without providing TINs, petitioners cannot properly claim any Section 151 exemptions for their children.

Section 7701(a)(41) defines the term "TIN" for purposes of the *Internal Revenue Code* to mean "the identifying number assigned to a person under section 6109." Section 6109(d) specifies that the SSN issued to an individual is the identifying number of the individual, except as otherwise specified under applicable regulations. The regulations provide that an individual required to furnish a TIN must use an SSN unless the individual is not eligible to obtain an SSN. See Sec. 301.6109l(a)(ii)(A) and (B), Proced. & Admin. Regs. The regulations further specify that "Any individual who is duly assigned a Social Security number or who is entitled to a Social Security number will not be issued an IRS individual taxpayer identification number." Sec. 301.6109-1(d)(4), Proced. & Admin. Regs.

SSNs are issued by the Social Security Administration of the U.S. Department of Health and Human Services (the SSA) upon application by a citizen, qualified alien, or by a parent on behalf of a qualified child. See generally 20 C.F.R. Secs. 422.101 to 422.112 (2000). The issuance of an SSN entails several consequences, including (i) the creation of a record at the SSA of that person's earnings for purposes of determining the old-age and other benefits to which the person may be entitled, and (ii) establishing a unique numerical identifier for the individual for use by a variety of governmental and private entities. When the SSN was first chosen as the identification number for tax purposes, the rationale for the choice was that most people already had an SSN and thus the use of that preexisting number would relieve taxpayers of an additional burden. See H. Rept. 1103, 87th Cong., 1st Sess. 3 (1961); S. Rept. 1102, 87th Cong., 1st Sess. 3 (1961), 1961-2 C.B. 475.

II. The Religious Freedom Restoration Act of 1993

Petitioners assert that requiring them to furnish SSNs for their children as a condition to obtaining the dependency exemptions is an unconstitutional intrusion on the free exercise of their religion. The First Amendment to the Constitution provides, in relevant part, that: "Congress shall make no law respecting an establishment of religion, OR PROHIBITING THE FREE EXERCISE THEREOF." (Emphasis added.)

In *Bowen v. Roy*, 476 U.S. 693 (1986), the Supreme Court considered whether a Federal statute requiring applicants for Federal welfare assistance to obtain and furnish SSNs for their children was constitutional as applied to two Native American applicants who held a religious belief that the use of the number would harm their daughter's spirit. Part III of the opinion of Chief Justice Burger, joined by two other Justices, rejected the strict scrutiny test applied by the trial court, concluding that there is no violation of the Free Exercise Clause of the First Amendment when the Government demonstrates "that a challenged requirement for government benefits, neutral and uniform in its application, is a reasonable means of promoting a legitimate public interest." Id. at 708. The four dissenting Justices would have required the Government to show that its refusal to accommodate the appellants' religious objection to the use of SSNs served a compelling State interest.

In *Employment Div. v. Smith*, 494 U.S. 872 (1990), the Supreme Court reviewed a claim that the Free Exercise Clause permitted the ingestion of a prohibited drug, peyote, in the context of the worship of the Native American Church. In so doing, the Court held that a "neutral, generally

Continued

Exhibit 5-4 Tax Court Opinion—Concluded

applicable law need not be justified by a compelling governmental interest even if the law has the incidental effect of burdening a particular religious practice." Id. at 886.

In response to *Smith,* Congress enacted the Religious Freedom Restoration Act of 1993 (RFRA), Pub. L. 103-141, Sec. 2, 107 Stat. 1488, 42 U.S.C. Secs. 2000bb to 2000bb-4 (1994). A person whose religious exercise is burdened in violation of the RFRA "may assert that violation as a claim or defense in a judicial proceeding and obtain appropriate relief against the government." RFRA, 42 U.S.C. Sec. 2000bb-1(c). A claimant under the RFRA must show that the Government "substantially burdened" his or her free exercise of religion. RFRA, 42 U.S.C. Sec. 2000bb-1(a). Upon such a showing, the Government must demonstrate that the application of the burden to the person (i) is in furtherance of a compelling governmental interest and (ii) is the least restrictive means of furthering that compelling interest. RFRA, 42 U.S.C. Sec. 2000bb-1(b). The Government's burden is both of production and persuasion. RFRA, 42 U.S.C. Sec. 2000bb-2(3).

III. Substantial Burden

Petitioners seek dependency exemptions which, over a number of years, may be worth several thousands of dollars to them. In order to secure this benefit, which is available to similarly situated parents, petitioners must obtain and use SSNs for their children. Respondent concedes this would violate a central tenet of petitioners' religion. Thus, petitioners' argument that the SSN requirement imposes a cognizable burden on their freedom of religion may find some support under First Amendment case law. See *Thomas v. Review Bd.,* 450 U.S. 707, 717-718 (1981) ("Where the State conditions receipt of an important benefit upon conduct proscribed by a religious faith * * * a burden upon religion exists."). But see *Patterson v. Commissioner,* T.C. Memo. 1989-193, affd. without published opinion 896 F.2d 544 (2d Cir. 1990) (imposing higher tax rates on taxpayer who could not divorce or legally separate because of his religious beliefs was not an unconstitutional burden on his free exercise rights). In re *Turner,* 193 Bankr. 548 (Bankr. N.D. Cal. 1996) (requiring use of SSN on bankruptcy forms does not impose a "substantial burden" under the RFRA on form preparer with religious objections to use of the number). Nevertheless, we do not find it necessary to determine whether petitioners' free exercise of religion is substantially burdened by the SSN requirement because, as discussed below, respondent has satisfied the compelling interest test.

IV. Compelling Government Interest Test

Under the RFRA, the Government may impose a substantial burden on the free exercise of religion if it demonstrates that the application of the burden is the least restrictive means of achieving a compelling governmental interest. See RFRA, 42 U.S.C. Sec. 2000bb-1(b) (1994); *Adams v. Commissioner,* 110 T.C. 137 (1998), affd. 170 F.3d 173 (3d Cir. 1999). We find that the Government has a compelling interest in effectively tracking claimed dependency exemptions. Through cross-matching of the SSNs respondent can easily identify whether an SSN has been claimed on another return for the year, thereby detecting erroneous or fraudulent claims. For example, SSNs make it easier for the IRS to determine whether divorced parents are both trying to claim their children as dependents. Congress acknowledged this benefit in 1994, when it eliminated an exception to the TIN requirement for dependents below a certain age.

The requirement that TINs be provided with respect to each dependent claimed on a tax return has significantly reduced the improper claiming of dependents. Requiring that TINs be supplied regardless of the age of the dependent will further reduce the improper claiming of dependents. [H. Rept. 103-826, at 196 (1994) (discussing Sec. 742(b) of the Uruguay Round Agreements Act, Pub. L. 103-465, 108 Stat. 4809, 5010 (1994)).]

* * *

We have considered all of the other arguments made by petitioners and, to the extent we have not addressed them, find them to be without merit.

In accordance with these findings, we hold that petitioners are not exempt from furnishing SSNs for their children in claiming them as dependents.

Decision will be entered for respondent.

Using the same citation conventions, the general and permanent citations, respectively, for a Tax Court memorandum decision would appear as follows.

General
Nicholls, Walter J., T.C. Memo. 1995–291, where:
    T.C. Memo is a reference to a Tax Court Memorandum decision.
    1995 is the year of the decision.
    291 is the decision number.

Permanent RIA
Nicholls, Walter J., RIA T.C. Memo. ¶ 95,291, where:
    RIA T.C. Memo is the RIA Tax Court Memorandum reporter.
    ¶ 95,291 is the paragraph number.

Permanent CCH
Nicholls, Walter J., 69 TCM 3042 (1995), where:
    69 is the volume number.
    TCM is the CCH Tax Court Memorandum reporter.
    3042 is the page number.
    (1995) is the year of the decision.

One can observe from the RIA citation that the opinion was issued in 1995 because all of the Tax Court Memorandum Decisions for that year are included in the RIA reporter using paragraph numbers that begin with "95."

As we observed with respect to the regular Tax Court decisions, the temporary citation becomes obsolete when the permanent bound edition of the memorandum reporter is published.

Besides the traditional published sources for Tax Court decisions, these items also are available on computer tax services such as RIA Checkpoint, Lexis, Kleinrock's, etc. All of the computer services reference the general citation, and most give the parallel RIA and CCH reporter citations.

Tax Court Rule 155

When a court reaches a tax decision, it normally will not compute the tax that is due to the government or the refund that is due to a taxpayer. The computation of this amount is left to be determined by the IRS and the taxpayer. The court will compute the tax only if the government and the taxpayer cannot agree. When the Tax Court reaches a decision without calculating the tax, the decision is said to be entered under *Rule 155.* See *Estate of Wayne-Chi Young v. Commissioner,* 110 T.C. 24, for an example of when the Tax Court will enter a decision under Rule 155. For Tax Court decisions prior to 1974, this practice was referred to as *Rule 50.*

Scope of Tax Court Decisions

The Tax Court may examine an entire tax return for a taxpayer whose case it is hearing. On the other hand, the District Court and Court of Federal Claims can address only the specific issue or issues that are involved in the case. If a taxpayer wants only a specific issue (or issues) litigated in a case, then the District Court or Court of Federal Claims may be a better forum for him than the Tax Court.

District Courts

The U.S. **District Courts** are another trial-level forum that hears tax cases. Unlike the Tax Court, however, the District Courts hear cases involving legal issues based on the entire United States Code, not just the *Internal Revenue Code*. District Court judges typically are generalists, rather than specialists in Federal tax laws. The same District Court judge might render opinions concerning matters of tax law, civil rights, bank robbery, interstate commerce, kidnapping, and fraud.

The District Courts are further distinguished from the Tax Court in that a taxpayer who disagrees with the IRS may take his or her case to the appropriate District Court only after paying the disputed tax liability; thus, in the typical District Court taxation case, the taxpayer sues the government for a refund of the disputed tax liability.

Numerous District Courts are located throughout the United States, each assigned a geographical area. The designated district can be as small as one city (New York City) or as large as the largest state (Alaska). Typically, the taxpayer will request a hearing before the District Court that has jurisdiction over the location in which he or she lives or conducts business.

District Court cases are heard before one judge, not a panel of judges. In the appropriate District Court, the taxpayer can request a jury trial concerning a tax case (or certain other Federal matters). This opportunity may be useful if the taxpayer wants to argue an "emotional" issue rather than a technical one, or if the taxpayer or his or her associates are particularly credible witnesses (and thus have a good chance of winning a jury trial). Limited to decisions concerning questions of fact, juries apparently occasionally can be persuaded in a tax case to hold for the taxpayer when a judge might not be so inclined.

Because the District Courts are general in nature and do not specialize in tax matters, over time, their decisions can vary significantly among the districts. Some of their decisions have important precedential value and can be relied on by the tax researcher; however, many of these decisions are poorly structured or poorly conceived from a technical standpoint, and represent candidates for overturn on appeal. The tax researcher must examine these decisions carefully to assess their probable use as a precedent before using them to help solve a client's tax problem.

Locating District Court Decisions

District Court tax decisions are published in three different reporters. West Publishing includes such cases in its *Federal Supplement Series;* citations for these cases include the "F.Supp." abbreviation. The series contains all decisions of the District Courts designated for publication, including those for the numerous nontax cases. Most university and law school libraries subscribe to the *Federal Supplement Series*. However, it is a waste of money for the tax researcher to subscribe to this series to obtain just the tax decisions that are rendered in the District Courts. Instead, the tax researcher can use special tax case reporters that include only tax decisions selected from all of the decisions of the Federal courts except the Tax Court. (As we discussed earlier, the Tax Court's Regular and Memorandum Decisions are published in specialized reporters, so they do not present a budgeting problem of this sort.)

RIA's specialized tax reporter is titled *American Federal Tax Reports,* abbreviated in citations as **"AFTR."** Currently, the second series of this reporter is in use, with

"2d" added to indicate that the cases therein usually relate to the current *Internal Revenue Code*. Accordingly, the abbreviation AFTR2d is commonly used. CCH's specialized Federal tax case reporter is known as *United States Tax Cases,* which is abbreviated as **"USTC"** in traditional citations. Do not confuse this abbreviation with that for the U.S. Tax Court, which we have identified as "T.C." Occasionally, the West citation (F.Supp.) is referred to as the primary citation for a case, and the CCH and RIA reporters are used for secondary citations. The AFTR2d and USTC reporters each publish 1,200–1,500 tax cases per year from courts other than the U.S. Tax Court.

Besides the traditional published primary and secondary court reporters, electronic court reporters are also available. For example, Kleinrock's publishes tax decisions as part of its computer service. The computer-based reporters have their own citations, and they usually cross-reference one or more of the standard printed reporters (West, RIA, CCH). An illustration of various citations for a District Court case follows.

Court Reporters
West: *Barber, Lori,* 85 F.Supp. 967 (N.D.C.A., 2000)
RIA: *Barber, Lori,* 85 AFTR2d 2000-879 (N.D.C.A., 2000)
CCH: *Barber, Lori,* 2000-1 USTC ¶ 50,209 (N.D.C.A., 2000)
Kleinrock: *Barber, Lori,* KTC 2000-45 (N.D.C.A., 2000)

Each of these citations indicates both the specific District Court that heard the case and the year in which the opinion was issued. Given publication time lags, however, this may not match the year in which the reporter volume was published. Unless necessitated by such a delay, a proper citation need not include in the parentheses the year in which the opinion was issued, in all but a West citation.

Notice that more than one volume of the USTC reporter was published by CCH in 1994, as indicated by the volume number, and that this reporter uses paragraph numbers to organize the opinions. Other elements of the citations are familiar. A complete citation for this case, using traditional form, would appear as follows.

Barber, Lori, 85 F.Supp. 967; 85 AFTR2d 2000-879; 2000-1 USTC ¶ 50,209; KTC 2000-45 (N.D.C.A. 2000)

COURT OF FEDERAL CLAIMS

The U.S. **Court of Federal Claims** is the newest of the trial-level courts. It was created on October 1, 1982, by the Federal Courts Improvement Act (P.L. 97-164). In this act, the U.S. Court of Claims and the U.S. Court of Customs and Patent Appeals were reorganized into two new courts. The trial division of the U.S. Court of Claims became the new U.S. Claims Court, and the remaining divisions of both courts became the new Court of Appeals for the Federal Circuit, discussed later. The forum was renamed the U.S. Court of Federal Claims in 1992. Sixteen judges are appointed to the Court of Federal Claims. Its jurisdiction lies in hearing cases concerning all monetary claims against the Federal government, only one type of which is in the form of tax refunds. Thus, the taxpayer must pay the disputed tax and sue the government for a refund in order for the case to be heard in the Court of Federal Claims. Similarly, like the District Court but unlike the Tax Court, the Court of Federal Claims is composed of judges who, with only a few exceptions, are not specialists in technical tax law. The Court of Federal Claims does not allow jury trials on any matter.

The U.S. Court of Federal Claims is a national court located in Washington, D.C. However, because the Court of Federal Claims judges periodically travel to the major cities of the country and hear cases in these various locations, in a manner similar to that of the Tax Court, one need not go to Washington, D.C., to present a case before the Court of Federal Claims.

Moreover, because the Court of Federal Claims is a national court that must follow the decisions only of the Federal District of the Court of Appeals, it is not bound by the geographical Circuit Courts of Appeals that have ruled on similar cases, nor by the Court of Appeals for the circuit in which the taxpayer works or resides. This may be important to a taxpayer whose circuit has held adversely to his or her position on the disputed issue: if the case were presented to the appropriate District Court, or to the Tax Court (recall the *Golsen* rule), the precedent of the adverse ruling would be adopted by those trial courts, but the Court of Federal Claims is not so bound.

Locating Court of Federal Claims Decisions

Before October 1982, all U.S. Court of Claims decisions concerning both tax and nontax issues were published in West's *Federal Reporter,* second series (this reporter is now in its third series). Citations to the reporter use the abbreviations "F.2d" or "F.3d," as the case may be. Current decisions of the U.S. Court of Federal Claims can be found in West's primary reporter, *U.S. Court of Federal Claims,* which can be cited by using the abbreviation "Fed. Cl." In addition, tax decisions of the old U.S. Court of Claims and the new U.S. Court of Federal Claims are available through several secondary published and electronic reporters. U.S. Court of Federal Claims decisions are published in CCH's *United States Tax Cases* (USTC), RIA's *American Federal Tax Reports* 2d (AFTR2d), and other places.

Examine the following proper primary and secondary citations for decisions of the U.S. Court of Federal Claims. All of the elements of these citations are familiar to us. As is most often the situation, when a decision is issued and published in the same year, one need not be redundant in identifying the given year in the body of the citation because the reader can infer the year from other aspects of the listing. A complete citation of the case would include references to all of the publications, in the form indicated previously.

Court Reporters
West: *Bennett, Courtney,* 30 Fed. Cl. 396 (1994)
CCH: *Bennett, Courtney,* 94-1 USTC ¶ 50,044 (Fed. Cl., 1994)
RIA: *Bennett, Courtney,* 73 AFTR2d 94-534 (Fed. Cl., 1994)
Kleinrock: *Bennett, Courtney,* KTC 1994-647 (Fed. Cl., 1994)

As a general tax court, the U.S. Court of Federal Claims has generated decisions that cannot easily be anticipated. Practitioners usually should pursue a case in the U.S. Court of Federal Claims when the applicable U.S. District and U.S. Tax Court decisions are adverse to the taxpayer, or when a nontechnical matter lies at the heart of the taxpayer's case.

COURTS OF APPEALS

The first level of Federal appellate courts is the U.S. **Courts of Appeals.** Like the District Court and Court of Federal Claims, the Courts of Appeals consider issues in both tax and nontax litigation, although the Courts of Appeals generally will hear only cases that involve a question of law. Seldom will a Circuit Court of Appeals challenge the trial court's findings as to the facts.

Congress has created thirteen Courts of Appeals: eleven are geographical, in that they are responsible for cases that originate in designated states; one is assigned to Washington, D.C.; and one is known as the Court of Appeals for the Federal Circuit. This last court hears tax and other cases that originate only in the Court of Federal Claims. The other Courts of Appeals consider tax and nontax issues brought from the Tax Court or a District Court for an assigned geographical region.

The eleven geographical Courts of Appeals are organized into geographical *circuits,* each of which is assigned a number. Practitioners commonly refer to the circuit courts by this number. For example, the Court of Appeals designated to hear cases that originate in Seattle typically is referred to as the Ninth Circuit Court of Appeals. Exhibit 5–5 shows the jurisdiction of each of the Courts of Appeals. Approximately twenty judges have been appointed to each of the circuit courts. Typically, a three-judge panel hears a Court of Appeals case. Jury trials are not available in these courts.

A Court of Appeals decision carries precedential weight because each circuit is independent of the others and must follow only the decisions of the U.S. Supreme Court. Because the Supreme Court hears only about a dozen tax cases annually, the Court of Appeals, in most situations, represents the final authority in Federal tax matters. Thus, a researcher generally must follow the holding of a tax decision issued by the Court of Appeals for the circuit in which the client works or resides if the controlling facts or issues of law are sufficiently similar.

Decisions by the circuit court in which the taxpayer works or resides should be given great consideration, even if the researcher has found that another circuit court

Exhibit 5–5
Circuit Court Jurisdictions

Circuit	Assigned Jurisdiction
First	Maine, Massachusetts, New Hampshire, Puerto Rico, Rhode Island
Second	Connecticut, New York, Vermont
Third	Delaware, New Jersey, Pennsylvania, Virgin Islands
Fourth	Maryland, North Carolina, South Carolina, Virginia, West Virginia
Fifth	Canal Zone, Louisiana, Mississippi, Texas
Sixth	Kentucky, Michigan, Ohio, Tennessee
Seventh	Illinois, Indiana, Wisconsin
Eighth	Arkansas, Iowa, Minnesota, Missouri, Nebraska, North Dakota, South Dakota
Ninth	Alaska, Arizona, California, Guam, Hawaii, Idaho, Montana, Nevada, Oregon, Washington
Tenth	Colorado, Kansas, New Mexico, Oklahoma, Utah, Wyoming
Eleventh	Alabama, Florida, Georgia
D.C.	Washington, D.C.
Federal	U.S. Court of Federal Claims

has held in the taxpayer's favor in a similar case. For example, if a taxpayer lives in San Antonio, and the Fifth Circuit has held that an item similar to the taxpayer's does not qualify as a deduction, the deduction most likely should not be claimed, even if the Seventh or Eighth Circuit has held that the deduction is available. Under the *Golsen* rule, the unfavorable Fifth Circuit decision will apply to the taxpayer at the trial-court level, even though the U.S. Tax Court will be forced in this example to render opinions that are inconsistent among taxpayers.

If, in the same example, however, the Fifth Circuit had not yet ruled on the issue, and the favorable Seventh Circuit ruling is available, the researcher may be more comfortable in following the decision of the "outside" circuit. Prior decisions of Courts of Appeals are of great importance in the construction of subsequent decisions by another circuit, and the researcher rightly can place precedential value on the holdings of other circuits in anticipating the proper position for a client.

So, in general, the Court of Appeals decisions most important to a given taxpayer are those issued by the circuit in which he or she works or resides. In addition, however, these observations can be made: Second, Ninth, and D.C. Circuit decisions are especially important, because of numerous innovative, unusual, and controversial judicial interpretations of the tax laws, and because their jurisdictions include the two most populous states in the nation and the nation's capital.

Locating Court of Appeals Decisions

Court of Appeals decisions are reported in several general and specialized tax publications. All of the decisions of the various Courts of Appeals designated for publication are included in West's *Federal Reporter* (F.2d or F.3d). Most tax cases from the Courts of Appeals are published in the *United States Tax Cases* service (USTC), and in the *American Federal Tax Reports*. The familiar citation conventions are used in the following examples of primary and secondary citations for a Court of Appeals decision.

Court Reporters

West:	*Oxford Capital Corp.*, 211 F.3d 280 (CA-5, 2000)
RIA:	*Oxford Capital Corp.*, 85 AFTR2d 2000-1840 (CA-5, 2000)
CCH:	*Oxford Capital Corp.*, 2000-1 USTC ¶ 50,447 (CA-5, 2000)
Kleinrock:	*Oxford Capital Corp.*, KTC 2000-228 (CA-5, 2000)

Exhibit 5–6 reproduces a tax decision from the Court of Appeals.

SUPREME COURT

The U.S. **Supreme Court** is an appellate court and the highest court in the nation. Article III of the Constitution created the Supreme Court and extended to it judicial power "to all cases of law and equity, arising under this Constitution, the laws of the United States, and treaties. . . ." Thus, concerning all areas of Federal law, the Supreme Court is the final level of appeal and the sovereign legal authority.

The Supreme Court meets and hears cases only in Washington, D.C. If a taxpayer wants to have his or her case heard by the Supreme Court, the taxpayer and counsel must travel to the nation's capital to present the arguments. The Supreme Court is a nine-justice panel; all nine judges hear every case that the Court agrees to consider. The Court does not conduct jury trials.

Exhibit 5–6 Court of Appeals Decision

IMRE CZIRAKI; GIZELLA CZIRAKI, PETITIONERS–APPELLANTS v. COMMISSIONER OF INTERNAL REVENUE, RESPONDENT–APPELLEE.

UNITED STATES COURT OF APPEALS FOR THE NINTH CIRCUIT No. 99-70615; 87AFTR2d 2001-308; 2001-1 USTC ¶50,141. Filed December 22, 2000.

Appeal from a Decision of the United States Tax Court

Before: GOODWIN, HUG, and PREGERSON, Circuit Judges.

Imre and Gizella Cziraki (the "Czirakis") appeal the tax court's decision denying their casualty loss deduction in the amount of $220,000 for the 1992 tax year for damage to a dirt road on their farm land. Specifically, the Czirakis challenge the tax court's determination that this road was a "single identifiable property" (SIP) as this limits their casualty loss deduction to the road's basis. We have jurisdiction to review the final order of the tax court under 26 U.S.C. Section 7482, and we affirm. Because the parties are familiar with the factual and procedural history of the case, we will not repeat it here except as necessary to explain the disposition.

The question of whether a dirt road is a SIP or is part of the surrounding land is untechnical and factual and, thus, subject to our review for clear error. See *Condor Int'l. Inc. v. CIR,* 78 F.3d 1355, 1358 (9th Cir. 1996). Tax deductions are a matter of legislative grace, and as such the burden of proving a deductible loss and its amount is always upon the taxpayer. *Clapp v. Commissioner,* 321 F.2d 12, 14 (9th Cir. 1963). A casualty loss deduction is allowed under I.R.C. Section 165(a) for "any loss sustained during the taxable year and not compensated for by insurance or otherwise." In this context, the amount of loss taken into account is the lesser of (1) the difference between the fair market value of the property immediately before and after the casualty or (2) the taxpayer's adjusted basis of the property. I.R.C. Section 165(b); Income Tax Regs. Section 1.165-7(b)(1). A loss incurred in a trade or business is determined in this manner, but by reference to the "single identifiable property" damaged or destroyed. Income Tax Regs. Section 1.165-7(b)(2).

The Czirakis maintain that the dirt road had no basis and rather than being a SIP it was inextricably part of the land and so their casualty loss deduction for damage to the road should be limited by their basis in the land. The tax court characterized the dirt road as a SIP and accordingly limited the Czirakis' deduction to the basis in that road. In doing so, the tax court considered the time, effort, expense and resources spent on constructing the road. The court also correctly considered that a taxpayer may not borrow basis from unharmed property to increase the amount of a loss deduction for injury to other property. See *Rosenthal v. Commissioner,* 416 F.2d 491, 497-98 (2d Cir. 1969).

The tax court's finding that the dirt road was a SIP was not clearly erroneous. Accordingly, the decision of the tax court is AFFIRMED.

Endnotes
1. This disposition is not appropriate for publication and may not be cited to or by the courts of this circuit except as may be provided by 9th Cir. R. 36-3.
2. The Czirakis also contend that the tax court erred in commingling the basis in the dirt road and an adjacent asphalt road. If they are correct, then their entire deduction would be disallowed. Having noted that the Czirakis may have received a deduction to which they were not entitled, the Commissioner did not appeal the decision to allow the $6,844 deduction. Assuming the Czirakis prefer the limited deduction to no deduction at all, we leave the tax court's decision undisturbed.

A U.S. citizen does not have an automatic right to have his or her case heard by the Supreme Court. Permission to present the case must be requested by a **writ of certiorari.** If the Court decides to hear the case, the "certiorari is granted"; if it refuses, the "certiorari is denied." One must treat a Supreme Court decision as having the full force of the law; although Congress might repeal the challenged statute or the Federal administration might refuse to fund or enforce the underlying law and related activities, neither the citizen nor the government can appeal a Supreme Court decision.

As we have discussed, however, certiorari is granted in very few tax cases. Only about a dozen appeals relating to tax issues—state, local, and federal; income, property, sales, estate, and gift; individual, corporate, and fiduciary—are heard by the Supreme Court in a typical year. In most cases, those petitions granted involve an issue at conflict among the Federal circuits or a tax issue of major importance. For instance, the Court might hear a client's case concerning the inclusion in gross income of life insurance proceeds, if many similar cases had been brought before the various Federal courts and tremendous tax liabilities were under dispute, or if two or more of the circuits had issued inconsistent holdings on the matter.

In denying the petition for certiorari, the Supreme Court is not "upholding," or in any way confirming, a lower court decision. Rather, the Court simply does not find the appealed case to be interesting or important enough to consider during its limited sessions. The lower court's decision does stand, but one cannot infer that the decision necessarily is correct or that it should be followed in the future by other taxpayers whose situations are similar. These matters of open-fact tax planning must be analyzed using the tax researcher's professional judgment.

Locating Supreme Court Decisions

At least five different general and specialized reporters publish all of the tax-related Supreme Court decisions. CCH includes such cases in the *United States Tax Cases* service (USTC), and RIA publishes them in the *American Federal Tax Reports* (AFTR, AFTR2d, or AFTR3d). The Government Printing Office publishes the *United States Supreme Court Reports,* which contains all of the tax and nontax decisions of the Court. In common citation convention, references to this service are abbreviated as "U.S." In addition, West Publishing includes all Supreme Court decisions in the *Supreme Court Reporter* (S.Ct.).

In the following examples of proper citations, one can infer from the GPO and West citations that the case was heard by the Supreme Court, and any further reference to that forum (e.g., as USSC) would be redundant. In addition, if a case involves an issue of pre-1954 Code tax law, the first series of the AFTR service would be cited. Exhibit 5–7 is an example of a tax decision of the Supreme Court, reproduced from the USTC reporter.

Court Reporters

GPO: *Indianapolis Power & Light,* 493 U.S. 203 (1990)
West: *Indianapolis Power & Light,* 110 S.Ct. 589 (1990)
RIA: *Indianapolis Power & Light,* 65 AFTR2d 90-394 (USSC, 1990)
CCH: *Indianapolis Power & Light,* 90-1 USTC ¶ 50,007 (USSC, 1990)
Kleinrock: *Indianapolis Power & Light,* KTC 1990-53 (USSC, 1990)

CASE BRIEFS

Tax researchers have found that the construction of a concise **case brief** is of great value to them, both when they return to a client's research problem or planning environment after a period of time passes and in using the given case in constructing a

Exhibit 5–7 Supreme Court Decision Syllabus

SUPREME COURT OF THE UNITED STATES

Syllabus

O'GILVIE et al., Minors v. UNITED STATES

Certiorari to the United States Court of Appeals for the Tenth Circuit

Docket: 95-966, 95-977 - Decided December 10, 1996

519 U.S. 79; 117 S.Ct. 452

Petitioners, the husband and two children of a woman who died of toxic shock syndrome, received a jury award of $1,525,000 actual damages and $10 million punitive damages in a tort suit based on Kansas law against the maker of the product that caused decedent's death. They paid Federal income tax insofar as the award's proceeds represented punitive damages, but immediately sought a refund. Procedurally speaking, this litigation represents the consolidation of two cases brought in the same Federal District Court: the husband's suit against the Government for a refund, and the Government's suit against the children to recover the refund that the Government had made to the children earlier. The District Court found for petitioners under 26 U.S.C. Section 104(a)(2), which, as it read in 1988, excluded from "gross income," the "amount of any damages received . . . on account of personal injuries or sickness." (Emphasis added.) The court held on the merits that the italicized language includes punitive damages, thereby excluding such damages from gross income. The Tenth Circuit reversed, holding that the exclusionary provision does not cover punitive damages.

Held:

1. Petitioners' punitive damages were not received "on account of" personal injuries; hence the gross-income-exclusion provision does not apply and the damages are taxable. Pp. 2–11.

   (a) Although the phrase "on account of" does not unambiguously define itself, several factors prompt this Court to agree with the Government when it interprets the exclusionary provision to apply to those personal injury lawsuit damages that were awarded by reason of, or because of, the personal injuries, and not to punitive damages that do not compensate injury, but are private fines levied by civil juries to punish reprehensible conduct and to deter its future occurrence. For one thing, the Government's interpretation gives the phrase "on account of" a meaning consistent with the dictionary definition. More important, in *Commissioner v. Schleier*, 515 U.S. 323, this Court came close to resolving the statute's ambiguity in the Government's favor when it said that the statute covers pain and suffering damages, medical expenses, and lost wages in an ordinary tort case because they are "designed to compensate . . . victims," id., at ____, n. 5, but does not apply to elements of damages that are "punitive in nature," id., at ____. The Government's reading also is more faithful to the statutory provision's history and basic tax-related purpose of excluding compensatory damages that restore a victim's lost, nontaxable "capital." Petitioners suggest no very good reason why Congress might have wanted the exclusion to have covered these punitive damages, which are not a substitute for any normally untaxed personal (or financial) quality, good, or "asset" and do not compensate for any kind of loss. Pp. 2–8.

   (b) Petitioners' three arguments to the contrary—that certain words or phrases in the original, or current, version of the statute work in their favor; that the exclusion of punitive damages from gross income may be justified by Congress' desire to be generous to tort victims and to avoid such administrative problems as separating punitive from compensatory portions of a global settlement or determining the extent to which a punitive damages award is itself intended to compensate; and that their position is supported by a 1989 statutory amendment that specifically says that the gross income exclusion does not apply to any punitive damages in connection with a case not involving physical injury or sickness—are not sufficiently persuasive to overcome the Government's interpretation. Pp. 8–11.

2. Petitioners' two case-specific procedural arguments—that the Government's lawsuit was untimely and that its original notice of appeal was filed a few days late—are rejected. Pp. 12–14.

   66 F. 3d 1550, affirmed.

   BREYER, J., delivered the opinion of the Court, in which REHNQUIST, C.J., and STEVENS, KENNEDY, SOUTER, and GINSBURG, JJ., joined. SCALIA, J., filed a dissenting opinion, in which O'CONNOR and THOMAS, JJ., joined.

* * *

research analysis for another client. The reader should be careful, though, to distinguish this concise research tool from the case briefs required as part of the procedure of most court hearings. The latter is a lengthy document that includes a detailed analysis of all parts of the litigants' arguments.

A proper tax research case brief presents in summary fashion, ideally not exceeding one page, the facts, issue(s), holding, and analysis of the chosen court case. From such a brief, the researcher can discover in a very short period of time whether the full text of the case is of further use in the present analysis. If the briefed case does warrant further examination, the researcher can locate it (or any other cases that are cited in the brief itself) very quickly.

Study carefully the format of the case brief in Exhibit 5–8. Notice that the indicated tax research issues correspond with each of the analyses and holdings of the

Exhibit 5–8 Court Case Brief Illustrated

CITATION	*U.S. v. Stephen W. Bentson*, 947 F.2d 1353; 92-1 USTC ¶50,048; 68 AFTR2d 5773 (CA-9, 1991).
ISSUE(S)	(1) Does the IRS's failure to comply with the Paperwork Reduction Act (PRA) preclude a taxpayer from being penalized for failing to file a tax return and cause charges against him to be dismissed? (2) Could the IRS penalties be avoided because the Form 1040 had not been published in the *Federal Register*? (3) Could the IRS penalties be avoided because of a lack of proof that Bentson had failed to file returns?
FACTS	For the tax year 1982, Bentson filed a "protest tax return." He refused to supply information other than his name, address, social security number, and signature. The rest of his Form 1040 was filled with asterisks, and he attached a statement asserting that to supply other information violated his Fifth Amendment constitutional right. No tax returns could be located for 1983 and 1984. Bentson was charged by the IRS with three counts of willful failure to file tax returns. A District Court bench trial was held. After the close of the government's case, Bentson moved for dismissal, relying on *U.S. v. Kimball*, 896 F.2d 1218, vacated, 925 F.2d 356 (CA-9, 1991).
HOLDING	The District Court granted Bentson's motion as to the first count only. He was found guilty on two counts and sentenced to eight months incarceration followed by three years' probation, and a $2,000 fine. The Ninth Circuit affirmed the lower court's decision.
ANALYSIS	(1) Bentson argued the IRS failed to comply with the Paperwork Reduction Act and relied on the original *U.S. v. Kimball*. This decision was reversed in 1991 (see 925 F.2d 356). The Ninth Circuit held that the public protection provision of the Paperwork Reduction Act is not a defense to prosecution under IRC § 7203 (willful failure to file a return, supply information, or pay tax). (2) Bentson argued that Form 1040 and the instructions constitute a "rule" for purposes of the Administrative Procedures Act (APA) and therefore must be published in the *Federal Register* to be valid. The Ninth Circuit ruled this argument had no merit. (3) Bentson argued the IRS had not proved he did not file tax returns for 1983 and 1984. This argument was rejected because Bentson had already made a binding judicial admission to the contrary.

court, as indicated by the numbers of the brief's outline format. Finally, notice that citations to other cases, or to administrative proclamations, are complete and somewhat detailed, helping to facilitate further research.

THE INTERNET AND JUDICIAL SOURCES

The Internet and the World Wide Web provide a new way for tax researchers to access judicial sources of tax law. Many law schools, journals, tax publishers, and individuals have set up their own home pages (web sites) on the Internet. While not as user friendly as a commercial service, these home pages allow anyone with access to the Internet to locate many court decisions. Examples of some of these home pages that have links to other judicial sources are as follows.

Emory U. School of Law	**http://www.law.emory.edu**
Cornell U. School of Law	**http://www.law.cornell.edu**
U. of Texas School of Law	**http://www.utexas.edu/law**
Practitioners Publishing Co.	**http://www.ppcnet.com**
Will Yancey's Home Page	**http://www.willyancey.com**

COMPUTER TAX SERVICE EXAMPLE

The tax researcher can use an online computer tax service to find court cases of interest. If the researcher knows the case name or citation, he or she can enter it directly and obtain a copy of the case. However, if the case name or citation is not known, the researcher can use a computer query to find cases that have addressed the issue at hand.

Example 5–1 Your client is involved in a dispute with the IRS over the valuation for estate tax purposes of a closely held business. In the process of getting ready to go to the Tax Court on this matter, you have to hire an expert witness to justify the client's valuation of the business. During the interviews, one of the experts says that she will use the Capital Asset Pricing Model (CAPM) as the basis for her valuation. You are not sure what the CAPM is and how the courts will react to it. You therefore execute a computer search using RIA Checkpoint to see if there is any information available on the use of the CAPM in tax valuation. Exhibit 5–9 shows an example of a search query that could be used to find any court cases that have discussed the CAPM. Exhibit 5–10 shows a portion of a Tax Court Memorandum Decision (*Furman v. Comm.*, T.C. Memo. 1998-157) you found in which the Tax Court rejected the use of the CAPM in favor of another method. Thus, you decide to hire an expert familiar with the other method of valuation.

SUMMARY

The tax practitioner must possess a working knowledge of the Federal court system in order to address tax research problems. The researcher must understand the role of the courts in generating Federal tax law, the relationship of the courts to one

Exhibit 5-9
RIA Checkpoint CAPM Search Query

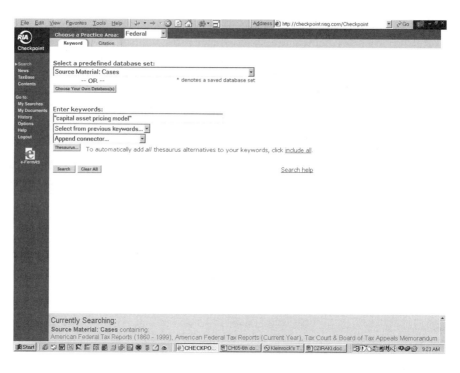

Exhibit 5-10
RIA Checkpoint CAPM Search Result

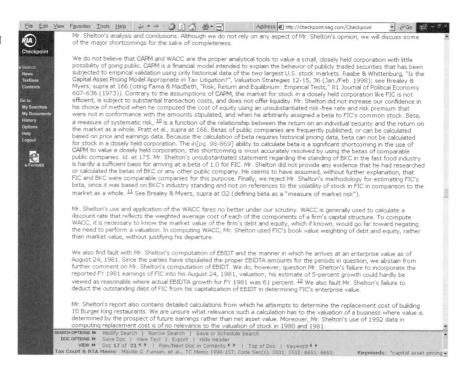

another, the constitution and jurisdiction of each court, where to locate an appropriate decision, and how to interpret that decision.

Exhibit 5–11 offers a summary of some of the attributes of the trial-level and appeals courts discussed in this chapter. Because of differences among courts, the tax adviser may be inclined to choose one of the trial-level courts over the others to accommodate the special needs or circumstances of the client.

Exhibit 5–12 summarizes the decisions available in each of the tax case reporter services discussed in this chapter. With the variety of tax publications available, choices must be made so that the practitioner's tax research budget can be used effectively, without sacrifice of his or her ability to solve the client's problems.

Finally, a number of observations concerning citation conventions can be made. Review the citation examples given in this chapter to verify the list shown in Exhibit 5–13 and to add your own observations to it.

TAX TUTOR

Reinforce the tax research information covered in this chapter by completing the online tutorials located at the Federal Tax Research web site:

http://raabe.swcollege.com

Exhibit 5–11 The Judicial Obstacle Course: Selected Attributes of Trial-level Courts

Item	Tax Court	District Court	Court of Federal Claims
Jurisdiction	Tax cases only	Legal issues based on entire *U.S. Code*	Monetary claims against U.S. government
Judges	Tax law specialists	Tax law generalists	Tax law generalists
Domain	National court, but judges travel	Limited geographical area	National court, but judges travel
Jury trial available?	No	Yes, if question of fact	No
Number of judges hearing case	One, reviewed by chief judge; *en banc* hearing for certain issues	One	One to five
Small Cases Division available?	Yes	No	No
Payment of tax	Trial, then payment	Payment, then trial	Payment, then trial
Precedents court must follow	Supreme Court; pertinent circuit court; Tax Court	Supreme Court; pertinent circuit court; own District court	Supreme Court; Federal Circuit Court; Court of Federal Claims

Exhibit 5–12 Court Decision Reporter Summary

I. By Reporter

Reporter, Common	Publisher, Common Abbreviation	Decisions Included
Primary Reporters		
T.C. (B.T.A.)	GPO	Regular Tax Court (BTA) decisions
TCM	CCH	Tax Court Memorandum decisions
RIA T.C. Mem. Dec.	RIA	Tax Court Memorandum decisions
F.Supp	West	District court decisions
Fed. Cl.	West	Court of Federal Claims decisions
F.3d (F.2d)	West	Court of Appeals and pre-1982 Court of Claims decisions
U.S.	GPO	All Supreme Court decisions
S.Ct.	West	All Supreme Court decisions
Secondary Reporters		
USTC	CCH	Tax cases from all Federal courts except the Tax Court
AFTR series	RIA	Tax cases from all Federal courts except the Tax Court
KTC	Kleinrock's	Tax cases from all Federal courts except the Tax Court

II. By Court

Court	Publisher	Citation Abbreviation	Reporter
Supreme Court			
All cases	West	S.Ct.	Supreme Court Reporter
	GPO	U.S.	U.S. Supreme Court Reports
Tax only	CCH	USTC	U.S. Tax Cases
	RIA	AFTR series	American Federal Tax Reports
	Kleinrock's	KTC	Kleinrock's Tax Cases
Court of Appeal			
All cases	West	F.3d (F.2d)	Federal Reporter, 3d (2d) series
Tax only	CCH	USTC	
	RIA	AFTR series	
	Kleinrock's	KTC	
Tax Court			
Regular	GPO	T.C.	Tax Court of the U.S. Reports
Memo	CCH	TCM	Tax Court Memorandum Decisions
	RIA	RIA T.C. MemDec.	RIA Tax Court Memorandum Decisions
	Kleinrock's	T.C. Memo	
District Courts			
All cases	West	F.Supp.	Federal Supplement Series
Tax only	CCH	USTC	
	RIA	AFTR series	
	Kleinrock's	KTC	
Court of Federal Claims			
All cases post-1982	West	Fed. Cl.	U.S. Court of Federal Claims
Tax only	CCH	USTC	
	RIA	AFTR series	
	Kleinrock's	KTC	

Exhibit 5–13
Citation Conventions and Observations

> The common form of a citation is as follows: case name–volume number–reporter–page number–court–year
>
> The AFTR second series began with 1954 IRC cases.
>
> The B.T.A. became the U.S. Tax Court in 1943.
>
> The U.S. Court of Claims became the U.S. Claims Court in 1982, and the U.S. Court of Federal Claims in 1992.
>
> *Unless* the case was published in a year different from that in which it was heard, the USTC volume number (and many AFTR page numbers) includes a reference to the year, so the year need not be repeated in the citation.
>
> The S.Ct. and U.S. citations imply that the case was heard in the Supreme Court, so the court abbreviation need not be repeated in the citation.
>
> The government need not be mentioned in a typical Tax Court citation.

KEY WORDS

By the time you complete this chapter, you should be comfortable discussing each of the following terms. If you need additional review of any of these items, return to the appropriate material in the chapter or consult the glossary to this text.

AFTR	Permanent Citation
Board of Tax Appeals	Regular Decision
Case Brief	Small Cases Division
Court of Federal Claims	Supreme Court
Courts of Appeals	Tax Court
District Court	Temporary Citation
En Banc	USTC
Golsen Rule	Writ of Certiorari
Memorandum Decision	

DISCUSSION QUESTIONS

1. Who can initiate a court case that deals with a tax matter—the taxpayer or the IRS?
2. Explain the general organization of the Federal court system for cases concerning Federal tax issues.
3. May a taxpayer take his or her tax case directly to the Supreme Court?
4. Who has the burden of proof in most cases involving the tax law? Why?
5. The U.S. Tax Court hears only certain types of cases. Identify those cases.
6. The U.S. Tax Court has undergone an evolution since it was founded. What happened to its structure in 1926, 1943, and 1969, respectively?
7. How many judges sit on the U.S. Tax Court? What is the length of time of the appointment of each judge?

8. The U.S. Tax Court is a national court that meets in Washington, D.C. Does this mean that the taxpayer and his or her attorney must travel to Washington to have a case heard?
9. May a taxpayer have a jury trial in the U.S. Tax Court?
10. What does the term sitting *"en banc"* mean?
11. Distinguish between a Regular and a Memorandum decision of the Tax Court.
12. The U.S. Tax Court is a national court that hears cases of taxpayers who may appeal to various geographical Courts of Appeals. How does the Tax Court reconcile the opposite holdings of two or more of these Courts of Appeals for taxpayers who work or reside in different parts of the country?
13. What is the Small Cases Division of the U.S. Tax Court? What is the maximum amount of the deficiency that can be the subject of a Small Cases hearing? Comment on the trial procedures in the Small Cases Division.
14. Where are regular Tax Court decisions published? Illustrate the elements of both a temporary and a permanent regular Tax Court citation. Explain what each part of the citation means.
15. Tax Court Memorandum decisions are not published by the Federal government. However, commercial reporters include these decisions. Illustrate the elements of both a temporary and a permanent citation for a Tax Court Memorandum decision, using both the CCH and RIA reporters. Explain what each part of the citation means.
16. What is the jurisdiction of a U.S. District Court?
17. Must the taxpayer pay the disputed tax deficiency to the government before his or her case will be heard in a District Court? In the U.S. Court of Federal Claims? In the U.S. Tax Court?
18. Which of the trial courts is most appropriate for a taxpayer who wishes to limit the judicial review of the relevant year's tax return to the specific issue(s) involved in the case?
19. Which of the trial courts would best serve a taxpayer litigating an issue of a technical tax nature? Why?
20. Is a Federal District Court a national court? How many judges hear a case brought before a Federal District Court?
21. Name the three court case reporters that publish tax and nontax District Court decisions. Illustrate the elements of a citation that might be found in each reporter. Explain what each part of the citation means.
22. Differentiate between a primary and a secondary case citation.
23. What type of cases are heard by the U.S. Court of Federal Claims?
24. How many judges are appointed to the U.S. Court of Federal Claims?
25. Is the U.S. Court of Federal Claims a national court? Must a taxpayer go to Washington, D.C., to present a case to this U.S. court?
26. Name the three court case reporters that publish U.S. Court of Federal Claims decisions. Illustrate the elements of a citation that might be found in each reporter. Explain what each part of the citation means.
27. Are the U.S. Courts of Appeals national courts? What type of cases do they hear?
28. Identify the circuit court that would hear the case of a taxpayer who lives or works in each of the following areas.
    a. Texas
    b. New York

Continued

c. California
d. Colorado
e. Illinois
f. A case that is appealed from the U.S. Court of Federal Claims

29. Each Court of Appeals has approximately twenty judges. How many of these judges hear a typical case?
30. Name the three court case reporters that publish Court of Appeals decisions. Illustrate the elements of a citation that might be found in each reporter. Explain what each part of the citation means.
31. Can a taxpayer have a jury trial before a Court of Appeals?
32. What is the highest court in the United States? What is its jurisdiction? Where does it hear cases?
33. How does one petition the Supreme Court to hear one's tax case?
34. How many justices are appointed to the Supreme Court? How many hear each case?
35. Why does the Supreme Court hear so few tax cases?
36. Differentiate between the Supreme Court's overturning of a lower court's decision, and its denial of a writ of certiorari.
37. Name the four court case reporters that publish Supreme Court decisions. Illustrate the elements of a citation that might be found in each reporter. Explain what each part of the citation means.
38. Is it possible for a taxpayer to have a jury trial before any of the trial courts? Before a Court of Appeals? Before the U.S. Supreme Court?
39. Discuss the precedential value of a Court of Appeals decision. Which Court of Appeals decisions are most important to a specific taxpayer?
40. In the (fictitious) citation *Gomez v. U.S.*, 102 T.C. 123 (1999), what does the "102" stand for? The "T.C."? The "123"?
41. Which court would have issued the (fictitious) *O'Dell v. U.S.*, 66 TCM 86 (2000) decision? What does each element in the citation mean?
42. In the citation *Simons-Eastern v. U.S.*, 354 F.Supp. 1003 (D.Ct., Ga, 1972), the "F.Supp." tells the tax researcher that the decision is from which court?
43. *By using only the citation*, state which court issued each of the following decisions. If you cannot determine which court by looking at the citation only, say so.
    a. *Davis v. U.S.*, 43 Fed. Cl. 92 (1999)
    b. *D.C. Crummey v. U.S.*, 68-2 USTC ¶ 12,541
    c. *U.S. v. Goode*, 86 AFTR2d 2000-7273
    d. *James v. U.S.*, 81 S.Ct. 1052 (1961)

EXERCISES

44. Find the court decision located at 100 T.C. 32.
    a. What court heard the case?
    b. Who was the judge(s)?
    c. In what year was the case decided?
    d. What was the issue(s) involved?

45. Find the court decision located at T.C. Memo. 2001-71.
    a. What court heard the case?
    b. Who was the judge(s)?
    c. In what year was the case decided?
    d. What was the issue(s) involved?
46. Find the court decision located at 81-1 USTC ¶ 9479.
    a. What court heard the case?
    b. Who was the judge(s)?
    c. In what year was the case decided?
    d. What was the issue(s) involved?
47. Find the court decision located at 2001-1 USTC ¶ 50,176.
    a. What court heard the case?
    b. Who was the judge(s)?
    c. In what year was the case decided?
    d. What was the issue(s) involved?
48. Find the court decision located at 67 AFTR2d 91-718.
    a. What court heard the case?
    b. Who was the judge(s)?
    c. In what year was the case decided?
    d. What was the issue(s) involved?
49. If your last name begins with the letters A–L, read and brief each of the following cases.
    a. *Sorensen*, T.C. Memo. 1994-175
    b. *Keller*, 84-1 USTC ¶ 9194

    If your last name begins with the letters M–Z, read and brief each of the following cases.
    c. *Washington*, 77 T.C. 601
    d. *Tellier*, 17 AFTR2d 633
50. If your last name begins with the letters A–L, read and brief each of the following cases.
    a. *Rownd*, T.C. Memo. 1994-465
    b. *Arnes*, 93-1 USTC ¶ 50,016

    If your last name begins with the letters M–Z, read and brief each of the following cases.
    c. *Willie Nelson Music Co.*, 85 T.C. 914
    d. *Independent Contracts, Inc.*, 73 AFTR2d 94-1406
51. Read and brief each of the following cases.
    a. *Gregory v. Helvering*, 55 S.Ct. 266 (1935)
    b. *Hunt*, T.C. Memo. 1965-172

RESEARCH CASES

52. Snidely Limited spent $1 million this year to upgrade its manufacturing plant, which had received several warnings from the state environmental agency about releasing pollution into the local river. Late in the year, Snidely received an as-

sessment of $700,000 for violating the state's Clean Water Act. After he negotiated with the State, which cost $135,000 in legal fees, Snidely promised to spend another $200,000 next year for more pollution control devices, and the fine was reduced to $450,000. How much of these expenditures can Snidely Limited deduct for tax purposes?

Partial list of research material: § 162; Rev. Rul. 76-130, 1976-1 C.B. 16; *Tucker,* 69 T.C. 675.

53. Last year, only four of thirty-two professional basketball teams turned a nominal accounting profit. Betty purchased such a team this year. Her taxable loss therefrom properly was determined to be $950,000. Can she deduct this loss?

    Partial list of research material: § 183; Reg. § 1.183-2; *Brannen,* 722 F.2d 695.

54. Herbert, a collector of rare coins, bought a 1916 Spanish Bowlero for $2,000 in 1984. He sold the coin for $4,500 in January 1997. Herbert retired from his loading dock job in June 1997 and began actively buying and selling rare coins. By December 1997, Herbert's realized gain from such activities was $21,500. What type of taxable income was January's $2,500 gain?

    Partial list of research material: § 1221; Rev. Rul. 68-634, 1968-2 C.B. 46; *Frankel,* 56 TCM 1156 (1989).

55. Steve is an usher at his local church. Can he deduct commuting expenses for the Sundays that he is assigned to usher for church services?

    Partial list of research material: § 170; Rev. Rul. 56-508, 1956-2 C.B. 126; *Churukian,* 40 TCM 475 (1980).

56. A new member of the San Diego Chargers wants the team to transfer $1,000,000 into an escrow account, in his name, for later withdrawal. The player suggests this payment in lieu of the traditional signing bonus. When is this income taxable to him?

    Partial list of research material: § 451; Rev. Rul. 70-435, 1970-2 C.B. 100; *Drysdale,* 277 F.2d 413.

57. Professor Stevens obtained tenure and promotion to full professor status many years ago. Yet, he continues to publish research papers in scholarly journals to satisfy his own curiosity and to maintain his professional prestige and status within the academic community. Publications are also necessary in order for Professor Stevens to receive pay raises at his university. This year, Dr. Stevens spent $750 of his own funds to travel to southern Utah to collect some critical pieces of data for his work. What is the tax treatment of this expenditure?

    Partial list of research material: § 162; *Zell,* 85-2 USTC ¶ 9698; *Smith,* 50 TCM 904.

58. The local electric company requires a $200 refundable deposit from new customers, in lieu of a credit check. Landlord Pete pays this amount for all of his new-to-town tenants. Can he deduct the $200 payments on his tax return?

    Partial list of research material: § 162; *Hopkins,* 30 T.C. 1015; *Waring Products,* 27 T.C. 921.

59. High-Top Financing charges its personal loan holders a 2 percent fee if the full loan principal is paid prior to the due date. What is the tax effect of this year's $50,000 of prepayment penalties collected by High-Top?

    Partial list of research material: § 61; *Hort,* 41-1 USTC ¶ 9354.

60. Cecilia died this year, owning mutual funds in her IRA worth $120,000. Under the terms of the IRA, Cecilia's surviving husband, Frank, was the beneficiary of

the account, and he took a lump-sum distribution from the fund. Both Cecilia and Frank were age 57 at the beginning of the year.
   a. How does Frank account for the inheritance, assuming that he rolls it over into his own IRA in a timely manner?
   b. Would your answer change if Frank were Cecilia's brother?

   Partial list of research material: § 408; Rev. Rul. 92-47, 1992-1 C.B. 198; *Aronson,* 98 T.C. 283 (1992).

61. During a properly declared U.S. war with Outer Altoona, Harriet, a single taxpayer, was killed in action. Current-year Federal taxable income to the date of Harriet's death totaled $19,000, and Federal income tax withholding came to $2,300.
    a. What is Harriet's tax liability for the year of her death?
    b. What documentation must accompany her final Form 1040?

    Partial list of research material: § 692; Rev. Proc. 85-35, 1985-2 C.B. 433; *Hampton,* 75-1 USTC ¶ 9315.

62. Jerry Baker and his adorable wife Hammi believe in the worship of the "Sea God." This is a very personal religion to Jerry and Hammi. To practice their beliefs, the Bakers want to take a two-week trip to Tahiti this year to worship their deity. The cost (airfare, hotels, etc.) of this religious "pilgrimage" is $5,250. Jerry wants to know if he can deduct the cost of this trip as a charitable deduction on the joint Form 1040, Schedule A.

    Partial list of research material: § 170 and *Kessler,* 87 T.C. 1285 (1986).

63. Willie Waylon is a famous country and western singer. As an investment, Willie started a chain of barbecue restaurants called Willie's Wonderful Ribs. Willie's friends and associates invested $500,000 in this venture. The restaurant chain failed, and the investors lost all their money. Because of his visibility and status in the entertainment community, Willie felt that he personally had to make good on the losses suffered by the investors, so he paid $500,000 to reimburse them all. What are Willie's tax consequences?

    Partial list of research material: § 162 and *Lohrke,* 48 T.C. 679.

64. Paul Preppie is an accountant for the Very Big (VB) Corporation of America, located in Los Angeles, California. When Paul went to work for VB, he did not have a college degree. VB required that Paul earn a B.S. degree in accounting, so he enrolled in a local private university's night school and obtained the degree. VB Corporation does not reimburse employees for attending night school, and because Paul attended a private university, the tuition and other costs were relatively expensive. Can Paul deduct any of the $5,500 he paid in tuition and other costs during the current tax year? Prepare (in good form) a research memorandum to the file. (See Chapter 2 for an illustration of the structure of a tax memo.)

65. Several years ago, Carol Mutter, a cash-basis taxpayer, obtained a mortgage from Weak National Bank to purchase a personal residence. In December 1999, $8,500 of interest was due on the mortgage, but Carol had only $75 in her checking account. On December 31, 1999, she borrowed $8,500 from Weak Bank, evidenced by a note, and the proceeds were deposited in her checking account. On the same day, Carol issued a check in the identical amount of $8,500 to Weak Bank for the interest due. Is the interest expense deductible for the 1999 tax year? Prepare (in good form) a research memorandum to the file. (See Chapter 2 for an illustration of the structure of a tax memo.)

66. Phyllis maintained an IRA account at the brokerage firm ABC. On February 11 of the current year, she requested a check for the balance of her account. She received the check made out in her name and deposited it the same day in a new IRA account at the brokerage firm XYZ. Phyllis then requested a check on May 8 from XYZ, which was deposited in another new IRA account 35 days later. Is the May 8 distribution taxable to Phyllis? Prepare (in good form) a research memorandum to the file. (See Chapter 2 for an illustration of the structure of a tax memo.)

67. Crystal Eros is a devout Pyramidist and a member of the Religious Society of Yanni, a Pyramidist organization. She adheres to the fundamental tenets of Pyramidist theology, including the belief that the Spirit of God is in every person and that it is wrong to kill or otherwise harm another person. Crystal's faith dictates that she not voluntarily participate, directly or indirectly, in military activities. Because Federal income taxes fund military activities, Crystal believes that her faith prohibits her from paying such taxes. Is there any legal substantiation for Crystal's position? Prepare (in good form) a research memorandum to the file. (See Chapter 2 for an illustration of the structure of a tax memo.)

68. Last year, your client, Robert Dinero, mailed an automatic extension for his tax return on April 15. He enclosed a check for $10,000 with the extension request. The IRS cashed the check on April 28. Later, the IRS assessed Robert late filing penalties of $2,900 because they claim he did not mail the extension request on time. On the same date, Robert mailed an income tax extension request and check to the State of California. The California check was cashed on April 16. You requested the IRS send you a copy of the extension request envelope showing the postmark: however, the IRS has lost it. The IRS recently attached Robert's bank account for the $2,900. You have known Robert for years, and he could be described as a good, law-abiding, taxpaying citizen. He always pays his taxes on time, has never been in trouble with the IRS, and is not a tax protester. Robert asks you to recommend whether or not he should engage a tax attorney and sue for a refund, knowing that the legal fees for such an action will probably exceed $10,000. Write a client letter to Robert explaining your findings. His address is 432 Lucre Street, Tecate, CA 91980.

69. Your client, Luther Lifo, is an auditing professor who runs a CPA review course. He comes to you with the following tax questions.

    Question One. Luther teaches CPA review courses on either a guaranteed or non-guaranteed basis. Under the guaranteed program, students pay higher tuition and, if they fail the CPA examination, are entitled to a full refund within two weeks of the release of the results. The CPA review course contracts require him to place the tuition in a set-aside escrow account until the students pass the exam; he established the savings account as a trust account for this purpose. The registration fee and tuition must be paid in full before the classes begin. Thus, students enrolled in the class that started in January 20x1 paid their tuition in December 20x0. In 20x0, Luther deposited registration fees and tuition, including $30,000 in guaranteed tuition payments for the winter 20x1 course, into a checking account. Also during 20x1, he paid refunds to guaranteed students who failed the 20x1 exams from that account. Does Luther report the $30,000 as income in

20x0 or 20x1? How are the refunds paid in 20x1 treated for tax purposes? State the authority for your conclusion.

Question Two. Luther is a majority shareholder in a corporation that owns an office building. He leases space in the building for use in his CPA review course. Luther pays approximately $20 per square foot in annual rent. The corporation leases the remaining space in the building to a LSAT, GMAT, SAT, and GRE review course run by other taxpayers for approximately $10 per square foot. Luther's main intent in negotiating the discounted lease was to secure the additional traffic generated by the other review courses in order the enhance the potential revenue for the CPA review course. What is the amount of rent that Luther can deduct in connection with the CPA review course? State the authority for your conclusion.

Write a client letter to Luther explaining your findings. The address is 321 Fifo Street, Temecula, CA 91980.

70. Austin Towers is a convicted former spy for the Soviet Union. Austin received a communication from a Soviet agent that $2 million had been set aside for him in an account upon which he would be able to draw. Austin was told that the money was being held by the Soviet Union, rather than in an independent or third party bank or institution, on petitioner's behalf. Over the next few years, Austin drew approximately $1,000,000 from the account. During that period, Austin filed annual tax returns with his wife showing taxable income of approximately $65,000 per year. Conduct appropriate research to determine Austin's tax liability for the $1,000,000 in spy fees. Write a client letter to Austin explaining your findings. His address is Lompoc Federal Prison, Cell #123, Lompoc, CA 93401.

71. The Reverend Shaman Oracle is an ordained minister in the Church of Prophetic Prophecy in Palm Desert, California. In the current year, Shaman receives payments from the church for his services of $150,000. Of this amount, the church designates $60,000 for compensation and $90,000 as a housing allowance. Shaman and his wife own a home and have actual expenditures during the year for the home of $72,000. The house is located in a well-established rental market, and the fair rental value of the home for the current year is $55,000. Shaman wants to know how he and his wife should report these amounts on their current year's tax return. Write a client letter to Shaman explaining your findings. His address is P.O. Box 1234, Palm Desert, California 92211.

Part 3

Computer Research Tools

Chapter 6:   Electronic and Printed Tax Services

Chapter 7:   Electronic and Printed Legal Services

Chapter 8:   Citators and Other Finding Devices

Chapter 9:   Tax Journals, Newsletters, and Internet News Sources

6

Electronic and Printed Tax Services

LEARNING OBJECTIVES

- Understand the advantages and disadvantages of published and electronic tax services
- Apply the research process to actual Federal research problems
- Know the major features of electronic tax services
- Know the major features of annotated and topical published tax services
- Use the keyword, cite, and contents searches to find relevant materials in electronic tax services
- Use the keyword, Code section, and court case methods to find relevant materials in the published tax services
- Apply the research process to state research problems
- Know which tax services are most appropriate for different research objectives

CHAPTER OUTLINE

Published Versus Electronic
   Currency
   Accessing Information
Computer Services
The Research Process
   Illustrative Example
   Approaching the Research Problem
   Assessing Computerized Tax Information
RIA Checkpoint
   Keyword Search
   Cite Search
      Code Search
      Case Search
   Contents Search
      Table of Contents Search
      Index Search
CCH Tax Research NetWork
   Keyword Search

   Cite and Contents Searches
   State Tax Search
Kleinrock
Published Services
Annotated Services
   Entering Compilation Volumes
   Keyword Search
   Code Section Search
      Code Volumes
   Case Name Search
   Other Pathways into the Compilations
   CCH Annotated Service
   RIA Compilations
Topical Services
   Nature of Topical Tax Services
   RIA *Coordinator* and *Analysis*

Chapter 6 Electronic and Printed Tax Services

Every tax researcher must have access to one or more commercial tax services. By organizing the vast array of primary and secondary sources of the tax law, these tax services facilitate more efficient, effective, and comprehensive research. Accordingly, the function of the commercial tax services is to act as an index for primary and secondary tax law source materials, not as an end in themselves. Generally, only reckless (or inadequately trained) tax researchers will confine their analysis to the commentary available in tax services. The tax services should efficiently direct the researcher to the germane primary sources of the controlling law. It is the professional duty of the researcher to undertake an evaluation of these sources. Furthermore, quality research is not completed until the latest developments in the relevant areas of the law have been assessed.

This chapter reviews the basic steps for developing effective and efficient tax research introduced in Chapter 2 while exploring the electronic and printed versions of the major tax services. First, the electronic tax services are presented as a group, and then the printed versions are discussed. Tax services offering legal as well as tax products are examined in Chapter 7.

PUBLISHED VERSUS ELECTRONIC

Traditionally, commercial tax services were classified into two general types, annotated and topical. **Annotated tax services** are organized by *Internal Revenue Code* section number. **Topical tax services,** on the other hand, divide the tax law into transactions and related subject matter with underlying tax principles as an organizing format. Published services are still organized in these two categories. While the electronic services developed from published services contain topical and annotated databases, the structure is less visible.

Virtually all tax information is available in various electronic forms. However, the presence of this information does not translate into more effective research. This is because voluminous information takes more time to sort, read, and comprehend, which can lead to information overload and inefficiency. All this information must be managed; otherwise, using computers for tax research will be less effective than using published tax services.

In addition, with the nationwide increase in computer use, access to electronic information can be delayed as a result of having to wait for terminals or slow Internet connections. Advancements in graphics for web pages have also caused a slowdown in accessing information as the user waits for images to load. It is sometimes faster, therefore, to look up the answer to a simple question in a desk copy of the CCH *Master Tax Guide* than to log on the computer and search for the solution. With these caveats aside, computers can greatly increase the efficiency and effectiveness of tax research through instant access to an abundance of primary sources and explanations of the tax law.

One of the greatest benefits of any electronic tax service is its ability to store immense amounts of information in a small physical space (or even off-site via online and Internet services) and then to find, organize, and display the information very quickly. Moreover, electronic tax services can link references to full-text documents, making retrieval of the relevant data virtually seamless. The methods of accessing this wealth of electronic information are essentially the same for CD-ROM, online, and Internet services.

Currency

A substantial advantage of the Internet and online services over their printed versions is the currency of the information provided. For published services, changes in the tax law must be processed by editors, printed, shipped, and then, with loose-leaf services, filed by the practitioner or employee. This can result in a substantial time lag, especially if the updates are not filed on a weekly basis. Further, there is the likelihood of human filing errors—and a page misfiled is information lost to the researcher. For services that are not loose-leaf, the practitioner must constantly refer to the supplements to ensure that the information read is up to date.

CD-ROMs overcome the drudgery of filing updates and the possibility of misfiled information. The cost, however, is that CD-ROM services are generally updated only monthly. Alternatively, most Internet services update in text on a daily or continuous basis. Keep in mind that daily updating does not necessarily mean that what happened yesterday will be accessible today. Processing time is still required. It does mean, however, that as soon as the information is processed it can be entered into the system. There is no further waiting.

Accessing Information

In defense of published tax services, books offer a level of browsing ability that cannot be attained with electronic services. With a published service, researchers can scan the binders to determine which one is related to their area of interest. They can flip through the pages until they find an entry that looks relevant or interesting. The computerized services are not structured to facilitate this type of browsing. Each document or section of explanation is treated as a separate retrievable document; access of a complete binder of information is generally not possible. This is a problem when the researcher knows the general area of interest but not the specifics. Thus, there can be a place for both published and electronic services in many research projects.

The most common entry to a published tax service is through its index. The usefulness of an index is limited by the perspicacity of the indexer. Frequently, a researcher cannot find the specific topic in the index because the terms the indexer uses are not the ones the researcher anticipates. In paper-based research, one must become efficient at using preorganized finding devices developed by third parties.

The keyword **full-text search** is the electronic version of the index. This technique can be much more powerful than a traditional index. A full-text search locates every occurrence of a word or phrase in everything from a single document to an entire collection of documents. It can be quick and easy when the appropriate search words or phrases are selected. The downside, however, is that *every* occurrence of the word or phrase may not be relevant to the research. The context of the words is not evaluated by the computer. It is, therefore, important for tax professionals to learn to construct searches in an effective manner. If the key words are very selective, the research may be precisely targeted. However, if the search terms are too narrow, they can miss important materials. This can result in reaching an inappropriate conclusion. If the terms are too broad, the information overload problem will materialize. An effective search saves time by relieving the researcher of the need to review materials that are not on point.

COMPUTER SERVICES

The number of tax resources offered in computer-compatible media has increased rapidly. Some tax services simply compile primary source information obtained from the government, while others originate information and include substantial analysis. CD-ROM tax resources are common, in part, due to their ability to replace large primary source tax libraries with just a few CDs. While the amount varies with the nature of the material and how much information the publisher chooses to put on a particular CD, the standard disk can hold more than 250,000 pages of text, or as much as 100 feet of bookshelf space.

CD-ROMs are particularly suited to maintaining archival information that a practitioner needs to access fairly frequently. An added advantage of a CD-ROM's storage ability is that the information is accessible through the computer without having to be online and without being loaded on the computer hard drive. Thus, valuable hard disk space is not usurped by the data contained on the CDs.

With CD-ROM services (as well as published services), the practitioner must be in physical possession of the product. If the practitioner is not at the same location as the CDs, access is unavailable. The Internet, in most situations, provides the practitioner access to information from any locality equipped with a computer and a modem. This means research can be performed at a client's office or late night at home. While practitioners can retrieve many free primary tax sources through the Internet, this free access cannot substitute for the need to have access to comprehensive tax services. Besides checking the validity of primary tax sources, tax services furnish various methods of searching the tax sources, editorial analysis and comments, organization, and an integration of the tax resources.

THE RESEARCH PROCESS

A sample research problem will be utilized to explore the major features of the electronic and published tax services. It is important that *you* attempt the illustrative research project using the tax services available to you. The procedural knowledge necessary to use these tax services efficiently can only be acquired through hands-on practice. The remainder of this chapter is designed to guide you through the basic tax services and is *not* a substitute for your actually using the services.

ILLUSTRATIVE EXAMPLE

The sample research project concerns the following situation.

Example 6-1 Our client, Ms. Sanski, an executive with International Marketing, was a guest professor at a local university for one semester. She found that one of the tenured professors, Dr. Nu, shared her interest in the acquisition and distribution networks for products during the European Renaissance. They decided to write a book on the subject and began working in March of the current year. Most of the documents they needed for the book, however, were located in Europe. In June, Ms. Sanski and Dr. Nu traveled to Italy, France, and Spain to examine documents germane to their book. Returning to the United States, they stopped in Washington, D.C., to gather more information at the Library of Congress. By the end of the current year, they expect to have collected most of the materials needed for writing the book. Ms. Sanski has incurred all of the expenses in obtaining these materials. Actual writing of the book will start next year and should be completed by the end of that year. When they have several chapters of the book written, they will contact a publisher. They hope the book will be in print within one year of completing the manuscript. Ms. Sanski wants to deduct all of the costs associated with data collection in the current year. Ms. Sanski asks you if it is possible to treat the costs as current business expenses.

APPROACHING THE RESEARCH PROBLEM

Regardless of the media used for tax research, the starting point in approaching any tax research problem is to formulate the tax question being asked. The research question for the example appears to be: How should the current expenses for a book that may be published in the future be treated for tax purposes? Should they be immediately expensed or capitalized and expensed as the revenues from the book are received? This first formulation of the research question should not be considered its final version. As research is performed, other issues will probably be identified that will require refinement of the question. Recall the iterative nature of tax research as discussed in Chapter 2 relative to Exhibits 2–1 and 2–2.

Gradually the research question is refined into its final state. However, this refinement does not guarantee that a definite answer will be found which controlling authority substantiates. The final conclusion may be that one solution appears more supportable than another, or that the IRS or the courts will interpret the facts and circumstances in a particular manner when making a decision. Remember that in most tax decisions professional judgment is required because the controlling law is imprecise and can be interpreted differently by the taxpayer and the IRS.

Based on the initial questions formulated, the main issue in this research project appears to be expensing versus capitalization of the author's prepublication business costs. Therefore, relevant keywords appear to be "author," "business expenses," "prepublication expenses," and "capitalization." Through a basic knowledge of the Code, we know that capitalization of costs is governed by § 263A, the uniform capitalization rules. Finally, in prior research of other topics, you have seen references to a case called *Hadley* that was about an author's prepublication expenses. The case is old, but it may have some bearing on situation.

ASSESSING COMPUTERIZED TAX INFORMATION

The key to effective tax research is finding the pertinent material necessary to formulate an informed conclusion about the optimum treatment of the transaction. How the electronic tax services are entered will determine how efficiently the relevant materials are found. Most of these services allow the researcher to choose whether to have retrieved documents presented in order of relevance to the search or listed by database sources. The latter lets the researcher decide which documents should be examined first. Regardless of the order displayed, a researcher unfamiliar with the topic should start with an editorial explanation of the topic. This overview of the topic will help identify the most pertinent elements of the project and introduce the primary tax law applicable to the topic. It is easy to gain access to the primary sources from the explanation because they are generally hyper-linked to their citations.

From this initial analysis, a researcher may decide that a new, more targeted search is warranted. Once the relevant primary sources are identified, but before they are carefully read, it is necessary to determine which of the sources are still good law by checking them through a citator (see Chapter 8 for a full discussion of citators). The fact that the tax service locates a document and places it high on the relevance list does not mean the researcher can assume it is still valid law. The last step is to read carefully the selected primary tax law sources that are germane to the tax question. After evaluating these sources, the optimum treatment for the item in question can be ascertained.

Keep in mind that the commercial providers of CD-ROM, online, and Internet tax services offer a plethora of tax products (databases) that can be bundled in a variety of ways. This chapter's description of the tax databases within any of the services may not be what is available to the reader. Each firm (or library) performs a cost–benefit analysis and purchases only those resources that it can afford and finds useful in its practice. The basic methodology described in this chapter should apply to whatever tax databases are available to the reader.

RIA CHECKPOINT

Electronic tax services can be entered using the three search methods: keyword, cite (Code section and case name), and content. How to use each method will be illustrated using **Checkpoint,** the Research Institute of America (RIA) Internet tax service. This is one of the most authoritative and well-known Internet tax services available. The general computer research methodology that applies to RIA Checkpoint also applies to its CD-ROM version, OnPoint. This presentation will be followed by less detailed examples of other electronic tax services.

RIA Checkpoint provides the full gambit of Federal tax information with several different product packages available. The most inclusive package includes all primary tax sources, *Federal Tax Coordinator 2d, United States Tax Reporter, Citator 2nd Series,* Warren, Gorham & Lamont (WG&L) journals, WG&L textbooks, IRS publications, etc. With so much information available it is important to limit a search to only those databases that are pertinent to the research project; otherwise, too many irrelevant documents will be retrieved. Hence, products like pension analysis and benefits analysis will be omitted from our project's search list.

Exhibit 6–1 shows the Opening search screen that appears after the RIA Checkpoint log-on screen. The choices on the left-hand toolbar screen allow a practitioner to begin researching or reading the most current tax news. The news library includes RIA *Tax Watch,* preview issues of *Federal Taxes Weekly Alert, International Weekly* and *State and Local Taxes Weekly,* plus lists of current topics in the latest issues of WG&L journals. *TaxBase,* a news database developed by Tax Analyst, provides current Federal, state, and international tax information through links to *Tax Notes Today, State Tax Today,* and *Worldwide Tax Daily.* Additionally, up-to-date data on state legislation is available through State Net.

Because we are starting a new search project, we can either select the Keyword, Citation, or Legislation file tab located at the top of the RIA screen. Let's start with a keyword search. We also need to choose a practice area (box above the search tabs, not visible in Exhibit 6–1). Given that our research involves a Federal income tax problem, we will select "Federal" as our practice area.

KEYWORD SEARCH

The Opening screen is the Keyword search screen (Exhibit 6-1). The entry box, "Select a predefined database set," allows the researcher to select a database for the search from a pull–down menu. The database set utilized in this research project is a more comprehensive version than that offered in the student RIA Checkpoint. This comprehensive set was chosen to demonstrate the extensive features available in RIA Checkpoint. To view all of the databases offered by the student version (or your library's or employer's subscription), click on the "Choose Your Own Database(s)" button shown in Exhibit 6–1.

For an initial search, the terms "author, business, and expense" were entered in the Keywords box of Exhibit 6–1 and "All Federal Databases," the default database, was searched. Over 600 documents were referenced on the Source Documents screen. As previously discussed, a full-text search looks for *"author"* anywhere in the text of the documents. It does not consider our desire that the document be about the taxation of business expenses of authors. The program literally searches for the term. Thus, every document about business expenses with the word "author" in it was identified. Regulations, for example, often have in their last paragraph "the au-

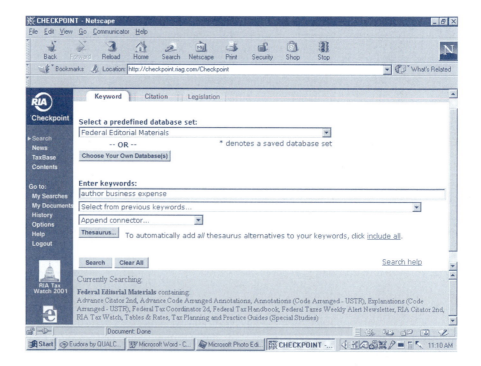

Exhibit 6–1
RIA Checkpoint Opening screen

thors of this Regulation are. . . ." If the Regulation discussed business expenses, it was included in the document list. The same would be true for documents containing comments about "the author." This problem would not occur with a published service because the indexers take into consideration the context of keywords. The indexers know that the researcher is not interested in the authors of the documents.

Due to the number of the documents retrieved, the search was modified by selecting "Federal Editorial Materials" as the database (see Exhibit 6–1). This database was selected because it was less likely to generate documents with irrelevant references to "authors." To change databases, the "Modify Search" option at the top of the Source Documents screen in Exhibit 6–2 was selected. This returns to the original search entries to permit modifications to be made. Running the search terms "author, business, and expense" with the new database still identified more than 60 documents. Consequently, the term "business" was replaced with "prepublication" to narrow the search. "Prepublication" was not merely added to the search words by using the "Narrow Search" option (top of screen, Exhibit 6–2) because it is likely that "prepublication" will appear in documents not containing the term "business." "Narrow Search" allows the researcher to further search the source documents already identified using additional terms.

Through this iterative research process, our final search terms became: "author," "prepublication," and "expense." These were entered into the Keywords box (see Exhibit 6–1) in no particular order. However, if an order is desired, parentheses are added. To indicate that the words constitute a phrase, "quotes" are used. For example, if we want *prepublication expenses* to be treated as a phrase, we would type quotes around the terms. The spaces between words imply an "and" connection. For our search we are going to use each of the three words as separate keywords.

Exhibit 6–2
RIA Checkpoint Initial Source Documents Screen

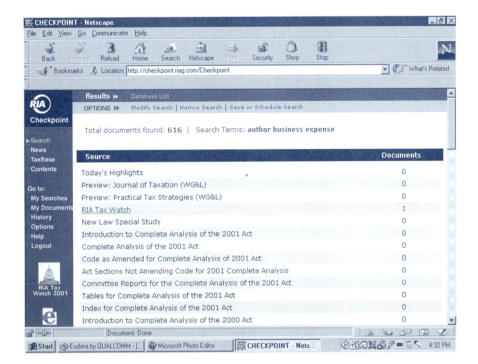

RIA Checkpoint will search for these exact words. If we want to search for author and authors, we need to enter "author*" where the asterisk is a holder for zero or more characters at the end of a word. For a complete list of connectors, click on the down arrow of the "append connectors" box (see Exhibit 6–1).

To have the search include words that are synonymous with the key terms, click on "include all" appearing at the end of the line following the "Thesaurus" button. Clicking on the "Thesaurus" button will bring up a screen with three boxes: "Terms in the query," "Alternatives," and "Current query." When a term in the "Terms in the query" box is highlighted, possible synonyms appear in the "Alternatives" box. The researcher may add individual terms to the query by highlighting them in the "Alternatives" box. The "Current query" box shows the additions to the search terms. For our search terms, we have clicked on the "include all" for all synonyms to be added to the query. Only the "expense" term elicited additions of synonymous. These additions appear in the Keywords box with vertical slashes between each term indicating an "or" connection for the synonyms. More information on formatting keyword entries can be found by clicking on "Search Help" in the lower right corner of the search screen (see Exhibit 6–1). The box directly below the Keywords entries retains previous keyword searches. These may be selected to rerun a search perhaps using a different database or when updating the research.

Using the database and search terms described, our search results in eight documents being identified in three sources: *Federal Tax Coordinator 2d, Annotations (Code Arranged – USTR),* and *Explanations (Code Arranged – USTR).* Through "Options," listed under the "Go to" selections in the left-hand toolbar (see Exhibit 6–1), the researcher may designate whether the results are presented by publication source (called table of contents order) or in relevance order. "Options" is also where the researcher may select what the start up practice area will be, set the level of Table of Contents, select display options, etc.

As mentioned, RIA provides two complete tax services in Checkpoint: *Federal Tax Coordinator 2d* and *United States Tax Reporter (USTR).* Both of these services have published counterparts that are described in more detail in the latter part of this chapter. The **Federal Tax Coordinator 2d,** RIA's flagship service, is a topical service, whereas the **United States Tax Reporter** is an annotated service. We will examine the references in both services to insure complete coverage of RIA Checkpoint.

Clicking first on *"Federal Tax Coordinator 2d"* in the Source Documents list reveals the summaries of two documents: "G-5464 Films, sound recordings, video tapes, books, etc." and "L-4110 Writers." After reading the summaries, it appears that both documents would pertain to our research project. Clicking on the title of the document will retrieve its full-text entry. Exhibit 6–3 reproduces the document "L-4110 Writers." The top portion of this screen denotes the location of this document within the *Federal Tax Coordinator 2d.* Clicking on "Go to first keyword" displays the first occurrence of any keyword. The keywords throughout the text are highlighted for easy identification. Also, any cites hyper-linked to full-text documents are indicated by colored type. Lastly, notice that the case we identified, *Hadley,* is cited in footnote 17 at the bottom of the document.

While browsing the text in the Document View screen (Exhibit 6–3), commands are available at the bottom of the screen that enable the researcher to move from one retrieved document to the next. The other commands at the bottom of the screen are self-explanatory with the exception of "View Text." By clicking on this command, the text is displayed full screen rather than having the document location denoted at

Exhibit 6–3

RIA Checkpoint Document: L-4110 Writers

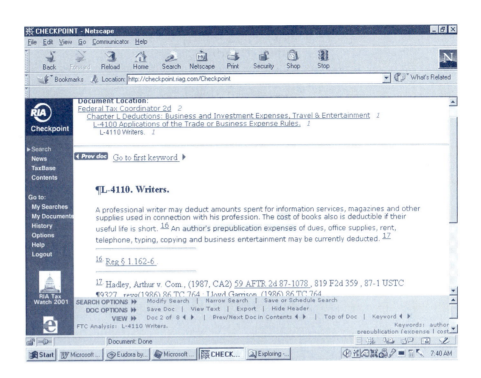

the top. It also removes any highlighting from the text. This option is useful when printing the document.

Returning to the Source Documents screen, we select *"Explanation – USTR."* The document summaries displayed are for "¶263A4.02 Property subject to UNICAP" and "¶263A4.163 Costs subject to UNICAP; pre-'94 rules." Clicking on the first title brings up the full-text document presented in Exhibit 6–4. Directly above the title of the document are a number of buttons which will lead the researcher to other documents related to this topic such as: annotations (Annot), the applicable Code sections (IRC), Regulations (Regs) and Committee Reports (Com Rpts). When comparing this document with the *Federal Tax Coordinator 2d* document in Exhibit 6–3, observe that these useful buttons are not present. This is because the *Federal Tax Coordinator 2d* is a topical service and the *USTR* is an annotated service.

Finally, we again turn to the Source Documents screen and select *"Annotations–USTR."* All of the annotations summarized seem to be pertinent to our research. Upon opening each annotation, the researcher will notice that many of the same buttons (IRC, Regs, Com Rpts.) appear above the annotation title. In addition, the Expl button will take the researcher to the explanation portion of the *USTR* related to the annotation. Each annotation has hyper-links to the related primary documents. Competent researchers will always read the primary documents and not rely on these exceeding brief **annotations** when resolving a tax question.

CITE SEARCH

Citation searches are another method for retrieving relevant documents in the tax services. To perform a search by Code section or case name, choose the Citation tab

Exhibit 6–4
RIA Checkpoint Document: ¶263A4.02 Property subject to UNICAP

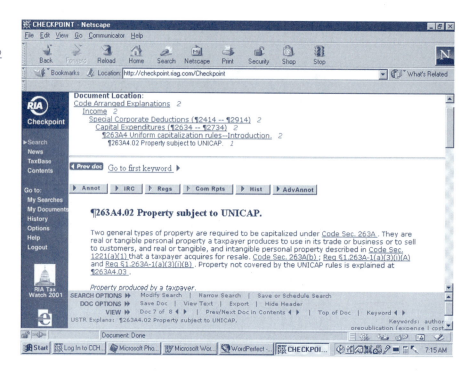

on the opening research screen (see Exhibit 6–1). At the top of the Citation Search screen in Exhibit 6–5 are buttons to retrieve templates for entering citations. The researcher can also scroll down the page until the desired template is reached. The templates make entering a citation simple because the format is provided.

Exhibit 6–5
RIA Checkpoint Citation Screen

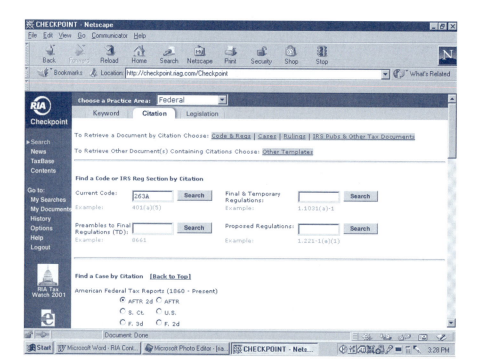

Code Search

To search by Code section, type the citation in the Current Code box as show in Exhibit 6–5 and click on "Search." The next screen presents document titles that match the Code search. Clicking on the only title shown retrieves the full text of § 263A. The initial screen is reproduced in Exhibit 6–6. The topmost part of the page contains the exact location of the Code section within the *Internal Revenue Code,* providing the subtitle, chapter, subchapter, part, and section numbers. On careful examination of Exhibit 6–6, you will see a symbol for the four compass directions. Clicking on this symbol brings up a box in which the exact cite of document line is displayed. This small box is visible in Exhibit 6–6 for the § 263A(a)(1)(A) subparagraph. This is quite helpful when examining long Code sections or Regulations with complex paragraphing structures.

Using the Code section as the beginning point for identifying related documents is simplified by use of the buttons located above the Code section title. These buttons will lead the researcher to explanations and annotations in the *United States Tax Reporter* (Expl and Annot), topical entries in the *Federal Tax Coordinator 2d* (FTC), and to relevant primary sources (Regs and Com Rpts). Through these links, the researcher finds many relevant documents. However, relying exclusively on Code section searches may be more time consuming than keyword searches when there are several Code sections involved in the research issue.

Case Search

Unlike the other major electronic citation services, RIA Checkpoint allows the researcher to enter either the name of the case or its citation. This is quite convenient when all you know is the name of the case. The templates for case names and citations are shown in Exhibit 6–7. While the search was conducted using only the *Hadley* case name, its citation is entered in Exhibit 6–7 to demonstrate the proper use

Exhibit 6–6
RIA Checkpoint
§ 263A Document

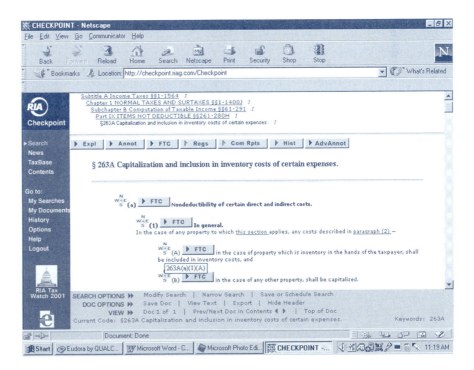

Exhibit 6–7
RIA Checkpoint Case Template Screen

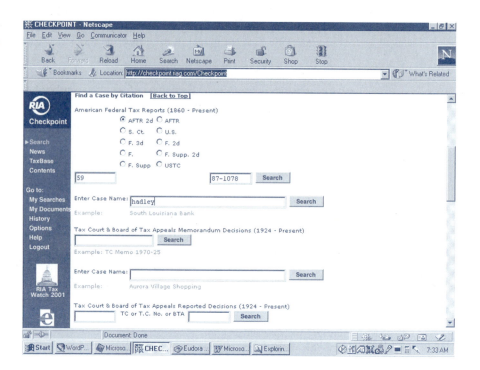

of the citation template. The next screen reports 11 *Hadley* documents were found in the AFTRs. Clicking on the "AFTRs" produces the list of cases shown in Exhibit 6–8. The *Hadley* case pertinent to this research is 59AFTR 2d 87-1078. Note that after the citation, Code Section 263 is listed. This helps in identifying the *Hadley* case of interest. Click on this citation, and the case appears in full text. The full RIA citation is given as the title for the document and, again, the Code section to which the case applies is provided. Since the *Hadley* case is from 1987, we should check this case through the citator (using the citator button provided) to make sure that it is still good law (see Chapter 8 for a detailed discussion of citators).

As was true for a Code section document, a case document may furnish entry into the tax services. The buttons leading to explanations that appeared on the Code Section screen are also present on the Case screen. With these buttons, the researcher is led to the case's annotations in the *United States Tax Reporter* or explanations where the case is cited in the *Federal Tax Coordinator 2d* service. Selecting either of these buttons will lead the researcher to documents retrieved in the previous keyword searches.

With a case or Code section search, the results are the specific case or section. These types of searches do not facilitate the retrieval of all documents that might be relevant to the research project. Case names or Code sections may be utilized as terms in keyword searches to locate relevant documents. It would be important in this type of search to include other keywords to ensure that every document containing the name or the Code section number is not retrieved. These latter searches follow the same steps as any keyword search.

Exhibit 6–8
RIA Checkpoint Case Source Screen

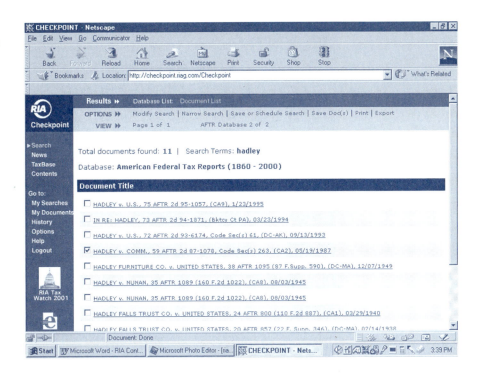

Contents Search

A third approach to electronic searches is a Contents search. This method basically treats the computerized tax services as if they are their counterpart paper services. Thus, the steps in performing this research are similar to those used in conducting research in published services.

The two content search methods are Table of Contents and Index searches. To start either in RIA Checkpoint, select "Contents" in the left-hand toolbar. The next screen, Exhibit 6–9, allows the researcher to select a database by clicking on the down arrow at the end of the box for "Show contents for" entry box.

Table of Contents Search

This search is similar to scanning the binders of the printed RIA tax services or leafing through the service's table of contents. After selecting *"Federal Tax Coordinator 2d"* from the database choices, a list of the published version's chapter titles appears (see Exhibit 6–10). For the illustrative research project, both "Chapter G Tax Accounting: Periods, Methods, Inventories, Installment Sales" and "Chapter L Deductions: Business and Investment Expenses, Travel & Entertainment" are relevant areas. Clicking on these will display the table of contents for the chapters. The researcher would continue to drill down through the contents until individual entries in the service are reached. This method can be very efficient when the researcher has a good idea of where in the services the relevant documents are likely to be located.

Exhibit 6–9
RIA Checkpoint Table of Contents Screen

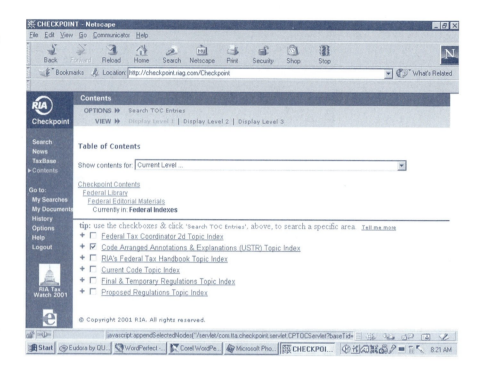

If the researcher is not sure which chapters may be relevant to the project, using the "Search TOC Entries" option at the top of the Table of Contents screen in Exhibit 6–9 may be helpful. After selecting up to 15 chapters (topics), a keyword search screen appears. The remaining searching is identical to a general keyword search where documents within the chapters are being searched for the keywords. It is not limited to the table of contents titles as might be presumed by the title of the option. Thus, using this method should lead to the same relevant documents as the general keyword method. The advantage of this option is that the researcher can limit the chapters of the tax service searched to only those that are pertinent to the issue being researched.

Index Search
Rather than selecting a service database, to perform an index search "Federal Indexes" is selected from the "Show contents for" pull-down menu (see Exhibit 6–9). The databases with indexes are listed at the bottom of Exhibit 6–9. Once a database is selected, the researcher has two options. Clicking on the database will display a listing of the alphabet. From this screen the researcher can select a letter and continue to drill down until the specific topic of interest and the documents are located. This method is similar to using an index for a published service.

The "Search TOC Entries" option is also available with index searches (see Exhibit 6–9). In this situation, the option searches the index entries. This differs from other keyword searches in that it is the index entries themselves and not the underlying documents that are being searched. The advantage of this approach is that the meaning of the words searched are relevant. This is because the entries within the indexes were created by individuals who considered the definitions of the words

Exhibit 6–10
RIA Checkpoint Table of Contents *Federal Tax Coordinator 2d* Screen

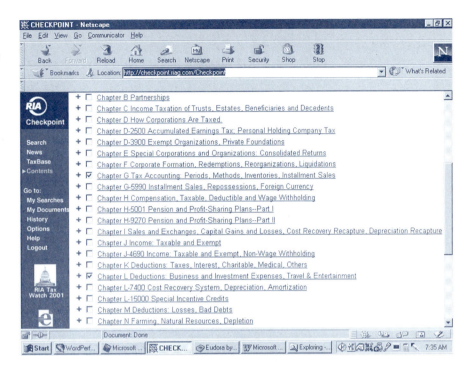

listed. Consequently, the keywords chosen for this type of search would likely be the same words the researcher would select for beginning a research project in a published service's index. Some researchers find it beneficial to start with an index search to help them identify effective terms for their general keyword searches.

CCH TAX RESEARCH NETWORK

Like RIA, Commerce Clearing House (CCH) has a CD-ROM and an Internet tax service. Again, the Internet service, which is called **Tax Research NetWork** (Net-Work), will be emphasized. While visually quite different, the searching methods utilized with NetWork are similar to those discussed in the RIA Checkpoint section. There are several differences, however, that will be illustrated.

The first screen after logging on provides a variety of database choices and search options. Current tax news is available through the open folder, "My CCH" (see Exhibit 6–11). The news can be personalized to focus on those areas of the tax law that are of particular interest to the practitioner. This time-saving feature alerts practitioners to tax law changes in their area of specialization without requiring that they wade through all news articles for the day.

KEYWORD SEARCH

CCH NetWork's opening screen assumes the researcher will be performing a keyword search. Accordingly, other types of searches require selection of buttons at the top of the screen. The keywords are entered in the box below these buttons. The

Exhibit 6–11
CCH Tax Research NetWork Opening Screen

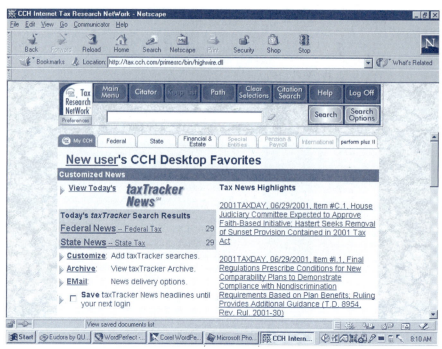

© 2001, CCH INCORPORATED. All Rights Reserved. Reprinted with permission from CCH Tax Research Network.

"Search Options" button to the right of the Keyword box enables the researcher to customize word searches. From this screen, the researcher may select from the following search methods: all terms (the default setting), any term, near (terms to be within 20 words of each other), exact phrase, or Boolean connectors. The number of documents retrieved can set from 1 to 9999 with the default at 50. The program will sort the documents retrieved by relevance unless the researcher selects otherwise. The program also automatically applies a thesaurus to the keywords. With the RIA Checkpoint, the researcher must select application of the thesaurus. Two other options of interest are "Selecting Recent Searches" (similar to "Select from previous keywords" in RIA Checkpoint) and "Date Restrictions." This latter option is especially convenient when the researcher is updating a previous research project.

Once the keywords and search options are entered, one of the database folders must be selected. The choices shown on Exhibit 6–11 are: Federal, State, Financial & Estate, Special Entities, Pension & Payroll, or International. The Perform Plus II tab offers access to Federal and state tax forms. For our project, the Federal database is selected. Within this folder there are a variety of resources groups, composed of numerous databases, from which to choose. Researchers have the option of selecting all the databases within a resource group or only those databases applicable to their project (see Exhibit 6–12). If a researcher decides to change the selection, clicking the "Clear Selections" button at the top of the screen removes all choices, and the selection process starts over again. The researcher can also just unmark the database boxes not desired.

To locate editorial explanations related to our research question, the *Federal Tax Service* and *Standard Federal Tax Reporter* were selected in Exhibit 6–12. As with RIA Checkpoint, CCH NetWork provides access to a topical service **(*Federal Tax*

Exhibit 6–12
CCH Tax Research NetWork Federal File Screen

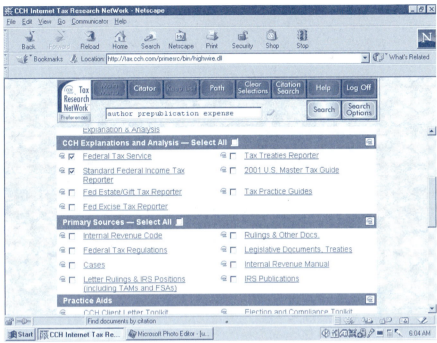

© 2001, CCH INCORPORATED. All Rights Reserved. Reprinted with permission from CCH Tax Research Network.

Service) and an annotated service *(Standard Federal Tax Reporter)*. However, unlike RIA, CCH's premier service is its annotated service. The **Standard Federal Tax Reporter** will be discussed in more detail in the Published Services section of this chapter. Since the *Federal Tax Service* is no longer available to new paper subscribers, it will not be described.

The result of the search is a document list presented in order of relevancy. Having the search results listed by type of publication, similar to the default presentation of RIA Checkpoint, is available through the "Preference" settings. The small "Preference" button is located under the CCH Tax Research NetWork logo (see Exhibit 6–11). At the top of the document list screen, CCH NetWork lists all of the terms searched, including those added by the thesaurus.

CITE AND CONTENTS SEARCHES

To search by Code section, case name, or other primary source, the researcher selects the Federal database folder on Exhibit 6–11 and the Primary Sources resource group on Exhibit 6–12. The "Citation Search" button at the top of Exhibit 6–12 is then selected. If the complete citation is known, it can be entered in proper format in the citation general box; otherwise, one of the templates supplied in Exhibit 6–13 is completed. To use the templates, however, the researcher must know the exact citation. Unlike RIA Checkpoint, names of cases may not be entered. Fortunately, if only the name of the case is known, the proper citation for a case is obtainable by selecting the "Citator" button at the top of the screen (see Exhibit 6–11).

A contents search of a database begins by clicking on the *title* of the database of interest in the listings in Exhibit 6–12. The next screen will furnish the table of contents

Exhibit 6–13
CCH Tax Research NetWork Citation Screen

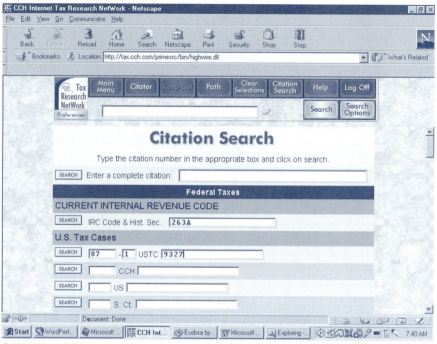

© 2001, CCH INCORPORATED. All Rights Reserved. Reprinted with permission from CCH Tax Research Network.

for the database. Continue to drill down in the same manner as in RIA Checkpoint until the documents of interest are recovered. The same documents can be located using this method as were retrieved using the keyword search. An index search is also supported by CCH NetWork. The last database listed on the Federal folder is Topical Indexes. The search is conducted by check marking this database and using a keyword search. Clicking on the Topical Index title will reveal the services contained within the Topical Index database. At this screen, the researcher can select individual services to keyword search. Rather than using keywords, the researcher can move through an index of the selected service. The statements in the RIA Checkpoint section regarding the usefulness of this method of searching apply to CCH NetWork as well.

STATE TAX SEARCH

All states impose taxes on their citizens, and the practitioner must consider the state tax implications of their clients' transactions. Each state has its own tax laws and administrative requirements that must be followed. CCH NetWork provides access to each state's tax Codes, administrative pronouncements, and court cases, depending on the subscription.

To facilitate a state search, the following simple research project will be used.

Example 6–2 The mayor and city council of a California city have contacted your firm regarding the current requirements for being designated an enterprise zone by the Trade and Commerce Agency. Specifically, the city council wants to know if their city could qualify as an "eligible area," given the changes that have occurred in recent years.

The steps in performing a State tax search are the same as in a Federal tax search. After selecting the State folder, the researcher chooses which state or states to include in the search. For this project only California is check marked in Exhibit 6–14. The keywords are entered with quotation marks to indicate that "enterprise zone" and "eligible area" are actually two phrases (see Exhibit 6–14). Running the search produces the five documents appearing in Exhibit 6–15— two are CCH explanations and three are California state laws. The CCH explanation entries provide a list of the state Code sections covered in the document. Within the documents, each state Code section reference is hyper-linked to its full text in a manner similar to the Federal folder of CCH NetWork.

KLEINROCK

Kleinrock Publishing is known for its affordable, easy-to-use **TaxExpert** CD-ROM. This service contains nearly a gigabyte of tax law sources on a single CD. Thus, not only is the TaxExpert comprehensive, it is also very portable. A student version is made available at an exceedingly reasonable price. Kleinrock has also launched an Internet service that features TaxExpert Online and supplies daily news bulletins. Lastly, Kleinrock carries Forms Library Plus. This is a complete Federal and state tax forms service (more than 30,000 pages of forms and instructions) available on one CD-ROM. These forms can be filled out on-screen and easily printed.

Upon loading the CD-ROM, the Main Menu screen appears offering Single Database Searches or Multiple Database Searches (Exhibit 6–16). Kleinrock's CD-ROM and Internet services have more than 20 databases containing editorial explanations and analysis of the tax law, primary sources, IRS pronouncements and

Exhibit 6–14
CCH Tax Research NetWork State Search Screen

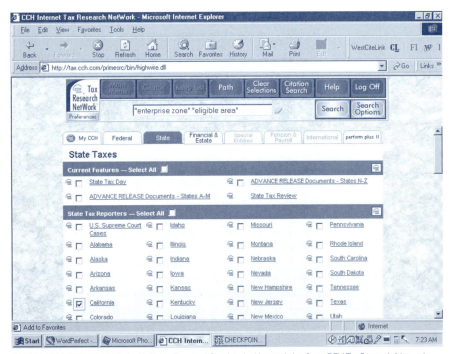

© 2001, CCH INCORPORATED. All Rights Reserved. Reprinted with permission from CCH Tax Research Network.

Exhibit 6–15
CCH Tax Research NetWork State Documents Screen

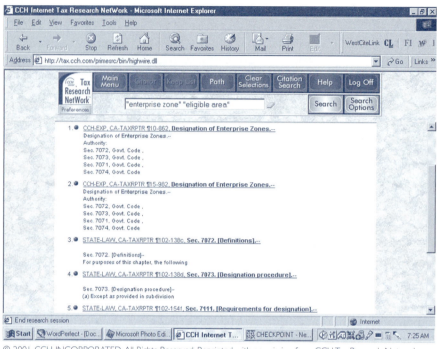

© 2001, CCH INCORPORATED. All Rights Reserved. Reprinted with permission from CCH Tax Research Network.

publications, U.S. tax treaties, and Congressional Committee Reports. A description of each database appears in the "Database Info" box when the researcher scrolls through the Single Database Search list on the CD-ROM version (Exhibit 6–16) and in the left-hand window frame of the online version (Exhibit 6–17).

Exhibit 6–16
Kleinrock CD-ROM Main Menu Screen

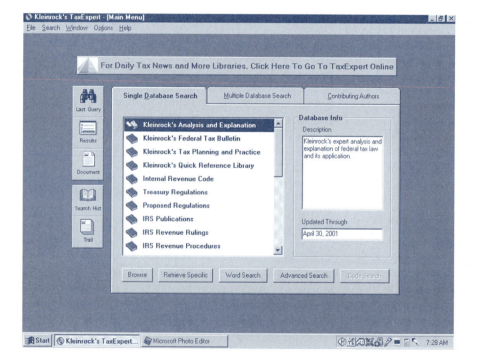

Exhibit 6–17
Kleinrock TaxExpert Online Homepage Screen

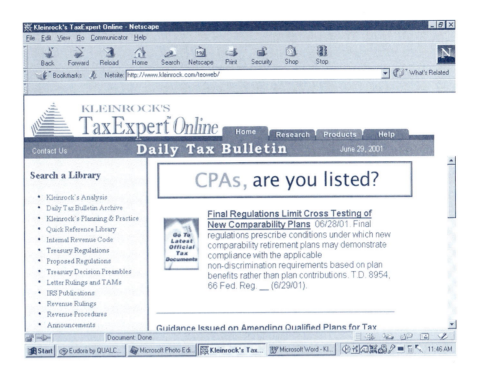

Kleinrock offers four methods for entering the database selected for the search: browse, retrieval by citation ("Retrieve Specific"), simple word search, and advance word search. Choosing the "Browse" button at the bottom of the CD-ROM screen in Exhibit 6–16, presents the table of contents for the selected database. The researcher may drill down until the topic or document of interest is located. For example, drilling through the "Analysis and Explanation" database reveals that it's structured as a topical tax service rather than an annotated service. In comparing the analysis and explanations of Kleinrock with those of RIA or CCH, Kleinrock's are reliable but less comprehensive. This should be expected because Kleinrock costs substantially less than the other two services and, when compared to RIA and CCH, Kleinrock is a relative newcomer to the analysis and explanation arena.

Returning to the CD-ROM Main Menu screen, the Multiple Database Search was chosen for the research problem in Example 6–1. The screen lists all of the possible databases available; the default setting is Select All. While the screen in the Internet version differs in appearance, it displays the same databases from which to choose. Once the databases are identified, the type of search is selected. Kleinrock supports a simple Word Search, Advanced Word Search, and a Code Search. Case name searches can be performed using the Word Search. We selected an Advanced Word Search in the Exhibit 6–18 CD-ROM screen, using "authors expenses" as the first group of keywords and "uniform capitalization" as the second set. The "and" connector was selected as the relationship between the word groups. Of the documents retrieved, three are of interest: an analysis of uniform capitalization rules, § 263A, and the *Hadley* case. Selecting the analysis document, the keywords can be located in the document by clicking on the "Query Words" button at the top of the document screen (see Exhibit 6–19).

Exhibit 6–18
Kleinrock CD-ROM
Advance Word Search
Screen

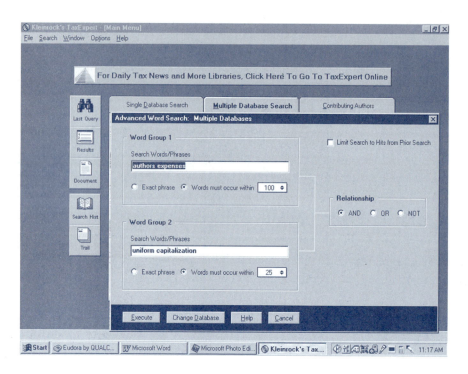

The last type of TaxExpert search allows the researcher to retrieve a specific document. This search starts at the CD-ROM Main Menu screen using the "Retrieve Specific" option. Depending on the database selected, the program provides an example of the proper format for entering the citation of the document desired. In the

Exhibit 6–19
Kleinrock CD-ROM
Document Screen

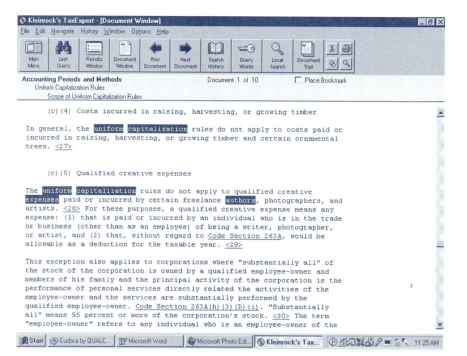

Multiple Database Search document option, the Code Search is just for locating documents containing references to a particular Code section. These searches return full-text documents. To search these documents for a discussion of the relevant terms, click on the "Local Search" button at the top of the screen in Exhibit 6–19. "Local Search" is very useful with any type of search where the researcher wants to find terms not specified in the original keywords search.

Across the top of the CD-ROM Main Menu is a button for connecting the researcher to TaxExpert Online (Exhibit 6–16) where the libraries and the daily tax news can be accessed. For those with subscriptions to the online version, clicking on one of the libraries in the left sidebar (Exhibit 6–17) will display the Main Online Search screen shown in Exhibit 6–20. This screen's appearance is very different from the CD-ROM Main Menu of Exhibit 6–16. "Step 1" lists the databases for a single database search as does the first tab in the CD-ROM version. "Step 2" provides for three of the possible search methods: simple word search, browse, or retrieval by citation. As with the CD-ROM, the program gives an example of the proper format for entering a citation depending on the database selected. The advanced search and multiple database search are available by clicking on "go" in the "Advanced Search" box. Using the Main Search screen of the online service reduces the buttons that must be selected and the boxes that need to be opened, thus simplifing the search process.

Although Kleinrock does not provide the extensive libraries and editorial explanations of CCH or RIA, it is easy to use and very affordable. It is a good choice in those situations where the practitioner is familiar with the tax topic and is looking for the authoritative sources to back up his or her conclusions. The CD-ROM is very popular with practitioners who want access to primary sources without having to open a book or connect to the World Wide Web.

Exhibit 6–20
Kleinrock Online Main Search Screen

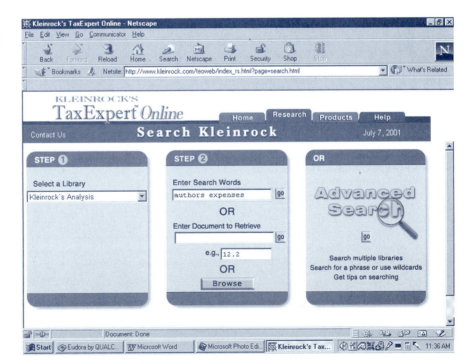

PUBLISHED SERVICES

As previously mentioned, there are two types of published tax services: Annotated, whose organization is based on the *Internal Revenue Code*, and Topical which is organized by transactions or related subject matter. Most, if not all, of these published tax services are available through electronic means. These services may be offered with other resources, such as tax journals, citators, and case law, at a lower bundled price, making the electronic versions an attractive choice. Consequently, paper services are disappearing from accounting offices and college libraries. It is increasingly difficult to justify having two versions of the same services when (1) the online and web-based services are updated daily, (2) they are accessible 24 hours a day from any location with a computer, and (3) they are offered at a lower price.

ANNOTATED SERVICES

There are two major published annotated tax services: the CCH *Standard Federal Tax Reporter* (CCH) and the *United States Tax Reporter* (RIA). The volumes of these services are called Compilations because they compile an editor's explanation and evaluation with the Code section, its recent committee reports, Regulations, and annotations of related court cases and administrative rulings. CCH also includes as part of its service two separate volumes containing the *Internal Revenue Code* and a two-volume citator series. While RIA also includes a two-volume *Internal Revenue Code*, its multi-volume citator series is available as a separate service.

ENTERING COMPILATION VOLUMES

Finding the relevant material needed to resolve a tax question is the key to tax research. How the Compilation volumes are entered will determine how quickly and efficiently the pertinent materials are found. Research in annotated services often follows the sequence enumerated in Exhibit 6–21. The Compilation volumes lead the researcher to primary sources of the tax law. The Code sections and Regulations are reproduced in full text in the Compilations, whereas cases and rulings are annotated in summary form. The full text of cases and rulings (other than those issued in

Exhibit 6–21 Using the Compilations Effectively

1. Efficiently enter the Compilation volumes and locate paragraphs that may be appropriate.
2. Skim the material, identifying the most pertinent elements of the primary tax law for the research.
3. Carefully read the paragraphs that apply directly to the research.
4. Find and analyze the relevant update materials and Citator materials.
5. Find and read all the primary materials (Code, Regulations, court cases, rulings, etc.) identified by the research.

the current period) will be found in the court case reporter series, the *Cumulative Bulletins,* or a Private Letter Ruling collection. The current year cases and rulings are generally provided as part of the tax service. The researcher should consult a citator to evaluate the status and value as precedent of the court cases or rulings relevant to the tax problem. Finally, quality research is not completed until the latest developments in the identified areas of the law have been assessed.

The tax services should efficiently direct the researcher to the controlling primary sources of the tax law. It is the professional duty of the researcher to undertake an evaluation of such sources. Exhibit 6–22 summarizes the three major methods of finding materials in the compilations: by keyword, Code section, and case name. How to use each method will be explored using the illustrative research project provided in Example 6–1. Using this example will facilitate comparisons of the published services with their electronic counterparts. The CCH *Standard Federal Tax Reporter* will serve as the primary service for this section. In those situations where the services differ, both RIA and CCH services will be presented to aid in comparison of the two services.

Exhibit 6–22 Accessing the Compilation volumes

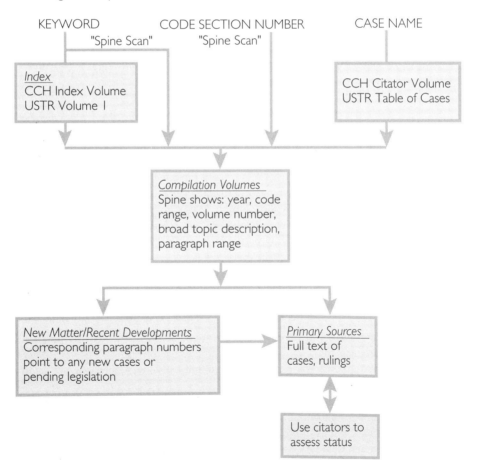

Keyword Search

The Compilation volumes of an annotated service can always be entered by Code section number, because the section numbers are printed on the spines of the volumes. However, if the tax topic is narrow or unfamiliar to the researcher, it usually is more efficient to begin directly with a keyword search in the service's Topic Index.

The list of keywords selected for a search in published services may differ from those chosen for an electronic keyword search. The main reason for this difference is the search method employed by each service. The meaning and context of the keywords will be relevant in the paper service index search. However, the researcher has to anticipate how the index creator categorizes and list the topics. Therefore, a variety of terms that are directly related to the tax question should be considered. This will increase the odds of finding the most relevant material related to the tax issue. Nevertheless, the selection should be limited to insure that the search does not become inefficient. For the tax research project in Example 6–1, the keywords chosen are "authors" "business expense" and "uniform capitalization rules." The term "prepublication" was not selected because it appears to be (and in fact is) too narrow.

The CCH Index provides great variety and specificity of keyword entries, thus using the index often requires significant research time. However, time spent in a thorough examination of the index to identify all pertinent material will pay off once the researcher moves into the Compilation volumes. To avoid false starts, **New Matters Index,** (**Recent Developments Index,** in RIA) should always be checked before investing a substantial amount of time on a specific research path. This will ensure that the information found in the Compilations is read in light of any recent changes in the tax law.

Using the excerpts in Exhibit 6–23, the CCH Index provides paragraph references for "expenses" and "uniform capitalization rules" as subheadings under "Authors." The heading "Business Expenses," had a subheading for "authors" which referenced the same paragraph as for "expenses" under "Authors." Since it provides no additional information, it is not included in the list. The "Uniform Capitalization Rules" heading also has a subheading for "authors" that references one of the paragraphs listed under the heading "Authors." In browsing through the other Uniform Capitalization Rules subheadings, we find the "creative property" entry that references some promising paragraphs (see Exhibit 6–23). This ability to browse is one of the advantages of the paper services.

In the edited RIA Index in Exhibit 6–24, the heading "Authors" also lists "expenses, story preparation" and "uniform capitalization rules" as subheadings. The general entry "Business Expenses" provides no direct reference that would apply to the facts in our research case. Lastly, the "Uniform Capitalization Rules" heading directs us to look under "Capitalization" where we find a listing for "authors." The differences in the keywords furnishing useful references in CCH versus RIA illustrates the need for the researcher to identify a variety of words descriptive of the topic being searched.

The paragraphs identified by the above keyword searches are similar to the paragraph numbers of the documents found using the Internet versions of these two services. For example, the Internet CCH search found an annotation discussing "author prepublication expenses" at ¶ 8521.1094, whereas the paper version leads to the annotation at ¶ 8521.1091 for "author expenses." These are close but not the same.

Exhibit 6–23 CCH Index Entries

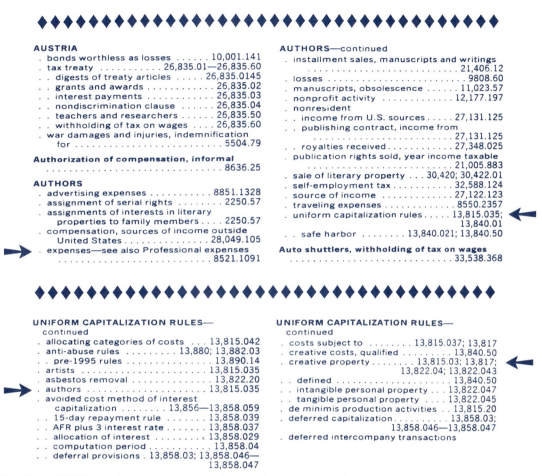

© 2001, CCH INCORPORATED. All Rights Reserved. Reprinted with permission from CCH *Standard Federal Tax Reporter*.

Upon examining the published list of annotations associated with ¶ 8521 reproduced in Exhibit 6–25, entries for both of these paragraphs are found. Also notice that within the CCH Explanation at the top of Exhibit 6–25, ¶ .05 addresses the production of creative property issue. This explanation was not identified by either of the keyword searches. This again demonstrates the advantage of being able to flip through the pages of a paper service.

After reading the explanations and annotations (step 3 in Exhibit 6–21) but before undertaking a thorough analysis of the primary sources (step 5 in Exhibit 6–21), the applicable updating materials should be examined. For CCH, the current citations are included in its New Matters volume (Exhibit 6–26) and for RIA they are in the Recent Developments volume (Exhibit 6–27). The CCH service contains two Cross Reference Tables, the Cumulative Index, and the Latest Additions to the Cumulative Index, whereas RIA has a single table. These tables use the Compilation paragraph

Exhibit 6–24 RIA Index Entries

Attorneys—Automobile   Capital—Capitalization

◆◆◆◆◆◆◆◆◆◆◆◆◆◆◆◆◆◆◆◆◆◆◆◆◆◆◆◆◆◆◆◆◆◆◆◆◆

Authors
- capital gains and losses . . . . . . **12,210(§1221);** *12,212;* 12,214.45; 12,215.45(5); **12,310(§1231);** *12,312*
- ➤ expenses, story preparation 1625.200
- income earned abroad by U.S. citizen, exclusion . . . . 9115.06(45)
- nonresident aliens (See Nonresident aliens, subhead authors)
- royalties (See Royalties, subhead authors)
- trade or business with U.S. . . . . . 8645.01(45)
- uniform capitalization rules . . . **263A0(§263A);** 263A4.02; 263A4.13; 263A5.01(45)
- withholding on . . . . 34,014.51; 34,015.51(70)

Capitalization (See also Capital expenditures)
—Cont'd
- uniform (UNICAP) . . . . **263A0(§363A)**
- . . additional costs 263A4.04
- . . allocation of costs 263A4.06
- . . . pre-1994 rules 263A4.165
- . . ancillary land development costs . . . . 263A5.02(5)
- . . anti-abuse rules 263A4.12
- . . artists . . . *163A2.01;* **263A0(§263A);** 263A4: 263A4.13; 263A5.01(45)
- . . authors . . . . **263A0(§263A);** *263A2.01;* *263A2.03;* 263A4.02; 263A4.13; 263A5.01(45) ⬅

and subparagraph numbers as links to the current materials. The CCH Compilation paragraphs are listed in numerical order in the left column and the paragraphs in which the new developments appear are in the right column. The Code sections are listed in the middle as heading for the listings. These Code headings permit researchers to review new developments in areas of interest without knowing paragraph cites. Researchers may also locate recent developments by checking the current materials topical indexes for relevant references. For our research project, we find no entries with respect to the pertinent paragraphs. Thus, we can assume, for the moment, that there are no new developments affecting our research. Accordingly, we turn to the primary sources to finish our research.

CODE SECTION SEARCH

Frequently, seasoned tax researchers will know the Code sections that apply to a client's tax question. They can find the appropriate Compilation material simply by using the Code section numbers printed on the spines of the Compilation binders. Since Regulation numbers correspond to their controlling Code sections, a Regulation can also lead directly into the appropriate Compilation materials. The Code and Regulation section numbers are also displayed prominently on the Compilation pages as Exhibit 6–25 demonstrates.

Another method of entering the Compilations is through a **spine scan**—scanning the volume contents listed on the spines of the service's binders. The broadest term on our keyword list for the Example 6–1 tax question, "business expenses" ("business deductions"), appears on the spines of both CCH and RIA volumes as a major division heading. Additionally, "capitalization" appears on the CCH volume containing § 263A.

After opening a binder, the researcher will notice the tab guides that delineate the major divisions of the volume. The Table of Contents found immediately after each tab guide furnishes a good overview of the Compilation paragraphs that follow. Further, it can lead the researcher to relevant Compilation materials.

Exhibit 6-25 CCH Annotation Entries

TRADE OR BUSINESS EXPENSES— § 162 [¶ 8500]   **21,933**

What Is a "Business"?

● ● *CCH Explanation*

with the property may be deductible under Code Sec. 212 as expenses incurred for the production or collection of income (see ¶ 12,523.361 et seq.). Rules applicable to the allowance of deductions for business use of homes and vacation homes are discussed at ¶ 14,854 et seq. As to the deductibility of a loss incurred on the sale of a residence that has been converted from personal use, see ¶ 10,103.352.

➡ **.05 Production of creative property.**—The uniform capitalization rules are applicable to the costs of producing tangible personal property, including films, sound recordings, video tapes, books and other similar property embodying words, ideas, concepts, images or sounds of the creator (Code Sec. 263A and ¶ 13,822.045). For example, the term tangible personal property specifically includes the costs of producing and developing books (Reg. § 1.263A-2(a)(2)(ii)).

Artistic entrepreneurs. As a general rule, a taxpayer engaged in the trade or business of being an artist, author or other artistic entrepreneur can deduct ordinary and necessary business expenses under Code Sec. 162 despite the uniform capitalization rules. An exception from the uniform capitalization rules exist for the qualified creative expenses of free-lance artists, authors and photographers or for the expenses of the corporation that they own (Code Sec. 263A(h)). It should be noted that when determining if the exception applies, i.e. whether the expense is paid or incurred in the business of being an artist, the originality and uniqueness of the item created is considered (Code Sec. 263A(h)(3)(C)(ii)). See ¶ 13,840.—CCH.

● ● ● *Annotations by Topic*

Airplane operation .1084	Household, running of .125
Artists and authors:	Illegal activities:
Actor .1085	Abortionist .1255
Artist .109	Arsonist .1257
➡ Author .1091	Bookmakers .1260
Entertainer .1092	Embezzlement .1262
Photographers .1093	Liquor sales .1264
➡ Prepublication expenses .1094	Lottery .1265
Screenwriter .1095	Numbers game .1266
Automobile racing .1101	Organized crime .1267
Bicycle racing .1102	Poker club .1268
Blood, selling of .1103	Protection .1269
Cable tv .1349	Income-producing property (reference to ¶ 12,523.01)
Campaigning for public office (reference to ¶ 8952.3555)	Insurance agent .128
Casual sales .112	Investors, relationship to business .1285
Computer software development .1122	Law student .1295
Computer use at home .1123	Lawyer .13
Consignee .1124	Limited partnerships .1344
Consultant .1125	Logging .131
Corporate officer/director .1126	Museum .1312
Designer .1201	Musician .1313
Distributorship .1205	Nurse .1314
Employees' expenses (reference to ¶ 8524.01)	Oil exploration .1315
Employee's side business .1207	Organizers .1319
Evidence .1209	Partnership payments after liquidation .132
Expansion costs .1333	Pre-opening/start-up expenses distinguished (reference to ¶ 12,371 et seq.)
Fiduciaries (nonprofessionals) .121	Public official .1334
Fishing boats .122	Radio time .1345
Gambling .123	Real estate:
Golf .124	Change in purpose for which property held .1355
Hobby of shareholder .1242	Commissions on real estate sales .1357
Hobby v. business (reference to ¶ 12,177)	
Horse racing .1245	

2001(3) CCH—Standard Federal Tax Reports   **Reg. § 1.162-1(b)(8) ¶ 8521.05**

© 2001, CCH INCORPORATED. All Rights Reserved. Reprinted with permission from CCH *Standard Federal Tax Reporter.*

Exhibit 6–26 CCH New Matters Entries

18 4-12-2001

Cumulative Index to 2001 Developments
(For Reports 1-18)
(See also Cumulative Index at page 75,251.)

| From Compilation Paragraph No. | | To New Development Paragraph No. |

◆◆◆

	.74	*Tarakci*, TCM—Regular telephone and cellular phone charges ordinary and necessary; deduction allowed 47,719
	.7636	Alaska Native Corporation not entitled to deduct repayment of tax-share—Letter Ruling 47,461
➤ 8521	.1084	Deduction, capitalization of aircraft airframe maintenance costs discussed; Rev. Proc. 99-49 modified—Rev. Rul. 46,218
	.1209	*Hunter* aff'd, CA-2 (¶50,098)—Transportation costs to and from libraries not incurred in connection with trade or business. Taxpayer on appeal to CA-2.
	.1209	*Sheehy* aff'd, CA-9 (unpub. op.)—Research and development expenses not deductible absent proof of business purpose 49,935
	.1475	*Ball*, TCM—Business deductions denied absent showing of trade or business 47,612
	.39	*Kurzet* aff'd, rev'd and rem'd, CA-10—On another issue 49,923
8522	.384	*Neonatology Associates, P.A.*, TC—Excess contributions to insurance plans not compensation to employees 47,601
	.386	Guidance on split-dollar arrangements issued; Rev. Rul. 55-747 revoked; Rev. Ruls. 64-328 and 66-110 modified—Notice 46,247
	.386	*Neonatology Associates, P.A.*, TC—Contributions to insurance plans established under sham VEBAs not deductible 47,601
	.3945	Corrections issued to Rev. Proc. 2001-3—Announcement 46,358
	.3945	Rev. Proc. 2000-3 amplified—Rev. Proc. 46,045
	.3945	Rev. Proc. 2000-3 superseded—Rev. Proc. 46,240
8523	.273	*Campbell*, TCM—Unsubstantiated business expense deductions denied 47,887

～～～～～～～～～～～

26 6-7-2001

Latest Additions to Cumulative Index to 2001 Developments
(For Reports 19-26)
(See also Cumulative Index at page 75,301.)

| From Compilation Paragraph No. | | To New Development Paragraph No. |

◆◆◆

Code Sec. 162—Trade or business expenses

8520	.028	Tax Court rejects capitalization of federal bank fees—Comment 48,716B
	.1521	Coporation had to capitalize fees to acquire loans—Letter Ruling 47,467
	.52	Expenses of trader partnership treated as trade or business expenses by partner—Letter Ruling 47,481
	.586	*Kudo* aff'd, CA-9 (unpub. op.)—On another issue 50,393
	.591	*Schachter* aff'd, CA-9 (unpub. op.)—Additional trade or business expenses denied 50,336
	.653	*Consolidated Manufacturing, Inc.* aff'd, rev'd and rem'd, CA-10—On another issue 50,400
➤ 8521	.26	*Martens* modified, aff'd *per curiam*, CA-5—Amounts loaned by shareholder to store not deductible 50,416
8522	.3945	Rev. Proc. 2001-3 modified—Rev. Proc. 46,414
	.3945	Rev. Proc. 2001-30 modified—Rev. Proc. 46,436
8524	.265	*Popov* aff'd, rev'd and rem'd, CA-9—On another issue 50,353
8526	.41	*Metrocorp, Inc.*, TC—Fees incurred in FDIC fund conversion currently deductible to acquiring bank 47,934
	.4234	*Metrocorp, Inc.*, TC—Fees incurred in FDIC fund conversion currently deductible to acquiring bank 47,934
	.4321	*Brincat*, TCM—Attorney's fees not deductible absent proof third-party's payments were on his behalf 47,976
8550	.255	*Popov* aff'd, rev'd and rem'd, CA-9—On another issue 50,353
	.269	Rev. Proc. 2001-3 modified—Rev. Proc. 46,414
	.269	Rev. Proc. 2001-30 modified—Rev. Proc. 46,436
8570	.146	Rev. Proc. 2001-3 modified—Rev. Proc. 46,414

Standard Federal Tax Reports   ¶ **8570**

© 2001, CCH INCORPORATED. All Rights Reserved. Reprinted with permission from CCH *Standard Federal Tax Reporter*.

Exhibit 6-27 RIA Recent Developments Entries

Cross Reference Table

From ¶	To ¶/page	Listed in Code Section Order
	IRC §220	**Retirement Savings (IRAs) for Certain Married Individuals—Prior Law**
2204.02	86,120	MSA changes highlighted. Adv Announc 2001-21
	IRC §263A	**Capitalization Rules for Inventory Costs**
➤ 263A5.01(17)	2001-2031	*Pelaez & Sons Inc aff:* Without discussion. CA
	IRC §274	**Disallowance of Certain Entertainment, Gift and Travel Expenses**
2745.01(10)	17.5	*Bishop:* Financial planner's unsubstantiated deduction claims. TCMem

Code Volumes

The *Internal Revenue Code* language appears twice in both the CCH and RIA services. It is reproduced in the Compilation volumes and again in its basic form in the separate Code volumes. These separate volumes allow the researcher to examine the Code itself more quickly than is possible in the lengthier Compilation materials.

The Code volumes support reference and cross-section functions. In addition, the volumes include historical notes that help trace the evolutionary development of the Code. They also contain cross-reference tables that facilitate the matching of current Code section numbers to their 1939 Code counterparts.

The Code volumes for both services include a topical index and a listing of tax legislation that has amended the Code. In its Code Volume II, the CCH service also reproduces portions of selected laws that are not part of the *Internal Revenue Code* but might have an incidental effect on tax liabilities. For instance, Code sections that address estate/gift taxes and Federal excise taxes also are included in the services' Code volumes, but are not in the Compilations. Both publishers sell estate/gift and excise tax services separately from their standard annotated income tax services.

CASE NAME SEARCH

The last method of entering the Compilation material is through a case name. Recall from Example 6-1 that the *Hadley* case was related to our research. Case names and IRS rulings often provide effective means of accessing compilation materials.

The CCH *Citator* is included as part of the *Standard Federal Tax Reporter* service. The citations in this service are listed alphabetically by case name. In addition to formal citations, the Compilation paragraph numbers where the case is annotated or cited are also given. The Exhibit 6-28 excerpt from the CCH *Citator* indicates that the *Arthur Hadley* case is referred to in ¶ 8521.1091. A decimal point in a CCH citation indicates that the reference is to an annotation paragraph in the

Exhibit 6–28 CCH Citator Entries

HAD	94,030	————CCH————

Haddock, Morris W. . . . . ¶12,177.751
   ● TC—Dec. 43,396(M); 52 TCM 638; TC Memo.
      1986-476
   Schell, TC, Dec. 49,789(M), 67 TCM 2692, TC
      Memo. 1994-164
Haddon, Mark R. . . . . ¶39,475.61, 39,560.34,
      39,651G.305
   ● TC—Dec. 48,808(M); 65 TCM 1714; TC Memo.
      1993-7
Haden Co. (See Trust Co. of Texas)
Haden Co. . . . . ¶5802.282
   ● SCt—Cert. denied, 314 US 622; 62 SCt 73
   CA-5—(aff'g BTA), 41-1 USTC ¶9331; 118 F2d 285
   Stackhouse, CA-5, 71-1 USTC ¶9352, 441 F2d 465
   DeFelice, CA-10, 67-2 USTC ¶9748, 386 F2d 704
   Killian Co., CA-8, 42-2 USTC ¶9487, 128 F2d 433
   Carroll-McCreary Co., Inc., CA-2, 42-1 USTC ¶9183,
      124 F2d 303
   DeFelice, TC, Dec. 28,030(M), 25 TCM 835, TC
      Memo. 1966-158
   ● BTA—Dec. 10,855-D; October 20, 1939

Haden, William F. . . . . ¶39,475.61
   ● TC—Dec. 43,481(M); 52 TCM 986; TC Memo.
      1986-539
   Befumo, TC, Dec. 47,680(M), 62 TCM 975, TC
      Memo. 1991-509
Haderlie, Verl W. . . . . ¶5901.47, 5901.50
   ● TC—Dec. 52,366(M); 74 TCM 1254; TC Memo.
      1997-525
   Sutter, TC, Dec. 52,784(M), 76 TCM 59, TC Memo.
      1998-250
Hadley, Arthur T. ¶8521.1091 ⬅
   ● CA-2—(rev'g TC), 87-1 USTC ¶9327; 819 F2d 359
   Keating, TC, Dec. 50,513(M), 69 TCM 2052, TC
      Memo. 1995-101
   Doubleday & Co., Inc., DC-NY, 89-2 USTC ¶9549,
      721 FSupp 436
   ● TC—Dec. 43,026(M); 51 TCM 948; TC Memo.
      1986-173
   Miller, David B., TC, Dec. 44,520(M), 54 TCM 1517,
      TC Memo. 1988-15
Hadley, Ben F. (See Thomas, Oscar L.)

© 2001, CCH INCORPORATED. All Rights Reserved. Reprinted with permission from CCH *Standard Federal Tax Reporter*.

Compilation. This is the same annotation paragraph identified by the keyword search using the terms "Authors, expenses" (see Exhibit 6–23).

Since RIA does not include its multi-volume citator as part of its *United States Tax Reporter* service, it furnishes a tax case **Finding List** in Volume 2. The Finding List arranges the court cases alphabetically and provides the Compilation paragraphs in which the cases are discussed. It also gives the reporter location where the full text of the case may be found (see Exhibit 6–29). A supplemental table of recent cases precedes the main table of cases. Keep in mind that the Finding List cannot function as a citator. It provides neither a detailed judicial history of the case nor a list of other cases in which the case is cited. It merely serves as an entry to the Compilations.

OTHER PATHWAYS INTO THE COMPILATIONS

Both of the annotated tax services provide a series of helpful finding lists. Each has finding list tables that correlate Regulations, Revenue Rulings, Treasury Decisions, Private Letter Rulings, and other references to the Compilation paragraphs. The CCH Finding Lists are located in the *Citator* Volume M–Z. The RIA ruling Finding Lists are in Volume 2 along with the case Finding List.

The CCH Revenue Ruling Finding List not only leads to the applicable Compilation paragraphs, but it also shows the history of the ruling and gives citations for

Exhibit 6–29 RIA Finding List Entries

MAIN TABLE OF CASES	HAGEMEYER

Haden, W. D., Est., *43,493 ..12,215.41(45)
Haden, W. D., Est., *53,250 ..12,215.37(15);
   12,215.41(10); 12,215.41(75); 79,007.56
Haden, W. D., Est.; Comm. v, (1955, CA5) 48
   AFTR 1831, 55-2 USTC ¶9639 ..12,215.37(15);
   12,215.41(10); 12,215.41(75); 79,007.56
Haden, William F., *86,539 ..66,515.03(22);
   66,535.02(5); 66,535.04(15)
➡ Hadley, Arthur T., *86,173 ..2635.07(35)
Hadley, Arthur T. v Comm., (1987, CA2) 59
   AFTR 2d 87-1078, 819 F2d 359, 87-1 USTC ¶9327
   ..2635.07(35)
Hadley, Ben F. (See Thomas, Oscar L.)

Hafner, John L., Tr. (See Fletcher, J. Gilmore, Tr.)
Hafner v U.S. (See Fletcher v U.S.)
Haft, Al, Sport Enterprises, Inc., *49,202
   ..1625.262(5)
Haft, Al, Sport Enterprises, Inc. v Comm.,
   (1951, CA6) 40 AFTR 709, 189 F2d 384, 51-1
   USTC ¶9292 ..1625.262(5); 66,515.08(30)
Haft, Alfred Lewis, (See Haft, Joyce T.)
Haft, Charles M., (1930) 20 BTA 431
   ..1655.025(10)
Haft, Harold, (1963) 40 TC 2 (A, 1967-2 CB 2) ..
   1625.007(95); 79,007.70(10)

court cases and other rulings that have cited it. Thus, it performs many of the same functions as the Revenue Rulings section of the RIA *Citator* (see Chapter 8 for a full discussion). The selections from the CCH Finding List reproduced in Exhibit 6–30 demonstrate a search chain, starting with a 1974 Revenue Ruling. The columns are displayed together here for the illustration. Each column is actually found on a different page in the CCH Revenue Ruling Finding List.

It is apparent from our review of the CCH and RIA Compilations that they include an immense amount of information useful to a tax researcher. Thus, it is important that the practitioner become familiar with the manner in which the services are organized and also be comfortable with the terminology employed by these services.

CCH ANNOTATED SERVICE

The CCH *Standard Federal Tax Reporter* is a multi-volume service whose binders are replaced each year. Each compilation volume is organized into several divisions with tab guides separating each division. As previously mentioned, at the beginning of each division is a summary paragraph, a table of contents for the division, and an overview commentary. The full text of each Code section is reproduced, usually followed by historical notes concerning its legislative evolution. Typically, this notation includes the relevant portion of Committee Reports from recent bills and citations for older underlying Committee Reports.

Exhibit 6–30 CCH Revenue Ruling Finding List Entries

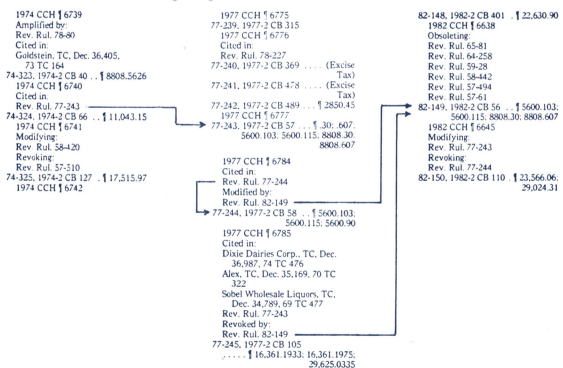

© 2001, CCH INCORPORATED. All Rights Reserved. Reprinted with permission from CCH *Standard Federal Tax Reporter*.

Following the Code section materials are the related final and temporary Regulations reproduced in full text. Proposed Regulations and proposed amendments to the existing Regulations are next. For each Code section and many of the Regulations, the CCH editors write easy-to-read explanations and analyses of the law. Lastly, annotations of court cases and rulings are reported by topic. The annotations can be voluminous because of numerous cases and rulings addressing an area of the law. Therefore, a detailed alphabetical index organizes the annotation entries. As can be seen in Exhibit 6–31, each of the components of the Compilation has a distinctive format for ease of recognition.

Exhibit 6–31 CCH *Standard Federal Tax Reporter* Format

—'86 Code—

Each Code section is reproduced in full and flagged as shown in the left margin. "Historical Notes" indicate whether there has been any amendment since 1954 and cite the location of other pertinent information such as Committee Reports. Code sections are always kept up-to-date. Amendments and changes are published promptly, and new pages are included in current Reports for insertion in the Compilations.

● *Regulations*

This "catch-line" always introduces Regulations. The full texts of all final and temporary Regulations follow the Code sections they construe. The Regulations are printed in larger type across the full width of the page.

> Full text Regulations standing in *proposed* form and *proposed amendments* to existing Regulations are reported in place in the Compilations, following the Code section they are intended to construe. Their unique presentation within boxes alerts readers to their status as proposals and to their relationship to existing Regulations.

Committee reports.—In the absence of Regulations, as in the case of recent legislation, controlling Committee Reports are frequently reproduced to indicate legislative intent. Code Section 195, located in Volume 4, is followed by Committee Reports. Note that Committee Reports are printed in double column format.

● ● *CCH Explanation*

> These editorial comments are set in larger type. They have their own "catch-line" and are enclosed within boxes to distinguish them from official contents. CCH Explanations lead into the digests of decisions and rulings, supply refinements of interpretation, and point out trends or conflicts among authorities.

● ● ● *Annotations by Topic*

Digests of decisions and rulings, called "annotations," are arranged by topic under the Code section and Regulations construed. Each large group of digests is preceded by a table indexing the annotations alphabetically.

The "catch-line" is centered. Annotations are arranged in double column format. The case name or ruling number, as well as the citation to the full text, is noted under each digest.

The numbers at the top and bottom of the Compilation page have a specific meaning. The top line of the page includes a centered heading with the Code section and the beginning Compilation paragraph number plus the page number. The page number is generally used only for filing the weekly updates in the loose-leaf binders. The bottom of the page shows the ending page Compilation paragraph number at the lower outside corner. Just inside the paragraph number is the Code or Regulation section that is the subject of the page. These features can be viewed in Exhibit 6–25.

RIA COMPILATIONS

While the RIA *United States Tax Reporter* is similar to the CCH *Standard Federal Tax Reporter* in many aspects, it does have some special features that deserve comment. RIA Compilations have a unique and functional paragraph numbering system. Code section numbers are incorporated into the paragraph numbers. Thus, paragraphs pertaining to a Code section will start with its section number. A single digit is added to the end of the Code section number, designating the nature of the material contained in the paragraph. Exhibit 6–32 summarizes the coding system employed by RIA, using IRC § 162 as an example. Reversing CCH, RIA paragraph numbers appear at the top of the Compilation pages with page numbers at the bottom.

TOPICAL SERVICES

Unlike the annotated tax services, topical tax services organize the tax law by subject matter or transactions; therefore, materials are presented together that are found in various nonadjacent Code sections. Hence, a topical tax service can be efficient in meeting the needs of the researcher in a typical client project. For example, a

Exhibit 6–32 RIA *United States Tax Reporter* Compilation Numbering System for § 162

Appending Digit	Type of Material	Comments	Example
0	Text of Code		1620
1	Committee Reports		1621
2	Regulations	Final and Temporary	1622
3	Proposed Regulations		1623
4	Explanations	RIA editorial commentary	1624
5	Annotations	Specific cases and rulings	1625
6	Procedural matters	Tax Court procedural material	1626
7	Miscellaneous items		1627
8	Prior law	Only if it is still relevant to some taxpayers	1628
9	Crossovers	Cross-reference materials to other Code sections	1629

client might need help with issues concerning shifting income among related taxpayers. The applicable law might include provisions relating to short-term trusts, low-interest loans, investments in taxable and tax exempt bonds or mutual funds, and life insurance. The annotated services would present this material by Code section number, making it more difficult for a practitioner to assemble an integrated picture of the many effects that the assignment-of-income doctrine might have in the client's situation. The topical tax service, on the other hand, would have a section that includes a discussion of provisions relating to general types of transactions, with analysis, suggested transaction structures, issues to consider, and problems to avoid.

NATURE OF TOPICAL TAX SERVICES

A topical approach to the tax law functionally integrates related Code sections and other primary and secondary sources of the Federal tax law, including court cases, administrative pronouncements, and general editorial commentary. The strength of topical services is their organization of materials into commonly encountered taxable events or types of transactions. However, like the Code, a topical service may incompletely address transactions that don't neatly fit into its organizational pattern. The editors of topical services cannot possibly address all of the tax ramifications of every type of transaction.

The various topical published tax services differ in their organization and the type of analysis they emphasize. If the organization of a given topical service suits a client's fact situation, the use of the service can be very effective. If not, using the service may be quite inefficient. Thus it is important, more so than is the case with an annotated service, to choose the right topical service for the specific research project or to use several services for different aspects of the same project.

Topical tax services typically have a variety of indexes and finding lists for their analytical materials, including keyword (topic), Code section, Regulations, rulings and administrative releases, and court case names. These indexes often parallel those available in annotated services. Also, like the annotated services, the topical services print the titles of their major divisions on the spines of the volume binders. The topical services are distinguished from each other chiefly by the structure of their material, not the structure of their indexes.

The following is a selective list of the titles of the more commonly used topical tax services.

Research Institute of America's *Federal Tax Coordinator 2d (Coordinator)*
Research Institute of America's *Analysis of Federal Taxes: Income (Analysis)*
Bureau of National Affairs' *Tax Management Portfolios (BNA Portfolios)*
Warren, Gorham & Lamont's *Federal Taxation of Income, Estates, and Gifts (Bittker & Lokken)*
West Group's *Mertens Law of Federal Income Taxation (Mertens)*

Survey the libraries you frequently use for research to determine which of these services are available for your use. The RIA *Coordinator* and *Analysis* are tax services and will be covered in this chapter. The *BNA Portfolios*, *Bittker & Lokken*, and *Mertens* are considered more legalistic and will be covered in Chapter 7.

As with the annotated services, we will use the authors prepublication expenses of Example 6–1 to learn how to conduct research with a topical tax service. Remember, it is important that you go to the library and follow the research steps outlined in this section. The illustrations are not substitutes for actually using the services.

RIA COORDINATOR AND ANALYSIS

The RIA *Federal Tax Coordinator 2d* is among the most comprehensive of the topical tax services. It divides the analysis of Federal income, gift, estate, and excise taxes into twenty-three chapters, designated by capital letters (A through W), contained in loose-leaf binders that are updated weekly. The RIA *Analysis of Federal Taxes: Income* is a condensed version of the *Coordinator* and covers only income tax issues. It is a more affordable option for the practitioners with a general tax practice.

For many researchers, the RIA services are an appropriate tool for commencing a tax research project. One of their strong points, particularly for researchers who have little experience in a specific subject area, is its general background discussions summarizing the major issues. Another valuable RIA feature is the hierarchical and distributed table of contents system. The titles for RIA's chapters are found on a table of contents page located at the front of every volume. At the beginning of each RIA chapter, a table of topics (Broad Reference Table) indicates, by paragraph number, the tax provisions that are discussed in that chapter. The Detailed Reference Table that follows gives greater detail of the chapter's contents. In these tables researchers can quickly scan the outline of topics to identify the paragraphs that are most germane to their research task. Finally, before the tax law analysis paragraphs are presented, a Treated Elsewhere Table alerts the researcher to other chapters and paragraphs of the service where related data can be found.

The RIA topical services can also be entered by the three major methods outlined for the annotated services: keywords, Code section, or case name. A spine scan using broad topics printed on the spines of the binders is also an option. Exhibit 6–33 reproduces edited sections of the Topic Index and Finding List for the Code. Notice that for our illustrative research, we can enter the topical service using the same key terms we used earlier, "authors, uniform capitalization rules."

As Exhibit 6–34 demonstrates, the RIA coverage of a tax topic consists of editorial explanations and analysis of the tax issues. Note that the primary sources are integrated into its explanation. This integration helps the researcher comprehend the interplay among the various primary sources and their relationship to the tax question. Besides primary sources, secondary law sources and citations to other paragraphs in the service are footnotes throughout the explanation. The researcher should always confirm the editorial explanations by reviewing the primary sources cited. The portions of the Code and Regulations relevant to the chapter topics are reproduced in an appendix following the chapter. Each Code section is followed by a history of its amendments in reverse chronological order. Lastly, RIA includes in its analysis in-text editorial comments. Such highlights are strictly observations by the editors and are not legal authority. Editorial comments are indicated with the special check-mark symbol. Exhibit 6–35 lists the four types of editorial comments found in the RIA services.

Exhibit 6-33 RIA Topic Index and Code Finding List

Main Topic Index		Internal Revenue Code Table	
Authors		Code Sec.	Discussed at ¶
→ . creative expenses and uniform capitalization rules	G-5800 et seq.	263(g)(2)	L-5986
→ . expenses	L-4110	263(g)(3)	L-5985
. identification numbers	S-1565	263(g)(4)(A)	L-5988
. nonresident aliens		263(g)(4)(B)	L-5988
.. compensation subject to 30 percent tax	O-10239	263(h)(1)	L-4224, P-5027
.. personal services as U.S. business	O-10502	263(h)(2)	L-4224, P-5027
. royalties on books printed in U.S	O-10937	263(h)(3)	L-4225
. self-employment tax	A-6084	263(h)(4)	L-4227, P-5027
. writer, defined, creative expenses and uniform capitalization rules	G-5804	263(h)(5)	L-4224
		263(h)(6)	L-4224, P-5027
♦♦♦♦♦♦♦♦♦♦♦♦♦♦♦♦♦♦♦♦		263(i)	N-3210
		263(i)(1)	N-3210
Uniform capitalization rules — Cont'd		263(i)(2)(A)	N-3210
. assembly costs	G-5802	263(i)(2)(B)	N-3210
.. retail costs	G-5537	263A	L-5800
. basis		263A(a)	H-10040, L-5600
.. allocation of administrative, service or support costs	G-5547	263A(a)(1)	G-5452
. bidding expenses for contracts awarded to taxpayer	G-5516; G-5517	263A(a)(1)(A)	G-5452
→ . books, property produced by taxpayer	G-5464	263A(a)(1)(B)	G-5452
. burden rates method, allocation of indirect costs	G-5490; G-5491	263A(a)(2)(A)	G-5453
. capitalizable indirect costs	G-5493 et seq.	263A(a)(2)(B)	G-5453, N-1075
		263A(b)	G-5464, H-10042
		263A(b)(1)	G-5461, H-10042, L-5600, 5915, 5920
		263A(b)(2)(A)	G-5476, H-10042, L-5600
		263A(b)(2)(B)	G-5479, L-5918
		263A(b)(2)(C)	G-5479
		263A(c)(1)	G-5466, L-5918
		263A(c)(3)	G-5518, 5519
		263A(c)(4)	G-5467, L-5918
		263A(c)(5)	L-5918
		263A(c)(5)(A)	G-5469

SUMMARY

Tax services are offered in print, on CD-ROM, online, and through the Internet. All have their advantages and disadvantages. No one medium is better than another, just as no one tax service is the best. Each medium and tax service has its place in tax research. Practitioners must determine which products and media they are most comfortable with and which fit the research requirements of their firm. Changes in technology and the tax services happen on a continuous basis. The same changes occur in the practitioner's business. Consequently, the practitioner's comfort level with products and technology and the research needs will change over time. Practitioners should evaluate their tax resource choices often, at least once a year when it is time to renew their services.

The annotated services are collections of various indexes and summaries of the primary sources of the Federal tax law organized around the *Internal Revenue Code*. The topical services organize their material along the logical threads that connect noncontiguous Code sections. While some services provide different features, all are most efficient when the organization of the service matches the issues in a client's tax situation. Research in a topical service, though, involves the extra step of finding the most efficient service with which to find the answer to the research problem. The tax researcher should employ tax services as gateways to the primary sources and not as a substitute for primary source research. Tax services can make the re-

Exhibit 6-34 RIA Explanations

¶ L-4108   Applications of Expense Rules

◆◆◆◆◆◆◆◆◆◆◆◆◆◆◆◆◆◆◆◆◆◆◆◆◆◆◆◆◆◆◆◆◆◆◆◆◆

wear. The actor didn't prove the need for specialized clothing or that his personal use of the clothing was de minimis.[9]

Payments to studio employees. Tips and rewards to studio employees for helping a motion picture star with clothes, speech, etc., are deductible.[10]

Chauffeur-bodyguard. Where a minor used his automobile and trailer dressing room in the performance of his movie contract, he could deduct a portion of wages paid to his chauffeur-bodyguard, but not the cost of driving to and from the studio.[11]

Physical training. Expenses of physical training paid by a stunt actor to keep in good physical condition are deductible[12] as are similar expenses incurred to keep in good physical condition.[13]

Dental work. An actor could deduct the cost of replacing teeth knocked out in making a prize fight motion picture as a business expense,[14] but not the cost of artificial teeth needed to correct a speech defect.[14.1]

observation: Dental work, though not deductible as a business expense, may qualify as a deductible medical expense subject to the medical expense limitations on deductions.

L-4109.1. Deductibility of musicians' business expenses.

A professional violinist was allowed to deduct the cost of food she provided at a reception following a recital at which she performed.[15]

A self-employed jazz musician was allowed to deduct the rent paid to a recording studio where demo audio and video tapes were recorded as well as payments to an engineer for mastering the final tracks of the tapes. The cost of stage clothes, which the court determined were not suitable for ordinary (offstage) use, and stage makeup, were also deductible.[15.1]

L-4110. Writers.

A professional writer may deduct amounts spent for information services, magazines and other supplies used in connection with his profession. The cost of books also is deductible if their useful life is short.[16] An author's prepublication expenses of dues, office supplies, rent, telephone, typing, copying and business entertainment may be currently deducted.[17]

A movie writer-producer-director could deduct expenses of a trip on which ideas for pictures were conceived and recorded.[18]

---

5. Rev Rul 76-130, 1976-1 CB 16.
6. O'Connor, Stanley, (1981) TC Memo 1981-151, PH TCM ¶ 81151, 41 CCH TCM 1191.
7. Hutchison, Charles, (1928) 13 BTA 1187, acq in part 1929-1 CB 22, nonacq in part 1929-1 CB 55; Denny, Reginald, (1935) 33 BTA 738, acq in part 1936-1 CB 7, nonacq in part 1936-1 CB 30.
8. Wilson, William, (1973) TC Memo 1973-92, PH TCM ¶ 73092, 32 CCH TCM 407, revd on other issue *sub nom* Linda Wilson v. Com., (1974, CA2) 34 AFTR 2d 74-5677, 500 F2d 645, 74-2 USTC ¶ 9630.
9. Green, James, (1989) TC Memo 1989-599, PH TCM ¶ 89599, 58 CCH TCM 606.
10. Goodrich, Olivia, (1953) 20 TC 323; Tracy, William, (1939) 39 BTA 578, acq 1939-2 CB 37.
11. Bartholomew, Frederick, (1944) 4 TC 349, acq & nonacq 1955-2 CB 4, petition dismd (1945, CA9) 34 AFTR 350, 151 F2d 534.
12. Hutchson, Charles, (1928) 13 BTA 1187, acq in part 1929-1 CB 22, nonacq in part 1929-1 CB 55.
13. Denny, Reginald, (1935) 33 BTA 738, acq in part 1936-1 CB 7, nonacq in part 1936-1 CB 30.
14. Denny, Reginald, (1935) 33 BTA 738, acq in part 1936-1 CB 7, nonacq in part 1936-1 CB 30.
14.1. Sparkman, Edward v. Com., (1940, CA9) 25 AFTR 285, 112 F2d 774, 40-2 USTC ¶ 9522.
15. Popov, Katia, (1998) TC Memo 1998-374, RIA TC Memo ¶ 98374, 76 CCH TCM 695, affd on other issue & revd on other issue (2001, CA9) 2001 WL 378330.
15.1. Genck, Valerie Jean, (1998) TC Memo 1998-105, RIA TC Memo ¶ 98105, 75 CCH TCM 1984.
16. Reg § 1.162-6.
17. Hadley, Arthur v. Com., (1987, CA2) 59 AFTR 2d 87-1078, 819 F2d 359, 87-1 USTC ¶ 9327, revg (1986) 86 TC 764; Lloyd Garrison, (1986) 86 TC 764.
18. Sandrich, Freda, (1946) PH TCM ¶ 46082, 5 CCH TCM 234.
19. Levy, Lou, (1958) 30 TC 1315, acq 1959-2 CB 5.

34,356   5/16/2001   RIA'S ANALYSIS OF FEDERAL TAXES: INCOME

---

search process more efficient and productive, but should not replace thorough review of primary sources and professional judgment.

TAX TUTOR

Reinforce the tax research information covered in this chapter by completing the online tutorials located at the Federal Tax Research web site:

http://raabe.swcollege.com

Exhibit 6–35
RIA Editorial Comments

illustration: To clarify the tax rules and problems discussed, with simple easy-to-follow illustrations.

caution: To warn of dangers which arise in particular tax situations and, where appropriate, to indicate what should be done.

recommendation: To provide specific, carefully studied guides to action which will keep taxes at a legal minimum.

observation: For professional analysis or commentary which is not part of cited authorities.

KEY WORDS

By the time you complete your work in this chapter, you should be comfortable discussing each of the following terms. If you need additional review of any of these items, return to the appropriate material in the chapter or consult the glossary at the end of this text.

Annotated Tax Service
Annotations
CCH *Federal Tax Service*
CCH *Standard Federal Tax Reporter*
CCH Tax Research NetWork
Finding List
Full-Text Searches
Kleinrock's TaxExpert

New Matters Index
Recent Developments Index
RIA *Analysis of Federal Taxes: Income*
RIA Checkpoint
RIA *Federal Tax Coordinator 2d*
RIA *United States Tax Reporter*
Spine Scan
Topical Tax Service

DISCUSSION QUESTIONS

1. What is the function of commercial tax services?
2. Compare and contrast the general format of an annotated tax service with that of a topical tax service.
3. What are some of the benefits of electronic tax services?
4. Because the Internet services tend to update on a daily or continuous basis, they are current up to the minute. Comment on this statement.
5. What is the equivalent to an index in an electronic tax service?
6. What are some potential problems with full-text searches?
7. Why would a practitioner subscribe to a tax service when most of the primary sources are available for free on the Internet?
8. Why is it important for you to actually try research projects with the various tax services?
9. If a research question is formulated correctly, the researcher will be able to find a definitive answer to the question. Comment on this statement.
10. The fact that a tax service located a document and placed it high on the relevance list means you can assume it is still valid law. Comment on this statement.
11. Why is it important to limit the databases searched when using an electronic tax service?

12. How can you determine which databases are included in your subscription to RIA Checkpoint?
13. What functions do "Modify Search" and "Narrow Search" perform?
14. Explain the functions of the following special symbols in a keyword search: ( ), " ", *
15. Which annotated and topical tax services are included in RIA Checkpoint?
16. What function does the "View Text" command perform?
17. What is the function of the directional symbol found in Code sections or Regulations reproduced in RIA Checkpoint? Why is it useful?
18. How does RIA Checkpoint differ from other electronic services with regards to case searches?
19. How does a "Search TOC Entries" differ when used in index searches and contents searches?
20. How is the news service on CCH's Tax Research NetWork different from RIA's Checkpoint news service?
21. Which annotated and topical tax services are included in NetWork?
22. How do the steps in a state tax search differ from a Federal tax search?
23. How is Kleinrock's TaxExpert different from the other tax services discussed in this chapter?
24. Compare Kleinrock's analysis and explanations with those of CCH or RIA. Why is this not surprising?
25. For what type of research is TaxExpert a good choice?
26. Why are the volumes of the annotated services called Compilation volumes?
27. What feature does the CCH *Standard Federal Tax Reporter* include in its service that RIA's *United States Tax Reporter* only offers as a separate service?
28. In using the annotated compilations effectively, why is finding and analyzing the relevant update materials performed before reading all the primary materials?
29. What are the three major methods of searching for materials in the compilations?
30. Why would the keywords chosen for an electronic search differ from those chosen for searches in the published versions of CCH and RIA?
31. What information is found in the CCH New Matters volume and the RIA Recent Developments volume?
32. What information would a researcher discover by performing a spine scan?
33. In reading a case you see a citation to a 1939 Code section. How do you find out what section number it is in the 1986 Code?
34. How does a researcher enter the RIA annotated service using a case name without using a citator?
35. Do the numbers at the top and the bottom of CCH's Compilations have the same meaning as those found in the RIA Compilations? Explain your answer.
36. Explain the paragraph numbering system used in the RIA annotated tax service.
37. How are the Code, Regulations, cases, and rulings presented in a topical tax service?
38. What are some of the beneficial features of the RIA *Coordinator 2d?*
39. Where are the Code sections relevant to a chapter's topic found in a topical service?
40. Published services are very different from electronic services. Therefore, the steps for computerized tax research are much different from those for published tax research. Comment on this statement.

EXERCISES

41. What are the four Source Materials included in the student version of RIA Checkpoint? How does your answer change if you use your school library's version of RIA Checkpoint?
42. Indicate the beginning year in which the following documents are included in RIA Checkpoint.
    a. Actions on Decisions
    b. Delegation Orders
    c. Notices
    d. Revenue Rulings
43. What Federal Editorial Materials have indexes in the student version of RIA Checkpoint? (Hint—Start with Contents) How does your answer change if you use your school library's version of RIA Checkpoint?
44. What TaxBase news databases are fully available through the student version of RIA Checkpoint? How does your answer change if you use your school library's version of RIA Checkpoint?
45. Using the IRS Phone Book provided through CCH NetWork, find the following. (Hint—the phone book is located on My CCH tab)
    a. The Washington State District Problems Resolution contact for the Seattle District
    b. Contacts for questions concerning § 3509
    c. The California State Board of Equalization Executive Director
    d. Contacts for questions concerning § 877
46. Using the CCH NetWork, indicate what is the most recent entry for the following.
    a. Volume of *Taxes—The Tax Magazine* available
    b. Revenue Procedure available through Advance Release Documents
    c. State Court of Appeals case in the Advance Releases Documents for the state of Ohio (Hint—use State tab)
    d. Volume of *Journal of Retirement Planning* Archive
47. Using the CCH Network Topical Indexes Database, determine the following.
    a. The listings for the letter "K" in the *Internal Revenue Code* index
    b. The number of listings under Bermuda in the *Tax Treaties Reporter*
    c. The letter "Q" in the *US Masters Tax Guide*
48. Under the Search Options of CCH NetWork, determine the following.
    a. What date restriction options are available?
    b. Which parts of a document may be searched?
49. Indicate the beginning year in which the following documents are included in Kleinrock TaxExpert.
    a. Announcements
    b. Proposed Regulations
    c. Notices
    d. Revenue Procedures
50. Using the browse option in Kleinrock TaxExpert, determine the location where each of following may be found.
    a. Tax Planning and Practice: Family tax planning: Planning around the Kiddie tax

Continued

b. Quick Reference Library: the current year's per diem rate
c. General information on feeder organizations of tax exempt entities in the Analysis and Explanation library
d. Ministers in the Market Segment Papers

51. Using the Internet version of Kleinrock TaxExpert, determine the function of each of these advanced search word operators and give an example of its use.
    a. The ? operator
    b. The <keywords> operator
    c. The * operator

52. Compare CCH NetWork, RIA Checkpoint, and Kleinrock TaxExpert on the following features.
    a. Default order of presenting search result documents
    b. Application of thesaurus
    c. Premier editorial service
    d. Index searches

53. Indicate the relevant Code section and the nature of the material found in each of the following CCH *Standard Federal Tax Reporter* paragraphs.
    a. ¶ 12,623.025
    b. ¶ 18,925
    c. ¶ 26,433.032
    d. ¶ 5,704.2892

54. Indicate the relevant Code section and the nature of the material found in each of the following RIA *United States Tax Reporter* paragraphs.
    a. ¶ 4,714.95
    b. ¶ 7,042.05
    c. ¶ 35,014.02
    e. ¶ 1,672.13

55. Indicate the relevant Code section and the nature of the material found in each of the following RIA *Federal Tax Coordinator 2d* paragraphs.
    a. ¶ A-5801
    b. ¶ N-2256
    c. ¶ E-5203
    e. ¶ V-2252

56. Locate the material on taxes as an expense in CCH's *Standard Federal Tax Reporter*.
    a. In what volume is the primary discussion?
    b. What is the paragraph number of the first Code section?
    c. What is the paragraph number of the fifth Regulation?
    d. What is the paragraph number of the state taxes discussion?
    e. What is the paragraph number of the first annotation?

57. Repeat Exercise 56 using RIA's *United States Tax Reporter* except substitute the following for part d.
    d. What is the paragraph number of the state and local taxes discussion?

58. Locate the discussion of Rev. Rul. 2000-05 in CCH's *Standard Federal Tax Reporter*.
    a. What is the number of the volume where you found this discussion?
    b. At what paragraph did you find this discussion?
    c. What is the subject matter of this discussion?

59. Repeat Exercise 58 using RIA's *United States Tax Reporter.*
60. Repeat Exercise 58 using RIA's *Federal Tax Coordinator 2d* and Rev. Rul. 2001-05.
61. Identify the paragraphs in the CCH *Standard Federal Tax Reporter* that include a discussion of the following cases.
    a. *Morton Zuckerman*
    b. *Shirley McVay Wiseman*
    c. *Sun Microsystems* (the 1995 decision)
    d. *William H. Roundtree* (Tax Court Memo decision)
62. Repeat Exercise 61 using RIA's *United States Tax Reporter.*
63. Repeat Exercise 61 using RIA's *Federal Tax Coordinator 2d.*
64. Where in RIA's *Federal Tax Coordinator 2d* is the information on the maximum per diem travel rates authorized to be paid by the Federal Government?

RESEARCH CASES

The following research cases may be answered using either the electronic or published services discussed in this chapter.

65. Candidate Feldman ran for Congress in 2000, raising $1.7 million for the campaign, including $300,000 in Federal matching amounts. Seven months after his opponent had been sworn into office, auditors discovered that Feldman had kept $150,000 of campaign proceeds for a personal vacation, taken immediately after the unsuccessful campaign. What are the tax consequences of this unexpected use of election funds?
66. Brian is required under a divorce decree to pay alimony of $1,000 per month and child suppport of $1,500 per month. Brian has only been paying $2,000 per month because he thinks the child support requirement is too high. On Brian's tax return, what portion of the payments does he treat as alimony and what part is considered child support? List the steps that you went through to reach your conclusion using two services (one having explanations organized as annotated and the other as topical).
67. Which of the following items qualifies for the child care credit claimed by the Rodriguez family?
    - Salary for nanny
    - Employer's share of FICA tax for nanny, paid by Rodriguez
    - Employee's share of FICA tax for nanny, paid by Rodriguez
    - Health insurance premiums on nanny, paid by Rodriguez
    - One half of nanny's hotel bill while on her own during a European vacation, paid by Rodriguez
    - Dry cleaning bills for nanny's clothes soiled by youngsters, paid by Rodriguez
68. Kenny has been a waiter at the Burger Pitt for four years. The Pitt treats its employees well, allowing them a 30 percent discount for any food that they buy and consume on the premises. This year, the value of this discount for Kenny amounted to $500 for days on which he was working and $150 for days when

he was not assigned to work but still stopped by during mealtimes. How much gross income must Kenny recognize this year with respect to the discount plan?

69. Ollie died this year in September, after a long illness. His wages prior to death totaled $15,000, and his state taxes thereon came to $600.
    a. Who must file Ollie's last tax return?
    b. How is the return signed?
    c. Who collects Ollie's $440 Federal refund?

70. When Fifi, a sheriff's deputy, was injured on the job, she was allowed under her contract with the state to choose between a $1,000 weekly sick-pay distribution and a $700 weekly workers' compensation payment. What must Fifi include in gross income with respect to her $1,000 weekly check?

71. Willie was tired of cleaning up the messes that his wife made in their house. One morning, he found a crumpled Kleenex on the bathroom vanity, so he disgustedly flushed it down the toilet. Unfortunately, the Kleenex was wrapped around Barbara's engagement ring, which she had removed the previous evening after cutting her finger while shoveling snow. Is the couple allowed a deductible casualty loss for Federal income tax purposes under IRC § 165?

72. Louella was born into a poor family that lives in a poor section of town. She recently got a job as wardrobe consultant at High Fashions, Ltd., a retailer of expensive women's clothing at an Elm Grove shopping mall. Can Louella claim a § 162 business expense deduction on her Federal income tax return for the cost and upkeep of the expensive Yves St. Laurent outfits that she is required to wear on the job?

73. Harriet purchased a variety of birth control devices during the year. To what extent, and under what circumstances, do such items qualify under § 213 for a medical expense deduction?

74. Phyllis sued Martin's estate and won a $65,000 settlement. She showed the probate court that she carried out her end of a compensatory arrangement with her companion, where under she provided "traditional wifely services" without benefit of matrimony during Martin's life in exchange for all of his estate. Martin left his entire estate to his faithful dog, via a trust. How much gross income is recognized by Phyllis?

75. How much gross income is recognized by Carol, who received $10,000 damages (two months' salary) for pain and suffering due to the school administration's critical reaction to her negative comments about ineffective recruiting of minority athletes?

76. Carol and Jerry, LLP, pay the monthly bill at the Good Eats Cafe. The two accountants eat lunch there every day and discuss business. Sometimes they invite friends who work at other CPA firms to join them so they can keep up with what is happening in the accounting community. Are these meals deductible?

77. Lila personally bought three insurance policies on her life. She borrowed $28,500 and prepaid the first five years' worth of annual payments on a whole life policy. In addition, she borrowed $4,200 and paid one of the two required premiums on a group term policy through her professional organization. Finally, she borrowed $3,000 and bought into a utilities mutual fund; principal and interest of the fund's assets were to be appropriated in a timely fashion by Lila to make payments on a five-premium endowment contract. Interest charges for the three loans were $3,500, $420, and $310, respectively. How much of this interest can Lila deduct?

78. CPA Joe reimburses a client for a $75,000 tax liability that is traceable to Joe's bad tax advice. For fear of increasing his already steep malpractice insurance premiums, Joe does not file a claim with the insurer. Can Joe deduct the $75,000 loss?
79. Gardener Toni lent Harry a new $500 lawn mower. Harry ruined the lawn mower, but replaced it with a $425 model. Later in the same year, Toni lent Harry $5,000 for bail, $3,000 to start a fencing operation, and $15 for a meal. According to Harry's parole officer, none of these items ever will be paid back. Can Toni deduct any of these losses?
80. Geraldine bought a Kandinsky for her art collection from a mail-order advertisement for $310,000. The painting, however, was actually painted by Kanske and, according to Geraldine's dealer, was not worth more than $3,100. What is her deductible loss upon discovery of the forgery?

EXTENSIVE CASE

81. Helen Hanks, who lives in San Francisco, California, has just been promoted to manager of the divisional office. However, the divisional office is located in Portland, Oregon. Helen's significant other, Tom Hunt, will be moving with her to Portland. Helen's children from a previous marriage will also be joining her in Portland. The children have been living with their father in Spain for the last year.

    Helen easily sells the San Francisco house in which she and Tom live. Helen is the sole owner of the house. However, she has a harder time finding the right home in Portland. Helen has to make several trips to Portland before buying a house under construction. It won't be available for occupancy for at least 20 days after she arrives in Portland. Tom accompanied Helen on the house hunting trips to give his opinion on the houses and to look for a new job.

    The actual move takes place as follows. The movers arrive on Wednesday to pack up Helen's and Tom's household items. Thursday, the movers pack up Helen's items from a storage unit located outside of the city and her sailboat. The movers then leave for Portland. Helen hires someone to drive her car to Portland; the driver leaves on Friday. On Saturday, after dropping Helen at the airport for her flight to Portland, Tom leaves to drive his car to Portland via Salt Lake City, Utah, where he visits his brother. Helen and Tom stayed in a hotel Wednesday to Friday while still in San Francisco and upon arriving in Portland until the house is ready for occupancy. The moving company stores their household items at its warehouse until Helen and Tom are ready to move in. Helen's children arrive two weeks after she and Tom have finally moved into the new house.

    Helen pays for all of the costs involved in selling the San Francisco home and moving Tom, the children, and herself to Portland in November of the current year. Helen's employer eventually reimburses her (in March of the next year) for 75 percent of all costs of moving the household items (Helen's and Tom's), Helen's car, and two house hunting trips. The employer also reimburses Helen for 50 percent of the total hotel and meal costs while she and Tom were in Portland and waiting for the completion of their home.

    Advise Helen on the tax consequences of the above events.

7

Electronic and Printed Legal Services

LEARNING OBJECTIVES

- Know the major features of legal services
- Use the search methodologies that are available with each of the legal services
- Understand the connectors, universal characters, and proximity commands applicable to each legal service
- Apply search methods to state research problems
- Know which legal services are most appropriate for different research objectives

CHAPTER OUTLINE

Lexis
    Selecting and Searching a Database
    Documents
    Academic Universe
BNA
    Portfolios
    Other Tax Products
        Portfolios Plus
        Tax Practice
        TaxCore
Tax Analysts
    TaxBase

    Other Tax Products
        OneDisc
        TaxLibrary.com
Westlaw
    Data and Access
    Searching Westlaw
    State Searches
Other Legal Services
    Mertens Service
    Bittker & Lokken Service
Internet Sites

continuing with the survey of tax research tools, this chapter examines the tax products available through legal service providers. The services covered in Chapter 6 were designed strictly for tax research, whereas the major services covered in this chapter, Lexis and Westlaw, were originally developed for attorneys to provide research capabilities in a wide variety of legal arenas. Therefore, they are oriented toward legal research. Since tax is one of the legal domains, legal services are amenable to tax research. Further, the service providers have in recent years begun adapting their products to be user friendly to tax practitioners in the accounting profession. Both Lexis and Westlaw offer individual bundling of products, and for their larger accounting firm clients, both create special web interfaces.

While there are numerous legal services that could be reviewed, the coverage in this chapter is limited to services most likely to be found in the "libraries" of tax practitioners. Only the tax products offered by these services will be discussed. Chapter 8 examines the case law products of these services, and Chapter 9 provides more detailed information regarding the tax news products available through the legal and tax services.

LEXIS

The amount of information available on the **LexisNexis** system is staggering. With more than 31,000 databases and 1.7 billion documents included in LexisNexis, it is possibly the world's largest full-text information source. About the only tax information not obtainable on Lexis is the CCH, Kleinrock, and Westlaw services.

Lexis, for legal (tax) sources, was started in 1973 and **Nexis,** for news, financial, and business information, was started in 1979. The LexisNexis services were initially offered on dedicated terminals because they were developed long before the universal use of personal computers. These services are now offered on the Internet with yearly, weekly, or daily subscriptions and on a pay-for-document credit card system. Documents can be retrieved for less than $10. Conducting the search is free.

SELECTING AND SEARCHING A DATABASE

Lexis is structured differently than the electronic services reviewed in Chapter 6. A researcher cannot search all the databases within the tax library, as is possible with the RIA and CCH services. Rather, Lexis is structured somewhat like a tree. The main libraries are located on the trunk of the tree, and the databases within the libraries are the various branches of the tree. At each level in the database selection process the branch is narrowing until the researcher reaches the end of the branch. For example, the opening screen in Exhibit 7–1 shows all the sources (major libraries) within Lexis. Selecting "Area of Law – By Topic" leads to a listing of searchable topics. As shown across the top of the search window in Exhibit 7–2, the drill down continued for several more iterations until a single database, BNA *Tax Management Portfolios,* was reached. Rather than drilling through the library lists, the researcher can search for a database or library by entering part or all of its title in the "Option 1: Find a Source" entry box (see Exhibit 7–1). A source search is possible at any point in the drilling down process as the Option 1 box appears on each screen until a single database is selected.

Exhibit 7–1

Lexis Opening Library Screen

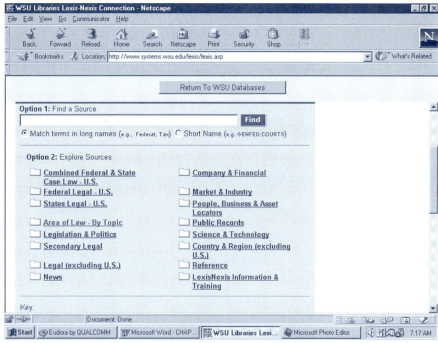

Reprinted with the permission of LexisNexis, a division of Reed Elsevier Inc.

Lexis offers the researcher a choice of natural language or **terms and connectors (Boolean)** types of searches (see Exhibit 7–2). With a **natural language** search, the tax question is entered in standard English (natural language) words, phrases, (entered within quotation marks), or sentences. The program determines the key terms for searching and relationships among the words (i.e., connectors to apply). This type of search is useful when the researcher is unsure as to which keywords would be the most effective.

Lexis supports numerous search connectors and **wildcard (universal) characters** in its terms and connectors searches. To review the connectors list click on "more" at the end of the "Use connectors to show relation of terms . . ." line below the search box (see Exhibit 7–2). This line appears only when "Terms and Connectors" is selected. Exhibit 2–10 in Chapter 2 also lists the most common connectors and their meaning. It is important to note that Lexis interprets a space between words as signifying a connection of words in a phrase and not as "and" in the usual sense. For example, if the researcher enters the words "kickback business deduction" with no connectors, Lexis will identify only documents with these three words appearing next to each other. To search for any occurrence of these words in the document, they must be entered with "and" in between them— "kickback and business and deduction."

Below the Search Term box are three additional options to improve the search results. The "Suggest Words and Concepts for Entered Terms" provides additional terms that could be added to the keyword terms selected by the researcher. These terms can be useful when the researcher is having trouble identifying appropriate keywords. The second option varies depending on whether terms and connectors or

Exhibit 7–2
Lexis Search Screen

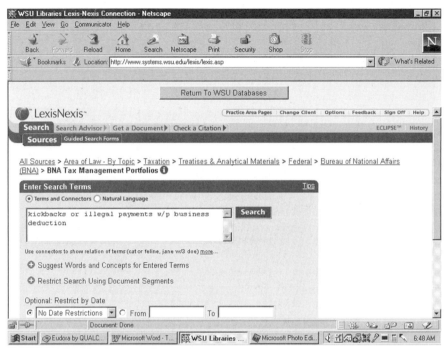

Reprinted with the permission of LexisNexis, a division of Reed Elsevier Inc.

a natural language search has been selected. With a terms and connectors search, the researcher may restrict the search to a particular segment of the document (see Exhibit 7–2). The segments range from title to footnotes. If a natural language search is selected, the researcher may restrict the search by requiring that certain terms appear anywhere in the document or in a specified document segment. The last option in the search window is a date restriction. The researcher selects either a previous period of time (previous year) or specifies a period (from . . . to . . .). The default is no date restriction. The date option is particularly beneficial when updating earlier research or when trying to locate tax law for a prior tax year.

Documents

Lexis offers four viewing choices for the documents identified by the search: Cite, KWIC, Full, or Custom. The Cite view in Exhibit 7-3 lists the citations for the retrieved documents. The partial sentences reproduced under each citation give the researcher an idea of how the keywords are used within the document. Although not visible in Exhibit 7–3, up to 10 retrieved document citations will be listed on the initial screen.

With **KWIC** (keyword in context) view in Exhibit 7–4, each document is presented on a separate screen. To move from one document to the next, click on the "next" arrow at the top of the screen. The keywords are displayed contextually in the document. The breadth of the context may be set by the researcher. Clicking once on "KWIC + 25" term brings up the screen to set the context. From one to 999 words can be displayed on either side of the highlighted keywords, the default being 25 words. Make sure the SuperKWIC is "On" when trying to set the number of context words in a natural language search.

Exhibit 7–3
Lexis Cite View Screen

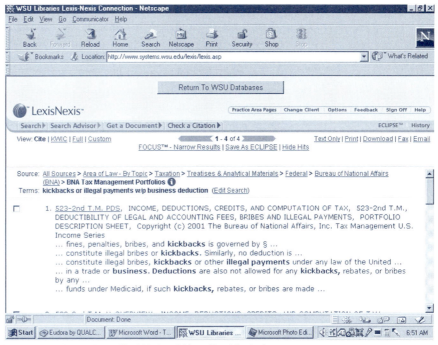

Reprinted with the permission of LexisNexis, a division of Reed Elsevier Inc.

Full view displays the full text of the document (cases, law, etc.) or a section of the document (treatises) with highlighted keywords. Lastly, the Custom view allows researchers to designate which parts of the documents are displayed. Thus, the

Exhibit 7–4
Lexis KWIC View Screen

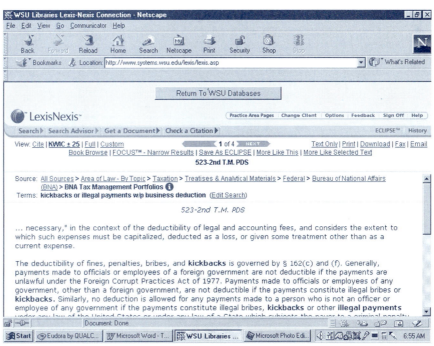

Reprinted with the permission of LexisNexis, a division of Reed Elsevier Inc.

Custom view is merely a modification of the Full view. If all segments are selected, the document view is Full. The list of segments choices are reproduced in Exhibit 7–5. The Custom view option saves the researcher time when printing or downloading a document. Only those segments of interest to the researcher need be included.

The Full view document screen in Exhibit 7–6 will be the basis for the remaining discussion of Lexis. The "Book Browse" feature (second line, document window) enables the researcher to browse the document as if it were in print. Browsing offers the research the ability to "flip through the pages" and find the area of interest without having to print the document. This can be more efficient when the researcher is acquainted with the document but does not remember the exact page where the pertinent information is located. The researcher can also identify the appropriate section by drilling down through the Table of Contents (middle, document text, Exhibit 7–6).

Finally, two unique features of Lexis accessible on Exhibit 7–6 are the "More Like This" and "More Like Selected Text" options (right end, second line, document window). Both of these options are offered only after an initial search has been completed. The "More Like This" derives core terms from documents with similar language patterns. Any or all of these words can be selected by the researcher as search terms. Additional terms or phrases and/or mandatory terms may also be included, as shown in Exhibit 7–7. The "More Like Selected Text" performs a similar search. A passage from a retrieved document is selected and entered into the search box by clicking on "More Like Selected Text." Mandatory terms may also be added (see Exhibit 7–8). The documents identified by this search will be utilizing the passage terms in a context similar to the original document. This helps to eliminate documents containing the terms of interest used in an entirely different context.

Exhibit 7–5
Lexis Custom View Options Screen

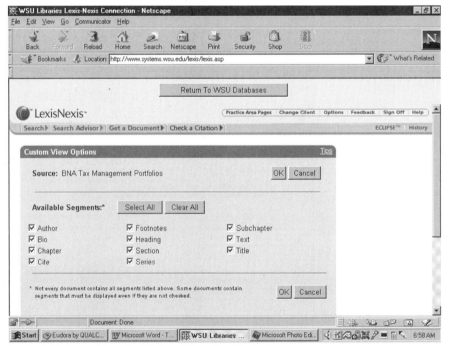

Reprinted with the permission of LexisNexis, a division of Reed Elsevier Inc.

Exhibit 7–6
Lexis Full View Screen

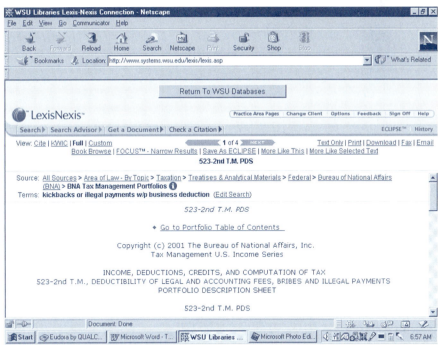

Reprinted with the permission of LexisNexis, a division of Reed Elsevier Inc.

ACADEMIC UNIVERSE

LexisNexis offers a customized version of its services to academic institutions and public libraries in its *Academic Universe* web site. The libraries and databases offered on *Academic Universe* vary with the subscription. Generally, primary tax documents and secondary news, law reviews, and journal articles are included. Given the nature of the secondary sources, *Academic Universe* receives a detailed review in Chapter 9, Journals, Newsletters and Internet News Sources.

To perform tax research using *Academic Universe*, select "Legal Research" on the opening screen. As can be seen in Exhibit 7–9, the Legal Research libraries pertaining to primary tax law would be Case Law and Codes & Regulations. One of the options offered under Case Law, Area of Law by Topic, appears promising. However, this choice leads to a dead end. Tax is not one of the topic areas listed. A more productive option is Tax Law found under Codes & Regulations. This library contains most of the primary tax sources (Code, Regulations, court cases, IRS pronouncements, etc.) and journals by several different publishers. Each of these databases are keyword searchable, but only one database may be searched at a time. This can cause a search on *Academic Universe* to be more time consuming than one on services that allow multiple database searches.

BNA

Tax Management, a subsidiary of **Bureau of National Affairs** (BNA), offers a wide range of products covering all areas of Federal taxes. However, it is best known as the publisher of the BNA *Tax Management Portfolios* (BNA *Portfolios*). These

Exhibit 7–7
Lexis More Like This Screen

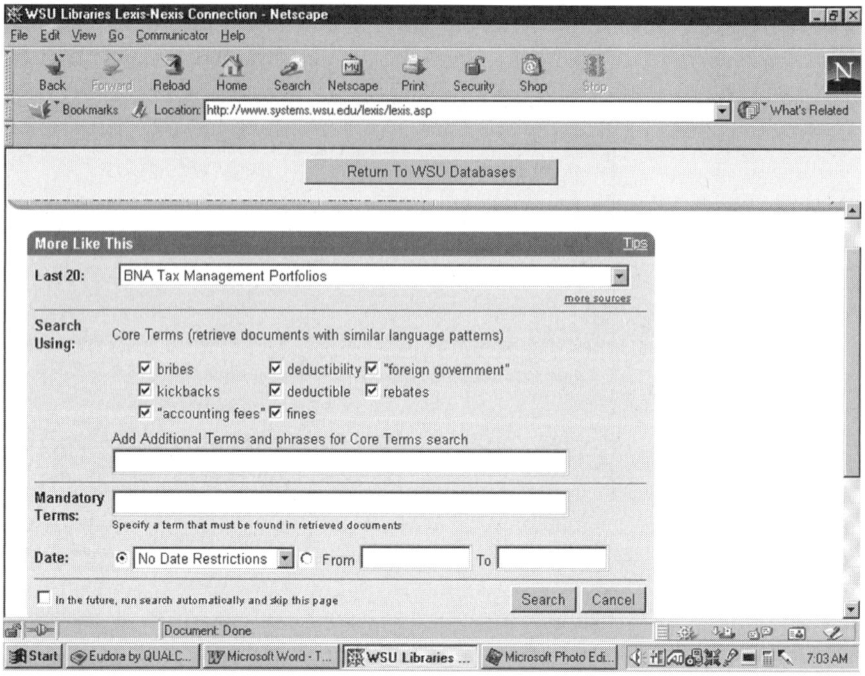

Reprinted with the permission of LexisNexis, a division of Reed Elsevier Inc.

portfolios are available in print, on CD-ROM, and on the Web. They are also included in Lexis, Westlaw, and their own online service, Portfolios Plus Library. BNA Tax Management has two other electronic tax services, Tax Practice Library and TaxCore, that will be briefly reviewed in this section.

Exhibit 7–8
Lexis More Like Selected Text Screen

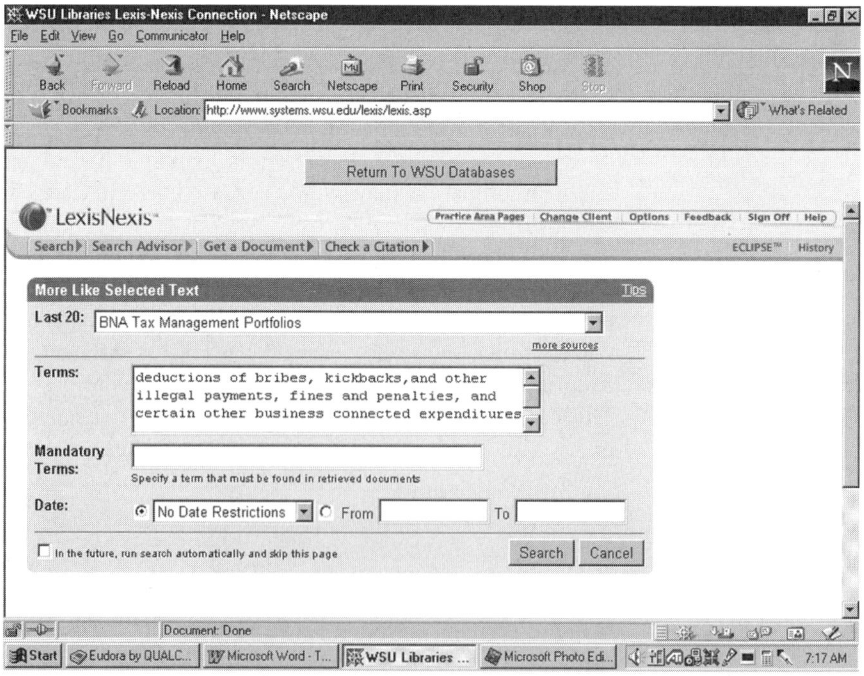

Reprinted with the permission of LexisNexis, a division of Reed Elsevier Inc.

Exhibit 7–9

Academic Universe Legal Research Categories

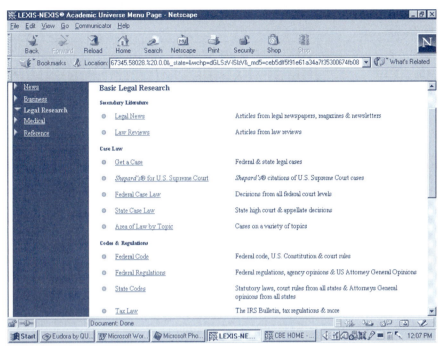

Reprinted with the permission of LexisNexis, a division of Reed Elsevier Inc.

PORTFOLIOS

The more than 280 BNA *Portfolios* are classified into three series: U.S. Income Tax; Estates, Gifts, and Trusts; and Foreign Income. The size of the *Portfolio* library varies as topics are added, deleted, or combined. While the number of *Portfolios* appears vast, the series is not truly comprehensive. As with any topical service, it would be impossible to cover every issue that a practitioner may encounter in the course of business.

Each BNA *Portfolio* begins with a Portfolio Description, which gives a brief overview of the topic and the order of presentation of the materials. In a printed version, the Table of Contents would follow the description. The remainder of the *Portfolio* contains three sections: (A) Detailed Analysis, (B) Working Papers, and (C) Bibliography and References. The printed page numbers of these sections are preceded by the letters (A, B or C) to indicate which portion of the *Portfolio* is being examined. The *Portfolio* sections are updated in response to important tax developments, and, when necessary, the complete *Portfolio* is rewritten.

The Detailed Analysis section is, as the title suggests, a comprehensive examination of the topic. It is written by one or more tax practitioners who are experts on the topic. Practitioners are the preferred authors because they are more sensitive to the information requirements of the service users. For this reason, *Portfolios* are a favorite research tool with practitioners. As with other topical services, the Code, Regulations, rulings, and court case opinions are integrated into the analysis with citations footnoted or included in the text (see Exhibit 7–10). In addition, the authors identify potential pitfalls, probable IRS positions, effective tax planning techniques, and alternative means of structuring transactions in a tax-favorable manner. The value of these insights will vary by author.

Exhibit 7-10 BNA *Portfolio* Detailed Analysis

Detailed Analysis

will terminate with respect to expenditures paid or incurred after December 31, 2000. For further discussion of §198, see 505 T.M., *Trade or Business and For-Profit Activity Deductions*.

V. Fines, Penalties, Bribes and Kickbacks: General

Prior to the Tax Reform Act of 1969,[682] the IRS and the courts denied deductions of bribes, kickbacks, and other illegal payments, fines and penalties, and certain other business connected expenditures if: (1) the taxpayer could not meet the "ordinary" requirement for a business deduction,[683] and/or; (2) such payments frustrated or violated public policy as expressed by federal or state statute (hereinafter the "public policy doctrine").[684] In endeavoring to apply the public policy doctrine, however, there was no simple criteria for determining when a given illegal payment or penalty violated or frustrated public policy.

The public policy doctrine rested essentially on a compromise between the goals of taxing net, rather than gross, income and avoiding the appearance of subsidizing illegal activities through tax deductions. Under the public policy rule, the courts held that expenditures recognized as ordinary and necessary expenses must, nonetheless, be denied deduction if they are illegal or closely connected with illegal activity.[685]

However, some courts were unwilling to disallow a deduction on public policy grounds when the taxpayer's expenditures had violated so-called "deadletter" laws, such as state liquor laws. Thus, some courts used the zeal with which state enforcement agencies prosecuted violations of illegal payment statutes as a factor in determining whether allowance of a deduction might violate public policy.[686] Also, beginning with *Pittsburgh Milk Co. v. Comr.*,[687] taxpayers had considerable success in arguing that allowances, discounts, and rebates made to certain customers, in violation of a state statute, should reduced a taxpayer's gross sales in determining gross income because taxes are imposed only on "income," and not on every conceivable type of receipt.[688]

Note: For a detailed analysis of the validity of the holding enunciated in *Pittsburgh Milk* after the Tax Reform Act of 1969, see X, below.

Finally, Congress recognized, in its 1969 deliberations, that "Public Policy . . . generally is not sufficiently clearly defined to justify the disallowance of deductions."[689] Therefore, the Tax Reform Act of 1969[690] amended §162(c)[691] (by, inter alia, adding subsections (c)(1) and (c)(2)) and added §§162(f)[692] and 162(g),[693] which stated the circumstances under which deductions for fines, penalties, bribes, and kickbacks will be disallowed. Thus, a business deduction paid or incurred after the enactment of the Tax Reform Act of 1969 cannot be denied solely on the grounds that the allowance of the deduction would frustrate a sharply defined public policy.[694] These provisions, which codified several of the most frequent applications of the public policy doctrine, are as follows:

---

[682] P.L. 91-172, 21902; 1969-3 C.B. 10, 147.

[683] *See Reffet v. Comr.*, 39 T.C. 869 (1963) (denying a deduction for contingent witness fees paid in an action for damages to the taxpayer's business, because such payments were not the "common and accepted [ordinary] means used by a coal operator or any other person in prosecuting an action for damages to his business," but not on public policy grounds); *Frederick Steel Co. v. Comr.*, 42 T.C. 13 (1964), *rev'd on other grounds*, 375 F.2d 351 (6th Cir. 1967) (finished steel jobber was denied a deduction for kickbacks to a customer's purchasing agent as payments in the nature of commercial bribes were not common [ordinary] in that segment of the steel industry); *United Draperies, Inc. v. Comr.*, 340 F.2d 936 (7th Cir. 1964), *aff'g*, 41 T.C. 451 (1963) (denying a deduction for kickbacks paid to vice-presidents of the trailer manufacturing companies the taxpayer supplied as kickbacks occurred but said they were not an ordinary means of securing or promoting business).

[684] In Rev. Rul. 62-194, 1962-2 C.B. 57, the IRS summarized these approaches to the illegal payment question.

[685] *See Comr. v. Heininger*, 320 U.S. 467, 473 (1943)(allowing deduction of attorney fees incurred by a mail-order dentist in the unsuccessful resistance of a fraud order issued by the Postmaster General, and finding that disallowance of an otherwise ordinary and necessary business expense was proper only when allowance would "frustrate sharply defined national or state policies proscribing particular types of conduct."); *Lilly v. Comr.*, 343 U.S. 90 (1952) (allowing deduction for kickbacks paid by an optician to the ophthalmologist who had referred patients to him to have their eyeglasses made, because no applicable state statute made such payment illegal and no public policy existed where such payments, however reprehensible, could frustrate; the taxpayer had only to show that the payments were ordinary and necessary to be allowed the deduction); *Tank Truck Rentals, Inc. v. Comr.*, 356 U.S. 30 (1958) (denying a deduction for fines incurred for intentional as well as innocent violations of a state motor vehicle maximum weight statute to a truck operator, and holding that the test of nondeductibility is always the severity and immediacy of the frustration resulting from allowance of the deduction); *Comr. v. Sullivan*, 356 U.S. 27 (1958) (allowing deduction for the rental and wage expenses of an illegal gambling operation under state law, because no federal statutory or regulatory disapproval of these expenses existed, and such expenses were ordinary and necessary business expenses and deductions were permitted "unless it is clear that the allowance is a device to avoid the consequence of violation of a law . . . or otherwise contravenes the federal policy expressed in a statute or regulation."); *Tellier v. Comr.*, 383 U.S. 687 (1963) (upholding the deductibility of legal fees incurred in unsuccessfully resisting a criminal prosecution for securities fraud on the ground that the employment of legal counsel for the defense against a criminal charge was not against public policy, and clarifying that the public policy doctrine related to a "sharply limited and carefully defined category" of situations where a deduction would frustrate an expressed governmental policy proscribing certain conduct).

[686] *Stacy v. U.S.*, 231 F. Supp. 304 (D. Miss. 1963). *See also Kane v. Comr.*, T. C. Memo. 1971-221 (allowing the deduction of a condiment purveyor's kickbacks to chefs and stewards despite an Illinois commercial bribery statute prohibiting such payments; such payments had not violated public policy for federal income tax purposes, because the state had neither taken any action against the taxpayer nor prosecuted anyone else, despite the widespread nature of the illegal practice; since no prior determination of guilt had been made, no public policy issue arose).

[687] 26 T.C. 707 (1956), *nonacq.*, 1959-1 C.B. 6, *acq.*, 1962-2 C.B. 5, *nonacq.*, 1976-2 C.B. 3, *acq.*, 1982-2 C.B. 2.

[688] The holding of *Pittsburgh Milk* has been followed in *Rosedale Dairy Co. v. Comr.*, T.C. Memo 1957-243; *Harmony Dairy Co. v. Comr.*, T.C. Memo 1960-109; *Atzingen-Whitehouse Dairy v. Comr.*, 36 T.C. 173 (1961), *acq.*, 1982-2 C.B. 1; *Bloomingdale Dairy Co., Inc. v. Comr.*, T.C. Memo 1961-117.

[689] S. Rep. No. 552, 91st Cong., 1st Sess. 274 (1969), H.R. Rep. No. 782, 91st Cong., 1st Sess. 309 (1969).

[690] P.L. 91-172, §902; 1969-3 C.B. 10, 147.

[691] Prior to the amendments made by the Tax Reform Act of 1969, §162(c) read as follows:

(c) Improper payments to officials or employees of foreign countries. No deduction shall be allowed under subsection (a) for any expenses paid or incurred if the payment thereof is made, directly or indirectly, to an official or employee of a foreign country, and if the making of the payment would be unlawful under the laws of the United States if such laws were applicable to such payment and to such official or employee.

[692] Pre-1969 TRA §162(f) was redesignated as §162(h).

[693] For a discussion of §162(g)(denial of deduction for treble damages under the antitrust laws), see 522 T.M., *Tax Aspects of Settlements and Judgments*.

[694] Regs. §1.162-1(a).

The Working Papers section of the BNA *Portfolios* is perhaps the service's most unique and useful feature. This portion includes practitioner checklists; reproduced IRS forms, occasionally filled in for an illustrative fact situation; computation worksheets; sample draft agreements and contract clauses; sample board or shareholder resolutions and employment contracts; reproductions of pertinent primary sources; and other practical materials that would assist the professional in implementing tax planning techniques and procedures.

The Bibliography section of a BNA *Portfolio* has a comprehensive listing of the primary (Official) and secondary (Unofficial) sources of the tax law utilized by the author(s) in the preparation of the *Portfolio*. Finally, this section of the *Portfolio* often includes a listing of journal articles and treatises that are relevant to the *Portfolio* topic.

The researcher may have access to electronic and/or published versions of the BNA *Portfolios*. Since searching electronic services is covered in other sections of this chapter, it will not be discussed here. The published BNA *Portfolios* have a comprehensive index to aid in the search process. For each series (Income, Estates, Gifts, & Trusts, and Foreign Income) the Master Index provides a list by topic and portfolio number all of the portfolios within the series. The topics section is a very broad-based index, whereas the numerical listing is like a table of contents for the series (see Exhibit 7–11). The Master Index is updated at least quarterly.

The Index also contains a Code section guide that traces specific Code sections to the various *Portfolios* within which it is discussed. The asterisk in front of the *Portfolio* title indicates that it contains primary coverage of this Code section topic. Lastly, *Portfolios* may by identified by IRS Forms and Publications Finding Table. This part of the Index identifies *Portfolios* discussing the item and/or reproducing the form, as Exhibit 7–11 indicates. It is particularly useful when the practitioner has questions regarding the proper completion of a particular form.

OTHER TAX PRODUCTS

BNA has three electronic services that have been developed for tax practitioners. These are Portfolios Plus Library, Tax Practice Library, and TaxCore. Of these three, Portfolios Plus Library is considered BNA's premier tax service.

Portfolios Plus

The backbone of **Portfolios Plus Library** (Portfolios Plus), as the name implies, is the BNA *Portfolios*. Access to primary sources, weekly news reports, practice tools, and a limited number of journals is also included in the subscription, as can be seen in Exhibit 7–12, the opening screen. From this screen, the researcher begins one of the following searches: Table of Contents, Indexes and Finding Aids, or Global Search. By clicking on "U.S. Income Series," under the Expert Analysis section, the major topic headings for this portfolio series appear. By drilling down, the researcher locates the portfolio and sections within the portfolio germane to the tax question (see Exhibit 7–13). This method is similar to using the BNA *Portfolios* published Index list of the *Portfolios* by number and then the table of contents of the selected *Portfolio*. Searching using the Index and Finding Aids is also very similar to using the published Index. Both index word searches and Code searches are possible.

The "Global Search," one of three word searches offered in Portfolios Plus, is the only one accessible from the opening screen. This keyword option lets the researcher search any combination or all of the databases at once. The other two

Exhibit 7-11 BNA *Portfolio* Index

INTERNAL REVENUE CODE SECTION — MASTER INDEX

◆◆◆◆◆◆◆◆◆◆◆◆◆◆◆◆◆◆◆◆◆◆◆◆◆◆

§162 - TRADE OR BUSINESS EXPENSES
Allocation and Apportionment of Expenses – Regs. §1.861-8 (F), 906
Amortization of Intangibles (US), 533
Bad Debts (US), 538
Cafeteria Plans (US), 397
Charitable Contributions by Corporations (US), 290
Choice of Entity (US), 700
Compensating Employees with Insurance (EGT), 828
Compensating Employees with Insurance (US), 386
* Deductibility of Legal and Accounting Fees, Bribes and Illegal Payments (US), 523
Deduction Limitations: General (US), 504
Deductions: Overview and Conceptual Aspects (US), 503
Employee Fringe Benefits (US), 394
Employee Plans – Deductions, Contributions and Funding (US), 371

◆◆◆◆◆◆◆◆◆◆◆◆◆◆◆◆◆◆◆◆◆◆◆◆◆

NUMERICAL FINDING LIST

520	Entertainment, Meals, Gifts and Lodging — Deduction and Recordkeeping Requirements
521-2nd	Charitable Contributions: Income Tax Aspects
522-2nd	Tax Aspects of Settlements and Judgments
523-2nd	Deductibility of Legal and Accounting Fees, Bribes and Illegal Payments
525	State, Local, and Federal Taxes
527	Loss Deductions
530-2nd	Depreciation: General Concepts; Non-ACRS Rules
531	Depreciation: MACRS and ACRS
533	Amortization of Intangibles

U.S. INCOME PORTFOLIOS—MASTER INDEX

◆◆◆◆◆◆◆◆◆◆◆◆◆◆◆◆◆◆◆◆◆

KICKBACKS
Deductibility, 504:A-78; 520:A-86; 523:A-55, A-57, A-60
Gross income, 501:A-182

KIDDIE TAX
See also TAX MANAGEMENT EGT PORTFOLIOS INDEX
Allocable parental tax, 507:A-13
AMT, 288:A-44(1), C&A:A-44(1); 507:A-42
Assignment of income doctrine, 502:A-90
Computation of, 507:A-12
Election to include in parent's gross income applicable children's gross income, 507:A-14
Net unearned income, 502:A-91; 507:A-12
—Inflation adjustments, 502:C&A:A-91
1997 TRA changes, 288:C&A:A-44(1); 507:A-42

KNOW-HOW, 557
See also PATENTS
Amortization of §197 intangible property, 533:A-6; 557:A-4, A-34; 561:A-57
Assignment of income doctrine, 557:A-41
Computer programs, classifying transfers of, Prop. Regs., 558:A-38(2)
Contingent payment sales, 557:A-42
Definition, 557:A-27
Depreciable property sales between related taxpayers, 557:A-39
Foreign corporation transfers, 557:A-34
Imputed interest, 557:A-38
Installment method sales, 557:A-38
Licenses, 557:A-32
OID, 557:A-38

◆◆◆◆◆◆◆◆◆◆◆◆◆◆◆◆◆◆◆◆◆◆◆◆◆◆◆◆◆◆◆◆◆◆◆◆◆◆◆

Forms and Publication Finding Table

Form Number	Title	Portfolio/Reference File
1040 (Sch. A) (Filled In)	Itemized Deductions	852 (EGT), Pub. 559; 540 (US), Pub. 908; 907 (F), Pub. 519
1040 (Sch. B) (Filled In)	Interest and Dividend Income	740 (US), Pub. 564; 852 (EGT), Pub. 559; 540 (US), Pub. 908
1040 (Sch. C) (Filled In)	Profit or Loss From Business	547 (US), Pub. 587
1040 (Sch. D) (Filled In)	Capital Gains and Losses (And Reconciliation of Forms 1099-B)	549 (US), Pub. 925; 594 (US), Pub. 523; 740 (US), Pub. 564; 540 (US), Pub. 908

keyword search options, "Search Words" and "Special Search," appear in the left toolbar (below Indexes and Finding Aids command) after choosing a database on the opening screen (see Exhibit 7–13). The results of the "Search Words" option can be viewed by titles or by documents. With the "Special Search," shown in Exhibit 7–14, the researcher is able to target an area of the tax law or a particular portfolio. A specific portion of the portfolio, Detailed Analysis or Working Papers, may also be designated. This is a convenient search method when the applicable portfolio is known, but the relevant sections need to be identified.

Exhibit 7–12
BNA Portfolios Plus Library Opening Screen

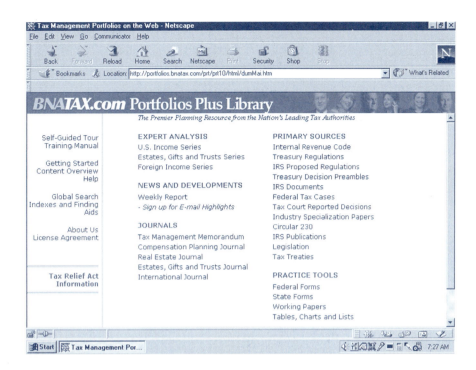

Tax Practice

The **Tax Practice Library** (Tax Practice) is a basic tax service furnishing access to primary sources, practice tools, and limited news sources. Rather than relying on the BNA *Portfolio Series,* Tax Practice has developed its own explanatory analysis.

Exhibit 7–13
BNA Portfolios Plus Library U.S. Income Series Screen

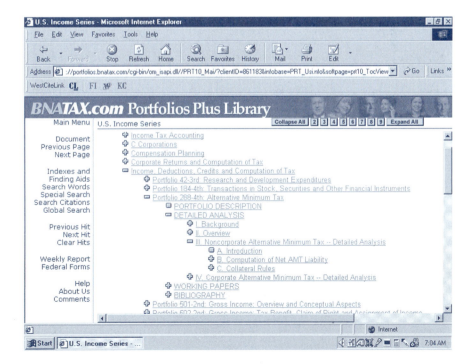

Exhibit 7–14
BNA Portfolios Plus Library Special Search Screen

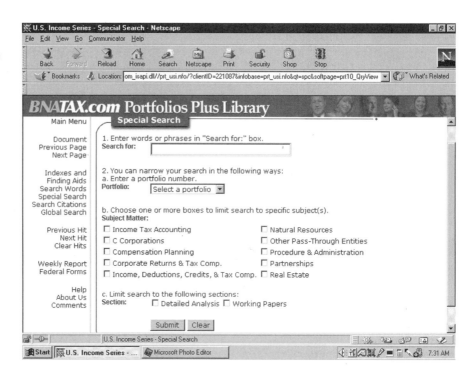

Other than offering fewer databases (no BNA *Portfolio* or journals), this service is almost identical to Portfolios Plus in its searching methods. Even the opening screens look similar.

TaxCore

Subscribers to several of BNA's news services, such as the *Daily Tax Report* (see Chapter 9 for description), receive **TaxCore** as part of their subscriptions. TaxCore provides the hyper-linked primary sources and tax-related documents discussed and cited in the news reports. It does not contain all primary sources, nor does it furnish explanations or analysis of the tax law. The source materials are archived to November 1997. TaxCore can be purchased without a subscription to a news service. Given the type of documents it contains and its limited nature, TaxCore would be a logical service to acquire without the news subscription only for those practitioners desiring access to materials issued by the government and private sectors that are difficult to obtain by any other means.

TAX ANALYSTS

Tax Analysts is a nonprofit entity organized to provide literary forums for the discussion of taxation. Tax Analysts disseminates timely and comprehensive state, Federal, and international tax information through its daily, weekly, and monthly print publications, scholarly books, and electronic database services. Its news publications such as *Tax Notes* are discussed in Chapter 9. This section will focus on their electronic tax services, TaxBase (professional and student version), OneDisc, and TaxLibrary.com.

TaxBase

TaxBase is the most comprehensive tax product in Tax Analysts' electronic line. It offers Federal *(Tax Notes Today),* state *(State Tax Notes),* and/or international tax *(Worldwide Tax Daily)* news updated daily, as well as numerous primary source databases and analysis/explanations of the law.

The databases are organized into three major libraries, U.S. Federal, U.S. State, and Worldwide, each of which is available by separate subscription. Consequently, these libraries must be searched separately. Also, some of the databases within these libraries must be separately searched. For example, each database listed under the U.S. Federal heading in Exhibit 7–15 would require a separate search. A practitioner subscribes to either the Basic Federal Research Library (Basic) or the Federal Research Library. The main difference between these two libraries is that Basic does not include the Chief Counsel Advice (including Private Letter Rulings) or the Court Opinion (more than 40,000 tax decisions) databases.

Exhibit 7–16 presents the keyword search screen for the Federal Research Library. Keywords, phrases, or multiple terms with connectors are permissible. As in the Lexis service, the program interprets a space between terms as signifying words in a phrase and not as the "and" connector. The "and" connector must be added to have the words searched as separate terms. Other recognized connectors are "and not" and "or." While sentence and paragraph proximity searching is offered, truncation symbols and universal, or wildcard, characters are not accepted. However, the program searches for root words and finds common variations such as plurals, different tenses, and possessives.

Exhibit 7–15
Tax Analysts TaxBase Opening Screen

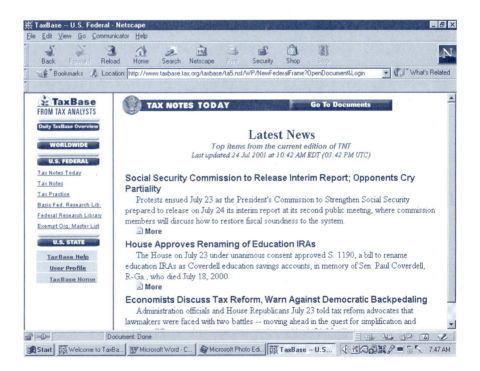

Exhibit 7–16
Tax Analysts TaxBase Federal Research Library Search Screen

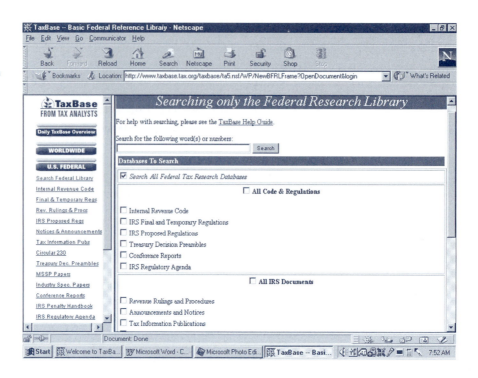

The databases in the Federal Tax Library are divided into sections. Any one to all of these sections are searchable at once, or the researcher may select individual sources within the sections. Another method for searching a single source is to select it in the left frame toolbar (see Exhibit 7–16). The table of contents displayed can be browsed in the same manner as a printed document. Keyword searches of the full text or just content titles are also possible methods of locating the document or section of interest. These keyword options are helpful when searching the *Federal Tax Baedeker* database *(Baedeker). Baedeker* is the 26-chapter analysis and explanation of the tax laws covering individuals, businesses, trusts, and estates included in TaxBase.

Tax Analysts offers a student version of TaxBase, free of charge, through its **TA Campus** web site at **http://tacampus.tax.org**. Professors may register for the Student TaxBase service for their students and themselves on a semester-by-semester basis. A registration code, which can be obtained by e-mailing or calling the contact person listed on the professor registration screen, is necessary. This is a valuable service that grants unlimited, 24-hour access to essentially the same news and research libraries that are included in TaxBase. Besides tax sources, TA Campus furnishes links to scholarship information, student organizations, career resources, and internship opportunities.

OTHER TAX PRODUCTS

OneDisc

Tax Analysts developed a single-disc tax product similar to the Kleinrock service discussed in Chapter 6. **OneDisc** contains an extensive list of primary sources (including Private Letter Rulings and key court decisions) and the explanations of

Exhibit 7–17
Tax Analysts OneDisc Opening Screen

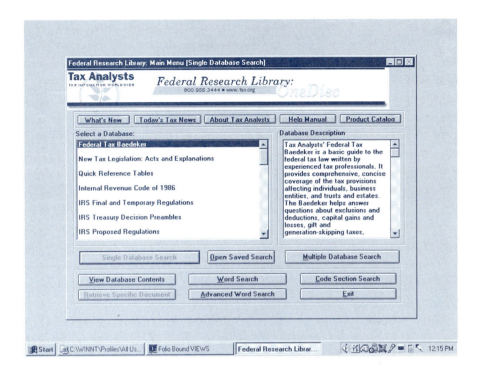

Baedeker. Also like Kleinrock, Tax Analysts offers this product to students at a substantially reduced price.

The opening screen of OneDisc is reproduced in Exhibit 7–17. All of the databases available on OneDisc are listed in the Select a Database box. A description of the database appears in the right window as the database title is highlighted in the left frame. After choosing a database (Single Database Search), the researcher must decide whether to View the Database Contents, Retrieve a Specific Document, or perform a search. The search options are a simple word search, advanced word search, or a Code section search. The advanced search supports Boolean connectors "and," "or," and "not" between two words/phrases and the "within paragraph" proximity command. Wildcard (universal) characters such as "*" and "?" are recognized. If the researcher wishes to search more than one database at a time, the "Multiple Database Search" is selected. This screen is designed to facilitate selecting from two to all of the databases for the search.

Double clicking on any of the database titles in the Select a Database window opens the entire database. This is a great feature for those practitioners who like to browse. The database is stored as one continuous document. Consequently, the contents can be browsed in the same manner as "flipping through the pages" in a book. Rather than browsing, the researcher can search the opened database using the "Query" button located on the left-hand toolbar shown in Exhibit 7–18. The menu bar Search command also offers the "Query" option on its pull-down menu. Templates specifically designed for document retrieval from the opened database are another option listed on the "Search" pull-down menu (see Exhibit 7–18). The "Contents" button on the left-hand toolbar allows the researcher to move through the table of contents of the opened database. Lastly, a search of the database's own index

Exhibit 7–18
Tax Analysts OneDisc
Database Screen

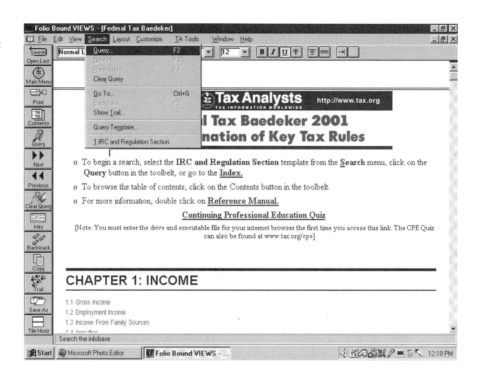

is possible by clicking on the highlighted word "Index" in the search instructions at the top of the database window.

Returning to the opening screen of Exhibit 7–17 by clicking on the "Main Menu" button on Exhibit 7–18, there are two button above the database box that merit explanations: "Tax News Today" and "What's New." Given that OneDisc is a CD-ROM, how is it possible to have daily tax news? Clicking on "Tax News Today" displays a link to TaxWire, the Tax Analysts free Internet daily tax news service. The other button, "What's New," is where the researcher can find out what has been added to the disc recently. This will vary depending on whether the practitioner's subscription includes monthly, quarterly, or yearly updates. This is valuable information when updating previous research for the latest developments. The database is keyword searchable, an expandable table of contents is provided, and browsing is possible. For items such as IRS rulings, the pronouncements are listed by Code section rather than issue date to facilitate searching.

TaxLibrary.com

Wanting to provide affordable basic research tools for sole practitioners and small firms, Tax Analysts created the **TaxLibrary.com** service. Subscriptions are offered on a yearly, 90-day, and monthly basis. Included in the web-based service is access to news, primary sources, and tax law explanations by *Baedeker*. The daily tax news is supplied by TaxWire and by the *Tax Practice*, a weekly magazine. The primary sources available are listed on the search screen in Exhibit 7–19. This is not a comprehensive tax library. Federal case law and Private Letter Rulings are excluded from the service and primary sources are updated monthly rather than daily to keep costs reasonable.

Performing a search in TaxLibrary.com is similar to TaxBase. Clicking on a database under the "Stacks" heading allows the same browsing capabilities as in

Exhibit 7–19
Tax Analysts
TaxLibrary.com
Search Screen

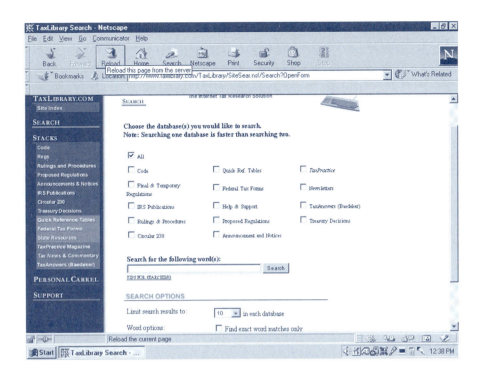

TaxBase. Selecting the "Search" heading opens the keyword screen. The researcher has the option of selecting from one to all of the databases for the keyword search. By marking a box at the bottom of the search screen, the researcher can require that exact word matches be retrieved (see Exhibit 7–19) or a thesaurus be applied to the keywords (not visible in Exhibit 7–19). The Tips For Searching located directly below the keyword entry box explains the connector options supported in TaxLibrary.com. Lastly, the number of documents retrieved per database may be set at 10, 50, 100, 200, or all. Setting the results to "all" can substantially increase the processing time of the search.

The results of the search are listed by database. Clicking on the title displays the full-text document. At the top of the Document screen in Exhibit 7–20 are several navigation buttons. Unlike most other services, the "Previous (Next) Document" button takes the researcher to the previous (next) document in the database, not the previous (next) document in the results list. The "Go to Stacks" button is for locating a particular document or going to a different database for a new search. The other "Go To" button will vary by database. This button will open a screen for performing a word search within the database. The remaining button, "Add to Personal Carrel," creates a space where the researcher can save search results, organize the materials, and add comments.

WESTLAW

The West Group, an important legal publisher, offers tax research capabilities electronically through its **Westlaw** service. This service is legally oriented because it was designed by attorneys for attorneys. Its orientation is evident in its structure and

Exhibit 7–20
Tax Analysts
TaxLibrary.com
Document Screen

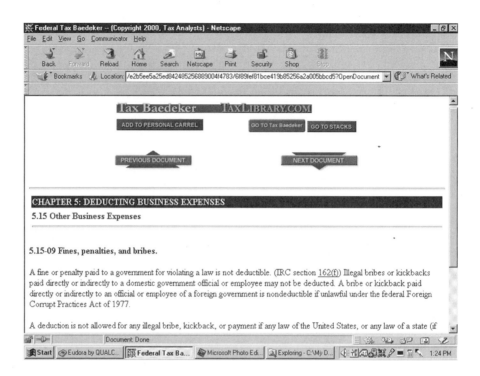

its emphasis on citators and citing. (Westlaw has several types of citators, whereas CCH and RIA offer only one type.) Due to this attorney orientation, Westlaw is less represented than RIA and CCH in accounting firms. However, many of the larger CPA firms subscribe to Westlaw, especially those that hire lawyers into their tax service groups. Virtually all lawyers are trained in law school on the Westlaw system.

DATA AND ACCESS

Westlaw contains nearly 15,000 databases with information provided by numerous sources. Included in its databases are BNA *Tax Management Portfolios,* Tax Analysts *Tax Notes,* all of the RIA products including the *Federal Tax Coordinator 2d* and its citator, Warren, Gorham & Lamont journals and treatises, all law school reviews, and various tax news services. The West Group's topical tax service, called *Mertens Law of Federal Income Taxation,* is also included in Westlaw. This service will be examined in the next section of this chapter.

As with Lexis, when Westlaw began in 1975, it required a dedicated online terminal. Now Westlaw is accessible via the Internet using a web browser by downloading WestMate software or by using Westlaw links to integrate it into a firm's intranet or portal. In 2000, Westlaw became accessible with wireless and mobile devices (Westlaw Wireless). Westlaw offers tailored bundling of the databases to its customers and even provides access to its services without requiring a subscription. Using a pay-as-you-go system (credit card required), researchers can retrieve documents as necessary from Westlaw.

A recent innovation of the West Group is customized Westlaw web sites to meet the specific professional needs of its different customers. Consequently, the appearance of the Westlaw service demonstrated in this chapter may vary from the customized site available to you through your school or your employer. The basic searching strategies discussed in this section, however, will be similar in all versions of Westlaw.

SEARCHING WESTLAW

When logging on to Westlaw, it may be necessary to enter a client name in order to proceed with the research project. This feature, included for the benefit of the tax professional, keeps track of the time spent on each search by client for billing purposes.

The Welcome screen (Exhibit 7–21) is divided vertically into two windows. The left-hand frame enables the researcher to immediately search for a document by citation, perform a citator search, or locate a database. The right-hand window is filled with the information about Westlaw and interesting legal news. Above the windows are the buttons for the various types of searches available with Westlaw. With the exception of KeyCite, each of the these is reviewed in this section. KeyCite is a citator and will be covered in Chapter 8, Citators and Other Finding Devices. Above these buttons are the file tabs for Westlaw, Westnews, and any personalized tabs established by the practitioner. In Exhibit 7–21, a tab for the "Tax" practice area has been created. Customizing the tabs is executed in "My Westlaw " (button located at the top right of the Welcome screen). Up to six personalized tabs may be added by selecting databases in the general, topical, Federal, or state jurisdictional areas. The tabs can be further personalized to furnish direct access to databases most commonly accessed.

The first type of search offered in Westlaw is the Find a Document (the "Find" button). If its citation is known, a document can be retrieved by typing the citation in the "Enter Citation" box in the left frame of Exhibit 7–22. Exact spacing and

Exhibit 7–21
Westlaw Opening Screen

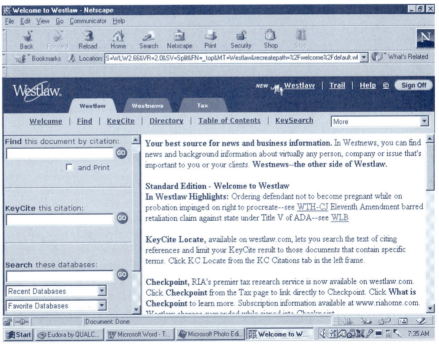

Source: Westlaw. Reprinted with permission.

punctuation is not necessary, but the exact citation must be known. Most Federal documents, topical materials, and law review or journal articles may be retrieved by citation. When the citation is not known, select one of the "Find" options, title, person, company, or database, shown in the lower left frame of Exhibit 7–22 or the program, Find Wizards (see bottom of right frame) will help the researcher select a database to search.

Another starting point for selecting databases to search is the Directory option. If the abbreviations of the databases desired are known, they are entered in the "Search These Databases" text box in the left frame of Exhibit 7–23. Up to 10 databases separated by commas or semicolons may be entered. Databases recently or frequently searched (favorite databases) are additional methods for selecting databases. The right frame of the Westlaw Directory screen in Exhibit 7–23 displays the expandable list of the directories. The researcher drills down through the directories until the database desired is reached. As Exhibit 7–24 shows, the database selected appears at the top of the Search screen. To determine what is included in combined databases, click on Scope in the left frame, and on the next screen click on Contents for a full listing of the items included.

On the Search screen (Exhibit 7–24), the researcher selects either a natural language or terms and connectors (Boolean) keyword query. A thesaurus is conveniently provided to help in selecting the best words for the search. It is not automatically applied, however; the synonyms must be added to the keywords by the researcher. The list of Westlaw connectors and expanders is similar to those of other services. Unlike other services, a space between two words is interpreted as an "or" not as an "and" or phrase connector. An "&" or the word "and" must be included to have an "and" connection. Westlaw also supports an expansive list of field restrictions such as judge, attorney, and references.

Exhibit 7–22
Westlaw Find Search Screen

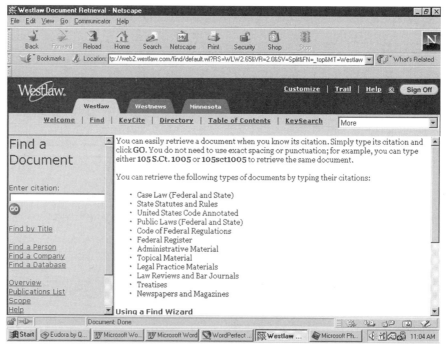

Source: Westlaw. Reprinted with permission.

Exhibit 7–23
Westlaw Directory Screen

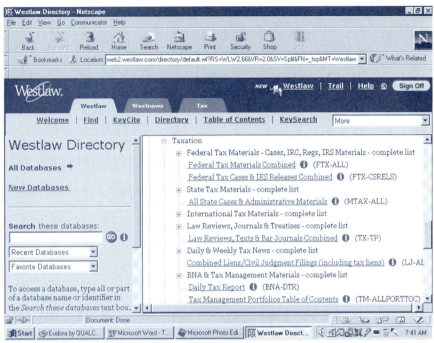

Source: Westlaw. Reprinted with permission.

Like the Directory, the Table of Contents offers an expandable list of categories containing publications with tables of contents. Drilling down through the categories expands the lists from the left frame to the right frame of the screen. Notice in Exhibit 7–25

Exhibit 7–24
Westlaw Directory Search Screen

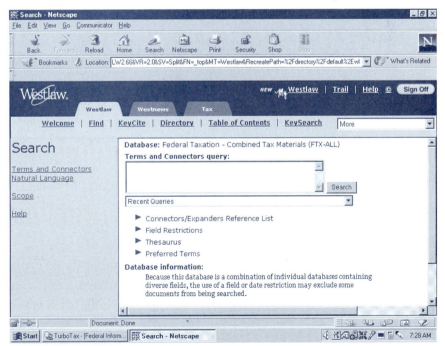

Source: Westlaw. Reprinted with permission.

Exhibit 7-25
Westlaw Table of Contents Search Screen

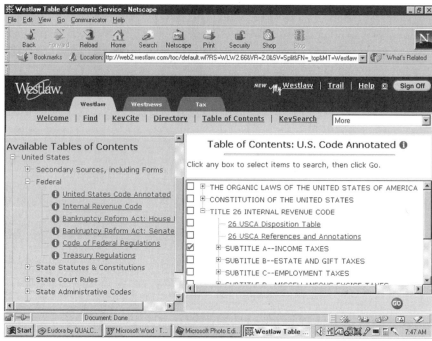

Source: Westlaw. Reprinted with permission.

that there are two sets of boxes before the various divisions of Title 26, *Internal Revenue Code*. Clicking on the small box containing the "+" will expand the subtitle, while clicking on the boxes farther to the left will mark these items as areas to be searched.

KeySearch is a new feature added to Westlaw in 2001. The West numbering system of key issues (topics) found in court cases is the backbone of this searching mode. The researcher identifies the legal topic within which the research problem lies either by searching the list of topics with the word search (left frame) or by drilling down through the topics presented in the right frame of Exhibit 7–26. KeySearch formulates a query based on the underlying terms for the topic and adds the key numbers associated with the topic. As seen at the bottom of Exhibit 7–27, the results are a list of search terms that the researcher can modify to insure the results will be relevant. This type of search is especially effective when the researcher is unfamiliar with that particular area of the tax law.

STATE SEARCHES

State research is performed using the same search methodologies as Federal searches. In the Directory, the state databases are located under the heading "U.S. State Materials." Selecting "Other U.S. States" subheading in Exhibit 7–28 displays the states in alphabetical order. The accessible legal topics are listed after choosing the state of interest. Tax materials will generally be one of the topics listed for each state. Rather than selecting "Other U.S. States," the researcher can select from the numerous topics under "U.S. State Materials" such as "Statutes & Legislative Services." This information is available for all states together and for individual states (see Exhibit 7–28). A third subheading leading to a complete list of state tax materials is "Taxation" under the heading "Topical Materials by Area of Practice" (see Exhibit 7–23).

Exhibit 7–26
Westlaw KeySearch
Screen

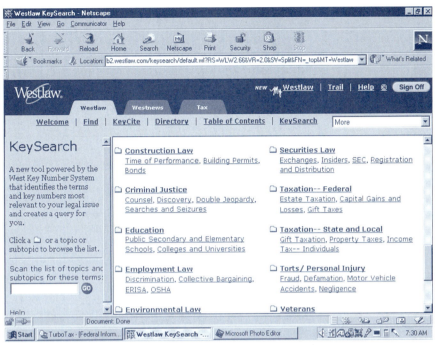

Source: Westlaw. Reprinted with permission.

Exhibit 7–27
Westlaw KeySearch
Search Screen

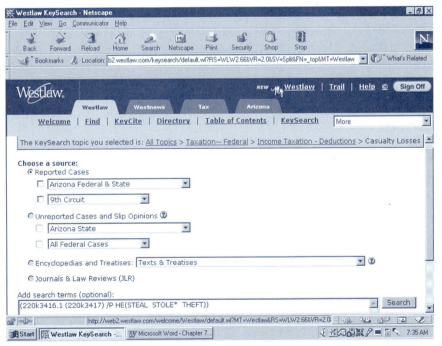

Source: Westlaw. Reprinted with permission.

Exhibit 7–28
Westlaw State Directory Screen

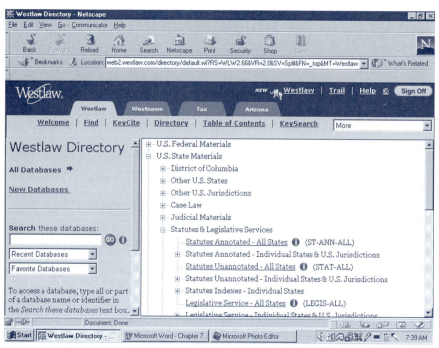

Source: Westlaw. Reprinted with permission.

With varying levels of drilling under these headings, tax materials for the state and primary documents germane to the research are retrieved.

The left frame of the Table of Contents Search screen reproduced in Exhibit 7–25 lists the state databases available for contents searches. Selecting any of the state databases produces a listing of the states. When a state is highlighted, its table of contents appears in the right frame of the window, as Exhibit 7–29 illustrates. A Municipal Codes database that holds the city statutes for some of the larger cities in the United States also exists.

Practitioners performing state research frequently will want to create State and/or Federal circuit case tab(s) for easy access to these databases. The tabs are created using the Jurisdictional categories in the My Westlaw customizing option.

OTHER LEGAL SERVICES

Various legal publishers have developed multi-volume bound *tax treatises* or loose-leaf services that are devoted to detailed analysis of various tax topics and narrow sets of tax issues. Such single-topic works can be effective research tools for practitioners with area specializations, but comprehensive research is seldom confined to just these works. Most of these publications are also available on CD-ROM, through Lexis, Westlaw, and other Internet tax services providers. Within the range of analysis that the authors have selected, the researcher may enjoy a detailed discussion of the law, including citations to primary or secondary sources. These services may be limited in range, but not in their quality.

Two legal-oriented tax services providing multi-volume and full-range coverage are *Mertens Law of Federal Income Taxation* and *Federal Taxation of Income,*

Exhibit 7–29
Westlaw State Table of Contents Screen

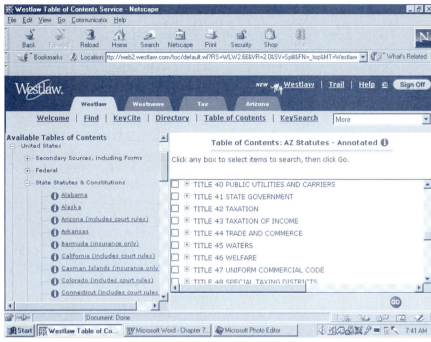

Source: Westlaw. Reprinted with permission.

Estates, and Gifts. These services are well known in the accounting and legal communities for their expert tax analysis and authoritative stature.

MERTENS SERVICE

Mertens Law of Federal Income Taxation *(Mertens),* developed by the West Group, is offered on Westlaw's Internet service and in a published format. It also has a one-disc CD-ROM version, Tax Link, that contains not only *Mertens* but also an annotated Code, Tax Court Rules, and issues of current newsletters. This version integrates with Westlaw, allowing the practitioner to access the full text of documents cited in the service. The published *Mertens* is rapidly being replaced in law and accounting offices and legal libraries with the electronic versions.

Mertens is a topical tax treatise organized in over 100 chapters, which are numbered from 1 to 63. Some numbers are reserved, and other chapters have number and letter designations (Chapters 55, 55A, and 55B). The published version is housed in a set of nineteen loose-leaf binders. *Mertens* is more legally oriented than the RIA or CCH tax services discussed in Chapter 6. Consequently, it is cited by courts more than the other tax services. This legal orientation is evidenced by the text material being heavily footnoted. On occasion there is more footnote material than text material on a *Mertens* page. These footnotes provide more than mere citations to the relevant primary tax law sources; often they annotate cases, quote freely from the Code, Regulations, and Committee Reports, or review legislative history.

In the front of each published *Mertens* volume, on yellow sheets, is the Cumulative Supplement. This is a collection of supplementary information that has accrued since the chapters in the volume were last revised. The supplements are updated monthly. Also monthly, one of the chapters in the service is rewritten to incorporate the supplemental materials. Therefore, to be certain of the current law, the supplements must be read. The Table of New or Changed Section Titles, which appears at the beginning of the Semiannual Supplement, provides a listing of sections that have changed since the main volume text was last updated. The Internet and CD-ROM versions have the same updating system as the published version. This means updates are not integrated into the text of the electronic service more frequently than in the published version. Therefore, the cumulative supplements must also be checked in the electronic versions to make sure that the explanations are up-to-date.

The *Mertens* service includes a Code Commentary, which furnishes contextual explanation of Code provisions. In addition, the service provides loose-leaf collections for both current Regulations and Revenue Rulings. The Code, Regulations, and Rulings volumes each contain Amendment Tables, which allow the researcher to trace the statutory or administrative evolution of any provision.

Finally, the service has "snapshot" versions of up to 10 previous years' Code, Regulations, and Rulings volumes. This extremely useful feature of the *Mertens* service can facilitate analysis of the evolution of a law. For a client whose prior years' tax returns are under audit or at trial, the tax practitioner can use this feature of *Mertens* to reconstruct the details of the primary law sources that applied at the date of the original return.

BITTKER & LOKKEN SERVICE

Warren, Gorham & Lamont, now an affiliate of RIA, is the publisher of ***Federal Taxation of Income, Estates, and Gifts,*** a treatise by Boris I. Bittker and Lawrence Lokken. The five-volume service is less comprehensive and more conceptual than many of the other topical tax services on the market. Its stated objective is "provid[ing] guidance and orientation [to income and transfer taxation] by emphasizing the purpose, structure, and principal effects of the *Internal Revenue Code,* without bogging down in the details." Due to its goals, the service sometimes reads like a collection of essays and journal articles rather than a systematic analysis of the workings of the Code. However, it is generally considered to be a leading authoritative treatise by professionals and even by the United States Supreme Court.

The treatise is updated three times a year, and one of the case-bound volumes is revised each year. Thus, the service is on a five-year cycle. The update volume is generally larger than the other volumes. Because the volumes are bound (precluding the use of replacement pages), the update materials can be disproportionately large as each volume nears the end of its five-year update cycle. The possibility of voluminous update materials means that when the researcher finds material of interest in the service, it is especially important to immediately check the current materials for the section or paragraph of interest to determine the status of the material in the main text. It would be a poor use of time to read the text thoroughly, only to learn from the new matters material that Congress or a recent court case has dramatically changed the relevant tax provisions.

The Bittker & Lokken service may serve as a good starting point for the researcher who needs to obtain an initial grasp of a selected area of the tax law. Its citations can provide easy access into the other tax services or immediately direct the practitioner to the primary sources of tax law. Currently, it stands somewhere between a one-volume treatise or textbook and a free-standing comprehensive topical tax service. This service is available in print, on CD-ROM, and on several Internet services such as Lexis, Westlaw, and RIA Checkpoint.

INTERNET SITES

As mentioned previously, most of the primary tax source documents are accessible free of charge on the Internet. The Federal government has numerous web sites to disseminate its documents to the general public. As will be discussed in Chapter 9, there are also many web sites maintained by companies, organizations, and individuals that have links to the government sites to facilitate retrieval of primary sources of the tax law. A list of web sites offering government documents is presented in Exhibit 7–30.

Exhibit 7–30 Web Sites for Tax Services

Information Available	Web Sites
Code of Federal Regulations	http://www.access.gpo.gov/nara/cfr
Congressional Record	http://www.access.gpo.gov/su_docs/aces/aces150.html
Digital Daily/current IRS tax info	http://www.irs.gov/
Dept. of Justice Tax Division	http://www.usdoj.gov/tax/
Fedworld FTP site	http://www.fedworld.gov/ftp.htm
Fedworld Info Network	http://www.fedworld.gov/
Federal Register	http://www.access.gpo.gov/su_docs/aces/aces140.html
Federal Tax Code	http://www.tns.lcs.mit.edu/uscode/
Financial Accounting Standards Board	http://www.fasb.org
GPO Access Databases	http://www.access.gpo.gov/su_docs/aces/aaces002.html
Highlights of Tax Provisions	http://www.irs.ustreas.gov/prod/hot/tax-law.html
House Ways and Means Committee Rpts	http://www.house.gov/ways_means/
Internal Revenue Bulletins	http://www.irs.ustreas.gov/prod/bus_info/bullet.html
Internal Revenue Service	http://www.irs.ustreas.gov
Joint Committee on Taxation	http://www.house.gov/jct/
Legislation on Internet	http://thomas.loc.gov/bss/d105/hot-subj.html
Senate Finance Committee	http://www.senate.gov/~finance/
Social Security Administration	http://www.ssa.gov
Tax Forms	http://www.irs.ustreas.gov/prod/forms_pubs/forms.html
Tax Regulations	http://www.irs.ustreas.gov/prod/tax_regs/index.html
U.S. Code, Title 26	http://www.law.cornell.edu/uscode/26/
U.S. House of Representatives	http://www.house.gov
U.S. Senate	http://www.senate.gov
U.S. Treasury Department	http://www.ustreas.gov
White House	http://www.whitehouse.gov

Exhibit 7–31
Web Sites for Commercial Tax Services

Commercial Services	Web Sites
Bureau of National Affairs (BNA)	http://www.bna.com OR
	http://www.bnatax.com
Portfolios Plus Library	http://portfolios.bnatax.com
TaxCore	http://subscript.bna.com/taxcore
Tax Practice Library	http://taxpractice.bnatax.com
Tax Management Resources (BNA)	http://www.taxmanagement.bna.com
Commerce Clearing House	http://tax.cchgroup.com
Tax Research NetWork	http://tax.cchgroup.com/network
LexisNexis	http://www.lexisnexis.com
Academic Universe	http://web.lexis-nexis.com/universe
Lexis	http://www.lexis.com
Nexis	http://www.nexis.com
Kleinrock	http://www.kleinrock.com
Research Institute of America	http://www.riag.com OR
	http://www.riahome.com
Checkpoint	http://checkpoint.riag.com/Checkpoint
Tax Analysts	http://www.tax.org OR
	http://www.taxanalysts.org OR
	http://www.taxanalysts.com
TaxBase	http://taxbase.tax.org
TA Campus	http://tacampus.tax.org
TaxLibrary.com	http://taxlibrary.com
West Group	http://www.westgroup.com
Westlaw	http://www.westlaw.com

The web sites for the tax services discussed in Chapter 6 and this chapter are listed in Exhibit 7–31.

SUMMARY

The market supports a variety of tax research products, all designed to facilitate locating relevant sources by practitioners. Whether the service is categorized as legal or tax, all have their place in tax research. The enormous databases of services such as Lexis and Westlaw make them very attractive. On the other hand, the ability to access materials on a single CD without having to connect to the Internet is appealing to many sole practitioners and small firms. There is a wide range of products between these extremes. The real problem for practitioners is which media and tax products best serve the needs of their business at a price they can afford. With technology and software advances occurring at a rapid pace, what seemed to be an innovative product when this text was written may be passé by the time it is printed. The ability to be flexible and quickly adjust the changing technology to business needs is important to the success of tax practitioners.

Chapter 7 Electronic and Printed Legal Services 229

TAX TUTOR

Reinforce the tax research information covered in this chapter by completing the on-line tutorials located at the Federal Tax Research web site:

http://raabe.swcollege.com

KEY WORDS

By the time you complete your work in this chapter, you should be comfortable discussing each of the following terms. If you need additional review of any of these items, return to the appropriate material in the chapter or consult the glossary to this text.

Academic Universe
Boolean
Bureau of National Affairs
Federal Taxation of Income, Estates, and Gifts
Federal Tax Baedeker
KWIC
Lexis
LexisNexis
Mertens Law of Federal Income Taxation
Natural Language
Nexis

OneDisc
Portfolios Plus Library
TA Campus
Tax Analysts
Tax Management Portfolios
Tax Practice Library
TaxBase
TaxCore
TaxLibrary.com
Terms and Connectors
Universal Characters
Westlaw
Wildcard Characters

DISCUSSION QUESTIONS

1. When were Lexis and Nexis started? What topic areas are covered by each?
2. What tax sources are not included in the Lexis offerings?
3. How is the database structure of Lexis different from the RIA and CCH tax services?
4. What is a natural language search and when is it useful?
5. What are the three additional options Lexis provides to improve keyword searches?
6. Explain the More Like This and the More Like Selected Text features in Lexis.
7. What is *Academic Universe?*
8. What are the various tax services offered by Bureau of National Affairs?
9. How is each volume of the BNA *Tax Management Portfolios* arranged?
10. Describe the manner in which main text materials are updated in the BNA *Tax Management Portfolios?*
11. Where are copies of primary sources such as the *Internal Revenue Code* found in the BNA *Tax Management Portfolios?*
12. Describe the BNA *Tax Management Portfolios* Index.

13. Discuss the three types of word searches available in Portfolios Plus Library.
14. What is TaxCore? What is its purpose?
15. What connectors and proximity searches are supported in TaxBase and OneDisc?
16. What is *Baedeker?* What services offer it?
17. When a database is opened in OneDisc, what are the various methods for locating pertinent documents?
18. What is the purpose of the Personal Carrel in TaxLibrary.com?
19. What tax services are available in Westlaw?
20. Which two legal services offer pay-for-document type services?
21. What are the types of searches available in Westlaw?
22. What are the various ways a space between two words can be interpreted by research programs?
23. How do searches for state tax laws differ from Federal searches when using Westlaw?
24. What makes the footnotes in *Mertens Law of Federal Income Taxation* unique?
25. Explain when the "snapshot" versions of previous years' Code, Regulations, and Rulings volumes in the *Mertens* service would be useful.
26. What is the scope or objective of *Federal Taxation of Income, Estates, and Gifts*?
27. Describe the manner in which the volumes of *Federal Taxation of Income, Estates, and Gifts* are updated. How often are new bound volumes published?

EXERCISES

28. Using Lexis, answer the following questions.
    a. What are the date restrictions available for a term search?
    b. In which libraries/databases can *Federal Taxation of Income, Estates, and Gifts* be found?
    c. What two Technical Advice Memorandums (Private Letter Rulings) issued in August and September 1999 discuss the Alternative Minimum Tax?
29. Using Lexis, answer the following questions.
    a. Selecting "Review the Most Current Documents" option on the Select a Path screen for Tax Analysts, what document is displayed and on what date was it created?
    b. What publishers have products listed in the State & Local subdivision for Treatise & Analytical Materials in the Taxation library?
    c. What is the volume and paragraph number where qualified residence interest is discussed in *Federal Taxation of Income, Estates, and Gifts?*
30. Using Lexis, answer the following questions.
    a. What sources are included in the Public Records folder found in the Taxation library (Area of Law by Topics)?
    b. Are the State & Local listings found in Treatise & Analytical Materials the same as the State & Local listings found in Multi-Source Groups? Explain your answer.
    c. What BNA Multi-state *Portfolio* discusses the state tax treatment of Net Operating Losses?

31. Using Lexis, answer the following questions.
    a. What are the subdivisions for Treatise & Analytical Materials found in the Taxation library?
    b. In a Terms and Connectors search, what segments are offered for limiting the search?
    c. When using the "w/n" proximity connector, what is the maximum number "n" can be? (Hint—Terms & Connectors needs to be selected in the Search Terms screen.)
32. Using *Academic Universe,* answer the following questions.
    a. What IRS pronouncements are included in the Tax Law database?
    b. In the Area of Law by Topic, what sources included in this database are more likely to include court cases on income taxes?
    c. What state sources are included in the Tax Law database?
33. Using BNA's *Tax Management Portfolios,* answer the following questions.
    a. Which *Portfolio(s)* discuss(es) the deductibility of gifts to clients?
    b. In the discussion about athletic scholarships found in Portfolio 517-1st: Scholarships and Educational Expenses, what Revenue Rulings are cited?
34. Using BNA's *Tax Management Portfolios,* answer the following questions.
    a. In what section of which *Portfolio* is there a discussion of the tax treatment of transfers of appreciated property to political parties?
    b. In which *Portfolio* do you find a worksheet sample of the § 173 election to capitalize newspaper circulation expenditures?
35. Using BNA's *Tax Management Portfolios,* answer the following questions.
    a. On what worksheet found in which *Portfolio* is there information on how to elect out of the alcohol fuel credit?
    b. In which *Portfolios* are the at-risk rules in § 49 covered?
36. Repeat Exercise 34 using Portfolios Plus Library. For each question, indicate your search method.
37. Using Portfolios Plus Library, answer the following questions.
    a. In the Primary Source Tax Treaties, what article on private pensions and annuities by J.P. Klein is listed as a bibliography reference?
    b. Perform a Global Search on clergy housing. How many IRS publication sources did your search find? Code sources? Regulation sources? List the sources.
    c. For a Regulation listed in (b.) above, go to the document section discussing clergy housing and click on the "Where am I" button. What information does it provide?
38. Using Tax Practice Library, answer the following questions.
    a. What practice aids are provided for corporate reorganizations? At what paragraph numbers are they located?
    b. What are the three credits that make up the alcohol fuels credit? Where did you find the information? At what paragraph are the credits discussed?
    c. In what paragraph is the minimum tax credit discussed?
    d. What is the nature of the practice aid found at paragraph 7110.100?
39. Using TA Campus, answer the following questions.
    a. The Treasury proposed regulations on March 1, 2000, regarding exempt organizations. What aspect of unrelated business income do the regulations address?

Continued

b. What does Announcement 2000-43 discuss?
c. What is in Chapter 20-232.1 of the IRS Penalty Handbook?
40. Using TA Campus, answer the following questions.
   a. In what chapter of *Federal Tax Baedeker* do you find a discussion of the alcohol fuel credit? On what tax form is the credit claimed?
   b. Who is the person responsible for Federal tax litigation issues (especially appeals) in the State Attorney General's office of your state?
   c. What are MSSP Papers? Find the MSSP on ministers computing self-employment taxes. What footnote items are hyper-linked to documents?
41. Using TA Campus, answer the following questions.
   a. What is contained in Treasury Decision 8760?
   b. *Tax Notes Today* issued a special report on Keogh Plans in February 2000. What is the title of the article, and who are the authors?
   c. What are BATF Regulations? What are the regulations under BATF regarding newspaper cuts? When was this regulation last revised?
42. Using OneDisc, answer the following questions.
   a. Can farmers have voluntary withholding from payments received from agencies?
   b. Run an Advanced Search with Multi-databases using the term "exempt organization" and the connector "and" with the second term "sponsorship." Run the same search requiring that "exempt organization" be an exact phrase and that "exempt organization" and "sponsorship" be within the same paragraph. Compare your search results.
   c. What Private Letter Ruling issued in 2000 determines the tax consequences of transferring subchapter S stock to ten trusts?
43. Using OneDisc, answer the following questions.
   a. Search the Industry Specialization Papers and Settlement guidelines using the query search using the terms "abandonment" and "asset." What do you find?
   b. Do recipients of pension and annuity distributions have the option of electing not to have taxes withheld? What code sections govern these withholding rules?
   c. What is listed in the What's New under Final and Temporary Regulations?
44. Using TaxLibrary.com, answer the following questions.
   a. What state resources are available for your state?
   b. Search Tax Practices for documents on the interaction of the Alternative Minimum Tax (AMT) and the kiddie tax. What do you find?
   c. How are the following conectors used in searching: @, *, ( ), " "
45. Using Westlaw, answer the following questions.
   a. What options are listed in the More pull-down menu?
   b. Where is the amortization of trademarks discussed in *Mertens Law of Federal Income Taxation?*
   c. Using the KeySearch, determine what the Key numbers 371k988.1 and 371k989 mean. (The subject under which these numbers appear is State Income Taxation of Corporate Dividends.)
46. Using Westlaw, answer the following questions.
   a. What symbol is used for the connector "but not"? Explain the use of the universal characters * and !. What does "+n" mean and how large can "n" be?

Continued

b. Using the Find search, find the article in Volume 54 of the *Tax Law Review* starting on page 171. What is the title of the article, and who is the author?

c. In the My Westlaw customizing command, what topics in the General choice tab options (besides Westlaw and Westnews) would contain government documents?

47. Using Westlaw, answer the following questions.
    a. What is the database identifier (database abbreviation) for the WG&L combined tax treatises database? How many treatises with Bittker as the first author are included in this database?
    b. Using the Directory search, find a Private Letter Ruling that discusses whether gifts (cash payments) to clients of a tax exempt organization who participate in a new program are taxable?
    c. Using Find the document by citation, determine what is the proper abbreviation for finding Code sections, Regulations, and Revenue Rulings.

48. Using Westlaw, answer the following questions.
    a. What synonyms does the Westlaw thesaurus provide for the following terms: kickback, casualty, and fuel?
    b. Using the Table of Contents search, determine what is in Article II of Chapter 7 of the San Antonio Municipal Code?
    c. What field restrictions are supported in a Terms and Connectors search?

49. Using *Mertens Law of Federal Income Taxation*, answer the following questions.
    a. The sale of a patent by the original individual inventor generally is treated as a capital gains transaction. Is this true even for a professional inventor? Where was the relevant discussion of the law found?
    b. According to the historical development discussion of patent sales, when were substantial liberalizing revisions made to this area of the tax law? The Commissioner announced that for years beginning prior to the effective date and after May 31, 1950, he would adhere to the position he had taken prior to the enactment of the §1235 changes. What did Congress do to foil the Commissioner's plan?
    c. In what Code section is the relevant discussion found for the following?
        Deduction of armed services uniforms
        Expenditures incurred in producing photographs
        Charitable contribution valuation of a business interest
        Redemption effects on Accumulated Earnings Tax

50. Use Bittker & Lokken's *Federal Taxation of Income, Estates, and Gifts* to answer the following questions.
    a. According to the Supreme Court case of *Diedrich v. CIR*, the payment of gift taxes by the donee may result in a taxable gain for the donor. State the circumstances that will cause this to happen. Where did you find this information? Provide from volume to the subparagraph number.
    b. What is the official citation for *Diedrich v. CIR?* Give the volume and page number of the *Iowa Law Review* that has a comment on this case.
    c. List the titles of the volume through subparagraph of Volume 13, Chapter 92, Paragraph 92.3, Subparagraph 92.3.2. What is the first sentence of Subparagraph 92.3.2?

RESEARCH CASES

Support your answers for each case with citations to primary tax law sources.

51. Three friends form a small manufacturing partnership, each owning equal interests. Their contributions to the start-up entity are as follows.

    Glen: Cash $10,000; equipment, FMV $5,000, basis $4000.

    Alex: Land with a small building, FMV $70,000, basis $20,000, recourse mortgage $55,000 (assumed by the partnership).

    Debra: Neither cash nor other property, just extensive and valuable business knowledge.

    Determine the partners' bases in their respective partnership interests, and the partnership's basis in each of the assets transferred to it. State a general rule for deriving such computations.

52. Can a business traveler to your town use the high-cost-city meal allowance for travel away from home overnight? What would the meal allowance be for a business trip to Washington, D.C.?

53. Nancy and Curtis had not spoken to each other since their mother's funeral in 1971. Nancy broke the family discord this year by selling Curtis a family heirloom, basis to her $10,000, for $1,700. What are the tax consequences of this transaction?

54. Zarco, a very profitable corporation, was owned by three shareholders, Julio, Tilly, and Martinez. Julio and Martinez purchased all of Tilly's Zarco Corporation stock for $50,000 and a $100,000 promissory demand note that was guaranteed by Zarco. Tilly demanded payment on the note, and Zarco, rather than Julio and Martinez, paid the note. What are the tax consequences of this transaction?

55. Dolores is a limited partner in the Houston Hopes partnership. This year, she was forced under the terms of the agreement to make a $50,000 contribution to capital because the general partners were unable to meet the operating expenses of the entity. Dolores's basis in the partnership prior to the contribution was $40,000, but her at-risk amount was zero because of her limited partner status and her prior-year pass-through losses. What is her at-risk amount after the $50,000 cash call?

56. Steve is an usher at his local church. May he deduct as a charitable contribution the commuting expenses for the Sundays that he is assigned to usher?

57. Phil is a used-car manager. To obtain advanced skills in management and marketing, he enrolls in the weekend MBA program at Montana State University, twenty miles from his home. Does Phil qualify for an educational credit? What items associated with Phil's education are deductible, assuming that he receives no reimbursements for any of them?

58. Jon and Mary have been married for twenty years. Without Mary's knowledge, Jon has been operating as a bookie at his local pub. This year's earnings from the operation were the highest ever. In fact, if Jon had reported any of the net gambling income, their joint Federal income tax liability would have increased by $140,000. When Jon finally is nabbed by the FBI, he is taken to jail. Mary is unable to locate any of Jon's earnings in bank or brokerage accounts. Can Mary fend off the IRS's charge that she should pay the $140,000 in tax, plus interest and penalties, from her salary as a physician?

59. Maria has an unusually strong constitution and the highest quality blood and plasma available for transfusion. She manages to stay healthy while donating

blood at the hospital two or three times a week. For each donation, the Blood Center pays Maria $175 for the blood. Maria drives forty miles round-trip to the hospital to make her donation. Moreover, she spends about $35 every month for vitamins and other pills prescribed by her physician to ensure that her general health and blood quality do not degenerate in light of her frequent donations. Last year, Maria quit all of her part-time jobs and now survives financially solely by these blood donations. Specify the tax consequences of this regular activity.

60. Chang, a brain surgeon, pays for the *Journal of Brain Research* under the three-year plan; he paid $3,000 this year for a three-year subscription to the weekly scientific journal, which charges $1,500 for an annual renewal. In what year(s) can Chang deduct this $3,000?

61. Handy Corporation assists its relocated executives by buying their homes if an acceptable deal cannot be struck before the move. Purchase is made at the appraised value. What is the nature of Handy's gain or loss on the subsequent sale?

62. Walt was convicted of murder and sent to prison for life. Walt continued to profess his innocence. His sister, Wanda, believed him, and after spending three years in law school and two years gathering facts, she proved that he was innocent. Walt and Wanda assigned the book, movie, and photo rights concerning their story to Warner Brothers for $500,000. How is this payment treated by Walt and Wanda?

63. Hugo was burying his (dead) dog when he unearthed 100,000 certificates of ITT bearer bonds, current value $4,000,000. He speculated that they had been placed there by the (also dead) former owner of Hugo's home, at a time when they were worth nearly $400,000. Hugo did not sell the bonds by the end of the year. Must Hugo recognize any gross income with respect to the bonds?

64. Karla is a single parent with two children ages 7 and 11. She is a full-time student and earns $12,000. Both of her children receive dividends and capital gains from mutual funds started for them by their grandparents. Karla has elected to include her children's income on her return for the kiddie tax computation. Since it is on her tax return, does her children's income affect the computation of Karla's earned income credit?

65. At gunpoint, Roger lent $2,000 from the cash register at his hardware store to four large youths who told Roger that they would set up their own store to compete with Roger's. Not having the phone number of any of the sprightly entrepreneurs, Roger could not recover any of the invested funds. Can Roger claim any deduction with respect to this loan? In what tax year?

66. Phyllis, a Virginia resident, owns some property in Florida. Every year, she travels to Florida (coincidentally, during baseball's spring training season) to inspect the property, initiate repairs, and look for new tenants and new properties in which to invest. She also attends about twenty ball games. Determine Phyllis's deductible travel expenses.

67. Bruce wanted to be an Olympic skater. His family paid $12,000 in 1998 and $14,000 in 1999 for travel and training expenses related to skating practices and competitions. Bruce made the 2000 U.S. Olympic team. The U.S. Olympic Committee is an exempt organization. How much of Bruce's expenses are deductible and when?

68. Harold installed a safe and an alarm system and bought a German shepherd dog to protect his vintage movie and video collection. What are his deductible items?

69. Donna's and Albert's children attend a parochial grade school. The school charges $1,500 annual tuition and $200 for uniforms for Donna's children, but only $500 tuition and $100 for uniforms for Albert's children because he is a member of the congregation. Albert contributed $800 to the church this year. Can Donna and Albert withdraw amounts out of their children's educational (IRA) savings accounts to pay for this private primary education? What is the amount of Albert's charitable contribution for the year?

70. Julie sings in the Seattle Symphony Chorus. The rules of the chorus require that its members wear traditional formal wear (i.e., $400 tuxedos for the men and $250 long black gowns for the women) during performances. In addition, because of her annual $15,000 contribution to the chorus's patron drive, Julie is a member of the symphony's board of directors. The board chooses the works to be performed, sites for the concerts, and the resident conductor. How much of Julie's $15,250 expenditures on behalf of the exempt orchestra this year can she deduct?

71. Tony, a single parent, spent $2,160 on after-school care for his 6-year-old son. Tony received $900 from the Department of Social Services (DSS) for child care as part of the welfare assistance program in which he is enrolled. In determining his child care credit, how much of the DSS payments are included in gross income, and what is the amount of Tony's child care costs for computing the child care credit?

ADVANCED CASES

These items require that you have access to research materials other than the Federal tax law and related services. For instance, you might need to refer to an international tax or multi-state service to prepare your solution for these cases. Consult with your instructor before beginning your work to be certain you have available to you all of the necessary research resources for the case(s) that you choose.

72. A friend of yours took a job in the air transportation industry. Knowing that you are taking tax courses, she asks you about the excise taxes that her firm must pay and some proposed changes in the deposit dates for those excise taxes. She is curious what the changes might be and whether the changes are in effect currently. Indicating that excise taxes for the air transportation industry are not generally covered in your research class, you tell your friend that you will see what you can find out about this for her. What do you learn about excise taxes for the air transportation industry?

73. Which of the following receipts are taxable to the state high school athletic association as unrelated business income?
    - Ticket revenues from the basketball tournaments
    - Advertising revenues from the programs sold at the tournaments
    - Subsidy from the state budget for the tournaments
    - Payment from Grand Central Limited to be the official sponsor of the tournaments

74. VanDelay, a citizen of the United States but a resident of Dulcinea, is an important sculptor. This year, he came to the United States to appear at a showing of his work in San Francisco. The United States has no tax treaty with Dulcinea. Does the $250,000 that VanDelay netted from the show qualify for the § 911 earned income exclusion?

75. Which of the following payments by International Partners, Inc., a Montana corporation, qualifies for the foreign tax credit?
    - Income tax paid to Germany, covered by an existing treaty
    - Income tax paid to Adagio, with which the United States has no income tax treaty
    - Value-added tax paid to Largetto, with which the United States has no income tax treaty
    - Oil extraction tax paid to Tedesco, with which the United States has no income tax treaty
    - Transportation tax paid to Santa Lucia, with which the United States has no income tax treaty. The tax is reduced dollar-for-dollar when International provides consulting services in designing Santa Lucia's new bullet train system. This year, International incurred $1 million in taxes but earned a $600,000 reduction for its services.

76. Heather had named Brenda the executrix of her estate. Brenda had no experience in this domain, but she filed the return, and the estate paid a Federal death tax of $2 million. This year, Heather's son Dylan, studying for a master's degree in taxation, discovered that Brenda had not reported any of Heather's realty in the gross estate and that an additional $250,000 in tax and interest was due. The IRS then assessed various penalties, totaling $30,000. How can the estate, now administered by Dylan, avoid this penalty?

77. Popular Inc. has its corporate headquarters, plants, and warehouses all located in Vermont. Until this year, all of its sales have been in Vermont. Its first out-of-state sale of $1 million (cost of sales, $300,000) is shipped by a common carrier trucking firm from Popular's warehouse to the purchaser's dock in Indiana. The truck stops for gasoline in New York and Ohio, and its driver spends a night in Ohio. To which states must Popular apportion income from the sale? How much income is taxed in each such state?

78. The Ohio Government Employees Credit Union (Union) was created by merging the Ohio Teachers Bank, the Ohio Transit Credit Association, and the Federal Government Workers Credit Bank. The stock issued by the merged entity is held by those having deposits in Union. The Union believes that it is not subject to the Ohio franchise tax (an income tax) because immunity is implied under the Supremacy Clause of the U.S. Constitution. The Union believes it is closely connected with the government and thus should be exempt from taxation. Is the Union correct in its conclusion that it is not subject to the Ohio franchise tax?

79. Tax Analysts reported that the country of Bhutan recently introduced an individual income tax. How are wages (including perks), Bhutan company dividends, interest, rental income, and cash crops taxed? Is the tax proportional or progressive? Do students receive any special treatment?

EXTENSIVE CASE

80. Thomas and Nicole Eirgo have been married for 20 years and have three children, Candice, age 18, and twin boys, Trevor and Julian, age 12. Nicole has an undergraduate degree in accounting and worked in public accounting while Thomas was obtaining his law degree. Five years ago they quit their jobs and

started TechKnow, a C corporation that develops legal and tax software specifically for accountants and lawyers with hi-tech clients. Thomas and Nicole work more than full time at TechKnow and have received only modest salaries. No dividends have been paid. The business has finally started to make substantial profits, but success, unfortunately, has brought problems. Thomas and Nicole have very different opinions regarding TechKnow's future. Thomas would like to continue to reinvest most of the profits for the development of software for other specialties, whereas Nichole would like to focus on the lines they have and enjoy their success by distributing some of the profits. Since they cannot come to an agreement, the earnings are being retained, and no new software is being developed.

These business disagreements are having a disastrous toll on their marriage. The only solution Thomas and Nicole see is to a divorce. As might be expected, Thomas and Nicole cannot decide on how to separate their ownership interests in TechKnow. Some options they are considering are redeeming Nicole's stock, having Thomas and/or the children buy the stock, or dividing the business in some manner between the two.

One thing Nicole has decided is to fulfill a lifelong dream of obtaining a doctorate degree in accounting. She will be entering a PhD program in the fall, at which time the divorce should be final. Since Candice will also be attending college, she will live in an apartment with her mother. Thomas will keep the house, and the boys will live with him. Thomas will pay Nicole alimony and child support while she and Candice are in school. The terms and amounts will be determined at the time the divorce is final.

Advise the Eirgos on the tax consequences of the above events. Support your conclusions with primary citations.

8

Citators and Other Finding Devices

LEARNING OBJECTIVES

- Understand the function of the citator in the tax research process
- Become adept at using the indexing systems in each of the most popular tax citators
- Know the abbreviation and reference conventions used by the most popular tax citators
- Efficiently use the update materials in the most popular tax citators
- Know the comparative strengths and weaknesses of the most popular tax citators
- Become familiar with the basic and advanced citator functions of Internet resources

CHAPTER OUTLINE

Basic Research Goals
Citators
    What Is a Citator?
    Commercial Citators
    RIA Citators
        RIA Citators *Organization*
        RIA Citators *Conventions*
        RIA Citators *Rulings*

CCH Citator
    CCH Citator *Conventions*
Shepard's and Lexis Citation Services
    Shepard's Citators
    Lexis Services
Westlaw Citator System
    KeyCite

Earlier chapters of this text discuss the tremendous number of legislative, administrative, and judicial sources of the tax law. This body of law is constantly changing because new laws are passed, administrative pronouncements are issued, judicial opinions are released, and old laws are superseded or overruled on a daily basis. This chapter addresses how tax practitioners can find the most up-to-date tax laws, cases, and administrative material in both published and electronic forms.

BASIC RESEARCH GOALS

The goals of tax research are to define the research problem, to find tax law that addresses the problem, to apply the law to the problem, to reach a conclusion about how the tax law affects the client, and to communicate the findings to the client. Research serves different functions at different points in this process. In the beginning, the researcher is trying to obtain a basic understanding of the tax law pertaining to the client's problem. Reading journal articles or other authoritative explanations of the law, such as those found in tax services, is helpful at this stage. Next the researcher wants to determine how the primary source of tax law, the *Internal Revenue Code,* applies to the client's situation. Once the applicable Code sections are identified, they must be interpreted. Remember, if the Code is clear, practitioners need look no further because it is of the highest authority. However, in most cases the Code is not clear, and practitioners turn to other primary tax law sources such as Regulations, rulings, or court cases to seek clarification. In this phase, the tax law is searched to find primary sources that interpret specific Code sections or contain facts resembling those in the client's case. Performing these research functions has been covered in Chapters 6 and 7. Finally, once an opinion is formed as to the optimum application of the law to the client's situation, the practitioner needs to confirm that the primary tax law being relied upon has not been affected by subsequent developments. How to verify whether primary sources are still good law is covered in this chapter. Lastly, the conclusions of the practitioner, based on the results of the research and verification of the sources, can then be communicated to the client by the methods covered in Chapter 10.

Both published and electronic tax research sources can be used to meet these goals with varying degrees of effectiveness. Some materials may only be accessible to the researcher in one source because either the publisher or the researcher's library supports only one type. Thus, the researcher should be familiar with a variety of tax services and both published and electronic sources.

CITATORS

Law relies heavily on precedent, and tax law is no exception. Virtually every time a case is decided, the judge who writes the opinion refers to other cases and administrative rulings for guidance. The law attempts to maintain continuity so people can anticipate the application of the law to their situations. Each appellate opinion sets a precedent that applies to later cases.

WHAT IS A CITATOR?

The law is constantly in a state of flux, and, again, tax law is no exception. The Code is changed frequently by passage of tax bills. Regulations are proposed, finalized, and withdrawn. Administrative rulings are issued, modified, superceded, and revoked or made obsolete by other changes in the tax law. A case decided at one level may be appealed by one or both parties. The higher court may overrule the lower court. Infrequently, a court may see a flaw in the reasoning it or another (equal or lower) court used to decide an earlier case or use a different reasoning to reach a distinct decision. When a court takes some action that relies on, rejects, or affects the holding of another case, it refers to that case in its opinion. All of this results in a tangle of inter-references among vast numbers of cases.

Along with statutory law, tax practitioners rely on administrative rulings and court decisions to interpret the law and argue the appropriate treatment of their clients' tax transactions. They must be able to determine if subsequent events have affected the validity of the law on which they rely. Thus, they need a tool to help them ascertain which rulings and cases are strong precedents and which have little to no value. One way would be to follow the reference threads from case to case or ruling to ruling, but this would be extremely tedious and would only identify earlier cases. Fortunately, citators do much of this work of following the threads in subsequent cases and summarize, in shorthand form, where the threads lead and what they mean.

A citator is a tool through which a tax researcher can learn the history of a case or ruling and evaluate the strength of its holdings. Before a researcher relies on the opinion in a case or analysis in a ruling, it is important to ascertain how later cases and rulings have treated the holdings. Thus, when a case or ruling relevant to a client's tax situation is found, this document's listing in the citator will indicate what later cases and rulings have said about its opinion. Some secondary sources such as law review articles may be included in the citators as well.

To avoid confusion, it is important to learn the specific terminology that describes references between cases. When one case refers to another case, it **cites** the latter case. The case making reference to another case is called the **citing case.** The case that is referenced is the **cited case.** The citing case will contain the name of the cited case and where the cited case can be found. The reference is called a **citation.** A **citator** is a service, in either published or electronic form, that indexes cited cases, gives full citations, and lists the citing cases and where each citing case can be found. A significant older case, one that establishes an important principle, may have been cited in hundreds of other cases. Thus, its entry in a citator would be extremely long and complex. A very recent or narrow case would have few cites and thus have a short entry.

A citator will not provide all types of information about a case or a ruling. For instance, it does not guide the researcher to documents related to the case or ruling that do not specifically cite it. While the *CCH Citator* will lead into its annotated service, the other citators do not provide this direct access to explanations. Citators do not indicate when a case or ruling is no longer effective because of changes in the Code, unless the Code itself specifically identifies the document. This is because citators are created by searching primary sources for cites to the case or ruling. You can perform the same type of search by using the case name or its official cite in a keyword search of a database containing all primary sources. Imagine what an arduous task this would have been before the advent of electronically searchable databases! It is amazing that there were citators long before there were computers. Given the tremendous number of court cases issued annually, the citator is a vital element in the practitioner's tax research process.

The various commercial citators organize the lists of citing cases in distinctive ways. Depending on the researcher's purpose, one citator may be more helpful than another. For example, one citator may only list citations that have a major impact on the logic or holding of the cited case. Another may list all citations. A researcher, initially checking to make sure a case has not been overruled, would prefer the former. The citations may be annotated to indicate the type of impact the citing case has on the cited case (e.g., modified, overruled, followed). A case may be considered at the trial and appellate levels and generate a decision at each level. Because each level of decision in a case may be cited in other documents, cases are generally organized by jurisdictional level. As each citator is discussed in this chapter, you should consider its suitability for specific research applications.

It is important for the practitioner to consider a case in context, to trace its judicially derived decision, and to monitor the reaction of subsequent court cases. This is even more important when the opinion is innovative. By using a citator properly, the practitioner reviews subsequent courts' reactions and determines the strength of the precedent established by the opinion. However, before turning to a case, the Code and Regulations that are the basis for the tax question being researched must be read and analyzed. Remember, cases and rulings are reviewed to provide guidance in interpreting the law.

When a case has been identified as pertinent to a research question, the first step in its review is an examination of the citator's lists of subsequent citing cases. For instance, say that a tax researcher has identified *Corn Products Refining Company* (a 1955 Supreme Court holding) as pertinent to a research project. The holding in the case might help or hurt the client's case. The task, then, is to find out how strong the holding in the *Corn Products* case is. The researcher must determine how subsequent cases evaluated the legal reasoning and findings of the *Corn Products* decision. In addition, the researcher must determine if changes in the Code made the case obsolete.

COMMERCIAL CITATORS

The three commercial citators that exclusively cover tax cases are updated frequently and on a regular schedule to keep their information current. The Commerce Clearing House (CCH) and Research Institute of America (RIA) citators are organized alphabetically by the case names. *Shepard's Federal Tax Citator* is organized by reference to the case reporter in which the case is reproduced. The CCH citations are *general*, directing the researcher to the first page of the citing case, whereas the other two citators have citations that are *local* (also called pinpoint), directing the researcher to the exact page where the cited case is mentioned in the citing case. For example, *Corn Products* (350 US 46) is cited in *Kraft, Inc.*, (30 Fed Cl 739) on page 820. The CCH citing is *Kraft, Inc.*, 30 Fed Cl 739, whereas the RIA citator has *Kraft, Inc.*, 30 Fed Cl 820.

These three commercial citators are available in published or electronic formats. CCH provides its citator as part of its *Standard Federal Tax Reporter* tax services, whereas the *RIA citator* is offered separately from its tax services. Both of these are available on CDs and through the Internet from each company's web site. *Shepard's Federal Tax Citator* is also offered through the Internet exclusively by LEXIS.

The discussion in this chapter concentrates on the three major tax citators, RIA, CCH, and Shepard's. The Westlaw KeyCite citator will also be reviewed. It does not, however, have a separate tax citator. The published versions of the citators are reviewed because these give a sense of the origins and evolution of citators, as well as some concept of the physical scope of the information contained in citators. The electronic versions tend to be just the paper publication in electronic form. While each of the citators can still be perused in published form, they may be offered exclusively in electronic formats in the near future. In the meantime we can still experience the musty charm of such books as the well-worn original *Prentice-Hall Citator,* published in 1941.

RIA CITATORS

The **Research Institute of America Citator** and **Citator 2nd Series** were formerly published by Prentice-Hall and then Maxwell Macmillan. Many practitioners still refer to this service as the *Prentice-Hall **(PH) Citators,*** however, the name "Prentice-Hall" was eliminated from the *Citator 2nd Series* as of Volume 3. In this text, the full series will be called the *RIA Citators,* with the older volumes referred to as the *PH Citators* and the newer volumes as *Citator 2d Series.*

The coverage of *RIA Citators* is comprehensive. Along with tax cases, Treasury Decisions and Administrative Pronouncements (hereafter referred to as Rulings) are evaluated. All District Court, Federal Claims, Court of Appeals, and Supreme Court cases reported in the AFTR, AFTR2d, and AFTR3d series are included, as well as Tax Court and Tax Court Memorandum decisions. Non-published cases such as the Small Claims division of the Tax Court, however, are not represented in the *RIA Citators.* An abbreviated list of the Rulings contained in the *RIA Citators* is provided in Exhibit 8–1. The citations for Rulings are found in the back of each citator volume.

RIA Citators Organization

The *RIA Citators* are divided into two series. The first series *(PH Citators)* consists of three bound volumes covering the Federal tax cases dated between 1863 and 1953. The second series *(Citator 2nd Series)* consists of three hard bound volumes, 1954–1977, 1978–1989, and 1990–1996, plus a soft bound volume for 1997–2000 and cumulative monthly supplements that cover from 2001 to the present. Exhibit 8–2 explains which volumes of the *RIA Citators* must be consulted, depending on when the case of interest was decided. Note that for older cases as many as eight volumes and supplements will need to be consulted. Thus, a substantial amount of valuable research time may be expended on a thorough citator search using the published volumes.

Each bound volume provides the history of cases that were decided during the period which the volume covers. Each volume also includes updates for cited cases that first appeared in previous volumes. One exception to this general organization scheme should be noted. Originally, Tax Court Memorandum decisions were not included in the citators. Thus, none of these cases are found in Volume 1 of the *PH Citators.* Initial entries for decisions issued during the period 1934–1941 are found in Volume 2 of the *PH Citators.*

Exhibit 8–1
RIA Citators Treasury Decisions and Rulings Abbreviations

Treasury Decisions and Rulings Cited In *RIA Citator*

Abridged List

Announc	Announcements
ARM	Appeals and Revenue Memorandum
ARR	Appeals and Revenue Recommendations
Ct D	Court Decisions
Del Order	Commissioner's Delegation Order
EO	Executive Orders
GCM	General Council Memorandums
IR	Internal Revenue News Releases
IT	Income Tax Unit Rulings
Letter Rulings	Private Letter Rulings
LO	Law Opinions
News Release	News Releases
Notice	Notices
OD	Office Opinions
PS	Processing Tax Division Rulings
Rev Proc	Revenue Procedures
Rev Rul	Revenue Rulings
TD	Treasury Decisions
TD Cir	Treasury Decision Circular
TDO	Treasury Decision Order
TIR	Technical Information Release

One of the significant advantages of the electronic version of the *RIA Citators* is that the need to consult multiple volumes is eliminated. The citations from the various published volumes are found with only one search. However, the *RIA Citators* offered electronically do not include the older *PH Citators;* only the *Citator 2nd Series* is available. Thus, if a case being cited was decided before 1954, the researcher must resort to the published versions of the *PH Citators*.

Exhibit 8–2
RIA Citators Organization

Consult Volumes

For Decisions Dated	PH Citator	Citator 2nd Series
1863–1941	1, 2, 3	1, 2, 3, 4 and supplements
1942–1947	2, 3	1, 2, 3, 4 and supplements
1948–1953	3	1, 2, 3, 4 and supplements
1954–1977	None	1, 2, 3, 4 and supplements
1978–1989	None	2, 3, 4 and supplements
1990–1996	None	3, 4 and supplements
1997–2000	None	4 and supplements
2001–present	None	supplements

The *Citator 2nd Series* can be accessed through the RIA Checkpoint Internet service using either the Citations folder tab or the Contents option (see Chapter 6, Exhibit 6–1). Selecting the Citation tab allows the researcher to enter a case either by name or citation and a ruling by citation (see Chapter 6, Exhibit 6–7). As shown in Exhibit 8–3, the document provides the location of the *Upjohn* case within the AFTR 2d series (at the top of the document), Code section addressed in the case, prior history of the *Upjohn* case, and its full citation. The three buttons just above the *Upjohn* case name access annotations of the case in the *United States Tax Reporter*

Exhibit 8–3
RIA Checkpoint Case Document

Results ▸▸   Database List   Document List   Document

Document Location:
American Federal Tax Reports (1860 - 2000)   1
  1981   1
    AFTR 2d Vol. 47   1
      47 AFTR 2D 81-593 (636 F.2d 1139) - 47 AFTR 2d 81-452 (630 F.2d 654)   1
        UPJOHN CO., ET AL. v. U.S., ET AL., 47 AFTR 2d 81-523 (101 S.Ct. 677), Code Sec(s) 7602, (S Ct), 01/13/1981
1

▸ Annot ▸ FTC ▸ Citator

UPJOHN CO., ET AL. v. U.S., ET AL., Cite as 47 AFTR 2d 81-523 (101 S.Ct. 677), 01/13/1981 , Code Sec(s) 7602

UPJOHN CO., ET AL., PETITIONERS v. U.S., ET AL., RESPONDENTS.

Case Information:

Code Sec(s):	7602
Court Name:	U.S. Supreme Court,
Docket No.:	No. 79-886,
Date Decided:	01/13/1981
Prior History:	Court of Appeals, (6th Cir.) 44 AFTR 2d 79-5179, reversed.
Disposition:	Decision for taxpayer.
Cites:	47 AFTR 2d 81-523, 449 US 383, 101 S Ct 677, 66 L Ed 2d 584, 81-1 USTC P 9138.

HEADNOTE

1. INTERNAL REVENUE SERVICE—Discovery of liability and enforcement of tax—authority in general—privileged communications. Attorney-client privilege attached to employee statements made to counsel during internal investigation of possible illegal payments. Privilege didn't apply to statements which weren't responses to questionnaires or interview questions. Communications were made by employees beyond control group, not taxpayer's officers and agents, but narrow interpretation of control group frustrated privilege. Privilege attached since information was furnished by employees acting within scope of employment and was otherwise unavailable from upper-echelon management.

Reference(s): 1981 P-H Fed. ¶39,650(15). Code Sec. 7602.

2. INTERNAL REVENUE SERVICE—Discovery of liability and enforcement of tax—authority in general—privileged communications. Work-product doctrine applied to IRS summons seeking memoranda prepared by taxpayer's general counsel during internal investigation of illegal payments. Government's substantial need or inability to locate equivalent information by questioning taxpayer's employees wasn't enough to mandate disclosure of attorney's mental processes. And memoranda based on employees' oral statements were otherwise protected by attorney-client privilege.

Reference(s): 1981 P-H Fed. ¶39,650(50). Code Sec. 7602.

OPINION

(Annot button), paragraph references of the case in the *Federal Tax Coordinator 2d* (FTC button), or the case's listing in the *Citator 2nd Series* (Citator button).

Using the Contents option to access the *Citator 2nd Series,* the researcher selects "Citator 2nd" in the Show Contents For pull-down menu in Exhibit 8–4. At this point, the researcher may either perform a keyword search on the case name using the Options > Search TOC Entries (at top of screen) or drill down to the case name after clicking on the Citator 2nd title (in background of Exhibit 8–4).

As previously stated, the published *RIA Citators* are not included as part of either of the RIA tax services, the *United States Tax Reporter* or the *Federal Tax Coordinator 2d*. Consequently, cases do not have paragraph references indicating where in the services the cases are reviewed. To find these paragraph references, the researcher must examine the Finding Lists provided in both services. The Finding Lists arrange the court cases alphabetically and give the reporter location where the full text of the case may be found, as well as the paragraph references. As discussed in Chapter 6, Finding Lists cannot function as a citator. They provide neither a detailed judicial history of the case nor a list of other cases in which the case is cited. They merely serve as an entry to the published tax services and as a method of locating a reproduction of the case.

RIA Citators Conventions

When the plaintiff in a tax case is the U.S. Government, Commissioner of Internal Revenue, Secretary of the Treasury, or an IRS District Director, the *RIA Citators* do not list the case under the plaintiff's name as is the traditional legal convention. This is because there are literally thousands of cases in which Eisner, Helvering, Burnet, or other Commissioners or Secretaries of the Treasury initiated the litigation. Rather,

Exhibit 8–4
RIA Checkpoint Contents Screen

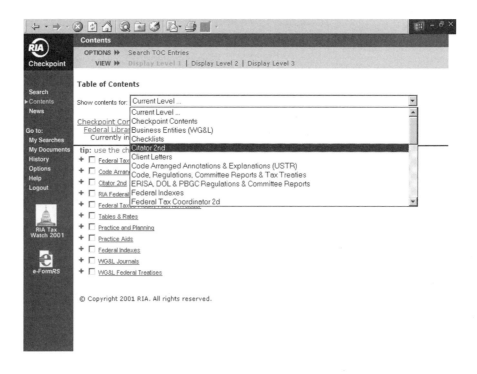

the *RIA Citators* list all cases in alphabetical order by the taxpayer's name. This convention greatly facilitates the researcher's search for specific cases.

To illustrate the *RIA Citators* conventions we will examine the *Upjohn* case already introduced in Exhibit 8–3. This case generated three separate opinions, and its course through the courts is one frequently encountered. It was first decided in 1978 by the U.S. District Court (41 AFTR2d 78-796), which found for the IRS. The taxpayer appealed to the U.S. Court of Appeals for the Sixth Circuit. This case, decided in 1979 (44 AFTR2d 79-5179), found for the IRS on most issues. The taxpayer appealed again, this time to the U.S. Supreme Court. The Supreme Court decided the case in the taxpayer's favor in 1981 (47 AFTR2d 81-523). Consequently, there are three separate entries in Exhibit 8–5 for this case in the *Citator 2nd Series,* Volume 2: the trial court, the appellate court, and the Supreme Court. Notice that the Court of Appeals case entry (44 AFTR2d 79-5179) is listed in the citator before the Supreme Court case (47 AFTR2d 81-523) and the trial court case entry (41 AFTR2d 78-796) is presented after the Supreme Court case. The Supreme Court citation of *Upjohn* is designated by a bold black bullet. Each of these courts wrote an opinion that can be cited by other cases. The Supreme Court opinion is the most likely to be cited, because it is the final decision on the issues. There is little reason for future decisions to cite the trial or appellate cases, since they were reversed.

Exhibit 8–5 *RIA Citator 2nd Series,* Volume 2, *Upjohn Case*

→ **UPJOHN CO., THE; U.S. v, 44 AFTR2d 79-5179, 600 F2d 1223 (USCA 6, 6-28-79)**
    r—Upjohn Co. v. U.S., 47 AFTR2d 81-523, 449 US 383, 101 S Ct 677, 66 LEd2d 584
    remg—Upjohn Co.; U.S. v, 41 AFTR2d 78-796 (DC Mich)
    Davis, Craig E.: U.S. v, 47 AFTR2d 81-948, 636 F2d 1039 (USCA 5) [See 44 AFTR2d 79-5182, 600 F2d 1228, n. 13]
    q—El Paso Co., The; U.S. v, 50 AFTR2d 82-5536, 682 F2d 538 (USCA 5) [See 44 AFTR2d 79-5182, 600 F2d 1228, n. 12]
    n—El Paso Co., The; U.S. v, 50 AFTR2d 82-5546, 682 F2d 550 (USCA 5) [See 44 AFTR2d 79-5182, 600 F2d

    q-1—Amerada Hess Corp.; U.S. v, 45 AFTR2d 80-589, 619 F2d 987 (USCA 10)
    e-1—Bonnell, Harold; U.S. v, 45 AFTR2d 80-730, 483 F Supp 1079 (DC Minn) [See 44 AFTR2d 79-5182, 600 F2d 1228, n. 13]

→ • **UPJOHN CO. v U.S., 47 AFTR2d 81-523, 449 US 383, 101 S Ct 677, 66 LEd2d 584 (1-13-81)**
    sr—Upjohn Co., The; U.S. v, 44 AFTR2d 79-5179, 600 F2d 1223 (USCA 6)
    f—Zolin, Frank S.; U.S. v, 63 AFTR2d 89-1487 (US) 109 S Ct 2625 [See 47 AFTR2d 81-526, 449 US 389]
    n—Young, Arthur, & Co.; U.S. v, 49 AFTR2d 82-1115, 82-1117, 677 F2d 222, 224 (USCA 2)
    e—Grand Jury 83-2, In re; U.S. v, 55 AFTR2d 85-367 (USCA 4) [See 47 AFTR2d 81-526, 449 US 389]
    e—Klein, Lee J., In re, 56 AFTR2d 85-6167 (USCA 7) [See 47 AFTR2d 81-530, 449 US 399]
    f—Aronson, Mitchell; U.S. v, 56 AFTR2d 85-6369, 610 F Supp 220 (DC Fla) [See 47 AFTR2d 81-526, 449 US 398]
    k—Hartz Mountain Industries, Inc. & Subs, 93 TC 525, 93 PH TC 264 [See 47 AFTR2d 81-526, 449 US 389]
    Mulvania, Richard L., 1984 PH TC Memo 84-369 [See 47 AFTR2d 81-526, 449 US 389]
    k-1—Doe, John v U.S.; 62 AFTR2d 88-5750, 487 US 214, 108 S Ct 2350
    l—Wyatt, Oscar S., Jr.; U.S. v, 47 AFTR2d 81-789, 637 F2d 295 (USCA 5)
    l—Moody, Shearn, Jr. v I.R.S., 48 AFTR2d 81-5172, 654 F2d 798 (CADC)

    l—Riewe, Daryl; U.S. v, 49 AFTR2d 82-1205, 676 F2d 420 (USCA 10)
    e-1—El Paso Co., The; U.S. v, 50 AFTR2d 82-5535—82-5536, 682 F2d 538 (USCA 5) [See 47 AFTR2d 81-526, 449 US 389]
    n-1—El Paso Co., The; U.S. v, 50 AFTR2d 82-5546, 682 F2d 550 (USCA 5)
    n-1—El Paso, Co., The; U.S. v, 50 AFTR2d 82-5546, 682 F2d 551 (USCA 5)
    l—Sealed Case, In re, 50 AFTR2d 82-5646, 82-5647, 82-5648, 82-5649, 676 F2d 808, 810, 811 (CADC)
    l—Newton, Willis H., In re, 52 AFTR2d 83-6309, 718 F2d 1021 (USCA 11)
    e-1—Liebman, Emanuel; U.S. v, 54 AFTR2d 84-5939, 84-5940, 742 F2d 809, 810 (USCA 3) [See 47 AFTR2d 81-526, 449 US 389]
    k-1—Olson, Robert G. v U.S., 63 AFTR2d 89-1170, 872 F2d 822 (USCA 8)
    g-1—Firestone Tire & Rubber Co., The v Dept. of Justice, 50 AFTR2d 82-5490 (DC DC)
    f-1—LSB Industries, Inc. & Subsidiaries v Comm., 51 AFTR2d 83-344, 556 F Supp 42 (DC Okla)
    e-1—Kilpatrick, William A.; U.S. v, 56 AFTR2d 85-6086, 85-6092—85-6093, 594 F Supp 1342, 1350 (DC Colo)
    g-1—Parker, Lyndon J.; U.S. v, 58 AFTR2d 86-5368 (DC Pa)
    f-1—Isherwood, Hunter & Diehm; Olive, Anthony P. v, 60 AFTR2d 87-5044, 656 F Supp 1173 (DC Virgin Islands)
    k-1—Holifield, Dallas L. v U.S., 62 AFTR2d 88-5764, 689 F Supp 867 (DC Wis)
    f-2—Young, Arthur, & Co.; U.S. v, 49 AFTR2d 82-1113, 677 F2d 219 (USCA 2)
    f-2—Delaney, Migdail & Young, Chartered v I.R.S., 60 AFTR2d 87-5515, 826 F2d 127 (CADC)
    e-2—Schenectady Svgs. Bk.; U.S. v, 49 AFTR2d 82-1056, 525 F Supp 650 (DC NY)

→ **UPJOHN CO.; U.S. v, 41 AFTR2d 78-796 (DC Mich, 2-23-78)**
    remd—Upjohn Co., The; U.S. v, 44 AFTR2d 79-5179, 600 F2d 1223 (USCA 6)

Examining the entries in Exhibit 8–5 reveals that after the *Upjohn* case name is the case's citation in RIA's AFTR2d series, followed by other reporter locations of the same case, called parallel citations. First, the official reporters (government publications) are listed and then other unofficial court reporters (commercial publishers). Citations to the USTC series, published by RIA's main competitor, CCH, are not supplied until the 1990 Volume of *Citator 2nd Series*.

The first entries after the case name provide the judicial history of the case. Symbols designate the effects of the higher courts' decisions on the holdings of lower courts that previously heard the case. The Appeals Court case (44 AFTR2d 79-5179) indicates that it was reversed (r-) by the Supreme Court and remanded (remg-) to the trial court. The Supreme Court case (47 AFTR2d 81-523) reversed (sr-) the Appeals Court's earlier decision. The trial court cite also indicates the remanding (remd-) of the case by the Appeals Court. The explanation of all the judicial history symbols for the cited cases is provided in Exhibit 8–6.

The symbols in Exhibit 8–7 apply to the citing case. These indicate the evaluation by the citing cases of the cited case. Hence, the "f" in front of the *Zolin, Frank; v U.S.*, in Exhibit 8–5 means that the *Frank Zolin* case followed the reasoning of the *Upjohn* case. Compare the Exhibit 8–5 published entry with the same entry from the RIA Checkpoint electronic service in Exhibit 8–8. In RIA Checkpoint, rather than using the notations, the entry states that *Frank Zolin* followed the reasoning of *Upjohn*. Providing words rather than symbols makes using the electronic version more efficient.

RIA Citators (published and electronic) first list the citations for cases that are in complete agreement with the cited case. These are indicated by the abbreviation "iv," short for the legal idiom "on all fours." Next, citing cases are listed that discuss the holdings or reasoning of the cited case but do not refer to a specific paragraph or headnote. There are six of these type cases listed for the Supreme Court *Upjohn* case in Exhibit 8–5.

The next cases are listed in order of the **headnote** issue that they address. As Exhibit 8–3 reveals, headnotes are the paragraphs in which the editors of the court reporter summarize the court's holdings on each issue. They appear before the text of the actual court case. The numbered headnotes for a specific case will not necessarily correspond among the various reporters, due to differences in the editors analyzing the relevant legal issues. Thus, when using headnote numbers to limit a citator search, the researcher must be cognizant of which court reporter headnote numbers are pertinent to each citator service. *RIA Citators* base headnote designations on the *American Federal Tax Reports* (AFTR and AFTR2d) series, which is also a product of RIA. For the *Upjohn* case, AFTR2d provides two headnotes. The researcher needs to make sure that with the *RIA Citators* the AFTR headnotes are utilized and not headnotes from other reporters, such as those published by West.

Within any of the citing groupings—all fours, no specific headnote, Headnote 1, Headnote 2, and so on—citing cases and rulings are listed in the following order.

- U.S. Supreme Court
- U.S. Courts of Appeal
- U.S. Court of Federal Claims (or predecessor court)
- U.S. District Court
- U.S. Tax Court (or predecessor court—BTA, regular and memorandum decisions)
- State courts
- Treasury Rulings and Decisions

Exhibit 8–6
RIA Citators Symbols for Cited Cases

SYMBOLS USED IN CITATOR COURT DECISIONS
Judicial History

a	affirmed by a higher court (Note: When available, the official cite to the affirmance is provided; if the affirmance is by unpublished order or opinion, the date of the decision and the court deciding the case are provided.)
App auth	appeal authorized by the Treasury
App	appeal pending (Note: Later volumes may have to be consulted to determine if the appellate case was decided.)
cert gr	petition for certiorari was granted by the U.S. Supreme Court
d	appeal dismissed by the court or withdrawn by the party filing the appeal
(G)	following an appeal notation, this symbol indicates that it was the government filing an appeal
m	the earlier decision has been modified by the higher court, or by a later decision.
r	the decision of the lower court has been reversed on appeal
rc	related case arising out of the same taxable event or concerning the same taxpayer
reh den	rehearing has been denied by the same court in which the original case was heard
reinst	a dismissed appeal has been reinstated by the appellate court and is under consideration again
remd	the case has been remanded for proceedings consistent with the higher court decision
remg	the cited case is remanding the earlier case
revg & remg	the decision of the lower court has been reversed and remanded by a higher court on appeal
s	same case or ruling
sa	the cited case is affirming the earlier case
sm	the cited case is modifying the earlier case
sr	the cited case is reversing the earlier case
sx	the cited case is an earlier proceeding in a case for which a petition for certiorari was denied
(T)	an appeal was filed from the lower court decision by the taxpayer
vacd	the lower court decision was vacated on appeal or by the original court on remand
vacg	a higher court or the original court on remand has vacated the lower court decision
widrn	the original opinion was withdrawn by the court
x	petition for certiorari was denied by the U.S. Supreme Court
•	Supreme Court cases are designated by a bold-faced bullet (•) before the case line for easy location

Certain notations appear at the end of the cited case line. These notations include:

(A)	the government has acquiesced in the reasoning or the result of the cited case
(NA)	the government has refused to acquiesce or to adopt the reasoning or the result of the cited case, and will challenge the position adopted if future proceedings arise on the same issue
on rem	the case has been remanded by a higher court and the case cited is the resulting decision

Exhibit 8–7
RIA Citators Symbols for Citing Cases

Evaluation of Cited Cases

- c   the citing case court has adversely commented on the reasoning of the cited case, and has criticized the earlier decision
- e   the cited case is used favorably by the citing case court
- f   the reasoning of the court in the cited case is followed by the later decision
- g   the cited and citing cases are distinguished from each other on either facts or law
- inap   the citing case court has specifically indicated that the cited case does not apply to the situation stated in the citing case.
- iv   on all fours (both the cited and citing cases are virtually identical)
- k   the cited and citing case principles are reconciled
- l   the rationale of the cited case is limited to the facts or circumstances surrounding that case (this can occur frequently in situations in which there has been an intervening higher court decision or law change)
- n   the cited case was noted in a dissenting opinion
- o   the later case directly overrules the cited case (use of the evaluation is generally limited to situations in which the court notes that it is specifically overturning the cited case, and that the case will no longer be of any value)
- q   the decision of the cited case is questioned and its validity debated in relation to the citing case at issue

The evaluations used for the court decisions generally are followed by a number. That number refers to the headnoted issue in the American Federal Tax Reports (AFTR) or Tax Court decision to which the citing case relates. If the case is not directly on point with any headnote, a bracketed notation at the end of the citing case line directs the researcher to the page in the cited case on which the issue appears.

A blank may appear in the evaluation space. Generally, this means that the citing court didn't comment on any of the legal issues raised in the cited case.

Citing cases within any court or ruling group are arranged in chronological order. The entries for the *Upjohn* case in Exhibit 8–5 illustrate this organization scheme.

In their listings, the *RIA Citators* (published and electronic) include all of the citing cases that mention the cited opinion. Therefore, the listings for important cases containing many issues can be several pages long. The headnote number references allow researchers to restrict their search to only those citing cases with issues that are relevant to their client's factual situation. Thus, if the researcher is interested in the issue described in the second headnote of the *Upjohn* case, only cases designated with a 2 in Exhibit 8–5 (*Young, Delaney,* and *Schenectady Savings Bank*) need be reviewed.

Many researchers prefer to start their analysis of a case with the most recent cases and work backward to earlier cases. In this way, they can quickly identify the present status of the cited case. For example, a steady stream of favorable references probably indicates that the precedent of the original case is still valid, whereas either a list of negative comments or a scarcity of references may indicate a weak or overruled decision. The citator portion of a research project is complete when the researcher is satisfied that the status of the case is sufficiently confirmed. At this point some of the citing cases should be examined because the facts of a client's situation are rarely identical to the cases initially located.

Exhibit 8–8
RIA Checkpoint Citation Screen

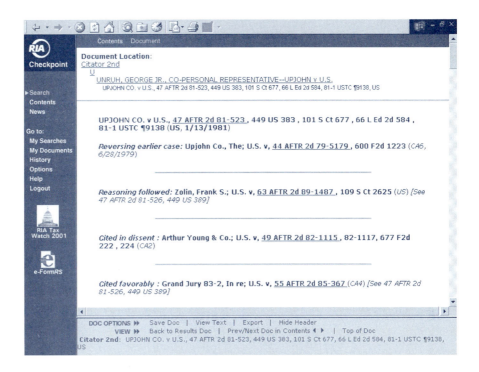

If the cases found initially support the client's position but the facts are somewhat different, the search should continue for a supportive case with more similar facts. Hence, those citations marked "k" or "cases reconciled," indicating that their facts or opinions are different from those of the cited case and require reconciliation, should be consulted. If the initial cases found have holdings adverse to a client's position, the practitioner should search for cases marked "g" or "cases distinguished," signifying that the citing case is distinguished from the cited case. These cases usually have found that their facts are actually different from those of the cited case, thus supporting a different holding. Some of these facts may resemble the facts of the practitioner's client and provide the desired support. Similarly, a case marked "l" or "cited generally" limits the holding of the cited case to a narrow set of facts. This may occur when a higher court has ruled differently on a case with somewhat similar facts or there has been a change in the tax law. Thus, the holding of the cited case may be inapplicable to the client's factual situation.

To complete the citator review for the *Upjohn* case, it is necessary to consult all subsequent bound volumes and paperback supplements. Exhibit 8–9 presents the citing cases in Volumes 3 and 4 of the *Citator 2nd Series* and the June 2001 supplement. All of these cases either followed the reasoning in the *Upjohn* case (f) or cited *Upjohn* favorably in their reasoning (e) but not to the extent of following it fully. From the number and support of citing cases we have reviewed, it is safe to conclude that the precedent of the *Upjohn* case is well established and the case is still good law.

RIA Citators Rulings

After identifying administrative rulings (Revenue Ruling, Revenue Procedure, Notice, etc.) that appear to support a client's tax position, it is critically important for a

Exhibit 8–9 *RIA Citator 2nd Series,* Updating, *Upjohn* Case

Volume 3 (1990 – 1996)	Volume 4 (1997 – 2000)	June 2001 Supplement
• **UPJOHN CO. v U.S.,** 47 AFTR 2d 81-523, 449 US 383, 101 S Ct 677, 66 L Ed 2d 584, 81-1 USTC ¶ 9138, (1-13-81) f—Holifield, Dallas L. v U.S., 66 AFTR 2d 90-5413, 909 F2d 203, (CA7). [See 47 AFTR2d 81-529, 449 US 396] f—Adlman, Monroe; U.S. v., 76 AFTR 2d 95-7191, (CA2), [See 47 AFTR2d 81-526, 449 US 389] f—Aramony, William; U.S. v. 78 AFTR 2d 96-5756, 88 F3d 1389, (CA4), [See 47 AFTR2d 81-526, 449 US 389] e—LeMaine, Reynald D. v. I.R.S., 71A AFTR 2d 93-4256, (DC MA). [See 47 AFTR2d 81-529, 449 US 395-396] f—Buckner, Roger C. v. U.S., 76 AFTR 2d 95-6656, (DC ID). [See 47 AFTR2d 81-526, 449 US 389] f—Palmer, Fred R.; U.S. v., et al. 76 AFTR 2d 95-6680, (DC ID). [See 47 AFTR2d 81-526, 449 US 389] f—Scott Paper Co v. U.S., 78 AFTR 2d 96-5670, 943 F Supp 499, (DC PA). [See 47 AFTR2d 81-526, 449 US 389] f—Matz, Jeffrey A. v. U.S., 78 AFTR 2d 96-6416, (DC AZ). [See 47 AFTR2d 81-526, 449 US 398] e—Fu Investment Co., Ltd., 104 TC 414, 104 TCR 247, [See 47 AFTR2d 81-526, 449 US 389] e—Bernardo, Bradford C. & Marybeth B., 104 TC (No. 33), 104 TCR 411, [See 47 AFTR2d 81-526, 449 US 389, cited at 93 TC 525] e-1—Mobil Corp.; U.S. v, 71 AFTR 2d 93-1876—93-1877, (DC TX) e-1—Kinney, Michael, M.D. v. U.S., 77 AFTR 2d 96-554, (DC FL) e-1—Chevron Corp; U.S. v., 77 AFTR 2d 96-1551, (DC CA) f-2—Rockwell Internat.; U.S. v, 65 AFTR 2d 90-840, 90-841, 897 F2d 1264, 1265, (CA3) e-2—Bell, Jack; U.S. v. 74 AFTR 2d 94-7273, 94-7275, (DC CA)	• **UPJOHN CO. v U.S.,** 47 AFTR 2d 81-523, 449 US 383, 101 S Ct 677, 66 L Ed 2d 584, 81-1 USTC ¶ 9138, (US, 1/13/1981) e—Massachusetts Institute of Technology; U.S. v., 80 AFTR 2d 97-7983, (CA1). [See 47 AFTR 2d 81-526, 449 US 389-390] e—Adlman, Monroe; U.S. v., 81 AFTR 2d 98-822, 98-823, 134 F3d 1196, 1197, (CA2), [See 47 AFTR 2d 81-526, 449 US 389] e—Frederick, Richard A.; U.S. v., 83 AFTR 2d 99-1872, 182 F3d 500, (CA7), [See 47 AFTR 2d 81-526, 449 US 389] e—Massachusetts Institute of Technology ;U.S. v., 79 AFTR 2d 97-596, (DC MA), [See 47 AFTR 2d 81-526, 449 US 389] e—Pribble, William C., Jr.; U.S. v., 79 AFTR 2d 97-1085, (DC MN), [See 47 AFTR 2d 81-530, 449 US 398] e—R.M. Dolgin, Inc; U.S. v., 81 AFTR 2d 98-808, (DC MO), [See 47 AFTR 2d 81-526, 449 US 389] e—Toliver, George T.; U.S. v., 81 AFTR 2d 98-543, 972 F Supp 1041, (DC VA), [See 47 AFTR 2d 81-526, 449 US 389] e—Boca Investerings Partnership v. U.S., 83 AFTR 2d 99-2317, (DC Dist Col), [See 47 AFTR 2d 81-526, 449 US 389] e—Boca Investerings Partnership v. U.S., 83 AFTR 2d 99-2314, (DC Dist Col), [See 47 AFTR 2d 81-526, 449 US 389] e—Jones, Harold W.; U.S. v., 84 AFTR 2d 99-6831, 99-6832, (DC SC), [See 47 AFTR 2d 81-526, 449 US 389] e—Hanna, John J. v. U.S., 80 AFTR 2d 97-7092, (Ct Fed Cl), [See 47 AFTR 2d 81-526, 449 US 389, cited at 63 AFTR 2d 89-1487, 491 US 562] e—Saba Partnership , et al, 1999 RIA TC Memo 99-2264, [See 47 AFTR 2d 81-526, 449 US 389, cited at 93 TC 525]	• **UPJOHN CO. v U.S.,** 47 AFTR 2d 81-523, 449 US 383, 101 S Ct 677, 66 L Ed 2d 584, 81-1 USTC ¶ 9138, (US, 1/13/1981) e—Segerstrom, Henry T. v. U.S., 87 AFTR 2d 2001-1154, (DC CA), [See 47 AFTR 2d 81-530, 449 US 398] e-1—Pomerantz, Gloria v. U.S., 87 AFTR 2d 2001-827, (DC FL)

researcher to determine if they are still in effect and represent the current view of the IRS. Due to the constant state of change in the tax law, rulings are continually being modified, superceded, or invalidated. As previously discussed, the *RIA Citators* include cites for Rulings in the back of each of its volumes (see Exhibit 8–1 for a list of Rulings covered by the *Citators*). The steps in checking the validity of a Ruling are the same as with a court case; however, the explanation symbols and citation organization are somewhat different. Exhibit 8–10 lists the notations for describing the judicial history of rulings. Exhibit 8–11 reproduces a page from the Treasury Decision and Ruling section of *Citator 2nd Series,* Volume 4. As this page demonstrates, the abbreviations of Exhibit 8–10 are utilized in evaluating the Rulings, in addition to the symbols for cited and citing cases given in Exhibits 8–6 and 8–7.

The pronouncements contained in the Treasury Decision and Ruling section of the *Citator 2nd Series* are presented in alphabetical order by type of ruling. The section starts with Announcements and ends with Treasury Decisions. Within each type of ruling the entries are presented in chronological order, as are the citing ruling for the entry. To the extent there are any cases citing the entry, they are listed after citing Revenue Rulings and before lesser pronouncements (such as Private Letter Rulings), as illustrated by Rev Rul 190, 1953-2 CB 303, in Exhibit 8–11. This ruling was followed (e) by Private Letter Ruling 9806007, reconciled with the *Daniela Aldea* case, and became obsolete with the issuance of Rev Rul 99-7. Examine Rev Rul 2000-4, also in Exhibit 8–11. It modifies (sm) and amplifies (ampfg) Rev Proc 99-49. This chronology emphasizes the importance of always checking pertinent pronouncements through a citator. What is currently good law may become unreliable at any point in the future.

Exhibit 8–10
RIA Citators Symbols for Cited Rulings

Symbols Used In Citator
Treasury Decisions and Rulings

Judicial History

The symbols and evaluations used for the treasury decisions and rulings are similar to those used for the court decisions, which are shown in pages v and vi, with some additions:

ampfd	amplified
ampfg	amplifying
clfd	clarified
clfg	clarifying
impmd	implemented
impmg	implementing
inap	inapplicable
ob	the cited boldface ruling has been declared obsolete by a later ruling, or has declared an earlier ruling obsolete
rescd	rescinded
rescg	rescinding
revkd	the IRS has revoked the cited ruling in light of its later position
revkg	the cited ruling is revoking the earlier ruling
supmd	supplemented
supmg	supplementing
supsd	the cited ruling has been superseded by a later ruling
supsdg	the cited ruling supersedes the earlier ruling
susp	the operation of the cited ruling is temporarily suspended

Note: Whenever possible, the rulings contain their official cites in the *Cumulative Bulletins*. Because of the proliferation of material, however, not all material is contained in that source. If there is no official location in the government's material, the cited ruling contains a reference to the *United States Tax Reporter* paragraph at which the ruling is reproduced.

CCH CITATOR

The *Commerce Clearing House Citator* (**CCH Citator**) is offered in print as an integral part of CCH's *Standard Federal Tax Reporter* (discussed in detail in Chapter 6) and is also available through CCH's Internet service Tax Research NetWork (NetWork) in the Federal Tax library and the U.S. Master Tax Guide Plus. It is not offered through any of the other major electronic services (such as Lexis, Kleinrock, or Westlaw).

The published *CCH Citator* differs dramatically from the *RIA Citators* on several points. First, the *CCH Citator* is housed in a two-volume, loose-leaf series with no bound volumes. The loose-leaf volumes are A to M and N to Z, with Rulings located in the back of the latter volume. Second, the main citator is updated yearly. Quarterly updates are filed in front of the A to M volume. The "[current year] Case Table" and the "Latest Additions to [current year] Case Table" located in the New Matters volume of the *Standard Federal Tax Reporter* tax service give the most recent case information. The latter is updated on a weekly basis.

These two points make citing a case or ruling in the *CCH Citator* far less time consuming than with the *RIA Citators*. However, the reason that the *CCH Citator* can be contained in just two loose-leaf binders is that it lists only those citing cases

Exhibit 8–11
RIA Citator 2nd Series,
Volume 4, Rulings
Citations

Rev Rul 99-14—Rev Rul 2000-41

Rev Rul 99-14, 1999 USTR ¶ 86,130
  e—Letter Ruling 199934002, 1999 USTR 86,806
  Notice 2000-15, 2000 USTR 86,379
  e—Notice 2000-20, 2000 USTR 86,428
  Rev Proc 99-26, 1999 USTR 86,616E
Rev Rul 99-15, 1999 USTR ¶ 86,149
Rev Rul 99-16, 1999 USTR ¶ 86,143, 1999 USTR (E&G)
  ¶ 144,336, 1999 USTR (Excise) ¶ 101,396
  s—IR- 1999-25, 1999 USTR ¶ 86,139, 1999 USTR (E&G)
    ¶ 144,334
Rev Rul 99-17, 1999 USTR ¶ 86,144
Rev Rul 99-18, 1999 USTR ¶ 86,170
  e—Rev Rul 99-24, 1999 USTR 86,588
  e—Rev Rul 99-38, 1999 USTR 86,790A
Rev Rul 99-19, 1999 USTR ¶ 86,187
Rev Rul 99-20, 1999 USTR (E&G) ¶ 144,340
  e—Rev Rul 2000-26, 2000 USTR (E&G) 20,030
Rev Rul 99-22, 1999 USTR ¶ 86,228
Rev Rul 99-23, 1999 USTR ¶ 86,221
  clfd—Announc 99-89, 1999 USTC ¶ 86,380
  e—Wells Fargo & Co and Subsidiaries v. Com., 86 AFTR
    2d 2000-5827, 224 F3d 888, (CA8)
  e—Notice 2000-12, 2000 USTR 86,329
Rev Rul 99-24, 1999 USTR ¶ 86,243
  e—Rev Rul 99-38, 1999 USTR 86,790A
Rev Rul 99-25, 1999 USTR ¶ 86,239
Rev Rul 99-26, 1999 USTR ¶ 86,270
Rev Rul 99-27, 1999 USTR ¶ 86,262, 1999 USTR (E&G)
  ¶ 144,342, 1999 USTR (Excise) ¶ 101,402
  s—IR- 1999-51, 1999 USTR ¶ 86,259
Rev Rul 99-28, 1999 USTR ¶ 86,268
  rc—IR- 1999-55, 1999 USTR 86,617
  revkg—Rev Rul 79-162, 1979-1 CB 116
Rev Rul 99-29, 1999 USTR ¶ 86,284
Rev Rul 99-30, 1999 USTR ¶ 86,301
Rev Rul 99-31, 1999 USTR ¶ 86,393
Rev Rul 99-33, 1999 USTR ¶ 86,362
Rev Rul 99-34, 1999 USTR ¶ 86,353
Rev Rul 99-35, 1999 USTR ¶ 86,342
Rev Rul 99-36, 1999 USTR ¶ 86,359, 1999 USTR (E&G)
  ¶ 144,352, 1999 USTR (Excise) ¶ 101,404
  rc—IR- 1999-70, 1999 USTR ¶ 86,358, 1999 USTR (E&G)
    ¶ 144,348
Rev Rul 99-38, 1999 USTR ¶ 86,377
Rev Rul 99-39, 1999 USTR ¶ 86,401
Rev Rul 99-40, 1999 USTR ¶ 86,399
  supsdg—Rev Rul 77-475, 1977-2 CB 476
  supsdg—Rev Rul 84-58, 1984-1 CB 254
  supsdg—Rev Rul 88-98, 1988-2 CB 356
Rev Rul 99-41, 1999 USTR ¶ 86,406
Rev Rul 99-42, 1999 USTR ¶ 86,428
Rev Rul 99-43, 1999 USTR ¶ 86,437
Rev Rul 99-44, 1999 USTR ¶ 86,434
Rev Rul 99-45, 1999 USTR ¶ 86,446
Rev Rul 99-46, 1999 USTR ¶ 86,467
Rev Rul 99-47, 1999 USTR ¶ 86,493
Rev Rul 99-48, 1999 USTR ¶ 86,485
  e—Rev Rul 2000-17, 2000 USTR 86,396
Rev Rul 99-49, 1999 USTR ¶ 86,499
  supsd—Rev Rul 2000-56, 2000 USTR ¶ 86,495
  supsdg—Rev Rul 98-59, 1998-2 CB 801
Rev Rul 99-50, 1999 USTR ¶ 86,500
  supsd—Rev Rul 2000-55, 2000 USTR ¶ 86,494
  supsdg—Rev Rul 98-58, 1998-2 CB 799
Rev Rul 99-51, 1999 USTR ¶ 86,514
Rev Rul 99-52, 1999 USTR ¶ 86,515
  e—Rev Rul 2000-52, 2000 USTR 87,125
Rev Rul 99-53, 1999 USTR ¶ 86,497, 1999 USTR (E&G)
  ¶ 144,363, 1999 USTR (Excise) ¶ 101,408
  rc—IR- 1999-96, 1999 USTR ¶ 86,496
  e—Rev Rul 2000-16, 2000 USTR 86,388
Rev Rul 99-54, 1999 USTR ¶ 86,524
  e—Rev Rul 2000-22, 2000 USTR 86,463
  e—Rev Rul 2000-31, 2000 USTR 86,699
  e—Rev Rul 2000-48, 2000 USTR 87,043
Rev Rul 99-55, 1999 USTR ¶ 86,525
Rev Rul 99-56, 1999 USTR ¶ 86,510
  rc—Westvaco corp. v U.S., 47 AFTR 2d 81-406, 639 F2d
    700, 225 Ct Cl 436, 81-1 USTC ¶ 9101, (12/31/1980)

Rev Rul 99-56—contd.
  rc—Weyerhaeuser Co & Subsidiaries v. U.S., 78 AFTR 2d
    96-5823, 92 F3d 1148, 96-2 USTC ¶ 50420, (CA Fed
    Cir, 8/2/1996)
  rc—Weyerhaeuser Co & Subsidiaries v. U.S., 74 AFTR 2d
    94-6049, 32 Fed Cl 80, 94-2 USTC ¶ 50471, (Ct Fed Cl,
    9/1/1994)
  revkg—Rev Rul 66-9, 1966-1 CB 39
  revkg—Rev Rul 73-51, 1973-1 CB 75
Rev Rul 99-57, 1999 USTR ¶ 86,511
  e—Notice 99-57, 1999 USTR 86,017
  e—TD 8883, 2000 USTR 86,528
Rev Rul 99-58, 1999 USTR ¶ 86,523
  e—TD 8898, 2000 USTR 86,869
Rev Rul 190, 1953-2 CB 303 ←
  ob—Rev Rul 99-7, 1999 USTR ¶ 86,059
  k—Aldea, Daniela, 2000 RIA TC Memo 2000-772
  e—Letter Ruling 9806007, 1998 USTR 86,339
Rev Rul 207, 1953-2 CB 442
  e—Munoz, Dean P., 2000 RIA TC Memo 2000-117
Rev Rul 2000-1, 2000 USTR ¶ 86,004
Rev Rul 2000-2, 2000 USTR (E&G) ¶ 144,364
  ob—Rev Rul 89-89, 1989-2 CB 231
Rev Rul 2000-3, 2000 USTR ¶ 86,056
Rev Rul 2000-4, 2000 USTR ¶ 86,031 ←
  sm & ampfg—Rev Proc 99-49, 2000 USTR ¶ 86,032
Rev Rul 2000-5, 2000 USTR ¶ 86,067
Rev Rul 2000-6, 2000 USTR ¶ 86,068
  sm—Rev Rul 88-36, 1988-1 CB 343, [in part]
Rev Rul 2000-7, 2000 USTR ¶ 86,091
  sm & ampfg—Rev Proc 99-49, 2000 USTR ¶ 86,032
Rev Rul 2000-8, 2000 USTR ¶ 86,092
  supsdg—Rev Rul 98-30, 1998-1 CB 1273
  e—Announc 2000-60, 2000 USTR 86,775
  e—Rev Rul 2000-35, 2000 USTR 86,770
Rev Rul 2000-9, 2000 USTR ¶ 86,073
Rev Rul 2000-10, 2000 USTR ¶ 86,098
Rev Rul 2000-11, 2000 USTR ¶ 86,103
Rev Rul 2000-12, 2000 USTR ¶ 86,117
  Notice 2000-15, 2000 USTR 86,379
Rev Rul 2000-13, 2000 USTR ¶ 86,135
Rev Rul 2000-14, 2000 USTR ¶ 86,136
Rev Rul 2000-15, 2000 USTR ¶ 86,125
Rev Rul 2000-16, 2000 USTR ¶ 86,123, 2000 USTR (Excise) ¶ 101,413
  rc—IR- 2000-14, 2000 USTR ¶ 86,122
Rev Rul 2000-17, 2000 USTR ¶ 86,126
  supmg—Rev Proc 92-19, 1992-1 CB 685, [in part]
Rev Rul 2000-18, 2000 USTR ¶ 86,144
Rev Rul 2000-19, 2000 USTR ¶ 86,145
Rev Rul 2000-20, 2000 USTR ¶ 86,154
Rev Rul 2000-21, 2000 USTR ¶ 86,178
Rev Rul 2000-22, 2000 USTR ¶ 86,179
  e—Rev Rul 2000-31, 2000 USTR 86,699
  e—Rev Rul 2000-48, 2000 USTR 87,043
Rev Rul 2000-23, 2000 USTR ¶ 86,188
Rev Rul 2000-24, 2000 USTR ¶ 86,210
Rev Rul 2000-25, 2000 USTR ¶ 86,220
Rev Rul 2000-26, 2000 USTR (E&G) ¶ 144,373
Rev Rul 2000-27, 2000 USTR ¶ 86,209
Rev Rul 2000-28, 2000 USTR ¶ 86,227
Rev Rul 2000-30, 2000 USTR ¶ 86,254, 2000 USTR (E&G)
  ¶ 144,377, 2000 USTR (Excise) ¶ 101,420
  rc—IR- 2000-39, 2000 USTR ¶ 86,253, 2000 USTR (E&G)
    ¶ 144,376
Rev Rul 2000-31, 2000 USTR ¶ 86,267
  e—Rev Rul 2000-48, 2000 USTR 87,043
Rev Rul 2000-32, 2000 USTR ¶ 86,265
Rev Rul 2000-33, 2000 USTR ¶ 86,302
Rev Rul 2000-34, 2000 USTR ¶ 86,292
Rev Rul 2000-35, 2000 USTR ¶ 86,303
Rev Rul 2000-36, 2000 USTR ¶ 86,304
Rev Rul 2000-37, 2000 USTR ¶ 86,305
Rev Rul 2000-38, 2000 USTR ¶ 86,306
  e—Rev Rul 2001-4, 2000 USTR 87,202, [See sec. 6.01(6)]
Rev Rul 2000-39, 2000 USTR ¶ 86,349
Rev Rul 2000-40, 2000 USTR ¶ 86,354
Rev Rul 2000-41, 2000 USTR ¶ 86,346

that the CCH editors believe will serve as useful guides in evaluating the cited case's effectiveness as precedent. Thus, the tax researcher is directed to those cases that may be most likely to develop, explain, criticize, or otherwise evaluate a rule of law. This is in contrast to the *RIA* (and *Shepard's*) *citators,* which list all of the cases that have mentioned the cited case. Although the latter practice provides a level of thoroughness that may be useful, the CCH editorial screening procedure guards against the possibility of being overwhelmed by the sheer volume of citing cases presented. The more selective CCH approach, of course, forces the researcher to rely on an editor's evaluation concerning the usefulness of the citing cases.

Another reason that the *CCH Citator* fits neatly in two volumes is that it covers only the Federal income tax decisions issued since 1913. Also, court decisions that are obsolete due to changes in the statutes are marked with a dagger symbol, and no citing cases are given for these cases. Estate and gift tax cases appearing in the USTC reporter (the CCH version of the AFTR) are listed by name, again with no citing cases provided (for example, see *William J. Upjohn*, Exhibit 8–12). Tax Court estate and gift cases are not even listed by name. This is because CCH has other complete citator services for the estate and gift cases and also for excise tax cases.

As Exhibit 8–12 illustrates, the *CCH Citator* acts as a Finding Table as well as a citator by providing paragraph references to where the entries are reviewed in the

Exhibit 8–12 CCH Published *Citator,* Upjohn Case

© 2001, CCH INCORPORATED. All Rights Reserved. Reprinted with permission from CCH *Standard Federal Tax Reporter.*

Standard Federal Tax Reporter. These references are also furnished in the electronic version found on NetWork (Exhibit 8–13). This feature reduces the searching time required to locate supplemental information regarding a case or ruling of interest. The tax service discussions help the researcher evaluate the case or ruling in the context of relevant Code sections, Regulations, and administrative sources of tax law. Recall that the *RIA Citators* do not include references to its tax services and Finding Lists must be referred to for these references.

In comparing Exhibits 8–9 *(RIA Citators)* and 8–12 *(CCH Citator)*, notice that the official reporter parallel citations appear in both citators. However, AFTR citations are not supported by the *CCH Citator*, whereas the *RIA Citators* after 1990 do include the USTC citations. This can cause problems when a journal article, for example, contains an AFTR2d cite for a case with a common taxpayer name, but the practitioner has access only to the *CCH Citator* and CCH court reporters.

Finally, the *CCH Citator* does not provide evaluations of the citing cases. This is a significant drawback of the citator. With a list of citing cases as long as that for the *Upjohn* case (Exhibit 8–12), knowing how each citing case interpreted to the *Upjohn* case could substantially reduce the number of cases the researcher reads.

CCH Citator Conventions

Cases in the *CCH Citator* are listed in strict alphabetical order with acronyms treated as separate words. Even business names that begin with a number are listed alphabetically as if the number were spelled out. For example, the 1244 Corporation would be listed under "T" for "twelve." The ampersand and connectors such as "and," "of," and "to," and legal conventions like "in re" and "in the matter of" are ignored, as is the word "the." Alphabetical order is maintained within the group of businesses whose names begin with a letter, as the excerpt in Exhibit 8–14 illustrates. If the taxpayer in

Exhibit 8–13

CCH NetWork *Citator*, *Upjohn* Case

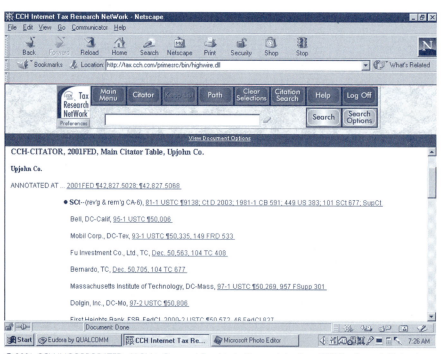

© 2001, CCH INCORPORATED. All Rights Reserved. Reprinted with permission from CCH Tax Research Network.

Exhibit 8–14

CCH Citator Case Order

```
A. P. Family Trust (See Wolan, Margaret, Trustee)
A. & P. Production Co. .............. ¶ 29,626.409
  • CA-5—(aff'g BTA), 41-2 USTC ¶ 9651; 122 F2d 192
  • BTA—Dec. 11,010-A; Feb. 9, 1940
A & P Water & Sewer Supplies, Inc. (See Tidewater
    Plumbing & Heating, Inc.)
A. & R. Concrete Co. (See Gilcrest Co., J. K. v. A. & R.
    Concrete Co.)
A. to Z. Equipment Corp.: Fidelity & Deposit Co. of
    Maryland v. (See Fidelity & Deposit Co. of
    Maryland v. A. to Z. Equipment Corp.)
A to Z Welding & Mfg. Co., Inc. ........ ¶ 40,580.21,
    42,283.738, 42,283.781
  • CA-8—(aff'g DC per curiam), 87-1 USTC ¶ 9109;
    803 F2d 932
    Buildwright Homes, Inc., BC-DC-Ohio, 95-1 USTC
    ¶ 50,173
    Goldsby, BC-DC-Ark, 92-1 USTC ¶ 50,118
    LaSalle Rolling Mills, Inc., CA-7, 87-2 USTC ¶ 9592,
    832 F2d 390
    Upton Printing Co., Inc., BC-DC-La, 90-2 USTC
    ¶ 50,392, 116 BR 66
    Frazier, DC-Va, 89-2 USTC ¶ 9495
    Casa Garcia, Inc., DC-La, 89-2 USTC ¶ 9426
    Condel, Inc.., BAP-9, 88-2 USTC ¶ 9555
    Young, Ltd., DC-Nev, 88-2 USTC ¶ 9397, 87 BR 635
    Heritage Village, DC-SC, 88-1 USTC ¶ 9234
    Cambridge Machined Products Corp., DC-Mass,
    87-2 USTC ¶ 9649
  • DC-Ark—86-1 USTC ¶ 9112; 58 BR 138
    LaSalle Rolling Mills, Inc., DC-Ill, 86-2 USTC ¶ 9723
    Gay Fire Equipment Co., Inc., DC-Ga, 86-1 USTC
    ¶ 9267

A.A. Electric Supply Co. (See Board of Education v.
    Bruce Electric Co.)
AAA Cycles (See Richman, R.R.)
AAA Delivery, Inc. (See Atkins, Everett W. v. Wells, Jr.,
    C.V.)
AAA Exterminators (See Lieb, Jr., William C.)
Aab, Raymond J. .................. ¶ 14,854.502
  • TC—Dec. 38,376(M); 42 TCM 1519; TC Memo.
    1981-620
    Storzer, TC, Dec. 39,099(M), 44 TCM 100, TC
    Memo. 1982-328
AABCO Building and Janitorial Services, Inc. .
    ................................. ¶ 39,060.78
  • DC-Ky—89-2 USTC ¶ 9604
Aagaard, Carl M. .......... ¶ 3100.095, 40,551G.36
  • TC—Dec. 42,043(M); 49 TCM 1278; TC Memo.
    1985-194
    Metcalf, TC, Dec. 42,388(M), 50 TCM 1077, TC
    Memo. 1985-487
Aagaard, Robert W. .......... ¶ 9604.10, 10,001.43,
    31,515A.079, 31,562.42, 31,562.47,
    32,263.3965
  • TC—Dec. 30,755; 56 TC 191; A. 1971-2 CB 1
    Richards, TC, Dec. 49,276(M), 66 TCM 707, TC
    Memo. 1993-422
    Delk, TC, Dec. 50,697(M), 69 TCM 2908, TC Memo.
    1995-265
    Thomas,, TC, Dec. 45,460, 92 TC 206
    DeNiro Est., TC, Dec. 41,962(M), 49 TCM 1004, TC
    Memo. 1985-128
    Andrews, TC, Dec. 37,916(M), 41 TCM 1533, TC
```

© 2001, CCH INCORPORATED. All Rights Reserved. Reprinted with permission from CCH *Standard Federal Tax Reporter.*

the case has the letter "A" in front of its name, such as A. & P. Production Co., it will precede all cases with double "A," such as A.A. Electric Supply Co., which would itself precede AAA Exterminators, which in turn would precede Aab, Raymond J. Thus, A to Z Welding is listed ahead of Aagaard, Robert W. Because the *CCH Citator* lists cases in "strict" alphabetical order, when you don't find a case listed where you expect it in the published version, be sure you are looking in the right place.

The names of cited cases are set in bold print, followed by paragraph number references to the *Standard Federal Tax Reporter* compilations (see Exhibits 8–12 and 8–13). The bold black bullets under the case name designate the court levels that have addressed a case. The highest level court to address the case is listed first, and the trial-level court is listed last. Hence, the citation for the *Upjohn* Supreme Court case is listed first followed by its citing cases, then the Sixth Circuit case followed by its citing cases, and lastly the District Court case. The advantage of this organization is that the researcher can easily determine the highest court that heard the case and the bullet headings clearly identify the levels of the court cases. The citing cases under each court decision are listed in reverse chronological order, with any Revenue Rulings addressing the case completing the citation entry. While this ordering allows the researcher to identify quickly the most recent cases that have cited the case of interest, it makes it more difficult to identify which cases are by the highest courts.

The *CCH Citator* provides information about the judicial history of the case. The reference for the Supreme Court case denotes that it reversed the Sixth Circuit's holding and remanded the case. The Sixth Circuit reference indicates it affirmed some holdings of the District Court decision and reversed and remanded on other issues. Since the *CCH Citator* does not supply evaluation symbols for citing cases, the researcher cannot determine if the Bell case followed, or explained, or distinguished itself from the *Upjohn* case.

Through CCH NetWork, there are three methods for accessing *Citator*. If the researcher knows either the case name or complete citation of a ruling or case, selecting the "Citator" button will display separate boxes in which to enter this information. When the researcher is unclear as to the proper form of the citation, the Citator templates will facilitate entering the data. For illustrative purposes, Exhibit 8–15 has entered the case name, complete citation, and cites using the case templates for the

Exhibit 8–15
CCH Tax Research NetWork *Citator*

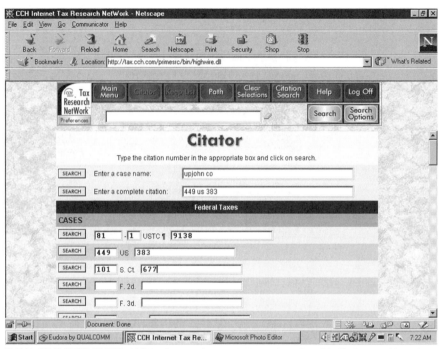

© 2001, CCH INCORPORATED. All Rights Reserved. Reprinted with permission from CCH Tax Research Network.

Upjohn case. A researcher would actually supply data for only one of these searches. Lastly, while the researcher is viewing a case on screen, selecting the "Citator" button will display the *Citator* entries for the case being examined.

SHEPARD'S AND LEXIS CITATION SERVICES

Over 125 years ago, Shepard's introduced the first citator as an aid to legal research. Since that time, Shepard's has developed citators for virtually every case reporter series, as well as for specialized areas of the law, such as **Shepard's Federal Tax Citator** for tax research. Because it developed citators and the breadth of its coverage, legal researchers often refer to the process of evaluating the validity of a case and locating additional authority via a citator as "**Shepardizing** the case."

Shepard's Citator services *(Shepard's Citator)* are currently available in print, on CD-ROM, and on the Internet exclusively through LexisNexis. Besides the *Shepard's Citator*, LexisNexis furnishes the Auto-Cite citator, Table of Authorities, and the LEXCITE search system. Each of these are useful tools to the researcher when verifying a case's value as precedent and the accuracy of the case citations.

Shepard's Citators

Shepard's Citator is the only major tax citator that is organized by case reporter series. Accordingly, the practitioner must know the court reporter citation for the case of interest, regardless of whether the paper or electronic version of the citator is used. This can be a problem if only the name of a case is known. Retrieving a document using the "Get a Document" button in Lexis also requires knowing the case citation. While viewing the retrieved case, however, clicking on the "Check a Citation" button will display the citation entry box of Exhibit 8–16 with the case's citation automatically filled in.

Exhibit 8-16

Shepard's Citator Search Screen on Lexis

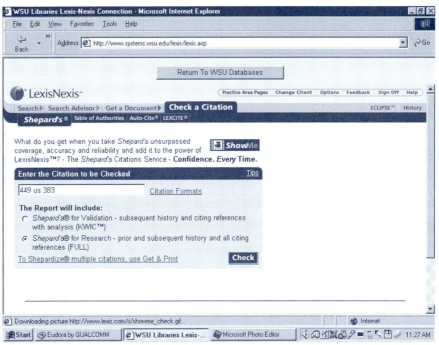

Reprinted with the permission of LexisNexis, a division of Reed Elsevier Inc.

When locating a citation in the published *Shepard's Citator,* first find the division of the citator for the court reporter of the case. Within each court reporter division, the cases are arranged in chronological order by volume number rather than in alphabetical order by the case name.

For each such volume, the *Shepard's Citator* lists, in bold print, the first page number of the cited cases. If more than one court opinion begins on the same page of the reporter volume, the *Shepard's Citator* distinguishes them as "Case 1" and "Case 2." After the page number, the case name and the year of the decision are given. The parallel citations follow in parentheses. The electronic version tends to provide a more extensive list of parallel citations. These features can be identified by examining Exhibit 8–17 (printed) and Exhibit 8–18 (electronic). The *Shepard's Citator* includes cases reported in all of the court case reporter series discussed in Chapter 5 as well as pertinent sections of the Code and Regulations. It also includes references to selected law review articles.

Citing cases follow the citation and history for the cited case. The judicial history of the cited case is given, indicating affirmation, reversals, dismissals, and so on. The *Shepard's Citator* also specifies the treatment (criticized, distinguished, explained, followed, etc.) and operation (amended, extended, revoked, etc.) of citing cases. The published version does not furnish the names of the citing cases, just their citation, whereas on Lexis the citing cases are listed by name and parallel citations are given.

Shepard's developed its own abbreviation system for evaluating the history and treatment by the citing cases. Exhibit 8–19 provides a listing of the evaluation symbols. The practitioner must take care not to mix up the symbols used by the *RIA Citators* with those of *Shepard's Citator*. For example, the symbol "d" in the *RIA Citators* means that the appeal was dismissed or withdrawn, whereas in *Shepard's Citator* "d" means that the citing case is distinguished from the cited case. Fortunately, the electronic versions

Exhibit 8–17

Shepard's Citator, Upjohn Case

Vol. 101		SUPREME COURT REPORTER (Tax Cases)			
Colo	d 63AF2d1169	103FRD^{3}66	563FS^{7}830	143FRD^{10}511	142FRD^{1}269
707 P2d353	f 63AF2d1483	103FRD^{5}66	567FS^{5}1360	f 143FRD^{10}518	142FRD^{1}411
Conn	65AF2d833	f 104FRD464	580FS^{5}1098	145FRD^{1}301	f 143FRD^{1}66
487 A2d1089	66AF2d5413	106FkD204	580FS^{6}1099	145FRD^{1}630	143FRD^{5}66
D C	71AF2d1876	106FRD^{1}205	587FS^{1}58	145FRD^{10}630	144FRD232
642 A2d118	71AF2d1877	118FRD^{10}247	589FS^{1}451	f 145FRD634	144FRD^{6}268
Fla	71AAF2d4256	139FRD^{1}8	589FS^{2}451	148FRD^{10}102	154FRD^{1}101
537 So2d647	74AF2d7273	139FRD^{3}8	598FS^{1}990	13BRW^{1}57	154FRD^{2}101

472 NW498	[50335	139FRD557	102FRD^{3}9	513FS^{1}522	805FS^{7}1305
—**677**—	118FRD196	144FRD^{3}604	102FRD^{9}11	557FS^{10}1058	805FS^{5}1306
Upjohn Co. v	133FRD324	152FRD^{3}3	102FRD^{10}11	562FS^{3}441	110FRD^{1}513
United States	Cir. DC	d 40BRW57	103FRD^{1}122	619FS^{11}1046	110FRD^{5}517
1981	654F2d^{10}798	d 79BRW98	106FRD^{5}38	619FS^{7}1047	114FRD^{1}695
(47AF2d523)	665F2d^{11}220	Cir. 2	106FRD^{6}38	656FS^{6}1173	e 114FRD^{5}696
(81UTC¶ 9138)	665F2d^{5}1220	670F2d386	110FRD^{10}690	d 692FS^{5}493	116FRD^{1}210
(449US383)	676F2d^{8}808	675F2d484	111FRD^{1}79	728FS^{11}102	116FRD^{3}210
(66LẼ584)	f 676F2d^{10}810	675F2d^{1}487	111FRD^{5}79	764FS^{1}343	118FRD^{5}587
s 44AF2d5179	686F2d^{2}32	675F2d^{2}487	111FRD^{6}80	766FS^{6}265	126FRD^{10}506
s 79UTC¶ 9457	686F2d^{3}33	d 675F2d^{3}488	112FRD103	766FS^{4}270	f 136FRD^{1}426
s 600F2d1223	737F2d^{1}98	d 675F2d^{6}488	112FRD391	766FS^{1}271	142FRD126
103SC^{1}1621	737F2d^{5}99	675F2d^{10}492	113FRD^{5}560	809FS^{1}363	144FRD^{1}70
103SC^{3}1621	737F2d^{2}101	677F2d^{1}219	114FRD^{6}644	815FS^{1}814	148FRD^{1}538
e 105SC^{15}1990	738F2d^{5}1369	f 677F2d^{4}220	117FRD^{1}525	834FS^{1}707	150FRD^{3}545
108SC2350	738F2d^{6}1369	j 677F2d222	121FRD10	841FS1398	152FRD80
f 109SC2625	826F2d127	700F2d^{5}827	121FRD^{1}200	848FS566	Cir. 5
f 109SC^{1}2626	f 838F2d^{5}1302	731F2d^{11}037	121FRD^{3}203	858FS54	637F2d295
47AF2d789	856F2d^{10}273	731F2d^{2}1037	121FRD^{10}639	858FS^{1}55	682F2d^{1}538
48AF2d5170	h 861F2d^{8}735	731F2d^{3}1037	125FRD386	859FS^{1}766	682F2d^{2}538
49AF2d1054	861F2d^{10}736	j 781F2d260	d 125FRD^{1}387	93FRD^{4}141	682F2d^{3}538
49AF2d1204	518FS^{1}680	825F2d679	128FRD35	103FRD^{3}409	682F2d^{6}539
j 50AF2d5530	518FS^{2}680	828F2d^{1}100	f 130FRD^{1}31	d 103FRD^{1}425	682F2d^{10}542
50AF2d5530	e 518FS^{5}681	828F2d^{3}100	f 131FRD^{1}377	103FRD^{6}430	682F2d^{8}544
51AF2d343	e 518FS^{7}681	888F2d^{10}12	f 131FRD^{3}377	f 109FRD687	j 682F2d550
d 52AF2d5537	571FS^{5}506	892F2d243	f 131FRD^{5}377	115FRD517	693F2d^{6}1242
52AF2d5537	f 654FS^{3}1364	926F2d^{1}1292	f 131FRD^{1}398	115FRD^{3}518	722F2d^{1}177
52AF2d6304	d 654FS1365	926F2d^{6}1294	f 131FRD^{5}404	125FRD^{9}615	822F2d^{1}524
54AF2d5938	f 672FS^{5}4	979F2d^{3}944	f 131FRD^{10}404	127FRD^{5}654	h 854F2d^{1}785
d 56AF2d6073	d 672FS^{5}5	992F2d452	f 131FRD^{6}405	130FRD^{1}570	927F2d875
e 56AF2d6367	705FS^{4}676	9F3d^{7}236	e 136FRD360	131FRD^{1}66	972F2d620
56AF2d6367	744FS^{8}1185	507FS^{5}112	137FRD^{10}644	132FRD^{1}395	f 43F3d^{9}970
58AF2d5368	857FS^{5}104	521FS^{1}640	140FRD^{10}304	f 134FRD^{5}123	556FS1155
60AF2d5042	100FRD^{6}24	525FS^{5}650	140FRD^{3}305	f 134FRD^{6}123	647FS118
60AF2d5513	100FRD^{6}438	553FS^{5}50	140FRD^{7}306	135FRD^{1}98	841FS1428
62AF2d5764	100FRD^{9}439	553FS^{9}51	143FRD^{3}46	139FRD^{10}614	f 89FRD^{6}600
	101FRD439	f 561FS1253	143FRD^{5}501	142FRD^{6}268	f 91FRD^{4}417

1612

of both citators use words to describe the evaluations rather than abbreviations, thus eliminating any confusion. In addition to the words, Lexis provides symbols for at-a-glance indications of the precedential status of a case: a red stop sign shape means "warning – negative treatment;" a yellow triangle means "caution – possible negative treatment;" and a green diamond shape with a plus in the center means "positive true – positive treatment."

Observe a small superscript number appearing immediately to the left of the page number in the published citing reference of Exhibit 8–17. This number indicates the headnote paragraph to which the citing court's analysis relates. The headnote numbering identification is available only for Federal tax cases appearing in the West court reporter series, the *Lawyers' Cooperative Edition* series and the *United States Supreme Court Reports,* but not for the AFTR court reporters. Surprisingly, no headnote notations are furnished in Lexis for the citing cases.

Shepard's Citator is one of the most comprehensive citators available to the tax researcher. For each cited case, the Shepard's analysis begins with all Supreme Court

Exhibit 8-18

Shepard's Citator, Upjohn Case Screen on Lexis

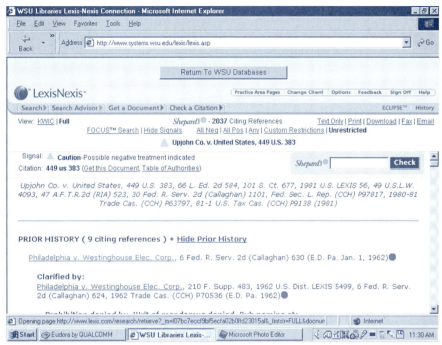

Reprinted with the permission of LexisNexis, a division of Reed Elsevier Inc.

citing cases and continues by Federal jurisdiction (Appeals Courts and District Courts), followed by the U.S. Court of Federal Claims, Tax Court, and various state courts. Within each of these citing groups, the citations are listed in chronological order in the published citator and reverse chronological in Lexis. As Exhibit 8-18 indicates, the number of citing case references can be staggering (see the upper center portion of the *Shepard's* window); there are over 2,000 for the *Upjohn* case. Due to the quantity of cases likely to be retrieved, Lexis allows the researcher to limit the case reference by various means.

Exhibit 8-18 was the result of selecting the "Full" view option. This view lists all of the prior history and subsequent appellate history. The prior history for the *Upjohn* case contains nine cases. All citing cases with or without attached analysis are presented, as well as statutes, law reviews, and legal periodicals citing the case of interest. The other view choice, "KWIC" (keyword in context) retrieved fewer than 200 citing references. This option is generally selected for validating the citation of interest. It presents the subsequent appellate history and only those citing cases with editorial analysis. Only one parallel citation for each citing case is provided. Even with these restrictions, the "KWIC" view may retrieve more cases than the researcher cares to review.

To reduce the number of cases retrieved, researchers may narrow the search by choosing to view cases containing only negative evaluations ("All Neg") or positive evaluations ("All Pos") or may limit the search by designating headnote issues, applying date restrictions, specifying jurisdictions, or selecting analysis categories ("Customize Restrictions"). All of these options are available with either the "Full" or the "KWIC" view (see Exhibit 8-18).

Exhibit 8–19
Shepard's Citator Symbols for Cited and Citing Cases

ABBREVIATIONS—ANALYSIS

History of Case

a	(affirmed)	The citing case affirms or adheres to the case you are Shepardizing.
cc	(connected case)	The citing case is related to the case you are Shepardizing, arising out of the same subject matter or involving the same parties.
Corr	(correction)	Error in prior treasury decision, revenue ruling or procedure pointed out and rectified.
D	(dismissed)	Same case or appeal therefrom dismissed.
m	(modified)	As a result of rehearing or appeal, the citing case modifies (changes in some way, including affirmance in part and reversal in part) the decision in the case you are Shepardizing.
PLR	(Prior Letter Ruling)	Prior Letter Ruling with same text reissued under a new letter ruling number.
r	(reversed)	The citing case reverses the case you are Shepardizing.
s	(same case)	The cited case involves the same litigation as the case you are Shepardizing, but at a different stage of the proceedings.
S	(superseded)	The decision in the citing case supersedes (has been substituted for) the case you are Shepardizing.
v	(vacated)	The citing case vacates (withdraws) the case you are Shepardizing.
US cert den in		Certiorari denied by U.S. Supreme Court.
US cert dis in		Certiorari dismissed by U.S. Supreme Court.
US cert gran in		Certiorari granted by U.S. Supreme Court.
US reh den in		Rehearing denied by U.S. Supreme Court.
US reh dis in		Rehearing dismissed by U.S. Supreme Court.
US app pndg		Appeal pending before the U.S. Supreme Court.

Treatment of Case

Acq	(acquiescence)	Acquiescence by Commissioner in reasoning or result of the cited case.
AcqR	(acquiescence, result only)	Acquiescence by Commissioner in result only, and not in the reasoning employed to reach such a result.
Amp	(amplified)	Previous revenue ruling or procedure expanded or extended to different factual situation.
c	(criticized)	The citing case disagrees with the reasoning/result of the case you are Shepardizing, although the citing court may not have the authority to materially affect its precedential value.
Clr	(clarification)	Clarification of prior revenue rule or procedure.
d	(distinguished)	The citing case is diferent from the case you are Shepardizing, involving either a dissimilar fact situation or a different application of the law.
e	(explained)	The citing case interprets or clarifies the case you are Shepardizing in a significant way.
f	(followed)	The citing case relies on the case you are Shepardizing as controlling or persuasive authority.
h	(harmonized)	The citing case is different from the case you are Shepardizing, but the citing court relies on the cited case after reconciling the difference or inconsistency.
j	(dissenting opinion)	The case you are Shepardizing is cited in a dissenting opinion.

Exhibit 8–19

Shepard's Citator Symbols for Cited and Citing Cases— Concluded

L	(limited)	The citing case restricts the application of the case you are Shepardizing, finding that its reasoning applies only in limited, specific circumstances.
Noacq	(nonacquiescence)	Nonacquiescence by Commissioner in reasoning or result of the cited case.
o	(overruled)	The citing case expressly overrules all or part of the case you are Shepardizing.
p	(parallel)	The citing case relies on the case you are Shepardizing by describing it as "on all fours" or "parallel" to the citing case.
q	(questioned)	The citing case questions the continuing validity or precedential value of the case you are Shepardizing because of intervening circumstances, including legislative or judicial overruling.
SLR	(subsequent Letter Ruling)	Subsequent Letter Ruling issued in same case.

Lexis Services

LexisNexis has developed its own citator, Auto-Cite, as well as providing *Shepard's Citator*. In addition, it furnishes the Table of Authorities and the LEXCITE search system. The services may be accessed through the "Check a Citation" button shown in Exhibit 8–16. Lexis itself may also be used as a citator.

Auto-Cite First offered in 1979, the **Auto-Cite** electronic citation service was originally available on Lexis only through its dedicated terminals. It is now part of the Lexis Internet service. Auto-Cite was designed by Lawyers Cooperative Publishing to help their editors check the validity of citations. Therefore, its primary objectives are to provide absolutely accurate citations, and to do so within 24 hours of receipt of each case. Not only is Auto-Cite beneficial in determining whether a case is still good law, it also allows researchers to check the standing of Revenue Rulings and Revenue Procedures.

The information retrieved by Auto-Cite includes the correct spelling of the case name, its official citation, the year of the decision, and all official and most unofficial parallel cites. The prior and subsequent case history focus on cases relevant to the case's value as precedent. Thus, Auto-Cite provides up-to-day (updated seven days a week), accurate information on cases that impact the strength of the cited case, whereas *Shepard's Citator* focus is on furnishing a comprehensive history of the case. Both identify citations making negative references, and Auto-Cite contains related article annotations from *American Law Reports* (ALR) and *Lawyers' Edition, 2d*.

Table of Authorities The **Table of Authorities** is a Shepard's service, but it is not like the previously discussed citator services. Citators provide a history of a particular case and a list of cases citing it. The Table of Authorities, on the other hand, lists cases that are cited within the case of interest. The list of cases cited is organized by jurisdiction. For each case, the name of the case and its citation with parallel cites is given. The Table of Authorities also provides an assessment of how the case of interest evaluated the cited case and the page on which the cited case is discussed. The cited case itself is evaluated by its prior history and a Shepard's symbol (stop sign, triangle, etc.) indicating the status of the cited case. Clicking on the symbol will shepardize the cited case. The Table of Authorities information is useful for finding deficiencies in a relevant case, whether or not it supports the client's preferred tax position. If the relevant case relies on other cases with negative or weak histories, the reasoning in a relevant case may be flawed. Hence, a case that itself has no negative history when cited and appears to be good law may be weak as precedent because it relies on cases that have been overruled or have other negative connotations.

LEXCITE When the researcher wants to search legal documents for references to a case of interest, **LEXCITE** is used. It is a search option designed to understand the "volume-reporter-page" convention of a citation. This format must be followed, but capitalization, internal spaces, and periods are optional, as long as the citation follows the basic format. Once the case has been cited in a document, LEXCITE will identify and highlight subsequent *id.* or *supra* references.

For the case citation entered, LEXCITE ascertains parallel citations and then searches for all of the embedded cite references in documents such as cases, law reviews, journals, legal newspapers, *Federal Register,* and *Cumulative Bulletins.* The LEXCITE feature actually searches the full text of the documents available in Lexis. Accordingly, the researcher is able to see the references to the case of interest in context and make a personal determination of how the case was evaluated in the document. One limitation should be mentioned, however; LEXCITE will not find references to case names only—a court reporter citation must be present for LEXCITE to identify the document as a source.

An advantage of using LEXCITE is that the practitioner can customize the search to retrieve documents that address only a particular point of law in the cited case by using other search terms in addition to the citation. The jurisdiction, such as only 9th Circuit Court of Appeals or only Missouri state court cases, can be specified. Date restrictions may also be imposed. This is particularly useful when searching secondary sources, such as legal newspapers and journals.

Lexis Lastly, a Lexis keyword search may be employed as a citator when only the name of a case and not its citation is known. A regular Lexis search on the case name will locate every occurrence of the name within the chosen library. If the taxpayer has a common name, there may be many irrelevant references retrieved by Lexis. If the case name is long, it is best to use essential parts of the name, so the search won't miss an occurrence because the case name has been shortened in the documents. Further, the search can be tailored by using other search terms in combination with the name, as described for LEXCITE.

WESTLAW CITATOR SYSTEM

As discussed in Chapter 7, **Westlaw** research service is structured for legal research. It was designed by attorneys for attorneys. Since case law is very important in most areas of law, taxation included, the citation applications are the centerpiece of the Westlaw service. Westlaw's citators are also very effective in validating statutes and administrative rulings.

Prior to July 1999, *Shepard's Citators* were available on both Lexis and Westlaw. In addition, Westlaw had developed its own major citator called KeyCite and offered other citator services such as the *RIA Citators.* With the loss of access to *Shepard's Citators,* Westlaw has reorganized its citators and now offers KeyCite as its comprehensive citator. KeyCite is only available through Westlaw. There is no published version. The *RIA Citators* are still furnished on Westlaw. Its operation is not substantially different than when accessed through the RIA Checkpoint service. Therefore, it will not be reviewed in this section.

KeyCite

As seen in Exhibit 8–20, the **KeyCite** citator is composed of four parts: KC History, KC Citations, Cite List, and Table of Authorities (TOA). Demonstrating just how "key" the KeyCite service is to Westlaw, it is accessible directly on the Westlaw Welcome screen (see Chapter 7, Exhibit 7–21) by entering a citation or by selecting the KeyCite tab on the Welcome screen and then entering a citation. As with *Shepard's Citator,* the citation of the document of interest must be known. Names of cases are not acceptable in KeyCite. Also like *Shepard's Citator,* the system has been designed to be flexible as to citation formats. Most formats are accepted as long as the general form of "volume-reporter-page" is used. The results of the citation search are the case in the right-hand window and the citations in the left-hand window (see Exhibit 8–20). The size of the windows is adjustable by the researcher.

KC History The direct and negative indirect history for the case in the right-hand window is retrieved when **KC History** is selected. The case's progress through the courts is listed first in the Direct History section. The editors indicate with words and symbols the effects of this progression. The symbols employed are similar to those in *Shepard's Citator.* A red flag warns that the case is no longer good law for at least one of its legal issues. A yellow flag means caution, the case has some negative

Exhibit 8–20
Westlaw KeyCite, *Upjohn* Screen

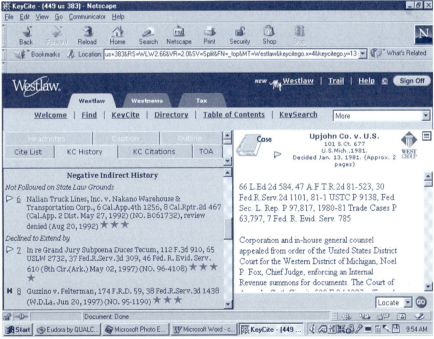

Source: Westlaw. Reprinted with permission.

history, but it has not been overruled. A Blue "H" indicates that the case has some history, and a green "C" means the case has no negative references.

Next is the negative indirect history, which includes any citing cases that adversely affect the precedent value of the case of interest. Phrases indicate whether the cases have criticized, distinguished, limited, questioned, or overruled the cited case's logic or holding. The negative cases are also evaluated as to whether they are still good law, using the same symbols as for the direct history (see Exhibit 8–20). Besides this evaluation, KC History determines the extent to which the citing cases discuss the cited case of interest. The symbols range from four stars to one star, with four denoting an extended examination of the case (usually more than a printed page in length) and one a brief reference (such as in a string of citations). Observe that the three citing cases in Exhibit 8–20 have either three or four stars, meaning they have a substantial discussion of the *Upjohn* case. Two have yellow flags (some negative history), and one has a blue "H" (some history). The final symbol found in KC History is quotation marks, indicating that the citing case has quoted the cited case. There is nothing comparable to the star and quote notations in any of the citators previously described in this chapter.

KC History allows the researcher to select a full history, negative history, or omit minor cases. This last option is a very useful filter for reducing the quantity of citing cases retrieved by Westlaw. It is not available with the other citators.

KC Citations For a comprehensive list of citing cases, select the **KC Citation** tab. The *Upjohn* case retrieves almost 2,700 citing cases, almost all of which are positive cites. The listing starts with the negative indirect history of the cited case. These will be the same negative cases retrieved by the KC History, but the most recent cases are presented first. The positive indirect history is organized by the depth of coverage, starting with the four star examinations and leading to the one star citing cases. The last group in the list contains secondary source references by law reviews, *American Law Reports,* administrative materials, *Mertens* tax service, etc.

Since the number of documents retrieved can be beyond ones ability to examine, KC Citations allows limitations to be placed on the search process by selecting the limit option. Exhibit 8–21 reproduces the limit option screen. The search may be narrowed by type of jurisdiction, type of document, and depth of treatment (number of stars). A keyword search is possible if the KC Citation list is less than 2,000 documents. This screen also allows the researcher to cause the headnotes for the cited case to be visible in the right-hand window when the case is being viewed. The headnotes are also itemized by key number on the left side of the limit option screen.

As discussed previously, the headnote paragraphs represent a summary of each significant legal issue in the case. The interpretation of "significant issues" will vary by the editorial staff of each court reporter. Compare the West's *Supreme Court Reporter* for the *Upjohn* case in Exhibit 8–22 with the RIA AFTR2d version in Exhibit 8–3. The editors of these court reporters analyzed the judicial opinions to different degrees of detail. While the West editors required ten headnotes to evaluate the law in the *Upjohn* case, the RIA editors needed just two. The drafting of headnotes and the breadth of the issue that each headnote addresses are a matter of the style and editorial policy of the entity that publishes the reporter.

Note the small keys and numbers in the headnotes in Exhibit 8–22. The West headnote system has a particularly valuable feature for finding law, the West Key Number System. The points of law articulated in a case are editorially classified into

Chapter 8 Citators and Other Finding Devices   267

Exhibit 8–21
Westlaw KC Citation Limits Screen

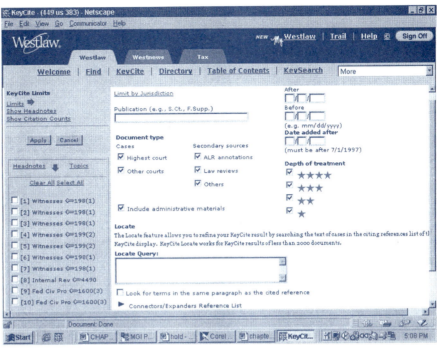

Source: Westlaw. Reprinted with permission.

Key Numbers that fit into an extensive system for organizing case law. West publishes a series of digests that organize the holdings of cases by Key Numbers. The Custom Digests are also accessible on Westlaw via the drop-down menu found in the "More" option (see Exhibit 8–20) on the toolbar. After drilling down through the Key Numbers and selecting a topic of interest, the screen in Exhibit 8–23 appears. This screen allows the researcher to customize the search by jurisdiction, date restrictions, and additional search terms. The order in which the headnotes are displayed may also be specified. The result of the search is a list of cases with headnotes key numbered to the issue.

Cite List The only information displayed by selecting the Cite List option is the full citation of the case, geographical location, and date of judgment. The full citation contains all official cites and a comprehensive list of unofficial cites. This option is selected when the researcher wants to check the spelling of the case name and verify the correctness of citations.

Table of Authorities The Westlaw Table of Authorities (TOA) performs the same function as the Shepard's version. However, the Westlaw TOA reports more information. Not only does it indicate where the case of interest cites other cases in supporting its reasoning, Westlaw denotes how much discussion was given to the case using its four-star depth of treatment symbols. Further, if the case of interest quotes other cases, this is designated with the quotation marks symbol. The cases listed in the TOA with negative history or that have been reversed or overruled are marked with either a yellow or red flag, making it easy for the researcher to determine the strength of the cases relied on by the case of interest.

Exhibit 8–22

West Publishing, *Supreme Court Reporter,* Headnotes for *Upjohn* Case

1. Witnesses ⟐198(1)

Purpose of attorney–client privilege is to encourage full and frank communication between attorneys and their clients and thereby to promote broader public interests in observance of law and administration of justice. Fed.Rules Evid. Rule 501, 28 U.S.C.A.

2. Witnesses ⟐198(1)

Attorney–client privilege rests on need for advocate and counselor to know all that relates to client's reasons for seeking representation if professional mission is to be carried out. ABA Code of Professional Responsibility, EC4–1.

3. Witnesses ⟐198(1)

Attorney–client privilege exists to protect not only giving of professional advice to those who can act on it but also the giving of information to lawyer to enable him to give sound and informed advice. Fed.Rules Evid. Rule 501, 28 U.S.C.A.; ABA Code of Professional Responsibility, EC4–1.

4. Witnesses ⟐199(2)

District court's test, of availability of attorney–client privilege, was objectionable as frustrating very purpose of privilege, insofar as test restricted availability of privilege to those corporate officers who played "substantial role" in deciding and directing corporation's legal response. Fed. Rules Evid. Rule 501, 28 U.S.C.A.

5. Witnesses ⟐199(2)

Where communications at issue were made by corporate employees to counsel for corporation acting as such, at direction of corporate superiors in order to secure legal advice from counsel, and employees were aware that they were being questioned so that corporation could obtain legal advice, such communications, consistently with underlying purposes of attorney–client privilege, were protected against compelled disclosure. Fed.Rules Evid. Rule 501, 28 U.S.C.A.

6. Witnesses ⟐198(1)

Attorney–client privilege only protects disclosure of communications, and it does not protect disclosure of underlying facts by those who communicated with attorney. Fed.Rules Evid. Rule 501, 28 U.S.C.A.

7. Witnesses ⟐198(1)

Application of privilege, such as attorney–client privilege, is determined on case-by-case basis. Fed.Rules Evid. Rule 501, 28 U.S.C.A.

8. Internal Revenue ⟐1451

Obligation imposed by tax summons remains subject to traditional privileges and limitations, and work–product doctrine does apply to IRS summonses. Fed.Rules Evid. Rule 501, 28 U.S.C.A.; Fed.Rules Civ.Proc. Rules 26(b)(3), 81(a)(3), 28 U.S.C.A.; 26 U.S.C.A. §§ 7402(b), 7602, 7604(a).

9. Federal Civil Procedure ⟐1600.2

Forcing attorney to disclose notes and memoranda of witness' oral statements is particularly disfavored, and rule accords special protection to work product revealing attorney's mental processes. Fed.Rules Civ. Proc. Rules 26, 26(b)(3), 28 U.S.C.A.

10. Federal Civil Procedure ⟐1600.2

Notes and memoranda sought by government were work products based on oral statements of witnesses, and where, if they revealed communications, protected by attorney–client privilege, and to extent they did not reveal communications, they revealed attorney's mental processes in evaluating the communications, and disclosure would not be required simply on showing of substantial need and inability to obtain equivalent without undue hardship, and stronger showing of necessity and unavailability by other means than was made by government or applied by magistrate would be necessary to compel disclosure. Fed.Rules Evid. Rule 501, 28 U.S.C.A.; 26 U.S.C.A. § 7602; Fed.Rules Civ.Proc. Rule 26(b)(3), 28 U.S.C.A.

SUMMARY

The tax researcher's job of sorting through the thousands of potentially pertinent Federal tax court cases is facilitated by citators, which can be either published or elec-

Chapter 8 Citators and Other Finding Devices

Exhibit 8–23
Westlaw Custom Digest Option Screen

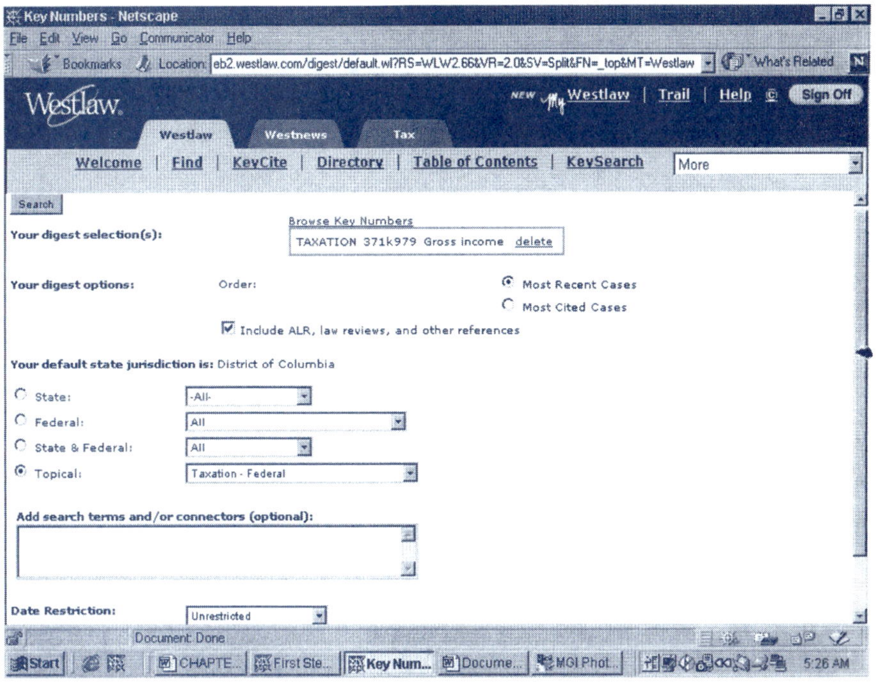

Source: Westlaw. Reprinted with permission.

tronic. When familiar with these research tools, the current status and precedential value of a specific case or ruling can be determined effectively and quickly. This determination is necessary for the researcher to evaluate the judicial and administrative sources of the tax law that pertain to a client's tax issue. The electronic services automate virtually all of the tedious mechanical aspects of Shepardizing cases and validating the formal correctness of citations. Further, they make the retrieval of cited and citing cases almost effortless. The overview of citators and the act of citing presented in this chapter demonstrate that research is not complete until all primary sources upon which the researcher is relying are found to be currently "good law."

TAX TUTOR

Reinforce the tax research information covered in this chapter by completing the on-line tutorials located at the Federal Tax Research web site:

http://raabe.swcollege.com

KEY WORDS

By the time you complete your work in this chapter, you should be comfortable discussing each of the following terms. If you need additional review of any of these items, return to the appropriate material in the chapter or consult the glossary at the end of this text.

Auto-Cite	KC History
CCH Citator	KeyCite
Citation	LEXCITE
Citator	*PH Citators*
Citator 2nd Series	*RIA Citators*
Cited Case	Shepardizing
Cites	*Shepard's Citator*
Citing Case	*Shepard's Federal Tax Citator*
Headnote	Table of Authorities
KC Citation	Westlaw

DISCUSSION QUESTIONS

1. What are the goals of tax research?
2. Describe the authority of the Code. What do practitioners do if the Code is not clear on an issue?
3. Why are subsequent cases important to the value of a prior case?
4. Describe the function of a citator in the tax research process.
5. Distinguish between the following terms: cited case, citing case, citation, and cites.
6. How may citators be organized?
7. Name the three most popular commercial tax citators, and indicate whether they are sold as part of a commercial tax service.
8. Explain the difference between a general directing and a local cite. Which service uses local directing cites?
9. What publishers have been associated with the *Citator* and *Citator 2nd Series?*
10. Name four types of Administrative Pronouncements included in the *RIA Citators?*
11. Explain the organization of the published *RIA Citators.*
12. What is the special treatment of Tax Court Memorandum decisions in Volume 2 of the *PH Citator?* What is the reason for this treatment?
13. What is a drawback in the coverage of cases in the electronic version of the *RIA Citators?*
14. What are the issues discussed in headnotes 1 and 2 of the *Upjohn* case?
15. The *RIA Citators* do not follow the traditional legal convention of listing cases under the plaintiff's name. What convention do they use? Why are the cases listed in this manner?
16. In what order do the *RIA Citators* list citations?
17. What are headnotes, and why do they have this name?
18. When is the citator portion of a research project finished?
19. Why are Revenue Rulings included in the *RIA Citators?* Where are they located, and how are they organized?
20. How many volumes are there in the *CCH Citator?* How are the volumes arranged?
21. How often are the CCH and the RIA citators updated?
22. What features of the *CCH Citator* facilitate its being housed in two volumes?
23. How are court decisions that are obsolete designated in the *CCH Citator?* What do the bold bullets indicate in the *CCH Citator?*

24. In the *CCH Citator,* what is the citation order for the courts hearing the same cited case? What is the *CCH Citator* convention for listing citing cases?
25. What does "Shepardizing" mean?
26. Compare the coverage and organization of *Shepard's Citators* with the RIA and CCH citator services.
27. With the *Shepard's Citator* a researcher can locate a case either by the case name or by its citation. Comment on this statement.
28. Is the citing case information the same in the published and the Lexis version of the *Shepard's Citator?*
29. What is the significance of the superscript number appearing immediately to the left of the page number in a citing reference in the published version of *Shepard's?* How is this feature indicated in the Lexis version?
30. What is Auto-Cite, who developed it, and what is its primary objective?
31. What is the function of a Table of Authorities? Why is it a useful research tool?
32. What is LEXCITE, and when would a researcher use this Lexis service?
33. What is KeyCite? What event in 1999 caused a reorganization of KeyCite?
34. How does the information provided by KC History differ from that retrieved using KC Citations?
35. What information regarding citing cases is provided by KeyCite that is not available from the other citation services discussed in this chapter?
36. Evaluate the following statement. The headnotes for a given case are set by the court and thus are consistent across court reporting services.
37. When is the West Key Number System useful to a researcher?
38. Compare the Shepard's (Lexis) Table of Authorities with the Westlaw version.
39. What important information does the Cite List provide? When is this option selected by a researcher?
40. What company was the first to introduce citators as legal aids?

EXERCISES

41. State which citator uses the following abbreviations/symbols and what each means.
    a. d
    b. r
    c. g
    d. h
    e. iv
    f. n
    g. p
    h. q
    i. x
42. State which citator uses the following abbreviations/symbols and what each means.
    a. SLR
    b. clfd
    c. reinst
    d. EO

Continued

e. Amp
f. ob
g. app
h. ARR
i. susp

43. Answer the following questions.
    a. Which published *RIA Citators* would need to be referenced for a case decided in 1945? Would all the information regarding this case be available through the RIA Checkpoint Internet service?
    b. Explain why there are three entries for the *El Paso Company* citing case under the *Upjohn* case in Exhibit 8–5.
    c. How have the most recent citing cases treated the *Upjohn* case?
    d. Explain the citator entry for Revenue Ruling 99–56?

44. In the published *RIA Citators*, find *Algernon Blair, Inc.*, under the letter "A" and under the letter "B."
    a. In what volume of what series do the cases initially appear?
    b. What reference does the Tax Court case listed under the Letter "A" make?
    c. Give the Prentice-Hall (PH) citation for the *Algernon Blair, Inc.*, case listed under letter "B."
    d. "[See 29 TC 1211]" is listed after the citing case of *Holmes Enterprises, Inc.* What does "See 29 TC 1211" mean?

45. Use the electronic *RIA Citators* to find *Algernon Blair, Inc. v Comm.* and *Algernon Blair, Inc. v U.S.*
    a. When using the Citation option to find the cases, what do you need to know besides the name of the cases to retrieve them?
    b. Use the Contents option to find the cases. How many entries are returned when a search of the TOC entries is performed on the *Citator 2d?* How many are actually entries for the cases of interest?
    c. Use the Contents option to find the cases. Drill down through the *Citator 2d* contents under the letter "A." In what case grouping do the cases appear? How many *Algernon Blair, Inc.*, cases are listed?

46. Locate Revenue Ruling 1979-162, and answer the following questions.
    a. What is its complete *Cumulative Bulletin* citation? Is it still a valid Revenue Ruling?
    b. What tax issue does the Revenue Ruling address?
    c. In what paragraph of the *Federal Tax Coordinator 2d* is this ruling discussed?
    d. In what paragraph of the CCH service was this ruling initially discussed?
    e. In what paragraph of the Code Arranged by Annotations (RIA Checkpoint) is this ruling discussed?

47. List in what order the following types of cases would be given under the "no specific headnotes" category of citations for a case found in the *RIA Citators*.
    - U.S. Courts of Appeal
    - Board of Tax Appeals
    - U.S. District Court
    - U.S. Court of Federal Claims
    - State courts
    - U.S. Supreme Court
    - U.S. Tax Court
    - Treasury Rulings and Decisions

Chapter 8 Citators and Other Finding Devices

48. Determine the order, from first to last, in which the following cases appear in the *CCH Citator*.
    - *Byron H. Gaar, Jr.*, 43 TCM 1425
    - *GBG, Inc.*, 43 TCM 169
    - *G. C. Services Corp.*, 73 TC 406
    - *William H. George*, 26TC 396
    - *G & G Records, Inc.*, 46 TCM 430
49. Locate *John Doe*, 74-1 USTC ¶ 9344, and answer the following questions.
    a. In what year was this decision rendered?
    b. What is the citation for *John Doe* in the F2d court reporter?
    c. What is the citation for *John Doe* in the AFTR2d court reporter?
    d. What was the court of original jurisdiction for this case?
50. In the *CCH Citator*, find *Algernon Blair, Inc.*, under the letter "A" and under the letter "B."
    a. Are these two the same case? Explain your response.
    b. Give the judicial history for *Algernon Blair, Inc.*, listed under the letter "B."
    c. What is the citation of the *Algernon Blair, Inc.*, case that is cited by Revenue Rulings? List the Revenue Rulings that cite this case.
    d. What is the citation of the *Algernon Blair, Inc.*, case that is cited by cases with banks as the taxpayers? List the banking cases that cite this case by name and citation.
51. Use both the *CCH Citator* and the *RIA Citators* to answer the following questions regarding the Tax Court case *Algernon Blair, Inc.*
    a. Which citator made it easier to identify how many Revenue Rulings were citing this case?
    b. What was the most recent citing Private Letter Ruling for each citator service? In which service was it easier to determine the most recent citing case?
    c. What year was the *Eastwood Mall, Inc.*, citing case decided? How did it evaluate *Algernon Blair, Inc.*, in its discussion? From which citator was it easier to obtain this information?
    d. In what paragraphs is the case discussed in the CCH tax service and the RIA tax services? From which citator was it easier to obtain this information?
52. Locate *City of New Britian*, 44 AFTR ¶ 798, using *Shepard's Citator*.
    a. What are the parallel citations for this case? In what year was this case decided?
    b. On what page does the case, *Estate of Romani*, 140 L. Ed. 2d 710, cite the *New Britian* case? What page would this be if you were using the *United States Supreme Court Reports* (U.S.)?
    c. The *Kimbell Foods, Inc.*, case, 99 S. Ct. 1448, discusses the *New Britian* case on two pages. What are the page numbers? Why does the *United States Supreme Court Reports* only indicate that the case is discussed on one page?
    d. What Lexis precedent symbol is associated with both the *Estate of Romani* and the *Kimbell Foods, Inc.* cases?
53. Locate *City of New Britian*, 1954 U.S. Lexis 2751, using Lexis Auto-Cite.
    a. What Lexis precedent symbol is associated with this case? What event caused the *New Britian* case to receive this symbol?
    b. What is this case's prior history?
    c. What publication cites this case in its discussion of the provisions of 31 USCS §§ 3713 and 9309?
    d. What citing cases are listed in the subsequent treatment history section?

54. Using LEXCITE, enter the following citation: 98 L. Ed. 520.
    a. In the "Enter more terms" type in the name of the case, *New Britian*. Which case is a Civil Action? Which case is a state Supreme Court Case?
    b. Limit the search to Court of Appeals cases for the circuit within which you live that were decided in the last 10 years. How many cases did you find? Give the citation for the most recent case.
    c. Use a five-year date restriction to limit the search. In what order are the documents listed?
    d. Perform the same search as (b) above except use the citation 347 U.S. 81. What are the results? Explain.
55. Using Lexis Table of Authorities, enter the following citation: 74 S. Ct. 367.
    a. What are the parallel citations for this case? In what year was this case decided?
    b. How many cases did it cite in developing its decision? Which cited cases have some type of warning associated with them?
    c. What are the jurisdictional levels in which the cases are divided?
    d. On which pages are the cases?
56. Use Shepard's on Lexis and Westlaw to locate *Algernon Blair, Inc.*, 441 F.2d 1379.
    a. How many citing decisions does Shepard's list? How many citing cases have warning or caution symbols?
    b. How many citing decisions does Westlaw list? How many citing cases have warning or caution symbols?
    c. What is the maximum depth of treatment the citing cases give *Algernon Blair, Inc.?* How many cases quote *Algernon Blair, Inc.?* Which service did you use to discover this information?
    d. What commercial tax services are listed as secondary sources in Westlaw? Name two journals listed as secondary sources in Shepard's.
57. Locate *Tank Truck Rentals, Inc.*, 78 S. Ct. 507, on Westlaw.
    a. What are official parallel citations for this case? In what year was this case decided?
    b. Use KC History. How many lower court cases are shown in the direct history? How was each treated?
    c. List the citing documents in the Negative Indirect History, and explain the depth of treatment by each.
    d. How many positive three- and four-star depth of treatment cases are listed for *Tank Truck Rentals, Inc.?* Of those cases, how many have warning or caution symbols marking them?
58. Use the Table of Authorities on Westlaw to find the following information for *Tank Truck Rentals, Inc.*, 78 S. Ct. 507.
    a. How many cases does *Tank Truck Rentals, Inc.*, cite in its decision?
    b. Which case(s) does it quote that has three stars for depth of treatment?
    c. How many of the cases cited in *Tank Truck Rentals, Inc.*, have warning or caution symbols? How does this make you feel about the reasoning in this case?
    d. How many different pages have discussion of cases?
59. Compare the headnotes for the *Upjohn* case reproduced in Exhibits 8–3 and 8–22.
    a. How many West headnotes are related to Code § 7602?
    b. How many RIA headnotes are related to Code § 7602?
    c. For what other areas of law (besides tax) does West provide headnotes?
    d. Why do you think RIA has so few headnotes and West has so many?

60. Find Revenue Rulings 1999-49 and 2000-56 in a citator of your choosing.
    a. What are their full citations?
    b. Are these rulings still valid? Explain your response by referring to their administrative history.
    c. What affect did these rulings have on previously issued rulings?
    d. What causes the history of these rulings?

RESEARCH CASES

For each of the research problems locate court cases or administrative pronouncements (Revenue Rulings, Revenue Procedures, etc.) that support your position. Provide a list of cases or administrative pronouncements citing your authority that demonstrate your authority is still good law.

61. Jamie's adjusted gross income is $31,000. During the year, she spent $250 of her own funds on birthday treats for the students in the second-grade class that she teaches. She bought these presents during a 75-mile round trip to a specialty educational toy store. Can she deduct any portion of these amounts?
62. Walter dies in California with an estate consisting mostly of real estate owned jointly with his wife, Wilma. At the time of his death there were large past due county assessments on most of the land. Wilma, the executrix of the estate, applied the valuation rules of Revenue Ruling 1959-60 to the land. She was in the process of negotiating down the assessments when the estate tax return was required to be filed. How does Wilma treat these liens on the estate tax return?
63. Peggy had been a heavy tobacco user until she joined the Norwood Tobacco Free Program. She had spent a substantial amount of money on nicotine patches and other non-prescription treatments without much success. Her father recently died from lung cancer. That really made her realize that to kick the habit she would need to get professional help before her habit created serious medical problems. While she is very pleased at being tobacco free for the first time in 10 years, she is wondering whether any of the vast amounts spent on the cure are deductible?
64. Sally sells her home to Bob and pays the $9,000 in points by offsetting this amount against her sale proceeds. Determine the tax effects on both parties.
65. Ethel and Rick spent $4,500 in allocable interest and taxes and $1,100 in advertising and maintenance for their "bed and breakfast" inn. This year's rental income from the inn came to $4,900. Determine the tax effects of conducting the B&B as a one-third part of Ethel and Rick's residence.
66. The parents of this year's "Annie" (she is age 8) spent $8,000 in travel expenses for auditions and rehearsals of the popular play. When she got the part, her parents were designated in the Broadway contract to receive one-half of her total earnings. Discuss the proper recognition of gross income and related deductions concerning this arrangement.
67. Barbara's psychologist recommended that Barbara divorce her husband, Tom. Tom's dress and eating habits had led to Barbara's serious neuroses. Are the costs of the divorce deductible to Tom? To Barbara?

68. Newark Marine Food Service sells hot lunches and snacks to the crews of ships that dock at the Port of Newark. According to custom, the officers of the visiting ships receive a five percent "commission" from all sales, so that Marine can retain its "exclusive rights" to the seamen's business. Are the commissions deductible by the shipping firms?

69. Clara works at the PamperU Hotel in Lake Tahoe. Clara's job is to provide relaxation demonstrations, teach yoga, provide massage therapy, and give lectures on stress management. Since Clara possessed no formal training in any of these subjects, she decided to attend seminars all over the United States on the topics related to her job. She also attended the local university and took physiology classes to learn more about the body and how it functions. Can Clara deduct these expenses as continuing educational expenses?

70. Joy accompanied her husband on a business trip to San Diego because he had been injured in a subway accident and could no longer drive an automobile. Joy was not associated with his business directly, but she did perform as his chauffeur on the trip. What is the tax treatment of Joy's incremental expenses for the trip?

71. After his divorce, Brown paid the expenses of maintaining the family home, which continued to be the principal residence of his ex-wife and their three daughters. He owned the house, but no longer lived there. Instead, he maintained another home as his principal residence. Can he claim head of household status, assuming that he is assigned the dependency exemptions for the daughters?

72. Alice, the chair of the School of Accountancy, entertains the faculty at her home each semester and has a holiday party at the end of December for the faculty and their families. When a faculty member is promoted or has a paper published in an exceptionally prestigious journal, she has a "social hour" at her house. She also sponsors a picnic for the faculty and graduate students at the start of the fall semester to let them get acquainted. To what extent are these expenses deductible?

73. Vandals caused $1,250 damage to Tricia's fully depreciated rental property. Determine her casualty loss or other deduction.

74. Buddy was injured by Matt in an automobile accident. The court awarded Buddy $30,000 in damages, but Matt was able to raise (and paid to Buddy) only $12,000. They both then considered the matter closed. Compute the amount of gross income to Buddy, and to Matt, from these transactions.

75. Con man Floyd sold Larry the Library of Congress for $15,000. Larry had embezzled the $15,000 he used to make the purchase from his employer.
    a. How much gross income should Larry and Floyd report as a result of these transactions?
    b. What is the tax treatment for Larry when he repays his (former) employer?

76. Reverend Ruth received an annual salary of $15,000 and a parsonage allowance of $6,000. She paid $4,000 rent on the home, and she spent $1,100 on housing-related purchases. What is her gross income from these items?

77. Jill received a research grant from the University of Minnesota in amounts of $10,000 for her time and $3,000 for related supplies and expenses. She purchased a $28,000 Audi the day after depositing the state's check. Jill is a candidate for a master's degree in philosophy and ethics. What is her gross income from the grant?

78. To what extent should Professor Dodd include in gross income the value of examination copies of books that he receives without charge from book publishers?

9

Journals, Newsletters, and Internet News Sources

LEARNING OBJECTIVES

- Become familiar with Internet sources of tax information
- Survey tax periodicals and the role they play in the tax research process
- Use correct citation form for printed and electronic tax materials
- Identify the most important electronic and print tax periodicals
- Examine various indexes to tax periodicals that can facilitate the task of locating pertinent journal articles

CHAPTER OUTLINE

Nature of Tax and Law Periodicals
Citing Print and Electronic Articles
Types of Tax Periodicals
    Annual Proceedings
    Scholarly Reviews
    Professional Tax Journals
    Tax Newsletters
Locating Relevant Tax Articles
    CCH *Federal Tax Articles*
    WG&L *Index to Federal Tax Articles*
    Shepard's Indexes
    LexisNexis *Academic Universe*
    Other Law and Accounting Indexes
    General Indexes
    Other Resources
Internet Sites

Tax journals and newsletters are secondary sources of the tax law. These periodicals take many forms, ranging from the strictest of law reviews, which accept no advertising of any sort, to newsletters in which the tax articles seem just an excuse for breaking up the advertising copy. Because articles are considered secondary sources, they generally should not be cited as the controlling authority, especially when primary sources supporting the position are available. With that caveat aside, researchers who ignore the tax periodicals might be accused, at best, of reinventing the wheel and, at worst, of professional malpractice. Such periodicals optimize research time by capitalizing on the author's expert judgments and references on a relevant topic, and by bolstering one's own argument during an audit or before a court, via a reference to the work of a noted tax authority.

NATURE OF TAX AND LAW PERIODICALS

Tax periodicals contain a variety of articles and news briefs that are designed to keep readers relatively knowledgeable of developments in specific or general areas of the tax law. These articles might contain, for example, an in-depth review of a recently decided court case, a broad analysis of the factors that should enter into the practitioner's decision on whether to make a certain tax accounting election, a mathematical analysis of the effects of a tax law modification on the overall economy, or a call for reform of a statute by a neutral (or biased) observer. Tax articles can suggest new approaches to tax problems, give guidance for solving complex problems, or just explain a new law in a readable form.

Any given periodical may contain an article that is right "on point" with research a practitioner is conducting. Through its references, the practitioner may be quickly led to pertinent primary sources of the law. In effect, the researcher is using the author of the article as a research associate, thereby saving hours of additional research.

Traditionally, citing articles in professional tax research is limited to two situations: (1) if the researcher is referring to the author's analysis and conclusions as stated in an article concerning, for instance, an interpretation of a Code section or court opinion; (2) if the researcher cannot find any controlling primary sources of law and a secondary source addresses the issue.

As discussed in several previous chapters, tax articles are now being cited more frequently in case opinions than in the past. When they are lacking both the appropriate primary law sources and adequate judicial staff, the authors of these opinions may draw on tax articles to support the views of the court. In any event, it is imperative that the researcher understands the practical implications of using secondary law sources.

CITING PRINT AND ELECTRONIC ARTICLES

A citation to a printed tax journal article should take the following standard form.

> Whittenburg, G. E., William A. Raabe and Martha Doran. "Optimize Early—And Penalty Free—IRA Distributions." 65 *Practical Tax Strategies* 1 (July 2000) at 5.

Notice the proper placement of capital letters, periods, and commas in the citation. Notice, too, that the volume and page numbers of the journal follow the citation conventions of court cases (i.e., volume number, journal, first page of article). The denotation "at 5" indicates that the researcher is referencing or quoting from a specific portion of the article. If the entire article were being referenced, the citation would merely contain the beginning page number of the article. For the citation above, this would be ". . . (July 2000) 4."

Unfortunately, the proper citation for articles found on the Internet is not as well established as for printed materials. Formats for citing resources on the Internet are in the same flux as the Internet itself. Thus, there is a lack of agreement among citation authorities as to the proper format for citing data found on the Internet. A problem that further complicates the issue is deciding how to characterize the Internet material to be cited. For example, is the material a journal article, a newsletter, or a report, who is the author, and when was the resource generated? Once this information is deciphered (and this deciphering may not be easy), a generally safe format of a citation is to follow that of a printed document, with additions or deletions as necessary. The following would be an acceptable format for a journal article found on the Internet.

> O'Neil, Cherie, Donald Samelson, and Matthew Wills. "The Business Auto Decision." *Journal of Accountancy Online* (February 2001). Retrieved April 23, 2001 from AICPA at: **http://www.aicpa.org/pubs/jofa/feb2001/index.htm**

Sites on the Internet are generally case and punctuation sensitive. Therefore, ignore normal grammar rules when providing uniform resource locators (URLs) and place no punctuation (such as a period or a comma) at the end of a URL. It is important to indicate the date on which the document was retrieved because documents and web site URLs may change or be removed over time.

TYPES OF TAX PERIODICALS

Tax periodicals can be categorized according to the depth of the coverage of their articles and the audience for which they are written. From the most extensive coverage to the least, they are as follows.

- Annual proceedings
- Scholarly reviews
- Professional journals
- Newsletters

Although each publication has its unique characteristics, several general characteristics of each category will be identified. This discussion will provide an initial introduction to the broad market of secondary source tax commentary.

ANNUAL PROCEEDINGS

A number of annual conferences for tax practitioners and academics are conducted every year. Usually sponsored by a professional organization, law school, or educational agency, these conferences last from two to five days. The agenda at these conferences may include any of the following: lectures, paper presentations with or without discussion, panel discussions, seminars, demonstrations, and luncheon addresses.

Often, the conference speakers allow the sponsoring agency to publish their presentations as **proceedings** of the meeting. These proceedings are distributed to the participants at the conference, and later to the general public in the form of a collection of articles. Most of these papers exhibit considerable depth of coverage and practical insight by the authors, and they can be a valuable resource for the tax researcher.

A few of the more established tax conferences include the following.

- New York University Institute on Federal Taxation had its first annual meeting in 1942.
- Penn State Tax Conference was established in 1946.
- University of Chicago Law School's Annual Federal Tax Conference first met in 1947.
- University of Southern California's Major Tax Planning Institute began in 1948.
- Tulane Tax Institute started in 1952.

The proceedings and indexes to these conferences are widely available. For example, CCH publishes the proceedings of the University of Chicago Law School's Annual Federal Tax Conference as an issue of *Taxes—The Tax Magazine*. Exhibit 9–1 provides an excerpt from the table of contents for the March 2001 issue of *Taxes*.

Exhibit 9–1 Table of Contents for *Taxes—The Tax Magazine*

TAXES

Vol. 79, No. 3   March 2001

CONTENTS

THE UNIVERSITY OF CHICAGO LAW SCHOOL'S

53RD ANNUAL FEDERAL TAX CONFERENCE

NOVEMBER 15-16, 2000

Conference Planning Committee

Jeffrey T. Sheffield, Chair, *Kirkland & Ellis*
Robert H. Aland, *Baker & McKenzie*
Sheldon I. Banoff, *Katten Muchin & Zavis*
Stephen S. Bowen, *Latham & Watkins*
Harvey L. Coustan, *Ernst & Young LLP*
Michael Duhl, *Deloitte & Touche LLP*
Howard Engle, *Arthur Andersen LLP*
Bradford L. Ferguson, *Sidley & Austin*
Thomas P. Fitzgerald, *Winston & Strawn*
Louis S. Freeman, *Skadden Arps Slate Meagher & Flom LLP*
Frank J. Gaudio, Jr, *PricewaterhouseCoopers LLP*
Marilyn Gerdes, *Sara Lee Corporation, Chicago*
Errol Golub, *KPMG LLP*
George B. Javaras, *Kirkland & Ellis*
Burton W. Kanter, *Neal Gerber & Eisenberg*
Richard M. Lipton, *McDermott Will & Emery*
James M. Lynch, *Winston & Strawn*
John B. Palmer III, *Foley & Lardner*
Julie A. Roin, *University of Chicago Law School*
Timothy C. Sherck, *Mayer Brown & Platt*
Douglas H. Walter, *Jones Day Reavis & Pogue*
Robert R. Wootton, *Sidley & Austin*
Lowell D. Yoder, *McDermott Will & Emery*

29 "1, 61, 83, Pay Me with Your E·qui·ty": Tax Problems Facing Service Firms (and Their Partners) Who Receive Stock or Options in Lieu of Cash Fees
By Sheldon I. Banoff

94 Compensating the Service Partner with Partnership Equity: Code Sec. 83 and Other Issues
By William R. Welke and Olga Loy

120 Applying the Property-Services Distinction in Corporate Transactions: The New Economy Tests the Limits
By Timothy C. Sherck and Wayne R. Luepker

146 The Emerging Hybrid Structure That Can Best Meet the Goals of Participants in an E-Commerce Start-up
By Barksdale Penick

169 Opening Pandora's Box: Who Is (or Should Be) a Partner?
By Eric Sloan and Christine Kraft

193 Tax Issues Arising in Connection with the Incorporation of an Ongoing Electronic Commerce Business
By John D. Rayis and David F. Levy

211 Characterizing the "New" Transfers of Intellectual Property
By Suresh T. Advani

231 The OECD Initiative: Harmful Tax Practices and Tax Havens
By Leslie B. Samuels and Daniel C. Kolb

© 2001 CCH INCORPORATED. All Rights Reserved. Reprinted with permission from *TAXES—The Tax Magazine*.

While some conferences select different areas of tax as the theme of the meetings each year, other annual conferences focus on a specialized area year after year. Examples of specialized tax conferences include the Non-profit Legal and Tax Conference held in March in Washington, D.C.; the Institute on Oil and Gas Law and Taxation, which meets in Dallas; the Great Western Tax and Estate Planning Conference of the National Law Foundation held in Las Vegas; the Asian Development Bank Organization's International Taxation Conference held in Japan; and the University of Miami Law Center's Heckerling Institute on Estate Planning held each January in Miami Beach.

SCHOLARLY REVIEWS

All major law schools and a few business schools produce publications referred to as **law reviews** or **academic journals.** These publications are edited either by faculty members or by graduate students under the guidance of the school's faculty. Most law reviews also use an outside advisory board comprised of practicing attorneys and law professors at other universities to aid in selecting and reviewing articles. The articles appearing in these publications are usually written by tax practitioners, academics, graduate students, or other noted commentators.

Many scholarly tax articles follow an introduction to the authors' chosen topics with a brief history of the law that is the subject of the review. The authors then present an analysis of the prevailing status of the selected area of the law, typically concentrating on a current case or recently issued Regulation to delineate the existing interpretation of the law. In most articles, the authors then discuss their own analysis of the precedents. The researcher may find analyses of this type useful in identifying the development of a point of law or in strengthening the client's similar case against the government. Due to the extensive references included as footnotes, law articles often run from 60 to more than 100 pages in length, prior to their publication in the law review.

Some law schools produce journals that are limited to a specific area of the law, such as constitutional or labor law, in addition to the regular multitopic law review. Most of the general law reviews feature one to three tax articles per year; however, some law reviews are dedicated exclusively to tax matters. The following are several of the law reviews that concentrate on taxation issues.

- *Akron Tax Journal* by University of Akron
- *The American Journal of Tax Policy* by University of Alabama (no longer published)
- *Boston University Journal of Tax Law* by Boston University (no longer published)
- *Ohio Tax Review* by Capital University
- *Florida Tax Review* by University of Florida
- *Tax Law Review* by New York University School of Law
- *Virginia Tax Review* by University of Virginia School of Law

Besides law schools, academic organizations such as the National Tax Association of (NTA) and the American Taxation Association (ATA) publish scholarly journals. (The web site for NTA is **http://www.ntanet.org** and for ATA the web site is **http://www.atasection.org**). While NTA membership is dominated by economists, the organization also includes attorneys, accountants, professors, businesspeople, and government employees with an interest in taxation. The articles appearing quarterly in its *National Tax Journal* and the proceedings from the NTA annual conference, published in *Proceedings of the Annual Conference,* tend to take an analytical or mathematical approach to identifying the broad economic and social implications of taxation on the population.

The ATA, a subdivision of the American Accounting Association, is composed chiefly of business school professors of taxation and tax professionals. It publishes two regular issues of *The Journal of the American Taxation Association (JATA)* and, like the NTA, the ATA prints a special conference supplement containing the papers presented at its yearly national conference. This journal is a research publication that offers a combination of taxation articles that employ (1) quantitative or analytical, (2) empirical, (3) theoretical, (4) legal, or (5) tax education methodologies in analyzing issues considered of interest to the tax community. Exhibit 9–2 presents the Table of Contents for a recent issue of *JATA.*

PROFESSIONAL TAX JOURNALS

A wide variety of **tax journals** are published for the purpose of keeping tax practitioners abreast of the current changes and trends in the tax law. This category of journals, commonly referred to as **professional journals** or **practitioner journals,** includes publications by professional organizations as well as commercial companies. Examples of the former are the AICPA's *Tax Adviser,* the ABA Section on Taxation's *Tax Lawyer,* and journals published by state CPA or law societies.

Because the commercial publications are numerous, the tax coverage of these journals can accommodate the needs of the general tax practitioner and those who specialize in a specific area of tax law. For example, journals such as Warren, Gorham & Lamont's *Journal of Taxation* and *Practical Tax Strategies* or Commerce Clearing House's *Taxes* cover a variety of tax areas, whereas journals such as Tax Management's *The Compensation Planning Journal* or Warren, Gorham & Lamont's *Journal of Taxation of Investments* cover singular topics. Further, the articles appearing in these journals also vary greatly in their coverage from very complex with an exceedingly narrow focus to extremely practical "how to" articles designed for immediate implementation. Exhibit 9–3 shows the table of contents for a specialized journal.

The editors of most professional journals presume that their readers have access to little, if any, other current tax resource material. Thus, any major change in the tax law or important Court tax decision will spawn numerous articles in the various periodicals on the same or similar topics. Accordingly, the Economic Growth and Tax Relief Reconciliation Act of 2001 caused a proliferation of journal articles aimed at apprising tax practitioners of various changes contained in the Act as well as offering analyses of the Act's impact on taxpayers and the economy. Many of the articles include hypothetical examples of relevant transactions, using specified dollar amounts, to explain or clarify major points.

To accommodate the tax practitioner's need for timely information, most of the multitopic tax journals are published monthly, whereas the more specialized tax journals tend to be issued on a quarterly basis. As will be discussed later in this chapter, most tax journals may be obtained through online services. The journals ensure the quality of their articles by accepting solicited and unsolicited articles prepared by appropriate tax experts. In each case, an editorial review board assesses the timeliness, accuracy, and readability of each article before it is accepted for publication.

Exhibit 9–2
Table of Contents
for *JATA*

Supplement 2000

The JOURNAL of the AMERICAN TAXATION ASSOCIATION

A Publication of the Tax Section of the American Accounting Association

2000 *JATA* Conference Supplement

Taxes and the Structure of Transactions

The Effect of Taxes on Acquisition Price and Transaction Structure
    Steven L. Henning, Wayne H. Shaw, and Toby Stock
    Discussant: Merle Erickson

The Effects of Goodwill Tax Deductions on the Market for Corporate Acquisitions
    Benjamin C. Ayers, Craig E. Lefanowicz, and John R. Robinson
    Discussant: Edward L. Maydew

Divestiture Structure and Tax Attributes: Evidence from the Omnibus Reconciliation Act of 1993
    Connie D. Weaver
    Discussant: Robert H. Trezevant

Joint Ventures between Nonprofit and For-Profit Organizations
    Richard C. Sansing
    Discussant: Shelley Rhoades-Catanach

Summaries of Papers in this Issue

Sponsored by
KPMG Peat Marwick Foundation

TAX NEWSLETTERS

The major tax services, discussed in Chapters 6 and 7, each include a **tax newsletter** as a part of their service. The Internet and online services tend to have daily newsletters, whereas the published services send the newsletters weekly. These newsletters help the

Exhibit 9–3
Table of Contents for
Journal of Taxation of Investments

Journal of Taxation of Investments

Volume 18, Number 2   Winter 2001

Qualified Small Business Stock Investments May Produce in
Significant Tax Benefits
Laura M. MacDonough, Richard D. Wehrheim, and Ian W. Ross   111

Internet Start-ups and the Use of Stock Options
Denis T. Rice   141

Developments Affecting Sales, Exchanges, and Basis—
2000 Brought a Good Crop of Important Decisions and Releases
Erik M. Jensen and Annette Nellen   155

Tax Incentives Encourage Brownfield Redevelopment
Beth S. Gotthelf and Tony R. Anthony   173

New Capital Gains Tax Legislation Encourages Venture Capital Investment
in Australia
Ann O'Connell   178

Corporate Finance Vehicles: Disaffiliating for Foreign Tax Credit Usage, Zero-Yield
Convertible Debt, Redeemable Preferred, *Custom Chrome*, and Other
Recent Developments / *Robert Willens*   192

Structured Investments: Debt Instruments on Which Interest Rates Reset
Before Maturity / *Frank R. Stong*   204

MARKET NOTES
    GOA Study Confirms Rapid Increase in AMT Impact
    Tracking Stock Still Popular Despite Clinton Proposals   209

subscriber keep abreast of important tax law developments. They are designed to give the practitioner both a capsule summary of tax law modifications and a reference to the paragraphs in the compilation materials that contain a more detailed analysis. Some of these newsletters also publish information concerning tax seminars and professional meetings, short reviews of (or citations for) selected current tax articles, and editorial highlights concerning recent tax developments. *TaxTracker News,* which is received by subscribers to CCH's web tax services, has a special feature that allows subscribers to customize the newsletter's coverage to the tax areas of interest to the subscriber. Several of the most popular commercial tax newsletters are listed in Exhibit 9–4. An example of a daily report, CCH *taxTracker News,* and a weekly newsletter, *Weekly Alert* published by RIA, are produced in Exhibits 9–5 and 9–6, respectively.

One of the most important newsletters is the BNA **Daily Tax Report.** Showing both breadth of topic and quality of analysis, the *Daily Tax Report* offers the subscriber up-to-date information concerning statutory, administrative, and judicial tax law developments that affect state, federal, and international taxation. In addition, the newsletter provides interviews with government officials, articles reviewing the day's events, and the full text of key documents discussed in the newsletter. In some instances these documents are not available from other tax services. Monthly indexes, including Private Letter Ruling and Code Section indexing, are provided

Exhibit 9–4 Selected Tax Newsletters from Major Publishers

Title	Frequency	Publisher
BNA *E-Commerce Tax Report*	Biweekly	Bureau of National Affairs
CCH Tax Day *News and Documents*	Daily	Commerce Clearing House
Daily Tax Bulletin	Daily	Kleinrock
Daily Tax Highlights and Documents	Daily	Tax Analysts
Daily Tax Report	Daily	Bureau of National Affairs
E-commerce Tax Alert	Monthly	Commerce Clearing House
Multistate Tax Report	Monthly	Bureau of National Affairs
RIA Tax Alert	Daily	Research Institute of America
State and Local Taxes	Weekly	Research Institute of America
State Tax Review	Weekly	Commerce Clearing House
Tax Features	Bimonthly	Tax Foundation
Memorandum	Biweekly	Bureau of National Affairs
Tax News Now	Continuously	Tax Analaysts
Tax Notes	Weekly	Tax Analysts
Tax Notes International	Weekly	Tax Analysts
Tax Notes Today	Daily	Tax Analysts
Taxes on Parade	Weekly	Commerce Clearing House
Tax Practice	Weekly	Tax Analysts
Tax Practice Series Bulletin	Biweekly	Bureau of National Affairs
taxTracker News	Daily	Commerce Clearing House
TaxWire	Continuously	Tax Analysts
Weekly Alert	Weekly	Research Institute of America
TM Weekly Report	Weekly	Bureau of National Affairs

Exhibit 9–5
Commerce Clearing House *taxTrackerNews*

New user's News — **CCH taxTracker News**℠ — April 20, 2001

The latest breaking federal and state tax news and documents customized just for you.

| ANALYSIS & COMMENTARY | TAX RESEARCH NETWORK | USER PREFERENCES |

[log off] New user, Welcome to Your **CCH taxTracker News** Page
You last checked your news on April 05, 2001. This news covers April 06, 2001 to April 20, 2001.

Contents

Federal News -- Federal Tax   50
State News -- State Tax   50
Click here to add tracker topics.
☐ Save taxTracker News headlines until your next login

Tax News Highlights:

2001TAXDAY, 04/20/2001, Item #C.2, JCT Releases "Blue Book" Explanation of Tax Bills Enacted in 106th Congress

2001TAXDAY, 04/20/2001, Item #J.3, Cayman Islands Corporation Bound by Closing Agreement; Letter Allegedly Modifying Settlement Offer Ineffective (Inverworld, Ltd., DC D.C.)

2001TAXDAY, 04/20/2001, Item #S.4, Washington--Use Tax; Sales Visits to State Created Nexus

Federal News -- Federal Tax

Text Only - Export to File - Add To KeepList

★ 2001TAXDAY, 04/20/2001, Item #C.1, Senate Moderates Press Leaders to Maintain $1.18 Trillion Tax Cut Limit,

Four moderate senators who helped the Senate pass a recommended tax cut of $1.18 trillion in the FY 2002 budget resolution (HConRes 83), sent a letter to Senate budget [continued . . .]

★ 2001TAXDAY, 04/20/2001, Item #C.2, JCT Releases "Blue Book" Explanation of Tax Bills Enacted in 106th Congress,

The Joint Committee on Taxation on April 19 released its "General Explanation of Tax Legislation Enacted in the 106th Congress" (JCS-2-01), which follows the chronological order of the [continued . . .]

★ 2001TAXDAY, 04/20/2001, Item #I.1, IRS Updates List of Countries for Which Foreign Residency Requirements Are Waived Due to Adverse Conditions (Rev. Proc. 2001-27),

The IRS has released an updated list of countries with respect to which the existence of adverse conditions during specified periods may excuse a taxpayer's failure to meet [continued . . .]

and are cumulated quarterly. Exhibit 9–7 illustrates the breadth of this newsletter's coverage.

The *Daily Tax Report* is available through Lotus Notes, the web, e-mail (summaries and table of contents), fax (table of contents), LexisNexis, and by paper subscription, which is hand-delivered in most major cities. It offers the equivalent of 30–50 pages of single-spaced printed copy every weekday. Because this is clearly too much to digest every day, the *Daily Tax Report* is organized to facilitate accessing only the material of greatest interest to the subscriber. While the content section lists only the title of each note by category (see Exhibit 9–7a), the highlights provide brief paragraphs describing the notes (see Exhibit 9–7b). Through the web, the listings in the contents and highlights sections are linked to the notes. Further, from the new notes or the highlights, the subscriber can access the actual government document on which the story is based (see Exhibit 9–7c).

Using Exhibit 9–7 documents, for example, selection of "IRS Releases First Annual Report On Structure, Activities Of APA Program" on the Contents Page or the "GG-2" box after the paragraph describing the same note on the Highlights Page will take the reader to the note. After reading the note on GG-2, the full text of the IRS Announcement 2000-35 can be examined by selecting the "L" box located at the

Exhibit 9–6 Research Institute Of America *Federal Taxes Weekly Alert*

Federal Taxes Weekly Alert

May 17, 2001
Volume 47, Number 21

■ Highlights ■

RIA Tax Watch 2001—for the latest tax-law developments: Hopes fade for quick bipartisan agreement on a Senate Finance Committee tax bill.

Tenth Circuit partially disagrees with Tax Court on inventory accounting issues: In a case involving inventory issues, the Tenth Circuit affirmed the Tax Court on the proper method to be used by a manufacturer to value inventory-related expenses but reversed and remanded for redetermination of the proper valuation of the inventory, which consisted of used automobile engines that repair shops returned to the taxpayer and which it remanufactured.

IRS allows GST tax-saving "reverse" QTIP election for estate that closed years ago: IRS has granted an estate that closed several years ago an extension to make a "reverse" QTIP election, with the result that the estate of the decedent's surviving spouse saved a significant amount of generation-skipping transfer tax.

New Special Study available on Checkpoint: A new Tax Planning & Practice Guide entitled "Tax Strategies for Handling a Stock Market Decline" is in the Federal Library under Practice and Planning. It explains tax strategies that lessen the damage of a stock market slide, whether investors hold stocks within or outside of retirement plan accounts and IRAs. It also explains how taxpayers currently receiving required distributions from traditional IRAs can cope with a market decline, and warns those who converted traditional IRAs to Roth IRAs when the stock market was higher of a tax trap that could cost them a 10% penalty even on a nontaxable withdrawal.

bottom of the note. The text of Announcement 2000-35 can also be reached from the Highlights Page by selecting the "Text L-28" box appearing after the description of the Announcement. This organization and the use of links allow the subscribers to tailor the amount of detail examined on a given tax topic.

A subscription to the *Daily Tax Report* includes access to Lotus Notes and Tax-Core, which are web-based sources of a wide variety of full-text primary tax materials. TaxCore is updated daily and has archived materials dating to November 1997. For practitioners not subscribing to the *Daily Tax Reports*, TaxCore may be obtained separately for a modest fee. The contents of TaxCore are described in Chapter 7.

As one would expect, receiving such extensive tax news on a daily basis is an expensive proposition. However, the *Daily Tax Report* (as well as many newsletters produced by other publishers) is available online to subscribers of various electronic tax research services. Thus, by subscribing to one of the major tax database systems, the practitioner has access to the *Daily Tax Report* at no incremental cost. To sample the *Daily Tax Report* or any other BNA tax publication, visit BNA's web site at **http://www.bnatax.com**.

Exhibit 9–7a
BNA *Daily Tax Report*
Contents

| Previous Page | Next Page | Search | Collapse |

BNA, Inc.

Daily Tax
REPORT

Contents
Highlights
Code Section
State Developments
International Taxes
Case Citations
   Alphabetically
   By issue date
Primary Source Material
   By BNA Issue Date
   By Agency Date
   By Document Type
   By IRC Section
IRS Transcripts
Tax Calendar

Publication
Information

▼ 03/31/2000
  ▼ **HIGHLIGHTS**
    ▼ In this Issue ...
       Highlights for this Issue
  ▼ **Lead Tax Report**
    ▼ APAs
       IRS Releases First Annual Report On Structure, Activities of APA Progra
    ▼ Electronic Commerce
       Panel Passes E-Commerce Report 10-8; Administration Officials All Vote
    ▼ Tax Legislation
       Finance Approves $248 Billion Tax Bill Providing Relief to Married Filer
  ▼ **Tax, Budget & Accounting**
    ▼ Accounting
       FASB Makes Progress on SPEs In Long-Running Consolidations Project
       FASB Decides More Issues on Changes To Rules on Transfer of Financial

---

Exhibit 9–7b
BNA *Daily Tax Report*
Highlights

Search

BNA, Inc.

Daily Tax
REPORT

Contents
Highlights
Code Section
State Developments
International Taxes
Case Citations
   Alphabetically
   By issue date
Primary Source Material
   By BNA Issue Date
   By Agency Date
   By Document Type
   By IRC Section
IRS Transcripts
Tax Calendar

Publication
Information

63
Friday March 31, 2000
ISSN 1522-8800

HIGHLIGHTS

E-Commerce Commission Narrowly Approves Report

After nearly a year of controversy, the Advisory Commission on Electronic Commerce narrowly approves, by a 10-8 vote, its report to Congress, showing support for changes to state taxing nexus that draw attacks from the Clinton administration and garner negative votes from all three federal officials on the 19-member commission. A representative of MCI Worldcom Inc. does not participate in the teleconferenced vote. Although the commission fails to achieve its congressionally required two-thirds majority consensus on all but two of the issues it addressed, Virginia Gov. Gilmore, the commission's chairman, immediately claims political victory, saying the commission is sending "a strong anti-tax report" to Congress, where some of its ideas are "already resonating" with lawmakers. GG-1 , Text L-47

IRS Releases First Annual Report on APA Structure, Activities

The number of completed advance pricing agreements involving a U.S. parent and foreign subsidiary, as opposed to a foreign parent and U.S. subsidiary, is almost equal, IRS says in its first annual report on APAs. The congressionally mandated study, released with Announcement 2000-35, says there were 91 APAs where the parent was U.S.-based and 90 APAs in which the parent was foreign. There also were two APAs involving partnerships and one involving a U.S. company and a possessions corporation subsidiary, IRS says. Of the 231 APAs completed since the program began, five industries have accounted for almost two-thirds of all completed accords--financial institutions and products; computer hardware, components, and related products, and computer software; chemicals and related products, pharmaceuticals, cosmetics; transportation equipment; and electrical equipment and components, the report says. GG-2, Text L-28

Reproduced with permission from *Daily Tax Report*, No. 63, web screen shots from the web notification service (March 31, 2000). Copyright 2000 by The Bureau of National Affairs, Inc. (800-372-1033) http://www.bna.com.

Exhibit 9–7c
BNA *Daily Tax Report* Article

Daily Tax
REPORT

No. 63
Friday March 31, 2000
ISSN 1522-8800

Page GG-2

Lead Tax Report

APAs
IRS Releases First Annual Report
On Structure, Activities of APA Program

The number of completed advance pricing agreements involving a U.S. parent and foreign subsidiary as opposed to a foreign parent and U.S. subsidiary is almost equal, the Internal Revenue Service said March 30 in its first annual report on APAs.

The congressionally mandated study, released with IRS Announcement 2000-35, said there were 91 APAs where the parent was U.S.-based and 90 APAs in which the parent was foreign.

There also were two APAs involving partnerships and one involving a U.S. company and a possessions corporation subsidiary. Eight APAs involved a U.S. company and foreign branches, while 27 completed agreements involved a foreign company and a U.S. branch.

The study, which covers APA statistics from fiscal years 1992 through 1999, was required under provisions of the Ticket to Work and Work Incentives Improvement Act of 1999 (P.L. 106-170), which included a provision providing APAs and related background materials the same Section 6103 confidentiality protection as tax returns.

Tangibles

Even though the APA Program is designed to address complex transfer pricing issues, a majority of the completed accords--138-- involved relatively less complicated sales of tangible property. The IRS report said 91 of the APAs were inbound situations and 47 were outbound situations.

◆◆◆

IRS said it used 12 different databases sold by four vendors to find comparable third-party transactions for APA analyses. The four vendors were Bureau van Dijk, Disclosure, Moody's, and Standard & Poor's.

In other areas, IRS in fiscal year 1999 recorded the first APA to be revoked or cancelled. There also was a record number of APA withdrawals--13--in fiscal year 1999, the service added.

Announcement 2000-35 is scheduled to appear in Internal Revenue Bulletin 2000-16, dated April 17, 2000.

Texts of Announcement 2000-35 and the IRS report are in Section L...

Reproduced with permission from *Daily Tax Report*, No. 63, web screen shots from the web notification service (March 31, 2000). Copyright 2000 by The Bureau of National Affairs, Inc. (800-372-1033) http://www.bna.com.

Tax Analysts publishes another set of important newsletters, including a daily tax news series available through **TaxBase** and the periodical *Tax Notes*. TaxBase is an Internet service comprised of several newsletter databases covering up-to-the-minute general *(Tax News Now)*, federal *(Tax Notes Today)*, state *(State Tax Today)*, and worldwide *(Worldwide Tax Daily)* tax news. It also provides access to an in-depth tax library. Tax Analysts developed a student version of TaxBase that is available free to students and professors through their campus web site: **http://tacampus.tax.org**. As discussed in Chapter 7, professors may register for this free service for their students and themselves by using the professor registration link on the opening page of the site. Through TaxBase, students will have access to *Tax Notes Today* as well as numerous primary sources (see Chapter 7 for a listing of sources available through TaxBase). As Exhibit 9–8 illustrates, the coverage of *Tax Notes Today* is as extensive as BNA's *Daily Tax Report*.

Exhibit 9–8

Tax News Now and *Tax Notes Today*

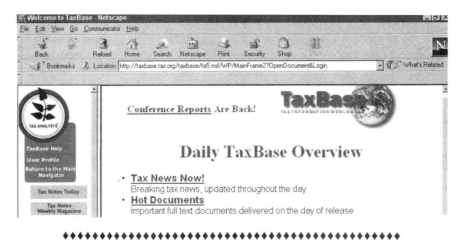

The contents of *Tax Notes,* published weekly, are similar to *Tax Notes Today* and the *Daily Tax Report* by BNA. In addition, *Tax Notes* includes in-depth analysis of court decisions, regulatory pronouncements, and policy-oriented research submitted by tax professionals and academics, as Exhibit 9–9 illustrates. Special sections provide news and practice tips just for accounting and tax practitioners. Each subscriber to the paper version of *Tax Notes* receives a fully searchable CD-ROM containing all the prior issues of *Tax Notes* except those for the most recent years (1972–1999 for 2001 subscriptions). The web version offers all of the paper version services plus online archives, links to full-text documents, PDF versions of all articles, full search capabilities, and multiple-user licenses.

Retrieving information in the web version of *Tax Notes* is similar to accessing the data in BNA's *Daily Tax Report.* Thus, to review an article the subscriber clicks

Exhibit 9–9

Tax Analysts *Tax Notes*

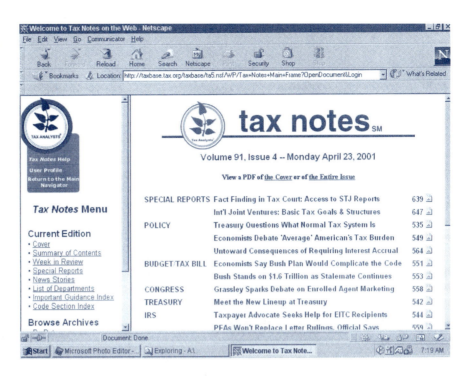

on the document icon after the page number. A document icon found within an article denotes that the preceding citation is linked to its full-text contents (see Exhibit 9–9). For example, the case *Investment Research Assocs. Ltd. v. Commissioner,* T.C. Memo. 1999-407, which is cited in the special report titled "Fact-Finding in the Tax

Court: Access to Special Trial Judge Reports," can be accessed by clicking on the document icon or by using the special *Tax Notes* document identification number "1999 TNT 242-7." The subscribers to the print version of *Tax Notes* use these unique document identification numbers to facilitate retrieval of the full-text documents through an online service such as Westlaw and Lexis.

Many other organizations, such as CPA firms, law firms, and special interest groups, issue newsletters either in print or through the Internet. These vary as to their coverage and quality as well as to their cost, but many are free to the general public. While all of the international CPA firms have newsletters, a few have very extensive letters available to the general public on special tax web sites. For a list of selected newsletters available through the Internet as well as sites offering links to a variety of tax and business newsletters, see Exhibit 9–10. As with any data on the Internet, the accessibility of these newsletters, their content, and quality is likely to change over time. Exhibit 9–11 illustrates a newsletter created by an international CPA firm.

Exhibit 9–10 Newsletter and News Web Sites

Accountants World	http://www.accountantsworld.com/taxcenter
AICPA	http://www.aicpa.org/news/index.htm
Andersen	http://www.arthurandersen.com/website.nsf/content/ MarketOfferingsTaxServices?OpenDocument
Beta Alpha Psi/ AccountingWEB Newswire	http://www.accountingweb.com
CPA Directory	http://www.cpa-finder.com
Delotte Touche, Tohmatsu	http://www.tax.deloitte.com
Ernst & Young	http://www.ey.com/global/gcr.nsf/International/ Welcome_-_Tax
Excite News Tracker	http://nt.excite.com/topics/business
IRS: The Digital Daily Newsstand	http://www.irs.ustreas.gov/ http://www.irs.ustreas.gov/prod/news/nandf.html
KPMG	by request at: http://www.kpmg.com
Lowtax Network	http://www.tax-news.com
McKenzie, Esq	http://www.mckenzielaw.com/#TAX
Michael Southon	http://www.freezineweb.com/tax.html
Newsletter Access	http://www.newsletteraccess.com
Organization Management, Inc.	http://www.taxexemptresources.com
Practitioners Publishing Co.	http://www.ppcnet.com/
PricewaterhouseCoopers	http://portal.pwcglobal.com
Tax Analysts Student TaxWire	http://tacampus.tax.org/

Exhibit 9–11
PricewaterhouseCoopers
Internet *Newsletter*

LOCATING RELEVANT TAX ARTICLES

The numerous published and computerized indexes available to tax researchers facilitate locating tax, business, and law journal articles that are pertinent to their research. However, the CCH *Federal Tax Articles* and the WG&L *Index to Federal Tax Articles* are the two indexes specifically designed for locating tax articles.

CCH *FEDERAL TAX ARTICLES*

The *Federal Tax Articles* index, published by Commerce Clearing House, has many outstanding features that make it one of the best tax indexes available. However, its most valuable feature is the concise abstracts furnished for each article cited in the index. Reading these abstracts helps the practitioner reduce the false starts that commonly occur when trying to find pertinent articles based solely on their titles. The framework for organizing these abstracts is the *Internal Revenue Code*. This organization also facilitates finding articles addressing the Code section under investigation by the researcher. Lastly, CCH updates this index monthly so the citations are timely. Because the *Federal Tax Articles* current volume is a loose-leaf service, the updates either replace existing pages or are added to the end of the binder. Twice a year the updates are cumulated. A Report Letter is also provided each month. The first few pages of each monthly issue highlight the articles added to the index and present new developments.

Every four to six years, the CCH cumulative bi-yearly reports fill the loose-leaf volume and require the publication of a bound volume. At this time the article abstracts are reorganized, and the various indexes are consolidated for the entire period. In the bound volumes, the cited articles with their abstracts are arranged alphabetically by title under each Code section heading. The article citations are preceded by a new paragraph number that is tied to the Code section.

Subsequently, a new loose-leaf volume is issued relative to the articles that are published after the issuance of the bound volume. CCH bound volumes cover 1954–1967, 1968–1972, 1973–1978, 1979–1984, and 1985–1989. A transfer binder is provided for 1990–1996, but as yet, these articles have not been reorganized and published in a bound volume. There is also a current loose-leaf binder that includes articles published in late 1996 and thereafter.

The more than 200 journals, law reviews, papers, and proceedings included in the index encompass Federal income, excise, estate, gift, and employment taxation. In the division called "Publishers and Publications," CCH provides the following information for each of the periodicals: publisher's name and address, frequency of publication, and the subscription cost. The cost of a single copy of each journal is also provided for those instances when the only source of a particular article is the publisher.

The main division of the index, called "Articles by Code Section," is where the full citation for each article and its abstract are located. This cumulative index gives Code section numbers with a brief description of the section as its headings. Articles can also be located by using the topic and author indexes. Each of these indexes refers the researcher to the "Articles by Code Section" division, through a system of paragraph numbering. The index's main cite number (i.e., to the left of the decimal point) provides the Code section paragraph number, and the numbers to the right of the decimal point refer to the specific article abstract. Using Exhibit 9–12 indexes, the article "E-Commerce and Tax Administration" under Code Section 6103 is referenced in the Index by Topic under "Internal Revenue Service—collection of taxes" as ¶ 4570.03 and in the Index by Author under "Roberts, Lauren" (and Brand, Phil) by the same number. Note that the paragraph number has no relation to the Code section number because this abstract is located in the current binder and not in a bound volume.

The *Federal Tax Articles* index does have one important drawback. As the loose-leaf volume accumulates a number of monthly updates, it becomes more difficult to use. As previously mentioned, twice a year the reports are consolidated and new paragraph numbers are assigned. These consolidated reports are maintained as separate sections in the loose-leaf binder. As of this writing, the current volume contained one yearly report for 1997 and 1998, three cumulative reports for 1999, and two cumulative reports for 2000. Thus, a researcher may examine up to eight separate Code section index reports for the years 1997–2000. The topic and author indexes are consolidated more frequently, and generally only two reports need to be examined.

WG&L INDEX TO FEDERAL TAX ARTICLES

Warren, Gorham & Lamont's ***Index to Federal Tax Articles*** provides citations and occasional summaries for articles covering Federal income, gift, and estate taxation or tax policy that appear in more than 350 periodicals. The index surveys not only

Exhibit 9-12
CCH *Federal Tax Articles*

3476   2000 Article Summaries—Reports 455-460   461 1-2001

¶ 4570   Confidentiality and disclosure of returns and return information (Code Sec. 6103)

.03 E-Commerce and Tax Administration. Phil Brand and Lauren Roberts. 31 Tax Adviser, May 2000, pp. 336-339.

Discusses the changes in tax administration that have occurred as a result of technological advancement. Describes the growth of the Internet and economic commerce, and considers its impact on government. Highlights the initial uses of "e-government" that focused on electronic tax return filing, refunds, tax payments, and dissemination of information. Describes advances in e-government, and presents some challenges. Addresses confidentially and other taxpayers' concerns. Considers tax compliance issues, noting how tax avoidance opportunities might arise. Discusses combined efforts of the private sector and the government in using e-commerce in the area of tax administration.

◆◆

461 1-2001   **Index by Topic**   **5071**
References are to Current Article paragraphs.

INTERNAL REVENUE SERVICE
. collection of taxes
.. bankruptcy...3324.016; 3326.014; 4206.038
.. closing agreements/offers in compromise
   ...3321.028; 3336.018; 3337.044; 3699.046;
   3875.02; 4211.048; 4211.05; 4354.052; 4354.054;
   4466.056; 4466.058; 4466.062
.. collection due process notice...4347.01
.. constitutional limitations...3690.034
.. criminal cases...4468.076
.. expense restrictions...3322.014
.. installment agreements...3685.014;
   4031.028; 4038.028; 4572.04
.. interest abatement...3505.012; 3878.01
.. IRS Restructuring and Reform Act...
   3885.756; 3885.758; 4051.012; 4060.01; 4215.014;
   4222.022; 4360.052
.. levy or foreclosure suit...3869.02; 4042.016;
   4206.038; 4207.01; 4573.026; 4574.018
.. litigation costs...3877.04
.. private debt collection...3868.036
.. procedures...3504.02; 3705.014; 3707.016;
   4042.016; 4461.012
.. Taxpayer Bill of Rights...3307.016; 3307.018;
   3334.058; 3340.026; 3340.028; 3340.03; 3503.032;
   3505.01; 3522.014; 3702.038; 3708.012
➤ .. technology, effect on...4570.03
.. third party contacts...4338.022
.. third party notification...4471.058
.. unauthorized disclosure of return
   information...3860.028
. criminal tax cases

INTERNAL REVENUE SERVICE—continued
.. oil and gas property...3417.02
.. practice before the IRS...3697.06
.. qualified retirement plans...3200.57;
   3579.648; 3579.664; 3581.038; 3750.682; 3750.70;
   3750.702; 3752.04; 3931.708; 3931.722; 4115.31
.. voluntary compliance...3700.056
.. voluntary disclosure policy...3515.02
. returns
.. disclosure of return information...3860.026
.. filing of...3311.04
.. unauthorized disclosure...3860.028
. rules and regulations
.. abusive exercise of authority...4365.042
.. accounting methods...3590.098; 3590.10;
   3602.026
.. amendment or revocation...4061.04
.. anti-abuse regulations...3229.056
.. interpretative...3520.258
.. retroactive application...4061.04

INVENTORIES
. accounting methods
.. clear reflection of income...4110.026;
   4276.028; 4277.032; 4502.12
.. inventory price index computation
   method...3600.018
. last-in, first-out...3764.02; 3764.022; 4510.034;
   4510.036
.. maintenance of inventories required...
   3404.022; 4407.03; 4503.026
.. valuation...3599.024; 4111.028; 4111.03

461 1-2001   **Index by Author**   **7075**
References are to Current Article paragraphs.

Rankin, Ken...3345.246; 3581.036; 3707.016;
4030.04; 4041.014; 4043.014; 4044.01; 4046.018;
4055.01; 4059.018

Rapkin, Stephanie G....3641.274

Rasman, Melissa B....3387.632; 3389.034

Raymond, Paul W....4207.01

Real, Frank J....3332.022

Reckers, Philip M.J....3700.056

Reid, Mark...4390.038

Reiff, Jonathan D....3663.072

Reifler, Stewart...3177.226

Reish, C. Frederick...3200.568; 3202.032; 3750.682;
3931.708; 3953.708

Renolds, Bruce...3466.01

Robbins, Andrew J....3294.02

Robbins, Angela Y....3225.036

Robbins, Kalyani...4062.80

Roberts, Elizabeth M....3769.052

Roberts, Jeffrey H....4153.014

Roberts, Lauren...4570.03 ⬅

Robertson, B. Ford...3169.156

Robertson, Bryan P....3550.254; 3839.012

Robinson, John R....3551.152

Robinson, Thomas R....4493.818

Robison, Jack...4084.072

Robitschek, Elizabeth...4177.032

Rocen, Donald T....4344.026; 4473.03

traditional tax journals, but also law reviews, major annual tax symposia, and certain economics, accounting, and finance journals. The *Index to Federal Tax Articles* is issued in bound volumes and includes permanent cumulations of references for the periods 1913–1974, 1974–1981, 1982–1983, 1984–1987, 1988–1992, and 1993–1996. A quarterly paperback cumulative supplement augments the main index volumes. Because the supplements are cumulative, the researcher need only consult one supplement for articles appearing in journals from 1997 to the present.

Unlike the CCH index, both the topic and the author indexes contain full article citations (see Exhibit 9–13). Using the full citations in the author index, the researcher can identify other current articles by the same author pertaining to a specific topic. Authors with several articles on the same topic are more likely to have an expertise in that field, and, thus, their analysis may be more effectual. Further, the custom of listing citations for each author and topic heading in reverse chronological order (rather than in alphabetical order) expedites finding the most recent publications.

The *Index to Federal Tax Articles* contains a user's guide that explains how to use the index, lists the more than 1,500 topical index subject headings, supplies a key to abbreviations of periodical titles, and lists the periodicals included in the first

Exhibit 9–13 Warren, Gorham & Lamont *Index To Federal Tax Articles*

2001 Spring Cumulative Supplement
Topical Index

Pension and Profit-sharing Plans—*Cont'd*

Individual Retirement Accounts—*Cont'd*

Using IRA for Home Purchase: A Tax Break To Avoid? Richard M. Walter and Sidney J. Baxendale, 65 Practical Tax Strategies No. 6, 343 (2000)

Retirement Plans: The Heir with the Biggest Pile of Money Wins, Steven E. Trytten, 52 University of Southern California Major Tax Planning Institute 16 (2000)

Optimize Early—And Penalty-Free—IRA Distributions, G. E. Whittenburg, William A. Raabe, and Martha Doran, 65 Practical Tax Strategies No. 1, 4 (2000)

Analyzing the Tax Effects of Distributions of Employer Stock From Qualified Retirement Plans, J. William Harden and David S. Hulse, 54 Journal of Financial Service Professionals No. 4, 44 (2000)

IRA Distributions to a Trust After the Death of the IRA Owner—Income or Principal? Jeremiah W. Doyle, 139 Trusts and Estates No. 9, 60 (2000)

How to Create Separate Accounts Within a Single IRA for Purposes of the Minimum Distribution Rules, Natalie B. Choate, 139 Trusts and Estates No. 9, 38 (2000)

IRS Letter Rulings Provide Insight Into Planning for IRAs, Christopher P. Bray, 27 Estate Planning No. 6, 266 (2000)

Software Review: *Pension & Roth IRA Analyzer* Software Calculates Distributions From Qualified Plans and IRAs, Donald H. Kelley, 27 Estate Planning No. 4, 189 (2000)

Asset Protection: Asset Protection for Retirement Plans and IRAs, Peter Spero, 27 Estate Planning No. 5, 229 (2000)

Revenue Ruling 2000-2—What Does It Mean for You? Marcia C. Holt, 139 Trusts and Estates No. 5, 16 (2000)

Index to Federal Tax Articles
Author Index

Whitman, Robert

Simplifying Estate Planning Documents: A New Idea for Reform, 12 Probate and Property No. 4, 61 (1998) (With Steven M. Fast)

Whittenburg, G. E.

Optimize Early-And Penalty-Free-IRA Distributions, 65 Practical Tax Strategies No. 1, 4 (2000) (With William A. Raabe and Martha Doran)

Power Swings to IRS on Assessment of Employer FICA Tax on Tipped Employees, 6 Journal of Taxation of Employee Benefits No. 6, 280 (1999) (With Devona D. Newport and William A. Raabe)

Investment Interest Expense Limitation: Making the Long-Term Capital Gain Election With the New 20 Percent Maximum Tax Rate, 16 Journal of Taxation of Investments No. 1, 44 (1998) (With James E. Williamson and Radie Bunn)

Assessment of Employer FICA Tax on Tipped Employees Limited by Recent Cases, 75 Taxes No. 3, 147 (1997) (With William Raabe and Alexis A. Wesbey)

Recent Rulings Enhance Pension Plan snd IRA Early Distribution Options, 4 Journal of Taxation of Employee Benefits No. 5, 216 (1997) (With William Raabe and Jennifer Deutsch)

Washington Watch: Tax Benefits of Giving an IRA to Charity, 14 Journal of Taxation of Investments No. 3, 277 (1997) (With N. A. Oestriech and James E. Williamson)

Whittenburg, Gerald E.

Wrong Plan Investments Can Create Unrelated Business Income Tax, 58 Taxation for Accountants No. 6, 350 (1997) (With William A. Raabe and James E. Williamson)

three volumes. Further, each cumulative volume and the current supplement lists not only the periodical titles but also the volumes and issue numbers searched for that volume. This information is useful, for example, when the practitioner is preparing an audit defense for a tax return of a prior year.

Whereas every citation in the CCH index is accompanied by an abstract, only articles judged by the compilers and Editorial Advisory Board to be of special interest are furnished a brief summary in the *Index to Federal Tax Articles*. Few articles receive this distinction.

SHEPARD'S INDEXES

Shepard's publishes two indexes that include tax articles appearing in legal documents, law reviews, and a limited list of legal periodicals. *Shepard's Law Review Citations* lists where selected articles have been cited in court case opinions, and *Federal Law Citations in Selected Law Reviews* furnishes where Federal cases and Code sections have been cited in law review articles.

Shepard's Law Review Citations provides a method of finding articles that have been cited in U.S. Supreme Court cases; lower Federal court opinions included in the *Federal Reporter* (Second Series and Third Series), the *Federal Supplement*, or the *Federal Rules Decisions;* and state court decisions recorded in the state reports or the national reporter system. To a limited extent, the service also indicates where other law reviews have cited the selected articles. The service currently has bound volumes covering 1957–1986, 1986–1990, and 1990–1995. The current supplement includes citations for 1996 to the present. The citations in these volumes are brief, giving only the volume of the review, abbreviated title, and page number.

The *Federal Law Citations in Selected Law Reviews* service lists where Supreme Court decisions and lower Federal court decisions are cited in selected law reviews. In addition, the service gives citations for the U.S. Constitution, the U.S. Code, Federal Regulations, and the Federal Court Rules. Consequently, citations for the *Internal Revenue Code* are included in the section for Title 26 of the U.S. Code, and tax regulations can be found in Title 26 of the U.S. Federal Regulations. Unfortunately, the list of selected law reviews is quite short when compared to other indexes' coverage. Fewer than 20 reviews are represented, and none of them are specifically tax law reviews.

LEXISNEXIS *ACADEMIC UNIVERSE*

Academic Universe, created by Congressional Information Service (a division of LexisNexis), provides web-based access to the offerings through an interface developed especially for academic institutions and public libraries. As illustrated in Exhibit 9–14, the home page is divided into three main parts: the left navigational panel, upper tool bar, and main search area. The navigational panel lists the universes available to the user through their provider. While there are seven universes, educational institutions need not subscribe to all of them. Only those covered under the subscription will appear in this panel. The universe pertinent to this chapter is the *Academic Universe*.

The tool bar in *Academic Universe* consists of five buttons: Home, Sources, How Do I, Overview, and Help. Sources presents an alphabetical searchable list of sources for the entire database. It also furnishes additional information about the

Exhibit 9–14
Academic Universe Home Page

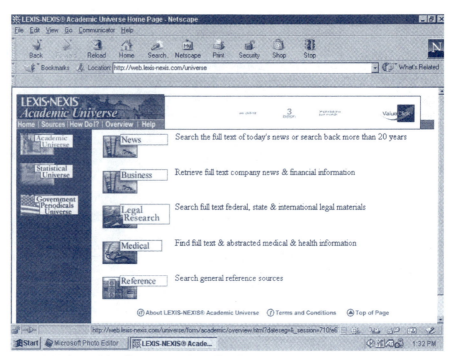

Reprinted with the permission of LexisNexis, a division of Reed Elsevier Inc.

publications, such as the years or issues accessible, how often published, and the publisher. The Overview contains a list of all of the categories available in the universe. Researchers may start their searches directly from this Overview page rather than from the main search area.

Besides information generally found through a Help button, *Academic Universe* includes examples of how to cite electronic references (using Modern Language Association and American Psychological Association formats) and explains how to decipher error messages.

To begin a search in *Academic Universe,* the researcher must select a library, a category, *and* specific source materials from within this category. A complete library or category cannot be searched with only one query. This is a disadvantage of *Academic Universe's* structure. For example, selecting "Legal Research" library in Exhibit 9–14 yields the categories listed in Exhibit 9–15. From this page a legal category must be chosen. Selecting "Legal News" displays the page for constructing a search.

There are two types of searches, Basic and Guided Search, available in many but not all of the libraries in *Academic Universe.* Where the Basic option is offered, such as in the news libraries and categories, it will appear as the default search method. Basic limits its search to headlines and lead paragraphs. This can cause few or no documents to be retrieved when the keywords do not appear in these two sections of a news article. The solution to this problem is to select Guided Search for the search. As can be seen in Exhibit 9–16, this option allows the user to designate a section or the full text of the article to be searched. It also prompts researchers to use Boolean searches and provides pull-down menus of connectors (see Chapter 2 for a list of Boolean connectors). To narrow the list of sources searched, retrieve the source list and use the check box option shown. Up to five of the individual publications can

Exhibit 9–15

Academic Universe Legal Research Categories

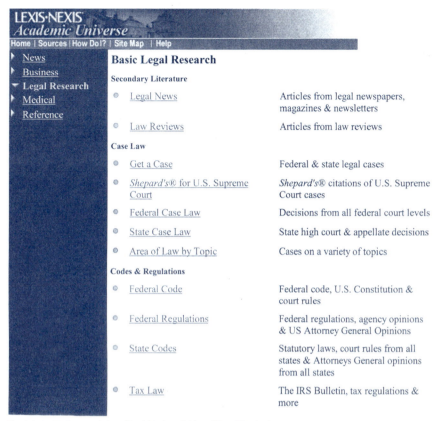

Reprinted with the permission of LexisNexis, a division of Reed Elsevier Inc.

be linked for the search. Once the publications are selected, click the "Paste to Search" button to have only those journals searched.

If the category "Tax Law" is selected rather than "Legal News," a different page for the search query is displayed. Since "Tax Law" uses a full-text search technique, the Basic search method is not an option. Click on the down arrow after the source box to reveal the specific source materials available for this search (see Exhibit 9–17). To view a brief description of each source, click on the "Tips" button in the upper right-hand corner of the screen. After selecting source material, more extensive information about each item is supplied by clicking on the blue button labeled "source list" on the right of the source search box. After selecting a source, the keyword and narrow search boxes are filled in with the search terms. Boolean connectors may be used in the keyword box. The narrow box terms in the Basic Search are considered to be connected to the key terms with an "and" connector. The Guided Search allows the researcher to designate the connector through pull-down menus. The date option allows the user to limit the time period searched with options ranging from items issued today to all available dates. Specific dates may also be selected by using the "From–To" boxes.

When the results from the search are too numerous or not on target for the research project, the user can modify the search by either editing the search or using FOCUS. These choices are listed at the top of the documents retrieved page. "Edit Search" will return to the query page where the user may edit the original query. A

Exhibit 9–16
Academic Universe
More Options

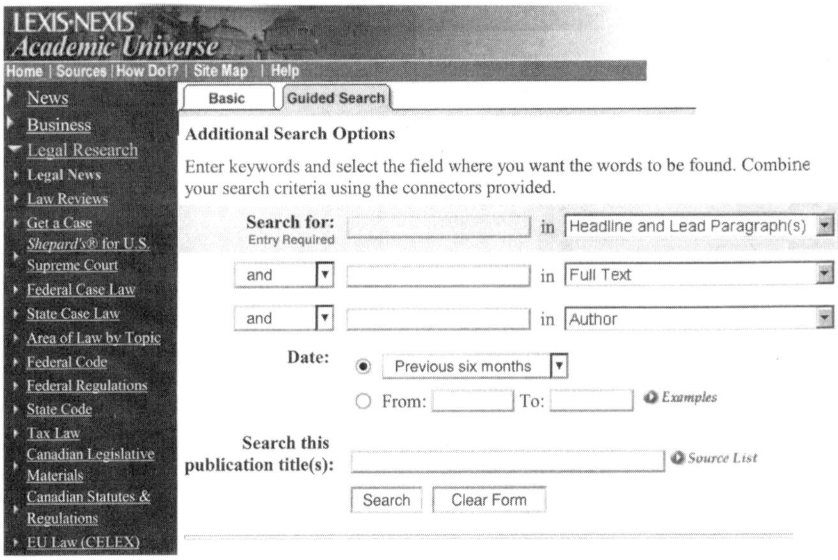

Reprinted with the permission of LexisNexis, a division of Reed Elsevier Inc.

new search will be run after the editing. FOCUS, on the other hand, restricts the additional terms search to the sources already retrieved by the original search. No new sources will be added to the list. Thus, by narrowing the search, this editing method is particularly useful when too many documents have been found on the target topic. Almost all of the documents retrieved through the *Academic Universe* searches are full text and may be downloaded, e-mailed, or printed from the browser by the user.

OTHER LAW AND ACCOUNTING INDEXES

Since it is not possible to review all the commercial indexes a practitioner might access, a few indexes have been selected to illustrate the variety of services available. Most of these services are available in print, CD-ROM, or online format; thus, they can accommodate the preference of any user. The print and CD-ROM versions tend to be updated monthly, whereas the online services are generally updated weekly. Many of the online services are accessible through LexisNexis or Westlaw.

The *Current Law Index* is published by the Information Access Company in cooperation with the American Association of Law Libraries. It catalogs more than 800 legal periodicals published in the United States and other English-speaking nations. Thus, it includes nearly all the periodicals referenced in the CCH or WG&L indexes, plus numerous other law publications that explore a variety of tax and nontax topics. This service provides five separate methods of locating pertinent tax articles—by topic, author, article title, case name, and statute. Article citations tend to appear much more quickly in the *Current Law Index* than in the CCH and WG&L services. On the other hand, it furnishes only article citations, lacking the article abstracts of CCH and, to a lesser extent, of WG&L. The current print supplements are bound yearly into two volumes, one for the subject indexing and the other for the author, title, case, and statute indexing. The *Current Law Index* is available in print, on CD-ROM (LegalTrac), and online through *Legal Resource Index,* Lexis and West-

Exhibit 9–17
Academic Universe Source Materials

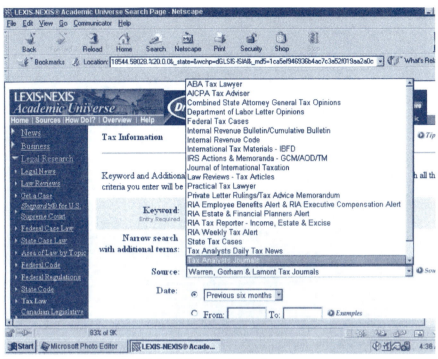

Reprinted with the permission of LexisNexis, a division of Reed Elsevier Inc.

law. The online services cover more journals and legal newspapers than the paper version, and they provide selected article abstracts.

The *Index to Legal Periodicals* (H.W. Wilson, publisher) is similar to the *Current Law Index* in the number and type of journals cataloged, methods of indexing article citations, and timely updates of the service. Articles indexed must be at least five pages in length, and notes and comments must be at least two pages in length. Books, book reviews, legislation, and jurisdictional surveys are also indexed. This index provides only citations for articles, with no abstracts in its print version. The *Current Law Index* is accessible in print, on CD-ROM, and online through Wilson-Web and Information Partners. Currently, H.W. Wilson Company is considering developing a full-text database for the *Index to Legal Periodicals*.

The advantage of these legal indexes is that the scope of periodical coverage is much larger than that of the dedicated tax indexes. However, both the *Current Law Index* and the *Index to Legal Periodicals* omit some accounting and other specialty-oriented journals.

GENERAL INDEXES

Sometimes practitioners want to start their research by obtaining an overall appreciation of a tax topic before confronting a detailed tax journal explanation. How does a practitioner locate tax-related articles written for the general public's consumption? One index that practitioners turn to is the H.W. Wilson *Business Periodicals Index*. It covers the *Wall Street Journal, New York Times,* and over 500 business periodicals, including a few professional tax journals. It is available in all three formats and access to full-text articles from over 250 journals can be added to the subscription.

Another general business index is *Business Source Elite* by EBSCO Publishing. It supplies citations and full-text articles from more than 1,000 journals and abstracts to more than 1,500 worldwide journals. A leaner version, *Business Source Plus,* has full-text articles from over 250 journals, with abstracts and indexing for nearly 700 journals worldwide. The *Premier* version, on the opposite end of the spectrum, has indexing and abstracts for more than 2,300 worldwide periodicals, with full-text access for more than 1,500 journals.

Lastly, many public and university libraries have ABI/FORM or a web database such as *ProQuest* published by UMI. Both of these catalog more than 1,000 periodicals (3,000 for *ProQuest*) with full text for a substantial portion of the journals. All citations are accompanied by an abstract. However, use of these products at university libraries may be limited to individuals affiliated with the school.

This review of available indexes for locating tax and tax-related articles is just a sampling of what is available. Furthermore, the CD-ROM and online service industry is growing and changing so rapidly that by the time this book is in print there will be many more worthwhile index databases for the interested practitioner to consider. An exceptional guide to online, portable, and Internet databases is the *Gale Directory of Databases,* published by Gale Research, Inc. This guide provides a descriptive summary for more than 14,000 databases that cover numerous and diverse disciplines, including that of tax law. It consists of two volumes; one covers online databases, and the other includes CD-ROM, diskette, magnetic tape, handheld, and batch access database products.

Each volume consists of three parts: database listings, producers, and vendors. The database listings gives details about the contents, costs, update frequency, producer contact, and vendor availability, while the producer and vendor listings provide contact information and lists of products obtainable through the producer or vendor. The directory is offered in a variety of media including print and online. Several universities have subscriptions.

OTHER RESOURCES

The BNA *Tax Management Portfolios,* discussed in detail in Chapter 7, also provide a source for locating pertinent tax articles. The bibliography located in Section C of most portfolios typically lists titles and citations of numerous articles that pertain to the subject of the portfolio. The citations are provided by year of publication, alphabetically by author. The new-material sheets for Section C update the bibliography listing. However, researchers should not rely on this feature of the BNA portfolios as their primary source for identifying relevant tax articles because the portfolios are uneven as to the magnitude, timeliness, and comprehensiveness of their bibliographies.

In addition, tax journals themselves can provide references to tax articles that can be of interest to the researcher. Many journals provide annual indexes (usually by topic, author, case name, and Code section) for their own articles. Occasionally, this index appears in each issue of the journal, in a rolling cumulative twelve-month format. Moreover, several of the journals regularly provide citations or summaries of articles that appear in some of their sister journals and even in their competitors' journals, presumably to facilitate the reader's efficient use of the entire tax literature.

The major tax services discussed in Chapters 6 and 7 include access to tax journal and newsletter articles. The number and variety of periodicals offered by the services varies greatly. For instance, The CCH Tax Research Network includes less than a dozen periodicals in its service, whereas LexisNexis provides access to thousands of periodicals in the business and legal areas as a part of its general service.

A number of other sources provide listings of current tax articles, but most of these would be better classified as tax update material rather than as a comprehensive research resource. Most of these finding lists are included as part of a weekly or monthly information newsletter that accompanies a general tax service or treatise, and they are intended merely as a "tickler" to make the practitioner aware of recent publications that might be of interest. Generally, they provide no article abstracts, they are not indexed by any attribute other than journal and title, and they are not accumulated or reorganized after a specified period. For instance, once a month, the RIA *Weekly Alert* includes a listing of selected current tax articles.

INTERNET SITES

A growing source of tax materials that literally changes daily is the Internet. Organizations, commercial enterprises, and individuals have web sites with links to valuable tax information. There is so much information available on the Internet that it can be overwhelming. A selected list of the vast number of tax-related web sites is given in Exhibit 9–18. (It does not repeat sites listed in Exhibit 9–10.) The web addresses in this list were accurate as of the date of publication, but by no means should be considered a comprehensive list.

SUMMARY

Tax journals and other periodicals not only help researchers locate primary sources of the tax law, but also enlighten them as to other ways of analyzing a tax issue. Tax articles can synthesize information from the Code, Regulations, and pertinent court cases into a more logical presentation, which may be useful as the practitioner identifies relevant tax issues or precedents during the research process or prepares for litigation on behalf of a client. Finally, such publications are an integral part of the means by which the tax professional remains current with respect to the evolution of the Federal tax law.

TAX TUTOR

Reinforce the tax research information covered in this chapter by completing the online tutorials located at the Federal Tax Research web site:

http://raabe.swcollege.com

Exhibit 9–18 Web Sites

Accounting Web	http://www.accountingweb.com
AICPA Tax Research	http://www.aicpa.org/pubs/jofa/aug97/taxsites.htm
Alan G. Kalman home page	http://pages.prodigy.net/agkalman
American Bar Association	http://www.abanet.org/tax/sites.html
American Taxation Association	http://www.atasection.org
Bureau of National Affairs	http://www.bnatax.com/prodhome/tax/dtr/links.htm
Essential Links	http://www.el.com/elinks/taxes
Kent Information Services	http://www.kentis.com/siteseeker/taxlink.html
Richard J. Joseph	http://www.bus.utexas.edu/~josephr/384/itaxsrcs.htm
Larry M. Elkin & Co.	http://www.elkin.com
Money Café	http://www.moneycafe.com/tax
My Biz Zone	http://www.mybizzone.net
Newsletter Access	http://www.newsletteraccess.com
Robert E. McKenzie, Esq.	http://www.mckenzielaw.com/
Sister States	http://www.sisterstates.com
Tax Analysts	http://www.taxanalysts.com or http://www.tax.org
Tax and Accounting Sites (Dennis Schmidt)	http://www.taxsites.com
Tax Gateways	http://www.angelfire.com/la/mansata/way.html
Tax Prophet	http://www.taxprophet.com
Tax Resources (Frank McNeil)	http://www.taxresources.com
Tax Web	http://irs.com
Tax World	http://www.taxworld.org
Thomas Legislative Information	http://thomas.loc.gov
UncleFed's Tax Board	http://www.unclefed.com
Will Yancey home page	http://www.willyancey.com

KEY WORDS

By the time you complete your work relative to this chapter, you should be comfortable discussing each of the following terms. If you need additional review of any of these items, return to the appropriate material in the chapter or consult the glossary to this text.

Academic Journals
Academic Universe
Daily Tax Report
Federal Tax Articles

Index to Federal Tax Articles
Law Reviews
Practitioner Journals
Proceedings

Professional Journals	Tax Newsletter
TaxBase	*Tax Notes*
Tax Journal	

DISCUSSION QUESTIONS

1. Why are tax journals and newsletters generally not cited as authority in professional tax research? However, when is it appropriate to cite tax journals or newsletters as authority in professional tax research?
2. What does the denotation "at 407" indicate in the citation of a journal?
3. Briefly describe each of the following.
    a. Annual proceedings
    b. Scholarly reviews
    c. Professional journals
    d. Newsletters
4. Name three major tax conferences and when they originated.
5. What are some of the distinctive characteristics of law reviews and academic journals?
6. Name two universities that currently publish tax-oriented journals or law reviews. Give the name of the journal or law review they publish.
7. What type of articles would a reader find in the *National Tax Journal* and *The Journal of the American Tax Association?* What organizations publish these journals?
8. What type of articles would you expect to find in *Taxes* versus the type you would expect to find in *Journal of Limited Liability Companies?* Which one of these would you expect to be published monthly and which quarterly?
9. Many tax services offer newsletters. How often are the online and printed newsletters made available to their subscribers?
10. Indicate the publication interval for the following newsletters and their publishers.
    - BNA E-Commerce Tax Report
    - *Daily Tax Bulletin*
    - *E-commerce Tax Alert*
    - *State and Local Taxes*
    - *Tax Features*
    - *Tax News Now*
11. Why is the *Daily Tax Report* one of the most important newsletters? What are the different sources available for accessing this newsletter?
12. Who publishes the *Daily Tax Report* and *Tax Notes?* How are the *Daily Tax Report* and *Tax Notes* similar? How are they different?
13. Why are documents cited in the printed version of *Tax Notes* given a unique Tax Analysts' document number?
14. Many organizations issue newsletters either in print or through the Internet. Provide the name of the organizations that have the following URLs.
    a. **http://www.cpa-finder.com**
    b. **http://tacampus.tax.org**
    c. **http://www.ppcnet.com**
    d. **http://www.tax-news.com**
    e. **http://portal.pwcglobal.com**

15. What is one of the most outstanding features of the CCH *Federal Tax Articles* that is not available in most other journal indexes? How does the organizational framework of the CCH *Federal Tax Articles* differ from the WG&L *Index to Federal Tax Articles?*
16. What are three methods that can be used to locate articles in the CCH *Federal Tax Articles?* Can these same three methods of locating an article be used with the WG&L *Index to Federal Tax Articles?* Explain your answer.
17. Where are full article citations found in the *Federal Tax Articles,* WG&L *Index to Federal Tax Articles,* and *Shepard's Law Review Citations?*
18. How frequently are the journal indexes *Federal Tax Articles* and *Index to Federal Tax Articles* updated?
19. What is included in *Shepard's Law Review Citations?* What is included in *Federal Law Citations in Selected Law Reviews?* How many law reviews are "selected" for this index?
20. What is *Academic Universe?* What special items are available in its Help menu?
21. In *Academic Universe,* what are the two types of searches available, and how do the two searches differ?
22. When a search in *Academic Universe* produces too many citations, the researcher can use either the edit or FOCUS commands to limit the search. How do these two commands differ?
23. Name three indexes that contain references to tax articles but are not dedicated to taxation. Indicate who publishes these indexes and whether they provide abstracts of articles or just citations. Indicate the formats in which the indexes are available.
24. What type of information is available in the *Gale Directory of Databases?*
25. Provide the name of the organizations that have the following URLs.
    a. http://www.taxexemptresources.com
    b. http://www.taxsites.com
    c. http://www.angelfire.com/la/mansata/way.html
    d. http://www.el.com/elinks/taxes
    e. http://www.atasection.org/
    f. http://www.ppcnet.com

EXERCISES

26. Who is the publisher of each of the following tax journals or newsletters?
    a. *Journal of Multisate Taxation*
    b. *Journal of Accountancy*
    c. *Worldwide Daily*
    d. *Real Estate Tax Digest*
27. Locate the 2000 edition for each of the following annual proceedings and provide the information requested.
    a. Institute on Federal Taxation (New York University): What is the annual proceeding number? Who is the publisher? What is the title of the Chapter 8 article? Who is the author?

Continued

b. Major Tax Planning Institute (University of Southern California): What is the annual proceeding number? Who is the publisher? What is the title of the Chapter 13 article? Who is the author?
28. Use CCH's *Federal Tax Articles* index to answer the following questions.
    a. For the 2000 summary reports 455–460, give the proper citation of the first article listed that discusses § 2031.
    b. Use the topic index of the 1990–1996 transfer binder to find the paragraph number and title of a 1995 article about converting an existing entity to a Limited Liability Company (LLC).
    c. Give the title of the September 2000 article listed for Eugene W. Seago. In what journal was it published?
    d. What is the date on the last update filed in your library's current binder of *Federal Tax Articles?* (Check behind the tab "Last Report Letter" to find the answer.)
29. Use CCH's *Federal Tax Articles* index to determine the publication schedule for the following journals.
    a. *CPA Journal*
    b. *Florida Law Review*
    c. *Today's CPA*
    d. *International Lawyer*
30. Use the WG&L *Index to Federal Tax Articles* to perform the following tasks. Include in your response the supplement and page number where each answer is located.
    a. Give the title of the 1996 article by Jane O. Burns that mentions "reclassification" in the title.
    b. Locate a 2000 article on holding offsetting positions in mark-to-market straddles by Hillary Johnson. Under what topical heading did you find an article? In what journal is the article printed?
    c. Who is the co-author with Philip J. Harmelink of a 2000 article discussing changing depreciation for rental real estate activities?
    d. In what year and by whom was an article in the *Taxes—The Tax Magazine* written on deducting education costs as medical expenses?
31. Find two current articles on transfers to controlled corporations (§ 351) using the CCH *Federal Tax Articles* index. Find two different articles using the WG&L *Index to Federal Tax Articles.*
    a. List the title of the articles and provide the index name, volume, and page number on which each citation was found.
    b. Compare the search strategies in using each index. Which one provides easier access?
32. Find an article on related party transactions that was presented at the Heckerling Institute of Estate Planning in 1997 using the CCH *Federal Tax Articles* index. Find the same article using the WG&L *Index to Federal Tax Articles.*
    a. List the article in standard citation format and provide the index name, volume, and page number on which the citation was found.
    b. Compare the search strategies in using each index. Which one provides easier access?

33. Find current articles written by Dr. Richard B. Toolson using the CCH *Federal Tax Articles* index. Now use the WG&L *Index to Federal Tax Articles* to determine the recent articles written by Dr. Toolson.
    a. List the titles of the articles and the journals in which they appeared, and provide the index name, volume, and page number on which each citation was found.
    b. Which index provided a more extensive list of articles by Dr. Toolson?
    c. What is the area of taxation covered by most of these articles?
    d. Compare the search strategies in using each index. Which one provides easier access?
34. Using the information collected in Exercises 31, 32, and 33, discuss the compatibility of the CCH *Federal Tax Articles* and the WG&L *Index to Federal Tax Articles* with the three methods of locating an article (by Code section, by author, and by topic).
35. Use *Shepard's Federal Tax Citations in Selected Law Reviews* to find law review citations for each of the following. List the most recent citation if more than one appears. Indicate in which volume it occurs.
    a. *United States Reports,* Vol. 528, 167
    b. *Federal Reporter 3rd Series,* Vol. 217, 162
    c. IRC § 401
    d. *Code of Federal Regulations for Income Taxes,* §301.7623-1(c)
36. Use *Shepard's Law Review Citations* to find the most recent volume cited for each of the following. List the volume and page number for the most recent citation.
    a. *Akron Law Review*
    b. *University of Richmond Law Review*
    c. *Taxes—The Tax Magazine*
    d. *Georgia Law Review*
37. Use *Academic Universe* Legal News category to answer each of the following questions.
    a. Using the Basic search option, determine on what day in 2000 the tax bill that repeals the ban of installment treatment for certain accrual accounting taxpayers was signed into law? In what newsletter did you find the answer?
    b. Repeat the installment sale search using the More Options and its full-text search. Did *Academic Universe* return the same list of articles? Explain why the list is or is not the same.
    c. Using the Basic search option, find articles by Rudolph J. Di Massa, Jr. on Chapter 13 bankruptcies published since 2000. List the title of the articles and the periodicals in which the articles were found.
    d. Repeat the Chapter 13 bankruptcy search using the More Options option and its author option. Did *Academic Universe* return the same list of articles? Explain why the list is or is not the same.
38. Use *Academic Universe* Legal News and Tax Law categories to answer each of the following questions.
    a. Using the Legal News category, determine in what IRS pronouncement the standard mileage tax rates for 2001 were announced. In what newsletter did you find this information?

Continued

b. Perform the same search using the Tax Law category instead of the Legal News. What set of source documents did you select in the Tax Law category? Did this selection return the same list of articles? Explain why the list is or is not the same.

c. Perform the same search as in part (b) above. In which two other sets of source documents were you able to find references to the IRS pronouncement?

d. What is the advantage of the search source options available in the Tax News category over the search source options in the Tax Law category?

39. Use *Academic Universe* to answer each of the following questions.
    a. What tax law reviews listed in the Scholarly Reviews section of this chapter are included in the Law Review category sources?
    b. What Warren, Gorham & Lamont journals are included in the Tax Law sources?
    c. What RIA products are included in the Tax Law sources?
    d. What tax law reviews are included in both the Law Review category and in the Law Review—Tax Articles sources of the Tax Law category? What does your answer to the previous question imply about searching these law reviews?

40. Locate the following articles and give the title and author(s) of the article.
    a. *Journal of Taxation*, Volume 93, October, p. 212
    b. *CPA Journal*, Volume 70, September, p. 15
    c. *Journal of Passthrough Entities*, Volume 4, March/April, p. 14
    d. *Taxes—The Tax Magazine*, Volume 79, February, p. 44

41. Use the most recent issue of the published newsletters to answer the following questions.
    a. What is the topic of the lead brief in "Policy Briefs" in *Tax Notes?*
    b. What is the topic of the first brief listed under "Highlight" in *Tax Management Weekly Report?*
    c. What is the topic of the first brief listed under "Tax Briefs" in *Taxes on Parade?*
    d. What is the lead article in *Weekly Alert?*

42. Use a computer journal index at your library that provides full-text access. Find a recent article on taxpayer noncompliance. Summarize the article and copy the first page of the article.

43. Using the *Gale Directory of Databases*, identify a tax library database that is offered on CD-ROM. List the name of the CD-ROM, vender, and cost of the database.

44. The BNA *Tax Management Portfolios* provide a bibliography in Section C of each portfolio. Find the portfolio which discusses the mark-to market rules of § 475. Give, in proper citation format, the most recent article listed in the bibliography. In what portfolio did you find the article?

45. Use Exhibit 9–18 to answer the following questions.
    a. Select one of the individual's home pages and list the major categories of links provided.
    b. Select one of the organization's web pages and list the major categories of links provided.

Continued

c. Using the data collected in (a) and (b) above, compare the two sites. Which one provided more useful links? Which one was easier to use?

RESEARCH CASES

46. For each of the following annual proceedings, provide the dates on which the most recent meeting took place and the title of the third article in the published proceedings.
    a. Institute on Federal Taxation (New York University)
    b. Annual Federal Tax Conference (University of Chicago Law School)
    c. Major Tax Planning Institute (University of Southern California)
    d. Tulane Tax Institute (Tulane University)

47. In the 1985–1989 CCH *Federal Tax Articles* index, under § 1221, Capital Assets Defined, is the article "TAXES—A Safe Harbor for Authors and Artists" 70 *Management Accounting* (August 1988) 12 by Israel Blumenfrucht. From reading the abstract, it appears that this article addresses the tax issues of your research project. However, it's a 1988 article, and you wonder if it's still relevant. Read the article and summarize what a taxpayer must do to elect the safe-harbor method. Determine whether this safe harbor is still available to authors and artists.

48. You were visiting the tax department of a CPA firm recently when you overheard two of the staff discussing "QTPs" and how distributions from them are now treated when "the credits" are involved. They mentioned that a tax act may have modified the treatment. You would like to know what "QTPs" are and what credits might affect the treatment of the distributions. Find two journal articles that discuss "QTPs" after the passage of the Economic Growth and Tax Relief Reconciliation Act of 2001. Write a one-page paper defining a "QTP" and describing the coordination of distributions from "QTPs" and educational credits and educational IRAs. Attach to your paper the first page of each article referenced.

49. It is 3 a.m. and your dog just ate your only copy of the Code. (Some dogs will eat anything!) Find a text version of the Code on the Internet and print § 61. Where did you find the Code? Who maintains the site? Send the site manager an e-mail message, expressing your appreciation for the manager's hard work in keeping the site up to date. Print your e-mail, and if you get an answer, print it also. Does the version of the Code you found use text hyperlinks? What happens when you click on a hyperlink? Download and print a copy of a page with hyperlinks, then click on several hyperlinks and print the page to which it links.

50. Through surfing on the Internet, you have seen some information about how the Economic Growth and Tax Relief Reconciliation Act of 2001 (EGTRA 2001) was beneficial or harmful to various states' ability to generate revenues from income taxes. Using *Academic Universe* or a similar service, find three newspaper articles published in your state that discuss how your state was affected by the EGTRA 2001. If your state does not have an income tax, select a nearby state's newspaper articles. Summarize the general consensus from these articles, and attach copies of the articles used in writing your one-page summary.

51. You are the research assistant for Dr. Jones, a newly hired tax professor in the accounting department. Dr. Jones is very anxious to submit a paper carved out of her dissertation. The paper is an empirical study of the tax and nontax costs

of certain accounting reporting decisions. Dr. Jones would like you to collect information on journals that would consider a paper of this type. She asks you to find information on the following journals: *Advances in Taxation, National Tax Journal,* and *The Journal of the American Taxation Association.* Using the Internet, find the information Dr. Jones will need to submit a manuscript to these three journals. Include in the information you provide the type of articles accepted for review, submission fees, number of copies to submit, and where to send the manuscript. Indicate what web sites you used to obtain the information.

52. Two Tax Court cases, *Martin Ice Cream Co. v. Commissioner,* 110 T.C. 189, and *Norwalk v. Commissioner,* T.C. Memo. 1998-279, have developed the concept of personal goodwill for owners or employees of corporations providing professional services. Using *Academic Universe* or a similar service, locate three articles on this topic. Write a one-page summary of the articles, focusing on how personal goodwill is useful upon liquidation of a corporation. Provide proper citation of the articles and attach a copy of the first page of the articles to the summary.

53. Use the Internet to locate the Committee Reports for the most recent tax act passed by Congress. Print the first page of the House, Senate, and Joint Conference reports. Indicate where you found the Committee Reports and who maintains the site.

54. Select three of the sites listed in Exhibit 9–18. Make a table showing the links each site provides. How much overlap is there? Determine the minimum number of sites you need to use to get the maximum amount of coverage. Out of your list, which site is the most essential?

55. Find five noncommercial web sites not listed in Exhibit 9–18 that provide useful tax information. List each site's address and what links to tax materials it provides.

Part 4

Implementing the Research Tools

Chapter 10: Communicating Research Results

Chapter 11: Tax Planning

Chapter 12: Working with the IRS

Chapter 13: Tax Practice and Administration: Sanctions, Agreements, and Disclosures

10

Communicating Research Results

LEARNING OBJECTIVES

- Produce a standard format for the construction of a file memorandum to contain the results of one's research efforts and professional judgment

- Develop other forms of communicating research results, including oral presentations and client letters

CHAPTER OUTLINE

Communications and the Tax Professional
The Heart of Tax Research Communication: The File Memo
Evaluating the Sources of Law
Client Letters
Comprehensive Illustration of Client File
Oral Presentations of Research Results

Once the practitioner has begun to develop effective tax research skills, he or she must hone them with practice—whether by working through tax research cases presented as a class exercise in a university course, or immediately beginning work for professional clients. Accordingly, the overriding purpose of this chapter is to provide the reader with guidance and opportunities to apply the research skills and examine the tax research resources that have been discussed in previous chapters.

In addition, this chapter will discuss the means by which the tax professional conveys the results of a tax research project—in other words, applying some of the judgment and communications skills required. Direction as to the proper format and content of memorandums to the file, of client letters, and of oral presentations is addressed, with development of professional skills the overriding goal.

COMMUNICATIONS AND THE TAX PROFESSIONAL

As we suggested in our initial discussions of the tax research process, illustrated in Exhibit 2–1, a tax research assignment often concludes with some form of communication by the tax professional. The audience for this communication often is the practitioner's supervisor or client, but tax-related communications can take many forms.

- A telephone call
- An informal discussion in person or via e-mail
- A letter prepared for reading by someone at least as familiar with the tax law as the writer
- A letter prepared for reading by someone less familiar with the tax law than is the writer
- A letter prepared for reading by someone who is essentially untrained in the tax law
- An article for publication in a newspaper or magazine directed at the general public
- An article for publication in a professional journal read by tax generalists
- An article for publication in a professional journal read by tax specialists
- A speech to a general audience
- A speech at a conference of tax professionals
- A memorandum to be read in the future by the writer or by a peer with similar training
- An appearance on a news broadcast or program with a serious tone
- An appearance on a broadcast with a less serious tone
- A posting on an Internet bulletin board or news group

For the most part, the tax professional's preparation for these communications is similar. For the purposes of this chapter, we assume that all of the pertinent tax research techniques developed in earlier parts of this text have been planned and conscientiously applied, so the practitioner is qualified and current enough with respect to prevailing tax law to address the audience in terms of the content of the communication. The challenge then becomes how to deliver this information in a manner that will be accepted and understood by the audience.

Actually, though, one's preparation for the delivery of tax communication must go far beyond obtaining control over the technical tax knowledge required for the assignment. As illustrated in Exhibit 10–1, communication truly occurs only when the

Exhibit 10–1 The Communication Process

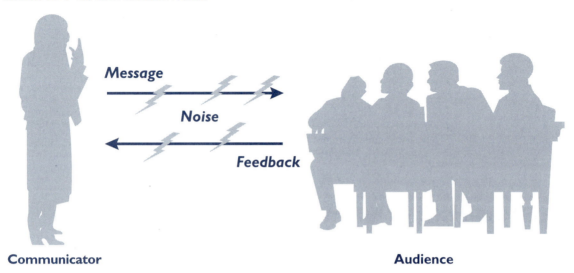

Communicator   **Audience**

message desired to be sent by the speaker or writer is received by the intended audience. Distractions of all sorts can make this process difficult to accomplish. Thorough research into the nature and expectations of the audience, factors that may interfere with the delivery of the message, and feedback and corrective measures must make up a critical part of the communicator's preparation.

Examples of "noise" that can disrupt the communications process include a mismatching of expectations as to the message, the chosen delivery method, the identity and nature of the sender and receiver of the message, other events competing for the attention of those involved, logistical difficulties, and technological problems. Feedback and corrective devices that can aid in accomplishing the delivery of the desired message include formal and informal evaluation processes, "real-time" opportunities such as question-and-answer periods and written comments received during the drafting of the document, and the sending and receiving of intended and unintended body language or other communicative signals.

Tax professionals generally are virtually untrained as to the application of communication methods in conveying tax messages, but this shortcoming can be remedied. The chief ingredients necessary to become an effective tax-content communicator are the desire to learn and improve as a communicator in general and the use of every opportunity possible to obtain and develop skills in the delivery of tax information. Given the nature of today's competitive tax profession, plenty of such opportunities for practice exist, and pressures from others who are competing for clients and promotions provide most professionals with more than enough motivation to make improvements in their communication skills a lifelong process.

We begin a more detailed review of the communication process with an examination of the most commonly encountered written communications demanded in the tax practice. The chapter concludes with a discussion of skills needed in delivering spoken communications. In either case, the structure of the communication follows the basic format delineated in Exhibit 10–2.

THE HEART OF TAX RESEARCH COMMUNICATION: THE FILE MEMO

The tax researcher spends most of his or her time reviewing primary and secondary sources of the Federal tax law, redefining pertinent issues, and attempting to discover additional facts concerning the client's situation. On completion of this review, the researcher must integrate the disparate results of the research process into a more usable form. Thorough practitioners generate a memorandum to the client's file for this purpose. This **file memorandum** is designed to:

- organize the facts, issues, and conclusions of the project,
- facilitate a review of the research activities by the practitioner's supervisors or colleagues, and
- allow for a subsequent examination of the research issue, by the original researcher or by his or her successor, with respect to the same or another client's identical or related fact situation.

Accordingly, the file memo should be constructed in a general, usable format that lends itself to a quick perusal of the pertinent tax facts and issues. Many accounting and law firms impose a standardized format. If the reader's employer has enacted no such requirement, he or she should consider adopting the format illustrated in Exhibits 2–6 and 10–3. A template for this memo format is available at the web site for this text.

Exhibit 10–2 The Structure of Technical Tax Communications

Element of the Message	Purposes	Comments
Introduction	Provide a roadmap for what is to come. Place the message in context. Generate audience interest, if necessary. Set the tone for the message.	**10% of allotted time/space.** Could include a story/anecdote, current news development, or "object lesson."
Body	Generally, the technical tax material is presented here. Usually follows an order suggested by the hierarchy of the sources of the tax law. Alternative ordering methods: historical, strengths/weaknesses, cost/benefit.	**80% of allotted time/space.** Must be brief, to the point, hard-hitting; not trite or condescending. Identify three to six key points that all readers/listeners must take away from the message.
Conclusion	Tie back to the introduction. Reinforce key elements of the message. Bring the presentation to a climax. Indicate next steps and follow-up action.	**10% of allotted time/space.** Tip off the reader/listener that the conclusion is starting, with "In closing," "To sum up," or "I'll conclude with...."

Exhibit 10–3 File Memorandum for Tax Research

Over & Short, CPAs
Brooklyn Park, MN

September 30, 20XX

Relevant Facts

The Browns live in South Dakota. They own their home and hold investments in the debt of several domestic corporations. The interest that they received on this debt was gross income to them. To diversify their portfolio, the Browns took out a sizable second mortgage on their home and applied a portion of the proceeds to some City of Chandler School Bonds. The remainder of the proceeds was used to expand the facilities of Mrs. Brown's dental clinic.

Specific Issues

How much of the mortgage interest paid can be claimed as an itemized deduction by the Browns?

Conclusions

That portion of the mortgage proceeds applied to the dental clinic generates an interest deduction to be claimed against clinic income on Schedule C. No other deduction is allowed.

Support

The Code disallows the deduction of interest on indebtedness that is incurred or continued to purchase or carry obligations, the interest on which is exempt from the Federal income tax. IRC § 265(a)(2). This provision denies the double benefit that would be enjoyed by the taxpayer who would receive tax-exempt income while simultaneously claiming an investment interest deduction for the interest expense paid, e.g., by incurring a bank loan and using the proceeds to purchase municipal bonds.

The IRS examines evidence to infer the intent of the taxpayer who is incurring the indebtedness. Under Rev. Proc. 72–18, 1972–1 C.B. 740, a taxpayer who purchases exempt bonds can claim an interest deduction if the debt in question has been incurred (1) for personal reasons (e.g., via a mortgage to finance the purchase of residential property) or (2) for valid business reasons, as long as the borrowing does not exceed legitimate business needs.

Continued

A file memo should include a brief introductory summary of the facts and issues that face the client. In all but the most complex instances, this statement should require no more than two paragraphs. Similarly, the rare file-memo footnote should be restricted to current developments, for example, with respect to an appeal relative to one of the critical cases that is cited in the memo or a statutory amendment.

The file memo then includes a listing of the tax issues that are in dispute and a matching conclusion for each identified issue. This format allows the subsequent reader to determine quickly whether each issue is "pro" or "con" for the taxpayer and limits the time required to sort through a number of such memos. In the support section, a detailed review and evaluation of controlling laws is derived, with full citations presented in the standard forms. The "meat" of the memo is presented here, and the strengths and weaknesses of both sides of the tax argument are developed and discussed. Finally, recommendations for subsequent actions with the client may be enumerated, and other strategies as to tax return or audit positions are identified.

Often, the gathering of the pertinent facts is the most challenging of the tax professional's tasks. Tax engagements typically begin with client contact in the form of

Exhibit 10–3 File Memorandum for Tax Research *(Concluded)*

Several court decisions have emphasized that the existence of such business motives must be documented clearly, as to both presence and amount. *Wisconsin Cheeseman v. U.S.*, 388 F.2d 420 (CA-7, 1968); *Bradford*, 60 T.C. 253 (1973); *Israelson v. U.S.*, 367 F.Supp. 1104 (D.Md., 1973). However, if the taxpayer's holdings of tax-exempt securities are deemed to be immaterial in amount, the § 265(a)(2) disallowance will not be invoked. *Indian Trail Trading Post, Inc. v. Comm.*, 503 F.2d 102 (CA-6, 1974). Typically, if the average adjusted basis of the exempt bonds does not exceed 2 percent of the average adjusted basis of the entire investment portfolio, the entire interest deduction is allowed. *Batten v. U.S.*, 322 F.Supp. 629 (E.D.Va., 1971); *Ball v. Comm.*, 54 T.C. 1200 (1970).

Mortgage indebtedness is a classic illustration of an investment that will generate deductible interest expenses for the taxpayer who holds exempt bonds. However, the timing of such a mortgage transaction must be monitored to exhibit the proper motives for the benefit of the IRS. In one case, the taxpayer paid for his home with cash. Only later was an investment program (that included municipal bonds) initiated and a residential mortgage secured. The IRS inferred that the mortgage proceeds were in indirect support of the exempt indebtedness, and the deduction for the mortgage interest was disallowed. *Mariorenzi v. Comm.*, 490 F.2d 92 (CA-8, 1974), 32 TCM 681 (1973). Had the taxpayer secured a mortgage before the home was completed, purchasing the exempt bonds out of savings, it appears that the deduction could have been preserved. The IRS has applied this doctrine outside of the Eighth Circuit, in PLR 8004129I.

Because the Browns live in the Eighth Circuit, the *Mariorenzi* doctrine prevails, and no itemized deduction is allowed at all, i.e., for that portion of the loan that is applied to the school bonds. Rev. Proc. 72-18 is insensitive to portfolio diversification motives, and no personal motive appears to exist that supports any other possible deduction. According to the logic of these precedents, the Browns should have sold the exempt bonds and then used the proceeds to finance their portfolio acquisitions.

Actions to Be Taken

Prepare letter, review results with client.

Suggest changes in portfolio holdings to re-gain the deduction.

Preparer: *Mary H. Polzin*

Reviewer: *Teri D. Cardwell*

---

a phone call or meeting, followed by an exchange of copies of pertinent documents such as letters, spreadsheets, trusts or wills, contracts, life insurance or annuity agreements, employer handbooks, and diaries or logbooks belonging to the client. In reality, though, the initial determination of the facts is likely to be incomplete.

- Taxpayers tend to see the dispute only from their side, so that facts and circumstances that may cast doubt on the ability to determine or document the pro-taxpayer position may be hidden or "forgotten."
- Taxpayers are not trained in the details of the technical tax law, so they may be unable to determine which documents or other evidence of the facts are important in determining the controlling tax law.
- For tax research that requires the full professional judgment and experience of the practitioner, there may be no clearly controlling tax statute or precedent, facts may be truly incomplete, or they may unfold as the evaluation of tax law occurs. The researcher may discover that issues of taxpayer motive, knowledge, or other circumstances turn on facts that were not immediately known to be critical.

Moreover, fact gathering often turns on such intangible factors as the reliability of the memories of the taxpayers and key witnesses, the ability of witnesses to withstand scrutiny in the deposition and testimony phases of the case, the unanticipated death or disappearance of key parties, the destruction of records due to casualty or computer mismanagement, and the tendency of some taxpayers to "fix the truth" after the fact. Recalling our language in Chapters 2 and 3, more research engagements entail closed-fact settings than open-fact situations by far, but those facts may be fairly difficult to determine and support in a manner that will satisfy the IRS or the courts. Such fact-gathering travails make for interesting anecdotes at conferences of tax practitioners, and they seldom are apparent from the clean, black-and-white statements of facts that accompany file memos and case briefs.

The tone and nature of the file memo should recognize that its readers will be restricted to fellow tax practitioners who are well versed in the Federal tax law. Thus, references to primary and secondary sources of the tax law should be frequent and complete, but usually limited to the tax case reporters that are available in the office of the researcher's firm. One must presume that the ultimate reader of the memo's comments will need no introduction to the hierarchy of the Federal tax system nor to statutory citation practices. In addition, it often is helpful to include pertinent references to one or more of the commercial tax services to which the researcher's firm subscribes, perhaps on a "sticky note" or other attachment to the memo, providing a clear paper trail to facilitate subsequent review and commentary concerning the tax issue.

Seldom will the researcher's efforts result in merely the preparation of a research memorandum to the file. In general, the memo will be accompanied in the file by briefs of one or more pertinent court cases or administrative pronouncements. (Review Exhibit 5–8 and your related class exercises concerning the format and content of a well-constructed court case brief.) In addition, many practitioners append to the file memo photocopies of or hot links to critical court case opinions, regulations or rulings, and journal articles, much of which features "highlighting," i.e., markup with a pastel marker. These practices were illustrated in Exhibit 10–3.

The authors recommend that practitioners restrict such appended material to only those resources that are of utmost importance to reduce both the associated client costs and the volume of the typical memo. In this regard, we believe that an effective statement of facts and issues, followed by a concise synthesis of the controlling law, is far more valuable than a mass of duplicated, small-print tax reference materials.

EVALUATING THE SOURCES OF LAW

The tax researcher will have made a number of judgments and creative applications concerning the client's fact situation before preparing the file memo. For instance, the researcher may select and eliminate competing issues and direct the research process onto one or more pathways to the exclusion of others. Nonetheless, in deriving an analysis of the various elements of the controlling sources of the tax law, the practitioner must choose from among a number of varied interpretations of the statute and of its (interpretive) regulations and court case opinions.

Often the researcher will be guided in this regard by the opinions of the most recent of the court cases discovered. Well-written case opinions typically provide a summary of the evolution of the pertinent tax law and a discussion of the competing interpretations thereof by the parties to the lawsuit. In this manner, the researcher regularly can obtain an indication of both the critical facts and issues that the court has identified in the present case and its interpretation as to the distinguishing features of seemingly relevant precedents. (In reality, most of these sections of the opinion are written by law clerks or law school students who obtain and retain their positions by preparing thorough and insightful file memos of their own!) Moreover, an increasing number of case opinions include lengthy dissenting or concurring opinions, from which the researcher can further identify the pertinent facts and issues relative to the opinion.

Lacking (or in lieu of) such judicial direction, the researcher's evaluation of the efficacy of a precedent or pronouncement often is guided by no more than a review of the hierarchy of the sources of the Federal tax law. (For a review of these sources, see Chapters 3 through 5.)

In addition, we offer the following points to be considered in the evaluation of a series of apparently conflicting tax laws.

- Regulations seldom are held to be invalid by a court. In the typical year, fewer than a dozen such holdings are issued. Thus, challenges to the provisions of a Regulation should be based on more than a simple challenge to the Treasury's authority or a self-serving competing interpretation of the statute offered by the taxpayer.
- Revenue Rulings and Revenue Procedures, however, are frequently modified or otherwise held to be invalid by a court. Accordingly, the taxpayer's attempted restructuring of the pertinent law in his or her favor with respect to such an administrative pronouncement is more likely to be heard openly by the court and, therefore, to be based on the weight of the competing arguments rather than simply on the Treasury's preemptive interpretive rights.
- The decisions of courts that are higher in the judicial hierarchy should receive additional precedential weight. Given an adequate degree of similarity in fact situations, district and circuit court opinions have direct bearing on the taxpayer only if they were issued in the corresponding jurisdiction. On the other hand, opinions of the Court of Federal Claims and Tax Court are binding on the taxpayer, even though they were issued with respect to a taxpayer who works or resides in another jurisdiction, unless they are overturned in a pertinent appeal.
- Thus, a taxpayer who works in Wyoming is not bound by decisions of, say, the Seventh Circuit or Alaska District courts. The practitioner should not feel restricted in a trial or appeal hearing by the doctrine of *stare decisis*. Conversely, an Alaska taxpayer's Court of Federal Claims decision is binding on the Wyoming citizen's Court of Federal Claims case. If this Court of Federal Claims decision was held in a manner that is detrimental to the Wyoming taxpayer, another trial court should be pursued.
- Other factors being equal, decisions of the Second, Ninth, and Federal Circuits should be assigned additional precedential value. Among other reasons, this additional weight can be attributed to the inclusion of the cities of New York and Washington and the state of California in these circuits. Typically, the Ninth Circuit is the first to introduce an innovative or otherwise unusual interpretation of the law, and the Second and Federal Circuits are authoritative in a more traditional vein.

- Older court decisions should be assigned a geometrically declining degree of importance unless (1) they are Supreme Court cases, (2) they are Second, Ninth, or Federal Circuit cases, or (3) they are the only precedents available. The roster and philosophical makeup of a court change over time and often reflect the changing societal culture and philosophies. Thus, recent case opinions are more likely to identify issues that are held to be critical by the sitting judges that the taxpayer will face, and they are likely to be better predictors of the outcome relative to the current taxpayer's issues.
- Tax journal articles are a useful source by which to identify current, critical tax issues. They also can be utilized in the formation of the practitioner's research schedule, because they often include both a comprehensive summary of the evolution of the controlling law and a thorough list of citations concerning prior interpretive court decisions.
- IRS agents are bound only by the Code, administrative pronouncements, and Supreme Court decisions. Some of the most difficult decisions a tax practitioner must face include those in which one must determine whether the time, effort, and expense of litigation will generate a reward that is sufficient to justify, in essence, the construction of new (judicial) tax law, that is, to overcome this narrow scope of the agent's concern.
- Court decisions are never completely predictable. Thus, even if absolutely all of the judicial precedent that is available supports the taxpayer's position, the court still may hold against him or her. Negative decisions may be the result of a poor performance by the attorney, other tax adviser, or witnesses that are heard by the court; changes in the makeup or philosophy of the members of the court; changes in societal mores, as reflected by the court; or an incorrect interpretation of the law by the court that hears the present case. The practitioner, however, can do little more than conduct a thorough tax research analysis concerning the case, identify convincing witnesses, and trust that justice will prevail.

CLIENT LETTERS

Our discussion to this point in the chapter has concentrated on the communication of tax research by the practitioner to him- or herself or to other tax professionals in a fairly sophisticated document—a memorandum to the file. We now shift the focus for the communication to a different audience, namely, the client, and to a different setting, the written or oral presentation.

By far the most common form of communication between the tax professional and his or her client is the telephone call. We must stress the danger inherent in placing too great a dependence on the phone call to convey the results of tax research, given the intricacies of both the fact situation and the (tax adviser's interpretation of) controlling law, in most professional situations. If the telephone must be used (perhaps because of time pressures or convenience) to convey tax research results, the practitioner should always send a fairly detailed follow-up **client letter,** in hard copy, not just e-mail, confirming his or her understanding as to the information that was conveyed and the actions that are to be taken as a result of the call.

Foremost among the attributes of the client letter is its brevity. Except in the most unusual circumstances, it should not exceed two pages. This rule should only be violated when the subject of the research is especially complex or grave, perhaps in anticipation of extended litigation or with respect to a more sophisticated client, where, for instance, one might be tempted to attach a copy (or a "client version") of the research file memo.

The brevity of the client letter is, most often, in response to the desire of the client for "the answer" that has been found concerning the extant tax issues. Clients do tend to see tax issues as black-and-white ones, and they want to know whether they will win or lose with the IRS. Of course, tax practitioners are aware of the colorful world that tax practice presents, and the various shades of emphasis and interpretation sometimes make the view quite murky. Thus, to accommodate the desire of the client, one typically must convey no more than the absolute highlights of the research process.

Another factor that leads to brief client letters is the tax practitioner's professional responsibilities. Responding to client questions is generally easier in a face-to-face meeting. Thus, most practitioners use the client letter to deliver the general conclusions of the research project and to request a follow-up meeting in which questions, comments, and the need for more detail can be addressed.

Exhibits 10–4 and 10–5 illustrate the format and content of typical client letters. The sole difference between these two letters is the degree of sophistication that is possessed by the receiving party.

In general, the client letter should be structured as follows, perhaps allowing one paragraph for each of the noted topics.

- Salutation/social graces/general conclusion
- Summary of the research project results
- Objective of the report
- Statement of facts and disclaimer as to the scope of the tax professional's knowledge base
- Summary of critical sources of law that lead to result
- Implications of the results
- Assumptions/limitations
- Closing/reference to follow-up meeting/social graces
- Attachments, if any (e.g., engagement letter, file memo, illustrative charts, bibliography), on a separate page

Effective written business communication often makes use of the following guidelines. Notice that most of these elements are present in each of the two sample client letters that we have included in this chapter.

- Make your main point(s) in the first paragraph of the communication.
- State a well-defined purpose for the document, and stick to it.
- Avoid "filler" language, e.g., "at the present time," "the fact that," "as you know," and "enclosed please find."
- Avoid cliches and trendy jargon, e.g., "interface," "input," "seamless," "hands-on," "state-of-the-art," and any number of sports analogies.
- Don't be afraid to revise the letter several times to improve its format or to expand or narrow (as needed) its content. In this regard, allow enough time for the preparation of the document in a professional manner.
- Use the social amenities to your advantage by spelling names correctly, keeping current on the recipient's promotions and current title, and adding handwritten messages at the beginning or end of the document.

Exhibit 10–4 Sample Client Letter—Sophisticated Client

> **Over & Short, CPAs**
> Brooklyn Park, MN
>
> November 19, 20XX
>
> M/M Dale Brown
> 2472 North Mayfair Road
> Fillingham, SD 59990
>
> Dear Dale and Rae,
>
> Thanks again for requesting my advice concerning the tax treatment of your interest expenses. I am sorry to report that only a portion of your expenses can be deducted this year.
>
> I have uncovered a series of court cases in which the IRS has prevailed over the taxpayer's requests for a deduction that is similar to yours. Unfortunately, the Tax Court's position is that interest such as yours is nondeductible, and additional litigation would be necessary to bring about a more favorable result for you.
>
> My efforts have concentrated on the treatment of interest expenses that are incurred by taxpayers who hold exempt bonds while maintaining a bank loan that requires interest payments.
>
> Over the last thirty years or so, a number of Circuit Court decisions have held that a taxpayer effectively must divest him- or herself of investments in such municipal bonds, regardless of portfolio diversification objectives, before a deduction for the interest payments to the bank is allowed. Fortunately, however, an exception exists relative to business-related loans, so that interest that is related to Rae's clinic will be allowed as a deduction. Conversely, that portion of the loan that relates to your school bond investment is nondeductible, even though it is secured by your residence.
>
> You may wish to reconsider your use of the mortgage for this purpose, as your tax advantages therefrom are somewhat limited. This appears to be more palatable for you than would be the alternative of expensive further (and, probably, fruitless) litigation of the issue.
>
> My conclusion is based upon the facts that you have provided me, and upon the efficacy of these somewhat dated court decisions. As you've requested, I've attached a copy of my research memo for you to read and from which you might develop subsequent inquiries.
>
> I'm sorry that the news from me wasn't more favorable. I look forward to seeing you, though, at the firm's holiday reception!
>
> Sincerely,
>
> *Mary H. Polzin,* for Over & Short, CPAs

- *Practice writing* until it becomes easier and more enjoyable for you to do. Word processing programs, with the editing and proofreading capabilities that they provide, will aid you in this task.

COMPREHENSIVE ILLUSTRATION OF CLIENT FILE

Exhibit 10–6 provides a comprehensive illustration of the two major elements of a client file: a client letter and a file memo. Notice the degree of correspondence between the two documents in that some portions of the client letter are no more than quotations or paraphrases of the file memo.

Exhibit 10–5 Sample Client Letter—Less Sophisticated Client

Over & Short, CPAs
Brooklyn Park, MN

November 19, 20XX

M/M Dale Brown
2472 North Mayfair Road
Fillingham, SD 59990

Dear Dale and Rae,

Thanks again for requesting my advice concerning the tax treatment of your interest expenses. I am sorry to report that only a portion of your expenses can be deducted this year.

My research has uncovered a series of successes by the IRS in convincing several important courts that interest such as yours should not be allowed as a deduction to reduce your taxes. Unfortunately, the court whose decision initially would prevail upon us would hold against you, and a series of court hearings, over two or three years or so, would be necessary for you to win the case.

This research has been restricted to situations that are similar to yours, that is, in which the taxpayer both owns a municipal bond and owes money to the bank from an interest-bearing loan.

It seems that the IRS would rather have you purchase the municipal bonds with your own money, rather than with the bank's. It maintains that you get a double benefit from the nontaxability of the school bond interest income and the deductibility of the interest expense that is paid to the bank. Thus, that portion of the interest that relates to the bond investment is not allowed. A business purpose for the loan salvages the deduction, however, so you can deduct the interest from the loan that relates to Dr. Rae's clinic.

You may just have to live with this situation, as the IRS has been winning cases like these for about thirty years. Yours is not likely to be the one that changes their mind, so you might reconsider your investment in the municipals in the near future.

My conclusion is based upon the facts that you have provided me, and upon the reliability of the court cases that I found.

I'm sorry that the news from me wasn't more favorable. I look forward to seeing you, though, at the firm's holiday reception!

Sincerely,

Mary H. Polzin, for Over & Short, CPAs

The remainder of the internal file for this hypothetical client would include, among many other possibilities, (1) an engagement letter, (2) a billing and collection history, (3) case, regulation, and ruling briefs that are pertinent to the file memo, and (4) reproductions of important analyses of the client's prevailing tax issues from treatises, journal articles, and other resources.

Each consulting firm or tax department has its own formatting requirements with respect to client files. As tax research becomes conducted almost exclusively using computer and telephone equipment, the temptation will be for the tax researcher to reduce the thickness of the client file, as duplications of controlling law and other precedent are deemed unnecessary. This paper reduction movement constitutes a laudable goal. Yet one must not shortchange the importance of the client file as a

Exhibit 10–6 Client File Illustration

CLIENT LETTER

Tax Jockeys Limited
Newport, RI

December 10, 20XX

Harold and Frieda van Briske
2000 Fox Point Heights
Whitefish Bay, RI 02899

Dear Harold and Frieda,

Congratulations on your recent marriage! I hope that you found your honeymoon at Club Med to be an enjoyable and memorable experience.

Thank you again for requesting my advice concerning the tax treatment of your pre-nuptial agreement. I understand that Frieda transferred some appreciated stock to Harold on the morning of the wedding, under the prenuptial agreement. I am happy to report that the transaction will not result in the imposition of any Federal tax for either of you.

My research has uncovered a series of successes by the IRS in convincing several important courts, including the Supreme Court, that an agreement such as yours is not supported by "full and adequate consideration," and, therefore, that it is to be treated as a gift. Although you did not intend for your property transfer to be a gift, the intent of the parties in such agreements does not control for Federal tax purposes.

Fortunately, however, the treatment of your transaction as a gift will result in the imposition of neither Federal income tax nor Federal gift tax upon you. Federal income tax is not imposed upon the transfer because gross income is not recognized by either the donor or donee when a gift is made. Although a gift has occurred, no gift tax is due, because the unlimited gift tax marital deduction neutralizes the transfer.

This research has been restricted to fact situations that are similar to yours, that is, in which, pursuant to a prenuptial agreement, a taxpayer surrendered his or her other marital rights in exchange for a sum of money or other property.

My conclusion is based upon the facts that you have provided to me and upon the reliability of the court cases that I found.

I look forward to seeing you at the Christmas Charity Ball!

Sincerely,

Karen J. Boucher, CPA, JD, MST, for Tax Jockeys Limited

FILE MEMO

December 10, 20XX

Tax Jockeys Limited
Newport, RI

Relevant Facts
On the morning of their wedding, Frieda gave to Harold $400,000 of appreciated stock, pursuant to a prenuptial agreement. Frieda's basis in the stock was $150,000. In exchange for these securities, Harold surrendered all other marital rights and claims to Frieda's assets, under the terms of the agreement. Harold and Frieda both are residents of Arizona.

Specific Issues
(1) What are the gift tax consequences of this exchange?
(2) What are the income tax consequences of this exchange?

Exhibit 10–6 Client File Illustration—*(Concluded)*

Conclusions
(1) Frieda incurs no gift tax liability as the agreement is executed and implemented.
(2) Asset basis carries over to Harold, the new owner of the securities. Neither Frieda nor Harold recognize gross income as a result of the exchange.

Support
Issue One
Donative intent on the part of the donor is not an essential element in the application of the gift tax. Reg. § 25.2511-1(g)(1).

The Supreme Court has held that prenuptial transfers in relinquishment of marital rights are not adequate and full consideration in money or money's worth for the transfer of property, within the meaning of IRC § 2512(b). *Merrill v. Fahs*, 324 U.S. 308, 65 S.Ct. 655 (1945); *Comm. v. Wemyss*, 324 U.S. 303, 65 S.Ct. 652 (1945); Reg. § 25.2512-8. However, the Second Circuit has held that a prenuptial agreement was acquired for valuable consideration and did not constitute a gift, for income tax (basis computation) purposes. *Farid-Es-Sultaneh v. Comm.*, 160 F.2d 812 (CA-2, 1947). This decision is not critical to the present analysis, though, because the van Briskes do not live in the Second Circuit, and because the somewhat dated decision may be aberrational.

Although the van Briske transaction resulted in a gift, no gift tax is imposed due to the application of the annual exclusion and the unlimited gift tax marital deduction. IRC §§ 2503(b) and 2523; Reg. § 25.2511-2(a); Rev. Rul. 69-347, 1969-2 C.B. 227.

IRC § 2501 imposes a tax on the transfer of property by gift; the gift tax is not imposed, though, upon the receipt of property by the donee. Rather, it is the transfer itself that triggers the tax. Since the prenuptial agreement here is enforceable by state law only when consummated by marriage, the transfer has not taken place until after the marriage occurred. Thus, the transfer appears to be eligible for the gift tax marital deduction, regardless of the timing of the transfer relative to the marriage ceremony on the wedding day. Even if the securities had been physically transferred to Harold prior to the completion of the ceremonies, the agreement was only enforceable after the couple was married. The IRS likely would not need or attempt to establish the exact moments of both (1) the transfer of the securities, and (2) the consummation of the marriage. *C.I.R. v. Bristol*, 121 F.2d 129 (CA-1, 1960); *Bradford*, 34 T.C. 1059 (1960, A); *Archbold*, 42 B.T.A. 453 (1940, A in result only); *Harris v. Comm.*, 178 F.2d 861 (1949).

Issue Two
Neither Harold nor Frieda recognize any gross income upon Harold's release of his marital rights. Gross income does not include the value of property that is acquired by gift. IRC §102(a); Reg. §1.102-1(a); Rev. Rul. 79-312; Rev. Rul. 67-221; *Howard v. C.I.R.*, 447 F.2d 152 (CA-5, 1971).

The transfer of securities is not deductible in any way by Frieda, but under the *Farid* decision, Harold's basis may be stepped up to fair market value. Recall our earlier comments, though, concerning the reliability of this precedent. *Illinois National Bank v. U.S.*, 273 F.2d 231 (CA-7, 1959), cert. den. 363 U.S. 803, 80 S.Ct. 1237 (1960); *C.I.R. v. Marshman*, 279 F.2d 27, cert. den. 364 U.S. 918, 81 S.Ct. 282 (1960); Rev. Rul. 79-312. In the typical gift situation, the donee takes the donor's income tax basis in the transferred property. IRC §§ 1015(a) and 1041(a)(1).

Actions To Be Taken
Prepare letter, review results with client.
Place copy of prenuptial agreement in the client file.
Alert the New York and New Jersey offices that their conclusions may differ, under the *Farid* decision.

Preparer: *Karen J. Boucher*
Reviewer: *Willie Schroeder*

roadmap by which to retrace the researcher's line of thinking that leads to the conclusions and recommendations evidenced in the file memo and client letter. Electronic equivalents of the mind-map of the researcher and of underlining or pastel highlighting of portions of lengthy legal documents must be developed.

Accordingly, every tax researcher must develop or work with a scheme by which to cross-reference the steps of the professional critical thinking model undertaken on the client's behalf. This might entail a listing of legal citations and computer files that would bear upon a reconstruction of the researcher's analysis, perhaps in the form of a decision tree or project management summary. Various software applications will be useful in this regard, not the least of which is the "footsteps" feature of many electronic tax research products, which records the detailed sequencing of commands and decisions made during the online or CD-based project. Regardless of the form this project diary takes, its importance for professional quality control cannot be overstated.

ORAL PRESENTATIONS OF RESEARCH RESULTS

Psychologists tell us that most people's greatest fear is speaking before groups of other people. Indeed, the thought of being the only one in the room who is standing, of having your listeners whispering their evaluations of you to each other, of having members of the audience taking notes on (or tape recording) your comments (certainly so that your errors of omission and commission can be parroted back at a later date), and of fielding extemporaneous questions is enough to bring many people to tears.

Yet public speaking is an important part of the tax practitioner's professional life. In many ways, it is the most accurate predictor of success. As politicians have long known, when one is delivering an oral presentation in an effective and professional manner, the audience becomes convinced that all of the other professional qualities that they desire from the speaker are also present. Conversely, an ill-prepared or ill-delivered message can do much to erode the audience's confidence in the speaker, not just with respect to the topic of the presentation, but in general.

Thus, it behooves the tax professional to develop skill in public speaking. In contexts that range from the presentation of an award to a colleague or the conduct of a staff meeting to the presentation of a keynote address at the annual tax conference of your peers, such skills can mean the difference between enhancing and damaging your reputation.

What is advised here is not a series of "tricks" to fool the audience into believing that you are more knowledgeable than you really are. Rather, we convey here some time-tested techniques leading to an effective communication of ideas—from one who has developed a secure base of knowledge in a subject to an audience with a specified background that has a desire to learn more about that subject. Whether making a presentation of one's results to a supervisor in one's own firm or elaborating on a research project with the client's board of directors, the communication of tax research results poses special problems that make a review of oral communications procedures all the more valuable. Specifically, we can make the following suggestions concerning **oral presentations** of tax research.

- General preparation for the talk should include a thorough, frank examination of the following set of questions by the presenter. Nearly all of these observations can be characterized as knowledge of the makeup of the audience.

Why me? Why was I asked to speak? What knowledge or celebrity do I bring to the event?

What do they want? What does the audience hope to take away from the presentation? Technical knowledge? Relief from stress? Inspiration? Skill development? Amusement or entertainment? Should I present an overview or a detailed technical update or analysis?

What is their attitude? Is the audience coming to the event curious or anxious to hear from me, or must they be persuaded of the relevance or importance of my topics?

From what should I stay away? Are there topics that are taboo for this audience, due to their age, experiences, or existing attitudes? One must not alienate the audience, wittingly or unwittingly, in any way if the message is to get across.

What do they already know? What is the knowledge base of the audience? It would be ideal to speak to a homogeneous audience, especially in the level of knowledge that it brings into the event, but this seldom is the case. One must decide, then, whether to aim at the median knowledge base, above, or below. The stakes are high in exercising this judgment, though, and either repeating what is common knowledge to the group, or presenting information at a high level that is accessible to only a few in the audience, can make communication impossible.

Who is the audience? Details as to the audience's demographic characteristics such as age, education and income level, political leanings, and so forth can be vital for tailoring one's style, presentation speed and media, references to literature and popular culture, and use of humor in an effective manner. Remember to play to as many members of the audience as possible, not just the majority of those in attendance or those who were involved directly in hiring or retaining your services.

- Be prepared in the technical aspects of your discussion, particularly the basic research. Spend most of your preparation time on your main points and conclusions rather than on the fine points. If you are caught without a piece of technical information, it is clearly better for you if that information is specific (so that you can refer the questioner to a more detailed reference or to a later, private conversation with you), rather than basic in nature.

- Resist the temptation to tell the audience all that you know about the subject. You almost certainly have neither the time nor the organizational abilities that are necessary to command the attention of the audience for that long a time. Direct your remarks to the highlights and general results of the research, and allow a questions-and-comments period in which more detailed subjects can be addressed. In this manner, you will provide the greatest amount of information to the greatest number of listeners in the audience.

- Use visual aids effectively. Handouts, overhead transparencies, or videotapes can serve to clarify or emphasize your key points (and, not incidentally, to transfer the "spotlight" of the presentation away from you). Most advisers recommend that you not look at the screen repeatedly, or read the text of the visual aid word for word along with the audience, but, rather, that you use the visual aid as a means of keeping the audience focused on the discussion points by the use of a pointer or other highlighter. Avoid a sequence that allows a "blank screen" for more than a second or two. Inexpensive computer software will assist you in preparing electronic presentations, slides, or transparencies, delivering your talk, and staying on schedule. If you are a regular on the lecture circuit, consider the purchase of an ink-jet or color laser printer with which to prepare your visual aids, or a moderately priced, easy to carry projector, so that you need not depend on conference center staff to present your slides.

Many speakers are tempted to overuse visual aids, especially because they are so easy to create, even at professional-quality levels, given today's software packages. Visual aids, though, generally should be used only for the following purposes.

- To illustrate things that are difficult to convey strictly with words by using a photograph, videotape, map, blueprint, or flowchart.
- To save time by consolidating ideas, committing to a time frame or strategy, or listing conflicting viewpoints or tactics.
- To create interest in a subject, perhaps by presenting the concept in a manner with which the audience is unfamiliar (e.g., an extra-large view, a view from "the other side of the issue," or an evolutionary time or growth line).
- To emphasize a point or concept by highlighting a graphic, picture, mnemonic, or list of key words or concepts.
- To organize the introduction, body, or conclusion of the presentation.
- To introduce humor to the event with a tasteful quotation or cartoon.
- To place ideas in the audience's memories, through a visual "take away" item.

Overhead transparencies, electronic presentations, or slides should be designed with care and diligence. When using this technology, as opposed to the hand-drawn flip chart or on-the-fly whiteboard drawing, one essentially is competing with professional graphic and television artists, and the audience will hold your efforts to these high standards. Most visual and graphic artists offer guidelines for presentation layouts, including the following.

- Use the slide to emphasize pictures, not text or numbers. Except to be able to point to a specific position on the page and keep the members of the audience in the same spot throughout the presentation, do not use transparencies to duplicate pages of text or spreadsheets with voluminous numbers. Employ graphs, charts, arrows, and other pictorial devices instead.
- When text is involved, use the "six and six" rule: No more than six lines of type, and no more than six words on a line. This directive will help to dictate the font chosen and the corresponding size of print.
- Keep the font style simple. Use sans serif or newspaper-type fonts, not script or modern fonts, unless corporate logos or other protected styles are used. Most designers recommend that no more than two colors of text be used on a slide and that the color scheme of the graphics blend well with that of the text. Be conservative—stick to the primary colors, colors of local sports teams, and multiple shades of gray, so as not to frustrate the duplication process for related handout materials.
- Similarly, try to use some background music if your available technology will support it at a professional-quality level. In this regard, select audio clips that do not draw attention to themselves, but are memorable in a more subtle way. Music can signal the start or end of a presentation or its subunits, a change in direction, or a specific idea (e.g., a Frank Sinatra clip sends a different message than does one by Jimi Hendrix or a New Age group).
- On the average, allow at least three minutes of spoken presentation for each slide. Accordingly, limit the number of your slides to the length of your talk in

minutes, divided by three. In this way, you will not overproduce your number of slides. If you want to provide your audience with a content outline, use some other medium, not the slides.
- Prepare for the worst: Number your slides and have hardcopy backups in case of emergency.

Without exception, determine ahead of the presentation how long your talk is supposed to be and be absolutely certain not to exceed it. You need to be fair to the other speakers, if any, who follow your presentation. Moreover, with very few exceptions, the audience also is aware of the schedule for the session, and if the speaker exceeds the allotted time, the audience, at best, will stop paying attention and, at worst, will become restless or angry. Because of their technical nature, most tax presentations should not exceed 45 minutes, and one-half of that time might be ideal for both speaker and audience.

Have an outline for your discussion that includes miniature versions of slides and transparencies and your business address, phone and fax numbers, and Internet addresses. Use the visual aids to convince the audience that you are following the outline. This will (1) ensure that you will cover the material that you desire, (2) build confidence among the audience as to your speaking abilities, and (3) convince yourself that you are doing a good job in leading the discussion of the assigned topic.

Rehearse your presentation, word for word, at least once. The most effective means of preparing yourself in this manner probably is with a video recorder, because your distracting mannerisms (e.g., clearing the throat repeatedly, saying the words "ah" or "you know" too often, or pounding on the lectern) quickly will become apparent. Lacking such a device, use an (audio) tape recorder. Family members or colleagues should not be used for this rehearsal.

Be kind to yourself in evaluating your video performance, but be observant for the following "I didn't know I did that" items.

- In all but the very largest presentation venues, get as physically close to the audience as you can, ideally removing the lectern, stepping down from the stage or platform, and moving to a series of different spots in the room throughout your speaking time.
- Eliminate nervous and visual distractions, such as jingling coins, playing with pen and marker tops, and adjusting clothing. Minimize the use of crossing your arms, pounding the table, and finger-pointing, reserving them as means of emphasizing key points or declaring victory over competing viewpoints.
- Vary the pitch of your voice, avoiding both a dry monotone and a "classic actor" dramatic approach. Many speakers talk too fast or too loud; check yourself throughout the talk on these matters. Test the microphone system before the audience arrives, so that you don't need to ask, "Can you hear me in the back?"
- Don't be afraid of silence. Pauses invariably seem longer to the speaker than they do to the audience, so don't let natural breaks in the talk add to your anxiety. In fact, well-paced pauses can relieve tension (both yours and the audience's), signal changes of pace, and allow you to emphasize the importance of certain ideas.
- Don't read directly from your outline, except for a selected quote of three lines or so from the material once or twice in the presentation. Try not to have a separate set of note cards, because the tendency again is to break your contact with the audience and hide behind the scripting device. Disguise your notes in the

form of comments on hard copies of transparencies and flip charts and notes in the margin of your copy of the outline. Keep your eyes up and on the audience.

Avoid references to administrative or "housekeeping" aspects of the event—leave these to be conveyed by the host of the event. Be enthusiastic and positive about your comments—don't apologize for a lack of discussion on a tangential point, a logistical snafu, or a misstatement of fact or law. The audience generally wants you to succeed, so don't undermine this trust with self-destructive comments. Don't refer to the schedule for the event or other timing issues, because they can distract the audience or otherwise detract from conveying your message (e.g., "Only 10 minutes to go," "We may be out of here early," "The previous speakers ran over into my time slot," or "I'll try to get through this quickly, so we can finish on time").

Rehearse the logistical aspects of the presentation, such as the lighting, projectors, or computer presentation software and terminals, before you begin to speak, ideally both the night before and one hour before your presentation. Have adequate numbers and varieties of markers, pointers, flip chart pads, and remote control devices. You don't want to encounter any surprises after it is too late to do anything about them! On your script, note cards, or transparency masters, make notes to yourself as to when, for instance, to pass out the handout material, turn on or turn off the projector, or refer to a flip chart.

Avoid clichés, such as opening with a joke, or saying, "It's a pleasure to be here." Don't take the risk of boring or offending the audience with a joke that (1) they may have heard already or (2) you may not tell effectively under pressure. This is not to suggest that you avoid humor altogether, however. Audiences, and speakers' reputations, thrive on it. If you are sure of your skill in this area, you might venture a joke, but it would probably be wiser to open with a "punch line" summary of some of the most interesting of your results or fact situations.

Have a "Plan B" ready to go—flexibility is the watchword of the effective speaker. If the time actually allowed for your talk is shorter than you had thought, due to a misunderstanding or unanticipated events, have a list of topics, videos, or slides that can be eliminated without changing the nature of the talk. Practice your question-and-answer-session skills, especially for occasions where there is more time available than you had anticipated. Do not mention any of these on-the-fly adjustments to the audience—make the changes, don't talk about them.

Observe audience body language, and use signals conveying interest, enthusiasm, boredom, or restlessness to your advantage. Make consistent eye contact with the audience, smile when appropriate, and take a few seconds at the completion of the presentation to accept the audience's show of thanks and savor your job well done.

SUMMARY

The tax professional must become proficient in communicating his or her research results. Recipients of these communications might include oneself or one's peers, via the file memorandum; the client, via a brief letter; or a number of other listeners, via an oral presentation. In each case, the practitioner must be sensitive to the needs, backgrounds, and interests of the recipients of the messages, without sacrificing professional demeanor or responsibilities.

TAX TUTOR

Reinforce the tax research information covered in this chapter by completing the online tutorials located at the Federal Tax Research web site:

http://raabe.swcollege.com

KEY WORDS

By the time you complete your work relative to this chapter, you should be comfortable discussing each of the following terms. If you need additional review of any of these items, return to the appropriate material in the chapter or consult the glossary to this text.

Client Letter   Oral Presentation
File Memorandum

TAX RESEARCH ASSIGNMENTS

As we have discussed them in this chapter, develop solutions and appropriate documentation for one or more of the problems that you have worked on in previous chapters or for the following fact situations. In this context, proper format and professional content are of equal importance, so that the development of the reader's tax research communication skills will be facilitated.

Specifically, as assigned by your instructor, prepare one or more of the following means of communicating your research results for your chosen problem or case.

- File memorandum
- Letter to tax-sophisticated client
- Letter to unsophisticated client
- Article for local business news weekly
- Speech to local chamber of commerce
- Article for *Taxation for Accountants*
- Speech to State Bar Association conference
- Presentation to client's board of directors
- Presentation to client's senior counsel
- Posting to the Internet Tax Forum for Practitioners
- Posting to the Internet Tax Help group for taxpayers

PROBLEMS

1. Professor White operates a popular bar review course as a sole proprietorship. He charges $1,000 tuition of each student, and he guarantees a full refund of the tuition if the student passes an in-course exam but does not pass the actual bar exam on the first try. White is bold enough to do this because the first-time-pass rate is more than 80 percent for the bar exam (as opposed to less than 15 percent for the CPA exam). He collected $50,000 tuition for his Fall 2002 review section, but he reported the gross receipts on his 2003 Form 1040, because the grades for those taking the fall review are not released until February 2003. Thus, White asserted that he had no constructive receipt of the tuition until February 2003. Is this treatment correct?
2. Lisa, usually a stay-at-home mother, went to the hospital one day for some outpatient surgery. She hired a babysitter for $35 to watch her four-year-old son while she was gone. What tax benefits are available to Lisa for this cash payment?
3. Same as 2, except that Lisa paid the sitter while she worked as a scout leader for the Girl Scouts.
4. Joan, a traveling sales representative, kept no formal books and records to summarize her gross receipts for the year, but she retained copies of all customer invoices and reported her gross income for the year from these totals. Is she liable for a negligence penalty under § 6662 for failing to keep any books and records?
5. Tex's credit union has provided him with financing to acquire his $200,000 home. The loan is set up as a three-year note with a balloon payment, but the credit union always renews the loan for another three years at the current interest rate. This year, the credit union renewed Tex's loan for the third time, charging $3,000 in points. In what year(s) can Tex deduct this $3,000?
6. Barb and Bob were one-fourth shareholders of a C corporation. When the entity had negative E&P, Barb and Bob secretly withdrew $200,000 in cash, hiding this fact from the other owners. How much gross income do Barb and Bob report?
7. Detail the tax effects to the Prasads of making the election to include their seven-year-old daughter's $10,000 unearned income on their current-year joint return.
8. Eighty percent of the Willigs' AGI comes from their submarine sandwich proprietorship. In 2003, the Willigs lost an IRS audit and owed $12,000 in 2001 Federal income taxes, all attributable to inventory computations in their business. Interest on this amount totaled $3,200. All amounts due were paid by the end of 2003. How much of the interest can the Willigs deduct on their 2003 Schedule C?
9. Al and Amy are divorced. In which of the following cases can legal fees be deducted?
    a. Al pays $5,000 to get the court to reduce his alimony obligation.
    b. Amy pays $5,000 to get the court to increase her alimony receipts.
    c. Al pays Amy's attorney fees in (b), as required by the original divorce decree.
10. Katie is a one-third owner of an S corporation. After a falling-out with the other shareholders, Katie signed an agreement early in January 2002. Under the terms of the agreement, Katie took $200,000 of her capital from the corporation and had eight months to negotiate a purchase of the stock of the other shareholders. She did not complete this task by the end of August 2002. Thus, contrary negotiations began and on March 1, 2003, Katie sold all of her shares to the remaining shareholders for a $2.5 million gain. For how many of these months does Katie report flow-through income from the S corporation?

11. Can an individual make a contribution to an IRA based on unemployment compensation proceeds received?
12. Duane paid his 1998 Federal income taxes in January 2001 in the amount of $10,000, and then paid $4,000 interest and penalties on this amount in May 2002. In April 2004, Duane filed a claim for refund of the $14,000, due to a sizable operating loss from his business in tax year 2003. Can he recover the 1998-related amounts?
13. After an audit was completed, IRS agent van Court informed Harris of the latter's $10,000 Federal income tax deficiency by leaving a summary memo on Harris's e-mail account. Harris shared this account with his mother, who read the mail first and in a panic confronted Harris with a two-hour "What's this all about?" interrogation. Did van Court violate Harris's right to privacy by using e-mail in this manner?
14. SlimeCo spent $250,000 to build storage tanks for its waste by-products. This is a recurring expenditure for SlimeCo, because once the tanks are filled, new ones must be built. When can SlimeCo deduct the $250,000?
15. Prudence was named a shareholder in her law firm, which operates as an S corporation. Her payments into the capital of the firm were to start in about nine months, when an audit would determine the full value of the firm and a new corporate year would commence. Paperwork with the pertinent state offices was completed, naming Prudence as a shareholder and director and adding her name to that of the firm. But Prudence left the firm eight months after the announcement, that is, before she paid any money for shares. Is Prudence liable for tax on her share of the entity's earnings for the eight months?
16. Laura deducted $8,100 in state income taxes on her 2001 Federal income tax return. Her refund, received in 2002 after all credits and the minimum tax, was $7,800 for these taxes.
    a. How much 2002 gross income must Laura recognize?
    b. How does your answer change if Laura's 2001 deduction was limited to $7,200, due to the application of IRC § 68?
17. Cal's son has been labeled a "can't miss" NBA prospect since junior high school. This year, while the son is a college freshman and classified as an amateur under NCAA rules, Cal spent $14,000 for special clothing, equipment, camps, and personal trainers to keep improving his son's skills. Can Cal deduct these items?
18. CPA Myrna forgot to tell her client Freddie to accelerate the payment of state income and property taxes in a year when Freddie was in an unusually high tax bracket. Upon discovering the error, the parties negotiated a $15,000 payment from Myrna (and her insurance company) to Freddie to compensate Freddie for Myrna's inadequate professional advice. Is this payment gross income to Freddie?
19. How much of the $100,000 interest that is paid on a loan from Everett National Bank can Ben deduct if he invests the loan proceeds in the following? Consider each item independently.
    a. South Chicago School District bonds
    b. AT&T bonds, paying $125,000 interest income this year
    c. Computer Futures, Inc., shares, a growth stock that pays no dividend this year
    d. A life insurance policy on Betty
20. Lilly leases a car that she uses solely for business purposes. The car would be worth $40,050 on the market, and Lilly paid $7,400 in lease payments this year. How are these items treated on her tax return?

RESEARCH CASES

21. Dave took a $100,000 cash withdrawal from his IRA. He bought $100,000 of Microcraft stock and, within the rollover period, transferred the stock to another IRA. Does Dave report any gross income?

22. Gold Partners wanted to complete a like-kind exchange just before it liquidated. Accordingly, it sold the real estate it meant to transfer to the other party, and a qualified intermediary held the resulting cash. When the intermediary found acceptable replacement realty, the intermediary transferred cash and the like-kind property directly to the partners, thereby liquidating Gold. Does § 1031 apply?

23. HelpCo pays Hank two $100,000 salaries per year, one through its WestCo subsidiary and one through its EastCo subsidiary. How do Hank and HelpCo treat his Social Security tax obligations?

24. Jack died three years after winning the lottery grand prize. He had elected to take the prize as a series of $500,000 payments for the rest of his life. Once the payment method was chosen, the annuity was not transferable to any other party, except for Jack's estate. According to IRS annuity tables, the present value of the remaining payments to be received by the estate was $8 million. How much should be included in Jack's Federal gross estate?

25. Karen files jointly in a year when she incurs $2,000 of job-related education expenses. No one else in her family incurred tax-favored education expenses this year. AGI is $80,000, and Karen's miscellaneous itemized deductions for employee business expenses total $400. How should Karen treat her education costs so as to maximize her Federal tax benefits for the year?

26. On December 6, Ed Grimely appeared on the game show, "The Wheel of Fate." As a result of his appearance, Grimely won the following prizes.

	Manufacturer's Suggested List Price	Fair Market Value	Actual Cost to the Show
All-expenses-paid trip to Hawaii	$8,432	$6,000	$5,200
One case of Twinkies	16	12	0
Seven music lessons for the calliope	105	35	0
One year of free haircuts	120	60	15

a. Assuming that Grimely received all of these prizes by the end of the year, compute his gross income from these prizes.
b. Will this amount change if Grimely refuses to accept the calliope lessons immediately after the program's taping session is completed?

27. Josh bought $120,000 worth of furnishings on his MasterCard in 2002, paying off the entire principal and interest in 2003. Interest charges of $7,800 relate to 2002 for the furnishings. How much can Josh deduct for interest relative to this transaction for 2002?

28. Rita's family had a history of heart disease. To reduce Rita's risk of future heart problems, and to enable her to lose about ten pounds, her physician recommended a rigid running program. Accordingly, Rita joined the Vic Tanny Health Club. One-fourth of her time at the club was spent on a supervised

running program. How much of her $450 annual fee is deductible as a medical expense?

29. Ellie owned five apartment buildings, each worth $200,000. For three of the buildings, she worked with employees to keep the property in good repair. This entailed maintaining electrical and plumbing fixtures, common areas, and walls and roofs, and providing janitorial services such as garbage removal, vacuuming, and rest room supplies. For the other two buildings, Ellie's lease required the tenants to perform this work. Can her estate claim a § 6166 estate tax deferral for any of the buildings?

30. HardCo spent $4 million this year on a new graphic design for its product, a yo-yo. Under the prior design, HardCo's name and logo only appeared on the box and wrapping paper, which were discarded by most customers once they started using the product. The new design displayed HardCo's name and newer, flashier logo on both sides of the yo-yo, with a paint that also made it glow in the dark. When can HardCo deduct the $4 million?

ADVANCED CASES

These items require that you have access to research materials other than the Federal tax law and related services. For instance, you might need to refer to an international tax or multistate service or to access Internet sources to prepare your solution for these cases. Consult with your instructor before beginning your work, so that you are certain to have available to you all of the necessary research resources for the case(s) that you choose.

31. Summarize the economic process requirements that apply for a multinational U.S. corporation electing an exclusion for Extraterritorial Income.

32. According to the Tax Foundation, what was Tax Freedom Day in 2002? How much of this time was spent with respect to tax liabilities and how much in meeting tax compliance costs? Which states bear the heaviest tax burden? The lightest? Per capita, how much annual total income and total tax does the U.S. citizen generate? What is the average U.S. citizen's average tax rate?

33. Chan's only transaction in the United States this year was to sell the biggest office building in Denver at a $100 million gain. Chan has no assets, offices, or employees in the United States. Can he be taxed on the gain? Why or why not?

34. As the result of a Federal audit, your 2001 Federal taxable income increased by $27,000. By when must you report this adjustment to your state's revenue department? What form is used for this purpose, where do you obtain it, and where is it to be filed?

35. Does your state provide a form with which to file for a manufacturer's exemption from sales/use tax? Which form is used for this purpose, where do you obtain it, and where is it to be filed?

36. For the current period, what is the short-term, quarterly compounded Federal AFR? Mid-term? Long-term exempt interest rate for computing loss carryforwards under §382?

37. SalesCo sold Tom a prepaid phone card for $100 in 2002. Tom used the phone card for communications services in 2003. When can your state collect sales/use tax from SalesCo for the sale to Tom?

38. GoodCo donated $40,000 of goods from its inventory to the Red Cross. Does your state require GoodCo to collect or pay sales/use tax on these donated goods?
39. The Downtown Wellness Clinic, a tax exempt organization, sells memberships to corporations so that their employees can work out before and after office hours. Three blocks away, the Power Up Fitness Center has similar facilities and also wants to sell memberships to corporate neighbors. Is the Clinic subject to Federal income tax on its membership sales?
40. Does America Online owe any corporate income tax to your state? Don't compute the tax, but determine whether AOL is subject to any obligation for the current year.
41. How much state and local income tax did Texas Ranger Alex Rodriguez owe to your state last year?
42. Find two government documents that discuss potential solutions to the so-called marriage penalty characteristic of the Federal income tax.

11

Tax Planning

LEARNING OBJECTIVES

- Identify several fundamental tenets of tax planning for optimizing tax liabilities
- Gain perspective as to the role of tax planning in tax practice
- Define and apply several key terms with respect to tax rate schedules
- Illustrate effective tax planning as found in today's tax profession

CHAPTER OUTLINE

Economics of Tax Planning, Avoidance, and Evasion
Tax Rate Terminology
    Tax Base
    Tax Rates
Tax Planning in Perspective
Fundamentals of Tax Planning
    Avoiding Income Recognition
    Postponing Income Recognition
    Changing Tax Jurisdictions
    Controlling Classification of Income
    Spreading Income among Related Taxpayers

Departing from the Fundamentals
Exploiting Inconsistencies in the Statute
    Inconsistencies between Transactions
    Inconsistencies between Taxpayers
    Inconsistencies between Years
Avoiding Tax Traps
    Statutory Tax Traps
    Judicial Tax Traps
Tax Planning Illustrations

In this chapter, we return to that element of the tax practice consisting of tax planning, as it was introduced in Chapter 1. A working knowledge of tax planning concepts is imperative for the researcher, because tax avoidance constitutes both (1) an important part of tax practice and (2) a prime motivation in the "open-fact" research context.

For most practitioners, tax research and planning represent the "glamor" end of the business. Properly accomplished tax planning (1) forces the client to identify financial goals and general means by which to achieve them, (2) allows the tax professional to exercise a higher degree of creativity than in any other part of the practice, and (3) affords the practitioner the greatest possible degree of control over the prescribed transactions and then tax consequences.

The tax planning process finds the tax professional in the roles of technical expert, friend, seer, and confessor priest for the client. It offers an opportunity for the most psychologically and financially rewarding work possible, in the context of a tax practice.

ECONOMICS OF TAX PLANNING, AVOIDANCE, AND EVASION

From both the Treasury and the taxpayer viewpoint, taxes can modify individual decisions. Taxes represent an additional cost of doing business or of accumulating wealth. Assuming that economists are correct in speaking about the ways in which a rational citizen makes day-to-day decisions, taxpayers employ tax planning techniques to accomplish the overall goal of wealth maximization.[1] Because taxes deplete the wealth of the taxpayer, planning behavior is designed to reduce the net present value of the tax liability. This is not the same as a simple reduction of taxes in nominal dollar terms, an objective that is so often assumed by laypeople, the media, and others, including too many tax advisors.

Example 11–1 Sharon can choose between two business plans. One will cost her enterprise $1,000 in taxes today. The other will cost the business $2,000 in taxes ten years from now. The plans are identical in all other ways. Prevailing interest rates average 10 percent. Because the present value of the taxes levied with respect to the second alternative are about $800, Sharon should choose the latter plan, that is, the one with the higher nominal dollar tax cost.

If prevailing interest rates average 5 percent during the 10-year planning period, the present value of the taxes levied under the second alternative would be about $1,225, so the first plan, the one that requires an immediate tax payment, should be adopted.

In one important sense, the Federal income tax is its own worst enemy. Taxpayers are rewarded more for finding ways to save taxes than for earning an equal amount in the marketplace. This incentive for tax planning is the result of two rules of tax law.

The first such rule is that the Federal income tax itself is not allowed as a deduction in determining taxable income. Consequently, reducing the amount of income taxes that are paid does not decrease one's allowable deductions and, hence,

---

1. We use "wealth" in its broadest sense here; that is, an individual may choose increased leisure time or other forms of so-called psychic income over traditional forms of wealth. Wealth, the accumulation of which constitutes the overall goal for the specified time period, thus can include measures of happiness, satisfaction, investment, and control over time and other resources.

does not trigger any further increase in taxable income. Instead, the full amount of any tax that is saved increases after-tax income; that is, the tax savings themselves do not constitute taxable income. Unlike most profit-seeking activities, tax planning produces benefits that are completely exempt from income taxation.

The second such rule allows a deduction for any business-related expenses that are incurred in connection with the determination of a tax. Most tax planning costs are deductible by business owners and sole proprietors, but only a few employee-individuals qualify for such a deduction. The net cost of a tax planning project, then, is its gross cost minus the amount of the reduction in the tax liability that is generated by the attendant deduction. In concise terms, the after-tax cost of tax planning can be expressed as follows.

$$ATC = BTC \times (1 - MTR)$$
where
ATC = after-tax cost
BTC = before-tax cost
MTR = marginal tax rate

In relating both rules to tax planning projects, one can see that such endeavors enjoy an economic advantage over most other profit-seeking activities. In evaluating most other investment projects, the decision maker must compare after-tax benefits with after-tax costs. Yet, for tax planning projects, the payoffs are tax free, while the costs usually remain tax-deductible. Thus, for tax planning activities, one effectively compares pretax benefits with after-tax costs.

Example 11-2 A corporate taxpayer, subject to a marginal state and Federal income tax rate of 40 percent, is considering two mutually exclusive alternatives. Alternative A is to hire a university accounting major for the summer at a cost of $2,000; his task would be to undertake research on a tax avoidance plan. If it is successful, the plan would save the corporation $1,600 in Federal income taxes. The probability of success for the plan is estimated at 80 percent. Alternative M is to hire a university marketing major for the summer at a cost of $1,800; her task would be to undertake research on a marketing plan. If it is successful, this plan would generate new revenues of $2,000. The probability of such success is estimated to be 85 percent. Which, if either, alternative should the corporation pursue?

	Alternative A	Alternative M
Before-tax cost	$2,000	$1,800
Tax reduction (40%)	− 800	− 720
After-tax cost	$1,200	$1,080
Possible pre-tax payoff	$1,600	$2,000
Probability of success	× 0.80	× 0.85
Expected pre-tax payoff	$1,280	$1,700
Tax on expected payoff (40%)	− 0	− 680
Expected after-tax payoff	$1,280	$1,020
Excess of after-tax payoff over after-tax cost	$ 80	$ (60)

Decision: Even though Alternative M offers a higher pretax payoff, a lower before-tax cost, and a higher probability of success, Alternative A should be accepted.

The facts of this example illustrate the apparent built-in economic bias of current tax law for tax planning projects, relative to other, seemingly more productive activities.

The analysis of Example 11–2, like most of the illustrations in this book, is based on a "marginal" viewpoint. Its purpose is to determine the effect of the transactions at issue, assuming that all other characteristics of the situation do not change. When it is viewed from this perspective, the after-tax cost of any deductible expenditure decreases if the marginal tax rate is increased. This fact may explain why lower income taxpayers, who are subject to lower marginal tax rates, engage in tax planning activities less often than do higher income taxpayers.

Example 11–3 Assume the same situation and opportunities as in Example 11–2, except that the corporation's marginal tax rate is 20 percent.

	Alternative A	Alternative M
Before-tax cost	$2,000	$1,800
Tax reduction (20%)	− 400	− 360
After-tax cost	$1,600	$1,440
Possible pre-tax payoff	$1,600	$2,000
Probability of success	× 0.80	× 0.85
Expected pre-tax payoff	$1,280	$1,700
Tax on expected payoff (20%)	− 0	− 340
Expected after-tax payoff	$1,280	$1,360
Excess of after-tax payoff over after-tax cost	$ (320)	$ (80)

Decision: Accept Alternative M, because it generates the lesser after-tax loss, or undertake neither (seemingly profitable) project.

TAX RATE TERMINOLOGY

The basic formula for computing a taxpayer's liability is

Tax Liability = Tax Base × Rate

Thus, in many respects, the function of a legislative body is to define adequately the appropriate tax base and construct a schedule of tax rates, so that the ensuing liabilities will be in accordance with the prevailing revenue and nonrevenue objectives of the tax system. Once a tax has been included in a society's tax structure, legislative efforts seem to focus on slight modifications of the existing tax base and rates; major overhauls, additions, or deletions to the structure rarely are considered. Tax reform legislation thus usually takes the form of "fine-tuning" the system rather than "changing channels" altogether.

TAX BASE

The income tax is the most modern of the taxes that are commonly found in contemporary industrialized societies. Allowing for the difficulties in constructing a definition for a virtually imaginary concept, most policymakers believe that a tax that is based on "ordinary taxable income," allowing deductions for the costs of earning such income and for certain personal expenditures, best reflects the capacity of the taxpayer to support government finance.

Previous efforts to base taxation on ability to pay have included taxes on individual consumption and wealth. Consumption taxes are supported by the rationale that the taxpayer receives personal benefit from society in accordance with the amount of goods and services that he or she exhausts during the period; thus, the government should appropriate its share of finances from what people take out of society's "kitty" for personal reasons, not from what they put into it, as is the case under income taxation.

Wealth or property taxes also have been structured to base levies on one's capacity to support the government. Most often, wealth taxes take the form of levies against the net holdings of tangible assets that are controlled by the taxpayer at a given time. In accounting terminology, the tax on the net tangible assets is assessed on what appears on the taxpayer's balance sheet at the end of the taxable year.

Tax Rates

Most tax scholars identify three distinct tax rate structures: proportional, progressive, and regressive, as illustrated in Exhibit 11–1. The classification of a rate structure depends on the trend of the tax rate as the tax base increases. Under a **proportional tax rate** system, the tax rate is constant; for example, it might stand at 29 percent of net wealth, over all possible values of the tax base. Most American sales and property taxes employ a proportional rate structure. Under a tax system

Exhibit 11–1
Alternative Tax Rate Structures: Graphic Illustrations and Applicable Schedules

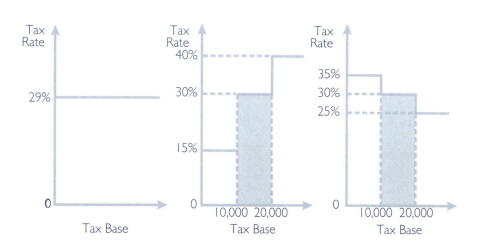

Proportional Rates		Progressive Rates		Regressive Rates	
Tax Base	Rate	Tax Base	Rate	Tax Base	Rate
All amounts	29%	1st $10,000	15%	1st $10,000	35%
		2nd 10,000	30	2nd 10,000	30
		3rd 10,000	40	3rd 10,000	25

with **progressive tax rates,** the applicable tax rate increases as the tax base grows larger. American income, estate, and gift taxes typically use nominally progressive rates. Finally, the tax rate decreases as the tax base grows larger under a system of **regressive tax rates.** Using the present scheme of classification, no American tax to date has employed a system of nominally regressive tax rates.

Example 11–4 In the typical year, Social Security taxes are imposed on employees at a flat rate (before credits), say, of 8 percent on all wages up to $90,000. For wages in excess of $90,000, there is no additional tax. Technically, this tax is proportional, because all covered wages (the tax base) are subject to the same rate of tax. However, many people regard Social Security taxes as being regressive, presumably because they tend to relate their analysis to all of one's income and not just to the statutory tax base. Under this view, because the marginal tax rate is zero on wages in excess of $90,000 for the year, the tax is both effectively and nominally regressive.

Many taxpayers confuse the appropriate meaning of their **marginal tax rate.** Typically, they assume that if a taxpayer is subject to a 36 percent marginal tax rate (i.e., 36 cents is payable in tax on the next dollar of taxable income), he or she owes 36 percent of the *entire* taxable income. One often hears people fall victim to this fallacy, when they state, "I wish I hadn't gotten that raise, because it threw me into a higher tax bracket!" The truth is that even under a system of progressive tax rates, one is never left worse off by earning more money. The higher marginal rates that apply to additional income affect only those increments; the tax liability on the original income layers does not change.

Such comments reflect a confusion on the part of the taxpayer concerning marginal tax rate and average tax rate. The **average tax rate** is a simple division of the total tax liability by the corresponding tax base.

Example 11–5 Lydia earned $30,000 this year. After applying various deductions, exclusions, and exemptions, though, Lydia's statutory taxable income is $21,000; further, the middle tax rate system of Exhibit 11–1 is in effect. Lydia's tax is computed as follows.

$$15\% \times \$10,000 = \$1,500$$
$$30\% \times 10,000 = 3,000$$
$$40\% \times 1,000 = \underline{400}$$
$$\text{Tax Liability} \quad \underline{\$4,900}$$

Lydia's marginal tax rate is 40 percent, but her average rate is only 23.33 percent ($4,900 tax due ÷ $21,000 taxable income).

The reader should make sure that he or she understands this distinction between marginal and average tax rates, because all tax planning analyses should be based on the marginal tax that the individual will pay or save by adopting a particular course of action. The average tax rate is an interesting statistic, but it is solely the marginal rate that affects the change in tax liability and any corresponding changes in taxpayer behavior.

Of course, this definition of statutory taxable income allows for certain deductions, exemptions, and exclusions from total receipts in determining the tax base for

Exhibit 11–2 Various Tax Rate Computations Illustrated

Lydia files a tax return for $30,000 of economic income and $9,000 of exemptions, exclusions, and deductions. Taxable income is $21,000. Tax liability is $4,900 under the prevailing rate system.

Marginal tax rate 40% (from tax rate schedule, middle system, Exhibit 11–1)

Average tax rates Nominal average rate: $4,900 / $21,000 = 23.33%

Effective average rate: $4,900 / $30,000 = 16.33%

the year. Often, because one has received tax-exempt income during the period and because of the tax base's exemptions and standard deduction, an individual controls more receipts than he or she legally must report as taxable income. In this case, the distinction between the nominal and effective average tax rates becomes important. The **nominal average tax rate** can be computed in Example 11–5 as the division of total tax liability by taxable income (i.e., 23.33 percent). However, before considering Lydia's exclusions, exemptions, and deductions, effectively she had command over $30,000 of income during the year, even though only $21,000 of this amount was defined technically as taxable income. Thus, Lydia's **effective average tax rate** of tax for the year can be found by dividing the total tax liability by "total," or economic, income. Here, the effective average rate of tax is only $4,900 ÷ $30,000 = 16.33 percent. Exhibit 11–2 summarizes the various tax rate computations that have been introduced in this section.

TAX PLANNING IN PERSPECTIVE

The entrepreneurial tax professional should not see tax planning as an end in itself. Rather, especially when dealing with individual clients, tax planning must be seen as part of two sets of major services provided by the practitioner, as illustrated in Exhibits 11–3 and 11–4. As we discussed in Chapter 1, tax planning is part of the entire menu of tax services that the tax professional makes available. Although the compliance and litigation aspects of the profession increasingly are shared with paraprofessionals (who prepare the bulk of tax returns for many professional firms) or attorneys (when a seemingly irresolvable conflict arises, usually between the client and the IRS), tax planning rightly is initiated by the well-educated and experienced tax practitioner.

Exhibit 11–3
Tax Planning in the Typical Tax Practice

TAX COMPLIANCE

| Tax Research | Tax Planning | Tax Litigation |

Exhibit 11–4
Tax Planning in the Client's Wealth Planning Process

EDUCATION PLANNING Trusts for Minors Special Investments		ESTATE PLANNING Asset Management Distributions and Control
RETIREMENT PLANNING Qualified Plans Nonqualified Plans Distributions Plans and Vehicles	**INCOME TAX PLANNING** Timing Tax Entity Exclusions and Deductions Income Classification Special Taxes Withholding Interest and Penalties	**INVESTMENT PLANNING** Risks Rewards Control Purchases/Sales Asset Allocation Regulations
CASH PLANNING Budgeting Finance		**RISK PLANNING** Insurance Security

Similarly, tax planning is but one of the various types of planning services that a tax professional offers to clients. As the U.S. population collectively ages, the importance of portfolio, estate, and retirement planning has increased. As the "baby boom echo" materialized in the early part of the twenty-first century, education planning again has taken center stage. Planning for cash and risk contingencies is mandatory for business clients, but even the most modestly endowed of individual clients can benefit from an introduction to such planning.

Thus, to the extent that the tax professional offers tax planning and counseling services, he or she must be facile with the rudiments of the planning process and with the dynamic nature of the evolution of the tax law as it affects planning engagements.

FUNDAMENTALS OF TAX PLANNING

As we noted in Chapter 1, tax planning is a completely legal means for saving taxes.[2] The basic objective of such planning is to arrange one's financial activities in a way that will reduce the present value of tax costs, such that maximum wealth accumulation can occur in the time period specified.

Opportunities for effective tax planning almost always are greater when tax effects are given consideration before transactions are finalized, rather than after they are completed. Decision makers should constantly be alert for tax-optimizing alternatives in the everyday conduct of their affairs. In other words, the first requirement for effective tax planning is **tax awareness** on the part of decision makers, rather than tax expertise by tax professionals.

---

2. Portions of this section are adapted from Raabe and Parker, *Tax Concepts for Decision Making* (St. Paul, MN: West Publishing Co., 1985).

Example 11–6 Russell and Phyllis Cohen, a married couple subject to a 30 percent marginal tax rate, currently are negotiating the purchase of their first home with the Hacienda Heights Construction Company, a land developer. The company has offered to sell the Cohens a selected house and lot at a price of $60,000, with a 20 percent down payment and 10 percent interest on annual payments over a five-year period. Under these terms, payments would be as follows.

Year	Beginning Balance	Interest	Principal	Total
0	$60,000	$ —	$12,000	$12,000
1	48,000	4,800	7,862	12,662
2	40,138	4,014	8,648	12,662
3	31,490	3,149	9,513	12,662
4	21,977	2,198	10,464	12,662
5	11,513	1,151	11,513	12,664
Totals		$15,312	$60,000	$75,312

The Cohens are aware that mortgage interest payments are tax-deductible and that the purchase price of a home is not. Thus, they make a counteroffer to purchase the home at a price of $54,445, with $12,000 down and 15 percent interest on annual payments over a five-year period. Under these new terms, Hacienda Heights receives the same cash payments (and gross income) as it did under the original terms. However, the amount of allowable deductions to the Cohens would be increased, with no change in total cash payments.

Year	Beginning Balance	Interest	Principal	Total
0	$54,445	$ —	$12,000	$12,000
1	42,445	6,367	6,295	12,662
2	36,150	5,423	7,239	12,662
3	28,911	4,337	8,325	12,662
4	20,586	3,088	9,574	12,662
5	11,012	1,652	11,012	12,664
Totals		$20,867	$54,445	$75,312

These results are not uncommon in a robust tax planning context. Often, decision makers can benefit by recognizing how the rearrangement of a planned transaction can produce tax savings, even if the economic substance of the transaction is left unaltered (or altered very little). The key, of course, is to pay close attention to the structural and transactional categories that have been established by Congress and the courts. In Example 11–6, by reclassifying a portion of their housing expenditures as (deductible) interest, rather than (nondeductible) principal, the Cohens were able to increase their allowable deductions and save taxes. Stated differently, the taxpayer's ability to conceptualize actions or events within stated legal definitions is of utmost importance.

Tax planning behavior can be characterized as falling into one or more of the general categories enumerated in Exhibit 11–5. Virtually every tax planning technique employed by the tax professional fits one or more of these overriding planning objectives.

AVOIDING INCOME RECOGNITION

Taxpayers often can reduce their exposure to taxation by avoiding the accumulation of gross income that must be recognized. This is not to suggest that a taxpayer should avoid accumulating real economic income. As long as marginal tax rates remain less than 100 percent, few people would be willing to go to that extreme. Rather, one usually should strive to obtain economic wealth in some manner that does not create recognized income under the tax law.

Example 11–7 Julie earned $3,500 when she sold the crop of fruits and vegetables that she grew, and she was subject to income tax on the full amount. Warren also grew a crop of produce of the same size, but he and his family ate the food. Thus, Warren recognized no gross income and paid no income tax relative to his gardening activities, but his family enjoyed $3,500 worth of fruits and vegetables.

Another method by which one can avoid obtaining recognized income is through the use of debt. Since neither the borrowing of money nor the receipt of funds that previously were lent generates gross income, taxpayers sometimes can use loans to avoid the recognition of taxable income on appreciated investments and enjoy the temporary use of the cash.

Example 11–8 Doug owns a tract of land that he acquired many years ago for $10,000. Currently, the land is worth $100,000. Doug needs $50,000 cash for a business venture. He is considering two alternatives: one is to sell half of the land and the other is to borrow the $50,000 by giving a mortgage on the land.

If Doug sells one-half of the land, he will recognize a $45,000 ($50,000 – 1/2 of $10,000) taxable gain. However, Doug recognizes no taxable income if he borrows the money, even though the amount that he borrows will be in excess of the basis of the land.

Example 11–9 Barbara Ward formed a new corporation by investing $100,000 cash. Following the advice of her tax consultant, Barbara designated $60,000 to be

Exhibit 11–5
Goals of Tax Planning Behavior

- Avoiding statutory income
- Postponing income recognition
- Changing tax jurisdictions
- Controlling the classification of income
- Spreading income among related taxpayers

used for the purchase of corporate stock and $40,000 as a loan to the corporation. In this way, if Barbara wants to receive large amounts of cash back from the corporation in the future, the entity simply will repay part or all of the loan principal to her, tax free, rather than making a large (taxable and nondeductible) dividend payment. Barbara also can direct the corporation to pay interest on the loan; such payments are deductible by the corporation. Of course, both interest and dividends are taxable to Barbara when she receives them.

Still another, and perhaps more obvious, way in which one can avoid the recognition of income for tax purposes is to take advantage of the many exclusions that the law permits. For example, an employee might arrange to receive certain nontaxable fringe benefits (such as health insurance) from the employer, in lieu of an equivalent value in (taxable) cash salary. This relationship should affect all negotiations as to compensation arrangements: the employer is indifferent between the two choices because both salary and fringe benefit payments are fully deductible against gross income, but the employee's after-tax wealth increases more where tax-free benefits are received.

Example 11-10 Lee Schrader, who is subject to a 40 percent overall marginal tax rate, is better off if she receives a tax-free fringe benefit than if she receives an equivalent raise in her salary.

	If Salary Increases	If Fringe Benefit Is Chosen
Value of compensation received	$2,000	$2,000
Tax on employee's compensation	− 800	
After-tax increase in employee's wealth	$1,200	$2,000

POSTPONING INCOME RECOGNITION

By delaying the recognition of income, one also delays the payment of the tax and, hence, can continue to enjoy the use of that tax money. Given the relatively higher interest rates that are anticipated in coming years, this delay takes on increased importance. At 12 percent annual interest, the present value of a $1,000 tax that is postponed for ten years is only $322. For longer periods and/or higher interest rates, the economic significance of the delay would be even greater. Appendix A includes a series of tables computing factors to reflect the time value of money.

Example 11-11 Agatha Fraser paid $1,000 for 4,800 Euros. At the same time, her sister, Betty, put $1,000 into a U.S. bank savings account. By the current year, the value of Agatha's Euros had increased to $1,800, and Betty's bank account had increased, due to interest accumulations, to the same amount. Since the increase in the value of the Euros was unrealized, Agatha had not been taxed yet on her $800 increase in economic wealth. On the other hand, Betty's increase was realized from interest that was credited annually to her account. Under the tax doctrine of *constructive receipt,* Betty had recognized gross income, accumulated over the nine-year planning period, of $800.

Example 11–12 Janie Heller owns land adjacent to her home that appreciated in value by $5,000 this year. However, because she did not sell the land, the appreciation in market value was not realized in a market transaction or recognized for income tax purposes. Janie has no recognized income from the land for that year.

Example 11–13 Janie Heller, of Example 11–12, paid interest of $4,000 on a mortgage that was used to finance her home and land investment. Janie can deduct the interest amount to offset the income that she derived from other investment sources in computing her taxable income. In effect, Janie is able to achieve a deliberate mismatching of current-year costs and unrealized revenues.

Example 11–14 Janie Heller, of Example 11–12, constructed an apartment building on her land, at a cost of $500,000, of which $475,000 was borrowed. By electing accelerated depreciation, which is based on the total $500,000 cost of the building rather than on Janie's $25,000 equity therein, Janie is able to take a depreciation deduction of about $24,000 in the construction year alone, nearly equal to her entire cash outlay for the current year.

CHANGING TAX JURISDICTIONS

Tax systems are not universal in breadth, nature, or application. Taxes are adopted by governmental jurisdictions, to be collected from those who live and do business within their boundaries. Often, by moving assets or income out of one tax jurisdiction and into another, tax reductions can be effected. Over time, governments tend to modify their tax systems to prevent the "leakage" of tax revenues through such cross-border transactions. Yet, in an effort to attract businesses and resulting jobs into their jurisdictions, governments often retain or create border incentives in the form of tax reductions that are limited in time or scope.

Example 11–15 The island country of Ricardo meets its revenue needs with tariffs on the fishing industry. Ricardo never has adopted an income tax system. Harris, a U.S. corporation, could build its new assembly plant through a wholly owned subsidiary incorporated and doing business only in Ricardo, thereby reducing its costs of conducting business because there is no income tax on executive salaries or annual profits. Perhaps by design, Ricardo has attracted new business, profits, jobs, and other benefits through its tax policies.

Example 11–16 State A includes in its statutory definition of taxable business income the interest paid on U.S. Treasury obligations. OneBank holds billions of dollars in Treasury notes, bills, and bonds, so, in an effort to reduce its tax costs, it creates a wholly owned subsidiary incorporated and doing business only in State B, which does not tax interest income. The subsidiary "repatriates" the interest to OneBank through quarterly dividend distributions, not taxed under the laws of State A. The economy of State A has been depleted because of its tax policy, but the taxpayer has responded with rational behavior in accord with its overall financial goals through judicious tax planning techniques.

CONTROLLING CLASSIFICATION OF INCOME

For Federal income tax purposes, several distinct categories of income, deductions, and credits are recognized. The most important of these are (1) ordinary income, which is fully taxable, and ordinary deductions, which decrease the tax base dollar for dollar; (2) investment or "portfolio" income, which usually is fully taxable except for tax-exempt state and local bond interest, and related expenses, which typically can be subtracted only against investment income; and (3) income from passive activities, such as the ownership of rental or "tax shelter" assets, which usually is fully taxable, and related expenses, which can be subtracted only against passive income.

In addition, a fourth classification of income and expenses should be identified. If the taxpayer is subject to the alternative minimum tax, preference and adjustment items, such as accelerated depreciation deductions, may be included, and other expenditures may not be available as deductions.

Effective tax planning often includes the proper identification or reclassification of income or expenditure items, using these statutory definitions.

Example 11–17 Phil Jankowski is the sole shareholder of a management consulting corporation. In addition, he has invested in tax shelter entities that are generating $40,000 per year in passive losses for him. According to the Code, such losses from passive activities cannot be applied as deductions to offset fully taxable income, for example, from Phil's salary or capital gain transactions. Accordingly, Phil cannot reduce current taxable income by the $40,000 passive loss from his tax shelter.

As the dominant shareholder of his corporation, however, Phil may be in a position to salvage the $40,000 deduction. If he reduces his salary from the corporation by $40,000 and takes instead from the corporation a $40,000 properly structured lease payment for the use of specified personal or real property that he owns but the corporation uses, like office equipment or automobiles, he may be able to create $40,000 in passive income from rental activities, against which the tax shelter loss can be offset.

Example 11–18 Matt Young Eagle is subject to the alternative minimum tax for the first time ever this year because he exercised the incentive stock options of his employer. Nonbusiness taxes paid and miscellaneous itemized deductions, among other familiar items, are not allowed as deductions when computing alternative minimum taxable income. Only certain tax credits are allowed against the AMT. Accordingly, Young Eagle should defer the payments of his fourth-quarter state income tax estimates and of the real estate tax on his home until next year, when the usual definitions of taxable income will apply to him again.

SPREADING INCOME AMONG RELATED TAXPAYERS

Because different types of legal entities are taxed separately and at different rates, an individual often can produce an overall tax savings by conducting various business and investment activities within separate taxpaying entities. The progressive nature of the various tax rate schedules further tends to increase the advantage of income splitting. This benefit might result from shifting income, either among different economic entities that are owned by the same individual or among the individual's family members. Accordingly, tax considerations often play an important role both in the selection of organizational forms for a business enterprise and in family financial arrangements.

Example 11–19 Bob and Lorraine Whitehead are currently providing for Lorraine's parents' retirement out of after-tax income. Given the Whiteheads' marginal income tax rate of 30 percent, $1,000 of pretax income is needed to produce $700 of savings [$1,000 − (0.30 of $1,000) = $700]. Assuming that the parents have a marginal income tax rate of only 18 percent, a transfer to them of $1,000 of pretax income, say, by the placement of income-producing assets into an appropriate trust, would raise the after-tax contribution to the parents' retirement to $820 [$1,000 − (0.18 of $1,000)].

Example 11–20 Sally Campbell is the sole shareholder and only employee of the Newark Corporation. The corporation's operating income this year is expected to be $125,000. Sally is subject to an overall marginal income tax rate of 30 percent. Sally wishes to know, considering only the Federal income tax, what amount of salary payments to her would produce the smallest combined tax for both herself and the corporation. Sally's income from other sources is sufficient to meet her living expenses and it precisely equals her total income tax deductions, so her taxable income is exactly equal to any salary that she receives from the corporation.

Currently, marginal corporate income tax rates do not exceed the 30 percent marginal individual tax bracket until corporate taxable income exceeds $75,000. Accordingly, the tax advisor should be certain to plan the corporation's compensation policy so that a corporate taxable income of at least $75,000 exists every year.

DEPARTING FROM THE FUNDAMENTALS

The general principles of tax planning that have been presented usually produce an optimal tax liability for the taxpayer. However, unusual circumstances may dictate that such principles should be violated purposely, to produce a desired effect. Again, however, the tax awareness of the parties is utmost in proper planning activities.

Example 11–21 Gretchen's manufacturing business is unincorporated. It has generated an operating loss of $265,000, which Gretchen can deduct on her tax return. Although there may be other tax uses for this loss, Gretchen may want to accelerate the recognition of other gross income into the current year, for example, by selling appreciated investments, exercising more sophisticated tax accounting elections, or simply sending out bills to customers in a more timely fashion. Economically, such income has been earned gradually by Gretchen, but it has had no tax effect yet because it has not been realized. Realization this year, however, will result in no tax liability for Gretchen because of the loss, so income acceleration should be considered.

Example 11–22 Brian's gross income is lower than he expected because of an unanticipated decrease in the sale of his homemade sandals. From a tax standpoint, it may be better to delay deductible expenditures of a discretionary or personal nature (e.g., advertising, medical expenses, and charitable contributions) until business picks up again. In this manner, the value of such deductions will increase, as will the marginal income tax rate to which he is subject.

Example 11–23 Dolores is subject to the alternative minimum tax this year, so her marginal tax rate is 24 percent, not the usual 36 percent. She might consider accelerating some gross income into the current year to take advantage of this structural decrease in her marginal tax rate. The tax advisor must be certain, though, to compare the present values of the resulting taxes, not just the nominal dollar amounts (i.e., the proper tax planning comparison is between the $32,400 and the $24,000), and Dolores should accelerate the gross income in this setting.

	If Regular Tax Applies, taxed next year	If AMT Applies, taxed this year
Nominal tax liability	$36,000	$24,000
Present value of tax liability	32,400	24,000

EXPLOITING INCONSISTENCIES IN THE STATUTE

INCONSISTENCIES BETWEEN TRANSACTIONS

Most forms of self-provided in-kind income go unrecognized for tax purposes. Often, the same items are not deductible, however, when they are purchased in market transactions. Thus, providing for one's own needs can be an important technique in managing the recognition of taxable income.

Example 11–24 Jerry has $50,000 in savings. If the money were invested in securities, the yield on his investment would be taxable, although no deduction would be allowed for his "personal" expense of renting a home. If the $50,000 were invested in a home for his own use, however, the net rental value of the home would escape taxation, since such in-kind value is not recognized as gross income under the law.

INCONSISTENCIES BETWEEN TAXPAYERS

Inconsistencies often exist between Code sections that control the recognition of income and those that control the allowance of deductions for the same items. When a transaction is between related taxpayers, such inconsistent treatments sometimes can be used to the taxpayers' advantage. The objective in such a situation usually is to structure the terms of the transaction so as to decrease taxable income to the taxpayer group as a whole.

Example 11–25 Marilyn is the sole owner-employee of a corporation. To the extent that the corporation pays dividends to Marilyn, she will recognize gross income, but the corporation will receive no deduction. To the extent that Marilyn is paid a reasonable salary, she will recognize gross income and the corporation will receive a deduction. To the extent that she receives certain employee fringe benefits, such as medical insurance, Marilyn is not required to recognize taxable income, and the corporation is allowed an ordinary business expense deduction. In summary, the payment of dividends increases combined taxable income of a shareholder and the corporation, the payment of salary does not change combined taxable income, and providing qualified fringe benefits reduces combined taxable income.

Example 11–26 Don and Ann Evans operate a farm, producing a net taxable income of about $30,000 per year. Their nondeductible expenses for housing average $12,000 per year.

The Evanses should consider forming a corporation and making a tax-free transfer of all of the farm property to the corporation, including their personal living quarters. As shareholders of the corporation, they could hire themselves as employees, with a requirement that they live on the business premises. The value of the lodging would not be taxable to the Evanses as individuals, under § 119 of the Code, but it would be deductible as a business expense of the corporation, thus reducing the corporation's taxable income before salaries to $18,000 ($30,000 − $12,000).

The Evanses then should have the corporation pay them reasonable salaries totaling $18,000. In this manner, taxable income of $18,000 would be taxed directly to them as individuals, and the corporation's taxable income would be reduced to zero, thus avoiding any double taxation. By using this combination of income splitting and an employee fringe benefit, the Evanses could effectively reduce their taxable income (i.e., from $30,000 to $18,000) by the amount of their lodging costs ($12,000), even though such costs are generally nondeductible by both self-employed persons and employees.

This result is based on the assumptions that $18,000 is a reasonable salary for the work that they perform, and that the requirement for living on the farm is for a bona fide business purpose (other than merely for tax avoidance).

INCONSISTENCIES BETWEEN YEARS

Another form of inconsistency concerns timing differences in the recognition of income and deductions. Such inconsistencies may relate to the transactions of one taxpayer, or they may concern two taxpayers engaging in a single transaction. In both cases, careful planning to take advantage of tax law inconsistencies can result in a considerable delay in the payment of taxes.

Example 11–27 Sarah Carter uses borrowed funds to acquire nondividend-paying corporate stocks. Appreciation on the stocks is not taxed until it is realized on the sale of the shares; yet, Carter might be able to claim investment-interest deductions for the interest that she pays on the borrowed funds.

Example 11–28 Harry Fischer is a 40 percent shareholder and junior executive of the Able Corporation. Harry's performance incentive bonus is set at 30 percent of the corporation's pre-tax earnings for the year. It is payable on January 31 of the following year.

Because the corporation is an accrual-basis taxpayer, the bonus is deductible in the year in which it is earned. As a cash-basis minority shareholder, however, Harry need not recognize the income until the following taxable year, (i.e., when he receives it). To the extent of Harry's bonus, the recognition of combined corporate and shareholder income thus is delayed for one year.

Example 11–29 Jane Summer is an employee of the Orange Corporation and is covered by the company's qualified pension plan. The corporation makes a contribution to the plan for Jane's retirement, which will occur in 30 years. Although Jane will not receive any gross income from the pension benefits until her retirement in 30 years, the corporation is entitled to a current-year business expense deduction.

AVOIDING TAX TRAPS

Ever since the enactment of the first income tax law, taxpayers have been trying to find ways to avoid such taxes. Likewise, Congress, the IRS, and the courts have enacted rules and doctrines to prevent, or at least restrict, various avoidance schemes. As a result, current tax law includes a maze of tax traps for the unwary.

STATUTORY TAX TRAPS

Many of the statutory provisions encountered in a tax planning context can best be understood when they are viewed as preventive provisions, that is, as rules designed by Congress to prevent certain techniques of tax avoidance. However, remember that any transaction that falls within the scope of a given provision, whether or not it is intended as part of a tax avoidance scheme, is subject to that provision. Thus, a basic knowledge of the tax system is necessary for the tax planner if certain disastrous pitfalls are to be avoided.

As we noted earlier in this chapter, income splitting between related taxpayers often can generate significant tax savings. To be effective for tax purposes, though, the income actually must be earned by the separate entities and not merely assigned by means of artificial transactions between them. Section 482 gives the IRS the power to reallocate both income and deductions among certain related taxpayers so as to reflect "true taxable income."

In applying § 482, the regulations indicate that the IRS's right to determine true taxable income is not limited to fraudulent or sham transactions, but also situations where income inadvertently has been shifted between controlled parties. The courts have held, however, that there truly must be a "shifting" of income before the IRS's power comes into play. Bona fide business transactions that bring tax advantages in their wake should not subject the related parties to reallocation. In concept, at least, § 482 can be applied by the IRS only where there has been some manipulation of income or deductions by the taxpayers.

Thus, while its boundaries are, in practice, both broad and sometimes hazy, § 482 does not prohibit the use of multiple entities for the purpose of earning income. It does, however, give the IRS a potent weapon with which to combat the artificial shifting of income between those entities.

Example 11–30 X and Y are two corporations that are fully owned by the same individual. X operates an international airline, and Y owns several hotels that are located in cities served by X. In conjunction with the advertising of its airlines, X often pictures Y's hotels. Although the primary benefit of the advertising is to X's airline operations, Y's hotels also obtain patronage by travelers who respond to the ads. X does not charge Y for the advertising. Because an unrelated hotel operator presumably would have been charged for such advertising, the IRS may make an allocation of income from X to Y to reflect the fair market value of the advertising services that were provided.

The Code restricts the amount of passive income that can be taxed at the (lower) marginal rates of one's dependent child who has not yet attained age 14, to less than $1,500 per year, an amount indexed for inflation. Any unearned income of the child that exceeds this amount is taxed to the child, but at the (higher) marginal rates of his or her parents. The purpose of this portion of the *Internal Revenue Code* is not to discriminate against children (who cannot vote in congressional elections), nor to place a higher tax burden on interest and dividend income, nor even to make the family the chief taxable unit in this country. Rather, the provision was enacted simply to discourage the shifting of taxable income from the higher tax brackets of the parent, through a temporary trust or some other accepted income-shifting vehicle, to the more favorable rates of the child, without any permanent loss by the parent of control over the use of the asset. Such tax planning techniques had been undertaken for many years, as a means (similar to that of Example 11–19) of accumulating after-tax contributions to an educational fund, by transferring income to the lowest marginal tax rates that were available within the family.

Whereas the objective of this part of the statute may be defensible by some, the broad provision that was enacted to implement it may create undue hardships in some circumstances, because it affects all taxpayers, not only those with the now-forbidden income-shifting motivation.

Example 11–31 Jimmy, age 7, received an inheritance from his grandmother's estate last year. Grandmother wanted Jimmy to attend a good graduate program in taxation someday, so she invested in high-income securities that produce about $12,000 in interest income annually. Jimmy's parents are to see that he accumulates this income for his education. The interest will be taxed at the parents' 40 percent marginal rate, however, and not at Jimmy's (zero and) 15 percent rate, so a smaller after-tax amount of this income will be available for this laudable educational purpose.

JUDICIAL TAX TRAPS

In the final analysis, the words of the tax law mean only what the courts say that they mean. Often, judicial decisions must be consulted to determine the allowable limits of various Code provisions.

Example 11–32 An employee-shareholder of a 50 percent family-owned corporation received an annual salary in excess of $1 million, an amount greater than that then paid to the heads of such corporations as General Motors and Sears.[3] Yet, despite IRS arguments to the contrary, the Tax Court upheld the entire amount paid as "reasonable" under the circumstances of the case because of the special talents and abilities that the employee brought to the corporation.

---

3. *Home Interiors and Gifts, Inc.*, 73 T.C. 92 (1980).

Example 11–33 A widow changed her will to disinherit her relatives and leave her assets to her attorney and his wife.[4] When the widow died, her relatives brought suit against the attorney, alleging that he had influenced the widow improperly through a personal relationship with her. The attorney paid them $121,000 to withdraw their litigation and deducted the payment as a business expense. The Tax Court upheld the deduction on the grounds that the payment was made for the purpose of maintaining the professional reputation of the lawyer.

On appeal, the Tax Court's decision was overturned. According to the appeals court, a taxpayer's reasons for paying do not determine whether the payment is deductible. Because the lawsuit arose from the attorney's personal relationship with the widow, the $121,000 settlement was deemed to be a personal, nondeductible cost.

Example 11–34 Housing is expensive in Japan. A unit of Mobil Oil owned the house that was used by its president, at his discretion, when he stayed in Japan.[5] The house would have rented for $4,400 a year in the United States, but in Tokyo its annual rental value was $20,000. The executive included it in income and paid tax on $4,400, the U.S. rental value. However, the IRS asserted that the full $20,000 should have been included in his gross income.

The U.S. Court of Claims agreed with the taxpayer, holding that the excess rental value was primarily of benefit to the company, rather than to the individual. The home's prestige value was held to be important to the employer because of social values that were peculiar to Japan, where, in the words of the court, "'face' is an almost tangible reality."

Two pervasive judicial doctrines that often limit the taxpayer's ability to employ effective planning techniques are the concepts of *business purpose* and *substance over form*. To be upheld for tax purposes, transactions must possess some nontax, or "business," purpose in addition to that of tax avoidance. Moreover, there is always the possibility that the court may ignore the form of a transaction if it perceives that such structural false colors cloud the actual substance of the arrangement.

Whenever a series of transactions results in significant tax savings, the IRS may attempt to apply the concept of substance over form by "telescoping" or "collapsing" several transactions into one. If it is upheld by a court, this *step-transaction doctrine* sometimes can negate what had been a good tax plan (where the steps were viewed as separate transactions). To guard against this possibility, the taxpayer should have a bona fide business purpose for each individual step in the transaction. Of course, documenting nontax purposes is usually much easier if the various transactions are separated by reasonable time spans, since they are then less likely to be viewed as component parts of an overall plan.

Example 11–35 Sandra is the sole shareholder of a real estate development corporation. On January 15, she purchased ten additional shares of stock from her corporation for $100,000. On the same day, she sold a tract of undeveloped land to the corporation for its fair market value of $100,000. To the corporation, the land will be inventory. For Sandra, it had been a capital asset, having been held for investment

---

4. *William J. McDonald, Jr.*, 592 F.2d 635, 78–2 USTC ¶ 9631, 42 AFTR2d 78–5797 (CA-2).
5. *Faneuil Adams*, 585 F.2d 106, 77–2 USTC ¶ 9613, 40 AFTR2d 77–5607.

purposes since its purchase ten years previously for $20,000. If these events are viewed as two separate transactions, Sandra will have increased the basis of her investment in the corporation by $100,000 and realized a fully taxable capital gain of $80,000 ($100,000 − $20,000). The corporation's basis in the land will be $100,000. Thus, if the corporation were to sell the land for, say, $110,000, its income therefrom would be only $10,000 ($110,000 − $100,000).

Alternatively, if these events are collapsed into a single transaction, Sandra's payment and receipt of cash would be ignored. Instead, she would be viewed as having given a tract of land in exchange for ten shares of stock of a corporation that she already controls. Under this single-transaction view, Sandra would recognize no taxable capital gain, and the corporation's basis in the stock would be the same as her prior basis, $20,000. Thus, if the corporation were to sell the land for $110,000, its ordinary income would be $90,000 ($110,000 − $20,000).

Taxpayers are restricted to the actual legal forms of the transactions in which they engage, but the IRS has the option of employing the step-transaction doctrine. Thus, the lack of any time lapse between the two transactions effectively gives the IRS its choice as to which interpretation it wishes to follow.

TAX PLANNING ILLUSTRATIONS

Consider several other examples of tax planning that are found in today's tax practice. Usually, a tax planning technique manifests at least one of the planning goals as listed in Exhibit 11–5. The best techniques meet two or more of those goals.

Example 11–36 Albert contributes the maximum amount for the year to an Education IRA for his daughter. No immediate deduction is allowed, but the earnings in the account never are taxed. Withdrawals similarly are excluded from gross income when they are used for education-related expenses. Result: *Avoiding statutory income.*

Example 11–37 Phil designates a portion of his monthly paycheck for medical and child care expenses. No payroll taxes are due on these amounts. Phil's employer reimburses him from these funds when it receives documentation from Phil that he incurred medical and babysitting expenses for the period. By using a "flexible spending plan" such as this one, Phil reduces his total tax liability and has more discretionary income for the year. Result: *Avoiding statutory income.*

Example 11–38 Mary Jane uses a depreciable asset in her business to generate net sales at a profit. The depreciation deductions shelter current sales income from tax, but because the tax basis of the asset is reduced accordingly, there is a greater gain computed when Mary Jane sells or retires the income-producing asset. Result: *Postponing income recognition.*

Example 11–39 Judy keeps a log of her travels so that she can document that she is a resident of Texas, not New York. As a result, Judy's state income tax liability is reduced significantly every year. Result: *Changing tax jurisdictions.*

Example 11–40 Because she is a citizen of the Cayman Islands and not the United States, Ingrid is subject to very low marginal estate and gift tax rates on her extensive portfolio and collectible holdings. Result: *Changing tax jurisdictions.*

Example 11–41 Fizzy Corporation holds some vacant land for potential expansion of its operating plant. By paving asphalt over the land and turning it into a parking lot, charging its executives a nominal fee so that they can park closer to their offices, Fizzy converts portfolio gain into passive income, which frees up deductions now suspended under the passive activity rules. Such passive income is taxed, however, only when Fizzy unilaterally decides to sell the vacant land. Result: *Controlling income classification. Postponing income recognition.*

Example 11–42 Ralph forms a partnership that borrows money and purchases an office building in Texas, which is the home state of none of the partners. The entity passes through net operating losses, made up chiefly of interest and depreciation deductions, which the partners use to offset their passive income from other sources. When the building is sold, state and local income and property taxes are relatively low under Texas law. Result: *Avoiding statutory income. Postponing income recognition. Changing tax jurisdictions. Controlling the classification of income. Spreading income among related taxpayers.*

Example 11–43 Carolyn sets up a charitable lead trust, under which the museum receives the trust's distributable net income for 15 years. Carolyn receives an immediate charitable contribution deduction, equal to the present value of the income stream that she has transferred to the museum. Then, the income producing property of the trust is deeded to Carolyn's granddaughter, thereby likely deferring any estate tax on the property for another 50 years. Result: *Avoiding statutory income. Postponing income recognition (and transfer tax). Spreading income among related taxpayers.*

Example 11–44 George renovates a downtown warehouse and turns it into condos and apartments. Because the building has some historic significance, George undertakes the rehabilitation so as to maximize his state and Federal tax credits for rehabilitation expenditures. Result: *Controlling income classification. Avoiding statutory income (creating tax credits).*

Example 11–45 Richie makes certain that he makes gifts every year of $11,000 to each of his relatives, thereby using the entire statutory annual gift tax exclusion. Result: *Avoiding statutory income (using transfer tax exclusions). Spreading income among related taxpayers.*

SUMMARY

The study of taxes can be viewed as an examination of various ways to optimize one's tax liability. Tax rules that otherwise might seem as dry as a mouthful of sawdust have a way of becoming interesting, stimulating, and challenging when one realizes their economic significance and the resulting implications on human behavior. Tax optimization, therefore, can be viewed both as the heart of professional tax work and as the most important aspect of taxation for nontax specialists.

TAX TUTOR

Reinforce the tax research information covered in this chapter by completing the on-line tutorials located at the Federal Tax Research web site:

http://raabe.swcollege.com

KEY WORDS

By the time you complete your work relative to this chapter, you should be comfortable discussing each of the following terms. If you need additional review of any of these items, return to the appropriate material in the chapter or consult the glossary to this text.

Average Tax Rate
Effective Average Tax Rate
Marginal Tax Rate
Nominal Average Tax Rate

Progressive Tax Rate
Proportional Tax Rate
Regressive Tax Rate
Tax Awareness

EXERCISES

1. Using the following codes, identify the basic approach(es) to tax avoidance that are used in each of the cases described below.

Av	=	Avoiding income recognition
Cl	=	Controlling the classification of income or expenditure
Ju	=	Changing tax jurisdictions
Po	=	Postponing income recognition
Sp	=	Spreading income among related taxpayers
None	=	None of the above

   a. Albert invests his savings in tax-exempt state bonds.
   b. Betty invests in nondividend-paying corporate stocks by using borrowed funds.
   c. Chuck lends $100,000 to his daughter on an interest-free demand note.
   d. Doris lends $10,000 to her son on a five-year note, bearing interest at the annual rate of 65 percent.
   e. Ed invests $100,000 of his savings in a home for his own use.
   f. Frankie invests in a mutual fund that purchases only the indebtedness of the state in which he lives.
   g. Grace invests in a mutual fund that purchases only the shares of U.S. corporations that pay no dividends, but whose share prices increase in value over a five-year time period.

2. Using the codes from Exercise 1, identify the basic approach(es) to tax avoidance that are used in each of the cases described below.

   a. Annie invests in a mutual fund that purchases only the shares of Colonnia corporations, a country that has no tax treaty with the United States.
   b. Burt moves his manufacturing plant to Mexico. Mexico has a tax treaty with the United States, but its labor and utility rates are much lower than is the case where Burt's Ohio plant now operates.

c. Cheryl moves her manufacturing plant to Allegro. Allegro has no tax treaty with the United States, and its labor and utility rates are much lower than is the case where Cheryl's Ohio plant now operates.
d. Donna fails to report on her tax return the interest earned on her savings account.
e. Evelyn has her controlled corporation pay her a salary instead of a dividend during the current year.
f. Flip operates his business as a regular corporation because of his high marginal tax rate. He plans to sell the corporation in five years.
g. Georgia grows most of her own food instead of taking a second job.

3. With respect to the system of coding used in Exercises 1 and 2, create one new illustration in each tax planning category.
4. How do taxes fit into the general economic goals of most taxpayers?
5. How might a tax advisor ignoring the present value approach to tax planning arrive at an improper conclusion? Illustrate.
6. Give some examples of U.S. taxes that employ proportional, progressive, and regressive rate structures.
7. Give an example of a transaction between two taxpayers in which an inconsistent treatment is afforded the two taxpayers. Explain how related taxpayers might structure a transaction to take advantage of this inconsistency.
8. Give an example to show when a taxpayer might consider shifting income from the ordinary classification to capital.
9. Name two types of tax traps and give an example of each.
10. How does the typical tax practitioner divide his or her time among planning, compliance, research, and litigation?
11. What planning engagements can the tax professional offer? Why is he or she in an ideal position to offer these services?
12. Summarize the most important planning services that a tax professional can offer to a client.
13. Why does tax planning analysis focus on the marginal tax rate?
14. When might a taxpayer undertake transactions seemingly opposite to the usual tax planning principles?
15. Higher income taxpayers tend to engage in tax planning more than do lower income taxpayers. Why?
16. Is the objective of tax planning always to minimize taxes? Explain.

PROBLEMS

17. Examples 11–2 and 11–3 in the text concern a decision between the same two mutually exclusive alternatives under identical conditions, except for the corporation's marginal tax rate. In Example 11–2, where the marginal tax rate was 40 percent, the conclusion was to accept Alternative A. In Example 11–3, where the marginal tax rate was 20 percent, the conclusion was to accept Alternative M.

    Determine the marginal tax rate at which the two alternatives would be economic equivalents, that is, they would generate the same excess after-tax payoff over after-tax cost. Your answer should be based on all of the conditions and assumptions as stated in Examples 11–2 and 11–3.

18. On creating a new 100 percent owned corporation, Ben was advised by his tax consultant to treat 50 percent of the total amount that was invested as a loan and 50 percent as a purchase of corporate stock. What tax advantage does this arrangement have over structuring the entire investment as a purchase of stock? Explain.
19. Julia currently is considering the purchase of some land to be held as an investment. She and the seller have agreed on a contract under which Julia would pay $1,000 per month for 60 months or $60,000 total. The seller, not in the real estate business, acquired the land several years ago by paying cash of $10,000. Two alternative interpretations of this transaction are (a) a price of $51,726 with 6 percent interest and (b) a price of $39,380 with 18 percent interest. Which interpretation would you expect each party to prefer? Why?
20. George, a high-bracket taxpayer, wishes to shift some of his own taxable income to his fifteen-year-old daughter, Debra, and is considering two alternative methods of doing so. One is to make a gift of the interest on some corporate bonds that he owns. The other is to make her a gift of the full principal amount of the bonds. Evaluate the pros and cons of each alternative.
21. Betty Smith has two sons, Bob and Jack. List several tax planning techniques that would allow Betty to transfer her full ownership in the family dry cleaning business to Bob and Jack, maximizing the wealth of all four taxpaying entities (Betty, Bob, Jack, and the company).

EXTENDED CASES

22. Should Ferris Corporation elect to forgo the carryback of its $60,000 year 2002 net operating loss? Ferris is subject to a 15 percent cost of capital. Corporate tax rates are as in IRC § 11.

    a.

Tax Year	Actual or Projected Taxable Income
2001	$700,000
2003	700,000

    b.

Tax Year	Actual or Projected Taxable Income
2001	$ 70,000
2003	700,000

    c.

Tax Year	Actual or Projected Taxable Income
2001	$ 70,000
2003	(70,000)
2004	(70,000)
2005	(70,000)
2006	700,000

23. Should Harris Corporation accelerate gross income into 2003, its first year subject to the alternative minimum tax? Harris is subject to a 15 percent cost of capital. The corporate AMT rate is a flat 20 percent, and Harris exceeds the annual AMT exemption phase out.

    a.

Tax Year	Actual or Projected Taxable Income
2004	Regular Tax $700,000
2005	Regular Tax $700,000

    b.

Tax Year	Actual or Projected Taxable Income
2004	AMT $700,000
2005	Regular Tax $700,000

    c.

Tax Year	Actual or Projected Taxable Income
2004	AMT $700,000
2005	AMT $700,000
2006	AMT $700,000
2007	AMT $700,000
2008	Regular Tax $700,000

24. Paris Corporation holds a $100,000 unrealized net capital gain. Should Paris accelerate the recognition of this gain, given a net capital loss carryforward in each of the following amounts? Paris is subject to a 15 percent cost of capital. Its marginal tax rate is 40 percent.
    a. $40,000
    b. $120,000

25. Maris Corporation put into service $100,000 of equipment that qualifies for its state's 10 percent research credit. To the extent that the credit is claimed, no cost recovery deductions are allowed. Maris is subject to a 15 percent cost of capital. If the credit were not claimed, the property would qualify for cost recovery deductions using a three-year life, straight line with no salvage value, and a half-year convention. The state's flat income tax rate is as follows.
    a. 2 percent
    b. 4 percent
    c. 8 percent

12

Working with the IRS

LEARNING OBJECTIVES

- Understand the organizational structure of the Internal Revenue Service and administrative procedures relative to the audit and appeals process
- Advise clients as to audit selection factors and probable litigation success
- Develop decision guidelines as to audit etiquette, working through the appeals system, and constructing taxpayer defenses

CHAPTER OUTLINE

Organization of the Internal Revenue Service
    IRS National Office
    IRS Service Centers
    Taxpayer Assistance Orders
    Local Taxpayer Advocates
Taxpayer Rights
The Audit Process
    Preliminary Review of Returns
        Mathematical/Clerical Error Program
        Unallowable Items Program
    Selection of Returns for Examination
        Discriminant Function System
        Taxpayer Compliance Measurement Program
        Other Selection Methods
        Chances of Audit

Examinations
    Correspondence Examinations
    Office Examinations
    Field Examinations
    Dealing with an Auditor
    Conclusion of Examination
    Thirty-Day Letter
    File a Protest or Go Straight to Court?
The Appeals Process
    Appeals Conference
    Ninety-Day Letter
    Entering the Judicial System

We have discussed various aspects of tax practice throughout this text, including both the principles of tax research and the structure of the judicial decision-making process. In this chapter, we will examine in more detail the workings of the **Internal Revenue Service** (IRS) and the **Treasury Department,** with an eye toward an overview of the elections and other opportunities and pitfalls that face the practitioner in working with these administrative bodies.

After all, when the researcher has decided that his or her client should prevail with respect to a specified tax issue, a challenge to the IRS must be issued and implemented. In this chapter, we present some of the procedural aspects of this course of action.

ORGANIZATION OF THE INTERNAL REVENUE SERVICE

The Department of the Treasury is responsible for administering and enforcing the internal revenue laws of the United States. However, most revenue functions and authority have been delegated by the Secretary of the Treasury to the **Commissioner of Internal Revenue.** The commissioner is the chief executive officer of the Internal Revenue Service and is appointed by the President of the United States. The Commissioner holds the responsibility for overall planning and for directing, coordinating, and controlling the policies and programs of the IRS.

The Internal Revenue Service is one of about a dozen bureaus within the Department of the Treasury. It was established by Congress on July 1, 1862, to meet the fiscal needs of the Civil War. At that time, the name of the agency was the Bureau of Internal Revenue. In 1953 the name was changed to the Internal Revenue Service.

Since 1962 the agency has undergone a period of steady growth as the means for financing government operations shifted from the levying of import duties on outsiders to one of internal taxation on U.S. citizens and businesses. This expansion increased substantially after 1913 with the ratification of the Sixteenth Amendment, which authorized the modern income tax on noncorporate entities.

Until 1951 the agency was organized on a type-of-tax basis (i.e., with income, alcohol and tobacco, etc., divisions), with jurisdictionally separate departments that were responsible for administering these different revenue sources. Since 1952 the agency has undergone five major reorganizations, including one in 1994 aimed at downsizing the organization. The most important aspects of these reengineering exercises have been the reorganization of the IRS along functional lines (i.e., into administration, operations, technical, planning, and inspection divisions), and the abandonment of the system of political appointments to positions other than that of the Commissioner and the Chief Counsel.

Another major restructuring effort was initiated in 1998, as a response to perceived abuses by the agency. Recognizing that most Commissioners serve only a short tenure and that the Treasury Department carries myriad duties, Congress believed that the addition of an IRS Oversight Board would improve the chances for the development of consistent long-term strategies and priorities. Private sector input is provided through the IRS Oversight Board, which functions as part of the Treasury Department. The Board has no authority to affect tax policy, to intervene in IRS personnel or procurement matters, or to affect the processing of individual tax cases. Its major duties include the following.

- Review and approve IRS mission, strategic plans, and annual planning documents.
- Review IRS operational functions, including modernization, outsourcing, and training efforts.
- Recommend to the President candidates for Commissioner.
- Review the process of selecting, evaluating, and compensating senior IRS executives.
- Review and approve the IRS annual budget request.
- Ensure the proper treatment of taxpayers.

The Board is designed to function like a corporate board of directors. It is made up of six members of the private sector, appointed to five-year terms by the President, and of the Treasury Secretary, the IRS Commissioner, and a representative of IRS employees.

IRS National Office

The IRS processes about 140 million tax returns every year, about 40 million of which are filed electronically. It collects almost $2 trillion in tax revenues and pays refunds to about 100 million taxpayers every year. Today, the IRS is an organization of about 100,000 employees. With the exception of the Department of Defense, it is the largest agency of the Federal government. It consists of a national office in Washington, D.C., and a large decentralized field organization. Its current mission statement is as follows, reflecting the "retail" and "service" orientation that the agency now has implemented.

Provide America's taxpayers top quality service by helping them understand and meet their tax responsibilities and by applying the tax law with integrity and fairness to all.

Exhibit 12–1 illustrates that the IRS is organized to facilitate both the processing of tax returns and the carrying out of its broader goals, using a "shared services" model like that used by most large businesses.

Exhibit 12–1 IRS National Office

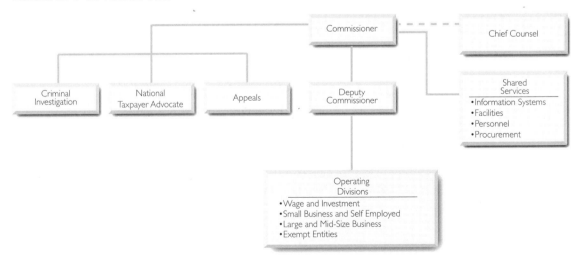

The IRS's national office is located in the District of Columbia. It is staffed by the office of the Commissioner of Internal Revenue, which includes a Deputy Commissioner and various chief officers and assistants to the Commissioner. The IRS Commissioner is appointed by the President to a renewable five-year term. He or she is the chief executive officer of the agency and is charged under § 7803(a) to administer, manage, conduct, direct, and supervise the execution of the Federal tax laws. The Commissioner's nomination is reviewed by the Senate. He or she must demonstrate some level of experience in the management of organizations. The Commissioner is the agency's final authority as to the interpretation of tax law.

The Chief Counsel is the agency's highest ranking legal adviser, and he or she reports to the Commissioner, relative to the administration and enforcement of the tax laws. In effect, the Chief Counsel is the IRS's attorney. Rulings and other written determinations are prepared by the Chief Counsel's office. The Chief Counsel represents the agency in Tax Court cases and often assists in preparing proposed legislation, treaties, regulations, and executive orders. Associate Chief Counsels are assigned duties relative to litigation, technical matters, international transactions, and finance and management.

The operating divisions of the IRS reflect the major types of tax return that the agency processes. Exhibit 12–2 provides estimates of the workload of each operating division.

The IRS also takes on national-level projects in working with taxpayers. Some of the most important of these recent initiatives include the following.

- Document matching, allowing a lower audit rate because deficiencies or refunds are sent out when data listed on a tax return does not match that on a corresponding source document, like a Form 1099 or W-2.
- Electronic filing, again to reduce error rates and improve compliance with the filing requirements and to enact a modernization of the agency's data processing functions.
- Extending the reach of the Earned Income Credit to more of the targeted low-income employees.
- Educating cash- and tip-oriented workers to comply fully with their filing requirements.

IRS SERVICE CENTERS

The first **Internal Revenue Service Center** was established in 1955 in Kansas City on a pilot basis. Later that same year, a second center was activated in Lawrence, Massachusetts. Additional service centers were established during the 1960s to meet the processing needs of the various geographic regions of the country. Today, 10 service centers serve the IRS regions. They are located at Andover, Massachusetts; Austin, Texas; Brookhaven, New York; Chamblee, Georgia; Covington, Kentucky; Fresno, California; Kansas City, Missouri; Memphis, Tennessee; Ogden, Utah; and Philadelphia, Pennsylvania.

The primary function of the service centers is to process and perform mathematical verifications of the massive volume of Federal tax returns. Statistical data are compiled at the IRS Data Center in Detroit, and special return-processing functions are performed at the National Computer Center in Martinsburg, West Virginia. In addition, **Computing Centers,** located in Detroit, Martinsburg, and Memphis, manipulate data collected from tax returns at **Processing Centers** in Austin,

Exhibit 12–2 IRS Operating Divisions

Tax Year 2000 estimates	Wage and Investment	Small Business and Self-Employed	Large and Mid-Size Businesses (Assets > $5 million)	Exempt Entities (Charities, Retirement Plans, Governments)
Type of return filed	1040 with only wage and investment income (no Schedules C, E, F, or Form 2106)	1040 Schedules C and F, Forms 1120, 1120S, and 1065	1040 Schedules C and F, Forms 1120, 1120S, and 1065	Form 990 and various payroll forms
Number of filers	90 million, 116 million taxpayers	45 million	210,000	3 million entities, 1.9 million pay tax
Annual income tax liabilities	$265 billion	$816 billion	$466 billion	$94 billion
Payroll taxes, withholdings paid	$38 billion	$562 billion	$712 billion	$198 billion
Notes	Fewer than half use a paid tax preparer. Only 2% earn >$100,000 per year, 85% earn <$50,000, 28% earn <$10,000	Pay in over 40% of all cash received by the IRS. 4–60 annual transactions with the IRS	Further organized into industry segments to handle complex filing requirements. About 10% are audited every year, some deal with IRS agents year-round	Control about $7 trillion in assets

Cincinnati, Kansas City, Memphis, and Ogden. About twenty-five **Customer Service Sites** deal with telephone and electronic contacts from taxpayers, in working with electronic filing of returns, and in answering telephone and online taxpayer inquiries.

TAXPAYER ASSISTANCE ORDERS

The **National Taxpayer Advocate** administers a taxpayer-intervention system, which is designed to resolve a wide range of tax administration problems that are not remedied through the agency's normal operating procedures or administrative channels. The Advocate reports directly to the Commissioner and works through a system of local Taxpayer Advocates, one of which is located in each state. The National Taxpayer Advocate has statutory authority to issue a **Taxpayer Assistance Order** (TAO) to suspend, delay, or stop actions where, in the determination of the Advocate, the taxpayer is suffering or about to suffer a significant hardship as a result of the manner in which the IRS is administering the revenue laws.[1]

1. § 7811.

"Hardships" refer to any circumstance that includes an immediate threat of adverse action for the taxpayer, his or her irreparable injury, a delay of more than 30 days in settling the taxpayer's account, or the incurring of significant costs (such as professional advisory fees) to handle the dispute. The IRS action that is the subject of a TAO must be such that it would offend one's sense of fairness, given all the related facts.

Typically, the TAO requires remedial actions, such as a release from the IRS's levy of specific property or the cessation of a collection activity, or it gives the IRS a deadline for action. A TAO is binding on the IRS, short of its rescission by the Advocate, the Commissioner, or a Deputy Commissioner.

A taxpayer applies for a TAO by filing Form 911, Application for Taxpayer Assistance Order (Taxpayer's Application for Relief from Hardship), reproduced as Exhibit 12–3.

LOCAL TAXPAYER ADVOCATES

The IRS uses local Taxpayer Advocates in a system designed to help resolve taxpayer problems or complaints that are not being satisfied through regular agency channels. The primary objective of the Advocate system is to provide taxpayers with a representative within the IRS who has access to the pertinent regional, district, or service center official. In addition, the program enables the IRS to identify its own organizational, procedural, and systematic problems and to take corrective action as needed.

The system is not intended to circumvent the existing IRS channels of managerial authority, established administrative procedures, and formal avenues of appeal. Rather, it is designed to ensure that taxpayer problems or complaints that have not been resolved adequately through such normal procedures are referred and controlled within the program. When a case is referred to a member of the National Taxpayer Advocate team, he or she will ensure that the problem is not lost or overlooked, and that it will be resolved as promptly and efficiently as is possible. If a case cannot be resolved within five working days after receipt of the statement of the problem or complaint, the taxpayer will be contacted by telephone, advised of the status of the case, and given the name and telephone number of the IRS employee who is responsible for the resolution of the problem. Typically, the Advocate system is used to resolve billing, procedural, computer-generated, and other problems that taxpayers cannot correct after one or more contacts with the IRS office that is handling the matter.

The National Taxpayer Advocate works through local team members who are responsible for the work that is conducted within his or her jurisdiction. Local advocates are independent from IRS examination, collection, and appeals functions. They are responsible only to the National Taxpayer Advocate.

TAXPAYER RIGHTS

Under three incarnations of the so-called *Taxpayer Bill of Rights,* taxpayers are guaranteed various rights to representation before the IRS, a recording of any proceedings, and an IRS explanation of its position relative to the pertinent disagreement. Specifically, the taxpayer has a right to know why the IRS is requesting information, exactly how the IRS will use the information it receives, and what might happen if

Exhibit 12–3 Application for Hardship Relief

OMB No. 1545-1504

Department of the Treasury – Internal Revenue Service

TAXPAYER ADVOCATE SERVICE

Application for Taxpayer Assistance Order (ATAO)

Form **911** (Rev. 3-2000)

Section I. — Taxpayer Information

1. Name(s) as shown on tax return
2. Current mailing address (Number, Street & Apartment Number)
3. City, Town or Post Office, State and ZIP Code
4. Your Social Security Number
5. Social Security No. of Spouse
6. Tax Form(s)
7. Tax Period(s)
8. Employer Identification Number (if applicable)
9. E-Mail address
10. Fax number
11. Person to contact
12. Daytime telephone number
13. Best time to call
14. Please describe the problem and the significant hardship it is creating. *(If more space is needed, attach additional sheets.)*

15. Please describe the relief you are requesting. *(If more space is needed, attach additional sheets.)*

I understand that Taxpayer Advocate employees may contact third parties in order to respond to this request and I authorize such contacts to be made. Further, by authorizing the Taxpayer Advocate Service to contact third parties, I understand that I will not receive notice, pursuant to section 7602(c) of the Internal Revenue Code, of third parties contacted in connection with this request.

16. Signature of taxpayer or corporate officer
17. Date
18. Signature of spouse
19. Date

Section II. — Representative Information (if applicable)

1. Name of Authorized Representative
2. Mailing Address
3. Centralized Authorization File Number (CAF)
4. Daytime telephone number
5. Fax number
6. Signature of Representative
7. Date

Cat. No. 16965S

Form **911** (Rev. 3-2000)

Exhibit 12–3 Application for Hardship Relief *(Concluded)*

Section III.   (For Internal Revenue Service only)

Taxpayer Name			Taxpayer Identification Number (TIN)		
1. Name of Initiating Employee	2. Employee Telephone Number	3. Operating Division or Function		4. Office	

5. How Identified & Received (Check the appropriate box)   6. IRS Received Date

    IRS Function Identified Issue as Meeting TAS Criteria
    ❏ (r) Functional referral (Functional area identified TP/Rep issue as meeting TAS criteria)
    ❏ (x) Congressional correspondence/inquiry not addressed to TAS but referred for TAS handling

    Taxpayer or Representative Requested TAS Assistance
    ❏ (c) Taxpayer or representative filed Form 911 or sent other correspondence to TAS
    ❏ (n) Taxpayer or representative called into a National Taxpayer Advocate (NTA) Toll-Free site
    ❏ (p) Taxpayer or representative called TAS (other than NTA Toll-Free)
    ❏ (s) Functional referral (Taxpayer or representative specifically requested TAS assistance)
    ❏ (w) Taxpayer or representative sought TAS assistance in a TAS walk-in area
    ❏ (y) Congressional corresp/inquiry addressed to TAS or any Congressional specifically requesting TAS assistance

7. TAS Criteria (Check the appropriate box)
    ❏ (1) Taxpayer is suffering or about to suffer a significant hardship
    ❏ (2) Taxpayer is facing an immediate threat of adverse action
    ❏ (3) Taxpayer will incur significant costs, including fees for professional representation, if relief is not granted
    ❏ (4) Taxpayer will suffer irreparable injury or long-term adverse impact if relief is not granted
    ❏ (5) Taxpayer experienced an IRS delay of more than 30 calendar days in resolving an account-related problem or inquiry
    ❏ (6) Taxpayer did not receive a response or resolution to their problem by the date promised
    ❏ (7) A system or procedure has either failed to operate as intended or failed to resolve a taxpayer problem or dispute with the IRS
    ❏ (8) Congressional Duplicate of any criteria or non-criteria case already in TAS or on TAMIS
    ❏ (9) Any issue/problem not meeting the above TAS criteria but kept in TAS for handling and resolution

8. Initiating Employee: What actions did you take to help resolve the problem?

9. Initiating Employee: State reason(s) why relief was not provided.

Section III Instructions (For Internal Revenue Service only)
1. Enter your name.
2. Enter your telephone number.
3. Enter your function (i.e.; ACS, Collection, Examination, Customer Service, etc.). If you are now part of one of the new Business Operating Divisions (Wage & Investment Income, Small Business/Self-Employed, Large/Mid-Size Business, Tax-Exempt/Govt Entity), enter the name of the division.
4. Enter the number/Organization Code for your office. (e.g., 18 for AUSC, 95 for Los Angeles).
5. Check the appropriate box that best reflects how the taxpayer informed us of the problem. For example, did TP call or write an IRS function or TAS? Did TP specifically request TAS assistance/handling or did the function identify the issue as meeting TAS criteria?
6. The IRS Received Date is the date TP/Rep first informed the IRS of the problem. Enter the date the TP/Rep first called, walked in or wrote the IRS to seek assistance with getting the problem resolved.
7. Check the box that best describes the reason/justification for Taxpayer Advocate Service (TAS) assistance and handling.
8. Indicate the actions you took to help resolve taxpayer's problem.
9. State the reason(s) that prevented you from resolving taxpayer's problem and from providing relief. For example, levy proceeds cannot be returned since they were already applied to a valid liability; an overpayment cannot be refunded since the refund statute expired; or current law precludes a specific interest abatement.

Section IV.   (For Taxpayer Advocate Service only)

1. TAMIS CF#	2. BOD/Client	3. How Recd Code	4. Criteria Code	5. IRS Recd Date	6. TAS Recd Date
7. Reopen Ind	8. Func/Unit Assigned	9. Employee Assigned	10. Major Issue Code	11. ATAO Code/Subcode	12. PSD Code
13. Special Case Code	14. Complexity Code	15. Outreach	16. Local Use Code ❏ TP _|_|_|_|_| ❏ Case _|	17. Relief Date	18. TAS Clsd Date
19. Cust Satisfact Cde	20. Root Cause Code				

Hardship ❏ Yes ❏ No	Taxpayer Advocate Signature	Date

Cat. No. 16965S   Form **911** (Rev. 3-2000)

the taxpayer does not submit the requested information. Accordingly, prior to an initial audit or collection interview, an IRS employee or officer must explain, orally or in written form, the pertinent aspects of the procedures to come.[2]

A taxpayer may be represented by an attorney, CPA, or other person who is permitted to represent a taxpayer before the IRS and who has obtained a properly executed power of attorney. Absent an administrative summons, a taxpayer cannot be required to accompany the representative to an interview. Moreover, if a taxpayer clearly states during an interview that he or she wishes to consult with such a representative, the interview is suspended until such counsel is secured.[3]

After meeting a 10-day notice requirement, the taxpayer is allowed to make a tape recording of the IRS interview, using the taxpayer's own equipment. Similarly, if the IRS intends to record an interview with a taxpayer or his or her representative, it must give a 10-day notice to the taxpayer. In addition, upon receiving a request from the taxpayer and a reimbursement for duplication costs, the IRS must make available to the taxpayer a transcript of the interview or a copy of its tape recording.[4]

To protect the rights of so-called innocent spouses on joint returns, the IRS must inform spouses of their joint and several liability for tax deficiencies, and both spouses must receive separately mailed notices as to audit, appeals, and Tax Court proceedings. This may be especially important where the spouses have divorced or separated subsequent to filing the original joint return.

The Service must inform taxpayers of their rights to representation in carrying out a dispute with the agency and of rights to suspend at any time an interview with IRS personnel so as to include their representatives.

With respect to noncriminal tax matters before the IRS or a Federal court, the common law privilege of confidentiality exists between a taxpayer and his or her tax practitioner, that is, one who is authorized to practice before the IRS. The privilege exists with respect to tax advice the practitioner has rendered. These provisions extend existing privilege protection previously only applicable between a taxpayer and his or her attorney. The privilege does not exist with respect to dealings with tax shelters.

THE AUDIT PROCESS

The U.S. Federal income tax system is based primarily on an assumption of self-assessment. All persons with taxable incomes that exceed a specific amount are required to prepare an accurate statement of annual income (i.e., an income tax return) and to remit in a timely fashion any amount of tax that is due. In a somewhat paternalistic sense, the IRS uses the examination of returns as an enforcement device to promote such voluntary compliance with the internal revenue laws. In a manner that is somewhat similar to the treatment by a parent of a child who is considering some forbidden behavior, the threat of an IRS audit encourages many taxpayers to report accurately their taxable incomes and to pay any tax liability that remains outstanding.

Because only a small number of tax returns can be audited each year, the IRS attempts to select for examination only those returns that will generate additional rev-

---

2. § 7521(b)(1).
3. §§ 7521(b)(2) and (c).
4. § 7521(a).

enues for the Treasury. It primarily relies on sophisticated statistical models and computer technology to identify those returns that possess the greatest revenue return for the agency's investment of audit resources. However, in addition to this scientific selection process, a number of returns are manually selected for examination at an examiner's discretion.

PRELIMINARY REVIEW OF RETURNS

All business and individual tax returns are reviewed routinely by IRS personnel for simple and obvious errors, such as the omission of required signatures and Social Security numbers, at one of the service centers. After this initial (often computer-based) review, income tax returns are processed through the IRS Automatic Data Processing (ADP) program.

One of the most important functions performed by the ADP program is the matching of the information recorded on a return with corresponding data received from third parties, for example, from an employer on Form W-2. This procedure, which is referred to as the Information Document Matching Program (IDMP), has uncovered millions of cases of discrepancies between the amount, say, of income that recipients have reported on tax returns and corresponding deductions or other information that has been transmitted by payors. In addition, the IDMP provides the IRS with a means by which to detect taxpayers who fail to file any return at all. In the typical year, about 5 million taxpayers are sent such failure-to-file inquiries as a result of the matching program.

ADP is also used to conduct the Service's Mathematical/Clerical Error Program. This process is designed to uncover relatively simple and readily identifiable problems that can be resolved easily through the mail.

Mathematical/Clerical Error Program

The Mathematical/Clerical Error Program is one of a number of special programs that are conducted at the service centers. This program checks every return for mathematical errors, recomputes the tax due after properly applying the numbers that are included in the return, and summarily assesses any additional tax that is due or allows refunds or credits based on (previously) miscomputed deductions or credits. A summary assessment may be made concerning any deficiency that results from a mathematical or clerical error.[5] Consequently, the IRS need not send the taxpayer a formal notice of deficiency (i.e., a ninety-day letter, as discussed subsequently in this chapter) before the additional tax is assessed.

When a mathematical or clerical error is identified by the service center, the IRS mails the taxpayer a corrected tax computation and requests that he or she pay the additional tax within 10 days of the date of the notice, or 21 days if the tax underpayment is less than $100,000. If the deficiency is paid within this period, no interest is charged on the underpayment. However, if the deficiency is not paid in a timely fashion, interest is imposed on the unpaid amount for a period that begins on the date of the notice and demand and ends on the date of payment.

A taxpayer may not petition the U.S. Tax Court with respect to a deficiency that results from a mathematical or clerical error. However, other administrative procedures will allow the taxpayer to contest the summary assessment without first paying the tax.

5. § 6213(b)(1).

The IRS must give an explanation of the asserted error to the taxpayer. After receiving this explanation, the taxpayer has 60 days within which to request that the additional tax be abated. If a request for abatement is made, the assessment will be canceled automatically. However, the return is then identified for further examination if the taxpayer cannot justify satisfactorily or substantiate the figures that were included on the original return.

When an error results in a taxpayer overpayment of the tax, the IRS usually sends a corrected computation of the tax, together with a brief explanation of the error and a refund of the excess amount that was paid.

The IRS does not consider such a contact that it makes with the taxpayer to be an examination. Therefore, a taxpayer who is contacted under Mathematical/Clerical Error Program is not entitled to the administrative remedies that are available to taxpayers who are involved in a formal examination.

In addition to this testing of mathematical computations, the ADP program is useful for verifying one's compliance with estimated tax payment requirements. As a result of utilizing this system, the IRS has discovered that thousands of taxpayers have not been complying with the statutory estimated tax requirements, and that others collectively have been claiming millions of dollars in payments that actually never were made.

Unallowable Items Program

The IRS conducts another program at each service center that is similar to the Mathematical/Clerical Error Program called the Unallowable Items Program. Under this program IRS personnel at each service center question items that have been included on individual income tax returns that appear to be unallowable by law. These items may be identified manually or on their face by computer, and include such return elements as an overstatement of the standard deduction, the claiming of an incorrect filing status, the deduction of Federal income taxes, or the deduction of lost (but not stolen) assets as a casualty loss.

If a return is identified as including an unallowable item, the IRS computes the seemingly necessary adjustment in taxes, and the taxpayer is notified by mail. Again, the IRS does not consider the contact that it makes with a taxpayer under the Unallowable Items Program to be an examination. Consequently, it treats an adjustment in this circumstance as a correction of a mathematical or clerical error, and the taxpayer is not sent a formal notice of deficiency.

If the taxpayer is able to explain the questioned item adequately, the assessment is abated. However, the case will be continued as a correspondence or office audit if the taxpayer's response is deemed unsatisfactory.

SELECTION OF RETURNS FOR EXAMINATION

Each year the IRS determines the approximate number and types of returns that it intends to audit. The national office then prepares an audit plan to allocate its personnel to achieve the desired audit coverage. The primary goal of the IRS in selecting a return for examination is to review only those returns that will result in a satisfactory increase in the tax liability.

Computer and manual methods are used to select returns for examination. Computer programs select certain returns for examination, based on the potential that exists for changes in the tax treatment of certain items on the return. Generally, this is done through the use of mathematical models, including correlations and discriminant functions. IRS personnel also manually select returns that they believe warrant special attention. The Service describes in nontechnical terms its selection procedures in its annual Publication 1.

Although an increasing amount of the initial IRS screening of the returns for audit is performed by computers, a most detailed selection procedure is employed manually in the Examination Division of the District Director's office, where the classification staff ultimately selects those specific cases that will be examined. The number of returns that finally is selected by the staff is based on the examination resource (and other) capabilities of the respective district offices.

Discriminant Function System

Once a return has been processed through the Service's ADP program, a magnetic tape that contains the information from each return, as prepared at the service center, is sent to the National Computer Center in Martinsburg, West Virginia. There, each return is rated by computer for its audit potential by means of a mathematical model, the **discriminant function formula** (DIF). This formula assigns numeric weights to certain (undisclosed by the IRS) return items, generating a composite score for the return. In this regard, the higher the DIF score, the greater the potential for a favorable-to-the-Treasury change to the return upon audit. Statistics provided by the Commissioner show a high correlation between DIF scores and such tax modifications.

When the computer selects a return that has a high probability for an adjustment, as indicated by a high DIF score, an employee at the service center manually inspects the return to confirm its audit potential. If an acceptable explanation for the DIF score cannot be found after this manual examination of the return and its attachments, including explanatory data that the computer did not consider, the return is forwarded to the Examination Division at the appropriate district office.

Taxpayer Compliance Measurement Program

The Taxpayer Compliance Measurement Program (TCMP) is a research program that is designed to furnish the IRS with statistics concerning the type and number of errors that are made on a representative sample of individual income tax returns. These statistics then are used to develop and update the DIF formulas. Under the TCMP procedures, 50,000–100,000 individual income tax returns are selected randomly for an extremely thorough examination, based on the ending digits of the taxpayer's Social Security number. These returns then are examined comprehensively to determine the degree of their accuracy as filed.

Unlike the treatment that is given returns that are selected for general audit, the TCMP examiner may not exercise any judgment in dealing with an item on the return. Every item must be substantiated, and all errors must be noted and corrected, regardless of their amount. This procedure is necessary to a determination of the actual error patterns that individual income tax returns exhibit, so that the statistics that underlie the DIF procedure are free from any major bias. TCMP audits last took place more than a decade ago, and they now are out of political favor. Thus, data underlying the assumption of the DIF procedure are quite dated and likely are significantly inaccurate in today's economy. Because of the stresses that the TCMP places upon taxpayers, this procedure has not been funded by the Treasury for almost two decades. This means that the data underlying the discriminant functions upon which returns are selected for audit are almost a generation old.

Other Selection Methods

In addition to the previously discussed computerized methods for identification of returns for IRS examination, returns may be selected manually, for a variety of reasons. An examination may be initiated, for instance, because of information that is provided by an informant or because the selected return is linked to another return that is currently under examination (e.g., a partner's return may be selected as a result of a partnership audit).

Moreover, some returns automatically are reviewed by IRS personnel because the reported taxable income, gross receipts, or total assets exceed a predetermined materiality amount. For instance, individual returns with total positive income of $50,000 or more, or partnership returns with gross receipts or gross income of $500,000 or more, can be selected in this manner. Finally, a return may be selected for examination because the taxpayer has filed a claim for refund or otherwise has indicated that an adjustment in the original amount of tax liability is necessary.

"Economic reality" factors can be considered by the IRS in selection of returns for audit, but only where the agency has some other evidence that the taxpayer has underreported taxable income for the year. For instance, manual selection of a return and an economic-reality review might occur when an IRS employee, reviewing data in three-filing-year periods, finds indications that income might be underreported or deductions might be overstated or misclassified. Some of the factors believed to be perused in an economic reality audit include the following. Some IRS officials maintain that the agency no longer uses economic reality audits.

- Significant increases in interest, dividend, and other investment income.
- Significant decreases in mortgage and other reportable interest paid.
- Significant variance in self-employment or farming income during the period, relative to industry norms.
- Business and other expenditures not seemingly justified by income levels.

Chances of Audit

Taxpayers often want to know what their overall probability of selection for an audit might be for a given year. In general, the IRS selects less than 1 percent of all returns for examination, and this figure includes the results of the mathematical error program. The chances for selection increase, though, if the taxpayer:

- claims tax shelter losses;
- claims office-in-the-home deductions;
- operates a cash-oriented business, such as a restaurant (both as an owner, selling food and drink for cash, and as a waiter, collecting tips) or repair/construction trade;
- claims business deductions that are excessive for the income level;
- has had prior-year returns that were audited and found incorrect; or
- claims itemized deductions that are excessive for the income level.

Relative to the last point, one should not hesitate to claim all legitimate deductions, but it is useful to know what raises the IRS's "red flag" for itemized deduction amounts.

The data in Exhibit 12–4 were current for calendar-year 1999 returns. They vary quite a bit from state to state, given differing income levels, types and deductibility of state and local taxes, and spending patterns. For instance, with respect to taxpayers with adjusted gross income between $100,000 and $200,000 in 1999, Florida residents averaged $4,440 in itemized deductions, while New Yorkers averaged $13,188.

Note also in Exhibit 12–4 the varying degrees to which taxpayers itemize deductions, approaching (but not attaining) 100 percent at upper income levels. Nonitemizers at upper income levels usually indicate the lack of a state income tax, a paid-up residence, or the presence of comprehensive health insurance coverage.

The probabilities of selection for audit in a recent tax year were as shown in Exhibit 12–5. IRS work plans indicate that audit rates are likely to be somewhat lower in the future than they have been historically.

EXAMINATIONS

After a return is selected for audit, an IRS agent schedules it for a review in either a correspondence, office interview, or field examination. The type of examination to which the taxpayer is subject generally is determined by the audit potential of the return, the nature of the asserted error, and the type of taxpayer.

CORRESPONDENCE EXAMINATIONS

Many times, IRS personnel at a service center or a district office will question only one or two items on a selected return. In these cases, an examination is typically conducted by telephone or mail. The IRS examiner will request that the taxpayer verify the questioned item of income, deduction, or credit by mailing copies of receipts, canceled checks, or other documentation to the district office or service center. If the taxpayer requests an interview, the issues become too complex, or the taxpayer is unable to communicate effectively in writing, the case is referred to the appropriate district office for resolution as an office or field examination.

District office personnel usually conduct **correspondence examinations.** However, service center staff will conduct such a review if the questioned item is an itemized deduction on an individual taxpayer's income tax return.

Exhibit 12–4 Average Itemized Deductions

AGI ($000)	0–15	15–30	30–50	50–100	100–200	200+
Medical	$ 7,500	$ 5,137	$ 4,992	$ 5,950	$10,494	$32,259
Taxes	1,963	2,200	2,991	4,918	9,262	36,592
Contributions	1,350	1,619	1,774	2,282	3,727	19,454
Interest	5,958	5,866	6,247	7,544	10,806	21,735
Total	11,511	10,627	11,770	15,228	23,500	64,996
Percent Itemizing	3.56%	14.64%	36.66%	69.58%	90.49%	92.46%

Exhibit 12–5
Various Audit Statistics

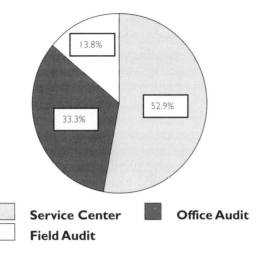

Individuals' returns filed	118,362,600	
Individuals' returns audited	1,519,243	1.28% of filed returns
Office audits	505,834	
Field audits	209,781	1.1% of Schedule Cs
		2.5% of corporate returns

Chances of Audit

Individual's Total Positive Income ($000)	Nonbusiness Returns	With Schedule C
0–25	1.39%	3.19%
25–50	0.70	2.57
50–100	0.77	2.57
100+	2.27	4.13
S Corporation		1.04
Partnership		0.59
Gift Tax		0.9
Estate Tax, Gross Estate ($000,000)		
0–1		6.83
1–5		18.88
5+		47.43

Average proposed tax and penalty assessment, individuals' returns

Office audit	$ 3,051
Field audit	15,942
Service Center (math/clerical)	1,714

"No change" audit report

Office audit, individuals' return	14%
Field audit, individuals' return	8
Service Center correspondence	35
Office audit, corporate return	24
Field audit, corporate return	47

A taxpayer who is subject to a correspondence examination is entitled to the same administrative and judicial appeal rights that are allowed to persons who are involved in office or field audits.

Issues that typically are addressed in the correspondence audit setting include itemized deductions for interest, taxes, charitable contributions, medical expenses, and simple miscellaneous deductions such as union dues.

OFFICE EXAMINATIONS

When a return that has been selected for examination involves one or more issues that will require some analysis and the exercise of the IRS personnel's judgment, rather than a mere verification of record-keeping requirements, the audit is usually conducted at the pertinent IRS district office. An office interview also will be scheduled if the examiner believes that an office examination is necessary to guarantee that the taxpayer's legal rights will be respected.

If the IRS decides to conduct an office examination, the taxpayer is asked to come to the district office for an interview and to bring any records and documents that will support the questioned items. Generally, the auditor is given very little time in which to prepare for the session, and the scope of the examination is limited to the items that are listed in the audit notification letter.

Office audits are usually confined to individuals' income tax returns that include no business income. However, in recent years, the IRS has increased the scope of some office audits to include a limited number of small business returns. Issues that typically are examined in an office audit setting include dependency exemptions; income from tips, rents, and royalties; income from partnerships, estates, and trusts; deductions for travel and entertainment; deductions for bad debts; and casualty and theft losses.

A field examination may be conducted in lieu of an office audit if it is difficult for the taxpayer to bring the requested records to the district office or if the taxpayer for some other valid reason requests that the audit be conducted on his or her premises.

FIELD EXAMINATIONS

Examinations that present complex issues that require more advanced knowledge of the internal revenue laws and accounting skills usually are conducted on the taxpayer's premises. A **field audit** is more comprehensive than a correspondence or office audit, and it usually is limited to an examination of corporation and individual business returns. In a field examination, the revenue agent reviews completely the entire financial operations of the taxpayer, including the business history of the taxpayer; the nature, amount, and location of taxpayer assets; the nature of the business operations; the extant accounting methods and system of internal control; and other financial attributes of the entity.

While an office audit ordinarily is limited to the items that are specified in the audit notification letter, a field examination may be open-ended. The agent is free to pursue any unusual items that are recorded in the tax return(s) or the records of the taxpayer (i.e., journals, ledgers, and worksheets) and to investigate other areas of which he or she may be suspicious.

The IRS prefers to conduct the field audit on the taxpayer's premises because the taxpayer's books and records may be more accessible and the agent will be better able to observe the taxpayer's business facilities and the scope of its operations. However, it is sometimes possible to have the audit conducted at the office of the taxpayer's representative instead. Only one such inspection of taxpayer books and records may be made for a tax year.[6] The Code includes a broad set of restrictions as to access to the taxpayer's physical office by the IRS.[7] Taxpayers refusing to admit IRS personnel are subject to a $500-per-refusal fine.[8]

The IRS uses a team approach in its field audits, known as the Coordinated Examination Program, when it examines the returns of large corporate taxpayers. During this type of examination, a large group of IRS agents will be used to investigate the operations of the taxpayer. Normally, such an investigation will span more than one IRS district as well.

Dealing with an Auditor

Most practitioners develop over time a list of "dos and don'ts" in negotiating with a government auditor. In the very best case, one will have dealt with the same auditor many times and will have become familiar with the nuances of that particular auditor's mode of operation. Whether this is the case or not, the following guidelines, dictated as much by common courtesy and decorum as by ethics and hardcore negotiating techniques, are likely to be useful.[9]

- Do conduct yourself courteously and professionally, showing that you have prepared yourself for the audit.
- Do review the strengths and weaknesses of your position before the agent arrives.
- Do cooperate with the auditor and promptly respond to all requests.
- Do establish internal timetables and responsibilities for completing the audit.
- Do provide the auditor with adequate work accommodations.
- Don't impede the audit process.
- Don't allow the auditor free access to and through the taxpayer's building.
- Don't let the agent browse through taxpayer information.
- Don't volunteer comments or information not requested by the agent.
- Don't attempt to bully or intimidate the auditor.
- Do assign one person to be the primary on-premises contact with the auditor—he or she cannot interview taxpayer employees on a random basis.
- Do verify the auditor's credentials before providing any information.
- Do request that all communications be in writing.
- Do keep track of time spent (by taxpayer, practitioner, and auditor) on the audit.
- Do meet at least daily with the auditor to review issues.
- Do agree to disagree on major irreconcilable issues.
- Do conduct a concluding conference to discuss audit recommendations.

6. § 7605(b).
7. § 7606.
8. § 7342.
9. Some of the material is adapted from a talk by Robert E. Dallman, "The Audit Process."

- Do obtain copies of all government workpapers affecting the potential assessment.
- Do request clarification of the rest of the appeals process.

CONCLUSION OF EXAMINATION

Upon the conclusion of the examination, the IRS auditor or agent must explain to the taxpayer any proposed adjustments to the tax liability. A written **Revenue Agent's Report** (RAR) is prepared by the agent and is given to the taxpayer. The RAR contains a brief explanation of the proposed adjustments and lists the balance due or the overpayment.

The RAR also includes a waiver of the restrictions on assessment, which the taxpayer is asked to sign if he or she agrees with the proposed modifications. This waiver will permit the IRS to assess any deficiency in tax immediately, without sending the taxpayer a formal notice of deficiency.

Even though the taxpayer may agree with the proposed adjustments to his or her return and sign the form, thereby indicating acceptance of the proposal, the case technically is not closed until the agent's report is reviewed and accepted by the district office review staff. Therefore, it is possible that an agreement that is worked out with the agent may not be accepted by the IRS.

After the taxpayer agrees to any increase in tax, he or she may either make an advance payment of the deficiency and accrued interest, to eliminate additional interest charges, or wait for a formal request for payment from the service center.

If the taxpayer disagrees with the agent's proposals, the IRS will make an immediate attempt to resolve the disagreement. The taxpayer normally will be given an opportunity to discuss the proposed adjustments with the agent's group supervisor or with an appeals officer. If an immediate interview is not possible or if the issues remain unresolved after such an interview, the taxpayer will receive a preliminary notice of deficiency, which is also referred to as a "thirty-day letter."

THIRTY-DAY LETTER

When the taxpayer does not agree with the agent's proposed adjustments, a **thirty-day letter** is issued. This correspondence formally notifies the taxpayer of the examiner's findings, requests that the taxpayer agree to the proposed adjustments, and informs the taxpayer of his or her appeal rights. If the taxpayer does not respond to the notice within 30 days, he or she will receive a statutory notice of deficiency, also known as a "ninety-day letter," discussed later in this chapter.

The taxpayer has 30 days from the date of the thirty-day letter to request a conference with an appeals officer. This request may be made orally with respect to an office examination or if the total proposed additional tax and penalties total $2,500 or less. The taxpayer's appeal must be in written form if the total proposed additional tax and penalties exceed $2,500,[10] and a formal protest, setting forth the specific facts and applicable law or other authority in support of the taxpayer's position, is required if the proposed tax and penalties exceeds $10,000.[11]

10. Reg. §§ 601.105(c)(2)(iii) and (d)(2)(iv).
11. Reg. §§ 601.105(d)(2) and 601.106(a)(1)(ii).

FILE A PROTEST OR GO STRAIGHT TO COURT?

In deciding whether to file a protest and request a hearing in the appeals office or to allow a ninety-day letter to be issued and skip directly to the courts for satisfaction, the taxpayer and his or her advisor must consider a number of factors.[12]

Factors in Favor of the Protest/Appeals Process

- An appeals officer can consider the hazards of litigation. This allows for the possibility of a settlement without the costs of litigation.
- The litigation path remains a possibility even if an appeal is pursued.
- The appeals process allows a further delay in the payment of the disputed tax. This can be an important criterion if (1) funds are not available with which to pay the tax, and (2) the taxpayer can earn more on the funds during the administrative period than is assessed in the form of interest.
- During the appeals process, the taxpayer will discover more of the elements of the government's position. In addition, the taxpayer will gain additional time in which to formulate or polish his or her own position.
- Recovery of some court costs and attorney fees is available if the court finds that the government's case was largely unjustified and all administrative remedies were attempted. Thus, working through the appeals process is required if any costs are to be recovered.

Factors in Favor of Bypassing Appeals

- The likelihood of the government finding and raising new issues during the appeal is eliminated.
- The government receives a psychological message that the taxpayer is firmly convinced of his or her position, and negotiating advantages for the taxpayer may result.
- The conclusion of the dispute, whether for or against the taxpayer, is expedited.

THE APPEALS PROCESS

To minimize the costs of litigation in both time and money, the IRS encourages the resolution of tax disputes through an administrative appeals process. If a case cannot be resolved at the examination level, the taxpayer is allowed to appeal to a separate division of the IRS, known as the **Appeals Division.**

The Appeals Division has the exclusive and final authority to settle cases that originate in a district that is located within its jurisdiction. This division is under the supervision of the Commissioner of the IRS, with input from the Chief Counsel. The appeals function provides the taxpayer with a final opportunity to resolve tax disputes with the IRS without incurring litigation. Its objective is to resolve tax controversies without litigation on a basis which is fair and impartial to both the government and the taxpayer.

---

12. Saltzman, *IRS Practice and Procedure,* Warren, Gorham & Lamont; ¶ 9.04(1).

Appeals Conference

The conference with the appeals officer is an informal proceeding. Although the appeals office may require allegations to be submitted in the form of affidavits or declarations under the penalty of perjury, testimony typically is not taken under oath.[13] The taxpayer, or his or her representative, meets with the appeals officer and discusses the dispute informally. According to the IRS's conference and practice rules, the appeals officer is to maintain a standard of strict impartiality toward the taxpayer and the government.

The appeals officer has the authority to settle all factual and legal questions that are raised in the examiner's report. He or she also can settle a tax dispute on the basis of the hazards of litigation. However, no settlement can be made that is based on the nuisance value of the case to the government.

The appeals officer may use a considerable amount of personal judgment in deciding how to handle the disputed issues of a case. He or she can split or trade issues where substantial uncertainties exist as to the law or the facts. On the other hand, the appeals officer may defer action on, or refuse to settle, a case or an issue to achieve greater uniformity concerning the application of the revenue laws and to improve the overall voluntary compliance with the tax laws.

Ninety-Day Letter

If the taxpayer and the IRS cannot agree on the proposed adjustments after an appeals conference, the regional director of appeals will issue a **statutory notice of deficiency.** The statutory notice is issued if the taxpayer does not request an appeals conference.[14]

A statutory notice of deficiency, commonly referred to as a **ninety-day letter,** must be sent to the taxpayer's last known address by certified or registered mail before the IRS can assess the additional taxes that it believes are due.[15] Once a formal assessment has been made, the IRS is entitled to collect and retain the tax. However, a statutory notice is not required relative to deficiencies that result from mathematical errors or from the overstatement of taxes that were withheld or paid as estimated taxes.

After the statutory notice of deficiency is mailed, the taxpayer has 90 days (150 days if the letter is addressed to a taxpayer who is outside the United States) to file a petition with the U.S. Tax Court for a redetermination of the deficiency. If such a petition is not filed in a timely fashion, the deficiency is assessed and the taxpayer receives a notice and demand for payment of the tax.[16] Once this 90-day period expires, the taxpayer cannot contest the assessment without first paying the tax, filing a claim for refund, and, if the claim is denied by the IRS, instituting a refund suit in a district court or the U.S. Court of Federal Claims.

Generally, no assessment or collection effort may be made during the 90-day period, or, if a Tax Court petition is filed, until after the decision becomes final.

A mailing of the statutory notice to the taxpayer's last known address is sufficient to commence the running of the 90-day period, unless the commissioner has

---

13. Reg. § 601.106(c).
14. A short-form notice often is issued relative to office audit disputes of no more than $5,000 per tax year.
15. §§ 6212(a) and 6212(b)(1).
16. § 6213(c).

been notified formally of a change of address.[17] The statute does not require actual notice; therefore, a notice that is sent by certified or registered mail to the proper address is effective, even though it is never received by the taxpayer him- or herself.[18]

After a case has been scheduled *(docketed)* for review in the Tax Court, the taxpayer is invited to attend a pretrial settlement conference with an appeals officer and an IRS attorney. However, this conference typically is offered only if the case was not considered previously by the appeals office and if no related criminal prosecution is pending. If the taxpayer and the IRS agree to settle the dispute at this stage, they will enter into a written agreement stipulating the amount of any deficiency or overpayment. This stipulation is filed with the Tax Court, which will enter a decision in accordance with the agreement. The Tax Court can levy a penalty of up to $5,000 if it determines that the taxpayer did not pursue the available administrative remedies prior to approaching the court.

ENTERING THE JUDICIAL SYSTEM

If a taxpayer cannot resolve his or her dispute with the IRS administratively, he or she may seek judicial relief. As we have discussed throughout this text, the taxpayer can choose from among the U.S. Tax Court, the pertinent District Court, and the U.S. Court of Federal Claims to initiate the lawsuit against the government.

The Tax Court will review the taxpayer's case, provided that he or she files a petition with the court within 90 days of the date of his or her statutory notice of deficiency. The District Courts and the Court of Federal Claims cannot hear the taxpayer's case unless he or she is suing for a refund. Consequently, the taxpayer first must pay the disputed tax, and then file an (unsuccessful) claim for refund to obtain a judicial review in either of these latter two forums.

Possibilities for appeal after completing the trial-level suit have been discussed in Chapters 2, 3, and 5. Exhibit 12–6 illustrates the appeals procedures, from the initial IRS examination to the final hearing before the Supreme Court. Exhibit 12–7 offers sample thirty- and ninety-day letters for the reader's perusal.

One should not consider tax litigation lightly, however. The additional costs to the taxpayer for attorney and accountant fees, in addition to filing and processing fees and the cost and time involved in gathering supporting documentation for the taxpayer's position, finding and coaching expert and other witnesses, and providing for one's own travel to the site of the hearing, make litigation a costly prospect. Given the right combination of facts and law, though, a suit might be the taxpayer's only chance to achieve an equitable solution.

Remember, nonetheless, that the IRS tends to litigate only cases that (1) it expects to win and (2) it expects will make good precedent to discourage other taxpayers. Moreover, because many taxpayers represent themselves before the Tax Court, procedural errors occur, usually to the detriment of the taxpayer. Thus, it is not surprising that the deck appears to be stacked against the taxpayer once he or she enters the judicial system, especially outside the Tax Court. The information in Exhibit 12–8 illustrates this situation.

---

17. See, for example, *Brown,* 78 T.C. 215 (1989), and *Weinroth,* 74 T.C. 430 (1980).
18. See, for example, *Lifter,* 59 T.C. 818 (1973), and *U.S. v. Ahrens,* 530 F.2d 781 (CA-8, 1976).

Exhibit 12–6 Income Tax Appeal Procedure

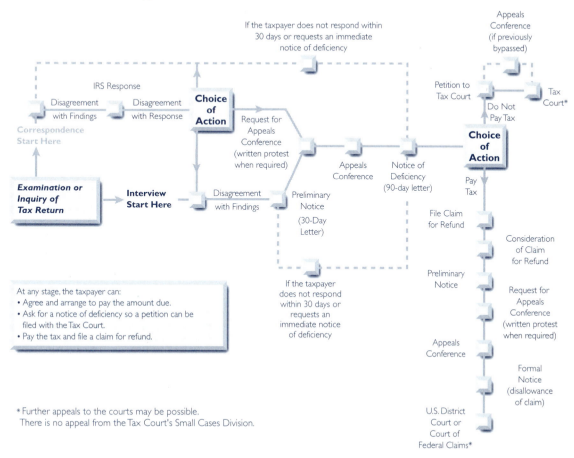

SUMMARY

In counseling clients, the tax professional must be aware of the organization and inner workings of the Internal Revenue Service. Strategic and tactical decisions as to how and when to appeal within the administrative system of the Service, assessing the strengths and weaknesses of the client's case, and determining available remedies can be made only with a thorough understanding of the agency and its operating style. Some of the most valuable advice that a client receives can be in the context of an audit selection letter or the handling of settlement alternatives thereafter.

TAX TUTOR

Reinforce the tax research information covered in this chapter by completing the on-line tutorials located at the Federal Tax Research web site:

http://raabe.swcollege.com

Exhibit 12–7 Sample Thirty- and Ninety-Day Letters

Notice of Adjustment—Thirty-Day Letter

Internal Revenue Service   Department of the Treasury
Date:
Social Security or Employee Identification Number:
Tax Year Ended:
Person to Contact:
Contact Telephone Number:
Contact Address:

Dear

Enclosed are two copies of our report explaining why we believe adjustments should be made in the amount of your tax. Please look this report over and let us know whether you agree with our findings.

If you accept our findings, please sign the consent to assessment and collection portion at the bottom of the report and mail one copy to this office within 30 days from the date of this letter. If additional tax is due, you may want to pay it now and limit the interest charge; otherwise, we will bill you. (See the enclosed Publication 5 for payment details.)

If you do not accept our findings, you have 30 days from the date of this letter to do one of the following:

1. Mail us any additional evidence or information you would like us to consider.
2. Request a discussion of our findings with the examiner who conducted the examination. At that time you may submit any additional evidence or information you would like us to consider. If you plan to come in for a discussion, please phone or write us in advance so that we can arrange a convenient time and place.
3. Discuss your position with the group manager or a senior examiner (designated by the group manager), if an examination has been held and you have been unable to reach an agreement with the examiner.

If you do not accept our findings and do not want to take any of the above actions, you may write us at the address shown above or call us at the telephone number shown above within 30 days from the date of this letter to request a conference with an Appeals Officer. You must provide all pertinent documentation and facts concerning disputed issues to the examiner before your case is forwarded to the Appeals Office. If your examination was conducted entirely by mail, we would appreciate your first discussing our findings with one of our examiners.

The Appeals Office is independent of the District Director. The Appeals Officer, who had not examined your return previously, will take a fresh look at your case. Most disputes considered by Appeals are resolved informally and promptly. By going to Appeals, you may avoid court costs (such as the United States Tax Court filing fee), clear up this matter sooner, and prevent interest from mounting. An Appeals Officer will promptly telephone you and, if necessary, arrange an appointment. If you decide to bypass Appeals and petition the Tax Court, your case will normally be assigned for settlement to an Appeals Office before the Tax Court hears the case.

Under Internal Revenue Code Section 6673, the Tax Court is authorized to award damages of up to $5,000 to the United States when a taxpayer unreasonably fails to pursue available administrative remedies. Damages could be awarded under this provision, for example, if the Court concludes that it was unreasonable for a taxpayer to bypass Appeals and then file a petition in the Tax Court. The Tax Court will make that determination based upon the facts and circumstances of each case. Generally, the Service will not ask the Court to award damages under this provision if you make a good faith effort to meet with Appeals and to settle your case before petitioning the Tax Court.

Exhibit 12–7 Sample Thirty- and Ninety-Day Letters *(Continued)*

The enclosed Publication 5 explains your appeal rights.

If we do not hear from you within 30 days, we will have to process your case on the basis of the adjustments shown in the examination report. If you write us about your case, please write to the person whose name and address are shown in the heading of this letter and refer to the symbols in the upper right corner of the enclosed report. An envelope is enclosed for your convenience. Please include your telephone number, area code, and the most convenient time for us to call, in case we find it necessary to contact you for further information.

If you prefer, you may call the person at the telephone number shown in the heading of this letter. This person will be able to answer any questions you may have. Thank you for your cooperation.

Sincerely yours,

District Director

Enclosures:
Examination Report (2)
Publication 5
Envelope

Notice of Deficiency—Ninety-Day Letter

Internal Revenue Service   Department of the Treasury
District Director
Date:
Social Security or Employer Identification Number:
Tax Year Ended and Deficiency:
Person to Contact:
Contact Telephone Number:

Dear

We have determined that there is a deficiency (increase) in your income tax as shown above. This letter is a NOTICE OF DEFICIENCY sent to you as required by law. The enclosed statement shows how we figured the deficiency.

If you want to contest this deficiency in court before making any payment, you have 90 days from the above mailing date of this letter (150 days if addressed to you outside of the United States) to file a petition with the United States Tax Court for a redetermination of the deficiency. To secure the petition form, write to United States Tax Court, 400 Second Street, NW, Washington, D.C. 20217. The completed petition form, together with a copy of this letter must be returned to the same address and received within 90 days from the above mailing date (150 days if addressed to you outside of the United States).

The time in which you must file a petition with the Court (90 or 150 days as the case may be) is fixed by law and the Court cannot consider your case if your petition is filed late. If this letter is addressed to both a husband and wife, and both want to petition the Tax Court, both must sign the petition or each must file a separate, signed petition.

If you dispute not more than $50,000 for any one tax year, a simplified procedure is provided by the Tax Court for small tax cases. You can get information about this procedure, as well as a petition form you can use, by writing to the Clerk of the United States Tax Court at 400 Second Street, NW, Washington, D.C. 20217. You should do this promptly if you intend to file a petition with the Tax Court.

Continued

Exhibit 12–7 Sample Thirty- and Ninety-Day Letters *(Concluded)*

You may represent yourself before the Tax Court, or you may be represented by anyone admitted to practice before the Court. If you decide not to file a petition with the Tax Court, we would appreciate it if you would sign and return the enclosed waiver form. This will permit us to assess the deficiency quickly and will limit the accumulation of interest. The enclosed envelope is for your convenience. If you decide not to sign and return the statement and you do not timely petition the Tax Court, the law requires us to assess and bill you for the deficiency after 90 days from the above mailing date of this letter (150 days if this letter is addressed to you outside the United States).

If you have questions about this letter, please write to the person whose name and address are shown on this letter. If you write, please attach this letter to help identify your account. Keep the copy for your records. Also, please include your telephone number and the most convenient time for us to call, so we can contact you if we need additional information.

If you prefer, you may call the IRS contact person at the telephone number shown above. If this number is outside your local calling area, there will be a long distance charge to you.

You may call the IRS telephone number listed in your local directory. An IRS employee there may be able to help you, but the contact person at the address shown on this letter is most familiar with your case.

Thank you for your cooperation.

Sincerely yours,

Commissioner
By

Enclosures:
Copy of this letter
Statement
Envelope

District Director

Exhibit 12–8 Taxpayer and Government Victories In Tax Litigation

Forum	Percent of Partial Taxpayer Victories	Percent of Total Taxpayer Victories	Percent of Total Government Victories
U.S. Tax Court, Small Cases Division	49.0	5.0	46.0
U.S. Tax Court, all other	64.0	3.0	33.0
U.S. District Court	11.6	23.2	65.2
U.S. Court of Federal Claims	12.2	14.3	73.5

Chapter 12 Working with the IRS

KEY WORDS

By the time you complete your work relative to this chapter, you should be comfortable discussing each of the following terms. If you need additional review of any of these items, return to the appropriate material in the chapter or consult the glossary to this text.

Appeals Division
Commissioner of Internal Revenue
Computing Center
Correspondence Examination
Customer Service Site
Discriminant Function Formula
Field Audit
Internal Revenue Service
Internal Revenue Service Center

National Taxpayer Advocate
Ninety-Day Letter
Office Audit
Processing Center
Revenue Agent's Report
Statutory Notice of Deficiency
Taxpayer Assistance Order
Thirty-Day Letter
Treasury Department

DISCUSSION QUESTIONS

1. Why must the tax professional be cognizant of how tax law administration works?
2. What are the major functions of the national office of the IRS?
3. What are the chances of having a tax return audited this year?
4. What techniques other than the random selection of returns for audit does the IRS use in its enforcement function?
5. Why might it be desirable to settle with an agent, rather than to continue by appealing to a higher level within the IRS?
6. Relate some of the "audit etiquette" tactics that you have heard taxpayers or tax professionals discuss.
7. Which of the following methods is used to select tax returns for audit? More than one answer may be correct.
   a. DIF procedures
   b. Random samples
   c. Amount of gross income
   d. Type of income, for example, business or wages
8. Which type of audit is used most often to substantiate the reported items of income or deduction for individuals who have only wages?
   a. Field
   b. Office
   c. Correspondence
   d. Home
9. A revenue agent may do which of the following in an attempt to negotiate a settlement after the completion of an audit? More than one answer may be correct.
   a. Attempt to settle an unresolved issue based on the hazards of litigation.
   b. Settle a question of fact.
   c. Reach an agreement that will be accepted unconditionally by the District Director.
   d. Turn the case over to the Appeals Division.

10. When an agreement cannot be reached with a Revenue Agent, a letter is transmitted stating that the taxpayer has 30 days to do which of the following?
    a. File a suit in the U.S. Tax Court.
    b. Request an administrative appeal.
    c. Pay the tax.
    d. Find additional facts to support his or her position.
11. A statutory notice of deficiency gives the taxpayer 90 days to do which of the following?
    a. Pay the tax.
    b. Request an administrative appeal.
    c. File a suit in the U.S. Tax Court.
    d. File a protest.
12. Consider the IRS's system of Taxpayer Advocates.
    a. When might a tax adviser request a hearing with a local Advocate?
    b. What types of issues does an Advocate address?
13. Distinguish among the various means by which the IRS selects a tax return for examination. For this purpose, examine the criteria of:
    a. scope of review
    b. probability of selection
    c. preservation of taxpayer constitutional rights
14. Add two items to the "dos and don'ts" list included in the discussion of audit etiquette.
15. Suggest other information documents that the IRS computers could add to the IDMP.
16. Identify several items that you believe are included in the prevailing DIF model.

EXERCISES

17. Distinguish among the various types of examinations that the IRS conducts relative to individual income tax returns, namely, office, correspondence, field, and TCMP audits. For this purpose, examine the criteria of:
    a. scope of review
    b. type of documentation that typically is required of the taxpayer
    c. use of IRS personnel time and other resources
    d. opportunity for agent to use professional judgment in resolving issues
18. Respond to a client's comment: "We have a better than even chance of winning in the Tax Court, according to an article I read. Let's sue the government!"
19. With respect to the Small Cases Division of the U.S. Tax Court, which statement is true?
    a. The taxpayer (but not the IRS) can appeal a contrary judgment.
    b. The IRS (but not the taxpayer) can appeal a contrary judgment.
    c. Either the IRS or the taxpayer can appeal a contrary judgment.
    d. Neither the IRS nor the taxpayer can appeal a contrary judgment.
20. How should the tax professional advise a client whose charitable contributions are double that of the U.S. norm for his or her income level?

PROBLEMS

21. The President of the United States has hired you to assist in a trim-the-fat program with respect to the Federal government. He has asked you to recommend specific steps to downsize the bureaucracy of the IRS, from the national office through the district headquarters, by 15 percent. Draft a memo to the President summarizing your recommendations. Augment your memo with diagrams supporting your proposals.

22. The IRS has issued a summons for the tax file held by CPA Ann Whitman for her clients the Harberts. The file consists of paper and electronic spreadsheets in which Hartman detailed some tax computations using assumptions that the IRS would find to be "too aggressive." In addition, the file includes notes from meetings with the Harberts, income and balance sheet data as to their personal assets, and other technical correspondence, including e-mail messages. In a memo to the tax research file, summarize the current status of the law as to whether the privilege of confidentiality protects these documents from the government.

13

Tax Practice and Administration: Sanctions, Agreements, and Disclosures

LEARNING OBJECTIVES

- Identify various penalties that may be applied to tax practitioners who fail to perform as directed by the Internal Revenue Service, and related computations of interest charges
- Identify various penalties that may be applied to taxpayers whose returns reflect improper amounts, and related computations of interest charges
- Understand the application of the statutes of limitations, and taxpayer–government agreements that may be made with respect thereto

CHAPTER OUTLINE

Taxpayer Penalties
  Civil Penalties
    Failure to File a Tax Return
    Failure to Pay Tax
    Accuracy-Related Penalty
    Civil Fraud
    Failure to Make Estimated Payments
    Individuals
    Corporations
    Failure to Make Deposits of Taxes or Overstatements of Deposits
    Giving False Information with Respect to Withholding
    Filing a Frivolous Return
    Other Civil Penalties
    Reliance on Written Advice of the IRS
  Criminal Penalties
    Nature of Criminal Penalties
    Criminal Tax Offenses
    Defenses to Criminal Penalties

Penalties on Return Preparers
  Definition of Return Preparer
  Definition of Return Preparation
  Preparer Disclosure Penalties
  Preparer Conduct Penalties
    Endorsing or Negotiating a Refund Check
    Understatements Due to Unrealistic Positions
    Willful Understatement
    Organizing Abusive Tax Shelters
    Aiding and Abetting Understatement
    Aiding or Assisting in the Preparation of a False Return
    Disclosure or Use of Information by Return Preparers
    Conflict among Taxpayer and Preparer Penalty Provisions

Injunctions
  Action to Enjoin Income Tax Return Preparers
  Action to Enjoin Promoters of Abusive Tax Shelters

Interest
  Interest–Computation Conventions
  Applicable Interest Rate

Statutes of Limitations
  Nature of Statutes of Limitations
  Assessment
    Irregular Returns
    Acceleration, Extension, and Carryback Effects
    IRS-Requested Extensions
  Collection
  Claim for Refund or Credit
    Limitations Period
    Other Extensions
    Amount of the Credit or Refund
  Suspension of Period of Assessment and Collection
  Mitigation of Statute of Limitations

Statutory Agreements
  Closing Agreements
  Offers in Compromise

The adversarial nature of the Federal tax system has become apparent throughout this text, especially in Chapter 12. The revenue system is based on the notion of self-assessment, but the failure of the taxpayer to comply in detail with the requirements of the structure can lead to painful negotiations with the Internal Revenue Service and prolonged litigation.

Yet, the Treasury need not wait for a resolution of the disputed tax issues alone to collect revenues. Penalties and interest play an ever-increasing role in the makeup of the Federal tax system—in many cases, the accumulated penalties and interest assessed by the IRS equal 50 percent of the disputed tax or more.

Interest charges are made by the Treasury so that the taxpayer gains no advantage or disadvantage with respect to the time value of money in deciding how to handle a tax dispute—to the extent that interest rates are developed to parallel those of the rest of the financial market, both parties are indifferent as to cash flow issues, and the negotiations can center on the tax issues alone. In Chapter 11, we discussed the role of present values in assisting taxpayers to make these decisions in an economically prudent manner.

Penalties have become more prominent in the Federal tax system for several reasons. The tax professional must incorporate into the research model the penalty-based "costs" of being too aggressive in taking a tax return or litigation position, and convey the computations of those costs to the client.

- In an environment where nominal tax increases are politically unpopular, penalty increases can supplement revenues in a manner that is acceptable to the public.
- Politics aside, penalties increase the tax cost of negotiating with the Treasury and may discourage challenges to tax precedents that are not founded in sound tax law.
- Penalties can bolster the self-assessment process by discouraging taxpayers from behaviors that the Treasury wishes to repress, such as working with tax shelters and ignoring filing deadlines and requirements.
- As professional tax preparers and advisors play a more important role in the development of tax return positions, the behavior of such third parties also must be controlled, both in keeping a free flow of information between the government and the taxpayer and in interpreting the tax law in an objective manner.

We conclude this chapter with a review of alternatives and strategies available to taxpayers in making various compromises and other agreements with the IRS as a result of the examination process. In today's tax practice, the professional must have a full working knowledge of the details of the tax administration process, so as best to serve clients and the fisc.

TAXPAYER PENALTIES

To promote and enforce taxpayer compliance with the U.S. voluntary self-assessment system of taxation, Congress has enacted a comprehensive array of penalties. Tax penalties may involve both criminal and civil offenses. Criminal tax penalties are imposed only after the usual criminal process, in which the taxpayer is entitled to the same constitutional guarantees that are given to nontax criminal defendants. Normally, a criminal penalty provides for imprisonment. Civil tax penalties are collected in the same manner as other taxes, and they usually only provide for monetary fines. Criminal and civil penalties are not mutually exclusive; therefore, a taxpayer may be liable under both types of sanctions.

Civil Penalties

The Code imposes two types of **civil penalties.** *Ad valorem penalties* are additions to tax that are based on a percentage of the delinquent tax. Unlike assessable penalties, ad valorem penalties are subject to the same deficiency procedures that apply to the underlying taxes. *Assessable penalties* typically are expressed as a flat dollar amount. Because of the lack of jurisdiction by the Tax Court or a specific statutory exemption, assessable penalties are not subject to review by the Tax Court. Note that the Code characterizes tax penalties as additions to tax; thus, they cannot subsequently be deducted by the taxpayer.

Civil penalties are imposed when the tax statutes are violated (1) without **reasonable cause,** (2) as the result of **negligence** or intentional disregard of pertinent rules, or (3) through a willful disobedience or outright **fraud.** The most important civil penalties include the following.

- Failure to file a tax return
- Failure to pay tax
- Failure to pay estimated income taxes
- Negligence, fraud, or substantial understatement of income tax
- Substantial understatement of the tax liability
- Failure to make deposits of taxes or overstatement of such deposits
- Giving false information with respect to withholding
- Filing a frivolous return

Failure to File a Tax Return

When a taxpayer fails to file a required tax return, a penalty is imposed unless it is shown that the failure is due to some reasonable cause and not to the taxpayer's willful neglect. The penalty is 5 percent of the amount of the tax, less any prior payments and credits, for each month (or fraction thereof) that the return is not filed. The maximum penalty that may be imposed is 25 percent (or five months' cumulative penalty).[1] A fraudulent failure to file is subject to a 15 percent monthly penalty, to a 75 percent maximum.[2]

If the taxpayer's failure to file is due to willful neglect, there is a minimum penalty for a failure to file an income tax return within 60 days of the due date, including extensions. This minimum penalty is the lesser of $100 or the full amount of taxes that are required to be shown on the return. The penalty does not apply if the failure is due to reasonable cause.[3] This penalty is applied in lieu of, rather than in addition to, some other penalty.

No statutory or administrative definition exists for the term "reasonable cause." However, some courts define it to include such action as would prompt an ordinary, intelligent person to act in the same manner as did the taxpayer, under similar circumstances. One of the most commonly encountered examples of reasonable cause is the reliance on the advice of competent tax counsel. Other examples of reasonable cause that the *Internal Revenue Manual* describes include the following.[4]

---

1. § 6651(a)(1).
2. § 6651(f).
3. § 6651(a)(3).
4. IRM Audit, § 4562.2(a).

- A timely mailed return that is returned for insufficient postage.
- Death or serious illness of the taxpayer or his or her immediate family.
- Destruction of the taxpayer's residence, place of business, or records by fire or other casualty.
- Proper forms were not furnished by the IRS.
- Erroneous information was obtained from IRS personnel.
- A timely mailed return was sent to the wrong district.
- An unavoidable absence by the taxpayer.
- An unavoidable inability to obtain records necessary to compute the tax.
- Some other inability to obtain assistance from IRS personnel.

However, the penalty will not be excused for any of the following reasons.

- The taxpayer lacks the necessary funds with which to pay the tax.[5]
- The taxpayer was hospitalized and suffered from an illness that was not incapacitating.[6]
- Lost or destroyed records were not necessary to the completion of the return.[7]
- The taxpayer was incarcerated.[8]
- The taxpayer allegedly was ignorant of the laws.[9]

To avoid the penalty, the taxpayer must meet the burden of proof that the failure to file (or to pay) was due to reasonable cause. In these situations, the IRS's determination of the penalty is presumed to be correct.

Failure to Pay Tax

If a taxpayer fails to pay either a tax that is shown on his or her return or an assessed deficiency within ten days of an IRS notice and demand, a penalty is imposed. The 10-day period becomes 21 days when the tax due is less than $100,000. The penalty is 0.5 percent of the required liability, after adjusting for any prior payments and credits, for each month (or fraction thereof) that the tax is not paid—but it increases to 1 percent of the underpaid tax per month after notice from the IRS.[10] The maximum penalty that may be imposed is 25 percent of the outstanding tax. This penalty does not apply if the failure to pay is attributable to a reasonable cause, or to the failure to pay an estimated tax for which there is a different penalty.

For this purpose, reasonable cause is defined in a manner that is identical to that discussed in conjunction with the failure-to-file penalty, except that, if an individual is granted an automatic filing extension, reasonable cause is presumed to exist, provided that the balance due does not exceed 10 percent of the total tax.[11]

The failure-to-file penalty is reduced by the 0.5 percent failure-to-pay penalty for any month in which both apply. Thus, no more than a 5 percent total (nonfraud) penalty typically can be assessed against a taxpayer for any month. Nonetheless, after rendering sufficient notice to the taxpayer, the IRS can assess both the failure-to-pay and the failure-to-file penalties.

---

5. *Langston,* 36 T.C.M. 1703 (1977).
6. *Hernandez,* 72 T.C. 1234 (1979).
7. *Long,* 37 T.C.M. 733 (1978).
8. *Jones,* 55 T.C.M. 1556 (1988).
9. *Lammerts Estate v. Comm.,* 456 F.2d 681 (CA–2, 1972).
10. § 6651(a)(2). After 1999, the monthly penalty rate is cut in half for taxpayers paying delinquent taxes under an installment agreement.
11. § 6654(a)(1)(B)(i).

A taxpayer can avoid the failure-to-file penalty if an extension of the return's due date is granted by the IRS. However, with the two exceptions that we just discussed, the failure-to-pay penalty is imposed when the total amount of the tax is not paid by the unextended due date of the return.

Example 13–1 John Gray, a calendar-year taxpayer, filed his 2002 income tax return on October 10, 2003, paying an amount due of $1,000. On April 1, 2002, John had obtained a four-month extension of time in which to file his return. However, he could not assert a reasonable cause for failing to file the return by August 15, 2003 (the extended due date), nor did he show any reasonable cause for failing to pay the tax that was due on April 15, 2003. Gray's failure to file was not fraudulent. As a result, Gray is subject to a $35 failure-to-pay penalty and a $135 failure-to-file penalty, determined as follows.

Failure to pay

Underpayment	$1,000
Penalty percentage	× .005
Penalty per month outstanding	$ 5
Months (or fractions thereof) for which required payment was not made	× 7
Failure-to-pay penalty	$ 35

Failure to file

Underpayment	$1,000
Penalty percentage	× .05
Penalty per month outstanding (before reduction)	$ 50
Months (or fractions thereof) for which return was not filed	× 3
Unreduced penalty	$ 150
Less: concomitant failure-to-pay penalty (i.e., for August–October) [3 months × (.005 × $1,000)]	− 15
Failure-to-file penalty	$ 135

Accuracy-Related Penalty

Major penalties relating to the accuracy of the return data, including the existing negligence penalty and the penalty for substantial understatement of income tax liability, are combined in a single Code section. This consolidation of related penalties into a single levy eliminates the possibility of the stacking of multiple penalties when more than one type of penalty applies to a single understatement of tax.

The **accuracy-related penalty** amounts to 20 percent of the portion of the tax underpayment that is attributable to one or more of the following.

- Negligence or disregard of applicable Federal tax rules and Regulations
- Substantial understatement of income tax
- Substantial valuation overstatement
- Substantial overstatement of pension liabilities
- Substantial understatement of estate and gift tax valuation

The penalty applies only where the taxpayer fails to show either a reasonable cause for the underpayment or a good-faith effort to comply with the tax law.[12] When the

---

12. § 6662.

accuracy-related penalty applies, interest on the penalty accrues from the due date of the return, rather than merely from the date on which the penalty was imposed.

Occasionally, a valuation overstatement penalty is encountered. This 20 percent penalty applies when an asset value has been overstated on a return, for example, to substantiate a charitable contribution deduction. It is assessed when the valuation used is 200 percent or more of the actual value, resulting in an underpayment of over $5,000 ($10,000 for C corporations).

Similarly, a 20 percent transfer valuation understatement penalty is assessed where the claimed value is 50 percent or less than the asset's actual value, resulting in an underpayment of over $5,000. The rate of both penalties is 40 percent if a gross valuation misstatement is made, that is, the income tax valuation was at least 400 percent of actual value, or the transfer tax value was 25 percent or less of actual.[13]

The practitioner is likely to encounter two of the elements of this penalty most frequently: (1) negligence or disregard of rules and (2) substantial understatement of tax. In the first penalty, "negligence" includes any failure to make a reasonable attempt to comply with the provisions of the Code.[14] This might occur when the taxpayer fails to report gross income, overstates deductions, or fails to keep adequate records with which to comply with the law. "Disregard" includes any careless, reckless, or intentional disregard of the elements of the tax law.[15]

The negligence component of the penalty is waived where the taxpayer has made a good-faith attempt to comply with the law, as indicated by a full disclosure of the nonfrivolous position that may be contrary to that of the IRS. Such disclosure is made by completing Form 8275, reproduced as Exhibit 13–1, and attaching it to the return. If the return position is contrary to the language of a Regulation, Form 8275-R is used.

The second commonly encountered penalty, substantial understatement of income tax, occurs if the determined understatement exceeds the greater of (1) 10 percent of the proper tax liability or (2) $5,000 ($10,000 for a corporation other than an S corporation or a personal holding company).[16] The amount that is subject to this penalty is reduced if the taxpayer either has substantial authority for the position that was taken in the return, or makes a full disclosure of the position taken in the return, on Form 8275 or 8275-R. More specifically, the taxpayer is not subject to this penalty where the weight of **substantial authority** for his or her position exceeds that supporting contrary positions.[17]

For this purpose, "substantial authority" includes the Code, Regulations (proposed and temporary), court decisions, administrative pronouncements, tax treaties, IRS information and press releases, IRS Notices and Announcements, Letter Rulings, Technical Advice Memoranda, General Counsel Memoranda, Committee Reports, and "Blue Book" explanations of tax legislation. Substantial authority does not include conclusions reached in tax treatises, legal periodicals, and opinions rendered by tax professionals.[18]

Clearly, greater weight will be placed on the Code and temporary Regulations than will be assigned to Letter Rulings and IRS Notices, but the derivation of a

13. § 6662(h).
14. § 6662(c).
15. § 6662(c).
16. § 6662(d)(1).
17. § 6662(d)(2)(A) and (B).
18. Reg. § 1.6661–3(b)(2).

Exhibit 13-1 Disclosure Statement

Form **8275**
(Rev. May 2001)
Department of the Treasury
Internal Revenue Service

Disclosure Statement

Do not use this form to disclose items or positions that are contrary to Treasury regulations. Instead, use Form 8275-R, Regulation Disclosure Statement. See separate instructions.

▶ Attach to your tax return.

OMB No. 1545-0889

Attachment Sequence No. **92**

Name(s) shown on return | Identifying number shown on return

Part I — General Information (see instructions)

	(a) Rev. Rul., Rev. Proc., etc.	(b) Item or Group of Items	(c) Detailed Description of Items	(d) Form or Schedule	(e) Line No.	(f) Amount
1						
2						
3						

Part II — Detailed Explanation (see instructions)

1

2

3

Part III — Information About Pass-Through Entity.
To be completed by partners, shareholders, beneficiaries, or residual interest holders.

Complete this part only if you are making adequate disclosure for a pass-through item.

Note: *A pass-through entity is a partnership, S corporation, estate, trust, regulated investment company (RIC), real estate investment trust (REIT), or real estate mortgage investment conduit (REMIC).*

1 Name, address, and ZIP code of pass-through entity	2 Identifying number of pass-through entity
	3 Tax year of pass-through entity / / to / /
	4 Internal Revenue Service Center where the pass-through entity filed its return

For Paperwork Reduction Act Notice, see separate instructions.   Cat. No. 61935M   Form **8275** (Rev. 5-2001)

weighted average among all of the competing positions with respect to a given tax question is not likely to be easily obtained.

Civil Fraud

If any part of an underpayment of tax is attributable to fraud, a substantial civil penalty is imposed. In addition, the taxpayer may be liable for a criminal penalty, which we will discuss later in this chapter. The civil fraud penalty is 75 percent of the underpayment that is attributable to the fraud.[19]

If any part of an underpayment is attributable to fraud, only the fraud penalty may be imposed with respect to that amount.[20] Neither the failure-to-file nor the failure-to-pay penalty, nor the civil accuracy-related penalty, is assessed in these circumstances. However, the penalty for underpayment of estimated tax (discussed here) may still be assessed, and interest is assessed from the (extended) due date of the return.

Fraud is not defined in either the Code or the Regulations. One long-standing judicial definition of fraud describes it as "... actual, intentional wrongdoing ... the intent required is the specific purpose to evade a tax believed to be owing."[21] This definition has been expanded to include acts that are done without a "bad or evil purpose." In *U.S. v. Pomponio,* the Supreme Court held that "willfulness," which is a crucial element of fraud, is present when the taxpayer's actions constitute "... a voluntary, intentional violation of a known legal duty."[22] Consequently, the taxpayer's deceptive or misleading conduct distinguishes fraud from mere negligence, or from other actions that are taken to avoid taxation, and not the presence of some (inherent or documented) evil purpose.

If a taxpayer is convicted of criminal fraud, he or she cannot contest a civil fraud determination. However, a charge that the taxpayer is guilty of criminal fraud may be contested when a civil fraud determination has been upheld. In a criminal fraud case, the IRS must prove "beyond a shadow of any reasonable doubt" that the taxpayer's actions were fraudulent. In a civil fraud case, there must be "clear and convincing evidence" that the taxpayer committed fraud.

Under an all-or-nothing rule, if the IRS establishes that any portion of an underpayment is attributable to fraud, the entire underpayment is treated as attributable to fraud, and the penalty applies to the entire amount due.[23] Ordinarily, the evidence that indicates that a taxpayer's conduct was fraudulent is circumstantial. Thus, the court must infer the taxpayer's state of mind from the evidence. Examples of fraud include the following.

- Keeping two sets of books, one in English and one in Japanese.[24]
- Making false accounting entries.[25]
- Destroying books or records.[26]
- Concealing assets or sources of income.[27]

---

19. §§ 6663(a) and (b).
20. § 6663(b).
21. *Mitchell v. Comm.,* 118 F.2d 308, 310 (CA–5, 1941).
22. 97 429 U.S. 10, S.Ct. 22 (1976).
23. § 6663(b).
24. *Noro v U.S.,* 148 F.2d 696 (CA–5, 1945).
25. *U.S. v Lange,* 161 F.2d 699 (CA–7, 1947).
26. *U.S. v Ragen,* 314 U.S. 513, 62 S.Ct. 374 (1942).
27. *Gendelman v U.S.,* 191 F.2d 993 (CA–9, 1952).

- Consistently understating income or overstating deductions.[28]
- Purposely avoiding the making of business records and receipts.[29]

Failure to Make Estimated Payments

A penalty is imposed on both individuals and corporations who fail to pay quarterly estimated income taxes. This penalty is based on the amount and duration of the underpayment, and the rate of interest that currently is established by the Code. This rate, for instance, was 7 percent late in 2001. Unlike the similar interest computation, however, this penalty is computed without any daily compounding and is not deductible.

The penalty is calculated separately for each quarterly installment. Each penalty period begins on the date on which the installment was required, and it runs through the earlier of either the date that the amount is paid or the due date for filing the return. Any overpayment is first applied to prior underpayments and the excess is credited to later installments.[30]

Individuals

An individual's underpayment of estimated tax is computed as the difference between the amounts that were paid by the quarterly due dates, and the least of (1) 90 percent of the tax that is shown on the current year's return; (2) 100 percent of the prior year's tax; and (3) 90 percent of the tax that would be figured by annualizing the income that was earned during the year, up to the month in which the quarterly payment is due.[31] For this purpose, unless the taxpayer can prove otherwise, taxes that are withheld are considered to have been remitted to the IRS in equal quarterly installments.[32]

The underpayment penalty will not apply if less than $1,000 in underwithheld tax is due, or if the total payments that are made by the applicable installment date are equal to an amount that would have been required on that date if the estimated tax (1) was based on the tax that is shown on the previous year's return (i.e., using 100 or 110 percent), or (2) equaled 90 percent of the tax, computed on the basis of the annualized income for the period that ends on the installment date.[33] In addition, an individual can avoid the estimated tax underpayment penalty if (1) the preceding taxable year included 12 months, (2) the individual did not have any tax liability for the preceding year, and (3) he or she was a citizen or resident of the United States throughout the preceding taxable year.

The IRS can waive the estimated tax underpayment penalty (but not the penalty that is based on the outstanding interest attributable thereto) (1) if the failure to make the payment was due to a casualty, disaster, or other unusual circumstance where it would be inequitable to impose the penalty, or (2) if the failure was due to reasonable cause rather than willful neglect during the first two years after the taxpayer retires, attains age 62, or becomes disabled.[34] The fourth installment penalty is waived

---

28. *Holland v. U.S.*, 348 U.S. 121, 75 S.Ct. 127 (1954) and *Ragen*, op.cit.
29. *Garispy v U.S.*, 220 F.2d 252 (CA–6, 1955).
30. §§ 6654(b) and 6655(b).
31. § 6654(d). The rule is 110 percent of the prior-year tax if that year's AGI > $150,000. This percentage was 112 for 2001.
32. § 6654(g).
33. §§ 6654(e)(1) and (2).
34. § 6654(e)(3).

if the corresponding tax return is filed with full tax payment by the end of the first month after the tax year-end (January 31 for calendar-year taxpayers).

Corporations

An underpayment on the part of a corporation is defined as the difference between the amount of the installment that would be required to be paid if the estimated tax was equal to 100 percent of the tax that is shown on the return (or, if no return was filed, 100 percent of the actual tax that is due), and the amount that was actually paid on or before the prescribed payment date.[35]

The underpayment penalty will not apply if less than $1,000 in tax is due, or if the total payments that are made by the applicable installment date are equal to the least of

1. 100 percent of the nonzero amount of tax that is shown on the corporation's tax return for the preceding year, provided that the preceding year contained 12 months;
2. 100 percent of the current-year tax liability; or
3. 100 percent of the tax that is due using a seasonal installment method, or annualizing the current year's income received for (a) the first two or three months, relative to the installment that is due in the fourth month of the tax year, (b) the first three, four, or five months, for the installment that is due in the sixth month, (c) the first six, seven, or eight months, for the installment that is due in the ninth month, or (d) the first nine, ten, or eleven months, for the installment that is due in the twelfth month as elected.[36]

Exception 1 does not apply to a "large corporation," that is, one that had a taxable income of $1 million or more in any of its three immediately preceding taxable years. To avoid an underpayment penalty, a large corporation must remit quarterly estimated tax payments that are equal to its current year's tax liability, or it must meet Exception 3, as discussed.[37]

Failure to Make Deposits of Taxes or Overstatements of Deposits

The Code requires employers to collect and withhold income and Social Security taxes from their employees. Amounts that are withheld are considered to be held in a special trust fund for the United States, and they must be deposited in a government depository on or before certain dates prescribed by the statute and Regulations. An employer who does not have either the inclination or sufficient funds with which to meet its deposit obligations may be tempted to postpone the making of these deposits, that is, to "borrow" from the government the cash provided by employees. Consequently, the Code imposes heavy civil and criminal penalties on those who are responsible for the failure to make a timely deposit of the withheld funds.[38] A responsible party may be an officer or board member of a corporation rather than the corporation itself, even for charities and other exempt entities.

If an employer fails to deposit on a timely basis taxes that were withheld from employees, a penalty equal to a percentage of the underpayment is imposed. This rate varies from 2 to 15 percent, depending on when the failure is corrected.[39] The

---

35. § 6655(b)(1).
36. §§ 6655(d), (e), and (f).
37. §§ 6654(d)(2) and (g)(2). The prior-year exception can be used in making the first-quarter installment, however. § 6654(d)(2)(B).
38. § 6656.
39. § 6656(b)(1).

penalty may be avoided where the taxpayer can show that his or her actions were due to reasonable cause and not to willful neglect.

If any person who is required to collect, truthfully account for, and remit employment taxes willfully fails to do so, a penalty equal to 100 percent of the tax is imposed.[40] Therefore, when a corporate employer does not pay to the government employment taxes that it withheld from an employee, the IRS effectively may collect the tax from those who are responsible for the corporate actions, such as the corporate directors, president, or treasurer.[41]

In addition to the civil penalties that have been discussed, criminal penalties may be imposed in an aggravated case of nonpayment.

Giving False Information with Respect to Withholding

All employees are required to give their employer a completed Form W-4, Employee Withholding Allowance Certificate. This form notifies the employer of the number of withholding exemptions that the employee is entitled to claim. The employer then calculates the amount of tax that must be withheld from each employee. A civil penalty of $500 is imposed on any person who gives to his or her employer false information with respect to withholding status or the number of exemptions to which he or she is entitled. This penalty is not imposed where there was a reasonable basis for the taxpayer's statement. Moreover, the IRS may waive all or a part of the penalty if the actual income taxes that are imposed are not greater than the sum of the allowable credits and estimated tax payments.[42]

The Regulations require that employers who receive a Form W-4 from an employee, on which he or she claims more than 10 exemptions, must submit a copy of the form to the IRS.[43]

Filing a Frivolous Return

A separate $500 civil penalty is assessed when the taxpayer is found to have filed a frivolous return.[44] Returns of this sort have been used to assert that the taxpayer's Fifth Amendment rights are violated by tax return disclosures,[45] that the taxpayer objects to the use of his or her tax receipts for defense or other uses,[46] that the government can collect taxes only in gold-based coins and certificates (which no longer circulate freely in the United States), or some other argument. Specifically, the penalty applies when the return:

- does not contain information by which to judge the completeness of the taxpayer's self-assessment (e.g., if the return is blank);
- contains information or statements that on their face indicate that the self-assessment requirement has not been met (e.g., a "tax protestor" statement is attached); or

---

40. § 6672(a).
41. § 7809(a).
42. § 6682.
43. Reg. § 31.3402(f)(2)–1(g).
44. § 6702.
45. *Welch v. U.S.*, 750 F.2d 1101 (CA–1, 1985).
46. *Fuller v. U.S.*, 786 F.2d 1437 (CA–9, 1986).

- otherwise takes positions that are frivolous or are meant to impede the administration of the tax law, for example, it takes a return position contrary to a decision of the U.S. Supreme Court, or it is not presented in a readable format.

Other Civil Penalties

A variety of other civil penalties may be imposed on taxpayers who fail to comply with the Code. Most of these penalties involve a specialized area of the tax law and ordinarily are not encountered by taxpayers. Consequently, one should be aware of the existence of such sanctions and refer to the Code and Regulations when working in such a specialized field to identify the events that might trigger such penalties.

Reliance on Written Advice of the IRS

The Secretary of the Treasury must abate any civil penalty or addition to tax that is attributable to the taxpayer's reliance on erroneous written advice furnished by an IRS officer or employee. This abatement is available only with respect to advice given in response to a specific request by the taxpayer, and it is negated if the IRS error was made due to a lack of information provided by the taxpayer.[47]

CRIMINAL PENALTIES

In addition to the civil penalties that we have discussed so far, the Code prescribes a number of **criminal penalties** for certain acts of taxpayer noncompliance. The criminal penalties are intended "to prohibit and punish fraud occurring in the assessment and collection of taxes."[48] They are imposed only after the implementation of the constitutional criminal process, under which the taxpayer is entitled to the same rights and privileges as other criminal defendants.

Nature of Criminal Penalties

Criminal and civil penalties are not mutually exclusive. Consequently, a taxpayer may be acquitted of a criminal tax offense, but still be liable for a corresponding civil tax penalty.

The IRS bears a greater burden of proof with respect to a criminal case. Moreover, the taxpayer holds the right to refuse to answer inquiries that are made by the IRS in a criminal setting if he or she would suffer a loss of some constitutional right by answering.

Ordinarily, criminal prosecutions are limited to flagrant offenses for which the IRS believes it is virtually certain to obtain a conviction. As a result, the IRS usually limits its charges to the civil penalty provisions. In the typical context, according to Section 100 of the *IRS Law Enforcement Manual IX*, criminal prosecutions are limited to cases in which (1) the additional tax that will be generated from a successful prosecution is substantial, (2) the crime appears to have been committed in three consecutive years, or (3) the taxpayer's flagrant or repetitive conduct was so egregious that the IRS believes that it is virtually certain to obtain a conviction. As a result, the IRS usually will not engage in a criminal prosecution when the taxpayer's noncompliance can be corrected by imposing civil penalties.

---

47. IR–88–75 (4/88) and § 6404(f).
48. *U.S. v. White*, 417 F.2d 89, 93 (CA–2).

Criminal Tax Offenses

The principal criminal offenses that are addressed by the Code include the following.

- Willful attempt to evade or defeat a tax (i.e., tax evasion)—a felony offense that is punishable by a fine that is not to exceed $100,000 ($500,000 for corporations) and/or imprisonment for a period that is not to exceed five years.[49]
- Willful failure to collect, account for, and remit any tax, by any person who is required to do so—a felony offense that is punishable by a fine that is not to exceed $10,000 and/or imprisonment for a period that is not to exceed five years.[50]
- Willful failure to file a return, supply information, or pay tax or estimated tax—a misdemeanor offense that is punishable by a fine that is not to exceed $25,000 ($100,000 for corporations) and/or imprisonment for a period that is not to exceed one year (five years and felony status for returns relative to cash received by a business).[51]
- Willful making, subscribing, or aiding or assisting in the making of a return or other document that is verified by a declaration under the penalties of perjury, and that the person does not believe to be true and correct as to every material matter—a felony offense that is punishable by a fine not to exceed $100,000 ($500,000 for corporations) and/or imprisonment for a period that is not to exceed three years.[52]
- Willful filing of any known-to-be-false or fraudulent document—a misdemeanor offense that is punishable by a fine that is not to exceed $10,000 ($50,000 for corporations) and/or imprisonment for a period not to exceed one year.[53]
- Disclosure or use of any information that is furnished to a person who is engaged in the business of preparing tax returns, or providing services in connection with the preparation of tax returns, for purposes other than the preparation of the return—a misdemeanor offense that is punishable by a fine not to exceed $1,000 and/or imprisonment for a period not to exceed one year.[54]

In addition to the penalties that we have just described, the Code prescribes a number of other criminal penalties that ordinarily are not encountered on a regular basis. Most of these penalties involve a specialized area of the tax law. Consequently, one should be aware of the existence of such sanctions and refer to the Code and Regulations when working in such a specialized field to identify them.

Defenses to Criminal Penalties

The standard for conviction in a criminal case is establishment of guilt beyond a reasonable doubt. With respect to criminal tax cases, taxpayers have had some success in presenting one or more of the following defenses—that is, to establish some doubt in the minds of the court or the jury.

- Unreported income was offset fully by unreported deductions.[55]
- Unreported income was in reality a gift or some other excludible receipt.[56]

---

49. § 7201.
50. § 7202.
51. §§ 7203 and 6050I.
52. § 7206.
53. § 7207.
54. § 7216.
55. *Koontz v. U.S.*, 277 F.2d 53 (CA–5, 1960).
56. *DiZenzo v. Comm.*, 348 F.2d 122 (CA–2, 1965).

- The taxpayer was confused or ignorant as to the applicable law—one cannot intend to violate the tax law if he or she does not know what that law is.[57]
- The taxpayer relied on the erroneous advice of a competent tax advisor.[58]
- The taxpayer has a mental disease or defect, so could not have acted willfully to violate the tax law.[59]
- The statute of limitations (discussed later in this chapter) has expired.
- The taxpayer enters a plea bargain and accepts conviction on a lesser offense.

PENALTIES ON RETURN PREPARERS

Individuals who prepare income tax returns or refund claims for compensation are subject to a number of disclosure requirements and penalties for improper conduct in the preparation of those documents. These provisions were added to the Code after Congress found that about one-half of all taxpayers utilized some form of professional assistance in preparing their income tax returns. Moreover, a significant percentage of returns that were prepared by return preparers indicated some fraud potential.

The return preparer penalties apply only to income tax returns. Most of them are mild, ranging from $50 for the failure to furnish an identification number to $1,000 for the aiding and abetting of an understatement of a tax liability. However, as these sanctions may be applied cumulatively, their magnitude can become more substantial. In addition, the criminal penalties that may be imposed on the return preparer provide for substantial monetary fines and jail terms.

We discussed some of these rules in Chapters 1 and 2. For both taxpayer and tax preparer, the penalty system "encourages" a lawful application of the tax rules by all, by raising the cost of the tax when specific requirements are violated.

DEFINITION OF RETURN PREPARER

An income tax **return preparer** (ITRP) is any person who prepares for compensation, or employs one or more persons to prepare for compensation, all or a substantial portion of a tax return or claim for income tax refund.[60] An ITRP can be an employer, employee, or a self-employed person. This distinction is important because certain penalties are imposed only on a selected type of preparer. For instance, only an employee preparer is subject to a negligence or fraud penalty, unless the employer participated in the wrongdoing. To determine whether the employer or employee return preparer (or both) is liable for a certain penalty, the Regulations that relate to that penalty must be consulted.

A person must prepare an income tax return for compensation if he or she is to be subject to the return preparer sanctions. If a return is prepared gratuitously, the preparer is not an ITRP. The preparer also must prepare all or a substantial portion of a return if the ITRP sanctions are to apply. In determining whether the work that has been performed by the party is substantial, a comparison must be made between the length and complexity of the prepared schedule, entry, or other item and the total liability or refund claim.

---

57. *U.S. v. Critzer,* 498 F.2d 1160 (CA–4, 1974).
58. *U.S. v. Phillips,* 217 F.2d 435 (CA–7, 1954).
59. *U.S. v. Erickson,* 676 F.2d 408 (CA–10, 1982).
60. § 7701(a)(36).

The Regulations adopt two objective safe harbors in determining the constitution of a substantial portion of a return or claim. If a schedule, entry, or other item involves amounts that are (1) less than $2,000 or (2) less than $100,000 and also less than 20 percent of the gross income (or adjusted gross income, where the taxpayer is an individual) that is shown on the return, then the item is not substantial.[61]

DEFINITION OF RETURN PREPARATION

In constructing a definition of the ITRP, one first must define the domain of *return preparation*. Return preparation includes activities other than the mere physical completion of a return. The IRS asserts that tax advisors, planners, software designers, and consultants are all tax preparers, even though they may only review the return or give the taxpayer instructions on its completion. According to the Regulations, one who furnishes a taxpayer or other preparer with "sufficient information and advice so that completion of the return or claim for refund is largely a mechanical matter" is an ITRP.[62] However, an advisor is not an ITRP when the advice is given with respect to completed transactions or for other than tax return filing purposes.

A person is not an ITRP merely because he or she:[63]

- furnishes typing, reproducing, or other clerical assistance;
- prepares a return or refund claim of his or her regular employer or of an officer or employee of the employer;
- prepares as a fiduciary a return or claim for refund; or
- prepares a claim for refund during the course of an audit or appeal.

PREPARER DISCLOSURE PENALTIES

Five different **preparer penalties** may be imposed on those who do not comply with certain disclosure requirements.[64]

- A penalty of $50 for each return may be imposed on an (employer of an) ITRP if the taxpayer is not given a complete copy of the return when it is presented to him or her for signature.
- A penalty of $50 for each return may be imposed on an employee ITRP if he or she fails to sign the return.
- A penalty of $50 for each return will be imposed on an (employer of an) ITRP if the preparer's identification number or that of his or her employer, or both, is not listed on each completed return.
- A penalty of $50 for each failure will be imposed on an (employer of an) ITRP if he or she does not retain a copy of all returns that he or she prepared. Alternatively, he or she may retain a list of all of the taxpayers and their identification numbers for whom returns were prepared for the previous three years.
- A penalty of $50 for each failure to retain, and $50 for each item that is omitted, is imposed on an (employer of an) ITRP who does not retain records that indi-

---

61. Reg. § 301.7701–15(b)(2).
62. Reg. § 301.7701–15(a)(1).
63. § 7701(a)(36)(B).
64. § 6695.

cate the name, identification number, and place of work of each preparer who is employed during the 12-month period that begins on July 1 of each year.

In each instance, the maximum penalty for any calendar year is $25,000.

Preparer Conduct Penalties

The Code contains a number of civil and criminal penalties that may be imposed on return preparers relative to their misconduct. The civil penalties were added to the Code because Congress found that a significant number of return preparers were engaging in improper practices, such as guaranteeing refunds or having taxpayers sign blank returns. However, except for the criminal penalty of aiding and assisting in the preparation of a false return, there were no lesser sanctions that could be applied to return preparers who were guilty of misconduct.

Civil penalties that may be imposed on preparers relate to:

- endorsing or negotiating a refund check;
- negligent understatement or intentional disregard of rules and Regulations;
- willful understatement of tax liability;
- organizing, or assisting in organizing, or promoting and making or furnishing statements with respect to an abusive tax shelter;
- aiding and abetting the understatement of a tax liability; and
- disclosure or use of return information for other than return preparation.

Return preparers have always been subject to criminal prosecution for willful misconduct. The two principal criminal preparer penalties involve those who:

- aid or assist in the preparation or presentation of a false return, affidavit, claim, or other document,[65] or
- disclose or use information for other than return preparation purposes.[66]

Endorsing or Negotiating a Refund Check

An income tax return preparer may not endorse or otherwise negotiate an income tax refund check that is issued to another person. A preparer who violates this rule is subject to a $500 penalty.[67]

Understatements Due to Unrealistic Positions

A tax preparer incurs a $250 penalty for each occurrence of an understatement of tax due to the taking of an unrealistic position in the return. This criterion is not subject to a materiality threshold. Rather, where there is no **realistic possibility** that the preparer's position will be maintained on its merits, the penalty simply applies.[68] The levy will be waived if the return includes a disclosure of the preparer's nonfrivolous position, or if the preparer has acted in good faith in preparing the return.

For this purpose, a realistic possibility exists where a reasonable and well-informed analysis by a person knowledgeable in the tax law would result in the conclusion that there was at least about a one-in-three likelihood that the position would

---

65. § 7206(2).
66. § 7213(a)(3).
67. § 6695(f).
68. § 6694(a).

be upheld on its merits. Thus, this criterion does not require certainty nor, indeed, even a preponderance of the evidence. Most likely, the party whose likelihood of sustaining the position is being measured is an appropriate judicial forum.

This penalty also is applied where the preparer fails to make adequate inquiries of the taxpayer relative to information that appears to be incomplete or incorrect.[69] The penalty is assessed only on the preparer who is required to sign the return.

Willful Understatement

A preparer is subject to a $1,000 penalty if any part of an understatement of a taxpayer's liability is attributable to the preparer's willful attempt in any manner to understate the liability, or to the reckless or intentional disregard of IRS rules or Regulations.[70] A preparer is considered to have willfully attempted to understate the tax in this manner if he or she disregards information that has been supplied by the taxpayer, or by any other person, in an attempt wrongfully to reduce the taxpayer's levy.

The willful understatement penalty is not imputed to the employer of the return preparer unless the employer also participated in the wrongdoing. The penalty focuses only on the conduct of the actual ITRP.

It is possible that both the willful and unrealistic position understatement penalties will apply to the same return. A penalty for willful understatement of liability may be based on an intentional disregard of the pertinent rules and Regulations. If a penalty is collected under the unrealistic-position penalty rule, the amount that may be collected under the willful-understatement penalty rule is reduced by a corresponding amount.

Organizing Abusive Tax Shelters

A civil penalty may be imposed on any person who organizes or assists in organizing, or (even indirectly) participates in the sale of any interest in, a tax shelter, and who makes or furnishes a statement regarding an expected tax benefit that the person knows or has reason to know is either false or fraudulent, or a gross valuation understatement.[71]

For this purpose, a gross valuation understatement is a statement of the value of any property or service that exceeds 200 percent of the amount that is determined to be its correct value, if the value of the property or service is directly related to the amount of any allowable deduction or credit.[72] Accordingly, there does not need to be an understatement of tax before this penalty can be applied. The penalty can be triggered without an IRS audit, and it can be based only on the shelter's offering materials.

The amount of the penalty is the greater of $1,000 or 100 percent of the gross income that is derived, or is to be derived, by the taxpayer from the project. The IRS may waive all or a portion of the penalty that is attributable to a gross valuation understatement if there was a reasonable basis for the valuation, and it was made in good faith.[73]

Although the penalty is not aimed specifically at tax preparers, but rather at the tax shelter industry itself, professional tax advisors may be subject to the penalty because they often assist in organizing tax shelter projects.

---

69. § 6694(a)(2).
70. § 6694(b).
71. § 6700.
72. § 6700(b)(1).
73. §§ 6700(a)(2) and (b)(2).

Aiding and Abetting Understatement

The Code imposes a civil penalty on any person who aids or assists, or procures or advises, in the preparation or presentation of any portion of a return or other tax-related document, if he or she knows or has reason to believe that the return or other document will be used in connection with any material tax matter, and that this use will result in the understatement of another person's tax liability.[74] This penalty may also be imposed on a person who acts in violation of the statute through a subordinate (e.g., an employee or agent) by either ordering or causing the subordinate to act, or knowing of and not attempting to prevent the subordinate from acting, wrongfully.[75]

The amount of the penalty is $1,000 ($10,000 for corporations) for each understating taxpayer. This penalty may be imposed only once per year for each understating taxpayer who is serviced by the ITRP. However, it may be imposed in addition to other penalties. Thus, the preparer may also be prosecuted under the criminal statutes.[76]

Aiding or Assisting in the Preparation of a False Return

A criminal penalty may be imposed on any person who willfully aids or assists in the preparation of a return or other document that is false as to any material matter. This penalty is the criminal equivalent to the civil penalty for aiding and abetting the understatement of any tax liability.

A person who is convicted of violating this statute is guilty of a felony and is subject to imprisonment for up to three years and/or may be fined an amount that cannot exceed $100,000 ($500,000 for corporations). This is one of the most severe tax preparer penalties under the Code.[77]

The persons who are prosecuted under this statute usually are accountants or other return preparers. However, a person who supplies false information that is used in the preparation of a return may also be subject to this penalty. The penalty can be assessed when it is merely a false tax-related document (like a Form 1099 or W-4), and not a tax return, that is prepared.

Disclosure or Use of Information by Return Preparers

The Code imposes a civil penalty on any return preparer who discloses or uses any tax return information for other than the purpose of preparing a tax return. This penalty amounts to $250 per improper use; a preparer's maximum penalty for any calendar year is $10,000. The Code also imposes a criminal penalty on any return preparer who knowingly or recklessly discloses or uses any tax return information for other than the specific purpose of preparing a tax return. One who is convicted of violating this statute is guilty of a misdemeanor and is subject to imprisonment for not more than one year and/or may be fined an amount that cannot exceed $1,000.[78]

The definition of a tax return preparer for purposes of this criminal penalty is broader than that under the civil preparer statutes. For instance, a clerical assistant who types or otherwise works on returns that are completed by the preparer is a "tax return preparer" for purposes of this provision; however, he or she would not be considered to be an ITRP for purposes of the civil preparer penalty statutes.

---

74. § 6701(a).
75. § 6701(c).
76. § 6701(b).
77. § 7206(2).
78. §§ 6713 and 7216(a).

The preparer, as here defined, may disclose information that is obtained from the taxpayer without being subject to the civil or criminal penalty if such disclosure is pursuant to any other provisions of the Code, or to a court order.

See Exhibit 13–2 for a summary of the most important of the civil and criminal penalties that may apply to taxpayers, preparers, and shelter distributors.

Conflict among Taxpayer and Preparer Penalty Provisions

Exhibit 13–3 illustrates the possibility for conflict between a taxpayer and his or her preparer, with respect to the taking and disclosure of a position on a return. No taxpayer substantial-understatement penalty is incurred if the substantial-authority criterion is met; that is, the taxpayer's position has the highest probability for success in a hypothetical court proceeding with respect to the disputed issue. With respect to nonfrivolous positions, no penalty is incurred if the substantial-authority test is failed but a Form 8275 disclosure is made on the return. At first glance, this criterion comes close to a "more likely than not" or greater-than-50-percent standard. Yet, where there are more than two defensible positions with respect to the disputed issue, this is not the case.

Example 13–2 Josie's return includes the claiming of a deduction that is contrary to an extant Revenue Ruling. Because of a new court decision in another circuit that is favorable to the deduction, Josie believes that there is a 70 percent chance that she would prevail in a suit relative to the deduction. No substantial-understatement penalty will apply to Josie, whether she wins or loses in court, and she need not disclose in any way her variance from the government position on her return.

Example 13–3 Continue with the facts of Example 13–2, except assume that Josie believes the following probabilities exist with respect to a court's treatment of her deduction, as supported by substantial authority.

Full support for her position	40%
Partial deduction allowed	35%
No deduction allowed	25%

No substantial-understatement penalty will apply to Josie, whether she wins or loses in court, and she need not disclose in any way her variance from the government position on her return. The weight of substantial authority for her position exceeds that supporting any other contrary position.

Example 13–4 Return to the facts of Example 13–2, except assume that Josie believes that she has a 40 percent probability of success in a court hearing. To avoid any substantial-understatement penalty, Josie must attach a Form 8275 to the return, revealing where and how she has deviated from the government's position relative to the deduction.

This discussion begs the question of how the typical lay taxpayer would arrive at the table of probabilities necessary to determine whether an additional Form 8275 disclosure would be necessary. It is clear that the substantial-authority criterion needs refinement to make it applicable to all but the most educated of taxpayers.

To avoid the preparer penalty for understatement-due-to-an-unrealistic-position, a one-in-three *realistic possibility* must exist that the return position will prevail on

Exhibit 13-2 Summary of Tax-Related Penalties

Criminal and civil penalties are not mutually exclusive, so a taxpayer or a preparer may be liable for both. Unlike civil penalties, which are collected in the same manner as would be true for the regular tax, criminal penalties are imposed only after the completion of the normal criminal process, in which the defendant is entitled to a number of constitutional guarantees and other rights, i.e., he or she is deemed to be innocent until proven guilty.

IRC Section	Type of Infraction	Penalty
Civil Penalties		
6694(a)	Understatement due to unrealistic position	$250 per return
6694(b)	Willful understatement of liability	$1,000 per return
6695(a)	Failure to furnish copy to taxpayer	$50 per failure
6695(b)	Failure to inform taxpayer of certain record-keeping requirements or to sign return	$50 per failure
6695(c)	Failure to furnish identifying number	$50 per failure*
6695(d)	Failure to retain copy or list	$50 per failure*
6695(e)	Failure to file correct information return	$50 per failure to file; $50 per omitted item*
6695(f)	Negotiation or endorsement of refund checks	$500 per check
6700	Organizing (or assisting in doing so) or promoting and making or furnishing statements with respect to abusive tax shelters	Greater of $1,000 or 100% of gross income derived by preparer from the project
6701	Aiding and abetting an understatement of tax liability	$1,000 per return; $10,000 per return if taxpayer is a corporation
6713	Improper disclosure or use of return data	$250 per improper use; annual maximum $10,000

*Annual maximum penalty = $25,000.

IRC Section	Type of Infraction	Penalty
Criminal Penalties		
7201	Attempt to evade or defeat tax	Felony; fine of not more than $100,000 ($500,000 if a corporation) and/or imprisonment for not more than five years
7202	Willful failure to collect or pay over a tax	Felony; fine of not more than $10,000 and/or imprisonment for not more than five years
7203	Willful failure to file return, supply information, or pay tax	Misdemeanor; fine of not more than $25,000 ($100,000 if a corporation) and/or imprisonment for not more than one year (five years relative to cash received by a business)
7204	Fraudulent statement or failure to make statement to employees	Fine of not more than $1,000 and/or imprisonment for not more than one year
7205	Fraudulent withholding exemption certificate or failure to supply information	Fine of not more than $1,000 and/or imprisonment for not more than one year
7206	Fraud and false statements	Felony; fine of not more than $100,000 ($500,000 if a corporation) and/or imprisonment for not more than three years
7206(2)	Aid or assistance in the preparation or presentation of a false return, claim, or other document	Felony; fine of not more than $100,000 ($500,000 if a corporation) and/or imprisonment for not more than three years
7207	Fraudulent returns, statements, or other documents	Fine of not more than $10,000 ($50,000 if a corporation) and/or imprisonment for not more than one year
7210	Failure to obey summons	Fine of not more than $1,000 and/or imprisonment for not more than one year
7212	Attempts to interfere with administration of internal revenue laws	Fine of not more than $5,000 and/or imprisonment for not more than three years
7216	Disclosure or use of information by preparer of return	Misdemeanor; fine of not more than $1,000 and/or imprisonment for not more than one year

Exhibit 13–3
Comparing Taxpayer and Preparer Penalties, Non-Tax-Shelter Disputes

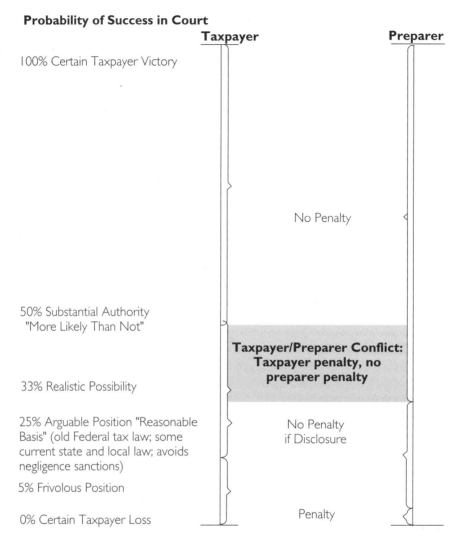

its merits. Lacking that level of likely success, a nonfrivolous position must be supported by a Form 8275 disclosure thereof.

Thus, the two penalties discussed here apply different disclosure criteria, and therein lies the possibility for preparer–taxpayer conflict. In many cases, the preparer will be likely to overstate the probability of success with respect to the disputed issue, because the no-disclosure-necessary level of certainty is lower for avoiding the preparer penalty than is the case for avoiding the taxpayer penalty. Again, one must conclude that further refinement of the penalty provisions is necessary, because the purpose of the tax law certainly is not to place the taxpayer at odds with his or her professional representative.

Under previous law, any *arguable position* taken in good faith on a return would be sufficient to avoid a taxpayer penalty. Thus, with respect to prior-year audits and concerning applications of state laws that may have retained the previous standards, the picture in Exhibit 13–3 can get even more complex.

INJUNCTIONS

The IRS is empowered to seek **injunctions** against two classes of persons of interest to our discussion: (1) income tax return preparers and (2) promoters of abusive tax shelters. An injunction is a judicial order that prohibits the named person from engaging in certain specified activities. The courts have broad authority to structure any injunctive relief that is granted to fit the circumstances of the case as appropriate.

ACTION TO ENJOIN INCOME TAX RETURN PREPARERS

The IRS may seek an injunction against an ITRP who is guilty of certain misconduct to prohibit him or her from engaging in such misconduct or from practicing as a return preparer.

Before such an injunction can be issued, however, the preparer must have (1) violated a preparer penalty or a criminal provision of the Code, (2) misrepresented his or her eligibility to practice before the IRS, (3) guaranteed the payment of any tax refund or the allowance of a credit, or (4) engaged in other fraudulent or deceptive conduct that substantially interferes with the administration of the tax laws.

In addition, it must be shown that the injunctive relief is appropriate to prevent the conduct from recurring. An injunction to prohibit the preparer from acting as an income tax return preparer may be obtained if the court finds that the preparer continually or repeatedly has engaged in misconduct, and that an injunction prohibiting such specific misconduct would be effective.[79]

ACTION TO ENJOIN PROMOTERS OF ABUSIVE TAX SHELTERS

The IRS may obtain an injunction against a person who is guilty of promoting abusive tax shelters, or of aiding and abetting an understatement of the tax liability, to prohibit him or her from engaging in such conduct or activities. Before such an injunction is issued, a court must find that injunctive relief is appropriate to prevent this conduct from recurring.[80]

INTEREST

The Code provides for the payment of interest on underpayments and overpayments of tax, at an adjustable rate, compounded daily. The objective of these provisions is to compensate offended parties for the use of their funds. Moreover, the interest charge eliminates the benefits that taxpayers (or the government) could obtain by adopting aggressive positions in the creation or processing of tax returns in order to postpone or avoid the payment of their taxes.

INTEREST–COMPUTATION CONVENTIONS

Interest on underpayments is payable at a federally specified rate, from the last date that is prescribed for the payment of the tax to the date on which the tax is actually

---

79. § 7407.
80. § 7408.

paid. The last date that is prescribed for payment of the tax is usually the unextended due date of the return that reports the amount of tax that is due.[81]

Interest is compounded on a daily basis.[82] Thus, given an interest rate that equals or exceeds about 15 percent, the obligation of the taxpayer or government could double in five years. The IRS has published interest-factor tables in Revenue Procedure 95-17, which automatically calculate the daily compounding for various rates of interest.[83]

The rate of interest that is used for underpayments and overpayments is adjusted quarterly to reflect the federal short-term interest rate for the first day of the quarter.[84] The new prevailing rate is published in a timely fashion, typically in a Revenue Ruling.

The interest rate on underpayments is set at one percentage point higher than that for overpayments. Thus, the taxpayer is subject to an interest rate that is higher than that which applies to the government. Large corporations add two more percentage points to the underpayment rate. Corporate overpayments in excess of $10,000 earn interest at only a discounted rate. Exhibit 13–4 documents the various IRS rates of interest that applied to over- and underpayments occurring through 2001.

Where the taxpayer is subject to both underpayment and overpayment computations for the same time period, whether the prior disputes involve income, transfer, or employment taxes, the amounts due and payable to the government are netted and a zero interest rate applies to those amounts.

Example 13–5 Mary Brown, a calendar-year taxpayer, filed her 2002 tax return and showed a balance due of $1,000. The return was filed on June 30, 2003, pursuant to a properly executed extension of time to file, and the tax was paid in full with the return. The prevailing IRS interest rate that applies to Brown's underpayment was 8 percent. She must pay about $17 of interest with her return, determined as follows.

Total tax outstanding	$ 1,000
Factor from Rev. Proc. 95–17, for 8% interest and 76 days' late payment	× .016795189
Interest assessed	$ 16.80

If Brown does not remit the interest that she owes when she files the return, interest will accrue, on both the tax and the $17 of interest itself, until the obligation is paid in full. If this amount is paid within ten days of the receipt of an IRS notice and demand for payment, however, no further interest accrues.

Interest accrues on the full amount of the tax liability that is appropriate under the Code, regardless of the amount of tax that is entered on the return. Moreover, interest is imposed on an assessable penalty, additional amount, or addition to the tax if these amounts are not paid within 10 days of the date on which the IRS requests

---

81. §§ 6601(a) and (b).
82. § 6622(a).
83. 1995–9 IRB 13.
84. § 6621.

Exhibit 13–4 IRS Overpayment and Underpayment Interest Rates

Period		Rate
Prior to July 1975		6%
July 1, 1975	– January 31, 1976	9
February 1, 1976	– January 31, 1978	7
February 1, 1978	– January 31, 1980	6
February 1, 1980	– January 31, 1982	12
February 1, 1982	– December 31, 1982	20
January 1, 1983	– June 30, 1983	16*
July 1, 1983	– December 31, 1984	11*
January 1, 1985	– June 30, 1985	13*
July 1, 1985	– December 31, 1985	11*
January 1, 1986	– June 30, 1986	10*
July 1, 1986	– December 31, 1986	9*

Period		Over-payment Rate*†	Under-payment Rate*†	Large Corporation Underpayment Rate*	Rate for Corporation Overpayments >$10,000*
January 1, 1987	– September 30, 1987	8%	9%		
October 1, 1987	– December 31, 1987	9	10		
January 1, 1988	– March 31, 1988	10	11		
April 1, 1988	– September 30, 1988	9	10		
October 1, 1988	– March 31, 1989	10	11		
April 1, 1989	– September 30, 1989	11	12		
October 1, 1989	– March 31, 1991	10	11		
April 1, 1991	– December 31, 1991	9	10	12%	
January 1, 1992	– March 31, 1992	8	9	11	
April 1, 1992	– September 30, 1992	7	8	10	
October 1, 1992	– June 30, 1994	6	7	9	
July 1, 1994	– September 30, 1994	7	8	10	
October 1, 1994	– December 31, 1994	8	9	11	
January 1, 1995	– March 31, 1995	8	9	11	6.5
April 1, 1995	– June 30, 1995	9	10	12	7.5
July 1, 1995	– March 31, 1996	8	9	11	6.5
April 1, 1996	– June 30, 1996	7	8	10	5.5
July 1, 1996	– April 15, 1998	8	9	11	6.5
April 16, 1998	– December 31, 1998	7	8	10	5.5
January 1, 1999	– April 15, 1999	6	7	9	4.5
April 16, 1999	– April 15, 2000	7	8	10	5.5
April 16, 2000	– April 15, 2001	8	9	11	6.5
April 16, 2001	– June 30, 2001	7	8	10	5.5
July 1, 2001	– December 31, 2001	6	7	9	4.5

*Daily compounding required.
†After 1998, noncorporate taxpayers use the second column for both under- and overpayments. Corporations still receive one percentage point less with respect to their smaller overpayments; i.e., the first column applies.

its payment. Interest on penalties generally is imposed only from the date of this IRS notice and demand, and not from the due date of the return. However, the fraud, accuracy-related, and failure-to-file penalties run from the (extended) due date of the return.[85]

No interest is charged on criminal penalties or delinquent estimated tax payments. However, recall that a nondeductible penalty is imposed in lieu of interest with respect to delinquent estimated tax payments. This penalty is computed in the same manner as would be the required interest, except that daily compounding of the penalty is not required.

In general, the IRS has no authority to forgive the payment of interest. Consequently, a taxpayer will be required to pay the total amount of interest assessed on any underpayment, even though the delinquency was attributable to a reasonable cause, including an IRS loss of records and the illness, transfer, or leave of a pertinent IRS employee. However, the IRS can abate such interest where it is attributable to an error or delay caused by an employee or officer of the IRS in response to the taxpayer's filing a claim on Form 843. Such a delay cannot be traceable to an interpretation of the tax law, but rather must relate to nondiscretionary, administrative, or managerial duties of procedure or return processing, including an IRS loss of records and the illness, transfer, or leave of a pertinent IRS employee.[86]

The government is required to pay interest at the applicable Federal rate to any taxpayer who has made an overpayment of tax. Interest on an overpayment runs from the date of the overpayment to the date on which the overpayment is credited against another tax liability, or, in the case of a refund, to a date that is not more than 30 days before the date of the refund check.

However, the IRS is allowed a specific period in which it may refund an overpayment without incurring interest. This interest-free period runs for 45 days after the unextended due date of the return or, if the return is filed after its due date, for 45 days after it is actually filed. If the refund is not made within this 45-day period, interest begins to accrue from the later of (1) the due date of the return or (2) the date on which the return was actually filed.[87]

Example 13–6 Joan Jeffries, a calendar-year taxpayer, filed her 2002 Federal income tax return on October 1, 2003. Her return showed an overpayment of $2,500, for which Jeffries requested a full refund. If the IRS refunds the $2,500 overpayment on or before November 14, 2003, no interest will be due from the government. However, if the refund is paid after November 14, 2003, interest will accrue from October 1, 2003, through a date that is not more than 30 days before the date of the refund check. (In any event, interest does not accrue as of April 16, 2003, for Joan.)

The date that is stated on the government's refund check determines whether the overpayment is refunded within the 45-day interest-free period. The date on which the refund is actually received does not control for this purpose. Thus, an interest-free refund may be paid, even though it is not received by the taxpayer until the 45-day period has expired.

---

85. § 6601(e)(2).
86. § 6404(e) and Rev. Proc. 87–42, 1987–2 CB 589.
87. § 6611(e).

APPLICABLE INTEREST RATE

Different rates are used with respect to IRS overpayments and underpayments after 1986, as is evident in Exhibit 13–4. The overpayment rate (paid by the IRS) is two percentage points greater than the Federal short-term interest rate, compounded daily, and the underpayment rate (paid to the IRS) is three percentage points greater than the same Federal rate.

Large corporations pay interest at two percentage points higher than the usual underpayment rate. Corporations receive interest on overpayments at 1½ percentage points lower than the usual overpayment rate, where the overpayment exceeds $10,000. Under- and overpayment rates are determined for the beginning of each calendar quarter, using the Federal rates in effect for the first month of that quarter.

STATUTES OF LIMITATIONS

The Code establishes a specific period of time, commonly referred to as a **statute of limitation,** within which all taxes must be assessed and collected and all refund claims must be made. After the pertinent statute of limitations expires, certain actions may not be taken, because the expiration establishes an absolute defense for the party against whom legal action is brought. In other words, a taxpayer cannot be required to pay taxes that he or she rightfully owes if these taxes are not assessed and collected within the time periods that the Code has established.

NATURE OF STATUTES OF LIMITATIONS

Although the statute of limitations appears to be a legal loophole that rewards delinquent taxpayers who avoid detection, Congress believes that, at some point, the right to be free of stale claims must prevail over the government's right to pursue them. If the statutes permitted the lapse of an extended period of time between the initiation of a claim and its pursuit, the defense could be jeopardized because witnesses might have died or disappeared, memories might have faded, and records or other evidence might have been lost. Moreover, some statutes of limitations are designed solely to protect the government (e.g., the statute of limitations on credits or refunds). A number of such statutes limit the time period within which assessment, collection, and claim for refund or credit activities must be conducted.[88]

ASSESSMENT

Assessment of an internal revenue tax generally must be made within three years of the later of the date that the return was actually filed or the unextended due date of the return. A return that is filed prior to its due date, for this purpose, is deemed to be filed on its due date. The assessment period for a return that is filed after the due date starts on the day that follows the actual filing date, regardless of whether the return is delinquent or the due date was extended properly.

---

88. § 6501.

The period in which a tax may be assessed is extended to six years if the taxpayer omits from his or her reported gross income an amount that is greater than 25 percent of the reported gross income.[89] For this purpose, § 61 gross income is used in the 25 percent computation, with two exceptions. First, the gross income of a business is *not* reduced by cost of sales. Second, income that is omitted from the return is ignored for purposes of constructing the base for the 25 percent test, if the omission is disclosed in the return or in an attached document.[90]

Although the limitations period will be extended for a substantial omission of income, it (surprisingly) is not extended where the taxpayer has overstated the amount of his or her deductions, regardless of the amount of the overstatement.

Irregular Returns

A tax may be assessed at any time when a taxpayer files a false or fraudulent return with the intent to evade tax liability.[91] Once the fraudulent return is filed, the limitations period remains open indefinitely. A later filing of a nonfraudulent amended return will not start the running of the three- (or six)-year limitation period.[92]

When a taxpayer fails to file a return, the tax may be assessed at any time. For this purpose, one's failure to file need not be willful. A taxpayer who innocently or negligently fails to file is still subject to an unlimited period of assessment for the tax.[93]

Acceleration, Extension, and Carryback Effects

Generally, the filing of an amended return does not affect the length of the limitations period. However, the limitations period is extended by 60 days if the IRS receives, within 60 days of the expiration of the applicable statute of limitations, an amended return that shows the taxpayer owes an additional tax.[94] This provision was enacted to discourage taxpayers from waiting until the limitations period on an assessment was about to expire before submitting an erroneous amended return. Prior to the enactment of this provision, it was beneficial for the taxpayer to wait to file an amended return this way, because the IRS would not have enough time to assess more tax if an examination of the original return uncovered additional unreported errors or omissions.

The usual three-year assessment period can be reduced to 18 months if a request for a prompt assessment is filed with the IRS.[95] This request usually is made for an income tax return of a decedent or an estate, or for a corporation that is in the midst of a dissolution. Generally, a prompt assessment is requested when all of the involved parties wish to accelerate the final determination of the tax liability.

A deficiency for a carryback year that is attributable to the carryback of a net operating loss, capital loss, or unused research or general business credit can be assessed at any time before the expiration of the limitations period for the year in which the loss occurred or the credit originated. This extension in the period of assessment for the carryback year is necessary to ensure that there is adequate time to

---

89. § 6501(e)(1)(A).
90. §§ 6501(e)(1)(A)(i) and (ii).
91. § 6501(c)(1).
92. *Badaracco v. Comm.*, 464 U.S. 386, 104 S.Ct. 756 (1984).
93. § 6501(c)(3).
94. § 6501(c)(7).
95. § 6501(d).

process the refund claim and to allow the IRS to examine the return that gave rise to the carryback item.[96]

The period for assessment is not extended when a net operating loss, capital loss, or unused credit is carried forward.

IRS-Requested Extensions

An extension of the period of limitations typically will be requested by the IRS when an audit or an appellate review cannot be completed until after the statute of limitations expires. The taxpayer is not bound to agree with such a request, but such a refusal may prompt the IRS to stop negotiations prematurely and assess a deficiency against the taxpayer. Although the issuance of a statutory notice of deficiency does not preclude the taxpayer from obtaining a negotiated settlement with the IRS, he or she will be required to undertake a more costly procedure and file a petition with the U.S. Tax Court or pay the assessment and file a claim for refund. Consequently, a taxpayer normally should not refuse to sign a waiver of the statute of limitations, as requested by the IRS, unless the agent has completed the examination and there exist one or more unagreed-upon issues that the taxpayer is ready to litigate.

COLLECTION

All taxes must be collected within 10 years after a timely assessment has been made.[97] **Collection** can be made either by IRS levy or by the agency's commencement of an action in court. If the tax is not collected administratively by levy within the 10-year period, the IRS must commence an action in court to reduce the assessment to a judgment before the statute of limitation expires. Once a judgment for the assessed tax is awarded, the tax may be collected at any time after the normal period of collections has expired. Thus, collection is not barred after the 10-year period expires, provided that the IRS has obtained a timely judgment against the taxpayer.

The taxpayer and the IRS may agree to an extension of the normal collection period. The IRS will request such an extension whenever the taxpayer has agreed to extend the period of limitations for assessment of the tax. In addition, the taxpayer may request an extension to allow additional time in which to (raise and) submit any delinquent taxes. If the taxpayer agrees to extend the period of limitation on collections, the IRS may agree not to seize and sell the taxpayer's property to satisfy the tax liability.

The 10-year period of limitations begins only after an assessment is made. If an assessment can be made at any time, for example, because the taxpayer failed to file a return or filed a fraudulent return, the tax may be collected within 10 years of the date of assessment, regardless of when it eventually is made.

CLAIM FOR REFUND OR CREDIT

A taxpayer must file a timely and valid claim at the service center for the district in which the tax was paid to receive a refund or credit of an overpayment of tax. The claim should be made by individuals on Form 1040X, Individual Amended Income Tax Return, and by corporations on Form 1120X, Corporate Amended Income Tax Return.

---

96. §§ 6501(h) through (k).
97. § 6502(a)(1).

Generally, an overpayment can be refunded or credited only to the person who was subject to the original tax. However, the IRS can apply overpayments to delinquent support obligations and certain certified nontax debts that are owed to the Federal government. Refunds in excess of $2,000,000 may not be made until they have been reviewed by the Joint Committee on Taxation.[98]

A taxpayer who reports a net operating loss, capital loss, or credit carryback can accelerate the processing of the refund by filing an Application for Tentative Carryback Adjustment on Form 1045 (for individuals) or Form 1139 (for corporations). The IRS has 90 days from the later of the date on which the application was filed or the last day of the month in which the return for the loss is due to examine the application and accept or deny the claim.[99] However, if the application is denied, the taxpayer cannot bring a suit for recovery of the overpayment, because the IRS's determination is only tentative. Instead, the taxpayer must file a refund claim on the appropriate form and wait for six months from the date on which the claim was filed, or until the IRS denies the refund claim, before legal action can be started.

Before a refund or credit can be issued, the IRS must review the taxpayer's claim. Even if the Commissioner agrees that the taxpayer has overpaid a tax, he or she has no authority to refund or credit the overpayment unless the taxpayer files the claim within the allowable period. Any refund of an overpayment that is made after the period for filing a timely claim is considered erroneous and a credit is considered void.

Limitations Period

A taxpayer who has filed a return must file a claim for credit or refund within three years of the date on which the return was filed or two years of the date on which the tax was paid, whichever is later. If the taxpayer did not file a return (e.g., because taxes were withheld from the taxpayer's wages, but the taxpayer did not file a return because his or her taxable income did not exceed the applicable exemptions and standard deduction), the claim for credit or refund must be made within two years of the date on which the tax was paid.[100]

The period within which a claim for credit or refund may be filed is extended when the taxpayer and the IRS agree to extend the statute of limitations on assessments. A claim can be filed within six months after the expiration of the extended assessment period.[101]

Other Extensions

The limitations period also can be extended where an overpayment results from a business bad debt or from a discovery of worthless securities.[102] A claim for refund or credit that is attributable to losses sustained from worthless securities or business bad debts may be filed within seven years from the date that the return was due, without regard to any extension for filing the return. This period is extended further if the debt or loss increases a net operating loss carryback, since the taxpayer will be entitled to three additional years for the filing of a claim that is based on the carryback.[103]

---

98. § 6405(a).
99. § 6411(b) and Reg. § 1.6411–1(b).
100. § 6511(a).
101. § 6511(c)(2).
102. § 6511(d).
103. § 6511(d)(2)(A).

This provision was enacted because the determination of the date on which a debt or share of stock becomes worthless is a question of fact that may not be determined until after the year in which the loss actually occurred. If taxpayers were not allowed additional time in which to file refund claims for these items, they could incur substantial losses without the receipt of any tax benefits, because the deductions must be taken in the taxable year of the loss, not in a later year.

The period for filing a claim for refund is extended when the claimed overpayment results from the carryback of a net operating loss, capital loss, or certain credits. If a claim for credit or refund is attributable to the carryback of a net operating loss, net capital loss, or business credit, it can be filed within three years of the extended due date of the return for the year in which the losses occurred or the credits originated, rather than within three years of the due date of the return for the carryback year. Again, this provision was enacted because the existence and amount of these items might not be known until after the expiration of the usual three-year period for filing the claim.

Amount of the Credit or Refund

If a claim for refund or credit is filed in a timely fashion, the amount of the taxpayer's refund or credit is limited to the portion of the tax that was paid during the three immediately preceding years, plus the period of any extension for filing the return.[104] The amount of tax that is subject to the claim may include amounts that were withheld and estimated payments that were made more than three years before the date on which the claim was filed, because these amounts are all deemed to have been paid on the due date of the return.

If a claim is filed after the three-year period, the amount of any refund or credit is limited to the portion of the tax that was paid during the two years that immediately precede the filing of the claim. This two-year period also is effective if a claim is filed for a year in which a return was not filed. Because this claim relates only to a two-year period, it may not protect payments that were made with the original return.

SUSPENSION OF PERIOD OF ASSESSMENT AND COLLECTION

Usually, a tax must be assessed within three years after the filing of a tax return, and it must be collected within six years of the assessment. However, under certain circumstances, the running of the statutes of limitations on assessment or collection is suspended.

When the IRS mails a statutory notice of deficiency (i.e., a ninety-day letter) to the taxpayer, the assessment and collection period is suspended for 150 days (210 days if the letter is addressed to a person who is outside the United States).[105] The statutes of limitations on assessment and collection also are suspended when a case is pending before the U.S. Tax Court. This suspension period begins when the taxpayer files a petition in the Tax Court contesting the deficiency, and it continues until 60 days after the decision of the Tax Court becomes final.

When a taxpayer submits an offer in compromise for consideration by the IRS, the statute of limitations on assessment is suspended. This suspension period begins

---

104. § 6511(b)(2)(A).
105. § 6503(a)(1).

when the offer is submitted, and it continues until one year after the offer is terminated, withdrawn, or formally rejected.[106]

In addition to the circumstances just discussed, the statute of limitations also can be suspended when:[107]

- the taxpayer's assets are in the custody of the court;
- the taxpayer is outside the United States for six or more consecutive months;
- the taxpayer's assets are wrongfully seized;
- a fiduciary or receiver is appointed in a bankruptcy case;
- the IRS is prohibited under bankruptcy law from any assessment or collection of a tax; or
- the collection of excise or termination taxes on certain retirement plans or private foundations are suspended.

MITIGATION OF STATUTE OF LIMITATIONS

Generally, the IRS cannot make an assessment and a taxpayer cannot obtain a refund after the statute of limitations has expired. However, §§ 1311 through 1314 of the Code include a complex set of rules designed to prevent the taxpayer or the IRS from taking advantage of an oncoming expiration of the period of limitations on assessment, collection, or refunds.

When an error has been made in the inclusion of an item of income, allowance, or disallowance of a deduction or other tax treatment of a transaction that affects the basis of property, the mitigation provisions will allow a submission of the error to be corrected, even though the normal period of limitations has expired for that year.

STATUTORY AGREEMENTS

The Code provides for two types of agreements that may be used to resolve tax disputes, namely, closing agreements and offers in compromise.

CLOSING AGREEMENTS

A **closing agreement** is a formal, written agreement that is made between a taxpayer and the IRS. It is the only agreement that the Code recognizes as being binding. Once it is approved, a closing agreement is final and conclusive on the part of both the government and the taxpayer, unless there is a showing of fraud, malfeasance, or a misrepresentation of a material fact, by either party.[108]

The purpose of a closing agreement is either (1) to enable the taxpayer and the IRS to resolve, finally and completely, a tax controversy for any period prior to the date of the agreement and to protect the taxpayer against the reopening of the matter at a later date; or (2) to determine a matter in a tax year that arises after the date of the agreement.

---

106. Reg. § 301.7122-1(f).
107. §§ 6503(b) through (f). That section also contains other, less frequently encountered suspension possibilities.
108. § 7121(b).

The IRS is authorized to enter into a closing agreement in any case where there appears to be a benefit to the government in closing the case permanently and conclusively, or if the taxpayer demonstrates a need to close the case and the government's interests are not harmed. Typically, a closing agreement is used in cases where the IRS and the taxpayer have made mutual concessions relative to the case, and it is necessary or desirable to bar further actions by either party. Such an agreement also may be used when a corporation is winding up its business affairs or when a taxpayer needs some authentic evidence of his or her tax liability, say, to satisfy creditors.

As a matter of practice, the IRS discourages the use of closing agreements because of their finality. Moreover, the IRS would have a difficult time processing a large number of requests for these agreements. Consequently, it prefers to use a number of informal agreements that may not resolve conclusively the tax dispute that is under examination, or that may not provide for the same degree of finality as would a closing agreement. Examples of such informal agreements include (1) Form 870, Waiver of Restrictions on Assessment and Collection of Deficiency in Tax and Acceptance of Overassessment; and (2) Form 870-AD, Offer of Waiver of Restrictions on Assessment and Collection of Deficiency in Tax and of Acceptance of Overassessment. Form 870 is reproduced in Exhibit 13–5.

OFFERS IN COMPROMISE

The Commissioner can make an **offer in compromise** for any civil or criminal case that does not involve sales of illegal drugs, prior to the time that the case is referred to the Justice Department for prosecution or defense. Once the case is referred to the Justice Department, however, the U.S. Attorney General has the final authority to compromise the case.[109] Compromise proposals entailing more than $50,000 in tax also must be supported by an opinion of the Chief Counsel.

In this context, the government will compromise a case only if there is doubt as to the liability or collectibility of the assessed tax. The IRS will not enter into a compromise with the taxpayer if the liability has been established by a valid judgment, and if there is no doubt as to the ability of the IRS to collect the amounts that are due.

A compromise agreement may cover the principal amount of tax, plus any corresponding interest or penalties. Ordinarily, the IRS will not compromise a criminal tax case unless it involves a violation of a regulatory provision of the Code or of a related statute that was not deliberately violated with an intent to defraud.

Although the IRS has complete authority to compromise most civil and criminal cases, there are certain cases that, as a matter of policy, it will not settle. These cases involve tax questions referred to as **prime issues.** If a case involves a prime issue, the IRS will not compromise its position. The taxpayer's only alternatives for resolving the issue in such a situation are (1) to concede the matter fully or (2) to proceed to litigate the matter.

Generally, the IRS designates a topic as a prime issue when the matter may be subject to taxpayer abuse and clearly threatens the IRS's ability to guard the currency. A list of prime issues is published in Volume 4 of the *Internal Revenue Manual*.

---

109. § 7122(a).

Exhibit 13–5 Taxpayer/IRS Agreement

Form **870** (Rev. March 1992)	Department of the Treasury — Internal Revenue Service **Waiver of Restrictions on Assessment and Collection of Deficiency in Tax and Acceptance of Overassessment**	Date received by Internal Revenue Service

Names and address of taxpayers *(Number, street, city or town, State, ZIP code)*	Social security or employer identification number

Increase (Decrease) in Tax and Penalties

Tax year ended	Tax	Penalties			
	$	$	$	$	$
	$	$	$	$	$
	$	$	$	$	$
	$	$	$	$	$
	$	$	$	$	$
	$	$	$	$	$
	$	$	$	$	$

(For instructions, see back of form)

Consent to Assessment and Collection

I consent to the immediate assessment and collection of any deficiencies *(increase in tax and penalties)* and accept any overassessment *(decrease in tax and penalties)* shown above, plus any interest provided by law. I understand that by signing this waiver, I will not be able to contest these years in the United States Tax Court, unless additional deficiencies are determined for these years.

YOUR SIGNATURE → HERE		Date
SPOUSE'S SIGNATURE →		Date
TAXPAYER'S REPRESENTATIVE HERE →		Date
CORPORATE NAME →		
CORPORATE OFFICER(S) SIGN HERE	Title	Date
	Title	Date

Catalog Number 16894U Form **870** (Rev. 3-92)

However, this portion of the manual is not released to the general public, so its exact contents are not known. One issue that is known to be on the list of prime issues, though, concerns the deductibility of rent payments for a gift-leaseback arrangement when the payments are made to a reversionary short-term trust.

A compromise agreement relates to the entire liability of the taxpayer, and it conclusively settles all of the issues for which an agreement is to be made. It is a legally enforceable promise that cannot be rescinded unless there has been a misrepresentation of the assets of the taxpayer by falsification or concealment, or a mutual mistake relative to a material fact. Consequently, a taxpayer cannot decide later to bring a suit for refund with respect to any item that is so compromised. Moreover, if a taxpayer defaults on a compromise agreement, the IRS may collect the original tax liability, less any payments that were actually made, or sue to enforce the agreement.

An offer in compromise is typically made via Form 656, Offer in Compromise, and it must be accompanied by a comprehensive set of the taxpayer's financial statements. The offer may be revoked or withdrawn at any time prior to its acceptance. Form 656 is reproduced in Exhibit 13–6.

SUMMARY

In dealing with tax underpayments, the stakes include more than just the disputed tax. Interest charges accrue, and both the taxpayer and tax advisor can be subjected to significant amounts of civil and criminal penalties. Restrictions on the actions of the taxpayer and practitioner are expressed using such ambiguously defined terms as *reasonable cause* and *substantial authority,* such that the lay taxpayer is expected to project accurately the final holding of a judicial forum. Such is the condition of a tax system under which tax rates virtually cannot be raised, yet revenue needs continue to escalate. The tax professional must include these sanctions in the research process, communicating their effects to the client as needed.

TAX TUTOR

Reinforce the tax research information covered in this chapter by completing the on-line tutorials located at the Federal Tax Research web site:

http://raabe.swcollege.com

KEY WORDS

By the time you complete your work relative to this chapter, you should be comfortable discussing each of the following terms. If you need additional review of any of these items, return to the appropriate material in the chapter or consult the glossary to this text.

Accuracy-Related Penalty	Closing Agreement
Assessment	Collection
Civil Penalty	Criminal Penalty

Continued

Exhibit 13–6 Offer in Compromise

IRS
Department of the Treasury
Internal Revenue Service
www.irs.gov
Form 656 (Rev. 5-2001)
Catalog Number 16728N

Form 656
Offer in Compromise

IRS RECEIVED DATE

Item 1 — Taxpayer's Name and Home or Business Address

Name

Name

Street Address

City   State   ZIP Code

Mailing Address *(if different from above)*

Street Address

City   State   ZIP Code

DATE RETURNED

Item 2 — Social Security Numbers

(a) Primary _____

(b) Secondary _____

Item 3 — Employer Identification Number *(included in offer)*

_____

Item 4 — Other Employer Identification Numbers *(not included in offer)* _____

Item 5 — To: Commissioner of Internal Revenue Service

I/We (includes all types of taxpayers) submit this offer to compromise the tax liabilities plus any interest, penalties, additions to tax, and additional amounts required by law (tax liability) for the tax type and period marked below: (Please mark an "X" in the box for the correct description and fill-in the correct tax period(s), adding additional periods if needed).

❑ 1040/1120 Income Tax — Year(s) _____

❑ 941 Employer's Quarterly Federal Tax Return — Quarterly period(s) _____

❑ 940 Employer's Annual Federal Unemployment (FUTA) Tax Return — Year(s) _____

❑ Trust Fund Recovery Penalty as a responsible person of (enter corporation name) _____ , for failure to pay withholding and Federal Insurance Contributions Act Taxes (Social Security taxes), for period(s) ending _____ .

❑ Other Federal Tax(es) [specify type(s) and period(s)] _____

Note: If you need more space, use another sheet titled "Attachment to Form 656 Dated _____ ." Sign and date the attachment following the listing of the tax periods.

Item 6 — I/We submit this offer for the reason(s) checked below:

❑ **Doubt as to Liability** — "I do not believe I owe this amount." You must include a detailed explanation of the reason(s) why you believe you do not owe the tax in Item 9.

❑ **Doubt as to Collectibility** — "I have insufficient assets and income to pay the full amount." You must include a complete Collection Information Statement, Form 433-A and/or Form 433-B.

❑ **Effective Tax Administration** — "I owe this amount and have sufficient assets to pay the full amount, but due to my exceptional circumstances, requiring full payment would cause an economic hardship or would be unfair and inequitable." You must include a complete Collection Information Statement, Form 433-A and/or Form 433B **and** complete Item 9.

Item 7

I/We offer to pay $ _____ (must be more than zero). Complete item 10 to explain where you will obtain the funds to make this offer.

Check one of the following:

❑ **Cash Offer (Offered amount will be paid in 90 days or less.)**

Balance to be paid in: ❑ 10; ❑ 30; ❑ 60; or ❑ 90 days from written notice of acceptance of the offer.

❑ **Short-Term Deferred Payment Offer (Offered amount will be paid in MORE than 90 days but within 24 months from written notice of acceptance of the offer.)**

$_____ within_____ days (not more than 90 — See Instructions Section, **Determine Your Payment Terms**) from written notice of acceptance of the offer; and

beginning in the _____ month after written notice of acceptance of the offer, $_____ on the _____ day of each month for a total of _____ months. (Cannot extend more than 24 months from written notice of acceptance of the offer.)

❑ **Deferred Payment Offer (Offered amount will be paid over the life of the collection statute.)**

$_____ within_____ days (not more than 90 — See Instructions Section, **Determine Your Payment Terms**) from written notice of acceptance of the offer; and

beginning in the first month after written notice of acceptance of the offer, $_____ on the _____ day of each month for a total of _____ months.

NOTE: Signature(s) of taxpayer required on last page of Form 656

Fraud
Injunction
Negligence
Offer in Compromise
Preparer Penalties
Prime Issues

Realistic Possibility
Reasonable Cause
Return Preparer
Statute of Limitations
Substantial Authority

DISCUSSION QUESTIONS

1. When should prevailing interest rates bear on tax decision making?
   a. The taxpayer is contemplating litigation in either the Tax Court or the Court of Federal Claims.
   b. An understatement of estimated tax payments is discovered late in the tax year.
2. What is the role of the statute of limitations in the Federal income tax system?
3. Indicate whether each of the following statements is true or false.
   a. The government never pays a taxpayer interest on an overpayment of tax.
   b. Penalties may be included as an itemized deduction on an individual's tax return.
   c. An extension of time for filing a return results in an automatic extension of the time in which the tax may be paid.
   d. The IRS can compromise on the amount of tax liability if there is doubt as to the taxpayer's ability to pay.
   e. The statute of limitations for assessment of taxes never extends beyond three years from the filing of a return.
   f. There is no statute of limitations relative to a taxpayer's claim for a refund.
4. Indicate whether, after both parties sign a Form 870, the following result(s) occur. More than one answer may be correct.
   a. The taxpayer still may appeal to a higher level of the IRS.
   b. The interest on the assessment stops accruing immediately.
   c. The agreement is binding on both the taxpayer and the IRS.
   d. The tax must be paid, but a suit for refund can be filed in the District Court or U.S. Court of Federal Claims.
5. Ace filed her 1998 income tax return on January 25, 1999. There was no material understatement of income on her return, and the return was properly signed and filed. The statute of limitations for Ace's 1998 return expires on:
   a. January 25, 2002
   b. April 15, 2002
   c. January 25, 2005
   d. April 15, 2005
6. Blanche filed her 1993 income tax return on April 4, 1999. On December 14, 1999, she learned that 100 shares of stock that she owned had become worthless in 1998. Since she did not deduct this loss on the 1998 return, Blanche intends to file a claim for refund. This claim must be filed by no later than April 15,
   a. 2000
   b. 2003
   c. 2005
   d. 2006
   e. There is no expiration date for the statute of limitations in this context.

7. Carl purposely omitted from his 1998 tax return $40,000 of the gross receipts that he collected as the owner of a saloon. His 1998 return indicated collective gross receipts of $25,000. The IRS no longer can pursue Carl with the threat of a collection of the related tax, interest, and penalties, as of April 15,
   a. 2000
   b. 2003
   c. 2005
   d. 2006
   e. There is no expiration date for the statute of limitations in this context.
8. Diane accidentally omitted from her 1998 tax return $40,000 of the gross receipts that she collected as the owner of a saloon. Her 1998 return indicated collective gross receipts of $25,000. The IRS no longer can pursue Diane with the threat of a collection of the related tax, interest, and penalties, as of April 15,
   a. 2000
   b. 2003
   c. 2005
   d. 2006
   e. There is no expiration date for the statute of limitations in this context.
9. List some of the liabilities and penalties that the Code imposes on tax preparers.
10. How has Congress used tax penalties to discourage the development of certain tax shelters?
11. Distinguish between or among the following.
    a. Offer in compromise and closing agreement
    b. Failure to file and failure to pay
    c. Criminal and civil penalties
    d. Injunction, suspension, and mitigation
    e. Assessment, collection, and claim

EXERCISES

12. Construct a scenario in which the tax advisor should recommend that the client terminate the challenge of the IRS with the following.
    a. Lawsuit
    b. Offer in compromise
    c. Closing agreement
    d. Appeals conference
    e. Office audit
    f. Correspondence audit
13. The client's return is found to include fraudulent data. Which of the following could the IRS charge with a preparer penalty?
    a. Taxpayer
    b. Partner of the accounting firm that prepared the return
    c. Employee of the client, who provided the accounting firm with the fraudulent data
    d. Staff member of the accounting firm, who used the fraudulent data to prepare the return and did not verify its accuracy
    e. Secretary of the accounting firm, who made copies of the fraudulent return

14. The client's return is found by the U.S. Tax Court to have included improper business deductions. The court agreed that the taxpayer's position had some statutory and judicial merit, but it held for the government nonetheless. Which of the following could the IRS charge with a preparer penalty?
    a. Taxpayer
    b. Partner of the accounting firm that prepared the return
    c. Employee of the client, who provided the accounting firm with the deduction data
    d. Staff member of the accounting firm, who used the deduction data to prepare the return
    e. Secretary of the accounting firm, who made copies of the return
15. Discuss the role of the penalty system in the conduct of a client's tax research.
16. Define and illustrate the following terms or concepts.
    a. Fraud
    b. Negligence
    c. Reasonable cause
    d. Lack of reasonable cause
    e. Civil penalty conviction
    f. Criminal penalty conviction
17. Discuss which penalties, if any, the tax advisor might be charged with in each of the following independent circumstances. In this regard, assume that the tax advisor
    a. provided information about the taxpayer's Federal income tax returns to the pertinent state income tax agency.
    b. provided information about the taxpayer's Federal income tax returns to the pertinent county's property tax agency.
    c. provided information about the taxpayer's Federal income tax returns to the FBI, which was interested in gathering evidence concerning the client's alleged drug dealing activities.
    d. suggested to the client various means by which to acquire excludible income.
    e. suggested to the client various means by which to conceal cash receipts from gross income.
    f. suggested to the client means by which to improve her cash flow by delaying for six months or more the deposit of the employees' share of Federal employment taxes.
    g. suggested to the client means by which to improve her cash flow by delaying for six months or more the deposit of the employer's share of Federal employment taxes.
    h. kept in his safe deposit box the concealed income of item (e).
    i. suggested that the client invest in a real estate tax shelter.
    j. provided a statement of assurance as to the accuracy of the financial data that is included in the prospectus of a real estate tax shelter.
    k. suggested to the promoters of a real estate tax shelter that a specific accounting technique, not recognized by generally accepted accounting principles, should be used to construct the prospectus.
    l. failed, because of pressing time conflicts, to conduct the usual review of the client's tax return. The IRS discovered that the return included fraudulent data.

Continued

m. failed, because of pressing time conflicts, to conduct the usual review of the client's tax return. The IRS discovered a mathematical error in the computation of the taxpayer's standard deduction.
18. What is a prime issue, and why is it designated as such?
19. For the completion and filing of his 2002 Federal income tax return, Ron retains the services of a tax preparer. Because of a particularly hectic tax preparation season, the preparer does not complete and file the return until June 2003. Is Ron excused from the failure to file and pay penalties under the reasonable cause exception?

PROBLEMS

20. Lefty, a calendar-year taxpayer subject to a 34 percent marginal tax rate, claimed a charitable contribution deduction of $15,000 for a sculpture that the IRS later valued at $10,000. The applicable overvaluation penalty is:
    a. $0
    b. $100 (minimum penalty)
    c. $340
    d. $1,700
    e. Some other amount

21. Righty, a calendar-year taxpayer subject to a 34 percent marginal tax rate, claimed a charitable contribution deduction of $170,000 for a sculpture that the IRS later valued at $100,000. The applicable overvaluation penalty is:
    a. $0
    b. $100 (minimum penalty)
    c. $4,760
    d. $5,950
    e. Some other amount

22. Shorty, a calendar-year taxpayer subject to a 34 percent marginal tax rate, claimed a charitable contribution deduction of $400,000 for a sculpture that the IRS later valued at $150,000. The applicable overvaluation penalty is:
    a. $0
    b. $17,000
    c. $21,250
    d. $10,000 (maximum penalty)
    e. Some other amount

23. Baldy, a calendar-year taxpayer subject to a 34 percent marginal tax rate, claimed a charitable contribution deduction of $600,000 for a sculpture that the IRS later valued at $100,000. The applicable overvaluation penalty is:
    a. $0
    b. $34,000
    c. $68,000
    d. $10,000 (maximum penalty)
    e. Some other amount

24. Slim, who is subject to a 50 percent marginal gift tax rate, made a gift of a sculpture to Red, valuing the property at $7,000. The IRS later valued the gift at $15,000. The applicable undervaluation penalty is:
    a. $1,000
    b. $800

Continued

c. $100 (minimum penalty)
d. $0
e. Some other amount

25. Tiny, who is subject to a 50 percent marginal gift tax rate, made a gift of a sculpture to Blondie, valuing the property at $80,000. The IRS later valued the gift at $150,000. The applicable undervaluation penalty is:
    a. $8,750
    b. $7,000
    c. $1,000 (minimum penalty)
    d. $0
    e. Some other amount

26. Fuzzy, who is subject to a 50 percent marginal gift tax rate, made a gift of a sculpture to Pinky, valuing the property at $100,000. The IRS later valued the gift at $250,000. The applicable undervaluation penalty is:
    a. $10,000 (maximum penalty)
    b. $18,750
    c. $15,000
    d. $0
    e. Some other amount

27. Jumbo, who is subject to a 50 percent marginal gift tax rate, made a gift of a sculpture to Curly, valuing the property at $100,000. The IRS later valued the gift at $500,000. The applicable undervaluation penalty is:
    a. $10,000 (maximum penalty)
    b. $80,000
    c. $40,000
    d. $0
    e. Some other amount

28. Kim underpaid her taxes by $15,000. Of this amount, $7,500 was due to negligence on her part because her record-keeping system is highly inadequate. Determine the amount of any negligence penalty.

29. Compute Dana's total penalties. She underpaid her tax by $50,000 due to negligence, and by $150,000 due to civil fraud.

30. Trudy's AGI last year was $50,000. Her Federal income tax came to $16,000, which she paid through a combination of withholding and estimated payments. This year, her AGI will be $170,000, with a projected tax liability of $46,000, all to be paid through estimates. Ignore the annualized income method. Compute Trudy's quarterly estimated payment schedule for the year, assuming that she wants to make the minimum necessary payments to avoid any underpayment penalties.

31. When Maggie accepted employment with Martin Corporation, she completed a Form W-4, listing fourteen exemptions. Since Maggie was single and had no exemptions, she misrepresented her tax situation in an attempt to increase her cash flow. To what penalties is Maggie exposed?

32. What is the applicable filing period under the statute of limitations in each of the following independent situations?
    a. No return was filed by the taxpayer.
    b. The taxpayer incurred a bad debt loss that she failed to claim.
    c. A taxpayer inadvertently omitted a large amount of gross income.
    d. Same as part (c), except that the omission was deliberate.
    e. A taxpayer inadvertently overstated her deductions by a large amount.

33. Kold Corporation estimates that its 2002 taxable income will be $900,000. Thus, it is subject to a flat 34 percent income tax rate and incurs a $306,000 liability. For each of the following independent cases, compute the minimum quarterly estimated tax payments that will be required from Kold to avoid an underpayment penalty.
    a. Taxable income for 2001 was ($100,000). Kold carried back all of its loss to prior years and exhausted the entire net operating loss in creating a zero 2001 liability.
    b. For 2001, taxable income was $200,000 and tax liability was $68,000.
    c. For 2000, taxable income was $2 million and tax liability was $680,000. For 2001, taxable income was $200,000 and tax liability was $68,000.

34. Mimi had $40,000 in Federal income taxes withheld in 2002. Due to a sizable amount of itemized deductions, she figured that she had no further tax to pay for the year. For this reason and because of personal problems, and without securing an extension, she did not file her 2002 return until July 1, 2003. Actually, the return showed a refund of $2,400, which Mimi ultimately received. On May 10, 2006, Mimi filed a $16,000 claim for refund of her 2002 taxes.
    a. How much of the $16,000 will Mimi rightfully recover?
    b. How would your analysis differ if Mimi had secured from the IRS an automatic four-month extension of time for filing her 2002 return?

RESEARCH CASES

35. The Church of Freedom encourages its members to file "tax protestor" returns with the IRS, objecting to both (a) the government's failure to use a gold standard in payment of tax liabilities, and (b) its sizable expenditures for social welfare programs. These returns routinely are overturned by the tax court as frivolous, with delinquent taxes, penalties, and interest due, and the church has engaged in a long-standing, sometimes ugly battle with the IRS over various constitutional rights. Meanwhile, church members continue to file returns in this manner.

    Ellen overheard church members talking about "roughing up" the IRS agents who were scheduled to conduct an audit of various members' returns. She went to the IRS and informed them of the danger that they might encounter. At the IRS's direction, Ellen then took a key clerical job at church headquarters. In this context, she had access to useful documentation and over a period of a few months gave to the IRS copies of church mailing lists and computer disks. She also helped tape record key conversations among church leaders and search the church's trash for other documents. In other words, Ellen helped the IRS build a case of civil and criminal tax fraud against the church and various members.

    All of these materials were given voluntarily to Ellen by church leaders in her context as an employee. Church members never suspected that she was working with the IRS. After delivering the various materials to the IRS, Ellen quit her job with the church and severed all communications with the IRS.

Chapter 13 Tax Practice and Administration: Sanctions, Agreements, and Disclosures   433

After the parties were charged with fraud, the government's case was found to be insufficiently supported by the evidence, and no penalties were assessed. Afterward, church leaders sued Ellen in her role as IRS informant, charging that she had violated their First Amendment rights of free association and their Fourth Amendment rights against illegal search and seizure. Government employees are immune from such charges, but Ellen was only an informant to the IRS and not its employee. Can the church collect damages from Ellen for informing on them?

36. Butcher attended meetings of tax protestors for many years in which the constitutionality of the Federal income tax and its means of collection were routinely challenged. Members of various protestor groups were provided with materials to assist them in preparing returns such that little or no tax would be due on the basis that, for instance, only gold- or silver-backed currency need be submitted to pay the tax or that a tax bill had originated in the Senate rather than the House of Representatives. Some of the groups maintained that no returns need be filed by individuals at all on the grounds that the current law supporting a Federal income tax violates various elements of the U.S. Constitution.

    The U.S. Tax Court routinely overturned such means of avoiding the tax, charging that such protestor returns were frivolously filed and charging the protestors with delinquent taxes, interest, and a variety of negligence and other accuracy-related penalties, especially where taxpayers failed to file altogether. The results of these cases never were discussed in the meetings that Butcher attended, though. Thus, although he never joined any of the groups, Butcher felt comfortable with the arguments of the protestor groups and never filed a Federal income tax return for himself or his profitable sole-proprietorship carpentry business.

    When the IRS discovered his failure to file and charged him with tax, interest, and penalties, Butcher went to the tax library and found that judicial precedent and administrative authority were stacked against him. He asked the court for relief from the civil fraud penalties related to his failure to file and failure to pay tax on the basis of his good-faith belief that the tax protestor information he had received was an acceptable interpretation of the law. Under this argument, a taxpayer cannot be found to willfully have failed to file and pay if he or she had a good-faith belief that no such requirement was supported by the Constitution. Should Butcher be required to pay civil fraud penalties?

37. Compute the overvaluation penalty for each of the following independent cases involving the taxpayer's reporting of the fair market value of charitable contribution property. In each case, assume a marginal income tax rate of 30 percent.

	Taxpayer	Corrected IRS Value	Reported Valuation
a.	Individual	$ 10,000	$ 20,000
b.	C Corporation	10,000	30,000
c.	S Corporation	10,000	30,000
d.	Individual	100,000	150,000
e.	Individual	100,000	300,000
f.	C Corporation	100,000	500,000

38. Compute the undervaluation penalty for each of the following independent cases involving the executor's reporting of the value of a closely held business in the decedent's gross estate. In each case, assume a marginal estate tax rate of 50 percent.

	Reported Value	Corrected IRS Valuation
a.	$12,000	$ 15,000
b.	50,000	90,000
c.	50,000	150,000
d.	50,000	200,000

39. Chang wants to claim a cost recovery deduction for the acquisition of masterwork paintings to be hung in the reception area of her dental office. The paintings were specially chosen because of their tendency to relax the patients who would be viewing them, thereby facilitating the conduct of Chang's business. Chang lives and works in the Fifth Circuit. A recent Eleventh Circuit case seems to support such a deduction, in limited circumstances. Complete the following chart, indicating for each independent assumption the actions that Chang can take without incurring the civil penalty for substantial understatement of taxes, but still maximizing her legitimate deductions for the year.

Probability of Success in Court	Claim the Deduction?	File a Form 8275 Disclosure?
80%		
40		
20		
2		

40. Continue with the facts of Research Case 39. Now assume that you are Chang's tax advisor. You wish to eliminate any chance of incurring a preparer civil unrealistic-position penalty. Indicate the actions that you would recommend that Chang take.

Probability of Success in Court	Claim the Deduction?	File a Form 8275 Disclosure?
80%		
40		
20		
2		

41. Your client, Lee Ann Harkness, has been accused of criminal tax fraud. A high school dropout, she received hundreds of thousands of dollars over the years from Bentley, an elderly gentleman, in exchange for love and companionship. When Bentley died and Harkness was left out of the will, she sued the estate for compensatory payments earned throughout her years of attending to Bentley. The government now accuses Harkness of fraud in failing to file income and self-employment tax returns for the open tax years. Construct a defense on Harkness's behalf.

42. The Scooter Company, owned equally by Julie (chair of the board of directors) and Jeff (company president), is in very difficult financial straits. Last month, Jeff used the $100,000 withheld from employee paychecks for Federal payroll and income taxes to pay off a creditor who threatened to cut off all supplies. To keep the company afloat, Jeff used these government funds willfully for the operations of the business, but even that effort was not enough. The company missed the next two payrolls, and today other creditors took action to shut down Scooter altogether. From whom and for how much will the IRS assess in taxes and penalties in the matter?

Appendices

Appendix A: Time Value of Money Tables   436

Appendix B: Standard Tax Citations   440

Appendix C: IRS Circular 230   444

Appendix A

Time Value of Money Tables

CONTENTS

Future Value of $1   437
Future Value of an Annuity of $1 in Arrears   437
Present Value of $1   438
Present Value of an Annuity of $1 in Arrears   439

Future Value of $1

Periods	4%	6%	8%	10%	12%	14%	20%
1	1.040	1.060	1.080	1.100	1.120	1.140	1.200
2	1.082	1.124	1.166	1.210	1.254	1.300	1.440
3	1.125	1.191	1.260	1.331	1.405	1.482	1.728
4	1.170	1.263	1.361	1.464	1.574	1.689	2.074
5	1.217	1.338	1.469	1.611	1.762	1.925	2.488
6	1.265	1.419	1.587	1.772	1.974	2.195	2.986
7	1.316	1.504	1.714	1.949	2.211	2.502	3.583
8	1.369	1.594	1.851	2.144	2.476	2.853	4.300
9	1.423	1.690	1.999	2.359	2.773	3.252	5.160
10	1.480	1.791	2.159	2.594	3.106	3.707	6.192
11	1.540	1.898	2.332	2.853	3.479	4.226	7.430
12	1.601	2.012	2.518	3.139	3.896	4.818	8.916
13	1.665	2.133	2.720	3.452	4.364	5.492	10.699
14	1.732	2.261	2.937	3.798	4.887	6.261	12.839
15	1.801	2.397	3.172	4.177	5.474	7.138	15.407
20	2.191	3.207	4.661	6.728	9.646	13.743	38.338
30	3.243	5.744	10.063	17.450	29.960	50.950	237.380
40	4.801	10.286	21.725	45.260	93.051	188.880	1469.800

Future Value of an Annuity of $1 in Arrears

Periods	4%	6%	8%	10%	12%	14%	20%
1	1.000	1.000	1.000	1.000	1.000	1.000	1.000
2	2.040	2.060	2.080	2.100	2.120	2.140	2.220
3	3.122	3.184	3.246	3.310	3.374	3.440	3.640
4	4.247	4.375	4.506	4.641	4.779	4.921	5.368
5	5.416	5.637	5.867	6.105	6.353	6.610	7.442
6	6.633	6.975	7.336	7.716	8.115	8.536	9.930
7	7.898	8.394	8.923	9.487	10.089	10.730	12.916
8	9.214	9.898	10.637	11.436	12.300	13.233	16.499
9	10.583	11.491	12.488	13.580	14.776	16.085	20.799
10	12.006	13.181	14.487	15.938	17.549	19.337	25.959
11	13.486	14.972	16.646	18.531	20.655	23.045	32.150
12	15.026	16.870	18.977	21.385	24.133	27.271	39.580
13	16.627	18.882	21.495	24.523	28.029	32.089	48.497
14	18.292	21.015	24.215	27.976	32.393	37.581	59.196
15	20.024	23.276	27.152	31.773	37.280	43.842	72.035
20	29.778	36.778	45.762	57.276	75.052	91.025	186.690
30	56.085	79.058	113.283	164.496	241.330	356.790	1181.900
40	95.026	154.762	259.057	442.597	767.090	1342.000	7343.900

Present Value of $1

Periods	4%	5%	6%	8%	10%	12%	14%	16%	18%	20%	22%	24%	26%	28%	30%	40%
1	0.962	0.952	0.943	0.926	0.909	0.893	0.877	0.862	0.847	0.833	0.820	0.806	0.794	0.781	0.769	0.714
2	0.925	0.907	0.890	0.857	0.826	0.797	0.769	0.743	0.718	0.694	0.672	0.650	0.630	0.610	0.592	0.510
3	0.889	0.864	0.840	0.794	0.751	0.712	0.675	0.641	0.609	0.579	0.551	0.524	0.500	0.477	0.455	0.364
4	0.855	0.823	0.792	0.735	0.683	0.636	0.592	0.552	0.516	0.482	0.451	0.423	0.397	0.373	0.350	0.260
5	0.822	0.784	0.747	0.681	0.621	0.567	0.519	0.476	0.436	0.402	0.370	0.341	0.315	0.291	0.269	0.186
6	0.790	0.746	0.705	0.630	0.564	0.507	0.456	0.410	0.370	0.335	0.303	0.275	0.250	0.227	0.207	0.133
7	0.760	0.711	0.665	0.583	0.513	0.452	0.400	0.354	0.314	0.279	0.249	0.222	0.198	0.178	0.159	0.095
8	0.731	0.677	0.627	0.540	0.467	0.404	0.351	0.305	0.266	0.233	0.204	0.179	0.157	0.139	0.123	0.068
9	0.703	0.645	0.592	0.500	0.424	0.361	0.308	0.263	0.225	0.194	0.167	0.144	0.125	0.108	0.094	0.048
10	0.676	0.614	0.558	0.463	0.386	0.322	0.270	0.227	0.191	0.162	0.137	0.116	0.099	0.085	0.073	0.035
11	0.650	0.585	0.527	0.429	0.350	0.287	0.237	0.195	0.162	0.135	0.112	0.094	0.079	0.066	0.056	0.025
12	0.625	0.557	0.497	0.397	0.319	0.257	0.208	0.168	0.137	0.112	0.092	0.076	0.062	0.052	0.043	0.018
13	0.601	0.530	0.469	0.368	0.290	0.229	0.182	0.145	0.116	0.093	0.075	0.061	0.050	0.040	0.033	0.013
14	0.577	0.505	0.442	0.340	0.263	0.205	0.160	0.125	0.099	0.078	0.062	0.049	0.039	0.032	0.025	0.009
15	0.555	0.481	0.417	0.315	0.239	0.183	0.140	0.108	0.084	0.065	0.051	0.040	0.031	0.025	0.020	0.006
16	0.534	0.458	0.394	0.292	0.218	0.163	0.123	0.093	0.071	0.054	0.042	0.032	0.025	0.019	0.015	0.005
17	0.513	0.436	0.371	0.270	0.198	0.146	0.108	0.080	0.060	0.045	0.034	0.026	0.020	0.015	0.012	0.003
18	0.494	0.416	0.350	0.250	0.180	0.130	0.095	0.069	0.051	0.038	0.028	0.021	0.016	0.012	0.009	0.002
19	0.475	0.396	0.331	0.232	0.164	0.116	0.083	0.060	0.043	0.031	0.023	0.017	0.012	0.009	0.007	0.002
20	0.456	0.377	0.312	0.215	0.149	0.104	0.073	0.051	0.037	0.026	0.019	0.014	0.010	0.007	0.005	0.001
21	0.439	0.359	0.294	0.199	0.135	0.093	0.064	0.044	0.031	0.022	0.015	0.011	0.008	0.006	0.004	0.001
22	0.422	0.342	0.278	0.184	0.123	0.083	0.056	0.038	0.026	0.018	0.013	0.009	0.006	0.004	0.003	0.001
23	0.406	0.326	0.262	0.170	0.112	0.074	0.049	0.033	0.022	0.015	0.010	0.007	0.005	0.003	0.002	
24	0.390	0.310	0.247	0.158	0.102	0.066	0.043	0.028	0.019	0.013	0.008	0.006	0.004	0.003	0.002	
25	0.375	0.295	0.233	0.146	0.092	0.059	0.038	0.024	0.016	0.010	0.007	0.005	0.003	0.002	0.001	
26	0.361	0.281	0.220	0.135	0.084	0.053	0.033	0.021	0.014	0.009	0.006	0.004	0.002	0.002	0.001	
27	0.347	0.268	0.207	0.125	0.076	0.047	0.029	0.018	0.011	0.007	0.005	0.003	0.002	0.001	0.001	
28	0.333	0.255	0.196	0.116	0.069	0.042	0.026	0.016	0.010	0.006	0.004	0.002	0.002	0.001	0.001	
29	0.321	0.243	0.185	0.107	0.063	0.037	0.022	0.014	0.008	0.005	0.003	0.002	0.001	0.001	0.001	
30	0.308	0.231	0.174	0.099	0.057	0.033	0.020	0.012	0.007	0.004	0.003	0.002	0.001	0.001		
40	0.208	0.142	0.097	0.046	0.022	0.011	0.005	0.003	0.001	0.001						

Present Value of an Annuity of $1 in Arrears

Periods

	4%	5%	6%	8%	10%	12%	14%	16%	18%	20%	22%	24%	26%	28%	30%	40%
1	0.962	0.952	0.943	0.926	0.909	0.893	0.877	0.862	0.847	0.833	0.820	0.806	0.794	0.781	0.769	0.714
2	1.886	1.859	1.833	1.783	1.736	1.690	1.647	1.605	1.566	1.528	1.492	1.457	1.424	1.392	1.361	1.224
3	2.775	2.723	2.673	2.577	2.487	2.402	2.322	2.246	2.174	2.106	2.042	1.981	1.923	1.868	1.816	1.589
4	3.630	3.546	3.465	3.312	3.170	3.037	2.914	2.798	2.690	2.589	2.494	2.404	2.320	2.241	2.166	1.879
5	4.452	4.330	4.212	3.993	3.791	3.605	3.433	3.274	3.127	2.991	2.864	2.745	2.635	2.532	2.436	2.035
6	5.242	5.076	4.917	4.623	4.355	4.111	3.889	3.685	3.498	3.326	3.167	3.020	2.885	2.759	2.643	2.168
7	6.002	5.786	5.582	5.206	4.868	4.564	4.288	4.039	3.812	3.605	3.416	3.242	3.083	2.937	2.802	2.263
8	6.733	6.463	6.210	5.747	5.335	4.968	4.639	4.344	4.078	3.837	3.619	3.421	3.241	3.076	2.925	2.331
9	7.435	7.108	6.802	6.247	5.759	5.328	4.946	4.607	4.303	4.031	3.786	3.566	3.366	3.184	3.019	2.379
10	8.111	7.722	7.360	6.710	6.145	5.650	5.216	4.833	4.494	4.192	3.923	3.682	3.465	3.269	3.092	2.414
11	8.760	8.306	7.887	7.139	6.495	5.988	5.453	5.029	4.656	4.327	4.035	3.776	3.544	3.335	3.147	2.438
12	9.385	8.863	8.384	7.536	6.814	6.194	5.660	5.197	4.793	4.439	4.127	3.851	3.606	3.387	3.190	2.456
13	9.986	9.394	8.853	7.904	7.103	6.424	5.842	5.342	4.910	4.533	4.203	3.912	3.656	3.427	3.223	2.468
14	10.563	9.899	9.295	8.244	7.367	6.628	6.002	5.468	5.008	4.611	4.265	3.962	3.695	3.459	3.249	2.477
15	11.118	10.380	9.712	8.559	7.606	6.811	6.142	5.575	5.092	4.675	4.315	4.001	3.726	3.483	3.268	2.484
16	11.652	10.838	10.106	8.851	7.824	6.974	6.265	5.669	5.162	4.730	4.357	4.033	3.751	3.503	3.283	2.489
17	12.166	11.274	10.477	9.122	8.022	7.120	6.373	5.749	5.222	4.775	4.391	4.059	3.771	3.518	3.295	2.492
18	12.659	11.690	10.828	9.372	8.201	7.250	6.467	5.818	5.273	4.812	4.419	4.080	3.786	3.529	3.304	2.494
19	13.134	12.085	11.158	9.604	8.365	7.366	6.550	5.877	5.316	4.844	4.442	4.097	3.799	3.539	3.311	2.496
20	13.590	12.462	11.470	9.818	8.514	7.469	6.623	5.929	5.353	4.870	4.460	4.110	3.808	3.546	3.316	2.497
21	14.029	12.821	11.764	10.017	8.649	7.562	6.687	5.973	5.384	4.891	4.476	4.121	3.816	3.551	3.320	2.498
22	14.451	13.163	12.042	10.201	8.772	7.645	6.743	6.011	5.410	4.909	4.488	4.130	3.822	3.556	3.323	2.498
23	14.857	13.489	12.303	10.371	8.883	7.718	6.792	6.044	5.432	4.925	4.499	4.137	3.827	3.559	3.325	2.499
24	15.247	13.799	12.550	10.529	8.985	7.784	6.835	6.073	5.451	4.937	4.507	4.143	3.831	3.562	3.327	2.499
25	15.622	14.094	12.783	10.675	9.077	7.843	6.873	6.097	5.467	4.948	4.514	4.147	3.834	3.564	3.329	2.499
26	15.983	14.375	13.003	10.810	9.161	7.896	6.906	6.118	5.480	4.956	4.520	4.151	3.837	3.566	3.330	2.500
27	16.330	14.643	13.211	10.935	9.237	7.943	6.935	6.136	5.492	4.964	4.525	4.154	3.839	3.567	3.331	2.500
28	16.663	14.898	13.406	11.051	9.307	7.984	6.961	6.152	5.502	4.970	4.528	4.157	3.840	3.568	3.331	2.500
29	16.984	15.141	13.591	11.158	9.370	8.022	6.983	6.166	5.510	4.975	4.531	4.159	3.841	3.569	3.332	2.500
30	17.292	15.373	13.765	11.258	9.427	8.055	7.003	6.177	5.517	4.979	4.534	4.160	3.842	3.569	3.332	2.500
40	19.793	17.159	15.046	11.925	9.779	8.244	7.105	6.234	5.548	4.997	4.544	4.166	3.846	3.571	3.333	2.500

Appendix B

Standard Tax Citations

Statutory

Constitution	U.S. Const. art. I, § 8, cl. 2.
	U.S. Const. amend, XIV, § 2.
Code	§ 101(b)(2)(B)(ii).
Public Laws	P.L. 99-514 Act § 1563.

Administrative

Regulation	Reg. § 1.162-5(a)(1).
Treasury Decision	T.D. 8175, 1988-1 C.B. 191.
Temporary Regulation	Reg. § 1.469-4T(c)(2).
Proposed Regulation	Prop. Reg. § 1.1176(b)(2).
Revenue Ruling	Rev. Rul. 2000-7, 2000-1 C.B. 712.
Revenue Ruling (temporary)	Rev. Rul. 2000-7, 2000-9 I.R.B. 712.
Revenue Procedure	Rev. Proc. 2001-21, 2001-1 C.B. 742.
Letter Ruling	Ltr. Rul. 200130042.
Technical Advice Memo	TAM 200002006.
Notice	Notice 2001-30, 2000-1 C.B. 989.
Notice (temporary)	Notice 2001-30, 2001-14 I.R.B. 989.
Announcement	Announcement 2001-11, 2001-4 I.R.B. 432.

Judicial

Board of Tax Appeals:	
GPO reporter	*Estate of D. R. Daly,* 3 B.T.A. 1042 (1926).
Tax Court Regular:	
(temporary citation)	*Arnes, John,* 102 T.C. ___ , No. 5 (1994).
Tax Court Regular:	
GPO reporter	*Arnes, John,* 102 T.C. 553 (1994).
Tax Court Memo:	
General (unpublished)	*Dixon, Michel,* T.C. Memo. 1999-310.
CCH reporter	*Dixon, Michel,* 78 TCM 462 (1999).
RIA reporter[1]	*Dixon, Michel,* RIA T.C. Memo. ¶ 99,310.
Kleinrock's	*Dixon, Michel,* T.C. Memo. 1999-310.
District Court:	
West reporter	*Barber, Lori,* 85 F.Supp. 2d. 967 (N.D.C.A., 2000).
CCH reporter	*Barber, Lori,* 2000-1 USTC ¶ 50,209 (N.D. C.A., 2000).
RIA reporter[1]	*Barber, Lori,* 85 AFTR2d 2000-879 (N.D. C.A., 2000).
Kleinrock's	*Barber, Lori,* KTC 2000-45 (N.D.C.A., 2000)
Court of Federal Claims:	
West reporter	*Bennett, Courtney,* 30 Fed. Cl. 396 (1994).
CCH reporter	*Bennett, Courtney,* 94-1 USTC ¶ 50,044 (Fed.Cl., 1994).
RIA reporter[1]	*Bennett, Courtney,* 73 AFTR2d 94-534 (Fed.Cl., 1994).
Kleinrock's	*Bennett, Courtney,* KTC 1994-647 (Fed.Cl., 1994).
Court of Appeal:	
West reporter	*Home of Faith,* 39 F.3d. 263 (CA-10, 1994).
CCH reporter	*Home of Faith,* 94-2 USTC ¶ 50,570 (CA-10, 1994).
RIA reporter[1]	*Home of Faith,* 74 AFTR2d 94-5608 (CA-10, 1994).
Kleinrock's	*Home of Faith,* KTC 1994-564 (CA-10, 1994).

1. Before 1992 this reporter was published by Prentice-Hall (P-H).

Supreme Court:
 GPO reporter   *Indianapolis Power & Light,* 493 U.S. 203 (1990).
 West reporter   *Indianapolis Power & Light,* 110 S.Ct. 589 (1981).
 CCH reporter   *Indianapolis Power & Light,* 90-1 USTC ¶ 50,007 (USSC, 1990).
 RIA reporter[1]   *Indianapolis Power & Light,* 65 AFTR2d 90-394 (USSC, 1990).
 Kleinrock's   *Indianapolis Power & Light,* KTC 1990-53 (USSC, 1990).

Books

W. Raabe, G. Whittenburg, D. Sanders, and J. Bost, *West's Federal Tax Research,* 6th ed. (Cincinnati: South-Western Thomson Learning, 2002).

Journals

G. Whittenburg, R. Bunn, and C. Venable, "New Law Expands Tax Breaks for Paying Education Costs," *Practical Tax Strategies* (August 2001), p. 79.

Capitalization

Proper nouns and words derived from them are capitalized while common nouns are not. The names of specific persons, places, or things are proper nouns. All other nouns are common nouns. Examples of proper nouns include:

 the Congress
 the Code
 Section 172(a)
 the Regulations
 Regulations Section 1.102-1
 the President
 the Fifth Circuit
 the Tax Court
 a Revenue Ruling
 a Private Letter Ruling

Italics

In handwritten or typed papers <u>underlining</u> represents italics. The titles of books, magazines, newspapers, pamphlets, court cases, and tax services are shown in italics. Examples of items that are italicized include:

 The Wealth of Nations
 Journal of Taxation
 New York Times
 AICPA Code of Conduct
 Circular 230
 Statements on Responsibility in Tax Practice
 Gregory v. Helvering
 Cumulative Bulletin
 Standard Federal Tax Reports
 Federal Tax Coordinator 2d

Note: Do not italicize the titles of legal documents such as the U.S. Constitution and the U.S. Code.

Lists

A list is an independent clause followed by a colon with each item in the list separated by a comma.

> The College of Business Administration has five departments: Accounting, Finance, Information Systems, Management, and Marketing.

Displayed Lists

Displayed lists are used to make items easy to scan by the reader. Such lists should be introduced with an independent clause or by a complete sentence ending with a period. Examples of items that it would be appropriate to display in list form would include:

- steps to solve a problem,
- rules,
- proposals to be discussed,
- checklists,
- recommendations, and
- procedures.

Periods are not used in lists unless the items in the list are complete sentences. The items in a list should be in the same form (i.e., nouns, phrases, clauses, or sentences). If the items in a list are to be numbered, use an arabic number followed by a period for each item. If the items are not numbered, say, because the list is not prioritized or sequential, consider using a bullet to draw the reader's attention to the items in the list (as shown above).

Other Systems

Many professions and academic disciplines have developed unique systems of citing published material. Examples of the more common style manuals include:

> *U.S. Government Printing Office Style Manual*
> *The Chicago Manual of Style*
> *MLA Handbook for Writers of Research Papers*
> *The Bluebook, A Uniform System of (legal) Citations*
> *Publication Manual of the American Psychological Association*

In addition to the manuals listed above, there are style manuals published for accounting, biology, chemistry, geology, linguistics, mathematics, medicine, and physics.

Appendix C

IRS Circular 230

Treasury Department Circular No. 230 (Rev. 7-94)

Regulations Governing the Practice of Attorneys, Certified Public Accountants, Enrolled Agents, Enrolled Actuaries, and Appraisers before the Internal Revenue Service

Department of the Treasury
Internal Revenue Service

Title 31 Code of Federal Regulations, Subtitle A, Part 10, revised as of July 1, 1994

Regulations Governing the Practice of Attorneys, Certified Public Accountants, Enrolled Agents, Enrolled Actuaries, and Appraisers before the Internal Revenue Service

Treasury Department Circular No. 230 (Rev. 7-94)

This publication contains the revision of Treasury Department Circular No. 230 appearing in 31 F.R. 10773, dated August 13, 1966, and includes the following amendments:

Amendment appearing in 31 F.R. 12638, dated September 27, 1966, which adds omitted section heading § 10.58.

Amendments appearing in 31 F.R. 13992, dated November 2, 1966, which add subparagraphs (b) and (c) to § 10.57 and add a sentence at the end, and as a continuation, of paragraph (c) of § 10.51.

Amendments appearing in 31 F.R. 13205, dated August 19, 1970, which are intended primarily to clarify the language of certain provisions of the regulations, strengthen certain conflict of interest and disciplinary provisions, and update statutory references.

Amendment appearing in 36 F.R. 8671, dated May 11, 1971, which corrects error in the August 19, 1970, amendments, which incorrectly added a new sentence to subparagraph 10.3(c) rather than subparagraph 10.3 (e).

Amendments appearing in 42 F.R. 38350, dated July 28, 1977, which eliminate outdated terms and provisions, and which increase the restrictions on practice by former Government employees.

Amendments appearing in 44 F.R. 4940, dated January 24, 1979, which prescribe rules permitting the expansion of advertising and solicitation provisions of the regulations governing practice by attorneys, certified public accounts, enrolled agents and others who represent clients before the Internal Revenue Service.

Amendments appearing in 44 F.R. 4944, dated January 24, 1979, which prescribe rules to permit enrolled actuaries to engage in practice before the Internal Revenue Service in connection with the provisions of the Internal Revenue Code involving pension plans under the Employee Retirement Income Security Act of 1974 (ERISA).

Amendments appearing in 49 F.R. 6719, dated February 23, 1984, which clarify who may prepare a tax return and furnish information to the Internal Revenue Service, and set standards for providing opinions used in the promotion of tax shelter offerings.

Amendments appearing in 50 F.R. 42014, dated October 17, 1985, which implement section 156 of the Deficit Reduction Act of 1984, 98 Stat. 695, to provide for the disqualification of appraisals and appraisers' testimony in connection with Treasury Department or Internal Revenue Service proceedings with respect to any appraiser who has been assessed an aiding and abetting penalty under 26 U.S.C. 6701(a) after July 18, 1984.

Amendments appearing in 51 F.R. 2875, dated January 22, 1986, which require that those who are enrolled to practice before the Internal Revenue Service renew their enrollment on a periodic basis. A condition of eligibility for renewal of enrollment will be the satisfaction of continuing professional education requirements. In addition, the amendments modify the regulations reflecting the transfer to the Office of Director of Practice of certain functions formerly performed by the Commissioner of Internal Revenue relative to the enrollment of individuals who wish to practice before the Internal Revenue Service.

Amendments appearing in 57 F.R. 41093, dated September 9, 1992, which relate to the provisions of the regulations addressing advertising and solicitation by those eligible to practice before the IRS, which were occasioned by judicial determinations impacting on the subject.

Amendments appearing in 59 F.R. 31523, dated June 20, 1994, which establish tax return preparation standards and prescribe the circumstances under which a practitioner may be disciplined for violating those standards, limit the use of contingent fees for preparing tax returns, clarify that certain existing restrictions governing limited practice before the IRS apply to all individuals who are eligible to engage in limited practice before the IRS, establish expedited proceedings to suspend individuals from practice before the IRS in cases in which certain determinations have been made by independent bodies, and permit attorneys and certified public accountants in good standing to obtain or retain enrolled agent status.

PART 10—PRACTICE BEFORE THE INTERNAL REVENUE SERVICE

Sec.
10.0 Scope of part.

Subpart A — Rules Governing Authority to Practice

10.1 Director of Practice.
10.2 Definitions.
10.3 Who may practice.
10.4 Eligibility for enrollment.
10.5 Application for enrollment.
10.6 Enrollment.
10.7 Representing oneself; participating in rulemaking; limited practice; special appearances; and return preparation.
10.8 Customhouse brokers.

Subpart B — Duties and Restrictions Relating to Practice Before the Internal Revenue Service

10.20 Information to be furnished.
10.21 Knowledge of client's omission.
10.22 Diligence as to accuracy.
10.23 Prompt disposition of pending matters.
10.24 Assistance from disbarred or suspended persons and former Internal Revenue Service employees.
10.25 Practice by partners of Government employees.
10.26 Practice by former Government employees, their partners and their associates.
10.27 Notaries.
10.28 Fees.
10.29 Conflicting interests.
10.30 Solicitation.
10.31 Negotiation of taxpayer refund checks.
10.32 Practice of law.
10.33 Tax shelter opinions.
10.34 Standards for advising with respect to tax return positions and for preparing or signing returns.

Subpart C — Rules Applicable to Disciplinary Proceedings

10.50 Authority to disbar or suspend.
10.51 Disreputable conduct.
10.52 Violation of regulations.
10.53 Receipt of information concerning attorneys, certified public accountants, enrolled agents, or enrolled actuaries.
10.54 Institution of proceeding.
10.55 Conferences.
10.56 Contents of complaint.
10.57 Service of complaint and other papers.
10.58 Answer.
10.59 Supplemental charges.
10.60 Reply to answer.
10.61 Proof; variance; amendment of pleadings.
10.62 Motions and requests.
10.63 Representation.
10.64 Administrative Law Judge.
10.65 Hearings.
10.66 Evidence.
10.67 Depositions.
10.68 Transcript.
10.69 Proposed findings and conclusions.
10.70 Decision of the Administrative Law Judge.
10.71 Appeal to the Secretary.
10.72 Decision of the Secretary.
10.73 Effect of disbarment or suspension; surrender of card.
10.74 Notice of disbarment or suspension.
10.75 Petition for reinstatement.
10.76 Expedited suspension upon criminal conviction or loss of license for cause.

Subpart D — Rules Applicable to Disqualification of Appraisers

10.77 Authority to disqualify; effect of disqualification.
10.78 Institution of proceeding.
10.79 Contents of complaint.
10.80 Service of complaint and other papers.
10.81 Answer.
10.82 Supplemental charges.
10.83 Reply to answer.
10.84 Proof, variance, amendment of pleadings.
10.85 Motions and requests.
10.86 Representation.
10.87 Administrative Law Judge.
10.88 Hearings.
10.89 Evidence.
10.90 Depositions.
10.91 Transcript.
10.92 Proposed findings and conclusions.
10.93 Decision of the Administrative Law Judge.
10.94 Appeal to the Secretary.
10.95 Decision of the Secretary.
10.96 Final order.
10.97 Petition for reinstatement.

Subpart E — General Provisions

10.98 Records.
10.100 Saving clause.
10.101 Special orders.

Authority: Sec. 3, 23 Stat. 258, secs. 2-12, 60 Stat. 237 *et seq.*; 5 U.S.C. 301, 500, 551-559, 31 U.S.C. 1026; Reorg. Plan No. 26 of 1950, 15 FR 4935, 64 Stat. 1280, 3 CFR, 1949-1953 Comp., p. 1017.

Source: Treasury Department Circular 230, Revised, 31 FR 10773, Aug. 13, 1966, unless otherwise noted.

Editorial Note: Nomenclature changes affecting this part appear at 57 FR 41095, Sept. 9, 1992.

§10.0 Scope of part.

This part contains rules governing the recognition of attorneys, certified public accountants, enrolled agents, and other persons representing clients before the Internal Revenue Service. Subpart A of this part sets forth rules relating to authority to practice before the Internal Revenue Service; subpart B of this part prescribes the duties and restrictions relating to such practice; subpart C of this part contains rules relating to disciplinary proceedings; subpart D of this part contains rules applicable to disqualification of appraisers; and Subpart E of this part contains general provisions, including provisions relating to the availability of official records.

[59 FR 31526, June 20, 1994]

Subpart A — Rules Governing Authority To Practice

§10.1 Director of Practice.

(a) *Establishment of office.* There is established in the Office of the Secretary of the Treasury the office of Director of Practice. The Director of Practice shall be appointed by the Secretary of the Treasury.

(b) *Duties.* The Director of Practice shall act upon applications for enrollment to practice before the Internal Revenue Service; institute and provide for the conduct of disciplinary proceedings relating to attorneys, certified public accountants, enrolled agents, enrolled actuaries and appraisers; make inquiries with respect to matters under his jurisdiction; and perform such other duties as are necessary or appropriate to carry out his functions under this part or as are prescribed by the Secretary of the Treasury.

(c) *Acting Director.* The Secretary of the Treasury will designate an officer or employee of the Treasury Department to act as Director of Practice in the event of the absence of the director or of a vacancy in that office.

[31 FR 10773, Aug. 13, 1966, as amended at 51 FR 2878, Jan. 22, 1986]

§10.2 Definitions.

As used in this part, except where the context clearly indicates otherwise:

(a) *Attorney* means any person who is a member in good standing of the bar of the highest court of any State, possession, territory, Commonwealth, or the District of Columbia.

(b) *Certified Public Accountant* means any person who is duly qualified to practice as a certified public accountant in any State, possession, territory, Commonwealth, or the District of Columbia.

(c) *Commissioner* refers to the Commissioner of Internal Revenue.

(d) *Director* refers to the Director of Practice.

(e) *Practice before the Internal Revenue Service* comprehends all matters connected with a presentation to the Internal Revenue Service or any of its officers or employees relating to a client's rights, privileges, or liabilities under laws or regulations administered by the Internal Revenue Service. Such presentations include preparing and filing necessary documents, corresponding and communicating with the Internal Revenue Service, and representing a client at conferences, hearings, and meetings.

(f) *Practitioner* means any individual described in §10.3 (a), (b), (c), or (d) of this part.

(g) A *return* includes an amended return and a claim for refund.

(h) *Service* means the Internal Revenue Service.

[59 FR 31526, June 20, 1994]

§10.3 Who may practice.

(a) *Attorneys.* Any attorney who is not currently under suspension or disbarment from practice before the Internal Revenue Service may practice before the Service upon filing with the Service a written declaration that he or she is currently qualified as an attorney and is authorized to represent the particular party on whose behalf he or she acts.

(b) *Certified public accountants.* Any certified public accountant who is not currently under suspension or disbarment from practice before the Internal Revenue Service may practice before the Service upon filing with the Service a written declaration that he or she is currently qualified as a certified public accountant and is authorized to represent the particular party on whose behalf he or she acts.

(c) *Enrolled agents.* Any person enrolled as an agent pursuant to this part may practice before the Internal Revenue Service.

(d) *Enrolled Actuaries.* (1) Any individual who is enrolled as an actuary by the Joint Board for the Enrollment of Actuaries pursuant to 29 U.S.C. 1242 may practice before the Internal Revenue Service upon filing with the Service a written declaration that he/she is currently qualified as an enrolled actuary and is authorized to represent the particular party on whose behalf he/she acts. Practice as an enrolled actuary is limited to representation with respect to issues involving the following statutory provisions.

Internal Revenue Code (Title 26 U.S.C.) sections: 401 (qualification of employee plans), 403(a) (relating to whether an annuity plan meets the requirements of section 404(a)(2)), 404 (deductibility of employer contributions), 405 (qualification of bond purchase plans), 412 (funding requirements for certain employee plans), 413 (application of qualification requirements to collectively bargained plans and to plans maintained by more than one employer), 414 (containing definitions and special rules relating to the employee plan area), 4971 (relating to excise taxes payable as a result of an accumulated funding deficiency under section 412), 6057 (annual registration of plans), 6058 (information required in connection with certain plans of deferred compensation), 6059 (periodic report of actuary), 6652(e) (failure to file annual registration and other notifications by pension plan), 6652(f) (failure to file information required in connection with certain plans of deferred compensation), 6692 (failure to file actuarial report), 7805(b) (relating to the extent, if any, to which an Internal Revenue Service ruling or determination letter coming under the herein listed statutory provisions shall be applied without retroactive effect), and 29 U.S.C. 1083 (relating to waiver of funding for nonqualified plans).

(2) An individual who practices before the Internal Revenue Service pursuant to this subsection shall be subject to the provisions of this part in the same manner as attorneys, certified public accountants and enrolled agents.

(e) *Others.* Any individual qualifying under §10.5(c) or §10.7 is eligible to practice before the Internal Revenue Service to the extent provided in those sections.

(f) *Government officers and employees, and others.* An individual, including an officer or employee of the executive, legislative, or judicial branch of the United States Government; officer or employee of the District of Columbia; Member of Congress; or Resident Commissioner, may not practice before the Service if such practice would violate 18 U.S.C. 203 or 205.

(g) *State officers and employees.* No officer or employee of any State, or subdivision thereof, whose duties require him to pass upon, investigate, or deal with tax matters of such State or subdivision, may practice before the Service, if such State employment may disclose facts or information applicable to Federal tax matters.

[31 FR 10773, Aug. 13, 1966, as amended at 35 FR 13205, Aug. 19, 1970; 36 FR 8671, May 11, 1971; 44 FR 4946, Jan. 24, 1979; 59 FR 31526, June 20, 1994]

§10.4 Eligibility for enrollment.

(a) *Enrollment upon examination.* The Director of Practice may grant enrollment to an applicant who demonstrates special competence in tax matters by written examination administered by the Internal Revenue Service and who has not engaged in any conduct which would justify the suspension or disbarment of any attorney, certified public accountant, or enrolled agent under the provisions of this part.

(b) *Enrollment of former Internal Revenue Service employees.* The Director of Practice may grant enrollment to an applicant who has not engaged in any conduct which would justify the suspension or disbarment of any attorney, certified public accountant, or enrolled agent under the provisions of this part and who, by virtue of his past service and technical experience in the Internal Revenue Service has qualified for such enrollment, as follows:

(1) Application for enrollment on account of former employment in the Internal Revenue Service shall be made to the Director of Practice. Each applicant will be supplied a form by the Director of Practice, which shall indicate the information required respecting the applicant's qualifications. In addition to the applicant's name, address, educational experience, etc., such information shall specifically include a detailed account of the applicant's employment in the Internal Revenue Service, which account shall show (i) positions held, (ii) date of each appointment and termination thereof, (iii) nature of services rendered in each position, with particular reference to the degree of technical experience involved, and (iv) name of supervisor in such positions, together with such other information regarding the experience and training of the applicant as may be relevant.

(2) Upon receipt of each such application, it shall be transmitted to the appropriate officer of the Internal Revenue Service with the request that a detailed report of the nature and rating of the applicant's services in the Internal Revenue Service, accompanied by the recommendation of the superior officer in the particular unit or division of the Internal Revenue Service that such employment does or does not qualify the applicant technically or otherwise for the desired authorization, be furnished to the Director of Practice.

(3) In examining the qualification of an applicant for enrollment on account of employment in the Internal Revenue Service, the Director of Practice will be governed by the following policies:

(i) Enrollment on account of such employment may be of unlimited scope or may be limited to permit the presentation of matters only of the particular class or only before the particular unit or division of the Internal Revenue Service for which his former employment in the Internal Revenue Service has qualified the applicant.

(ii) Application for enrollment on account of employment in the Internal Revenue Service must be made within 3 years from the date of separation from such employment.

(iii) It shall be requisite for enrollment on account of such employment that the applicant shall have had a minimum of 5 years continuous employment in the Service during which he shall have been regularly engaged in applying and interpreting the provisions of the Internal Revenue Code and the regulations thereunder relating to income, estate, gift, employment, or excise taxes.

(iv) For the purposes of paragraph (b)(3)(iii) of this section an aggregate of 10 or more years of employment, at least 3 of which occurred within the 5 years preceding the date of application, shall be deemed the equivalent of 5 years continuous employment.

(c) *Natural persons.* Enrollment to practice may be granted only to natural persons.

[31 FR 10773, Aug. 13, 1966, as amended at 35 FR 13205, Aug. 19, 1970; 42 FR 38352, July 28, 1977; 51 FR 2878, Jan. 22, 1986; 59 FR 31526, June 20, 1994]

§10.5 **Application for enrollment.**

(a) *Form; fee.* An applicant for enrollment shall file with the Director of Practice an application on Form 23, properly executed under oath or affirmation. Such application shall be accompanied by a check or money order in the amount set forth on Form 23, payable to the Internal Revenue Service, which amount shall constitute a fee which shall be charged to each applicant for enrollment. The fee shall be retained by the United States whether or not the applicant is granted enrollment.

(b) *Additional information; examination.* The Director of Practice, as a condition to consideration of an application for enrollment, may require the applicant to file additional information and to submit to any written or oral examination under oath or otherwise. The Director of Practice shall, upon written request, afford an applicant the opportunity to be heard with respect to his application for enrollment.

(c) *Temporary recognition.* Upon receipt of a properly executed application, the Director of Practice may grant the applicant temporary recognition to practice pending a determination as to whether enrollment to practice should be granted. Such temporary recognition shall not be granted if the application is not regular on its face; if the information stated therein, if true, is not sufficient to warrant enrollment to practice; if there is any information before the Director of Practice which indicates that the statements in the application are untrue; or which indicates that the applicant would not otherwise qualify for enrollment. Issuance of temporary recognition shall not constitute enrollment to practice or a finding of eligibility for enrollment, and the temporary recognition may be withdrawn at any time by the Director of Practice.

(d) *Appeal from denial of application.* The Director of Practice, in denying an application for enrollment, shall inform the applicant as to the reason(s) therefor. The applicant may, within 30 days after receipt of the notice of denial, file a written appeal therefrom, together with his/her reasons in support thereof, to the Secretary of the Treasury. A decision on the appeal will be rendered by the Secretary of the Treasury as soon as practicable.

(Sec. 501, Pub. L. 82-137, 65 Stat. 290; 31 U.S.C. 483a)

[31 FR 10773, Aug. 13, 1966, as amended at 42 FR 38352, July 28, 1977; 51 FR 2878, Jan. 22, 1986]

§10.6 Enrollment.

(a) *Roster.* The Director of Practice shall maintain rosters of all individuals:

(1) Who have been granted active enrollment to practice before the Internal Revenue Service;

(2) Whose enrollment has been placed in an inactive status for failure to meet the requirements for renewal of enrollment;

(3) Whose enrollment has been placed in an inactive retirement status;

(4) Who have been disbarred or suspended from practice before the Internal Revenue Service;

(5) Whose offer of consent to resignation from enrollment to practice before the Internal Revenue Service has been accepted by the Director of Practice under §10.55 of this part; and

(6) Whose application for enrollment has been denied.

(b) *Enrollment card.* The Director of Practice will issue an enrollment card to each individual whose application for enrollment to practice before the Internal Revenue Service is approved after the effective date of this regulation. Each such enrollment card will be valid for the period stated thereon. Enrollment cards issued individuals before February 1, 1987 shall become invalid after March 31, 1987. An individual having an invalid enrollment card is not eligible to practice before the Internal Revenue Service.

(c) *Term of enrollment.* Active enrollment to practice before the Internal Revenue Service is accorded each individual enrolled, so long as renewal of enrollment is effected as provided in this part.

(d) *Renewal of enrollment.* To maintain active enrollment to practice before the Internal Revenue Service, each individual enrolled is required to have his/her enrollment renewed as set forth herein. Failure by an individual to receive notification from the Director of Practice of the renewal requirement will not be justification for circumvention of such requirement.

(1) All individuals enrolled to practice before the Internal Revenue Service before November 1, 1986 shall apply for renewal of enrollment during the period between November 1, 1986 and January 31, 1987. Those who receive initial enrollment between November 1, 1986 and January 31, 1987 shall apply for renewal of enrollment by March 1, 1987. The first effective date of renewal will be April 1, 1987.

(2) Thereafter, applications for renewal will be required between November 1, 1989 and January 31, 1990, and between November 1 and January 31 of every third year subsequent thereto. Those who receive initial enrollment during the renewal application period shall apply for renewal of enrollment by March 1 of the renewal year. The effective date of renewed enrollment will be April 1, 1990, and April 1 of every third year subsequent thereto.

(3) The Director of Practice will notify the individual of renewal of enrollment and will issue a card evidencing such renewal.

(4) A reasonable nonrefundable fee may be charged for each application for renewal of enrollment filed with the Director of Practice.

(5) Forms required for renewal may be obtained from the Director of Practice, Internal Revenue Service, Washington, DC 20224.

(e) *Condition for renewal: Continuing Professional Education.* In order to qualify for renewal of enrollment, an individual enrolled to practice before the Internal Revenue Service must certify, on the application for renewal form prescribed by the Director of Practice, that he/she has satisfied the following continuing professional education requirements.

(1) *For renewed enrollment effective April 1, 1987.* (i) A minimum of 24 hours of continuing education credit must be completed between January 1, 1986 and January 31, 1987.

(ii) An individual who receives initial enrollment between January 1, 1986 and January 31, 1987 is exempt from the continuing education requirement for the renewal of enrollment effective April 1, 1987, but is required to file a timely application for renewal of enrollment.

(2) For renewed enrollment effective April 1, 1990 and every third year thereafter. (i) A minimum of 72 hours of continuing education credit must be completed between February 1, 1987 and January 31, 1990, and during each three year period subsequent thereto. Each such three year period is known as an enrollment cycle.

(ii) A minimum of 16 hours of continuing education credit must be completed in each year of an enrollment cycle.

(iii) An individual who receives initial enrollment during an enrollment cycle must complete two (2) hours of qualifying continuing education credit for each month enrolled during such enrollment cycle. Enrollment for any part of a month is considered enrollment for the entire month.

(f) *Qualifying continuing education — (1) In General.* To qualify for continuing education credit, a course of learning must:

(i) Be a qualifying program designed to enhance the professional knowledge of an individual in Federal taxation or Federal tax related matters, i.e. programs comprised of current subject matter in Federal taxation or Federal tax related matters to include accounting, financial management, business computer science and taxation; and

(ii) Be conducted by a qualifying sponsor.

(2) *Qualifying programs. (i) Formal programs.* Formal programs qualify as continuing education programs if they:

(A) Require attendance;

(B) Require that the program be conducted by a qualified instructor, discussion leader or speaker, i.e. a person whose background, training, education and/or experience is appropriate for instructing or leading a discussion on the subject matter of the particular program; and

(C) Require a written outline and/or textbook and certificate of attendance provided by the sponsor, all of which must be retained by the attendee for a three year period following renewal of enrollment.

(ii) *Correspondence or individual study programs (including taped programs).* Qualifying continuing education programs include correspondence or individual study programs completed on an individual basis by the enrolled individual and conducted by qualifying sponsors. The allowable credit hours for such programs will be measured on a basis comparable to the measurement of a seminar or course for credit in an accredited educational institution. Such programs qualify as continuing education programs if they:

(A) Require registration of the participants by the sponsor;

(B) Provide a means for measuring completion by the participants (e.g., written examination); and

(C) Require a written outline and/or textbook and certificate of completion provided by the sponsor which must be retained by the participant for a three year period following renewal of enrollment.

(iii) *Serving as an instructor, discussion leader or speaker.*

(A) One hour of continuing education credit will be awarded for each contact hour completed as an instructor, discussion leader or speaker at an educational program which meets the continuing education requirements of this part.

(B) Two hours of continuing education credit will be awarded for actual subject preparation time for each contact hour completed as an instructor, discussion leader or speaker at such programs. It will be the responsibility of the individual claiming such credit to maintain records to verify preparation time.

(C) The maximum credit for instruction and preparation may not exceed 50% of the continuing education requirement for an enrollment cycle.

(D) Presentation of the same subject matter in an instructor, discussion leader or speaker capacity more than one time during an enrollment cycle will not qualify for continuing education credit.

(iv) *Credit for published articles, books, etc.*

(A) Continuing education credit will be awarded for publications on Federal taxation or Federal tax related matters to include accounting, financial management, business computer science, and taxation, provided the content of such publications is current and designed for the enhancement of the professional knowledge of an individual enrolled to practice before the Internal Revenue Service.

(B) The credit allowed will be on the basis of one hour credit for each hour of preparation time for the material. It will be the responsibility of the person claiming the credit to maintain records to verify preparation time.

(C) The maximum credit for publications may not exceed 25% of the continuing education requirement of any enrollment cycle.

(3) *Periodic examination.* Individuals may establish eligibility for renewal of enrollment for any enrollment cycle by:

(i) Achieving a passing score on each part of the Special Enrollment Examination administered under this part during the three year period prior to renewal; and

(ii) Completing a minimum of 16 hours of qualifying continuing education during the last year of an enrollment cycle.

(g) *Sponsors.* (1) Sponsors are those responsible for presenting programs.

(2) To qualify as a sponsor, a program presenter must:

(i) Be an accredited educational institution;

(ii) Be recognized for continuing education purposes by the licensing body of any State, possession, territory, Commonwealth, or the District of Columbia responsible for the issuance of a license in the field of accounting or law;

(iii) Be recognized by the Director of Practice as a professional organization or society whose programs include offering continuing professional education opportunities in subject matter within the scope of this part; or

(iv) File a sponsor agreement with the Director of Practice to obtain approval of the program as a qualified continuing education program.

(3) A qualifying sponsor must ensure the program complies with the following requirements:

(i) Programs must be developed by individual(s) qualified in the subject matter;

(ii) Program subject matter must be current;

(iii) Instructors, discussion leaders, and speakers must be qualified with respect to program content;

(iv) Programs must include some means for evaluation of technical content and presentation;

(v) Certificates of completion must be provided those who have successfully completed the program; and

(vi) Records must be maintained by the sponsor to verify completion of the program and attendance by each participant. Such records must be retained for a period of three years following completion of the program. In the case of continuous conferences, conventions, and the like, records must be maintained to verify completion of the program and attendance by each participant at each segment of the program.

(4) Professional organizations or societies wishing to be considered as qualified sponsors shall request such status of the Director of Practice and furnish information in support of the request together with any further information deemed necessary by the Director of Practice.

(5) Sponsor agreements and qualified professional organization or society sponsors approved by the Director of Practice shall remain in effect for one enrollment cycle. The names of such sponsors will be published on a periodic basis.

(h) *Measurement of continuing education coursework.* (1) All continuing education programs will be measured in terms of contact hours. The shortest recognized program will be one contact hour.

(2) A contact hour is 50 minutes of continuous participation in a program. Credit is granted only for a full contact hour, i.e. 50 minutes or multiples thereof. For example, a program lasting more than 50 minutes but less than 100 minutes will count as one contact hour.

(3) Individual segments at continuous conferences, conventions and the like will be considered one total program. For example, two 90-minute segments (180 minutes) at a continuous conference will count as three contact hours.

(4) For university or college courses, each semester hour credit will equal 15 contact hours and a quarter hour credit will equal 10 contact hours.

(i) *Recordkeeping requirements.* (1) Each individual applying for renewal shall retain for a period of three years following the date of renewal of enrollment the information required with regard to qualifying continuing professional education credit hours. Such information shall include:

(i) The name of the sponsoring organization;

(ii) The location of the program;

(iii) The title of the program and description of its content, e.g., course syllibi and/or textbook;

(iv) The dates attended;

(v) The credit hours claimed;

(vi) The name(s) of the instructor(s), discussion leader(s), or speaker(s), if appropriate; and

(vii) The certificate of completion and/or signed statement of the hours of attendance obtained from the sponsor.

(2) To receive continuing education credit for service completed as an instructor, discussion leader, or speaker, the following information must be maintained for a period of three years following the date of renewal of enrollment:

(i) The name of the sponsoring organization;

(ii) The location of the program;

(iii) The title of the program and description of its content;

(iv) The dates of the program; and

(v) The credit hours claimed.

(3) To receive continuing education credit for publications, the following information must be maintained for a period of three years following the date of renewal of enrollment:

(i) The publisher;

(ii) The title of the publication;

(iii) A copy of the publication; and

(iv) The date of publication.

(j) *Waivers.* (1) Waiver from the continuing education requirements for a given period may be granted by the Director of Practice for the following reasons:

(i) Health, which prevented compliance with the continuing education requirements;

(ii) Extended active military duty;

(iii) Absence from the United States for an extended period of time due to employment or other reasons, provided the individual does not practice before the Internal Revenue Service during such absence; and

(iv) Other compelling reasons, which will be considered on a case-by-case basis.

(2) A request for waiver must be accompanied by appropriate documentation. The individual will be required to furnish any additional documentation or explanation deemed necessary by the Director of Practice. Examples of appropriate documentation could be a medical certificate, military orders, etc.

(3) A request for waiver must be filed no later than the last day of the renewal application period.

(4) If a request for waiver is not approved, the individual will be so notified by the Director of Practice and placed on a roster of inactive enrolled individuals.

(5) If a request for waiver is approved, the individual will be so notified and issued a card evidencing such renewal.

(6) Those who are granted waivers are required to file timely applications for renewal of enrollment.

(k) *Failure to comply.* (1) Compliance by an individual with the requirements of this part shall be determined by the Director of Practice. An individual who fails to meet the requirements of eligibility for renewal of enrollment will be notified by the Director of Practice at his/her last known address by first class mail. The notice will state the basis for the non-compliance and will provide the individual an opportunity to furnish in writing information relating to the matter within 60 days of the date of the notice. Such information will be considered by the Director of Practice in making a final determination as to eligibility for renewal of enrollment.

(2) The Director of Practice may require any individual, by first class mail to his/her last known mailing address, to provide copies of any records required to be maintained under this part. The Director of Practice may disallow any continuing professional education hours claimed if the individual concerned fails to comply with such requirement.

(3) An individual who has not filed a timely application for renewal of enrollment, who has not made a timely response to the notice of non-compliance with the renewal requirements, or who has not satisfied the requirements of eligibility for renewal will be placed on a roster of inactive enrolled individuals for a period of three years. During this time, the individual will be ineligible to practice before the Internal Revenue Service.

(4) During inactive enrollment status or at any other time an individual is ineligible to practice before the Internal Revenue

Service, such individual shall not in any manner, directly or indirectly, indicate he or she is enrolled to practice before the Internal Revenue Service, or use the term "enrolled agent," the designation "E. A.," or other form of reference to eligibility to practice before the Internal Revenue Service.

(5) An individual placed in an inactive status may satisfy the requirements for renewal of enrollment during his/her period of inactive enrollment. If such satisfaction includes completing the continuing education requirement, a minimum of 16 hours of qualifying continuing education hours must be completed in the 12 month period preceding the date on which the renewal application is filed. Continuing education credit under this subsection may not be used to satisfy the requirements of the enrollment cycle in which the individual has been placed back on the active roster.

(6) An individual placed in an inactive status must file an application for renewal of enrollment and satisfy the requirements for renewal as set forth in this section within three years of being placed in an inactive status. The name of such individual otherwise will be removed from the inactive enrollment roster and his/her enrollment will terminate. Eligibility for enrollment must then be reestablished by the individual as provided in this part.

(7) Inactive enrollment status is not available to an individual who is the subject of a discipline matter in the Office of Director of Practice.

(l) *Inactive retirement status.* An individual who no longer practices before the Internal Revenue Service may request being placed in an inactive status at any time and such individual will be placed in an inactive retirement status. The individual will be ineligible to practice before the Internal Revenue Service. Such individual must file a timely application for renewal of enrollment at each applicable renewal or enrollment as provided in this part. An individual who is placed in an inactive retirement status may be reinstated to an active enrollment status upon filing an application for renewal of enrollment and providing evidence of the completion of the required continuing professional education hours for the enrollment cycle. Inactive retirement status is not available to an individual who is the subject to a discipline matter in the Office of Director of Practice.

(m) *Renewal while under suspension or disbarment.* An individual who is ineligible to practice before the Internal Revenue Service by virtue of disciplinary action is required to meet the requirements for renewal of enrollment during the period of ineligibility.

(n) *Verification.* The Director of Practice may review the continuing education records of an enrolled individual and/or qualified sponsor in a manner deemed appropriate to determine compliance with the requirements and standards for renewal of enrollment as provided in this part.

(Approved by the Office of Management and Budget under control number 1545-0946)

[51 FR 2878, Jan. 22, 1986]

§10.7 Representing oneself; participating in rulemaking; limited practice; special appearances; and return preparation.

(a) *Representing oneself.* Individuals may appear on their own behalf before the Internal Revenue Service provided they present satisfactory identification.

(b) *Participating in rulemaking.* Individuals may participate in rulemaking as provided by the Administrative Procedure Act. See 5 U.S.C. 553.

(c) *Limited practice* — (1) *In general.* Subject to the limitations in paragraph (c)(2) of this section, an individual who is not a practitioner may represent a taxpayer before the Internal Revenue Service in the circumstances described in this paragraph (c)(1), even if the taxpayer is not present, provided the individual presents satisfactory identification and proof of his or her authority to represent the taxpayer. The circumstances described in this paragraph (c)(1) are as follows:

(i) An individual may represent a member of his or her immediate family.

(ii) A regular full-time employee of an individual employer may represent the employer.

(iii) A general partner or a regular full-time employee of a partnership may represent the partnership.

(iv) A bona fide officer or a regular full-time employee of a corporation (including a parent, subsidiary, or other affiliated corporation), association, or organized group may represent the corporation, association, or organized group.

(v) A trustee, receiver, guardian, personal representative, administrator, executor, or regular full-time employee of a trust, receivership, guardianship, or estate may represent the trust, receivership, guardianship, or estate.

(vi) An officer or a regular employee of a governmental unit, agency, or authority may represent the governmental unit, agency, or authority in the course of his or her official duties.

(vii) An individual may represent any individual or entity before personnel of the Internal Revenue Service who are outside of the United States.

(viii) An individual who prepares and signs a taxpayer's return as the preparer, or who prepares a return but is not required (by the instructions to the return or regulations) to sign the return, may represent the taxpayer before officers and employees of the Examination Division of the Internal Revenue Service with respect to the tax liability of the taxpayer for the taxable year or period covered by that return.

(2) *Limitations.*

(i) An individual who is under suspension or disbarment from practice before the Internal Revenue Service may not engage in limited practice before the Service under §10.7(c)(1).

(ii) The Director, after notice and opportunity for a conference, may deny eligibility to engage in limited practice before the Internal Revenue Service under §10.7(c)(1) to any individual who has engaged in conduct that would justify suspending or disbarring a practitioner from practice before the Service.

(iii) An individual who represents a taxpayer under the authority of §10.7(c)(1)(viii) is subject to such rules of general applicability regarding standards of conduct, the extent of his or her authority, and other matters as the Director prescribes.

(d) *Special appearances.* The Director, subject to such conditions as he or she deems appropriate, may authorize an individual who is not otherwise eligible to practice before the Service to represent another person in a particular matter.

(e) *Preparing tax returns and furnishing information.* Any individual may prepare a tax return, appear as a witness for the taxpayer before the Internal Revenue Service, or furnish information at the request of the Service or any of its officers or employees.

[59 FR 31526, June 20, 1994]

§10.8 Customhouse brokers.

Nothing contained in the regulations in this part shall be deemed to affect or limit the right of a customhouse broker, licensed as such by the Commissioner of Customs in accordance with the regulations prescribed therefor, in any customs district in which he is so licensed, at the office of the District Director of Internal Revenue or before the National Office of the Internal Revenue Service, to act as a representative in respect to any matters relating specifically to the importation or exportation of merchandise under the customs or internal revenue laws, for any person for whom he has acted as a customhouse broker.

Subpart B — Duties and Restrictions Relating to Practice Before the Internal Revenue Service

§10.20 Information to be furnished.

(a) *To the Internal Revenue Service.* No attorney, certified public accountant, enrolled agent, or enrolled actuary shall neglect or refuse promptly to submit records or information in any matter before the Internal Revenue Service, upon proper and lawful request by a duly authorized officer or employee of the Internal Revenue Service, or shall interfere, or attempt to interfere, with any proper and lawful effort by the Internal Revenue Service or its officers or employees to obtain any such record or information, unless he believes in good faith and on reasonable grounds that such record or information is privileged or that the request for, or effort to obtain, such record or information is of doubtful legality.

(b) *To the Director of Practice.* It shall be the duty of an attorney or certified public accountant, who practices before the Internal Revenue Service, or enrolled agent, when requested by the Director of Practice, to provide the Director with any information he may have concerning violation of the regulations in this part by any person, and to testify thereto in any proceeding instituted under this part for the disbarment or suspension of an attorney, certified public accountant, enrolled agent, or enrolled actuary, unless he believes in good faith and on reasonable grounds that such information is privileged or that the request therefor is of doubtful legality.

[31 FR 10773, Aug. 13, 1966, as amended at 57 FR 41095, Sept. 9, 1992]

§10.21 Knowledge of client's omission.

Each attorney, certified public accountant, enrolled agent, or enrolled actuary who, having been retained by a client with respect to a matter administered by the Internal Revenue Service, knows that the client has not complied with the revenue laws of the United States or has made an error in or omission from any return, document, affidavit, or other paper which the client is required by the revenue laws of the United States to execute, shall advise the client promptly of the fact of such noncompliance, error, or omission.

[42 FR 38352, July 28, 1977, as amended at 57 FR 41095, Sept. 9, 1992]

§10.22 Diligence as to accuracy.

Each attorney, certified public accountant, enrolled agent, or enrolled actuary shall exercise due diligence:

(a) In preparing or assisting in the preparation of, approving, and filing returns, documents, affidavits, and other papers relating to Internal Revenue Service matters;

(b) In determining the correctness of oral or written representations made by him to the Department of the Treasury; and

(c) In determining the correctness of oral or written representations made by him to clients with reference to any matter administered by the Internal Revenue Service.

[35 FR 13205, Aug. 19, 1970, as amended at 42 FR 38352, July 28, 1977; 57 FR 41095, Sept. 9, 1992]

§10.23 Prompt disposition of pending matters.

No attorney, certified public accountant, enrolled agent, or enrolled actuary shall unreasonably delay the prompt disposition of any matter before the Internal Revenue Service.

§10.24 Assistance from disbarred or suspended persons and former Internal Revenue Service employees.

No attorney, certified public accountant, enrolled agent, or enrolled actuary shall, in practice before the Internal Revenue Service, knowingly and directly or indirectly:

(a) Employ or accept assistance from any person who is under disbarment or suspension from practice before the Internal Revenue Service.

(b) Accept employment as associate, correspondent, or subagent from, or share fees with, any such person.

(c) Accept assistance from any former government employee where the provisions of §10.26 of these regulations or any Federal law would be violated.

[44 FR 4943, Jan. 24, 1979, as amended at 57 FR 41095, Sept. 9, 1992]

§10.25 Practice by partners of Government employees.

No partner of an officer or employee of the executive branch of the U.S. Government, of any independent agency of the United States, or of the District of Columbia, shall represent anyone in any matter administered by the Internal Revenue Service in which such officer or employee of the Government participates or has participated personally and substantially as a Government employee or which is the subject of his official responsibility.

[31 FR 10773, Aug. 13, 1966, as amended at 35 FR 13205, Aug. 19, 1970]

§10.26 Practice by former Government employees, their partners and their associates.

(a) *Definitions.* For purposes of §10.26: (1) *Assist* means to act in such a way as to advise, furnish information to, or otherwise aid another person, directly of indirectly.

(2) *Government employee* is an officer or employee of the United States or any agency of the United States, including a *special government employee* as defined in 18 U.S.C. 202(a), or of the District of Columbia, or of any State, or a member of Congress or of any State legislature.

(3) *Member of a firm* is a sole practitioner or an employee or associate thereof, or a partner, stockholder, associate, affiliate or employee of a partnership, joint venture, corporation, professional association or other affiliation of two or more practitioners who represent non-Government parties.

(4) *Practitioner* includes any individual described in §10.3(e).

(5) *Official responsibility* means the direct administrative or operating authority, whether intermediate or final, and either exercisable alone or with others, and either personally or through subordinates, to approve, disapprove, or otherwise direct Government action, with or without knowledge of the action.

(6) *Participate* or *participation* means substantial involvement as a Government employee by making decisions, or preparing or reviewing documents with or without the right to exercise a judgment of approval or disapproval, or participating in conferences or investigations, or rendering advice of a substantial nature.

(7) *Rule* includes Treasury Regulations, whether issued or under preparation for issuance as Notices of Proposed Rule Making or as Treasury Decisions, and revenue rulings and revenue procedures published in the Internal Revenue bulletin. *Rule* shall not include a *transaction* as defined in paragraph (a)(9) of this section.

(8) *Transaction* means any decision, determination, finding, letter ruling, technical advice, contract or approval or disapproval thereof, relating to a particular factual situation or situations involving a specific party or parties whose rights, privileges, or liabilities under laws or regulations administered by the Internal Revenue Service, or other legal rights, are determined or immediately affected therein and to which the United States is a party or in which it has a direct and substantial interest, whether or not the same taxable periods are involved. *Transaction* does not include *rule* as defined in paragraph (a)(7) of this section.

(b) *General rules.* (1) No former Government employee shall, subsequent to his Government employment, represent anyone in any matter administered by the Internal Revenue Service if the representation would violate 18 U.S.C. 207 (a) or (b) or any other laws of the United States.

(2) No former Government employee who participated in a transaction shall, subsequent to his Government employment, represent or knowingly assist, in that transaction, any person who is or was a specific party to that transaction.

(3) No former Government employee who within a period of one year prior to the termination of his Government employment had official responsibility for a transaction shall, within one year after his Government employment is ended, represent or knowingly assist in that transaction any person who is or was a specific party to that transaction.

(4) No former Government employee shall, within one year after his Government employment is ended, appear before any employee of the Treasury Department in connection with the publication, withdrawal, amendment, modification, or interpretation of a rule in the development of which the former Government employee participated or for which, within a period of one year prior to the termination of his Government employment, he had official responsibility. However, this subparagraph does not preclude such former employee for appearing on his own behalf or from representing a taxpayer before the Internal Revenue Service in connection with a transaction involving the application or interpretation of such a rule with respect to that transaction: *Provided,* That such former employee shall not utilize or disclose any confidential information acquired by the former employee in the development of the rule, and shall not contend that the rule is invalid or illegal. In addition, this subparagraph does not preclude such former employee from otherwise advising or acting for any person.

(c) *Firm representation.* (1) No member of a firm of which a former Government employee is a member may represent or knowingly assist a person who was or is a specific party in any transaction with respect to which the restrictions of paragraph (b)(1) (other than 18 U.S.C. 207 (b)) or (b)(2) of this section apply to the former Government employee, in that transaction, unless:

(i) No member of the firm who had knowledge of the participation by the Government employee in the transaction initiated discussions with the Government employee concerning his becoming a member of the firm until his Government employment is ended or six months after the termination of his participation in the transaction, whichever is earlier;

(ii) The former Government employee did not initiate any discussions concerning becoming a member of the firm while participating in the transaction or, if such discussions were initiated, they conformed with the requirements of 18 U.S.C. 208(b); and

(iii) The firm isolates the former Government employee in such a way that he does not assist in the representation.

(2) No member of a firm of which a former Government employee is a member may represent or knowingly assist a person who was or is a specific party in any transaction with respect to which the restrictions of paragraph (b)(3) of this section apply to the former employee, in that transaction, unless the firm isolates the former Government employee in such a way that he does not assist in the representation.

(3) When isolation of the former Government employee is required under paragraphs (c)(1) or (c)(2) of this section, a statement affirming the fact of such isolation shall be executed under oath by the former Government employee and by a member of the firm acting on behalf of the firm, and shall be filed with the Director of Practice and in such other place and in the manner prescribed by regulation. This statement shall clearly identify the firm, the former Government employee, and the transaction or transactions requiring such isolation.

(d) *Pending representation.* Practice by former Government employees, their partners and associates with respect to representation in specific matters where actual representation commenced before publication of this regulation is governed by the regulations set forth in the June 1972 amendments to the regulations of this part (published at 37 FR 11676): *Provided,* That the burden of showing that representation commenced before publication is with the former Government employees, their partners and associates.

[42 FR 38352, July 28, 1977, as amended at 57 FR 41095, Sept. 9, 1992; 59 FR 31527, June 20, 1994]

§10.27 Notaries.

No attorney, certified public accountant, enrolled agent, or enrolled actuary as notary public shall with respect to any matter administered by the Internal Revenue Service take acknowledgments, administer oaths, certify papers, or perform any official act in connection with matters in which he is employed as counsel, attorney, or agent, or in which he may be in any way interested before the Internal Revenue Service (26 Op. Atty. Gen. 236).

[31 FR 10773, Aug. 13, 1966, as amended at 57 FR 41095, Sept. 9, 1992]

§10.28 Fees.

(a) *Generally.* A practitioner may not charge an unconscionable fee for representing a client in a matter before the Internal Revenue Service.

(b) *Contingent fees for return preparation.* A practitioner may not charge a contingent fee for preparing an original return. A practitioner may charge a contingent fee for preparing an amended return or a claim for refund (other than a claim for refund made on an original return) if the practitioner reasonably anticipates at the time the fee arrangement is entered into that the amended return or claim will receive substantive review by the Service. A contingent fee includes a fee that is based on a percentage of the refund shown on a return or a percentage of the taxes saved, or that otherwise depends on the specific result attained.

[59 FR 31527, June 20, 1994]

§10.29 Conflicting interests.

No attorney, certified public accountant, enrolled agent, or enrolled actuary shall represent conflicting interests in his practice before the Internal Revenue Service, except by express consent of all directly interested parties after full disclosure has been made.

[31 FR 10773, Aug. 13, 1966, as amended at 57 FR 41095, Sept. 9, 1992]

§10.30 Solicitation.

(a) *Advertising and solicitation restrictions.* (1) No attorney, certified public accountant, enrolled agent, enrolled actuary, or other individual eligible to practice before the Internal Revenue Service shall, with respect to any Internal Revenue Service matter, in any way use or participate in the use of any form of public communication containing (i) A false, fraudulent, unduly influencing, coercive, or unfair statement or claim; or (ii) a misleading or deceptive statement or claim.

Enrolled agents, in describing their professional designation, may not utilize the term of art "certified" or indicate an employer/employee relationship with the Internal Revenue Service. Examples of acceptable descriptions are "enrolled to represent taxpayers before the Internal Revenue Service," "enrolled to practice before the Internal Revenue Service," and "admitted to practice before the Internal

Revenue Service." Enrolled agents and enrolled actuaries may abbreviate such designation to either EA or E.A.

(2) No attorney, certified public accountant, enrolled agent, enrolled actuary, or other individual eligible to practice before the Internal Revenue Service shall make, directly or indirectly, an uninvited solicitation of employment in matters related to the Internal Revenue Service. Solicitation includes, but is not limited to, in-person contacts and telephone communications. This restriction does not apply to (i) Seeking new business from an existing or former client in a related matter; (ii) communications with family members; (iii) making the availability of professional services known to other practitioners, so long as the person or firm contacted is not a potential client; (iv) solicitation by mailings; or (v) non-coercive in-person solicitation by those eligible to practice before the Internal Revenue Service while acting as an employee, member, or officer of an exempt organization listed in sections 501(c)(3) or (4) of the Internal Revenue Code of 1954 (26 U.S.C.).

Any targeted direct mail solicitation, i.e. a mailing to those whose unique circumstances are the basis for the solicitation, distributed by or on behalf of an attorney, certified public accountant, enrolled agent, enrolled actuary, or other individual eligible to practice before the Internal Revenue Service shall be clearly marked as such in capital letters on the envelope and at the top of the first page of such mailing. In addition, all such solicitations must clearly identify the source of the information used in choosing the recipient.

(b) *Fee information.* (1) Attorneys, certified public accountants, enrolled agents, or enrolled actuaries and other individuals eligible to practice before the Internal Revenue Service may disseminate the following fee information:

(i) Fixed fees for specific routine services.
(ii) Hourly rates.
(iii) Range of fees for particular services.
(iv) Fee charged for an initial consultation.

Any statement of fee information concerning matters in which costs may be incurred shall include a statement disclosing whether clients will be responsible for such costs.

(2) Attorneys, certified public accountants, enrolled agents, or enrolled actuaries and other individuals eligible to practice before the Internal Revenue Service may also publish the availability of a written schedule of fees.

(3) Attorneys, certified public accountants, enrolled agents, or enrolled actuaries and other individuals eligible to practice before the Internal Revenue Service shall be bound to charge the hourly rate, the fixed fee for specific routine services, the range of fees for particular services, or the fee for an initial consultation published for a reasonable period of time, but no less than thirty days from the last publication of such hourly rate or fees.

(c) *Communications.* Communication, including fee information, may include professional lists, telephone directories, print media, mailings, radio and television, and any other method: *Provided,* that the method chosen does not cause the communication to become untruthful, deceptive, unduly influencing or otherwise in violation of these regulations. It shall be construed as a violation of these regulations for a practitioner to persist in attempting to contact a prospective client, if such client has made known to the practitioner a desire not to be solicited. In the case of radio and television broadcasting, the broadcast shall be pre-recorded and the practitioner shall retain a recording of the actual audio transmission. In the case of direct mail communications, the practitioner shall retain a copy of the actual mailing, along with a list or other description of persons to whom the communication was mailed or otherwise distributed. Such copy shall be retained by the practitioner for a period of at least 36 months from the date of the last transmission or use.

(d) *Improper associations.* An attorney, certified public accountant, enrolled agent, or enrolled actuary may, in matters related to the Internal Revenue Service, employ or accept employment or assistance as an associate, correspondent, or subagent from, or share fees with, any person or entity who, to the knowledge of the practitioner, obtains clients or otherwise practices in a manner forbidden under this section: *Provided,* That a practitioner does not, directly or indirectly, act or hold himself out as an Internal Revenue Service practitioner in connection with that relationship. Nothing herein shall prohibit an attorney, certified public accountant, or enrolled agent from practice before the Internal Revenue Service in a capacity other than that described above.

[44 FR 4943, Jan. 24, 1979, as amended at 57 FR 41095, Sept. 9, 1992]

§10.31 Negotiation of taxpayer refund checks.

No attorney, certified public accountant, enrolled agent, or enrolled actuary who is an income tax return preparer shall endorse or otherwise negotiate any check made in respect of income taxes which is issued to a taxpayer other than the attorney, certified public accountant or enrolled agent.

[42 FR 38353, July 28, 1977, as amended at 57 FR 41095, Sept. 9, 1992]

§10.32 Practice of law.

Nothing in the regulations in this part shall be construed as authorizing persons not members of the bar to practice law.

[31 FR 10773, Aug. 13, 1966. Redesignated at 42 FR 38353, July 28, 1977]

§10.33 Tax shelter opinions.

(a) *Tax shelter opinions and offering materials.* A practitioner who provides a tax shelter opinion analyzing the Federal tax effects of a tax shelter investment shall comply with each of the following requirements:

(1) *Factual matters.* (i) The practitioner must make inquiry as to all relevant facts, be satisfied that the material facts are accurately and completely described in the offering materials, and assure that any representations as to future activities are clearly identified, reasonable and complete.

(ii) A practitioner may not accept as true asserted facts pertaining to the tax shelter which he/she should not, based on his/her background and knowledge, reasonably believe to be true. However, a practitioner need not conduct an audit or independent verification of the asserted facts, or assume that a client's statement of the facts cannot be relied upon, unless he/she has reason to believe that any relevant facts asserted to him/her are untrue.

(iii) If the fair market value of property or the expected financial performance of an investment is relevant to the tax shelter, a practitioner may not accept an appraisal or financial projection as support for the matters claimed therein unless:

(A) The appraisal or financial projection makes sense on its face;

(B) The practitioner reasonably believes that the person making the appraisal or financial projection is competent to do so and is not of dubious reputation; and

(C) The appraisal is based on the definition of fair market value prescribed under the relevant Federal tax provisions.

(iv) If the fair market value of purchased property is to be established by reference to its stated purchase price, the practitioner must examine the terms and conditions upon which the property was (or is to be) purchased to determine whether the stated purchase price reasonably may be considered to be its fair market value.

(2) *Relate law to facts.* The practitioner must relate the law to the actual facts and, when addressing issues based on future activities, clearly identify what facts are assumed.

(3) *Identification of material issues.* The practitioner must ascertain that all material Federal tax issues have been considered, and that all of those issues which involve the reasonable possibility of a challenge by the Internal Revenue Service have been fully and fairly addressed in the offering materials.

(4) *Opinion on each material issue.* Where possible, the practitioner must provide an opinion whether it is more likely than not that an investor will prevail on the merits of each material tax issue presented by the offering which involves a reasonable possibility of a challenge by the Internal Revenue Service. Where such an opinion cannot be given with respect to any material tax issue, the opinion should fully describe the reasons for the practitioner's inability to opine as to the likely outcome.

(5) *Overall evaluation.* (i) Where possible, the practitioner must provide an overall evaluation whether the material tax benefits in the aggregate more likely than not will be realized. Where such an overall evaluation cannot be given, the opinion should fully describe the reasons for the practitioner's inability to make an overall evaluation. Opinions concluding that an overall evaluation cannot be provided will be given special scrutiny to determine if the stated reasons are adequate.

(ii) A favorable overall evaluation may not be rendered unless it is based on a conclusion that substantially more than half of the material tax benefits, in terms of their financial impact on a typical investor, more likely than not will be realized if challenged by the Internal Revenue Service.

(iii) If it is not possible to give an overall evaluation, or if the overall evaluation is that the material tax benefits in the aggregate will not be realized, the fact that the practitioner's opinion does not constitute a favorable overall evaluation, or that it is an unfavorable overall evaluation, must be clearly and prominently disclosed in the offering materials.

(iv) The following examples illustrate the principles of this paragraph:

Example (1). A limited partnership acquires real property in a sale-leaseback transaction. The principal tax benefits offered to investing partners consist of depreciation and interest deductions. Lesser tax benefits are offered to investors by reason of several deductions under Internal Revenue Code section 162 (ordinary and necessary business expenses). If a practitioner concludes that it is more likely than not that the partnership will not be treated as the owner of the property for tax purposes (which is required to allow the interest and depreciation deductions), then he/she may not opine to the effect that it is more likely than not that the material tax benefits in the aggregate will be realized, regardless of whether favorable opinions may be given with respect to the deductions claimed under Code section 162.

Example (2). A corporation electing under subchapter S of the Internal Revenue Code is formed to engage in research and development activities. The offering materials forecast that deductions for research and experimental expenditures equal to 75% of the total investment in the corporation will be available during the first two years of the corporation's operations, other expenses will account for another 15% of the total investment, and that little or no gross income will be received by the corporation during this period. The practitioner concludes that it is more likely than not that deductions for research and experimental expenditures will be allowable. The practitioner may render an opinion to the effect that based on this conclusion, it is more likely than not that the material tax benefits in the aggregate will be realized, regardless of whether he/she can opine that it is more likely than not that any of the other tax benefits will be achieved.

Example (3). An investment program is established to acquire offsetting positions in commodities contracts. The objective of the program is to close the loss positions in year one and to close the profit positions in year two. The principal tax benefit offered by the program is a loss in the first year, coupled with the deferral of offsetting gain until the following year. The practitioner concludes that the losses will not be deductible in year one. Accordingly, he/she may not render an opinion to the effect that it is more likely than not that the material tax benefits in the aggregate will be realized, regardless of the fact that he/she is of the opinion that losses not allowable in year one will be allowable in year two, because the principal tax benefit offered is a one-year deferral of income.

Example (4). A limited partnership is formed to acquire, own and operate residential rental real estate. The offering material forecasts gross income of $2,000,000 and total deductions of $10,000,000, resulting in net losses of $8,000,000 over the first six taxable years. Of the total deductions, depreciation and interest are projected to be $7,000,000, and other deductions $3,000,000. The practitioner concludes that it is more likely than not that all of the depreciation and interest deductions will be allowable, and that it is more likely than not that the other deductions will not be allowed. The practitioner may render an opinion to the effect that it is more likely than not that the material tax benefits in the aggregate will be realized.

(6) *Description of opinion.* The practitioner must assure that the offering materials correctly and fairly represent the nature and extent of the tax shelter opinion.

(b) *Reliance on other opinions* — (1) In general. A practitioner may provide an opinion on less than all of the material tax issues only if:

(i) At least one other competent practitioner provides an opinion on the likely outcome with respect to all of the other material tax issues which involve a reasonable possibility of challenge by the Internal Revenue Service, and an overall evaluation whether the material tax benefits in the aggregate more likely than not will be realized, which is disseminated in the same manner as the practitioner's opinion; and

(ii) The practitioner, upon reviewing such other opinions and any offering materials, has no reason to believe that the standards of paragraph (a) of this section have not been complied with.

Notwithstanding the foregoing, a practitioner who has not been retained to provide an overall evaluation whether the material tax benefits in the aggregate more likely than not will be realized may issue an opinion on less than all the material tax issues only if he/she has no reason to believe, based on his/her knowledge and experience, that the overall evaluation given by the practitioner who furnishes the overall evaluation is incorrect on its face.

(2) *Forecasts and projections.* A practitioner who is associated with forecasts or projections relating to or based upon the tax consequences of the tax shelter offering that are included in the offering materials, or are disseminated to potential investors other than the practitioner's clients, may rely on the opinion of another practitioner as to any or all material tax issues, provided that the practitioner who desires to rely on the other opinion has no reason to believe that the standards of paragraph (a) of this section have not been complied with by the practitioner rendering such other opinion, and the requirements of paragraph (b)(1) of this section are satisfied. The practitioner's report shall disclose any material tax issue not covered by, or incorrectly opined upon, by the other opinion, and shall set forth his/her opinion with respect to each such issue in a manner that satisfies the requirements of paragraph (a) of this section.

(c) *Definitions.* For purposes of this section:

(1) *Practitioner* includes any individual described in §10.3(e).

(2) A *tax shelter*, as the term is used in this section, is an investment which has as a significant and intended feature for Federal income or excise tax purposes either of the following attributes:

(i) Deductions in excess of income from the investment being available in any year to reduce income from other sources in that year, or

(ii) Credits in excess of the tax attributable to the income from the investment being available in any year to offset taxes on income from other sources in that year. Excluded from the term are municipal bonds; annuities; family trusts (but not including schemes or arrangements that are marketed to the public other than in a direct practitioner-client relationship); qualified retirement plans; individual retirement accounts; stock option plans; securities issued in a corporate reorganization; mineral development ventures, if the only tax benefit would be percentage depletion; and real estate where it is anticipated that in no year is it likely that deductions will exceed the tax attributable to the income from the investment in that year. Whether an investment is intended to have tax shelter features depends on the objective facts and circumstances of each case. Significant weight will be given to the features described in the offering materials to determine whether the investment is a tax shelter.

(3) A *tax shelter opinion*, as the term is used in this section, is advice by a practitioner concerning the Federal tax aspects of a tax shelter either appearing or referred to in the offering materials, or used or referred to in connection with sales promotion efforts, and directed to persons other than the client who engaged the practitioner to give the advice. The term includes the tax aspects or tax risks portion of the offering materials prepared by or at the direction of a practitioner, whether or not a separate opinion letter is issued or whether or not the practitioner's name is referred to in the offering materials or in connection with the sales promotion efforts. In addition, a financial forecast or projection prepared by a practitioner is a tax shelter opinion if it is predicated on assumptions regarding Federal tax aspects of the investment, and it meets the other requirements of the first sentence of this paragraph. The term does not, however, include rendering advice solely to the offeror or reviewing parts of the offering materials, so long as neither the name of the practitioner, nor the fact that a practitioner has rendered advice concerning the tax aspects, is referred to in the offering materials or in connection with the sales promotion efforts.

(4) A *material* tax issue as the term is used in this section is

(i) Any Federal income or excise tax issue relating to a tax shelter that would make a significant contribution toward sheltering from Federal taxes income from other sources by providing deductions in excess of the income from the tax shelter investment in any year, or tax credits available to offset tax liabilities in excess of the tax attributable to the tax shelter investment in any year;

(ii) Any other Federal income or excise tax issue relating to a tax shelter that could have a significant impact (either beneficial or adverse) on a tax shelter investor under any reasonably foreseeable circumstances (e.g., depreciation or investment tax credit recapture, availability of long-term capital gain treatment, or realization of taxable income in excess of cash flow, upon sale or other disposition of the tax shelter investment); and

(iii) The potential applicability of penalties, additions to tax, or interest charges that reasonably could be asserted against a tax shelter investor by the Internal Revenue Service with respect to the tax shelter. The determination of what is material is to be made in good faith by the practitioner, based on information available at the time the offering materials are circulated.

(d) For purposes of advising the Director of Practice whether an individual may have violated §10.33, the Director of Practice is authorized to establish an Advisory Committee, composed of at least five individuals authorized to practice before the Internal Revenue Service. Under procedures established by the Director of Practice, such Advisory Committee shall, at the request of the Director of Practice, review and make recommendations with regard to alleged violations of §10.33.

(Sec. 3, 23 Stat. 258, secs. 2-12, 60 Stat. 237 *et seq.;* 5 U.S.C. 301; 31 U.S.C. 330; 31 U.S.C. 321 (Reorg. Plan No. 26 of 1950, 15 FR 4935, 64 Stat. 1280, 3 CFR, 1949-53 Comp., p. 1017))

[49 FR 6722, Feb. 23, 1984; 49 FR 7116, Feb. 27, 1984; 59 FR 31527, 31528, June 20, 1994]

§10.34 Standards for advising with respect to tax return positions and for preparing or signing returns.

(a) *Standards of conduct* — (1) *Realistic possibility standard.* A practitioner may not sign a return as a preparer if the practitioner determines that the return contains a position that does not have a realistic possibility of being sustained on its merits (the realistic possibility standard) unless the position is not frivolous and is adequately disclosed to the Service. A practitioner may not advise a client to take a position on a return, or prepare the portion of a return on which a position is taken, unless —

(i) The practitioner determines that the position satisfies the realistic possibility standard; or

(ii) The position is not frivolous and the practitioner advises the client of any opportunity to avoid the accuracy-related penalty in section 6662 of the Internal Revenue Code of 1986 by adequately disclosing the position and of the requirements for adequate disclosure.

(2) *Advising clients on potential penalties.* A practitioner advising a client to take a position on a return, or preparing or signing a return as a preparer, must inform the client of the penalties reasonably likely to apply to the client with respect to the position advised, prepared, or reported. The practitioner also must inform the client of any opportunity to avoid any such penalty by disclosure, if relevant, and of the requirements for adequate disclosure. This paragraph (a)(2) applies even if the practitioner is not subject to a penalty with respect to the position.

(3) *Relying on information furnished by clients.* A practitioner advising a client to take a position on a return, or preparing or signing a return as a preparer, generally may rely in good faith without verification upon information furnished by the client. However, the practitioner may not ignore the implications of information furnished to, or actually known by, the practitioner, and must make reasonable inquiries if the information as furnished appears to be incorrect, inconsistent, or incomplete.

(4) *Definitions.* For purposes of this section:

(i) *Realistic possibility.* A position is considered to have a realistic possibility of being sustained on its merits if a reasonable and well-informed analysis by a person knowledgeable in the tax law would lead such a person to conclude that the position has approximately a one in three, or greater, likelihood of being sustained on its merits. The authorities described in 26 CFR 1.6662 - 4(d)(3)(iii), or any successor provision, of the substantial understatement penalty regulations may be taken into account for purposes of this analysis. The possibility that a position will not be challenged by the Service (e.g., because the taxpayer's return may not be audited or because the issue may not be raised on audit) may not be taken into account.

(ii) *Frivolous.* A position is frivolous if it is patently improper.

(b) *Standard of discipline.* As provided in §10.52, only violations of this section that are willful, reckless, or a result of gross incompetence will subject a practitioner to suspension or disbarment from practice before the Service.

[59 FR 31527, June 20, 1994]

Subpart C — Rules Applicable to Disciplinary Proceedings

§10.50 Authority to disbar or suspend.

Pursuant to 31 U.S.C. 330(b), the Secretary of the Treasury after notice and an opportunity for a proceeding, may suspend or disbar any practitioner from practice before the Internal Revenue Service. The Secretary may take such action against any practitioner who is shown to be incompetent or disreputable, who refuses to comply with any regulation in this part, or who, with intent to defraud, willfully and knowingly misleads or threatens a client or prospective client.

[59 FR 31528, June 20, 1994]

§10.51 Disreputable conduct.

Disreputable conduct for which an attorney, certified public accountant, enrolled agent, or enrolled actuary may be disbarred or suspended from practice before the Internal Revenue Service includes, but is not limited to:

(a) Conviction of any criminal offense under the revenue laws of the United States, or of any offense involving dishonesty, or breach of trust.

(b) Giving false or misleading information, or participating in any way in the giving of false or misleading information to the Department of the Treasury or any officer or employee thereof, or to any tribunal authorized to pass upon Federal tax matters, in connection with any matter pending or likely to be pending before them, knowing such information to be false or misleading. Facts or other matters contained in testimony, Federal tax returns, financial statements, applications for enrollment, affidavits, declarations, or any other document or statement, written or oral, are included in the term "information."

(c) Solicitation of employment as prohibited under §10.30 of this part, the use of false or misleading representations with intent to deceive a client or prospective client in order to procure employment, or intimating that the practitioner is able improperly to obtain special consideration or action from the Internal Revenue Service or officer or employee thereof.

(d) Willfully failing to make a Federal tax return in violation of the revenue laws of the United States, or evading, attempting to evade, or participating in any way in evading or attempting to evade any Federal tax or payment thereof, knowingly counseling or suggesting to a client or prospective client an illegal plan to evade Federal taxes or payment thereof, or concealing assets of himself or another to evade Federal taxes or payment thereof.

(e) Misappropriation of, or failure properly and promptly to remit funds received from a client for the purpose of payment of taxes or other obligations due the United States.

(f) Directly or indirectly attempting to influence, or offering or agreeing to attempt to influence, the official action of any officer or employee of the Internal Revenue Service by the use of threats, false accusations, duress or coercion, by the offer of any special inducement or promise of advantage or by the bestowing of any gift, favor or thing of value.

(g) Disbarment or suspension from practice as an attorney, certified public accountant, public accountant, or actuary by any duly constituted authority of any State, possession, territory, Commonwealth, the District of Columbia, any Federal court of record or any Federal agency, body or board.

(h) Knowingly aiding and abetting another person to practice before the Internal Revenue Service during a period of suspension, disbarment, or ineligibility of such other person. Maintaining a partnership for the practice of law, accountancy, or other related professional service with a person who is under disbarment from practice before the Service shall be presumed to be a violation of this provision.

(i) Contemptuous conduct in connection with practice before the Internal Revenue Service, including the use of abusive language, making false accusations and statements knowing them to be false, or circulating or publishing malicious or libelous matter.

(j) Giving a false opinion, knowingly, recklessly, or through gross incompetence, including an opinion which is intentionally or recklessly misleading, or a pattern of providing incompetent opinions on questions arising under the Federal tax laws. False opinions described in this paragraph include those which reflect or result from a knowing misstatement of fact or law; from an assertion of a position known to be unwarranted under existing law; from counseling or assisting in conduct known to be illegal or fraudulent; from concealment of matters required by law to be revealed; or from conscious disregard of information indicating that material facts expressed in the tax opinion or offering material are false or misleading. For purposes of this paragraph, reckless conduct is a highly unreasonable omission or misrepresentation involving an extreme departure from the standards of ordinary care that a practitioner should observe under the circumstances. A pattern of conduct is a factor that will be taken into account in determining whether a practitioner acted knowingly, recklessly, or through gross incompetence. Gross incompetence includes conduct that reflects gross indifference, preparation which is grossly inadequate under the circumstances, and a consistent failure to perform obligations to the client.

(Sec. 3, 23 Stat. 258, secs. 2-12, 60 Stat. 237 *et seq.*; 5 U.S.C. 301; 31 U.S.C. 330; 31 U.S.C. 321 (Reorg. Plan No. 26 of 1950, 15 FR 4935, 64 Stat. 1280, 3 CFR, 1949-53 Comp., p. 1017))

[31 FR 10773, Aug. 13, 1966, as amended at 35 FR 13205, Aug. 19, 1970; 42 FR 38353, July 28, 1977; 44 FR 4946, Jan. 24, 1979; 49 FR 6723, Feb. 23, 1984; 57 FR 41095, Sept. 9, 1992; 59 FR 31528, June 20, 1994]

§10.52 Violation of regulations.

A practitioner may be disbarred or suspended from practice before the Internal Revenue Service for any of the following:

(a) Willfully violating any of the regulations contained in this part.

(b) Recklessly or through gross incompetence (within the meaning of §10.51(j)) violating §10.33 or §10.34 of this part.

[59 FR 31528, June 20, 1994]

§10.53 Receipt of information concerning attorneys, certified public accountants, enrolled agents, or enrolled actuaries.

If an officer or employee of the Internal Revenue Service has reason to believe that an attorney, certified public accountant, enrolled agent, or enrolled actuary has violated any provision of this part, or if any such officer or employee receives information to that effect, he shall promptly make a written report thereof, which report or a copy thereof shall be forwarded to the Director of Practice. If any other person has information of such violations, he may make a report thereof to the Director of Practice or to any officer or employee of the Internal Revenue Service.

[31 FR 10773, Aug. 13, 1966, as amended at 57 FR 41095, Sept. 9, 1992]

§10.54 Institution of proceeding.

Whenever the Director of Practice has reason to believe that any attorney, certified public accountant, enrolled agent, or enrolled actuary has violated any provision of the laws or regulations governing practice before the Internal Revenue Service, he may reprimand such person or institute a proceeding for disbarment or suspension of such person. The proceeding shall be instituted by a complaint which names the respondent and is signed by the Director of Practice and filed in his office. Except in cases of willfulness, or where time, the nature of the proceeding, or the public interest does not permit, a proceeding will not be instituted under this section until facts or conduct which may warrant such action have been called to the attention of the proposed respondent in writing and he has been accorded opportunity to demonstrate or achieve compliance with all lawful requirements.

[31 FR 10773, Aug. 13, 1966, as amended at 57 FR 41095, Sept. 9, 1992]

§10.55 Conferences.

(a) *In general.* The Director of Practice may confer with an attorney, certified public accountant, enrolled agent, or enrolled actuary concerning allegations of misconduct irrespective of whether a proceeding for disbarment or suspension has been instituted against him. If such conference results in a stipulation in connection with a proceeding in which such person is the respondent, the stipulation may be entered in the record at the instance of either party to the proceeding.

(b) *Resignation or voluntary suspension.* An attorney, certified public accountant, enrolled agent, or enrolled actuary, in order to avoid the institution or conclusion of a disbarment or suspension proceeding, may offer his consent to suspension from practice before the Internal Revenue Service. An enrolled agent may also offer his resignation. The Director of Practice, in his discretion, may accept the offered resignation of an enrolled agent and may suspend an attorney, certified public accountant, or enrolled agent in accordance with the consent offered.

[31 FR 10773, Aug. 13, 1966, as amended at 35 FR 13206, Aug. 19, 1970; 57 FR 41095, Sept. 9, 1992]

§10.56 Contents of complaint.

(a) *Charges.* A complaint shall give a plain and concise description of the allegations which constitute the basis for the proceeding. A complaint shall be deemed sufficient if it fairly informs the respondent of the charges against him so that he is able to prepare his defense.

(b) *Demand for answer.* In the complaint, or in a separate paper attached to the complaint, notification shall be given of the place and time within which the respondent shall file his answer, which time shall not be less than 15 days from the date of service of the complaint, and notice shall be given that a decision by default may be rendered against the respondent in the event he fails to file his answer as required.

[31 FR 10773, Aug. 13, 1966, as amended at 42 FR 38353, July 28, 1977]

§10.57 Service of complaint and other papers.

(a) *Complaint.* The complaint or a copy thereof may be served upon the respondent by certified mail, or first-class mail as hereinafter provided; by delivering it to the respondent or his attorney or agent of record either in person or by leaving it at the office or place of business of the respondent, attorney or agent; or in any other manner which has been agreed to by the respondent. Where the service is by certified mail, the return post office receipt duly signed by or on behalf of the respondent shall be proof of service. If the certified matter is not claimed or accepted by the respondent and is returned undelivered, complete service may be made upon the respondent by mailing the complaint to him by first-class mail, addressed to him at the address under which he is enrolled or at the last address known to the Director of Practice. If service is made upon the respondent or his attorney or agent of record in person or by leaving the complaint at the office or place of business of the respondent, attorney or agent, the verified return by the person making service, setting forth the manner of service, shall be proof of such service.

(b) *Service of papers other than complaint.* Any paper other than the complaint may be served upon an attorney, certified public accountant, or enrolled agent as provided in paragraph (a) of this section or by mailing the paper by first-class mail to the respondent at the last address known to the Director of Practice, or by mailing the paper by first-class mail to the respondent's attorney or agent of record. Such mailing shall constitute complete service. Notices may be served upon the respondent or his attorney or agent of record by telegraph.

(c) *Filing of papers.* Whenever the filing of a paper is required or permitted in connection with a disbarment or suspension proceeding, and the place of filing is not specified by this subpart or by rule or order of the Administrative Law Judge, the paper shall be filed with the Director of Practice, Treasury Department, Washington, D.C. 20220. All papers shall be filed in duplicate.

[31 FR 10773, Aug. 13, 1966, as amended at 31 FR 13992, Nov. 2, 1966; 42 FR 38354, July 28, 1977]

§10.58   Answer.

(a) *Filing.* The respondent's answer shall be filed in writing within the time specified in the complaint or notice of institution of the proceeding, unless on application the time is extended by the Director of Practice or the Administrative Law Judge. The answer shall be filed in duplicate with the Director of Practice.

(b) *Contents.* The answer shall contain a statement of facts which constitute the grounds of defense, and it shall specifically admit or deny each allegation set forth in the complaint, except that the respondent shall not deny a material allegation in the complaint which he knows to be true, or state that he is without sufficient information to form a belief when in fact he possesses such information. The respondent may also state affirmatively special matters of defense.

(c) *Failure to deny or answer allegations in the complaint.* Every allegation in the complaint which is not denied in the answer shall be deemed to be admitted and may be considered as proved, and no further evidence in respect of such allegation need be adduced at a hearing. Failure to file an answer within the time prescribed in the notice to the respondent, except as the time for answer is extended by the Director of Practice or the Administrative Law Judge, shall constitute an admission of the allegations of the complaint and a waiver of hearing, and the Administrative Law Judge may make his decision by default without a hearing or further procedure.

[31 FR 10773, Aug. 13, 1966, as amended at 42 FR 38354, July 28, 1977]

§10.59   Supplemental charges.

If it appears that the respondent in his answer, falsely and in bad faith, denies a material allegation of fact in the complaint or states that the respondent has no knowledge sufficient to form a belief, when he in fact possesses such information, or if it appears that the respondent has knowingly introduced false testimony during proceedings for his disbarment or suspension, the Director of Practice may thereupon file supplemental charges against the respondent. Such supplemental charges may be tried with other charges in the case, provided the respondent is given due notice thereof and is afforded an opportunity to prepare a defense thereto.

§10.60   Reply to answer.

No reply to the respondent's answer shall be required, and new matter in the answer shall be deemed to be denied, but the Director of Practice may file a reply in his discretion or at the request of the Administrative Law Judge.

[31 FR 10773, Aug. 13, 1966 as amended at 42 FR 38354, July 28, 1977]

§10.61 Proof; variance; amendment of pleadings.

In the case of a variance between the allegations in a pleading and the evidence adduced in support of the pleading, the Administrative Law Judge may order or authorize amendment of the pleading to conform to the evidence: *Provided,* That the party who would otherwise be prejudiced by the amendment is given reasonable opportunity to meet the allegations of the pleading as amended; and the Administrative Law Judge shall make findings on any issue presented by the pleadings as so amended.

[31 FR 10773, Aug. 13, 1966, as amended at 42 FR 38354, July 28, 1977]

§10.62 Motions and requests.

Motions and requests may be filed with the Director of Practice or with the Administrative Law Judge.

[31 FR 10773, Aug. 13, 1966, as amended at 42 FR 38354, July 28, 1977]

§10.63 Representation.

A respondent or proposed respondent may appear in person or he may be represented by counsel or other representative who need not be enrolled to practice before the Internal Revenue Service. The Director may be represented by an attorney or other employee of the Internal Revenue Service.

§10.64 Administrative Law Judge.

(a) *Appointment.* An Administrative Law Judge appointed as provided by 5 U.S.C. 3105 (1966), shall conduct proceedings upon complaints for the disbarment or suspension of attorneys, certified public accountants, or enrolled agents.

(b) *Powers of Administrative Law Judge.* Among other powers, the Administrative Law Judge shall have authority, in connection with any disbarment or suspension proceeding assigned or referred to him, to do the following:

(1) Administer oaths and affirmations;

(2) Make rulings upon motions and requests, which rulings may not be appealed from prior to the close of a hearing except, at the discretion of the Administrative Law Judge, in extraordinary circumstances;

(3) Determine the time and place of hearing and regulate its course and conduct;

(4) Adopt rules of procedure and modify the same from time to time as occasion requires for the orderly disposition of proceedings;

(5) Rule upon offers of proof, receive relevant evidence, and examine witnesses;

(6) Take or authorize the taking of depositions;

(7) Receive and consider oral or written argument on facts or law;

(8) Hold or provide for the holding of conferences for the settlement or simplification of the issues by consent of the parties;

(9) Perform such acts and take such measures as are necessary or appropriate to the efficient conduct of any proceeding; and

(10) Make initial decisions.

[31 FR 10773, Aug. 13, 1966, as amended at 42 FR 38353, 38354, July 28, 1977]

§10.65 Hearings.

(a) *In general.* An Administrative Law Judge will preside at the hearing on a complaint furnished under §10.54 for the disbarment or suspension of a practitioner. Hearings will be stenographically recorded and transcribed and the testimony of witnesses will be taken under oath or affirmation. Hearings will be conducted pursuant to 5 U.S.C. 556. A hearing in a proceeding requested under §10.76(g) will be conducted *de novo.*

(b) *Failure to appear.* If either party to the proceeding fails to appear at the hearing, after due notice thereof has been sent to him, he shall be deemed to have waived the right to a hearing and the Administrative Law Judge may make his decision against the absent party by default.

[31 FR 10773, Aug. 13, 1966, as amended at 42 FR 38354, July 28, 1977; 59 FR 31528, June 20, 1994]

§10.66 Evidence.

(a) *In general.* The rules of evidence prevailing in courts of law and equity are not controlling in hearings on complaints for the disbarment or suspension of attorneys, certified public accountants, and enrolled agents. However, the Administrative Law Judge shall exclude evidence which is irrelevant, immaterial, or unduly repetitious.

(b) *Depositions.* The deposition of any witness taken pursuant to §10.67 may be admitted.

(c) *Proof of documents.* Official documents, records, and papers of the Internal Revenue Service and the Office of Director of Practice shall be admissible in evidence without the production of an officer or employee to authenticate them. Any such documents, records, and papers may be evidenced by a copy attested or identified by an officer or employee of the Internal Revenue Service or the Treasury Department, as the case may be.

(d) *Exhibits.* If any document, record, or other paper is introduced in evidence as an exhibit, the Administrative Law Judge may authorize the withdrawal of the exhibit subject to any conditions which he deems proper.

(e) *Objections.* Objections to evidence shall be in short form, stating the grounds of objection relied upon, and the record shall not include argument thereon, except as ordered by the Administrative Law Judge. Rulings on such objections shall be a part of the record. No exception to the ruling is necessary to preserve the rights of the parties.

[31 FR 10773, Aug. 13, 1966, as amended at 35 FR 13206, Aug. 19, 1970; 42 FR 38354, July 28, 1977]

§10.67 Depositions.

Depositions for use at a hearing may, with the written approval of the Administrative Law Judge be taken by either the Director of Practice or the respondent or their duly authorized representatives. Depositions may be taken upon oral or written interrogatories, upon not less than 10 days' written notice to the other party before any officer duly authorized to administer an oath for general purposes or before an officer or employee of the Internal Revenue Service who is authorized to administer an oath in internal revenue matters. Such notice shall state the names of the witnesses and the time and place where the depositions are to be taken. The requirement of 10 days' notice may be waived by the parties in writing, and depositions may then be taken from the persons and at the times and places mutually agreed to by the parties. When a deposition is taken upon written interrogatories, any cross-examination shall be upon written interrogatories. Copies of such written interrogatories shall be served upon the other party with the notice, and copies of any written cross-interrogatories shall be mailed or delivered to the opposing party at least 5 days before the date of taking the depositions, unless the parties mutually agree otherwise. A party upon whose behalf a deposition is taken must file it with the Administrative Law Judge and serve one copy upon the opposing party. Expenses in the reporting of depositions shall be borne by the party at whose instance the deposition is taken.

[31 FR 10773, Aug. 13, 1966, as amended at 42 FR 38354, July 28, 1977]

§10.68 Transcript.

In cases where the hearing is stenographically reported by a Government contract reporter, copies of the transcript may be obtained from the reporter at rates not to exceed the maximum rates fixed by contract between the Government and the reporter. Where the hearing is stenographically reported by a regular employee of the Internal Revenue Service, a copy thereof will be supplied to the respondent either without charge or upon the payment of a reasonable fee. Copies of exhibits introduced at the hearing or at the taking or depositions will be supplied to the parties upon the payment of a reasonable fee (Sec. 501, Pub. L. 82 - 137, 65 Stat. 290 (31 U.S.C. 483a)).

[31 FR 10773, Aug. 13, 1966, as amended at 42 FR 38354, July 28, 1977]

§10.69 Proposed findings and conclusions.

Except in cases where the respondent has failed to answer the complaint or where a party has failed to appear at the hearing, the Administrative Law Judge prior to making his decision, shall afford the parties a reasonable opportunity to submit proposed findings and conclusions and supporting reasons therefor.

[31 FR 10773, Aug. 13, 1966, as amended at 42 FR 38354, July 28, 1977]

§10.70 Decision of the Administrative Law Judge.

As soon as practicable after the conclusion of a hearing and the receipt of any proposed findings and conclusions timely submitted by the parties, the Administrative Law Judge shall make the initial decision in the case. The decision shall include (a) a statement of findings and conclusions, as well as the reasons or bases therefor, upon all the material issues of fact, law, or discretion presented on the record, and (b) an order of disbarment, suspension, or reprimand or an order of dismissal of the complaint. The Administrative Law Judge shall file the decision with the Director of Practice and shall transmit a copy thereof to the respondent or his attorney of record. In the absence of an appeal to the Secretary of the Treasury, or review of the decision upon motion of the Secretary, the decision of the Administrative Law Judge shall without further proceedings become the decisions of the Secretary of the Treasury 30 days from the date of the Administrative Law Judge's decision.

[31 FR 10773, Aug. 13, 1966, as amended at 42 FR 38354, July 28, 1977]

§10.71 Appeal to the Secretary.

Within 30 days from the date of the Administrative Law Judge's decision, either party may appeal to the Secretary of the Treasury. The appeal shall be filed with the Director of Practice in duplicate and shall include exceptions to the decision of the Administrative Law Judge and supporting reasons for such exceptions. If an appeal is filed by the Director of Practice, he shall transmit a copy thereof to the respondent. Within 30 days after receipt of an appeal or copy thereof, the other party may file a reply brief in duplicate with the Director of Practice. If the reply brief is filed by the Director, he shall transmit a copy of it to the respondent. Upon the filing of an appeal and a reply brief, if any, the Director of Practice shall transmit the entire record to the Secretary of the Treasury.

[31 FR 10773, Aug. 13, 1966, as amended at 42 FR 38354, July 28, 1977]

§10.72 Decision of the Secretary.

On appeal from or review of the initial decision of the Administrative Law Judge, the Secretary of the Treasury will make the agency decision. In making his decision the Secretary of the Treasury will review the record or such portions thereof as may be cited by the parties to permit limiting of the issues. A copy of the Secretary's decision shall be transmitted to the respondent by the Director of Practice.

[31 FR 10773, Aug. 13, 1966, as amended at 42 FR 38354, July 28, 1977]

§10.73 Effect of disbarment or suspension; surrender of card.

In case the final order against the respondent is for disbarment, the respondent shall not thereafter be permitted to practice before the Internal Revenue Service unless and until authorized to do so by the Director of Practice pursuant to §10.75. In case the final order against the respondent is for suspension, the respondent shall not thereafter be permitted to practice before the Internal Revenue Service during the period of suspension. If an enrolled agent is disbarred or suspended, he shall surrender his enrollment card to the Director of Practice for cancellation, in the case of disbarment, or for retention during the period of suspension.

§10.74 Notice of disbarment or suspension.

Upon the issuance of a final order disbarring or suspending an attorney, certified public accountant, or enrolled agent, the Director of Practice shall give notice thereof to appropriate officers and employees of the Internal Revenue Service and to interested departments and agencies of the Federal Government. Notice in such manner as the Director of Practice may determine may be given to the proper authorities of the State by which the disbarred or suspended person was licensed to practice as an attorney or accountant.

§10.75 Petition for reinstatement.

The Director of Practice may entertain a petition for reinstatement from any person disbarred from practice before the Internal Revenue Service after the expiration of 5 years following such disbarment. Reinstatement may not be granted unless the Director of Practice is satisfied that the petitioner, thereafter, is not likely to conduct himself contrary to the regulations in this part, and that granting such reinstatement would not be contrary to the public interest.

[31 FR 10773, Aug. 13, 1966, as amended at 35 FR 13206, Aug. 19, 1970]

§10.76 Expedited suspension upon criminal conviction or loss of license for cause.

(a) *When applicable.* Whenever the Director has reason to believe that a practitioner is described in paragraph (b) of this section, the Director may institute a proceeding under this section to suspend the practitioner from practice before the Service.

(b) *To whom applicable.* This section applies to any practitioner who, within 5 years of the date a complaint instituting a proceeding under this section is served —

(1) Has had his or her license to practice as an attorney, certified public accountant, or actuary suspended or revoked for cause (not including a failure to pay a professional licensing fee) by any authority or court, agency, body, or board described in §10.51(g); or

(2) Has been convicted of any crime under title 26 of the United States Code, or a felony under title 18 of the United States Code involving dishonesty or breach of trust.

(c) *Instituting a proceeding.* A proceeding under this section will be instituted by a complaint that names the respondent, is signed by the Director, is filed in the Director's office, and is served according to the rules set forth in §10.57(a). The complaint must give a plain and concise description of the allegations that constitute the basis for the proceeding. The complaint, or a separate paper attached to the complaint, must notify the respondent —

(1) Of the place and due date for filing an answer;

(2) That a decision by default may be rendered if the respondent fails to file an answer as required;

(3) That the respondent may request a conference with the Director to address the merits of the complaint and that any such request must be made in the answer; and

(4) That the respondent may be suspended either immediately following the expiration

of the period by which an answer must be filed or, if a conference is requested, immediately following the conference.

(d) *Answer.* The answer to a complaint described in this section must be filed no later than 30 calendar days following the date the complaint is served, unless the Director extends the time for filing. The answer must be filed in accordance with the rules set forth in §10.58, except as otherwise provided in this section. A respondent is entitled to a conference with the Director only if the conference is requested in a timely filed answer. If a request for a conference is not made in the answer or the answer is not timely filed, the respondent will be deemed to have waived his or her right to a conference and the Director may suspend such respondent at any time following the date on which the answer was due.

(e) *Conference.* The Director or his or her designee will preside at a conference described in this section. The conference will be held at a place and time selected by the Director, but no sooner than 14 calendar days after the date by which the answer must be filed with the Director, unless the respondent agrees to an earlier date. An authorized representative may represent the respondent at the conference. Following the conference, upon a finding that the respondent is described in paragraph (b) of this section, or upon the respondent's failure to appear at the conference either personally or through an authorized representative, the Director may immediately suspend the respondent from practice before the Service.

(f) *Duration of suspension.* A suspension under this section will commence on the date that written notice of the suspension is issued. A practitioner's suspension will remain effective until the earlier of the following —

(1) The Director lifts the suspension after determining that the practitioner is no longer described in paragraph (b) of this section or for any other reason; or

(2) The suspension is lifted by an Administrative Law Judge or the Secretary of the Treasury in a proceeding referred to in paragraph (g) of this section and instituted under §10.54.

(g) *Proceeding instituted under §10.54.* If the Director suspends a practitioner under this §10.76, the practitioner may ask the Director to issue a complaint under §10.54. The request must be made in writing within 2 years from the date on which the practitioner's suspension commences. The Director must issue a complaint requested under this paragraph within 30 calendar days of receiving the request.

[59 FR 31528, June 20, 1994]

Subpart D — Rules Applicable to Disqualification of Appraisers

Source: 50 FR 42016, Oct. 17, 1985, unless otherwise noted.

§10.77 Authority to disqualify; effect of disqualification.

(a) *Authority to disqualify.* Pursuant to section 156 of the Deficit Reduction Act of 1984, 98 Stat. 695, amending 31 U.S.C. 330, the Secretary of the Treasury, after due notice and opportunity for hearing may disqualify any appraiser with respect to whom a penalty has been assessed after July 18, 1984, under section 6701(a) of the Internal Revenue Code of 1954, as amended (26 U.S.C. 6701(a)).

(b) *Effect of disqualification.* If any appraiser is disqualified pursuant to 31 U.S.C. 330 and this subpart:

(1) Appraisals by such appraiser shall not have any probative effect in any administrative proceeding before the Department of the Treasury or the Internal Revenue Service; and

(2) Such appraiser shall be barred from presenting evidence or testimony in any such administrative proceeding. Paragraph (b)(1) of this section shall apply to appraisals made by such appraiser after the effective date of disqualification, but shall not

apply to appraisals made by the appraiser on or before such date. Notwithstanding the foregoing sentence, an appraisal otherwise barred from admission into evidence pursuant to paragraph (b)(1) of this section may be admitted into evidence solely for the purpose of determining the taxpayer's reliance in good faith on such appraisal. Paragraph (b)(2) of this section shall apply to the presentation of testimony or evidence in any administrative proceeding after the date of such disqualification, regardless of whether such testimony or evidence would pertain to any appraisal made prior to such date.

§10.78 Institution of proceeding.

(a) *In general.* Whenever the Director of Practice is advised or becomes aware that a penalty has been assessed against an appraiser under 26 U.S.C. 6701(a), he/she may reprimand such person or institute a proceeding for disqualification of such appraiser through the filing of a complaint. Irrespective of whether a proceeding for disqualification has been instituted against an appraiser, the Director of Practice may confer with an appraiser against whom such a penalty has been assessed concerning such penalty.

(b) *Voluntary disqualification.* In order to avoid the initiation or conclusion of a disqualification proceeding, an appraiser may offer his/her consent to disqualification. The Director of Practice, in his/her discretion, may disqualify an appraiser in accordance with the consent offered.

§10.79 Contents of complaint.

(a) *Charges.* A proceeding for disqualification of an appraiser shall be instituted through the filing of a complaint, which shall give a plain and concise description of the allegations that constitute the basis for the proceeding. A complaint shall be deemed sufficient if it refers to the penalty previously imposed on the respondent under section 6701(a) of the Internal Revenue Code of 1954, as amended (26 U.S.C. 6701(a)), and advises him/her of the institution of the proceeding.

(b) *Demand for answer.* In the complaint, or in a separate paper attached to the complaint, notification shall be given of the place and time within which the respondent shall file his/her answer, which time shall not be less than 15 days from the date of service of the complaint, and notice shall be given that a decision by default may be rendered against the respondent in the event there is failure to file an answer.

§10.80 Service of complaint and other papers.

(a) *Complaint.* The complaint or a copy thereof may be served upon the respondent by certified mail, or first-class mail as hereinafter provided, by delivering it to the respondent or his/her attorney or agent of record either in person or by leaving it at the office or place of business of the respondent, attorney or agent, or in any other manner that has been agreed to by the respondent. Where the service is by certified mail, the return post office receipt duly signed by or on behalf of the respondent shall be proof of service. If the certified mail is not claimed or accepted by the respondent and is returned undelivered, complete service may be made by mailing the complaint to the respondent by first-class mail, addressed to the respondent at the last address known to the Director of Practice. If service is made upon the respondent in person or by leaving the complaint at the office or place of business of the respondent, the verified return by the person making service, setting forth the manner of service, shall be proof of such service.

(b) *Service of papers other than complaint.* Any paper other than the complaint may be served as provided in paragraph (a) of this section or by mailing the paper by first-class mail to the respondent at the last address known to the Director of Practice, or by mailing the paper by first-class mail to the respondent's attorney or agent of record. Such mailing shall constitute complete service. Notices may be served upon the respondent or his/her attorney or agent of record by telegraph.

(c) *Filing of papers*. Whenever the filing of a paper is required or permitted in connection with a disqualification proceeding under this subpart or by rule or order of the Administrative Law Judge, the paper shall be filed with the Director of Practice, Treasury Department, Internal Revenue Service, Washington, D.C. 20224. All papers shall be filed in duplicate.

§10.81   Answer.

(a) *Filing*. The respondent's answer shall be filed in writing within the time specified in the complaint or notice of institution of the proceeding, unless on application the time is extended by the Director of Practice or the Administrative Law Judge. The answer shall be filed in duplicate with the Director of Practice.

(b) *Contents*. The answer shall contain a statement of facts that constitute the grounds of defense, and it shall specifically admit or deny each allegation set forth in the complaint, except that the respondent shall not deny a material allegation in the complaint that he/she knows to be true, or state that he/she is without sufficient information to form a belief when in fact he/she possesses such information.

(c) *Failure to deny or answer allegations in the complaint*. Every allegation in the complaint which is not denied in the answer shall be deemed to be admitted and may be considered as proved, and no further evidence in respect of such allegation need be adduced at a hearing. Failure to file an answer within the time prescribed in the notice to the respondent, except as the time for answer is extended by the Director of Practice or the Administrative Law Judge, shall constitute an admission of the allegations of the complaint and a waiver of hearing, and the Administrative Law Judge may make his/her decision by default without a hearing or further procedure.

§10.82   Supplemental charges.

If it appears that the respondent in his/her answer, falsely and in bad faith, denies a material allegation of fact in the complaint or states that the respondent has no knowledge sufficient to form a belief, when he/she in fact possesses such information, or if it appears that the respondent has knowingly introduced false testimony during proceedings for his/her disqualification, the Director of Practice may thereupon file supplemental charges against the respondent. Such supplemental charges may be tried with other charges in the case, provided the respondent is given due notice thereof and is afforded an opportunity to prepare a defense thereto.

§10.83   Reply to answer.

No reply to the respondent's answer shall be required, and any new matter in the answer shall be deemed to be denied, but the Director of Practice may file a reply in his/her discretion or at the request of the Administrative Law Judge.

§10.84   Proof, variance, amendment of pleadings.

In the case of a variance between the allegations in a pleading and the evidence adduced in support of the pleading, the Administrative Law Judge may order or authorize amendment of the pleading to conform to the evidence; provided, that the party who would otherwise be prejudiced by the amendment is given reasonable opportunity to meet the allegations of the pleading as amended, and the Administrative Law Judge shall make findings on any issue presented by the pleadings as so amended.

§10.85 Motions and requests.

Motions and requests may be filed with the Director of Practice or with the Administrative Law Judge.

§10.86 Representation.

A respondent may appear in person or may be represented by counsel or other representative. The Director of Practice may be represented by an attorney or other employee of the Department of the Treasury.

§10.87 Administrative Law Judge.

(a) *Appointment.* An Administrative Law Judge appointed as provided by 5 U.S.C. 3105, shall conduct proceedings upon complaints for the disqualification of appraisers.

(b) *Powers of Administrative Law Judge.* Among other powers, the Administrative Law Judge shall have authority, in connection with any disqualification proceeding assigned or referred to him/her, to do the following:

(1) Administer oaths and affirmations;

(2) Make rulings upon motions and requests, which rulings may not be appealed from prior to the close of a hearing except at the discretion of the Administrative Law Judge, in extraordinary circumstances;

(3) Determine the time and place of hearing and regulate its course and conduct;

(4) Adopt rules of procedure and modify the same from time to time as occasion requires for the orderly disposition of proceedings;

(5) Rule upon offers of proof, receive relevant evidence, and examine witnesses;

(6) Take or authorize the taking of depositions;

(7) Receive and consider oral or written argument on facts or law;

(8) Hold or provide for the holding of conferences for the settlement or simplification of the issues by consent of the parties;

(9) Perform such acts and take such measures as are necessary or appropriate to the efficient conduct of any proceeding; and

(10) Make initial decisions.

§10.88 Hearings.

(a) *In general.* The Administrative Law Judge shall preside at the hearing on a complaint for the disqualification of an appraiser. Hearings shall be stenographically recorded and transcribed and the testimony of witnesses shall be taken under oath or affirmation. Hearings will be conducted pursuant to 5 U.S.C. 556.

(b) *Failure to appear.* If either party to the proceeding fails to appear at the hearing after due notice thereof has been sent to him/her, the right to a hearing shall be deemed to have been waived and the Administrative Law Judge may make a decision by default against the absent party.

§10.89 Evidence.

(a) *In general.* The rules of evidence prevailing in courts of law and equity are not controlling in hearings on complaints for the disqualification of appraisers. However, the Administrative Law Judge shall exclude evidence which is irrelevant, immaterial, or unduly repetitious.

(b) *Depositions.* The deposition of any witness taken pursuant to §10.90 may be admitted.

(c) *Proof of documents.* Official documents, records, and papers of the Internal Revenue Service or the Department of the Treasury shall be admissible in evidence without the production of an officer or employee to authenticate them. Any such documents, records, and papers may be evidenced by a copy attested or identified by an officer or employee of the Internal Revenue Service or the Department of the Treasury, as the case may be.

(d) *Exhibits.* If any document, record, or other paper is introduced in evidence as an exhibit, the Administrative Law Judge may authorize the withdrawal of the exhibit subject to any conditions which he/she deems proper.

(e) *Objections.* Objections to evidence shall be in short form, stating the grounds of objection relied upon, and the record shall not include argument thereon, except as ordered by the Administrative Law Judge. Rulings on such objections shall be a part of the record. No exception to the ruling is necessary to preserve the rights of the parties.

§10.90 Depositions.

Depositions for use at a hearing may, with the written approval of the Administrative Law Judge, be taken either by the Director of Practice or the respondent or their duly authorized representatives. Depositions may be taken upon oral or written interrogatories, upon not less than 10 days' written notice to the other party before any officer duly authorized to administer an oath for general purposes or before an officer or employee of the Internal Revenue Service who is authorized to administer an oath in internal revenue matters. Such notice shall state the names of the witnesses and the time and place where the depositions are to be taken. The requirement of 10 days' notice may be waived by the parties in writing, and depositions may then be taken from the persons and at the times and places mutually agreed to by the parties. When a deposition is taken upon written interrogatories, any cross-examination shall be upon written interrogatories. Copies of such written interrogatories shall be served upon the other party with the notice, and copies of any written cross-interrogatories shall be mailed or delivered to the opposing party at least 5 days before the date of taking the depositions, unless the parties mutually agree otherwise. A party upon whose behalf a deposition is taken must file it with the Administrative Law Judge and serve one copy upon the opposing party. Expenses in the reporting of depositions shall be borne by the party at whose instance the deposition is taken.

§10.91 Transcript.

In cases where the hearing is stenographically reported by a Government contract reporter, copies of the transcript may be obtained from the reporter at rates not to exceed the maximum rates fixed by contract between the Government and the reporter. Where a hearing is stenographically reported by a regular employee of the Internal Revenue Service, a copy thereof will be supplied to the respondent either without charge or upon the payment of a reasonable fee. Copies of exhibits introduced at the hearing or at the taking of depositions will be supplied to the parties upon the payment of a reasonable fee (Sec. 501, Pub. L. 82 - 137, 65 Stat. 290 (31 U.S.C. 483a)).

§10.92 Proposed findings and conclusions.

Except in cases where the respondent has failed to answer the complaint or where a party has failed to appear at the hearing, the Administrative Law Judge, prior to making a decision, shall afford the parties a reasonable opportunity to submit proposed findings and conclusions and supporting reasons therefor.

§10.93 Decision of the Administrative Law Judge.

As soon as practicable after the conclusion of a hearing and the receipt of any proposed findings and conclusions timely submitted by the parties, the Administrative Law Judge shall make the initial decision in the case. The decision shall include (a) a statement of findings and conclusions, as well as the reasons or bases therefor, upon all the material issues of fact, law, or discretion presented on the record, and (b) an order of disqualification or an order of dismissal of the complaint. The Administrative Law Judge shall file the decision with the Director of Practice and shall transmit a copy thereof to the respondent or his attorney of record. In the absence of an appeal to the Secretary of the Treasury, or review of the decision upon motion of the Secretary, the decision of the Administrative Law Judge shall without further proceedings become the decision of the Secretary of the Treasury 30 days from the date of the Administrative Law Judge's decision.

§10.94 Appeal to the Secretary.

Within 30 days from the date of the Administrative Law Judge's decision, either party may appeal such decision to the Secretary of the Treasury. If an appeal is by the respondent, the appeal shall be filed with the Director of Practice in duplicate and shall include exceptions to the decision of the Administrative Law Judge and supporting reasons for such exceptions. If an appeal is filed by the Director of Practice, a copy thereof shall be transmitted to the respondent. Within 30 days after receipt of an appeal or copy thereof, the other party may file a reply brief in duplicate with the Director of Practice. If the reply brief is filed by the Director, a copy shall be transmitted to the respondent. Upon the filing of an appeal and a reply brief, if any, the Director of Practice shall transmit the entire record to the Secretary of the Treasury.

§10.95 Decision of the Secretary.

On appeal from or review of the initial decision of the Administrative Law Judge, the Secretary of the Treasury shall make the agency decision. In making such decision, the Secretary of the Treasury will review the record or such portions thereof as may be cited by the parties. A copy of the Secretary's decision shall be transmitted to the respondent by the Director of Practice.

§10.96 Final order.

Upon the issuance of a final order disqualifying an appraiser, the Director of Practice shall give notice thereof to appropriate officers and employees of the Internal Revenue Service and to interested departments and agencies of the Federal Government.

§10.97 Petition for reinstatement.

The Director of Practice may entertain a petition for reinstatement from any disqualified appraiser after the expiration of 5 years following such disqualification. Reinstatement may not be granted unless the Director of Practice is satisfied that the petitioner, thereafter, is not likely to conduct himself/herself contrary to 26 U.S.C. 6701(a), and that granting such reinstatement would not be contrary to the public interest.

Subpart E — General Provisions

§10.98 Records.

(a) *Availability*. There are made available to public inspection at the Office of Director of Practice the roster of all persons enrolled to practice, the roster of all persons disbarred or suspended from practice, and the roster of all disqualified appraisers. Other records may be disclosed upon specific request, in accordance with the disclosure regulations of the Internal Revenue Service and the Treasury Department.

(b) *Disciplinary procedures*. A request by a practitioner that a hearing in a disciplinary proceeding concerning him be public, and that the record thereof be made available for inspection by interested persons, may be granted if agreement is reached by stipulation in advance to protect from disclosure tax information which is confidential, in accordance with the applicable statutes and regulations.

[31 FR 10773, Aug. 13, 1966. Redesignated at 50 FR 42016, Oct. 17, 1985, and amended at 50 FR 42018, Oct. 17, 1985]

§10.100 Saving clause.

Any proceeding for the disbarment or suspension of an attorney, certified public accountant, or enrolled agent, instituted but not closed prior to the effective date of these revised regulations, shall not be affected by such regulations. Any proceeding under this part based on conduct engaged in prior to the effective date of these regulations may be instituted subsequent to such effective date.

[50 FR 42019, Oct. 17, 1985]

§10.101 Special orders.

The Secretary of the Treasury reserves the power to issue such special orders as he may deem proper in any cases within the purview of this part.

[31 FR 10773, Aug. 13, 1966. Redesignated at 50 FR 42016, Oct. 17, 1985]

Glossary

The following definitions pertain specifically to the manner in which the identified terms are used in a tax research context. Other uses for such terms are not examined.

A

ABA The professional organization for practicing attorneys in the United States, namely, the American Bar Association.

Academic journals Scholarly publications of law schools, business schools, and academic organizations. These publications are edited either by faculty members or by graduate students under the guidance of the school's faculty. The articles appearing in these publications are usually written by tax practitioners, academics, graduate students, or other noted commentators.

Academic Universe Created by Congressional Information Service (a division of LexisNexis). It is an Internet research service offered to academic institutions and public libraries. While the databases offered on Academic Universe vary with the subscription, it generally contains primary tax documents and secondary news, law review, and journal articles.

Accuracy-related penalty Civil tax penalty assessed where the taxpayer has been negligent in completing the return or is found to have acted with a disregard of IRS rules and regulations, a substantial understatement of the income tax, a substantial valuation or pension liability overstatement, or a substantial transfer tax valuation understatement. A 20 percent penalty usually applies to the pertinent understatement, and related interest accrues from the due date of the return, rather than the date on which the penalty was assessed.

Acquiescence A pronouncement by the IRS that it will follow the decision of a regular Tax Court case to the extent that it was held for the taxpayer. Announced in the *Internal Revenue Bulletin*. Modifies the citation for the identified case.

Action on Decision A memoranda prepared when the IRS loses a case in a court that recommends the action, if any, that the IRS should take in response to the adverse decision.

Administrative proceeding A hearing between the taxpayer and an administrative agency of the government, typically the Internal Revenue Service, in an audit or appeal setting.

Administrative sources Federal tax law that is created by the appropriate use of power that is granted to the Treasury Department by Congress. These sources of the law have a presumption of the authority of the statute, but they are subject to taxpayer challenge. Such sources include regulations, rulings, revenue procedures, and other opinions that are used by the Treasury Department or the Internal Revenue Service.

AFTR The citation abbreviation for the tax case reporter, *American Federal Tax Reports*. The first series of the reporter includes cases concerning pre-1954 Code litigation, and the second and third series include cases that address issues relative to the 1954 and 1986 Codes, respectively. Includes most tax case opinions issued by Federal courts other than the Tax Court.

AICPA The professional organization of practicing Certified Public Accountants in the United States, namely, the American Institute of CPAs.

Annotated tax service A commercial tax research reference collection, i.e., a secondary source of Federal tax law. Includes Code, Regulation and ruling analysis, judicial case notes, and other indexes and finding lists, organized by Code section number. The two most important annotated services are published by Commerce Clearing House and Research Institute of America.

Annotation An entry in (especially) an annotated tax service, indicating a summary of a primary source of the Federal tax law that is pertinent to one's research, e.g., a court case opinion digest or a reference to a controlling regulation.

Announcements and Notices The IRS issues Announcements and Notices concerning items of general importance to taxpayers.

Appeals Division The internal group of the Internal Revenue Service that has the greatest authority to come to a compromise solution with a taxpayer concerning a disputed tax liability. Can consider the "hazards of litigation" in its deliberations. Failure to reach an agreement at this level of the IRS's organization means that the only subsequent appeal by either party to the dispute must be before a court of law.

Assessment The process of the IRS fixing the amount of one's tax liability. Although the U.S. tax system exhibits some degree of self-assessment, the IRS has the ultimate authority to assess the liability of every taxpayer.

Auto-Cite A citator in Lexis. The primary objective of Auto-Cite is to provide accurate citations as soon as possible, within 24 hours of receipt of each case. Auto-Cite can also be used to determine whether cases, Revenue Rulings, and Revenue Procedures are still good law.

Average tax rate The percentage of a taxpayer's income that is paid in taxes (i.e., computed by dividing the current-year tax liability by the taxpayer's income). The average can be computed as a percentage of total taxable income (this generates the taxpayer's average nominal tax rate) or as a percentage of the taxpayer's total economic income (this generates the taxpayer's average effective tax rate).

B

Bittker & Lokken Federal Taxation of Income, Estates, and Gifts A topical tax service published by Warren, Gorham & Lamont in five volumes, dedicated to Federal income and transfer taxation. Supplemented annually, the service includes a topical index and Code section, Regulation, case name, and Revenue Ruling finding lists.

BNA *Daily Tax Report* A daily collection of the latest regulations, rulings, case opinions, and other tax law revisions, as well as news reports, press releases, congressional studies and schedules, interviews, and other items of interest to the tax practitioner. Available through the mail and on various electronic tax services. One of the most important tax newsletters published because of its breadth of topics and its quality of analysis. In addition, the newsletter provides interviews with government officials, articles reviewing the day's events, and the full text of key documents discussed in the newsletter.

BNA *Tax Management Portfolios* A topical tax service published by the Bureau of National Affairs in a collection of more than three hundred magazine-size portfolios, dedicated to U.S. income, foreign income, and estate and gift taxation. Prepared by an identified expert in the field, each portfolio includes a detailed analysis of the topic, working papers with which to implement planning suggestions, and a bibliography of related literature. Supplemented by a biweekly newsletter, the portfolio series includes a topical index and case name and Code section finding lists.

Board of Tax Appeals An earlier name for the U.S. Tax Court, which did not have full judicial status. Opinions are recorded in the Board of Tax Appeals reporter, the citation abbreviation for which is BTA.

Boolean A deductive logic search that allows for the intersection of terms by using connectors such as "or," "and," or "within # number of words."

Bulletin Index-Digest System A comprehensive index of matters that the IRS has published since 1952 in the *Internal Revenue Bulletin*.

Bureau of National Affairs A subsidiary of Tax Management. It offers a wide range of products covering all areas of Federal taxes. However, it is best known as the publisher of the *BNA Tax Management Portfolios* (BNA Portfolios). BNA Tax Management also has three electronic tax services: Portfolios Plus Library, Tax Practice Library, and TaxCore.

C

Case brief A concise summary of the facts, issues, holdings, and analyses of a court case. Used in a tax research context to allow subsequent review of the case by its author or another party. Includes complete citations of the briefed case, and other items addressed in the brief, to facilitate additional review when necessary.

CCH Citator A citator published by Commerce Clearing House that is part of the CCH *Standard Federal Tax Reporter*. The volumes of this looseleaf service are labeled A to L and M to Z with a Finding List for Rulings in the back of the M to Z volume. This service covers the Federal income tax decisions that have been issued since 1913.

CCH *Federal Tax Articles* A loose-leaf and bound index to Federal tax articles published by Commerce Clearing House. This index provides concise abstracts for each article cited in the index. The framework for organizing these abstracts is the *Internal Revenue Code*. More than 250 journals, law reviews, papers, and proceedings are included in the index.

CCH *Federal Tax Service* The topical tax service of Commerce Clearing House. Offered to new subscribers only on CD-ROMs or through the Internet. Explanatory text, called the analysis, is divided into sixteen major topic areas, designated A through P. The editors' comments and evaluations of the law are the basis of the main text, with footnotes used to direct researchers to primary sources.

CCH *Standard Federal Tax Reporter* The annotated service of Commerce Clearing House dedicated to Federal income, estate, and gift taxation. Includes a weekly newsletter, topical index, tax calendar, rate tables and schedules, practitioner checklists, and case name, Code section, Regulation, and Revenue Ruling finding lists. In addition, it provides a two-volume *Internal Revenue Code* and a two-volume *Citator*.

CCH Tax Research NetWork The Internet tax service provided by Commerce Clearing House. It can include all of the tax services available from CCH if the practitioner is willing to purchase these services.

CD-ROM system West, CCH, RIA, and several other vendors have made available a collection of tax statutes, Regulations, rulings, cases, and other primary-source materials readable by a computer in a CD-ROM format. The related software allows the researcher to conduct an electronic search of the pertinent materials without incurring online charges: subscribers receive a series of compact disks containing the source materials, and the software instructs the user which disks to insert into the CD-ROM reader at appropriate times.

Circular 230 An Internal Revenue Service publication detailing the requirements and responsibilities of those who prepare Federal tax returns for compensation. Includes educational, ethical, and procedural guidelines.

Citation A means of conveying the location of a document. Appendix B of this text offers a standard format for citations used by tax researchers.

Citator A research resource that presents the judicial history of a court case and traces the subsequent references to the case. When these references include the citing case's evaluations of the cited case's precedents, the research can obtain some measure of the efficacy and reliability of the original holding.

Citator 2nd Series Published by Research Institute of America (RIA). The *Citator 2nd Series* is composed of three bound volumes plus paperback supplements, which cover from 1954 to the present. This citator series includes the history of cases that have been decided since 1954 and updates for cited cases appearing in the previous series. Within each volume, the cases are arranged in alphabetical order.

Cited case With respect to a citator, the original case, whose facts or holding are referred to in the opinion of the citing case.

Cites When one case refers to another case, it cites the latter case.

Citing case With respect to a citator, the subsequent case, which includes a reference to the original (cited) case.

Civil penalty In a tax practice context, a fine or other judgment that is brought against a taxpayer or preparer for a failure to comply with one or more of the elements of the Federal tax law. Examples include penalties for failure to file a return or pay a tax in a timely fashion.

Client letter A primary means by which to communicate one's research results to the client. Includes, among other features, a summary of the controlling fact situation and attendant assumptions, a summary of the critical sources of the tax law that led to the researcher's conclusions, specific implications of the results of the project, and recommendations for client action.

Closed transaction A tax research situation is closed when all of the pertinent transactions have been completed by the taxpayer and other parties, such that the research issues may be limited to the proper nature and amount of disclosure to the government on the tax return or other document, and to preparation activities relative to subsequent government review.

Closing agreement A form with which the taxpayer and the IRS finalize their computations of a disputed tax liability.

Collateral estoppel The legal principle that limits one's judicial exposure relative to a disputed item to one series of court hearings. In a tax environment, the principle can present hardships for the taxpayer who wishes to raise additional issues during the course of a judicial proceeding.

Collection The process by which the IRS extracts an assessed tax liability from a taxpayer. Usually takes the form of the receipt of a check or other draft from the taxpayer, but can include liens or other garnishments of taxpayer assets.

Commissioner of Internal Revenue The chief operating and chief executive officer of the Internal Revenue Service. Holds the ultimate responsibility for overall planning and for directing, coordinating, and controlling the policies and programs of the IRS.

Committee Report A summary of the issues that were considered by the House Ways and Means Committee, Senate Finance Committee, or Joint Conference Committee, here relative to proposed or adopted changes in the language of the *Internal Revenue Code*. Useful in tax research as an aid to understanding unclear statutory language and legislative history or intent. Published in the *Internal Revenue Bulletin*.

Compilation Broadly, a collection of primary sources, editorial comments, and annotations in a tax service (i.e., its collection of volumes).

Computing Centers IRS service centers that manipulate data collected from tax returns.

Connectors In using an online database or CD-ROM service, connectors are employed to link various parts of a search command using Boolean logic. For instance, "or," "and," and "within" are used as connectors in various research services.

Contingent fees The practice under which a professional bases his or her fee for services upon the results thereof. The AICPA has held that the performance of services for a contingent fee can be unethical; one exception is available, though, where (as in tax practice) the results are subject to third-party actions (here the government, in an audit setting). Several states are relaxing this restriction, allowing CPAs to mix the form of their compensation between fixed and contingent fees.

Correspondence examination An audit of one's tax return that is conducted largely by telephone or mail. Usually involves a request for substantiation or explanation of one or more items on a tax return, such as filing status, exemptions, and itemized deductions for medical expenses, interest, taxes paid, charitable contributions, or miscellaneous deductions.

Court of Appeals A Federal appellate court that hears appeals from the Tax Court, Court of Federal Claims, or District Courts within its geographical boundaries. Organized into geographical circuits, although there are additional circuits for Washington, D.C., and for cases appealed from the Court of Federal Claims. Opinions are recorded in the *Federal Reporter,* various series, and in the AFTR and USTC tax case reporter series.

Court of Federal Claims A trial-level court in which the taxpayer typically sues the government for a refund of overpaid tax liability. Hears nontax matters as well in Washington, D.C. or in other major cities. Opinions are reported in the Court of Federal Claims reporter and in the AFTR and USTC case reporter series.

Criminal penalty A severe infraction of the elements of the Federal tax law by a taxpayer or preparer. Felony or misdemeanor status for tax crimes can be accompanied by substantial fines or jail terms. Examples of tax crimes include tax evasion and other willful failures to comply with the *Internal Revenue Code.*

Cumulative Bulletin An official publication of the IRS, consolidating the material that first was published in the *Internal Revenue Bulletin* in a (usually semiannual) hardbound volume. Publication alters the proper citation for the contents thereof.

Customer Service Sites IRS service centers that deal with telephone and electronic contacts from taxpayers, in working with electronic filing of returns, and in answering telephone and online taxpayer inquiries.

D

Determination Letter An IRS pronouncement issued by the local IRS District Director, relative to the agency's position concerning a straightforward issue of tax law in the context of a completed transaction.

Discriminant function formula A means by which, on the basis of probable return to the IRS in terms of collected delinquent tax liabilities, the Service selects tax returns for examination.

District Court A trial-level court that hears tax and nontax cases. Organized according to geographical regions. Jury trials are available. Opinions are reported in the *Federal Supplement Series* and in the AFTR and USTC tax case reporter series.

District Director The chief operating officer of one of the IRS's functional districts. A District Director manages the district's resources and all of its examination, collection, investigation, and taxpayer service activities.

E

Effective average tax rate The proportion of a taxpayer's economic income that was paid to the government as a tax liability (i.e., it is computed by dividing the tax liability by the taxpayer's economic income for the year). Economic income includes nontaxable sources of income, such as gifts and inheritances, and tax-exempt interest.

En banc When more than one Tax Court judge hears a case, the court is said to be sitting "en banc."

Enrolled agent One who is qualified to practice before the IRS by means other than becoming an attorney or CPA. Typically, one must pass a qualifying examination and meet other requirements to become an Enrolled Agent.

Ethical standards Boundaries of social or professional behavior, derived by the culture or its institutions. Tax ethics are described in various documents of governmental agencies or professional organizations.

F

Fact issue A tax research issue in which the practitioner must determine whether a pertinent question of fact was satisfied by the taxpayer; e.g., was an election filed with the government in a timely manner? What was the taxpayer's motivation underlying the redemption of some corporate stock?

Federal Tax Baedeker A 26-chapter analysis and explanation of the tax laws covering individuals, businesses, trusts, and estates included in the Tax Analyst's tax service TaxBase.

Field audit The review of a corporation or business tax return by an IRS agent. Typically involves more complex issues of law and/or fact than are the subject of a correspondence or office audit.

Open-ended in nature. The agent who conducts a field examination reviews all of the taxpayer's business and financial operations, accounting methods, and means of internal control.

File memorandum A primary means by which to communicate the results of a research project to oneself, one's supervisor, and/or one's successor. Includes, among other features, a statement of the pertinent facts and assumptions, a detailed outline (and citations of) controlling tax law, a summary of the researcher's conclusions, and a listing of action recommendations for the client to consider.

Finding list An index to primary tax law sources, such as court cases or Revenue Rulings, typically arranged alphabetically, and referring to paragraph or division citations in the tax service's compilations.

Fraud In a tax practice context, a taxpayer action to evade the assessment of a tax. Criminal fraud requires a willful intent by the taxpayer. The IRS bears the burden of proof relative to fraud allegations.

Full-text search A computerized version of a published index. A full-text search locates every occurrence of a word or phrase in every document available for the search.

G

General Counsel's Memorandum A memoranda generated upon the request of the IRS, typically as a means to assist in the preparation of Revenue Rulings and Private Letter Rulings.

General Regulation A regulation issued under the general authority granted to the IRS to interpret the language of the Code, usually under a specific Code directive of Congress, and with specific congressional authority.

***Golsen* rule** Tax Court decisions are appealed to the Court of Appeals for the taxpayer's place of work or residence. The decisions of the Courts of Appeal are not always consistent. Thus, when a taxpayer whose circuit has ruled on a given issue brings a case that includes that issue before the Tax Court, the Tax Court will follow the holding of the pertinent Circuit, even if the Tax Court disagrees with the holding, or if another circuit has issued a contrary holding. This can lead to contradictory Tax Court rulings, based solely upon the state of the taxpayer's residence.

H

Headnote Numbered paragraphs in which the editors of the court reporter summarize the court's holdings on each issue. These paragraphs appear in the court reporters before the text of the actual court case.

Hypertext A means of moving around within the documents of an electronic database by clicking on a mouse or keyboard where a special text color or character indicates that a related document is available. For instance, in reading a court case, the user might move to the opinion issued in another case cited in a footnote, or to a controlling Code section or Regulation that is cited in the document.

I

Independence The AICPA requires the CPA who renders an opinion relative to a client's financial statements to be (and to appear to be) independent from the client. This principle entails restrictions as to the CPA's direct and indirect financial dealings with the client.

InfoTax Provider of a CD-ROM tax research service, including Code and Regulations, court cases, and administrative pronouncements.

Injunction The action by which the IRS or a court prevents (enjoins) a taxpayer, preparer, or tax shelter distributor from undertaking a specified action (e.g., preparing tax returns for compensation or offering a tax shelter for sale).

Internal Revenue Bulletin An official weekly publication of the Internal Revenue Service that includes Announcements, Treasury Decisions, Revenue Rulings, Revenue Procedures, and other information of interest to the tax researcher.

Internal Revenue Code The primary statutory source of the Federal tax law, a collection of laws that have been passed by Congress and incorporated in Title 26 of the United States Code. The Code was last reorganized in 1954. It presently is known as the Internal Revenue Code of 1986. The chief subdivision of the Code is the section.

Internal Revenue Service A division of the Department of the Treasury, the Federal agency that is charged with the collection of Federal taxes and the implementation of other responsibilities that are conveyed by the *Internal Revenue Code*.

Internal Revenue Service Centers Locations at which the IRS receives and processes tax returns, distributes tax forms, and performs other specified functional activities in the administration of the Federal tax laws.

Internet A means by which millions of remote computer stations are connected and can be used by individuals at any such station. Search engines assist in finding pertinent materials, and download features allow users to view and obtain files from the remote locations. The Internet is organized chiefly using the World Wide Web, bulletin board and newsgroup systems, and file transfer protocols. The Internet is useful to the tax researcher as a means of finding primary and secondary source documents in a timely fashion, sharing tax newsletters and spreadsheets, and transferring data to and from taxing jurisdictions.

J

Judicial sources Certain Federal court decisions that have the force of the statute in constructing the Federal tax law. The magnitude of this authority depends upon the level and location of the courts that issued the opinions.

K

KC Citation A service in Westlaw that provides a comprehensive list of citing cases for the case of interest.

KC History A service in Westlaw that provides the direct and negative indirect history for cases. It allows the researcher to select a full history, negative history, or omit minor cases.

KeyCite (KC) A Westlaw citator that furnishes a comprehensive direct and indirect history for court cases. The indirect history includes secondary materials that have the cited case in their text. *KeyCite* allows the researcher to select a full history, negative history, or omit minor cases. This option is not available with the other citators.

Kleinrock's *TaxExpert* A CD-ROM and Internet tax research service provided by Kleinrock. It includes primary tax law sources plus an explanation of the law.

KWIC Key word in context.

L

Law issue A tax research question in which one must determine which provision of the Federal tax law applies to the client's fact situation. This entails the evaluation of various statutory, administrative, and judicial provisions with respect to the client's circumstances, e.g., is the client's charitable contribution subject to the 30 percent of adjusted gross income limitation?

Law reviews Scholarly publications of law schools. These publications are edited either by faculty members or by graduate students under the guidance of the school's faculty. Most law reviews also use an outside advisory board comprised of practicing attorneys and law professors at other universities to aid in selecting and reviewing articles. The articles appearing in these publications are usually written by tax practitioners, academics, graduate students, or other noted commentators.

Legislative Regulation A regulation by which the IRS is directed by Congress to fulfill a law-making function and to specify the substantive requirements of a tax provision.

LEXCITE A citator service of Lexis. For the case citation entered, it ascertains parallel citations and then searches for all of the cites in the case law documents. It will find embedded references to a variety of documents such as cases, law reviews, journals, Federal Register, and Revenue Rulings.

Lexis An Internet service for legal (tax) sources started in 1973 by LexisNexis.

LexisNexis One of the largest legal and news services available on the Internet. An online database resource that allows the researcher to access a database consisting of the text of court cases, administrative rulings, and selected law review articles and to search these files for tax (and other) law sources that may be relevant to the research problem.

Linking A method of moving among the documents of an electronic database, as indicated by the controlling software. See *hypertext*.

Local citation A citation that directs the researcher to the exact page where the cited case is mentioned in the citing case.

M

Marginal tax rate The proportion of the next dollar of gross income (or other increase in the tax base) that the taxpayer must pay to the government as a tax. Thus, the marginal tax rate conveys the proportionate value of an additional deduction, or the cost of an increase to the tax base. Tax-effective decisions must take into account the marginal (and not the average or nominal) tax rate.

Memorandum decision A decision of the Tax Court that, in the opinion of the chief judge, does not address any new issue of tax law. Accordingly, the government does not publish the opinion. Commerce Clearing House and Research Institute of America each publish annual collections of these Tax Court Memorandum decisions.

Mertens See West Group *Mertens Law of Federal Income Taxation*.

N

National Taxpayer Advocate Empowered to achieve a temporary delay in the normal enforcement procedures of the IRS, as specified in a Taxpayer Assistance Order.

Natural language A search where a tax question is entered in standard English (natural language) words, phrases, (entered within quotation marks) or sentences. The program determines the key terms for searching and relationships among the words (i.e., connectors to apply). This type of search is useful when the researcher is unsure as to which keywords would be the most effective.

Negligence In a Federal tax context, a (nonwillful) failure to exercise one's duty with respect to the *Internal Revenue Code* or to use a reasonable degree of expected or professional care. Examples include the unacceptable failure to attempt to follow the IRS's rules and Regulations in the preparation of a tax return for compensation.

New Matters Index Index of current developments in the tax law that is part of the CCH *Standard Federal Tax Reporer* published service. It contains two updating cross reference tables: a cumulative index and the latest additions to the cumulative index.

Nexis An Internet service for news, financial, and business information, started in 1979 by Lexis-Nexis.

Ninety-day letter A statutory notice from the IRS that the taxpayer has failed to pay an assessed tax. An issuance of such a letter usually indicates that the taxpayer has exhausted all of his or her appeal rights within the IRS and that the next forum for review will be a trial-level court. Strictly, the taxpayer has ninety days to petition the Tax Court to be relieved of the deficiency assessment. If no such petition is filed, the IRS is empowered to collect the assessed tax.

Nominal average tax rate Determined by an inspection of the applicable rate schedule. The average nominal rate at which the taxpayer's total taxable income is taxed is computed by dividing the taxpayer's total tax liability by his or her taxable income. Tax-exempt income is not included in the denominator of this fraction.

Nonacquiescence An announcement by the IRS that it will not follow the decision of a regular Tax Court decision that was adverse to the agency. Notation is included in the proper citation of the disputed case. Announced in the *Internal Revenue Bulletin*.

O

Offer in compromise The means by which the government offers to reduce the amount of an assessed tax, usually because of some doubt as to the "litigation-proof" magnitude or collectibility of the tax. A legally enforceable promise that cannot be rescinded, an offer in compromise relates to the entire liability of the taxpayer, and it conclusively settles all of the issues for which an agreement can be made.

Office audit The audit of a nonbusiness tax return that is conducted at an IRS district office. Usually requires some analysis and the exercise of the IRS personnel's judgment, rather than a mere inquiry or substantiation verification. Typically involves tip, rent, or royalty income, travel and entertainment deductions, and income from partnerships or other conduit entities.

OneDisc A Tax Analyst's single disc tax product similar to the Kleinrock service. It contains an extensive list of primary sources and the explanations of *Federal Tax Baedeker.*

Online system In a tax research context, a collection of the text of court case opinions, statutes, administrative rulings, and selected law review articles. These text files can be searched by the practitioner in an extremely fast and efficient manner to assist him or her in locating tax law sources that may be relevant to the disputed tax issue.

Open transaction A tax research issue is open when not all of the pertinent transactions have been completed by the taxpayer or other parties, such that the researcher can suggest to the client several alternative courses of action that will generate differing tax consequences.

Oral presentation A primary means of communicating the results of a research project to others by way of a telephone conversation or a more formal presentation system.

P

PH Citator The first series of citators, formerly published by Prentice-Hall and now published by Research Institute of America. The first series consists of three bound volumes that cover all of the Federal tax cases dated between 1863 and 1953.

Permanent citation A Tax Court citation issued to a Tax Court decision containing the case name, volume number, reporter page number, and the year of the decision.

Portfolios Plus Library A BNA electronic tax service includes the BNA *Portfolios*. Access to primary sources, weekly news reports, practice tools, and a limited number of journals is also included in the subscription.

Practice before the IRS The privilege to sign tax returns as preparer for compensation and to represent others before the IRS or in court in an audit or appeal proceeding. This privilege is granted by the IRS and controlled under *Circular 230.*

Practitioner journal Journals published by professional organizations and commercial companies. The objective of these journals is to keep tax practitioners abreast of the current changes and trends in the tax law.

Preparer penalties A series of fines and other levies by which the IRS encourages taxpayers and preparers to fulfill their responsibilities under the *Internal Revenue Code*. Examples include penalties for failure to sign returns, keep or furnish copies of returns, and provide required information to Federal agencies.

Primary authority An element of the Federal tax law that was issued by Congress, the Treasury or Internal Revenue Service, or a Federal court, and thus carries greater precedential weight than elements of the tax law issued by other parties.

Prime issues A series of disputed tax questions for which the IRS will not sign offers in compromise. Thus, the taxpayer's only alternatives are to satisfy the full assessed liability or to proceed with litigation. These issues are designated by the National Office of the IRS, as a policy matter, when it is believed that taxpayer abuse of the subject matter threatens the integrity or viability of the tax.

Private letter ruling A written determination published by the Internal Revenue Service relative to its position concerning the tax treatment of a prospective transaction. Strictly, it cannot be applied to any taxpayer other than the one who requested the ruling. Text or summaries thereof are included in various commercial tax services.

Problem Resolution Program An organizational means by which the IRS attempts to satisfy taxpayer complaints, inquiries, and disagreements, short of the appeals process or litigation. The taxpayer can employ the Problem Resolution Program when the usual agency channels do not produce the desired results. Typically, the program is used to resolve billing, procedural, computer-generated, and other problems that the taxpayer has not resolved after one or more contacts with the appropriate IRS office.

Proceedings The published versions of conference presentations. These proceeding are distributed to the participants at the conference and later to the general public in the form of a collection of articles.

Processing Centers IRS service centers that process Federal tax returns.

Professional journals Synonym for practitioner journal.

Progressive tax rate If the marginal rates of a tax rate schedule increase as the magnitude of the tax base increases, the schedule includes progressive tax rates.

Proportional tax rate If the marginal rates of a tax rate schedule remain constant as the magnitude of the tax base increases, the schedule includes proportional tax rates.

Proposed Regulation An interpretation or clarification of the provisions of a portion of the *Internal Revenue Code,* issued by the Treasury and available for comment (and possible revision) in a public hearing.

Q

Query A means of searching an electronic database. Includes a definition of the scope of the search and a specification of the targeted terms in which the researcher is interested, often employing connectors in the grammar of the query.

R

Realistic possibility The realistic possibility standard is met if analysis of the tax return position by a reasonable and well-informed person knowledgeable in the tax law(s) would lead such person to conclude that the position has approximately a one in three (or greater) likelihood of being sustained on its merits.

Reasonable cause A means by which a taxpayer or preparer can be excused from an applicable penalty or other sanction. For instance, if the taxpayer failed to file a tax return on a timely basis because of illness or if the underlying records were destroyed by natural cause, the taxpayer likely would be excused from the penalty (but not from the tax or any related interest) because of this reasonable cause.

Recent Developments Index Index of current developments in the tax law that is part of the RIA *United States Tax Reporter* published service. It has a single updating cross reference table.

Regressive tax rate If the marginal rates of a tax rate schedule decrease as the magnitude of the tax base increases, the schedule includes regressive tax rates.

Regular decision A decision issued by the Tax Court that generally involves a new or unusual point of law, as determined by the Chief Judge of the court.

Regulation An interpretation or clarification of the provisions of a portion of the *Internal Revenue Code,* issued by the Treasury under authority granted by Congress. Legislative Regulations directly create the details of a tax law. Both general and legislative Regulations carry the force of the statute, unless they are held to be invalid in a judicial hearing.

Return preparer Any person who prepares for compensation, or employs one or more persons to prepare for compensation, all or a substantial portion of a tax return or claim for income tax refund.

Revenue Agent's Report Prepared upon the completion of the examination of a tax return to explain to the taxpayer the sources of any adjustments to the reported tax liability. If the taxpayer agrees to this recomputation, the associated tax, penalty, and interest become due. Lacking such agreement, other aspects of the appeals process are undertaken.

Revenue Procedure A pronouncement of the Internal Revenue Service concerning the implementation details of a specific Code provision. Published in the *Internal Revenue Bulletin.*

Revenue Ruling A pronouncement of the Internal Revenue Service concerning its interpretation of the application of the Code (typically) to a specific taxpayer-submitted fact situation. Published in the *Internal Revenue Bulletin.* Can be relied upon as precedent by other taxpayers who encounter similar fact patterns.

RIA *Analysis of Federal Taxes: Income* Published by Research Institute of America. It is a condensed version of the RIA *Federal Tax Coordinator 2d* and covers only income tax issues. It is a more affordable option for practitioners with a general tax practice.

RIA Checkpoint The Internet tax service provided by Research Institute of America. This is one of the most authoritative and well known Internet tax services available. All services available from Research Institute of America may be accessed by subscription through Checkpoint.

RIA Citators The citator service published by Research Institute of America. It includes two series of citators, the *PH Citator* and the *Citator 2nd Series.*

RIA *Federal Tax Coordinator 2d* Comprehensive topical tax service published by Research Institute of America. The editors comments and evaluations of the law are the basis of the main text with footnotes used to direct researchers to primary sources. One of its strong points is its general background discussions summarizing the major issues.

RIA OnPoint CD resource that allows the researcher to access a database consisting of the text of court cases, administrative rulings, and selected tax treatises and analytical articles and to search these files for tax law sources that may be relevant to the research problem.

RIA *United States Tax Reporter* The annotated service of Research Institute of America dedicated to Federal income, estate, and gift taxation. Includes a weekly newsletter, topical index, tax calendar, rate tables and schedules, practitioner checklists, case name, Code section, Regulation, and Revenue Ruling finding lists. This tax service has a unique and functional paragraph numbering system. All paragraphs pertaining to a particular Code section incorporate that section number into the paragraph number. A single digit is added to the end of the Code section number, indicating the nature of the material contained in the paragraph.

S

Seamless Ability to perform a function with little or no effort. For example, the ability to retrieve references full-text through the computer by double clicking on the reference's title.

Secondary authority An element of the Federal tax law that was issued by a scholarly or professional writer, e.g., in a textbook, journal article, or treatise, and thus carries less precedential weight than elements of the tax law issued by primary sources.

Shepard's Citations The full coverage of Shepard's citators available through Westlaw.

Shepard's Citator The only major tax citator that is organized by case reporter series.

Shepard's Federal Tax Citator A citator available through Westlaw and Lexis, organized by reference to the case reporter and volume number in which the case is found. Thus, to use the citator, the practitioner must know the court reporter citation for the case of interest.

Shepardizing The process of evaluating the validity of a case and locating additional authority via a citator.

Small Cases Division The Tax Court allows taxpayers whose disputed tax liability does not exceed $50,000 to try the case before the court's Small Cases Division. Procedural rules of the division are somewhat relaxed, and taxpayers often represent themselves. The Small Cases Division decisions are not published, nor can either party appeal the holdings thereof.

Spine scan A method of entering published tax services by scanning the volume contents listed on the spines of the tax service binders.

Statute of limitations Provides the maximum amount of time within which one or both parties in the taxing process must perform an act, such as file a return, pay a tax, or examine a return. Various time limits apply relative to the *Internal Revenue Code,* although both parties can, by mutual agreement, extend one or more of these time limitations, if desired.

Statutory notice of deficiency Synonym for a ninety-day letter.

Statutory sources The Constitution, tax treaties, and the *Internal Revenue Code* are the statutory sources of the Federal tax law. They have the presumption of correctness, unless a court modifies or overturns a provision in response to a taxpayer challenge. In this regard, legislative intent and history can be important in supporting the taxpayer's case.

Substantial authority A taxpayer penalty may be incurred if a tax return position is taken and not disclosed to the IRS where no substantial authority (generally, statute, Regulation, court decision, or written determination) supports the position.

Supreme Court The highest Federal appellate court. Hears very few tax cases. Approves a *writ of certiorari* for the cases that it hears. Opinions are reported in the *U.S. Supreme Court Reports* (citation abbreviation, US); the *Supreme Court Reporter* (SCt); the *United States Reports, Lawyer's Edition* (LEd); the AFTR and USTC tax case reporter series; and various on-line services.

T

TA Campus A student version of the Tax Analyst's TaxBase tax service that is available free of charge.

Table of Authorities A service available through Westlaw and Lexis that lists cases that are cited within a case of interest.

Tax Analysts A nonprofit entity organized to provide literary forums for the discussion of taxation. It disseminates timely and comprehensive state, Federal, and international tax information through their daily, weekly, and monthly print publications, scholarly books, and electronic database services.

Tax authority Any source of the Federal tax law; in common usage, this term is used to refer to government agencies.

Tax avoidance The legal structuring of one's financial affairs so as to optimize the related tax liability. Synonym for tax planning.

Tax awareness The first requirement for effective tax planning on the part of decision makers. It requires decision makers to be alert for tax-optimizing alternatives.

Tax compliance An element of modern tax practice in which a practitioner works with a client to file appropriate tax returns in a timely manner and represents the client in administrative proceedings.

Tax Court A trial-level court that hears only cases involving tax issues. Issues regular and memorandum decisions. Meets in Washington, D.C. and in other major cities. Formerly called the Board of Tax Appeals. Regular opinions are reported in the *U.S. Tax Court Reports*. Memorandum opinions are published only by commercial tax services.

Tax ethics The application of ethical standards to the tax practice.

Tax evasion The reduction of one's tax liability by illegal means.

Tax journal A periodic publication that addresses legal, factual, and procedural issues encountered in a modern tax practice. As a secondary source of Federal tax law, analyses in tax journals can be used in support of a taxpayer's case before a government agency or, especially, before a court.

Tax litigation An element of modern tax practice in which a practitioner represents the client against the government in a judicial hearing.

Tax Management Portfolios See BNA *Tax Management Portfolios*

Tax newsletter A weekly, biweekly, or monthly publication or electronic document, often furnished as part of a subscription to a commercial tax service. Typically provides digest-style summaries of current court case rulings, administrative pronouncements, and pending or approved tax legislation cross-referenced to the organization system of the tax service. Helps the practitioner to keep current relative to the breaking developments in the tax community.

Tax Notes A weekly collection of the latest regulations, written determinations, case opinions, congressional studies, policy analyses, and other items of interest to the tax practitioner. Available through the mail and on various electronic tax services.

Tax planning Synonym for tax avoidance.

Tax practice Meeting the tax research, litigation, planning, and compliance needs of a client by a recognized tax professional.

Tax Practice Library A basic electronic tax service of BNA furnishing access to primary sources, practice tools, and limited news sources. Rather than relying on the BNA *Portfolio Series,* Tax Practice has developed its own explanatory analysis. Other than offering fewer databases (no BNA *Portfolio* or journals), this service is almost identical to Portfolio Plus in its searching methods.

Tax research An examination of pertinent sources of the Federal tax law in light of all relevant circumstances relative to a client's tax problem. Entails the use of professional judgment to draw an appropriate conclusion and the communication of such conclusions or alternatives at a proper level to the client.

Tax service A commercial tax reference including statutory, administrative, and judicial sources of Federal tax law. Structured to maximize the practitioner's ease of use via a variety of indexes and finding lists. Often includes the text of the pertinent tax authorities and relevant scholarly or professional commentary.

Tax treaty An act of Congress that addresses the application of certain *Internal Revenue Code* provisions to a taxpayer whose tax base falls under the taxing statutes of more than one country. Published, among other places, in the *Internal Revenue Bulletin*.

TaxBase Electronic newsletter published daily by Tax Analysts. It covers Federal, state, and worldwide tax news as well as court petitions and complaints and highlights of the daily tax news.

TaxCore Subscribers to several of BNA's news services receive this service as part of their subscriptions. It provides the hyperlinked primary sources and tax-related documents discussed and cited in the news reports. It does not contain all primary sources nor does it furnish explanations or analysis of the tax law. The source materials are archived to November 1997.

TaxLibrary.com An affordable basic electronic research service for sole practitioners and small firms created by Tax Analysts. Included in the web-based service is access to news, primary sources, and tax law explanations by *Federal Tax Baedeker*. The daily tax news is supplied by *TaxWire* and by the *Tax Practice* weekly magazine.

Taxpayer Assistance Order The taxpayer uses this request to engage an IRS Taxpayer Advocate to delay the implementation of an IRS action, such as a collection or seizure activity, where it appears that the taxpayer has received less than fair treatment through the administrative procedures of the agency.

Taxpayer Compliance Measurement Program A means by which the IRS develops its discriminant function formulae. The taxpayer's return is selected randomly for an extensive review, during which every item of income, credit, deduction, and exclusion is challenged by the government. The results of such reviews are used (other than to adjust the examined taxpayer's liability) to delineate criteria by which other taxpayers' returns will be selected for examination.

Technical Advice Memorandum A pronouncement of the National Office of the Internal Revenue Service stating the agency's position relative to the tax treatment of a taxpayer whose return is under audit. Text or discussion thereof may be included in the body of a commercial tax service.

Technical Memorandum A memoranda prepared in the production of a Proposed Regulation.

Temporary citation A Tax Court citation issued to a Tax Court decision containing the case name, volume number, reporter, the case number, and the year of the decision. The page number is not included because the opinion has not yet been published.

Temporary Regulation An administrative pronouncement of the IRS, typically concerning the application of a recently enacted or detailed provision of the tax law, especially where there is insufficient time to carry out the public-hearings process that usually accompanies the Regulations process. Temporary Regulations carry the force of law, although citations differ from those for permanent Regulations with regard to the prefix.

Terms and Connectors The LexisNexis form of a Boolean search.

Thirty-day letter A notice from the IRS formally notifying the taxpayer of the results of an examination of the return and requesting that the taxpayer agree to the proposed modifications to the tax liability. A taxpayer's failure to respond to the letter triggers the statutory notice of a tax deficiency, i.e., the ninety-day letter demanding the payment of the tax or a petition to the tax court.

Topical tax service A professional tax research reference collection, i.e., a secondary source of Federal tax law. Includes Code, Regulation, and ruling analysis; judicial case notes; and other indexes and finding lists organized by general topic. The most important topical tax services are published by the Research Institute of America and the Bureau of National Affairs.

Treasury Decision A Regulation that has not yet been formally integrated into the published tax Regulation collection.

Treasury Department The cabinet-level government agency that is responsible for administering and enforcing laws that affect the currency. The Treasury has assigned its responsibilities relative to the *Internal Revenue Code* to the Internal Revenue Service.

U

Unauthorized practice of law A prohibited aspect of modern tax practice by nonattorneys, entailing, e.g., the issuance of a legal opinion or the drafting of a legal document for the client, for which the practitioner could be subject to legal or professional penalties.

Universal characters Symbols that are holders for zero or more characters in searches. See *Connectors*.

U.S. Constitution Ultimate source of the Federal tax law.

USTC The citation abbreviation for the Commerce Clearing House reporter, *United States Tax Cases*. Includes most of the tax decisions of the Federal courts other than the Tax Court.

W

Warren, Gorham & Lamont's *Index to Federal Tax Articles* An index to Federal tax articles published by Warren, Gorham & Lamont. It provides citations and occasionally summaries for articles covering Federal income, gift, and estate taxation or tax policy that appear in over 350 periodicals. This index has permanent cumulation indexes provided in paper-bound volumes and is updated quarterly by paperback cumulative supplements. Both the topic and the author indexes contain full article citations.

West Group *Mertens Law of Federal Income Taxation* The topical tax service of the legal publisher West Group. This tax treatise service is designed chiefly by and for attorneys.

Westlaw An online database resource provided by West Group. Allows the researcher to access a database consisting of the text of court cases, administrative rulings, and selected law review articles and to search these files for tax (and other) law sources that may be relevant to the research problem.

Wildcard characters See *universal characters*.

World Wide Web A popular means by which to organize and present one's data to the Internet community. The IRS, various tax research services, and numerous law libraries offer World Wide Web home pages, such that tax professionals can find and search through the documents available on the computers of those hosting the Internet site.

Writ of certiorari Document issued by the Supreme Court indicating the Court will hear the petitioned case. If the case will not be heard, certiorari is said to be denied.

Written determination General description of IRS or Treasury pronouncements, including Revenue Rulings, Revenue Procedures, Private Letter Rulings, Technical Advice Memoranda, and Determination Letters.

Index

A

ABA Model Code of Professional Responsibility, 19–20
Abusive tax shelters
 action to enjoin promoters of, 413
 organizing, 408
Academic journals, 281
Academic Universe, 297
 LexisNexis, 205
Acceleration, extension, and carryback effects, 418
Access and data, Westlaw, 218–219
Accounting and law indexes, other, 300–301
Accounting principles, 13
Accuracy-related penalty, 396
Acquiescence, 104
Action on Decision (AOD), 108
Acts discreditable, 14
Administrative proceeding, 17
 departure from position previously concluded, 17
 knowledge of error, 18
Administrative regulations and rulings, 91–110
Administrative sources, 41

Advertising, 14
 and solicitation, 9
Advice to taxpayers, form and content of, 18
Advocates, taxpayer, local, 369
Agent, enrolled, 6
Agreement
 closing, 422, 422–423
 statutory, 422–425
 tax practice and administration, 392–425
AICPA Code of Professional Conduct, 10–14
Aiding and abetting understatement, 409
Aiding or abetting preparation of a false return, 409
American Bar Association (ABA), 5
American Federal Tax Reports (AFTR), 130
American Institute of Certified Accountants (AICPA), 5
Annotated services, 176–187
 CCH, 185–187
Annotated tax services, 153
Annotation, 161
Announcements and Notices, 108
Annual proceedings, 279

Answers to questions on returns, 15
Appeals
 conference, 383
 division, 382
 process, 382–385
Applicable interest rate, 417
Articles, citing print and electronic, 278–279
Aspects of preparing returns, procedural, 16
Assessment, 417
 and collection, suspension of period of, 421–422
Assistance, taxpayer, orders, 368–369
Audit(s)
 chances of, 376
 field, 379
 office, 379
 process, 372–377
Auditor, dealing with a, 380–381
Authority
 evaluated, 44
 locating, 41
 primary, 65
 secondary, 41, 65
 substantial, 397
Auto-Cite, 263
Average tax rate, 344

 effective, 345
 nominal, 345
Avoidance, tax, 4
 economics of, 340–342
Avoiding income recognition, 348–349
Avoiding tax traps, 355–358
Awareness, tax, 346

B

Base, tax, 342–343
Bittker & Lokken Service, 226
BNA (Bureau of National Affairs), 205–212
 Daily Tax Report, 285
 Portfolios, 207–209
 Portfolios Plus, 209
 Portfolios Plus Library, 209
 Tax Management Portfolios, 205
 Tax Practice Library, 211
 tax products, 209–212
 TaxCore, 212
Board of Tax Appeals, 121
Boolean, 201
Briefs, case, 136–139
Bulletin Index-Digest System, 105–107
 contents, 107
Burden of proof, 119

497

Bureau of National Affairs
(BNA), 205–212
Business ethics, 21

C

Carryback effects, 418
Case briefs, 136–139
Case name search,
compilation, 183–184
Case search, RIA
Checkpoint, 163
Cause, reasonable, 394
CCH annotated service,
185–187
CCH Citator, 253–258
conventions, 256
CCH Federal Tax Articles,
293–294
CCH *Federal Tax Service,* 169
CCH NetWork
cite and contents searches,
169–170
keyword search, 167–169
state tax search, 170–171
CCH *Standard Federal Tax
Reporter,* 169
CCH Tax Research Network,
167–171
CD-ROM system, 46
Certified public accountants,
tax research by, 23–25
Changing tax jurisdictions, 350
Checkpoint, 157
Chief Counsel Memorandum,
107–108
Circular 230, 5–10, 444–482
Citation, 241
permanent, 124
revenue ruling, 97–99
temporary, 124
Citator, 241, 243
defined, 241–242
Citator 2nd Series, 243
Citators, 240–268
and other finding devices,
239–268
commercial, 242–243
Prentice Hall (PH), 243
Cite search
CCH NetWork, 169–170
RIA Checkpoint, 161–165
Cited case, 241
Citing case, 241
Citing print and electronic
articles, 278–279
Civil fraud, 399
Civil penalties, 394–403
other, 403

Claim for refund or credit,
419–421
Classification of income,
controlling, 351
Client file, comprehensive
illustration, 324–328
Client information,
confidential, 13
Client letter(s), 322–324
Closed transactions, 4
Closing agreement(s),
422–423
Code search, RIA
Checkpoint, 163
Code section search,
compilation, 180–183
Code volumes, compilation,
183
Collateral estoppel, 38
Collection, 419
and assessment, suspension
of period of, 421–422
Commercial citators,
242–243
Commissioner of Internal
Revenue, 365
Commissions and referral
fees, 14
Committee report, 71
where to find, 73–74
Common legal terminology,
120
Communicating research
results, 314–333
Communication(s)
and the tax professional,
315–317
tax research, 317–320
Compilation(s)
code section search,
180–183
code volumes, 183
keyword search, 178–180
other pathways to, 184–185
RIA, 187
volumes, entering, 176–177
Compliance
measurement program,
taxpayer, 375
tax, 3
with standards, 13
Compromise, offers in,
423–425
Computer in tax research,
using a, 50
Computer research query,
constructing, 51
Computer services, 155
Computerized tax

information, assessing,
156–157
research, overview of,
45–53
service,
benefits of using, 46–49
example, 139
factors in choosing a,
49–50
Computing Centers, 367
Conclusion of examination,
381
Conclusions, developed, 44
Conference, appeals, 383
Confidential client
information, 13
Confidentiality, tax, 120
Connectors and terms
(Boolean), 201
Constitutional and legislative
sources, 64–83
Contents search, CCH
NetWork, 169–170
Contents search, RIA
Checkpoint, 165–167
Contingent fees, 9, 13
Controlling classification of
income, 351
Conventions
interest-computation,
413–416
legal, 119–121
Coordinator, RIA, and
analysis, 189–190
Corporations underpayment of
tax, 401
Correspondence examinations,
377–379
Court decision, departure
from position previously
concluded, 17
Court of Appeals decisions,
locating, 134
Court of Federal Claims, U.S.,
131–132
decisions, locating, 132
Court vs. protest, 382
Courts of Appeals, U.S.,
132–134
CPAs and other
nonattorneys, 25
Credit or refund
amount of, 421
claim for, 419–421
Criminal penalties,
403–405
defenses to, 404
nature of, 403
Criminal tax offenses, 404

Cumulative Bulletin, 96
Currency, 154
Customer Service Sites, 368

D

Daily Tax Report, 285
Data and access, Westlaw,
218–219
Database
Lexis, selecting and
searching, 200–202
selecting a, 52
Decision(s)
locating Court of Appeals,
134
locating Court of Federal
Claims, 132
locating District Court, 130
locating Supreme Court, 136
locating Tax Court, 124
memorandum, 123
regular, 123
Tax Court, 123
scope of, 129
Decisions, Treasury (TDs), 92
Defenses to criminal
penalties, 404
Deficiency, statutory notice
of, 383
Departing from tax planning
fundamentals, 352–353
Deposits
of taxes, failure to make,
401
overstatements of, 401
Determination letter, 102–103
Determination(s)
written, locating, 104
written, numbering system,
103–104
written, public inspection
of, 103
Disclosure or use of
information by return
preparers, 409
Disclosure penalties, preparer,
406
Disclosures, tax practice
and administration,
392–425
Discreditable acts, 14
Discriminant function
formula (DIF), 375
system, 375
District Courts, U.S., 130–131
decisions, locating, 130
Documents, Lexis, 202–205
Due diligence, 8

Index

E

Economics
  of tax avoidance, 340–342
  of tax evasion, 340–342
  of tax planning, 340–342
Effective average tax rate, 345
Effective date of regulations, 94
Electronic and printed legal services, 199–228
Electronic and printed tax services, 152–190
Electronic articles, citing, 278–279
Elements of tax practice, 3–5
En banc, 123
Endorsing or negotiating a refund check, 407
Enrolled agent, 6
Error program, mathematical/clerical, 373
Error, knowledge of, return preparation, 17
Establishing the facts, 36–38
Estimated payments, failure to make, 400
Estimates, use of, 16
Estoppel, collateral, 38
Ethical standards, 20
  other, 22
Ethics
  business, 21
  in tax practice, 5–20
  nonregulatory, 20–23
Evaluate authority, 44
Evasion, tax, 4
  economics of, 340–342
Examination(s)
  conclusion of, 381
  correspondence, 377–379
  field, 379–380
  IRS, 377–382
  office, 379
  selection of returns for, 374–377
Extension effects, 418
Extensions
  IRS-requested, 419
  other, 420

F

Fact issues, 38
Facts, establishing, 36–38
Failure to
  file a tax return, 394
  make deposits of taxes, 401
  make estimated payments, 400
  pay tax, 395
False information with respect to withholding, giving, 402
False return, aiding or abetting preparation of a, 409
Federal Court System, 118–136
Federal Tax Articles, 293
Federal Tax Baedeker, 214
Federal tax law, sources of, 65
Federal Taxation of Income, Estates, and Gifts, 226
Fees, contingent, 9
Field audit, 379
Field examinations, 379–380
File a tax return, failure to, 394
File, client, comprehensive illustration, 324–328
File memorandum, 317
Filing a frivolous return, 402
Finding devices, citators and other, 239–268
Finding list, 184
Form and content of advice to taxpayers, 18
Form of organization and name, 14
Fraud, 394
  civil, 399
Frivolous return, filing a, 402
Full-text search, 154
Fundamentals, departing from, 352–353

G

General Counsel's Memorandum (GCM), 108
General Indexes, 301–302
General regulations, 93
General standards, 12
Giving false information with respect to withholding, 402
Golsen rule, 123

H

Headnote, 248
History of U.S. taxation, 65–67
Hypertext, 48

I

Identifying the issues, 38–41
Income
  controlling classification of, 351
  spread among related taxpayers, 351–352
Income recognition
  avoiding, 348–349
  postponing, 349–350
Income tax return preparers, action to enjoin, 413
Inconsistencies
  between taxpayers, 353–354
  between transactions, 353
  between years, 354–355
  in the statute, exploiting, 353–355
Independence, 12
Index
  search, RIA Checkpoint, 166
  to Federal Tax Articles, 294
Indexes
  general, 301–302
  law and accounting, 300–301
Individuals underpayment of tax, 400
Information
  accessing, 154
  computerized tax, assessing, 156–157
  disclosure or use of by return preparers, 409
Injunctions, 413
Integrity and objectivity, 12
Interest, 413–417
Interest rate, applicable, 417
Interest-computation conventions, 413–416
Internal Revenue Bulletin (IRB), 96, 105
Internal Revenue Code, 38, 71, 74–80
  interpreting, 80–83
  organization of, 75–78
  where to find, 78–80
Internal Revenue Service, 365
  organization of, 365–372
Internal Revenue Service Center, 367
Internet, 46
  and judicial sources, 139
  news sources, 277–303
  sites, 227–228, 303
Interpretations, judicial, 117–139
Introduction to tax practice, 2–26
Irregular returns, 418
IRS
  Appeals Division, 382
  examination, other selection methods, 376
  National Office, 366–367
  practice before the, 6
  pronouncements, other, 104–110
  reliance on written advice of, 403
  Service Centers, 367–368
  web site search, 53
  working with the, 364–385
IRS-requested extensions, 419
Issues
  fact, 38
  identifying, 38–41
  law, 38
  prime, 423
Iterative process, tax research as, 39

J

Journals, 277–303
  academic, 281
  practitioner, 282
  professional, 282
  tax, 43, 282
Judicial interpretations, 117–139
Judicial sources, 41
  Internet and, 139
Judicial system, entering the, 384–385
Judicial tax traps, 356–358
Jurisdictions, tax, changing, 350

K

KC Citation, 266
KC History, 265
KeyCite, 265
Keyword search
  CCH NetWork, 167–169
  compilation, 178–180
  RIA Checkpoint, 158–161
Keywords, identifying, 51
Kleinrock's TaxExpert, 171–175
Knowledge of error:
  administrative proceedings, 18
  return preparation, 17
KWIC, 202

L

Law
  and accounting indexes, other, 300–301

evaluating sources of, 320–322
history of unauthorized practice of, 24
issues, 38
periodicals, nature of, 278
reviews, 281
unauthorized practice of, 23
Legal conventions, 119–121
Legal services
electronic and printed, 199–228
other, 224–226
Legislative process, 70–74
Legislative regulations, 93
Letter
client, 322–324
determination, 102–103
ninety-day, 383–384
thirty-day, 381
Letter rulings, 101–104
private, 101–102
LEXCITE, 264
Lexis, 200, 200–205, 264
Citation Services, 258–264
documents 202–205
selecting and searching a database, 200–202
Services, 263
LexisNexis, 47, 200
LexisNexis Academic Universe, 205, 297–300
Limitations
period, 420
statutes of, 417–422
mitigations of, 422
List, finding, 184
Litigation, tax, 4
Local taxpayer advocates, 369
Locating
authority, 41
Court of Appeals decisions, 134
Court of Federal Claims decisions, 132
District Court decisions, 130
relevant tax articles, 293–303
Supreme Court decisions, 136
Tax Court decisions, 124

M

Marginal tax rate, 344
Mathematical/clerical error program, 373
Memoranda, technical advice, 102
Memorandum decision, 123
Mertens Law of Federal Income Taxation, 225
Mertens Service, 225–226
Methodology, tax research, 35–53
Mitigation of statute of limitations, 422
Model Code of Professional Responsibility, 19–20
Morality, 21

N

Name, form of, 14
National Taxpayer Advocate, 368
Natural language, 201
Negligence, 394
Negotiating a refund check, 407
New Matters Index, 178
Newsletters, 277–303
tax, 283
Nexis, 200
Ninety-day letter, 383–384
Nominal average tax rate, 345
Nonacquiescence, 104
Nonattorneys, other, 25
Nonregulatory Ethics, 20–23
Notice of deficiency, statutory, 383
Numbering system, written determination, 103–104

O

Objectivity and integrity, 12
Offer(s) in compromise, 423–425
Office audits, 379
Office examinations, 379
OneDisc, Tax Analysts, 214–217
Online system, 46
Open transactions, 4
Oral presentations, 328
of research results, 328–332
Orders, taxpayer assistance, 368–369
Organization, form of, 14
Organizing abusive tax shelters, 408
Outline of the tax research process, 36–45
Overstatements of deposits, 401
Overview of computerized tax research, 45–53

P

Pay tax, failure to, 395
Payments, estimated, failure to make, 400
Penalties
civil, 394–403
other, 403
criminal, 403–405
defenses to, 404
nature of, 403
on return preparers, 405–412
preparer, 406
disclosure, 406
taxpayer, 393–405
Penalty
accuracy-related, 396
provisions, taxpayer and preparer, conflict among, 410
Period of assessment and collection, suspension of, 421–422
Period, limitations, 420
Periodicals
tax and law, nature of, 278
tax, types of, 279–281
Permanent citation, 124
PH Citators, 243
Planning, tax, 4, 339–359
economics of, 340–342
fundamentals of, 346–352
illustrations, 358–359
in perspective, 345–346
Portfolios, BNA, 207–209
Portfolios Plus Library, 209
Position
departure from, 17
unrealistic, understatements due to, 407
Possibility, realistic, 10, 407
Postponing income recognition, 349–350
Practice before the IRS, 6
Practice of law, unauthorized, 23
Practitioner journals, 282
Preliminary review of returns, 373–374
Prentice-Hall (PH) Citators, 243

Preparation of a false return, aiding or abetting, 409
Preparation, return, definition of, 406
Preparer(s)
conduct penalties, 407–412
disclosure penalties, 406
penalties, 406
return (ITRP), 405
definition of, 405–406
penalties on, 405–412
tax return, 7
Preparing returns, procedural aspects of, 16
Presentations, oral, 328
Primary authority, 41, 65
Prime issues, 423
Print articles, citing, 278–279
Private letter rulings, 101–102
Procedures, revenue, 99–100
Proceeding(s), 280
administrative, 17
annual, 279
Process
audit, 372–377
legislative, 70–74
Processing Centers, 367
Professional journals, 282
Professional tax journals, 282–283
Professional, tax, communications and, 315–317
Progressive tax rates, 344
Promoters of abusive tax shelters, action to enjoin, 413
Pronouncements, other IRS, 104–110
Proof, burden of, 119
Proportional tax rates, 343
Proposed regulations, 93
Protest vs. court, 382
Public inspection of written determinations, 103
Publications, miscellaneous, 108–110
Published services, 176
Published vs. electronic tax services, 153–154

Q

Query, 51
constructing a computer research, 51
Questions on returns, answers to, 15

Index

R

Rate(s)
  average tax, 344
  marginal tax, 344
  progressive tax, 344
  proportional tax, 343
  regressive tax, 344
  tax, 343–345
Realistic possibility, 10, 407
Reasonable cause, 394
Recent Developments Index, 178
Recognition, income,
  avoiding, 348–349
  postponing, 349–350
Recommendations
  communicated, 44
  developed, 44
Referral fees, 14
Refund check, endorsing or negotiating, 407
Refund or credit
  amount of, 421
  claim for, 419–421
Regressive tax rates, 344
Regular decision, 123
Regulation(s), 92–96
  and rulings, administrative, 91–110
  assessing, 95–96
  citing a, 94–95
  effective date of, 94
  general, 93
  legislative, 93
  locating, 96
  proposed, 93
  temporary, 93
Related taxpayers, spreading income among, 351–352
Reliance on written advice of IRS, 403
Report, committee, 71
  where to find, 73–74
Research
  goals, basic, 240
  Institute of America Citator, 243
  Institute of America Citator 2nd Series, 243
  problem, approaching the, 156
  process, 155–157
    illustrative example, 155–156
  results
    communicating, 314–333
    oral presentations of, 328–332

tax, 4
  by certified public accountants, 23–25
Responsibility, social, 21
Return preparation
  definition of, 406
  knowledge of error, 17
Return preparer (ITRP), 405
  definition of, 405–406
  disclosure or use of information by, 409
  penalties on, 405–412
Returns
  answers to questions on, 15
  for examination, selection of, 374–377
  irregular, 418
  preliminary review of, 373–374
  procedural aspects of preparing, 16
Revenue Agent's Report (RAR), 381
Revenue Procedures, 99–100
Revenue Rulings, 96–99
  citations, 97–99
  locating, 99
Review of returns, preliminary, 373–374
Reviews
  law, 281
  scholarly, 281–282
RIA *Analysis of Federal Taxes: Income,* 189
RIA Checkpoint, 51, 157–167
  case search, 163
  cite search, 161–165
  code search, 163
  contents search, 165–167
  index search, 166
  keyword search, 158–161
  table of contents search, 165
RIA Citators, 243–253
  conventions, 246
  organization, 243
  Rulings, 251
RIA compilations, 187
RIA *Coordinator* and *Analysis,* 189–190
RIA *Federal Tax Coordinator 2d,* 160
RIA *United States Tax Reporter,* 160
Rights, taxpayer, 369–372
Rule 101: Independence, 12
Rule 102: Integrity and Objectivity, 12

Rule 201: General Standards, 12
Rule 202: Compliance with Standards, 13
Rule 203: Accounting Principles, 13
Rule 301: Confidential Client Information, 13
Rule 302: Contingent Fees, 13
Rule 501: Acts Discreditable, 14
Rule 502: Advertising and Other Forms of Solicitation, 14
Rule 503: Commissions and Referral Fees, 14
Rule 505: Form of Organization and Name, 14
Rule, *Golsen,* 123
Rules and ethics in tax practice, 5–20
Rulings
  letter, 101–104
  private letter, 101–102

S

Sanctions, tax practice and administration, 392–425
Scan, spine, 180
Scholarly reviews, 281–282
Search
  case, RIA Checkpoint, 163
  case name, compilation, 183–184
  cite,
    CCH NetWork, 169–170
    RIA Checkpoint, 161–165
  code,
    RIA Checkpoint, 163
  section, compilation, 180–183
  contents,
    CCH NetWork, 169–170
    RIA Checkpoint, 165–167
  executing the, 52
  full-text, 154
  index, RIA Checkpoint, 166
  interpreted and refined, 52–53
  IRS web site, 53
  keyword,
    CCH NetWork, 167–169
    compilation, 178–180
    RIA Checkpoint, 158–161

state tax, CCH NetWork, 170–171
state, Westlaw, 222–224
table of contents, RIA Checkpoint, 165
Secondary authority, 41, 65
Selection of returns for examination, 374–377
Service(s)
  annotated, 176–187
  CCH annotated, 185–187
  computer tax, example, 139
  published, 176
  tax, 43
  topical, 187–190
Shelter, tax, organizing abusive, 408
Shepard's
  Citation Services, 258–264
  Citator, 258
  Federal Tax Citator, 258
  Indexes, 297
Shepardizing, 258
Small Cases Division, 123
Social responsibility, 21
Solicitation
  and advertising, 9
  other forms of, 14
Sources
  administrative, 41
  constitutional and legislative, 64–83
  judicial, 41
  Internet and, 139
  legislative and constitutional, 64–83
  of Federal tax law, 65
  of law, evaluating, 320–322
  statutory, 41, 65
Spine scan, 180
Spreading income among related taxpayers, 351–352
SSTS No. 1: Tax Return Positions, 15
SSTS No. 2: Answers to Questions on Returns, 15
SSTS No. 3: Certain Procedural Aspects of Preparing Returns, 16
SSTS No. 4: Use of Estimates, 16
SSTS No. 5: Departure from a Position Previously Concluded in an Administrative Proceeding or Court Decision, 17

SSTS No. 6: Knowledge of Error: Return Preparation, 17
SSTS No. 7: Knowledge of Error: Administrative Proceedings, 18
SSTS No. 8: Form and Content of Advice to Taxpayers, 18
Standards
  ethical, 20
  other, 22
  for tax services, statements on, 15–19
State searches, Westlaw, 222–224
State tax search, CCH NetWork, 170–171
Statements on standards for tax services, 15–19
Statute, exploiting inconsistencies in, 353–355
Statutes of limitations, 417–422
  mitigation of, 422
Statutory
  agreements, 422–425
  notice of deficiency, 383
  sources, 41, 65
  tax traps, 355–356
Substantial authority, 397
Supreme Court, U.S., 134–136
  decisions, locating, 136
Suspension of period of assessment and collection, 421–422

T

TA Campus, 214
Table of Authorities, 263
Table of contents search, RIA Checkpoint, 165
Tax Analysts, 212–217
  OneDisc, 214–217
  TaxBase, 213–214
  TaxLibrary.com, 216
Tax and law periodicals, nature of, 278
Tax Appeals, Board of, 121
Tax articles
  locating relevant, 293–303
  resources, other, 302–303
Tax avoidance, 4
  economics of, 340–342
Tax awareness, 346
Tax base, 342–343

Tax compliance, 3
Tax confidentiality privilege, 120
Tax, corporations underpayment of, 401
Tax Court
  decisions, 123
  locating, 124
  Rule 155, 129
  scope of, 129
  U.S., 121–129
Tax evasion, 4
  economics of, 340–342
Tax, failure to pay, 395
Tax, individuals underpayment of, 400
Tax information, computerized, assessing, 156–157
Tax journals, 43, 282
  professional, 282–283
Tax jurisdictions, changing, 350
Tax litigation, 4
Tax Management Portfolios, 205
Tax newsletters, 283–293
Tax Notes, 289
Tax offenses, criminal, 404
Tax periodicals, types of, 279–281
Tax planning, 4, 339–359
  economics of, 340–342
  fundamentals of, 346–352
  illustrations, 358–359
  in perspective, 345–346
Tax practice
  elements of, 3–5
  introduction to, 2–26
  Library, 211
  rules and ethics in, 5–20
Tax practice and administration: sanctions, agreements and disclosures, 392–425
Tax professional, communications and, 315–317
Tax rate(s), 343–345
  average, 344
  effective average, 345
  marginal, 344
  nominal average, 345
  progressive, 344
  proportional, 343
  regressive, 344
  terminology, 342–345

Tax research, 4
  as iterative process, 39
  by certified public accountants, 23–25
  communication, file memo, 317–320
  computerized, overview of, 45–53
  methodology, 35–53
  overview of computerized, 45–53
  process, outline of, 36–45
  using a computer in, 50
Tax Research Network, CCH, 167–171
Tax return
  failure to file, 394
  positions, 10, 15
  preparer, 7
  action to enjoin, 413
Tax service(s), 42
  annotated, 153
  computerized
    benefits of using, 46–49
    factors in choosing a, 49–50
  electronic and printed, 152–190
  example, computer, 139
  published vs. electronic, 153–154
  statements on standards for, 15–19
  topical, 153
    nature of, 188–189
Tax shelters, abusive, action to enjoin promoters of, 413
Tax traps
  avoiding, 355–358
  judicial, 356–358
  statutory, 355–356
Tax treaties, 67–70
Taxation, history of U.S., 65–67
TaxBase, 213–214, 289
  Tax Analysts, 213–214
TaxCore, 212
Taxes, failure to make deposits of, 401
TaxExpert, 171
TaxLibrary.com, Tax Analysts, 216
Taxpayer(s)
  advice to, form and content of, 18
  advocates, local, 369
  and preparer penalty

provisions, conflict among, 410
Assistance Order (TAO), 368–369
compliance measurement program (TCMP), 375
inconsistencies between, 353–354
penalties, 393–405
rights, 369–372
spreading income among related, 351–352
Technical advice memoranda, 102
Technical Memorandum (TM), 108
Temporary
  citation, 124
  regulations, 93
Terminology
  common legal, 120
  tax rate, 342–345
Terms and connectors (Boolean), 201
Thirty-day letter, 381
Topical services, 187–190
Topical tax services, 153
  nature of, 188–189
Transactions
  closed, 4
  inconsistencies between, 353
  open, 4
Treasury Decisions (TDs), 92
Treasury Department, 365
Treaties, tax, 67–70

U

U.S. Constitution, 67
U.S. taxation, history of, 65–67
Unallowable items program, 374
Unauthorized practice of law, 23
  history of, 24
Underpayment of tax
  corporations, 401
  individuals, 400
Understatement
  aiding and abetting, 409
  due to unrealistic positions, 407
  willful, 408
United States Tax Cases (USTC), 131

Universal (wildcard) characters, 201
Unrealistic positions, understatements due to, 407
Use of estimates, 16
Using a computer in tax research, 50

V

Volumes
　code, compilation, 183
　compilation, entering, 176–177

W

Westlaw, 217–224, 364
　Citator System, 264–268
　Cite List, 267
　data and access, 218–219
　searching, 219–222
　state searches, 222–224
　table of authorities, 267
WG&L *Index to Federal Tax Articles*, 294–297
Wildcard (universal) characters, 201
Willful understatement, 408
Withholding, giving false information with respect to, 402
Working with the IRS, 364–385
World Wide Web, 49
Writ of certiorari, 135

Written advice of IRS, reliance on, 403
Written determinations
　locating, 104
　numbering system, 103–104
　public inspection of, 103

Y

Years, inconsistencies between, 354–355